Politics of Latin America

Politics of Latin America

The Power Game

THIRD EDITION

Harry E. Vanden
Gary Prevost

New York   Oxford
OXFORD UNIVERSITY PRESS
2009

Oxford University Press, Inc., publishes works that further Oxford University's
objective of excellence in research, scholarship, and education.

Oxford   New York
Auckland   Cape Town   Dar es Salaam   Hong Kong   Karachi
Kuala Lumpur   Madrid   Melbourne   Mexico City   Nairobi
New Delhi   Shanghai   Taipei   Toronto

With offices in
Argentina   Austria   Brazil   Chile   Czech Republic   France   Greece
Guatemala   Hungary   Italy   Japan   Poland   Portugal   Singapore
South Korea   Switzerland   Thailand   Turkey   Ukraine   Vietnam

Published by Oxford University Press, Inc.
198 Madison Avenue, New York, New York 10016
http://www.oup.com

Oxford is a registered trademark of Oxford University Press

Library of Congress Cataloging-in-Publication Data

Vanden, Harry E.
Politics of Latin America : the power game / Harry E. Vanden, Gary Prevost. – 3rd ed.
    p. cm.
Includes bibliographical references and index.

ISBN 978-0-19-533998-7
1. Latin America–Politics and government. I. Prevost, Gary. II. Title.
JL960.V36 2008
320.98–dc22   20080180843

Printing number: 9 8 7 6 5 4 3 2

Printed in the United States of America
on acid-free paper

This work is dedicated to those who teach Latin American politics, with special thanks to those who showed us the way: Bryon Nichols and Gary Wynia, who taught Gary Prevost, and C. Neale Ronning, John C. Honey, and Mario Hernández Sánchez-Barba, who guided Harry Vanden.

CONTENTS

Maps and Tables

MAPS

TABLES

FREQUENTLY CITED ACRONYMS

AD	Democratic Action Party, Venezuela
AID	Agency for International Development, U.S. Department of State
AMNLAE	Association of Nicaraguan Women, Luisa Amanda Espinosa
ANDI	National Association of Industrialists, Colombia
APRA	American Popular Revolutionary Alliance, Peru
ARENA	National Republican Alliance, El Salvador
AUC	Autodefense Units of Colombia
ARENA	National Renovating Alliance, Brazil
BPR	People's Revolutionary Bloc, El Salvador
CACIF	Coordinating Committee of Agricultural, Commercial, Industrial, and Financial Associations, Guatemala
CBC	Christian Base Communities
CDR	Committees for the Defense of the Revolution, Cuba
CDT	Democratic Workers' Confederation, Chile
CGT	General Confederation of Labor, Argentina, Colombia
CIA	Central Intelligence Agency, U.S.
CNS	Coordinadora Nacional de Sindicatos, Chile
CONAIE	Confederation of Ecuadorean Indigenous Nationalities
COPEI	Social Christian Party, Venezuela
CORFO	Development Corporation, Chile
CPC	Confederation of Production and Commerce, Chile
CPD	Coalition of Parties for Democracy, Chile
CSTC	Trade Union Confederation of Colombian Workers
CTDC	Democratic Confederation of Colombian Workers
CTV	Confederation of Venezuelan Workers
CTC	Confederation of Cuban Workers
CUT	Unitary Labor Central, Brazil, Chile, Colombia

ECLA/ECLAC	Economic Commission for Latin America/and the Caribbean
EGP	Guerrilla Army of the Poor, Guatemala
ELN	Army of National Liberation, Colombia
ERP	Revolutionary Army of the People, Argentina
ERP	Popular Revolutionary Army, El Salvador
EZLN	Zapatista Army of National Liberation, Mexico
FAL	Armed Forces of Liberation, El Salvador
FALN	Armed Forces of National Liberation, Venezuela
FAR	Fuerzas Armadas Rebeldes, Guatemala
FARC	Revolutionary Armed Forces of Colombia, Colombia
FEDECAFE	National Federation of Coffee Growers, Colombia
FDNG	New Guatemala Democratic Front
FDR	Democratic Revolutionary Front, El Salvador
FMLN	Farabundo Martí National Liberation Front, El Salvador
FREPASO	Front for a Country in Solidarity, Argentina
FSLN	Sandinista Front for National Liberation, Nicaragua
FTAA	Free Trade Area of the Americas
GAM	Group of Mutual Support, Guatemala
IFI	International Financial Institution
IMF	International Monetary Fund
ISI	Import Substitution Industrialization
M-19	April 19 Movement, Colombia
M-26 July	July 26 Movement, Cuba
MAS	Movement Toward Socialism, Venezuela, Bolivia
MDB	Brazilian Democratic Movement
MERCOSUR/ MERCOSUL	Common Market of the Southern Cone
MINUGUA	United Nations Verification Mission, Guatemala
MIR	Revolutionary Movement of the Left, Chile, Peru, Venezuela, Colombia, Bolivia
MNC	Multinational Corporation
MNR	National Revolutionary Movement, Bolivia
MST	Landless Movement, Brazil
MVR	Fifth Republic Movement, Venezuela
NAFTA	North American Free Trade Agreement
NAM	Non-Aligned Movement
OAS	Organization of American States
PAC	Civil Defense Patrol, Guatemala
PAN	National Action Party, Mexico
PCC	Cuban Communist Party

PDC	Christian Democratic Party
PDS	Social Democratic Party, Brazil
PDVSA	Venezuelan National Petroleum Company
PJ	Justice [Peronist] Party, Argentina
PLF	Party of the Liberal Front, Brazil
PMDB	Brazilian Democratic Movement Party
PP	Patriotic Pole, Venezuela
PPD	Party for Democracy, Chile
PRD	Democratic Revolutionary Party, Mexico
PRI	Institutional Revolutionary Party, Mexico
PSDB	Brazilian Social Democratic Party
PSN	Nicaraguan Socialist Party
PT	Workers Party, Brazil
RN	National Renovation, Chile
UCR	Radical Civic Union, Argentina
UFCo	United Fruit Company
UNO	National Opposition Union, Nicaragua
UNT	National Workers Union, Venezuela
UP	Popular Unity, Chile
UP	Patriotic Union, Colombia
URNG	Guatemalan National Revolutionary Unity

PREFACE TO THE THIRD EDITION

The third edition of *Politics in Latin America* is animated by the same passions that guided the first two editions, our love and fascination for Latin America and how politics are practiced there. We were motivated to proceed to a third edition by the continuing positive reactions we received from students and the community of scholars who study Latin America and have adopted our textbook. We are most indebted to our students at the University of South Florida, Saint John's University, College of Saint Benedict, and Hamline University, who have provided invaluable commentary. We are also indebted to the previous country chapter authors who have so graciously updated their work for the new edition.

The new edition continues to focus on power politics and recent developments in the region, especially the election and reelection since 2002 of numerous progressive governments chosen by their populations to provide an alternative to the Washington-driven neoliberal policies of the 1990s. Since the publication of our last edition three years ago, the electoral victories of Evo Morales (Bolivia), Rafael Correa (Ecuador), and Daniel Ortega (Nicaragua) have continued the leftward drift of the region's politics.

In recognition of the significance of the victory of Morales as the country's first elected indigenous leader, we have added a country chapter on Bolivia by Waltruad Morales of the University of Central Florida. We also analyze the continuing power of the United States in the region manifested by the implementation of the Central American Free Trade Agreement (CAFTA), bilateral trade agreements with Chile and Peru, and the continued funding of Plan Colombia. Counteracting that U.S. power we analyze the role of various Latin American based initiatives, including the expansion of MERCOSUR, the Bolivarian Alternative, and The Bank of the South. As before, we also provide ongoing analysis of the role that previously marginalized groups such as women, gays and lesbians, Afro-Latinos, and the indigenous play in contemporary Latin American life, primarily through a myriad of groups and organizations that challenge Latin America's long-standing elites using the hard-won political openings achieved in recent years.

Many have helped us in this endeavor. We continue to learn and benefit from the voices and actions of Latin American peoples and from our many colleagues who study the region from around the world. In this regard we are especially grateful to

David Close who helped us update the Nicaragua chapter, Richard Stahler-Sholk who provided an update on the Zapatistas, Brian Larkin for his assistance in reworking the Religion chapter, and Shawn Schulenberg who contributed the new section on gays and lesbians contained in Chapter 5. Gary Prevost is especially indebted to the office staff of Saint John's University and the College of Saint Benedict. Special recognition goes to Suzanne Reinert for invaluable secretarial help and to student assistant Benjamin Hieserich, who updated many tables, including the appendices on electoral results. We are most indebted to Courtney Glass at the University of South Florida for updating the majority of tables in this edition.

We hope this new edition continues to meet the needs of the students and professors who use it and beg the indulgence of the reader for any errors we may have made. These, of course, remain our responsibility.

Harry E. Vanden
Tampa

Gary Prevost
Collegeville

PREFACE TO THE FIRST EDITION

This book is born from a great love and appreciation of Latin America and a fascination with how politics are conducted there. It is designed to convey a contemporary and, we hope, realistic understanding of politics and power in the region and is premised on the belief that politics in Latin America can only be understood after one gains an appreciation for the socio-economic-historical context in which the political game is played.

Our understanding of the region and its politics is far from complete, but is well informed by the scholars, writers, and teachers who have preceded us. In recognition of those on whose shoulders we stand, we dedicate this book to those professors who showed us the complexities that define politics in the region. Gary Prevost gratefully acknowledges the import of his teacher Gary Wynia and his excellent work, *The Politics of Latin American Development*. Harry Vanden expresses his profound thanks to those who guided and inspired his study of politics in the region: C. Neale Ronning, John C. Honey, and Mario Hernández Sánchez-Barba. Both authors also gratefully acknowledge the influence of a great many Latin American friends and colleagues and many excellent Latinamericanists from all of the Americas, Europe, and Asia.

We acknowledge the assistance of many people in the preparation of this book, beginning with our colleagues who wrote the country chapters: Wilber Chaffee, Nora Hamilton, Susanne Jonas, Eduardo Silva, and Aldo Vacs. We are indebted to the many scholars who provided helpful commentary on the manuscript and individual chapters including Mark Amen, Carlos Batista, Dan Buchanan, Robert Buffington, Ronald Chilcote, David Close, María Crummett, Ed Nesman, Festus Ohaebulam, Patrice E. Olsen, Lou Pérez, Eric Selbin, Ofelia Shutte, and Ward Stavig. Thanks are due to Ilene Frank for research and web assistance. We wish to express our appreciation to Dorothea Melcher, who not only read several chapters, but contributed significantly to sections of Chapter 2 on pre-Columbian and colonial history. Likewise, we are deeply indebted to Kwame Dixon for his assistance in the sections on slavery and Afro-Latins in Chapters 3, 4, and 5. We also gratefully acknowledge the editorial assistance of Linda Jarkesy and Lisa Grzan at Oxford University Press.

We are most indebted to Brendan Dwyer for constructing the maps in this work and to Betilde Muñoz and Patrice E. Olsen for completing the index. Kate Arroyo, Ahad Hayauddin, Betilde Muñoz, Xuan Luo, and Jennifer Nagel deserve special thanks for their important work in preparing tables and chronologies. At St. John's University Suzanne Reinert provided valuable office assistance including the typing of significant parts of the manuscript and maintenance of computer files. Erik Gerrits prepared the appendices on elections and government structures. Gary Prevost acknowledges the support of a Dillon Research Grant from St. John's University that enables him to conduct field research. Finally, we remind the reader that any errors or omissions fall on our shoulders alone.

Harry E. Vanden
Tampa

Gary Prevost
Collegeville

NOTES ON STUDYING POLITICS IN LATIN AMERICA

Latin America is a dynamic, complex, and rapidly changing reality. It ranges from small pastoral villages to two of the largest urban megalopolises on earth. Both democratic and dictatorial, its governments are sometimes replaced by voting in clean elections and other times by military coups. Although exciting to study, Latin America's complexity often challenges the ideas and intellectual approaches we use to study it—indeed, one approach alone is usually just not sufficient to understand what is going on there. The authors of this work maintain that it takes all the conceptual tools and insights that can be mustered to begin to understand such a complex reality. Because the political history of the nations that comprise Latin America has been quite different from that which developed in the United States, Canada, Britain, or Australia, most of us who study Latin American politics believe it is imperative to know this history because most political practices grew out of it. The authors speak of dictatorial *caudillos* and of authoritarian political culture, yet acknowledge the great political changes and democratic reforms that have also marked Latin American history. Each nation has a political history marked by periods of dictatorship and democracy. Each nation has struggled with the need to change social and economic structures and traditional economic practices that have vested most of the land in a few families and left the vast majority of citizens with no or little land or means of adequately sustaining themselves. Latin America has experienced more revolutions than any other part of the world, yet the conditions for the lower classes in most countries are arguably not much better than they were at the end of the colonial period in the early 1800s. As reflected in the two introductory chapters on broad historical periods in Latin America (Chapters 2 and 3) and the detailed political history provided for each of the ten country case studies presented here, the authors strongly believe that one cannot begin to understand Latin American politics without knowing the region's history. Equally, they know just how great the political variations have been and thus strongly believe that one must equally study the particular historical evolution of each country to comprehend its own brand of politics and see how it conforms to and diverges from general political trends and practices in the region. The often influential role of the United States in Latin American politics and Inter-American relations is also explored in Chapter 3. Similarly, there are certain events—such as the Mexican and Cuban revolutions—and certain figures—such as Victor Raúl Haya de la Torre of Peru, Juan Perón of Argentina, or Cuba's Fidel Castro—whose historical trajectories need to be studied because of their lasting influence in their own countries and the region as a whole.

It should further be noted that there are many ways of remembering or interpreting what went on before. Indeed, it has been suggested that much, or some part, of history has been written by the elite. Using the term perfected by the influential Italian thinker Antonio Gramsci, we would say that the "superstructure," or the culture and institutions controlled by the dominant class, have dictated much of the history that has been written. For instance, we now know that much that was written by such patriarchal European elites was but one version of what transpired. Class, gender, race, nationality, religion, and ideology all influence how we see an event and how we evaluate it. Slavery, one imagines, will always be seen somewhat differently by slave and slaveholder. And the descendants of each may keep many of their foreparents' views of things. The chapters in this book will endeavor to present a view of the present and past that is inclusive of views of native peoples, Africans who were brought as slaves, women, dominated classes, and others who were subordinated, as well as the more standard history written from the perspective of the dominant elites in Latin America and Europe. By incorporating more diverse views, the authors hope to supply a better and more complete picture of how the region evolved and what it is like today.

But history is not enough. Similarly, before we deploy specific concepts gleaned from the study of comparative politics, most students of Latin American politics believe that a great deal of the political behavior in the region has been heavily influenced by internal and international economic forces and that one cannot fully comprehend politics without understanding the economics of the region. The internal economies of the indigenous societies were totally disrupted by the conquest and the imposition of economic systems designed to export wealth to Europe and thus incorporate the Americas into the international system on terms favorable to Europe. Economic power was seized by the European elite. Thereafter, the structure and functioning of Latin American nations would be heavily influenced by their trade and commercial relations with more economically developed areas; their economies, societies, and political institutions would also be transformed by this external orientation. Latin America was to fit into the international system as a producer of primary (unfinished) goods such as sugar, tin, tobacco, copper, coffee, and bananas. According to classical Western capitalist theories of free trade economics, such trade was to be equally advantageous to peripheral areas such as Latin America as it was to metropolitan areas such as Europe and the United States. Yet, after World War II, a careful study of the terms of trade for Latin America by the Economic Commission for Latin America of the United Nations suggested just the opposite—that benefits from trading patterns were accruing primarily to the developed areas, not to Latin America. As scholars of Latin America and other social scientists studied the full implication of this phenomenon, they arrived at a theory that explained the continuing underdevelopment and dependency of Latin America. Dependency theory, as the paradigm came to be called, soon heavily dominated thinking among social scientists who studied Latin America. For most scholars, it became the principal way of understanding Latin American society, politics, development, and the region's relations with the outside world. This approach predominated from the late 1960s into the 1990s, supplanting many classical economic assumptions and displacing other theories of underdevelopment, such as modernization theory, which was championed by many U.S. scholars. Chapter 7 explores dependency theory in greater detail and makes the general argument that since economic and political power is so closely entwined in Latin America, an approach that combines both—political economy—is necessary.

But even if, as Karl Marx believed, economic relations form the basis for social structures, it is still necessary to examine those social structures carefully. Nor can economic relations be fully comprehended until elements of social, gender, race, and class relations are introduced. Family and gender relations, race, and subordination have all played key roles in the development of Latin American politics and economics. The subordinate position of indigenous peoples, Afro-Latins, and women has conditioned politics and been conditioned by them. Class is of equal importance, given the hierarchical nature of the societies that developed. The authors believe familiarity with these issues is necessary and thus have included one chapter on indigenous and African peoples (Chapter 4) and a second that explores the status of women and gender roles (Chapter 5).

The rise of fundamentalism in domestic politics in the United States, the Islamic resurgence in a variety of Muslim countries, and the rise of religious parties in India have once more brought religion to the center of the political stage. Yet in Latin America, the role of the Catholic Church and religion has always been an important factor in politics. For five centuries, the Church has remained the bulwark of the status quo in most countries. Yet, there have always been radicals in the Church who were not afraid to challenge entrenched political interests, even though most of the Church hierarchy usually worked hand in glove with the state. Such was the case in the sixteenth century when Chiapas Bishop Bartolomé de las Casas became a crusader against the enslavement of indigenous people. At the beginning of the nineteenth century two progressive priests—Hidalgo and Morelos—waged the first phase of the mass-based independence movement in Mexico. Standing Marx on his head, the most original Marxist thinker in Latin America, José Carlos Mariátegui, argued that religion could be a revolutionary force. Stimulated by his thought and progressive theological trends in Europe, the Peruvian priest Gustavo Gutiérrez developed a radical new theology of liberation. The advent of liberation theology and growing support for the radical transformation of socioeconomic structures by the Conference of Latin American Bishops after 1968 made religion a major political force for change in many countries in the region. Priests supported guerrilla groups, resisted dictatorships, became guerrillas themselves, and, in the case of four priests in Nicaragua, became part of the Sandinista government. Lay people formed participatory Christian Base Communities and used their faith as a potent political force. Meanwhile, more conservative Protestant evangelical groups converted millions of the faithful. The new flock was often exhorted not to be involved in (radical) politics or to support fellow Protestant (and usually conservative) candidates. It is difficult to comprehend the dynamics of Latin American politics without understanding the religious forces and factions at work there. Thus the authors have also included a chapter on religion (Chapter 6).

Democracy and dictatorship have been two contrasting themes running through Latin American history and the conduct of politics in each nation. Their dynamic and dialectical interaction have defined the political game and created unique political cultures in the region. Thus democracy and authoritarianism are explored in Chapter 8, as is Latin America's special brand of political culture.

Chapters 1–10 provide the context in which Latin American politics are played out. Different readers and instructors may choose to emphasize different areas; others may opt to also read an accompanying novel like Isabel Allende's *House of the Spirits*, *El Señor Presidente* by Miguel Angel Asturias, or Gabriel García Márquez's *One Hundred Years of Solitude*. Films and videos also illustrate many of these factors and bring figures like Juan and Eva Perón to life (*Evita*). The authors believe that astute students of the political game in Latin America must develop some appreciation for such background factors before they begin to focus on politics.

Most political scientists believe that politics concerns power and influence—how resources are allocated in a society. In his classic work, *Politics: Who Gets What, When, How*, Harold Lasswell suggests that the study of politics is the study of influence and the influential. In a context that is particularly relevant to Latin America, he argues that the "influential are those who get the most of what there is to get" and further adds that those who get the most are the elite, and the rest are the masses (Lasswell 1958, 13). He further invokes the early political economist David Ricardo to the effect that the distribution of wealth suggests one of the principal avenues of influence in a given society. Thus Lasswell notes that in the early part of the twentieth century, 2,500 individuals in Chile owned 50 million of the 57 million acres of privately held land in the nation (17). That is, the large landowners were dominant economically and could use this base to influence—if not dominate—the political process. The study of politics and the subfield of comparative politics has evolved considerably since the time Lasswell originally wrote these pages (the 1930s). At that time he and other social scientists in the United States were more willing to focus on concepts of class and the domination of wealth. That was before the advent of the Cold War and the dichotomization of the world into two opposing camps, with social science often reflecting each camp's dominant values. Social science in Latin America has been much more willing to use class and Marxist concepts in its study of the Latin American reality. This is reflected in the work of many Latin Americanists outside the region as well. In the United States comparative politics evolved from traditional–legalistic approaches that looked at history and constitutions, to behavioral approaches that studied interest groups and voting behavior and other quantifiable political actions to explain politics, to postbehavioral approaches that came to include policy analysis, aspects of dependency theory, and world systems analysis, as well as a postmodern literary/cultural deconstructionist analysis. Currently, political scientists in the United States are focusing a great deal of interest on rational choice theory. Yet, those conceptual tools most frequently employed by Latin Americanists who focus on politics do not usually include deconstruction (although there are exceptions among literary-oriented Latin Americanists and Latin American intellectuals) or rational choice theory. Conceptual approaches most often and most successfully employed include elitist analysis, class analysis, a pluralist analysis of interest groups, mass organizations and others who exercise power in the political process, analysis of voting and political preferences where conditions allow for relatively clean elections and free expression of opinion, dependency analysis and political economy, and a careful consideration of powerful groups like the military or armed guerrilla groups that have the capacity to use force to take power or heavily influence policy decisions. All of these are employed in this work. The authors also rely on the approach to understanding Latin American power relations developed by Gary Wynia in *The Politics of Latin American Development*.

Latin Americanists have followed their own evolution. As suggested earlier, they have found political history to be of great importance. From this they extracted useful political concepts such as *caudillismo*, *golpe de estado* (coup d'état), and *junta*. These and similar concepts like authoritarianism and *machismo* are, nonetheless, explained well by the concept of political culture as developed in comparative politics in the 1960s, during the time when behaviorism was dominant. In that political values and beliefs in Latin America are generally so different from those found in Anglo-American political cultures, special treatment is given to general outlines of Latin American political culture in Chapter 8. The authors examine the development of political values from family, gender, race, and class relations as well as historic factors. They do so in the confines imposed by class, authoritarian rule, and the use and abuse of power by those who rule. Later, the country chapter authors make frequent use of these concepts as they analyze the politics of individual nations. Of equal importance is a fundamental subtext in most writing about Latin American politics: Power rules, and absolute power rules absolutely. This is manifest in the title of a highly respected work on Guatemala by Richard Adams, *Crucifixion by Power*. Frequently it is not what the constitution says, it is the power of the dictator or the president to ignore the constitution, have congress amend it, or simply arrange for the nation's supreme court to make a favorable interpretation. Ultimately it may not be the constitution, elections, public opinion, civilian politicians, or the party system that decide the issues. Rather it may be a coup, as in Ecuador in 2000, or a political understanding with the military that allows the president to dismiss congress and the supreme court and rule on his own, as in Peru in 1992. In most Latin American countries there is always the possibility that naked power can and will be used. This has been the case since the conquistadores established their rule through brute force. Naked power—and violence—can be used by the government to suppress the rulers' political enemies, by the military to take over the government or threaten to do so, or by armed opposition groups that contend for power through the use of arms. One is here reminded of Mao Zedong's oft-quoted dictum—"power flows out of the barrel of a gun." Even when democratic processes are being followed, the threat of the use of force is often present. Thus the military can often veto policy decisions by a civilian government, as was the case in El Salvador and Guatemala for many years; the oligarchy can threaten to mobilize their friends in the military on their behalf; or, as is the case in Nicaragua and Colombia, the opposition groups that grew out of revolutionary organizations can threaten to take up arms again. At the local level the amount of power a large landowner can wield may be a more important factor in local politics than the election of a reformist in the last election or the composition of the government. The local notable's power allows him to manipulate the policy process, control public officials, pay off the local police, or hire his own armed guards and also heavily influence the electoral process—indeed, most likely the reformer would have never been elected. Yet the notable's power could be challenged by a well-organized popular organization like the Landless in Brazil or neutralized by the presence of an active guerrilla group like the Fuerzas Armadas Revolucionarias de Colombia (FARC) in Colombia.

In Latin America politics are dictated by power and the powerful. This book examines those who play the power game in separate chapters on political actors and political institutions (Chapter 9) and revolutions and change (Chapter 10). The way the game is played is conditioned by the historic, social, and economic factors mentioned previously, but it also has developed its own rules and practices. They are explored in these chapters, beginning with a discussion of how the constitution is often best described as an ideal to strive for rather than a basis for the rule of law.

Country chapters on Guatemala, Mexico, Argentina, Brazil, Chile, Cuba, Nicaragua, Colombia, Venezuela, and Bolivia follow. They provide specific examples of how the power game is played in ten different Latin American nations. This is a representative—but not inclusive—sampling of the Latin American political reality. Each of the Latin American nation-states has developed its own way of conducting politics. Reference is made to some key events in the countries not included in the case studies, but it was not possible to fully explore the particular political nuances of all aspects of national politics in each country. Those who carefully study general trends and how they develop in the included case studies will, however, have a good basis to explore how politics are conducted elsewhere in Latin America.

Bibliography

Adams, Richard. *Crucifixion by Power*. Austin: University of Texas Press, 1970.

Allende, Isabel. *House of the Spirits*. New York: A. Knopf, 1985.

Asociación Latinoamericano de Sociología, Centro de Estudios sobre America, Editorial Nueva Sociedad. *Sistemas políticos: poder y sociedad (estudios de caso en América Latina)* [Political Systems: Power and Society (Latin American Case Studies)]. Caracas: Editorial Nueva Sociedad, 1992.

Asturias, Miguel. *El Señor Presidente*. New York: Antheneum, 1987.

Borón, Atilio A. *Reflexiones sobre el poder, el estado y la revolución*. [Reflections on Power, State and Revolution] Córdoba, Argentina: Espartaco Córdoba, 2007.

Eckstein, Susan, ed. *Power and Popular Protest: Latin American Social Movements*. Updated and expanded edition. Berkeley: University of California Press, 2001.

García Márquez, Gabriel. *One Hundred Years of Solitude*. New York: Harper & Row, 1970.

Lasswell, Howard D. *Politics: Who Gets What, When, How*. New York: Meridian Books, The World Publishing Company, 1958.

Mills, C. Wright. *The Power Elite*. New York and London: Oxford University Press, 1956.

Wynia, Gary. *The Politics of Latin American Development*. New York: Cambridge University Press, 1990.

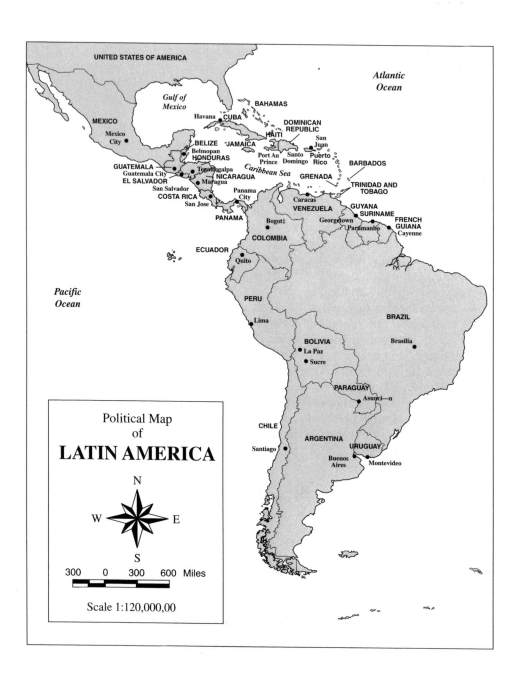

UNITED STATES OF AMERICA

Atlantic Ocean

Gulf of Mexico

BAHAMAS

Havana • CUBA

DOMINICAN REPUBLIC

MEXICO

Mexico City •

HAITI

San Juan

BELIZE   JAMAICA
Belmopan
HONDURAS   Port Au   Santo   Puerto
                        Prince   Domingo Rico

BARBADOS

GUATEMALA
Guatemala City
EL SALVADOR
San Salvador

Tegucigalpa
NICARAGUA
Managua

Caribbean Sea

GRENADA

TRINIDAD AND TOBAGO

COSTA RICA
San Jose

Panama City

Caracas

VENEZUELA   GUYANA
                        SURINAME
PANAMA   FRENCH
            Bogotá   Georgetown   GUIANA
                      Paramaribo   Cayenne
            COLOMBIA

ECUADOR

Quito

PERU

Pacific Ocean

Lima

BRAZIL

BOLIVIA
• La Paz   Brasilia •
• Sucre

PARAGUAY

Asunción •

CHILE

ARGENTINA   URUGUAY

Santiago •

Buenos   Montevideo
Aires

Political Map
of
LATIN AMERICA

N
W   E
S

300   0   300   600   Miles

Scale 1:120,000,00

ONE

An Introduction to Twenty-First Century Latin America

Latin America—a term coined by a Frenchman—is not a homogeneous part of the world that just happens to lie south of the border that runs from Florida to California. It is an immense region that is striving to establish its place in the world in the twenty-first century.

A diverse area of thirty-four nations and peoples that includes Mexico, Central America, the Caribbean nations, and South America and surrounding islands, Latin America is home to some 580 million people (10 percent of the world's population) who well represent the rich racial and cultural diversity of the human family. Its people include Amero-Indians from pre-Columbian civilizations, such as the Incas, Aztecs, and Maya; Europeans from such countries as Spain and Portugal (but also England, France, Holland, Italy, Poland, and Germany); West Africans from areas such as what is now Nigeria, the Congo, and Angola; Jews from Europe and elsewhere; Arabs and Turks from countries such as Lebanon, Syria, Egypt, and Turkey; Japanese; Chinese; and different peoples from the Indian subcontinent. These and other racial and cultural groupings have combined to create modern nations rich in talent and variety. The dynamic way that the races have combined in Latin America even led one observer to predict that the Latin American region would be the birthplace of the fusion of the world's major racial groupings into a new *raza cosmica*—a cosmic race.

Latin America is a place where women can be elected president, an Indian woman from Guatemala can be awarded the Nobel Prize and later run for the presidency, a Japanese president from Peru can receive the highest approval ratings in recent history only to be indicted some years later, and an Arab can be elected president of Ecuador only to be replaced briefly by his female vice president.

Latin America still has some places where the siesta follows the large mid-day meal. More commonly, the modern Latin American has a heavy meal in an urban setting and returns to the job for a full afternoon of work. The rapid pace of globalization, urbanization, commercialization, industrialization, and political mobilization continues to radically change the face of the region. Colombia, Nicaragua, Brazil, and Costa Rica still gear much of their economies around the export of excellent coffee. Meanwhile, Mexico is making more and more automobiles and automobile components as a result of the North American Free Trade Agreement (between Mexico, Canada, and the United States); Brazil is selling its passenger planes, jet trainers, and modern fighter aircraft in the globalized international market while it is developing a common market in the Southern Cone of South America (*Mercosur*); new clothing assembly plants are moving to Nicaragua and Guatemala; and Costa Rica is manufacturing Intel chips and exporting software for hospital administration.

Latin America and the Caribbean constitute an enormous and extremely rich region. The area ranges from the Bahamas, Cuba, and Mexico in the north to Argentina and Chile's southern tip in Tierra del Fuego some 7000 miles to the south. *El continente*, as the region is called by many of its Spanish-speaking inhabitants, is extremely diverse in geography and population. It encompasses hot and humid coastal lowlands, steamy interior river basins, tropical rain forest, highland plateaus, coastal deserts, fertile lowlands, and high mountain peaks of some 8000 meters (24,000 feet).

The term *Latin America* is an ingenious attempt to link together most of this vast area. Strictly speaking, it refers to those countries in the Western Hemisphere south of the United States that speak Spanish, Portuguese, and French.[1] In a more general sense, it also includes the English- and Dutch-speaking parts of the Caribbean and South America as well as Belize in Central America.[2] The focus of this book will be on the Latin part of the region, although the English- and Dutch-speaking countries will be included in some of the maps and tables and are occasionally referred to for the sake of comparison.

Geography

Latin America is huge and diverse; it runs from 32.5° north latitude to 55° south latitude. With a total area of 8 million square miles (20 million km²), it is one of the largest regions of the world. Taken on the whole, it is almost as large as the United States and Canada combined and larger than Europe.

The climatic and topographic diversity of Latin America is remarkable. Its range of environments is greater than in North America and Europe: rain forests, savanna grasslands, thorn scrub, temperate grasslands, coniferous forests, and even deserts. Plateaus extend down from the United States into Mexico and Central America. The Andes extend from the Caribbean island of Trinidad to Tierra del Fuego at the southern tip of South America and form the largest mountain chain on earth. They are most prominent as they parallel the west coast of South America. Many peaks are over 18,000 feet; Mount Aconcagua in northern Argentina reaches almost 24,000 feet and is the highest point in the Western Hemisphere. Snow-capped peaks can

TABLE 1. Basic Statistics for Latin America, Canada, and the United States

Countries	Estimated Total Population (2007) (Thousands)*	Annual Population Growth Rate %*	% Urban Population*	Cities with 100,000 or More Inhabitants***	Per Capita Gross National Income (US $$)*	Life Expectancy at Birth*	Literacy Rate (15+ Years old)*	% Labor Force Female ***	Infant Mortality Rate (per 1000 Live Births)*
Argentina	39,531	1	90.4	34	5,340	75.3	97.2	43 ***	12.6
Bolivia	9,525	1.8	65.1	8	1,087	65.6	86.7	46^^^	54.0***
Brazil	191,791	1.3	85.2	222	5,502	72.4	88.6	43**	22.6**
Chile	16,635	1	88.2	24	7,679	78.6	95.7	36*	7.9*
Colombia	46,156	1.3	73.3	37	2,763	72.9	90.4	42*	15.9*
Costa Rica	4,468	1.5	62.8	3	4,857	78.8	94.9	35**	9.7
Cuba	11,268	0	75.2	12	4,571	78.3	99.8	36**	5.3
Dominican Republic	9,760	1.5	68.2	3	3,109	72.2	87	42**	30.6
Ecuador	13,341	1.1	63.8	14	2,787	75	91	42*	22.1*
El Salvador	6,857	1.4	60.4	11	2,300	71.9	80.6	40**	25.0****
Guatemala	13,354	2.5	48.1	1	2,305	70.3	69.1	36****	39.0****
Haiti	9,598	1.6	40.1	4	489	60.9	55.6	43^^+	57
Honduras	7,106	1.9	47.4	2	1,290	70.2	80	33*	23
Nicaragua	5,603	1.3	59.8	5	946	72.9	76.7	45^^^	31.0^^^
Panama	3,343	1.6	72.4	3	4,726	75.5	93.1	37**	19.4*
Paraguay	6,127	1.8	59.7	3	1,543	71.8	93.5	39^^^	17.0**
Peru	27,903	1.2	73	17	3,138	71.4	87.9	41**	28.7*
Puerto Rico	3,991	0.5	98.1	8	14,720	78.7	94.8	43**	9.3*
Uruguay	3,340	0.3	92.2	1	5,644	76.4	98	45***	10.5
Venezuela	27,657	1.7	94	32	6,541	73.7	93	40****	15.5*
NAFTA countries									
Canada	32,876	0.9	80.3	57	38,360	80.7	99	47*	5.3**
Mexico	106,535	1.1	76.5	76	7,755	76.2	91.6	37*	18.1
United States	305,826	1	81.4	240	43,424	78.2	99.5	46*	6.8**

Sources: * Pan American Health Organization, *Basic Indicators 2007* (online: http://www.paho.org/english/dd/ais/BI-2007-ENG.pdf); ** *Regional Core Health Data Initiative Table Generator System 2005* (online:http://www.paho.org/English/SHA/coredata/tabulator/newTabulator.htm);
+ World Atlas, 2002, International Bank for Reconstruction and Development, p. 28.
** Statistics and Indicators on Women and Men. United Nations Statistics Division (http://unstats.un.org/unsd/demographic/products/indwm/tab5a.htm), August 28. 2006.
*** United Nations Statistical Division, *Demographic and Social Statistics, Population Density and Urbanization, Population of Capital Cities and Cities of 100,000 or More Inhabitants,* 2007.

* 2005. ** 2004. *** 2003. **** 2002. ^^^ 2001. ^^ 2000. ^ 1999.

be found from Venezuela in northern South America to Argentina and Chile in the south. A fault line that runs from California through the middle of Mexico and Central America and down the west coast of South America makes the region prone to earthquakes. Volcanoes are found in Mexico, the Caribbean, and Central and South America. Other major geographic areas include the Guiana Highlands in northern South America, the Brazilian highlands, and the Pampas in the south. River systems include the Orinoco in the north, the Río de la Plata in the south, and the mighty Amazon in the middle of the South American continent.

Even at the same latitude, one can find very different climates. *Altitudinal zonation*, as this phenomenon is called, refers to the range in altitude from sea level to thousands of feet that occurs as one travels as few as 50 miles horizontally. It makes for very different climates. Land from sea level to 3000 feet is termed *tierra caliente*; from 3000 to 6000 feet, *tierra templada*; from 6000 to 12,000 feet, *tierra fría*; and above 12,000 feet, *tierra helada*, which experiences frost, snow, and ice through all or most of the year. Even close to the equator, the temperature cools 3.7° F for each 1000 feet of altitude. Although at the same latitude, Quito, the capital of Ecuador at 9300 feet, has an average annual temperature of 54.6° F, while Ecuador's largest city, Guayaquil, located on the coast, has an average temperature of 78.2° F. Each zone is suitable for different crops. Tierra caliente, when it is humid, is usually ideal for tropical fruits, while tierra templada is suited for growing crops like coffee, potatoes (which can be grown up to 11,000 feet), corn, and coca plants. Because of the temperature variation, crops requiring very different climates, such as bananas (humid, tropical lowlands) and coffee (cooler, shaded highlands), can be grown in the same Caribbean island (Jamaica) or small Central American nation (Costa Rica, Nicaragua, or Guatemala). It is interesting to note that there are some crops that are extremely adaptive and can grow at a variety of altitudes. Corn is grown throughout Mexico, Central America, and the Andean region and formed an essential part of the classical Aztec, Mayan, and Incan economies. Coca cultivation has remained an essential part of agriculture in the area occupied by the Incan Empire (concentrated in Peru, Bolivia, and Ecuador but extending into Colombia, northern Chile, and Argentina). The cultivation and consumption of coca leaves has been an essential part of indigenous culture in most of the Andean region since pre-Incan times. The coca plant can live up to 40 years and produces the best leaves for chewing when grown at altitudes of 3000–4000 feet. Coca thrives in the shaded areas of the eastern Andean slopes, but it also can be grown at much higher altitudes or in the dryer mountainous regions such as the eastern Colombian Andes. It will also grow in hot, humid rain forests at much lower elevations. The leaves are not as good from these latter locations, but this is a less important consideration when they are used for a newer economic activity—the production of cocaine.

The Amazon is the second longest river in the world, carrying more water than any other. It runs from the jungles of eastern Peru for some 3900 miles to its mouth at the Atlantic Ocean. Large riverboats and many ocean-going ships with a draft of 14 feet or less can go as far as Iquitos, Peru, where they still transport all the heavy cargo for that jungle city.

Once There Were Rain Forests

During the first century, tropical rain forests covered 5 billion acres on our planet and represented 12 percent of the land surface. In the last 100 years alone, more than half that forest has been actively destroyed. The deforestation is extensive. According to one study, the size of the deforested areas rose from 78,000 km² in 1978 to 230,000 km² in 1988. By the mid-1990s, the annual deforestation rate was 15,000 km² per year and has continued to rise. In 2002, as we began the new millenium, over 50 million acres of tropical rain forest were lost every year. In Latin America, the Amazon basin alone houses the largest tropical rain forest in the world and contains one-fifth of the earth's freshwater, 20 percent of the world's bird species, and 10 percent of the world's mammals. More than 20 percent of the planet's oxygen is produced by the trees and plants in the area. Yet, as noted in Chapter 14, on Brazil, 14% of the rain forest has disappeared in a recent 10-year period. This trend has not decreased.

In 1964, a military government staged a coup and displaced the civilian government in Brazil. During their two decades in power, the development-minded military leadership built the Trans-Amazon Highway and embarked on a policy of exploiting the resources in the Amazon basin and encouraging settlement. During the 1960s, Peru's civilian president, Fernando Belaunde Terry, tried a similar developmentalist strategy for Peru's jungle area that lay on the eastern side of the Andes. However, most of the Peruvian settlers found the jungle's "green wall"[3] much more impenetrable than did their Brazilian counterparts. In Brazil, the migration into the Amazon was enormous. In 1960, there were 2.5 million people living in Brazil's six Amazon states. By the early 1990s, the population had grown to 10 million and continues to grow today. There are more than 18 million landless people in Brazil.

Rain forest in Costa Rica. *(Photo by Patrice Olsen)*

Thousands of landless peasants, rural workers, urban slum dwellers, entrepreneurs, and well-heeled Brazilian and foreign businesspeople arrived each day to see how they could carve a fortune from the land and resources in the forest. The land is often crudely torn open to search for gold, iron ore, or other minerals in places like the huge open-pit gold mine at Serra Pelada. Indigenous populations like the Yanomami are pushed farther into the jungle and even shot if they resist the encroachment on their ancesteral lands. When other local inhabitants, like rubber tapper Chico Mendes, try to resist the brutal destruction of the rain forest, they are often bullied by local officials, *fazenderos* (large landowners), or their hired henchmen or, as was Mendes's fate, assassinated.

The rain forest problem in Brazil alone is enormous. In 1998, the Brazilian government released figures indicating that destruction of the Amazon rain forest reached record levels in the mid-1990s. In 1994 and 1995, for example, an area larger than the state of New Jersey (7836 square miles) was destroyed. Indeed, according to a satellite imaging study by Brazil's National Institute of Space Research, 7010 square miles of Amazon rain forest were lost in 2001, and the figure increased to 9840 square miles in 2002. Not only is the rain forest cut down, but in classical slash-and-burn fashion, the vegetation is burned to prepare the land for agriculture or pasture. This means that not only are thousands of oxygen-producing trees lost every year, but enormous amounts of carbon dioxide are released into the atmosphere when the biomass is burned. This process is also accelerating in Central America and the rain forest in southern Mexico. Since 1960 almost 50 percent of Central American forests have been destroyed. Environmentalists see the resultant drastic reduction in oxygen production and dramatic increase in carbon dioxide as significant causal factors in the greenhouse effect linked to global warming.

As Latin America strives to develop and as its population grows, its ecosystems are put under increasing stress. In Haiti, the ecosystem has suffered severe stress because of the intense population density. Most of the trees have been cut down for building materials and firewood, and the number of birds throughout the region and other dependent species has been reduced drastically. In Haiti and elsewhere, the commercialization of agriculture, demographic pressure, and policies that favor large commercial producers over small peasant farmers are also combining to increase land degradation. This set the stage for a huge loss of life as rain and mud flowed uncontrolled down the hills and into heavily populated areas when a hurricane swept across Haiti in 2004. Deforestation, overgrazing, and overexploitation of the land are endangering entire ecosystems throughout the region. Desertification is advancing. It has been estimated that desertification and deforestation alone have affected about one-fifth of Latin America. As of 1995, some 200 million hectares of land—almost a third of the total vegetated land—were moderately or severely degraded.

The People

Latin America is endowed with enormous human resources. Its 580 million people come from all corners of the globe and are rich in their diversity and skills. Fertility rates are high in Latin America, and population growth rates have been some of the highest in the world. Currently, these rates have declined to about 2 percent per year. Even at this rate, the population will double approximately every 35 years.

The original inhabitants of the region crossed to the Western Hemisphere on the Bering land and ice bridge that once united Asia and North America. This happened some 20,000–35,000 years ago during the Ice Age. The Asian migration flowed into North America and then spread into the Caribbean and through Central America to South America. Varied indigenous civilizations grew up throughout the region. By the time the Spaniards and Portuguese arrived in the late 1400s and early 1500s, at least 50 million indigenous people lived in the region (some estimates are more than double this figure). Population concentrations included the Aztec civilization in Central Mexico, the Maya civilization in southern Mexico and northern Central America, and the Incan Empire in the west coast central Andean region in South America. Other groupings could be found throughout the region, including the Caribs, Taínos/Arawaks, Guaraní, and Araucanian. These peoples and their civilizations will be discussed more fully in the following chapter.

The Spanish and Portuguese were the first Europeans to arrive in Latin America. As they came in ever-increasing numbers, they began to populate the region as well. Informal and formal unions between Iberian men and indigenous women soon produced offspring, who came to be known as *mestizos*. Later, as the Amero-Indian population was drastically decimated and additional inexpensive labor was needed, Africans were brought to the hemisphere as enslaved peoples. At least 7 million survived the Middle Passage from western and southern Africa to Latin America and the Caribbean. The culture, religion, and cuisine they brought with them would forever change the face of the societies they helped to form. Indians, Europeans, and Africans populated Latin America during the first centuries. The fact that early Spaniards and Portuguese came without their families and claimed access to women in subordinate positions began a process of racial melding that continues to the present day. These pairings and their children were thrown together in dynamic new societies. *Mestizos, mulattos,* and *zambos* (the children of unions between Indians and Africans) appeared in growing numbers.

Most Latin Americans trace their ancestry to Amero-Indian, Iberian, and/or African sources. However, by the middle of the nineteenth century, there was a general realization that new laborers, artisans, and those with other skills could add to the growing nations. Most nations had outlawed slavery by the time of the Civil War in the United States. Brazil was the last; slavery was outlawed there in 1888. Thus, other sources of abundant and inexpensive labor were often needed. Chinese laborers were brought into Peru in the latter part of the nineteenth century. Thousands of Italians were lured to Argentina and southern Brazil to supply the labor for the growing agricultural and industrial production. Workers and indentured servants from India and the Chinese mainland were brought to the British Caribbean and British South America. Many Europeans came to their colonies or former colonies or from other nations to make their way in these new societies. French, Germans, Swedes, Irish, Poles, and others from Europe arrived on Latin American shores to make a better life or as refugees from famine, war, and revolution. European Jews came to seek opportunity and escape pogroms and persecution. Japanese came to southern Brazil and to other countries like Peru for better opportunities, often with their passages paid by the Japanese government (which wanted to alleviate population pressures on the home islands). Turks and Arabs came to explore new horizons. As the United States expanded its economic sphere into Latin America and the Caribbean, some U.S. citizens chose to stay in the lands where they went to make their fortunes. One, an early aviator who came to Peru, stayed to found what was that nation's best-known private airline, Faucett. The Spanish Civil War and World War II began a new wave of immigration from Spain and other countries taken over by the Fascists. Many Jews and others targeted by the Nazis owe their lives to the liberal immigration and visa policies of Latin American nations. (Ironically, as World War II was ending, Nazis, Fascists, and accused war criminals were often able to take advantage of these same liberal immigration policies and Argentine neutrality during World War II to make their way to countries like Argentina and Paraguay.) Today, new immigrants from Eastern Europe and elsewhere continue to arrive, to make their places in these dynamic new societies.

The Land

When the first Europeans arrived in the Western Hemisphere, they found abundant land and resources. Most of the native peoples incorporated the concept of the Andean earth mother *Pachamama*, the giver of all life. The land was a sacred trust, to be used with respect and care, and was not the property of any one person. Land either existed in a state of nature or was used or owned collectively by and for the whole community. It was never to be harmed or destroyed and always to be used for the benefit of all creatures. Thus, the native people used but did not abuse the land. Early reports suggest that food was in abundance and generally well distributed to the entire population.

The regime that the Iberians brought was far different. The crown, not the earth mother, was sovereign. Lands that had been inhabited by native peoples for thousands of years were unhesitatingly claimed for Spain and Portugal. Those who had been living on the land and working it were thought to have only those rights granted by the crown. Europeanization had begun. Hereafter, the land was to be used, owned, and abused for the benefit of the crown or its subjects. The native peoples, their needs, and their descendants were and would continue to be secondary and subordinate. The land and the people who lived in harmony with it would no longer be respected. There were empires to be carved and fortunes to be made.

At the time of the conquest, Spain and Portugal were very much dominated by feudal institutions. The landowning system was no exception. Both countries were dominated by huge feudal estates and powerful landlords. The peasants were poor and subordinate. This would be the basis of the system brought to the newly conquered lands. Initially, the Spanish and Portuguese monarchs gave huge land grants and grants to use the native peoples in a specific area. The *mercedes* (land grants, *sesmarias* in Brazil) and *encomiendas* (right to use the native peoples and the land on which they lived as long as the *encomendero* took responsibility for Christianizing them) were given to the *conquistadores* and others to whom the crown owed favors or debts. Thus, Europeans soon established domain over huge stretches of land and the people who lived on them. These initial grants were later turned into large landed estates, or *latifundios*, which were not too different from the huge feudal landed estates in the Iberian peninsula. Often ranging for hundreds of thousands of acres, they were frequently larger than whole counties. They were ruled over by the *patrón* and his family, who were the undisputed masters. The lowly *peon* was like a feudal serf and had little, if any, power or recourse, even after protective laws had been enacted. From colonial time to the present, the land tenure system reflected the nature and power configuration of the whole society. Well into the twentieth century the subordinate status of the peasant and agricultural laborer was maintained. Vestiges of this system were still in evidence in the 1970s. In many areas, the humble *campesino* was expected to approach the *patrón* with eyes cast down, bowing and scraping. As late as the 1960s, there were still instances of what had become a widespread practice in colonial times: *primera noche/prima nocta*, the landlord's right to spend the first night with newly married women on his estate.

In time, many of the *latifundios* were divided or otherwise changed and became modern-day large landholdings: *haciendas, fazendas* (in Brazil), and *estancias* (in Argentina). Still owned by one family and comprising hundreds, if not thousands, of hectares (1 hectare = 2.47 acres), these farms still control a disproportionate amount of the land and resources in the countryside. Their continued existence attests to the concentrated nature of land ownership in Latin America. Currently, land is also being concentrated in large commercial farms, including land used for sugar cane and other ethanol-producing crops.

The original indigenous population and later the *mestizos*, Africans, mulattos, *zambos*, and Europeans who became *campesinos* (anyone who owns or has control over the small or medium-sized land parcels they work) were left with the rest. Their holdings were never large and were further reduced by division through inheritance, illegal takings by large landowners, or the need to sell off part of the land to survive. The resulting small landholdings, or *minifundios*, were and are the most common type of agricultural unit. Comprising less than 10 hectares (24.71 acres), these small family farms afford a meager living during good times and near starvation during bad. In Colombia, traditionally they accounted for 73 percent of the farms, yet they covered only 7.2 percent of the agricultural area. In Ecuador in 1954, 0.04 percent of the landholdings accounted for 45.2 percent of the farmland; in contrast, the *minifundios* comprised 73 percent of the landholdings but only 7 percent of the land. In Guatemala, per the 1979 agrarian census, less than one-tenth of 1 percent of the landholdings comprised 22 percent of the land, while the largest 2 percent of the farms had 65 percent of the land. In El Salvador in 1971, 4 percent of the landowners (the *latifundistas*) owned 64 percent of the land, and 63 percent of the landowners (the *minifundistas* and *microfundistas*) had only 8 percent of the land. At the beginning of the 1980s, 40.9 percent of rural families were landless altogether; and land concentration is still continuing in many areas. In Brazil, 70 percent of the rural population did not own any land at all, but 1 percent of the country's farms (*fazendas*) occupied 43 percent of the arable land in the 1950s. This inequity continued and later engendered a growing movement of the Sem Terra—the Landless—in the 1980s. Their occupations of unused land have often met with brutal repression by local authorities and the *fazendero's* hired gunmen (see Table 2). The conflict was so intense that some 1600 Brazilians have been killed in land disputes since 1985.

TABLE 2. *Minifundios* and *Latifundios* in Select Countries: Traditional Landholding Patterns, 1970

	Minifundios		*Latifundios*	
	% of Farms	% of Land	% of Farms	% of Land
Argentina	43.2	3.4	0.8	36.9
Brazil	22.5	0.5	4.7	59.5
Colombia	64.0	4.9	1.3	49.5
Chile	36.9	0.2	6.9	81.3
Ecuador	89.9	16.6	0.4	45.1
Guatemala	88.4	14.3	0.1	40.8
Peru	88.0	7.4	1.1	82.4

Source: Michael Todaro, *Economic Development in the Third World.* 2nd ed. New York: Longman, 1985, p. 295.

The process of the fractionalization of small holdings has continued. The *microfundio*, a very small farm of less than two hectares, is unable to sustain a family. The food and income from this small holding must be supplemented by income from outside labor by one or more family members. The capitalization and commercialization of agriculture have put even greater stress on the *microfundistas* and many of the *minifundistas*. The reduction in demand for rural labor has forced many to abandon their holdings and flee to the cities in hope of better opportunities. In recent times, large-scale agricultural production has undergone a transformation. The heavy reliance on cheap labor and abundant land in the absence of mechanization is rapidly giving way to more capital-intensive production that relies on mechanization and more intensive use of irrigation (where necessary), chemical fertilizers, and the application of insecticides by aerial spraying. As has been the case in U.S. agriculture, land is also in the process of being consolidated into larger units that can most benefit from the efficiencies of large-scale production. This has signaled a move from the traditional agricultural economy to an integrated capitalist mode of production.[4] The large plantations and commercial farms devote more and more of their production to cash crops that are sold on the world market, while the production of basic foodstuffs for local consumption more frequently occurs on the small farms. Not surprisingly, the production of corn and grains for local consumption is decreasing amidst growing malnutrition. Fewer of the poor have the funds to augment their consumption of staples. Groups such as OxFam, Bread for the World, and Food First have noted the decrease in protein consumption among the poor with increasing alarm. More and more land is being used for the production of beef for export, yet few of the poor are able to afford beef or other meats more than a few times a year.

Although Latin America is industrializing and urbanizing at an amazing rate, agriculture is still very important. In 1990, agriculture still accounted for 40 percent of the exports for the region. The capitalization and commercialization of agriculture that have buttressed the consolidation and reconcentration of the land have radically decreased opportunities for labor and sharecropping in the countryside. Thirty-nine percent of the rural population in Brazil is now landless. There is also a high incidence of landlessness in Colombia, Ecuador, Guatemala, and Peru. Consequently, there are fewer opportunities for peasants and landless laborers to sustain themselves. Currently, more than 60 percent of the rural population live in poverty. Global economic forces are driving people off the land in record numbers. In Brazil, many flee to the Amazon region to mine gold or engage in a cycle of slash-and-burn agriculture that pushes them ever farther into the virgin rain forest. More generally, new rural refugees flock to the cities, where they try to establish themselves in the growing shantytowns that ring large urban centers.

The Cities Explode: Urbanization

Latin America is no longer the land of sleepy peasants and small villages. It has changed dramatically. Some three-quarters of the population now live in urban areas (see Table 1) compared to 41.6 percent in 1950. There are three cities in Latin America that are now larger than New York City. Mexico City alone has some 22 million people and is the largest city in the world. São Paulo, Brazil, has 18 million and is the third largest city in the world, and Buenos Aires, the capital of Argentina, has more than 12 million. By 1990 Latin America had forty cities with 1 million or more inhabitants. This was more than Canada and the United States combined. More than 140 million Latin Americans live in these modern megalopolises compared to fewer than 100 million in the United States. Urban areas in Latin America continue to explode with new people as more children are born and as millions flock to the bright city lights each year. Municipal services can in no way keep up with the steady stream of new arrivals. The streets are clogged with all types of vehicular traffic, and the air is polluted by thousands of cars, trucks, and buses. Mexico City has some of the most polluted air in the world. Oxygen is sold at booths on the street. Thousands suffer and many die from pollution-induced respiratory problems. Mexico City is immense and unmanageable. The quality of life for all too many of its residents is marginal. Nor is it easy to escape. It can take more than 2 hours to traverse it. São Paulo suffers from similar problems and has a very high crime rate. Other cities seem headed in this direction. As the growing middle class exercises its consumers' right to own private vehicles, gridlock is the norm in rush hour and parking is often near impossible. The impoverished masses endure long hours on crowded buses and vans. The congestion is sometimes alleviated by subways, but they rarely cover more than a few areas of the city and cannot keep up with the growing number of new neighborhoods and urban squatter settlements.

Often, a third or more of the population in the large cities live in slums and shantytowns. Of the 18 million people in greater São Paulo, close to 8 million live in the *favelas*, as the urban slums are called in Brazil. Because many of these new agglomerations often grow up quickly as unused land is illegally occupied, city services are often minimal or unavailable altogether. Living conditions are frequently horrible, with no running water, sewer, or trash collection (see Table 7 in Chapter 5). Sometimes the only electricity is provided by illegal taps to lines that run close to the neighborhood. Crime and violence are often at uncontrollable levels. Little, if any, police protection is available in most of the larger slums, and poor neighborhoods are often infiltrated by drug gangs and other types of organized crime. The rapidly growing Mara Salvatrucha and M 18 gangs control entire neighborhoods throughout El Salvador, Guatemala, and Honduras. Gangs often assert de facto control of specific slum neighborhoods, and the police are often reticent to enter unless in a concerted, massive action led by heavily armed special police. (See the Brazilian film *Tropa de Elite* for graphic depictions.) Slum areas are referred to as *barriadas, colonias, pueblos jovenes, villas de miseria,* or *tugurvios* in different Spanish-speaking countries and as *favelas* or *mocambos* in Brazil. They continue to grow dramatically. In these places, there is an abundance of misery and drugs, while hope is often in short supply.

Originally, towns in Spanish America were planned around gracious central plazas, often called the *Plaza de Armas* or *Zócalo.* Here, one would find a pleasant plaza with the church or cathedral, government buildings, and the palaces of prominent officials ringing it. Others of means and social standing would occupy neighborhoods adjacent to the center. The outskirts of the cities were reserved for the poor and marginalized. However, the once-majestic colonial centers are now generally overwhelmed with traffic problems and pollution. Towns in Portuguese America were not always planned affairs; often, they grew up around a fort or business center and then just grew. In all of Latin America, the worst slums are still generally found on the periphery of the cities, although poor neighborhoods and scattered makeshift dwellings can also be found inside traditional cities, as is the case in Rio de Janeiro. Many of the wealthy and upper middle class have also begun to flee the centers to populate more removed, attractive, exclusive neighborhoods characterized by high-walled, luxurious houses and high-rise condominiums staffed by numerous servants and well-armed private guards and with easy access to the newest in Latin American consumerism—the mall. Suburban-style *urbanizaciones* are also being constructed to cater to the housing needs of the rest of the growing middle class, which is also flocking to shopping centers and malls in growing numbers. The contrast between the lives of the urban poor and their middle- and upper-class fellow urbanites becomes ever more stark each day and has increased in much of the region with the turn to neoliberal economics.

Ironically, many are afraid to shop outside of the privately guarded malls and shopping centers. Fed by deteriorating socioeconomic conditions for the poor, urban crime and delinquency have grown dramatically in recent years. One can see the homeless and the hustlers living and sleeping on the streets in most of the major cities. Many middle- and upper-class drivers are even afraid to stop at traffic lights—particularly at night—in many areas for fear they will be robbed at knife- or gunpoint or even by street children who threaten with broken shards of glass. Sometimes the merchants and the police take matters into their own hands. Brazil in particular has become infamous for the way street children have been beaten, run off, and even killed in groups to clear the area and discourage their perceived criminal activity. Some 5 percent of Brazil's children live in the streets. Of these, more than 4000 were murdered between 1988 and 1991. Even Charles Dickens's impoverished souls would find life hard in the modern Latin American city.

Throughout Latin American society crime and violence are growing. Economic and social disparities, the suffering caused by International Monetary Fund–dictated economic adjustments and austerity, the ravages of globalization, a brand of free

Mexico City, 2000 *(Photo by Patrice Olsen)*

market economic policy called "neoliberalism" (see Chapter 7), narco trafficking, and the fallout from the guerrilla wars that have raged throughout the region all add to the general level of violence, which is now very high. For instance, El Salvador has one of the highest murder rates in the world at 55 per 100,000 per annum. Colombia was once higher at 80 murders per 100,000, while Brazil has 20 per 100,000. The cost in human suffering and lives is horrendous, and the economic cost is staggering. In 1998, the head of the Inter-American Development Bank reported that violence cost the region about $168 billion per year, or 14.2 percent of the regional economic product. Just in Brazil, the cost was $84 billion, or 10.5 percent of the gross domestic product. The figure for Colombia was 24.7 percent. Nor is Central America immune to the growing crime rates. Violent crime increased by 14 percent in the first half of 2004 alone in Guatemala. Throughout northern Central America violent street gangs, or *maras*, are on the rise. They got their start when thousands of Salvadoran and other street gang members from Los Angeles and elsewhere in the United States lost their residency because of criminal convictions and were deported to their home countries. Gang activity has been so virulent in El Salvador, Honduras and even Guatemala that their governments have engaged in heavy-handed, often violent crackdowns on the Mara Salvatrucha, M 18, and other gangs. Yet neither the police nor judicial authorities are able to stop the rapid growth of gangs (*maras*) in El Salvador, Guatemala , and Honduras, where they may include as many as 100,000 members. Also on the increase are violent kidnappings and car jackings in Mexico, Colombia, and elsewhere. The resultant personal insecurity and added economic expense weigh heavily on the region's future and cloud its growing dynamism. Crime and measures to combat it are consuming more of the region's gross national product (GNP) and slowing development. Many are now fleeing the cities to heavily guarded high-rises or gated suburban communities, or leaving their countries completely. More and more of the upper and middle class live in fear of their own countrymen and try to isolate themselves from the masses. There is a growing flow of refugees from gang persecution in Central America. The problem, and its causes, will need to be addressed before the region can realize its full potential.

Yet, the growing personal insecurity and environmental degradation that the region is suffering would seem to contradict an essential tenet of Latin American life—*Hay que gozar de la vida*, life is to be enjoyed. Many Latin Americans note that North Americans (meaning those who are from the United States) live to work and worry much too much about things. In contrast, Latin Americans work to live and *no se preocupan tanto*—do not worry so much. Whenever there is a bare modicum of economic security—and sometimes even when there is not—they live very well indeed. Life is an enjoyable experience to be savored. One rarely turns down an invitation to a social gathering and frequently enthusiastically dances till dawn at a *fiesta*. Of those with any means, it is common practice to stop for a coffee or lunch with friends and family, and most business meetings begin with a *cafecito* and talk of family and friends. Indeed, work is generally not the all-consuming activity it has become in the United States, Japan, and parts of Western Europe. However, when the pollution from the street makes it difficult to sit in sidewalk cafés and the frequency of attacks on nocturnal travelers makes it dangerous to go out at night, the very essence of Latin American existence is challenged. Many are even afraid to leave their houses unattended or in the hands of poorly paid servants because of the frequent break-ins and house takeovers. In countries like Colombia, Guatemala, and El Salvador and in cities like Mexico City, any person of means or position must also live in fear of kidnapping for ransom. Thus, rapid urbanization, industrialization, and the persistence of unresolved social and economic problems such as high unemployment, exploitation, and economic injustice have combined with rapid social and cultural change to produce conditions that threaten the very essence of the Latin American lifestyle. Yet, the indomitable Latin American spirit and passion for life propel "the continent" ever onward.

Notes

1. *Latin* here refers to modern languages that were derived from classical Latin: Spanish, Portuguese, and French in this case. Haiti is included as part of the region (indeed, it was the first country to gain independence—in 1804) and receives its fair share of attention and interest. Those areas still under French colonial rule receive much less attention. French colonies in Latin America include the Caribbean islands of Martinique, Guadeloupe, Saint Martin,

and Saint Pierre and Miquelon as well as French Guiana (site of Devil's Island) on the South American continent.

2. Although we will generally not include those areas that do not speak Spanish, Portuguese, or French in our study, it should be noted that the English-speaking part of the region includes not only Belize in Central America and Guyana in South America but also the Caribbean countries of the Bahamas, Barbados, Dominica, Grenada, Jamaica, Saint Kitts-Nevis, Saint Lucia, Saint Vincent and the Grenadines, and Trinidad and Tobago; English-speaking territories include Anguilla, Bermuda, Cayman Islands, Falkland Islands (which Argentina claims as Islas Malvinas), Montserrat, Turks and Caicos Islands, British Virgin Islands, and U.S. Virgin Islands. Dutch is spoken in the South American nation of Suriname and in the Caribbean Dutch islands of Aruba, Curaçao, Bonaire, Saba, Saint Eustatius, and Saint Maarten.

3. See the award-winning 1970 Peruvian film *La Muralla Verde* (written, produced, and directed by Armando Robles Godoy with Mario Robles Godoy) for a graphic depiction of the struggle with the jungle.

4. Because of the feudal nature of the original *latifundio* system and the way many small producers were primarily subsistence farmers who sold little, if any, of their production for the world market, many spoke of a dual rural economy with aspects of both feudal and capitalist modes of production. The integration into the capitalist world system that authors like Andre Gunder Frank emphasized in his *Capitalism and Underdevelopment in Latin America* (1967) has now become almost universal as the large farmers and plantations become ever more oriented to the production of cash crops for export and more and more of the smaller farmers are forced to sell their labor in the globalized national economy in order to survive.

Bibliography

Black, Jan Knippers, ed. *Latin America, Its Problems and Promise.* 4th ed. Boulder, CO: Westview Press, 2005.

Blouet, Brian W., and Olwyn M. Blouet. *Latin America and the Caribbean: A Systematic and Regional Survey.* 4th ed. New York: John Wiley and Sons, 2004.

Burch, Joann J. *Chico Mendes, Defender of the Rain Forest.* Brookfield, CT: Millbrook Press, 1994.

Dimenstein, Gilberto. *Brazil: War on Children.* London: Latin American Bureau, 1991.

Elkin, Judith. *The Jews of Latin America.* New York: Holmes and Meir, 1997.

Frank, Andre Gunder. *Capitalism and Underdevelopment in Latin America.* New York: Monthly Review, 1967.

Garrett, James L., ed. *A 2020 Vision for Food, Agriculture, and the Environment in Latin America.* Washington, DC: International Food Policy Research Institute, 1995.

Haralambous, Sappho, ed. *The State of World Rural Poverty: A Profile of Latin America and the Caribbean.* Rome: International Fund for Agricultural Development, 1993.

Hillman, Richard, ed. *Understanding Contemporary Latin America.* 3rd ed. Boulder, CO: Lynne Rienner, 2005.

Janvry, Alain de. *The Agrarian Question and Reformism in Latin America.* Baltimore: Johns Hopkins University Press, 1981.

Klich, Ignacio, and Jeffrey Lesser. *Arab and Jewish Immigrants in Latin America: Images and Realities.* London: F. Cass, 1998.

Levine, Robert. *Tropical Diaspora: the Jewish Experience in Cuba.* Gainesville: University Press of Florida, 1993.

Page, Joseph A. *The Brazilians.* New York: Addison-Wesley, 1995.

Place, Susan E., ed. *Tropical Rainforests: Latin American Nature and Society in Transition.* Revised and updated ed. Wilmington, DE: Scholarly Resources, 2001.

Preston, David, ed. *Latin American Development: Geographical Perspectives.* 2nd ed. Harlow, G.B.: Longman, 1996.

Rifkin, Jeremy. *Biosphere Politics: A New Consciousness for a New Century*. New York: Crown Publishers, 1991.

Skole, D. L., and C. J. Tucker. "Tropical Deforestation, Fragmented Habitat, and Adversely Affected Habitat in the Brazilian Amazon: 1978–1988." *Science* 260 (1993): 1905–1910.

Trigo, Eduardo J. *Agriculture, Technological Change, and the Environment in Latin America: A 2020 Perspective*. Washington, DC: International Food Policy Research Institute, 1995.

Vandermeer, John, and Ivette Perfecto. *Breakfast of Biodiversity: The Truth about Rainforest Destruction*. Oakland, CA: Food First, 1995.

Vasconcelos, José. *The Cosmic Race: A Bilingual Edition*. Baltimore: Johns Hopkins University Press, 1997.

FILMS AND VIDEOS

Bye, Bye Brazil. Brazil, 1980. A madcap introduction to Brazil.

Cidade de Deus/City of God. Brazil, 2003. Modern classic on (very) violent gang activity in largest slum in Rio de Janeiro.

Like Water for Chocolate. Mexico, 1992. Excellent portrait of Mexican family, food, and the daughter who stays at home to care for her mother.

Mexican Bus Ride. Mexico, 1951. Classic film by Spanish director Luis Buñuel on Mexico, life in Latin America, and the institution of the bus in Mexico and Latin America.

La Muralla Verde/The Green Wall. Peru, 1970 (video, 1990). An excellent film about a young Lima family that fights the bureaucracy and the jungle's green wall to colonize the Peruvian Amazon.

Pejote. Brazil, 1981. Gives a glimpse of the life of street children in a large Brazilian city. For more general city life, *Central Station*, Brazil, 1998.

Tropa da Elite Brazil, 2007. Graphically depicts how an elite police unit in Rio de Janeiro operates in the city's slums.

WEB SITES

http://lanic.utexas./edu Latin American Center Homepage, University of Texas.
www.blueplanetbiomes.org On rain forests in the Amazon.

DISPUTED BY
ENGLAND, RUSSIA
AND SPAIN

NEW
FRANCE

ENGLISH COLONIES

EFFECTIVE FRONTIER
OF SPANISH
SETTLEMENT

VICEROYALTY OF
NEW SPAIN

FLORIDA
Ceded to England.
1763–1783

ATLANTIC
OCEAN

Guadalajara •   • Mexico City

HAITI
(SAINT DOMINGUE)
Ceded to France, 1697

Guatemala •

JAMAICA
Conquered by
England, 1655

Santo
Domingo

Caracas •

VICEROYALTY OF
NEW GRANADA

Bogotá •

GUIANA

Separated from
Viceroyalty of Peru,
1717, 1739

Quito •

VICEROYALTY OF
PERU

VICEROYALTY OF
BRAZIL

Pernambuco •

PACIFIC
OCEAN

Lima •   • Cusco

Chuquisaca
La Plata; Sucre)
•

Salvador
(Bahia) •

Sao Paulo •

Rio de Janeiro
(Capital, 1763) •

VICEROYALTY
OF LA PLATA

Santiago •

Separated from
Viceroyalty of Peru,
1776

Map of
**COLONIAL
LATIN AMERICA**

N

W   E

S

0   500   1000 Miles

AUDIENCIA OF CHILE
Retained by
Viceroyalty of Peru,
1776

ANDES MTS.

Buenos
Aires •

CLAIMED BUT
NOT SETTLED
BY SPAIN

TWO

EARLY HISTORY

For many years, people in the Western Hemisphere have widely celebrated Columbus' 1492 "discovery" of what the Europeans called the "New World." Accordingly, Columbus Day is celebrated as a national holiday in the United States. More broadly, throughout the Americas, the year 1992 was celebrated as the 500th anniversary of the discovery of the "Americas"; but not all celebrated. Many native Americans banded together to solemnly mark the same period as 500 years of mourning because of the many injustices that the European invasion wrought on their people. Indeed, in the first 100 years of colonization, European rule attacked native religion and culture, razed temples and cultural centers to the ground, and forbade the practice of native religions. In so doing, the colonists attacked the very essence of the original Americans, called "Indians" because Columbus and the original explorers mistakenly believed they had reached the East Indies. Colonization was, as the French Antillean author Frantz Fanon suggests, a brutal, violent imposition of European on native. The effect of European rule was so devastating to the native peoples of Latin America that their numbers were reduced by as much as 90 percent during the first 100 years of European occupation.

There are several versions of how the Iberians treated the native people they encountered. The indigenous version is one of conquest, domination, and subordination. Yet, Spain maintained that it brought Christianity and Western civilization to the world it found. In contrast, England long propagated the Black Legend about the cruelties of Spanish colonial rule in the Americas and attributed much of the native population's decline to the barbarities they suffered at the hands of the Spaniards. Another explanation of this precipitous decline is found in several recent studies that make an ever stronger case for the disease theory of population decline—that is, the main cause of the radical decline in population of the original Americans was not the undeniable cruelty practiced by many of the Spaniards but the unstoppable epidemics of smallpox, measles, typhus, and other diseases that swept through the native population. The first Americans had not, it seems, acquired any natural immunity to these and other diseases the Europeans brought with them. Thus, they were ravaged by them. Many also argue this was the principal factor in the Spaniards' astounding conquest of millions of people with a few hundred *conquistadores*. Indeed, the diseases often spread so rapidly that they arrived before the Spaniards. Evaluating these different perspectives, one might conclude that the story does indeed sometimes change over time but that each new version adds to our understanding of the past. Not surprisingly, then, we find that our historical views of what happened in the sixteenth century are heavily colored not only by the cruelty that gave rise to the Black Legend but also by our present understanding of epidemiology.

People in the Americas before the Conquest

To understand the historical context in which political power is exercised in Latin America, we need to briefly trace the human past as it developed in the Americas. Human history did not begin when Europeans began arriving in the Western Hemisphere in large numbers after 1492. Indeed, the common ancestry of all racial groups who found their way to the Americas was neither European nor Asian. Currently, it is believed that the earliest humans emerged on the shores of Lake Victoria in East Africa some 3 million years ago. The famous Leakey family of anthropologists' discovery of tools and bone fragments from our most ancient human predecessors suggests an African birthplace of our species. From there, it is believed, humans spread south in Africa and north to the Middle East, Asia, and eventually Europe. Later, they crossed the land and ice bridge that spanned the Bering Strait during the Ice Age to move into the Americas.

Indigenous Civilization

The movement of peoples from Asia to North America occurred in waves and began as early as 40,000 years ago. It continued until about 8000 B.C.E. These immigrants first populated the Western Hemisphere and were the first Americans. They swept down from Alaska and spread across North America and into the Caribbean and Central America; from there they spread down the west coast of South America and then eastward across the continent. As their productive forces increased, they moved from a nomadic existence to one of sedentary agriculture. By 1500 B.C.E., there were villages of full-time farmers. Corn, beans, and squash became staples in Mesoamerica (the southern two-thirds of Mexico, all of Guatemala, and most of El Salvador, Belize, Honduras, and Nicaragua), while potatoes, manioc, and amaranth were dominant in areas of South America. The large numbers of different ethnic groups practiced sedentary or semi-sedentary agriculture. As they further developed their productivity, they formed larger groups: tribes, chiefdoms, and states. This also led to more concentrated political power.

Native American settlements were scattered throughout the region. The population did, however, become concentrated in three areas: present-day central Mexico, southern Mexico, and northern Central America; along the Pacific Coast; and in the Andean highlands in what is now Peru, Bolivia, and Ecuador. Here, agricultural production was sufficiently advanced to sustain a large, relatively concentrated population. Each of these areas eventually developed a dominant, centralized state civilization that came to be known, respectively, as Aztec, Mayan, and Incan. Smaller political groupings developed elsewhere.

Many aspects of these empires have influenced the culture and even the political organization of subsequent polities in these areas. In that little about these civilizations is usually included in most general courses, the following section presents a rudimentary description of their key aspects.

Large draft or meat animals that could be domesticated were not available to the native civilizations. In the west coast civilization in South America, the guinea pig was domesticated as a source of food and the llama was used as a pack animal and as a source of wool and meat. The Aztecs bred a small mute dog for food in Mexico. Unlike in Europe, there were no cattle, horses, or oxen.

The use of baskets and of stone, bone, and wood gave way to the development of pottery and more sophisticated stone (obsidian) weapons and tools and eventually to the use of bronze in the Aztec and Incan Empires. In the first more developed societies to emerge, such as the Olmecs and Toltecs in Mexico and the Mochica in coastal Peru, large temple-centered cities emerged. They were beautifully designed and employed sophisticated stone and adobe construction. Only in the thirteenth and fourteenth centuries did these city-centered societies begin to expand and form empires. They were still in the process of expansion when the Europeans arrived.

Our knowledge of these societies is incomplete, in part because there were few chronicles and inscriptions in Incan and pre-Incan civilizations on the west coast of South America and because many of the written texts, inscriptions, and chronicles that did exist for the Aztecs and Mayans were destroyed by the Europeans. The story of these peoples is only now being reconstructed through the laborious work of archaeologists and ethnologists from around the world.

The Maya. Mayan civilization flowered between 300 B.C.E. and 1100 C.E. During this time, Europe witnessed the disintegration of the Roman Empire, the rise of the Holy Roman Empire, and the beginning of the Middle Ages. Mayan civilization consisted of a series of city-states that developed in the Petén region of northern Guatemala, the Yucatan, and Chiapas. Their cities later spread into Belize and part of Honduras and eventually numbered about fifty. The Mayans developed what was then a very sophisticated native civilization. Their political–social organization was, however, hierarchical, with a king, nobles, and priests on top and the common people and slaves on the bottom; decision making was authoritarian.

In the original Mayan states, the common people lived in thatched roof huts, not unlike those of the poor Mayan peasants of today, and nourished themselves on a balanced diet consisting of beans, corn, and squash. These crops could be cultivated in the same field. Planting the corn first ensured that it grew upward toward the all-important sun; the beans then used the stalk of the corn to follow the same path, while the broad leaves of the squash spread out on the ground to shade the soil from the desiccating rays of the sun and inhibit the growth of weeds. Further, the beans added nitrogen to the soil as the corn and squash removed it. The Mayan calendar also specified times when the land was to lie fallow. Terraces were used in highland areas to increase land area and stop soil erosion.

It is currently believed that the Mayan peasants paid tribute to the political and religious rulers in the cities. They in turn engaged in warfare with other city-states to gain more riches and obtain additional tribute. They also established extended commercial relations with civilizations to the north and even used the sea as a trade route.

In about 900 C.E., Mayan civilization suffered a rapid decline. The major cities and ceremonial centers were eventually abandoned, to be reclaimed by the jungle. Current research suggests the causes for this disaster were probably the increasing wars among the Mayan states, civil wars, and soil exhaustion from overfarming, which had been induced by what evidently became unsustainable population density.

The Maya's accomplishments in astronomy, mathematics, ideographic writing, architecture, and art and their highly sophisticated calendar mark them as one of the most developed civilizations of their time. They had incorporated advances in timekeeping from the Toltec and Olmec and employed the resultant extremely accurate 365-day calendar of 18 months of 20 days with 5 additional days or "dead" days (which were considered unlucky). Their mathematical system used units of one, five, and twenty (which could be written as dots for ones and dashes for fives, with twenties denoted by position) and included a place value system employing a sign for zero. During their classical period, their calendar, astronomical observations, and use of zero as a place in written numbers marked their civilization as more advanced than any in Europe in these areas. Their hieroglyph-type writing recounted great events in their history and mythology and was carved or painted on their temples, pyramids, or upright stone *stelae* or recorded in their bark paper *codices*. Recent research suggests symbols for syllables were also sometimes used to phonetically sound out words. Although only four of the original glyph codices survived, an early Spanish transcription of the Quiche Mayan creation story, the Popol Vuh, is now part of world literature. Mayan civilization thrived in the classic period from 250 to 900 C.E. in the lowlands in northern Central America and southern Mexico. Great city-state centers like Tikal, Palenque, and Copan flourished.

Although there were occasional female rulers, the societies were patriarchal and the royal succession was decided through primogeniture. The kings and the nobles made up the ruling class but worked closely with the priests, who were also the astronomers and chroniclers as well as the theologians. Human sacrifice and bloodletting were integral parts of the ceremonial functions, with special importance placed on blood derived from puncturing the royal penis. The losers in a version of Mayan soccer were often beheaded or rolled down the steps of the great pyramids after being tied together as human balls.

Postclassical Mayan civilization lived on in the Yucatan centers like Chichén Itzá and Uxmal after other Mayan lands were conquered by the Spaniards beginning in 1527. As had been the case with the Aztecs, much of the remaining Mayan culture was destroyed by the Spanish authorities, who, despite some initial efforts by priests to preserve Mayan culture, eventually burned many invaluable codices as works of the devil, thus depriving the Mayan people of a good part of their history and heritage. Perhaps because of the strength and sophistication of culture, Mayan resistance to European domination lived on in more remote areas for centuries and bubbled to the surface occasionally. The Caste Wars in the Yucatan in the nineteenth century (isolated pockets of rebellion lasted into the twentieth century),

Rising some 45 meters out of the jungle in the Petén region of Guatemala, the Temple of the Jaguar in Tikal is one of the greatest Mayan structures. Apparently used for ceremonial purposes, it dates from the Classical Mayan period and was constructed about 700 A.D. (*Photo by H. Vanden*)

the indigenous support for some guerrilla groups in the Guatemalan highlands in the 1980s, and the Zapatista uprising in Chiapas in the 1990s were more recent manifestations. Mayan languages are still spoken in these areas, and some religious practices are still honored.

The Aztecs. The Aztecs replaced previous native civilizations like that of Teotihuacan and the Toltecs in central Mexico and the Olmecs in eastern Mexico and incorporated many of the values, knowledge, and technology of their predecessors' cultures. By the time Hernán Cortés arrived in central Mexico in 1519, there were perhaps 25 million inhabitants in the region (there is some controversy as to the exact number here and elsewhere in the region). The Aztecs, who migrated from northern Mexico, arrived in the Valley of Mexico in the early 1200s. They were relegated to marshy land not occupied by any other ethnic group. There, they established their capital, Tenochtitlán, on an island in Lake Texcoco about 1325. As their myths explain, they picked the spot because they saw the promised sign of an eagle clutching a snake perched atop a cactus (this symbol graces the Mexican flag).

The Aztec capital became very populous; it had between 150,000 and 200,000 inhabitants by the time of the conquest. As many as 60,000 came to an open-air market each day. Aztec civilization was characterized by military prowess, which extended control beyond the mountains ringing the Valley of Mexico through most of central Mexico and as far south as the Guatemalan border. Once they subjugated other peoples, the Aztecs forced them to pay tribute but did not directly occupy their land save in times of rebellion. Their frequent military campaigns provided many prisoners from the loose-knit empire. Aztec traders and merchants ranged far and wide. The thriving merchant class lived well. There were large houses for the nobility and the priests, palaces for the emperor, monumental limestone-covered pyramids, temples and other public buildings, and thatched roof huts for the commoners. Agriculture and trade provided the economic base for the society, which had also developed a well-respected artisan class. The common people consumed corn, beans, and vegetables garnished with chili sauces as their daily meals. The nobility and emperor had diets that included abundant fowl, venison, and the drink reserved solely for them—chocolate. Aztec civilization excelled in engineering, architecture, astronomy, and mathematics. Based on earlier achievements of the Toltecs and Maya, the Aztecs adopted the same 365-day calendar, divided into 18 months of 20 days, with 5 additional or "hollow" days added. The calendar also marked the beginning and end of religious rituals. A type of pictorial writing had been developed that was linked to some phonic elements and was found in their codices, or paperlike books. They did elaborate metal work in gold and silver but not iron. Like other civilizations in the Americas, the Aztecs had not yet learned how to work hard metals and did not use the wheel, nor, as noted before, had nature provided draft animals or beasts of burden.

Power was concentrated and vertical. The Aztec polity was a hierarchical theocracy headed by an emperor who was assisted by four great lords. Next came the politically powerful priests and nobles. The power of the ruler was not unlike that exercised by Mexican leaders in the last two centuries. The ruler exercised power absolutely and often despotically. The new Aztec emperor was chosen by a tribal council, where priests, state officials, and warriors dominated. He was chosen from among the sons, brothers, or nephews of the previous ruler. When Cortés arrived in 1519 and began to subjugate the Aztecs, Moctezuma II was the ruler. He had succeeded his uncle.

By the late fifteenth century, the number of private estates belonging to the nobles had begun to grow, with the subsequent conversion of small farmers into farm workers and tenant farmers. Slavery was a recognized institution and, as in African society, was used as a punishment for a variety of offenses. There was continuing incentive for the frequent wars and uprisings that occurred within the empire. The continuing conflicts provided an almost constant flow of prisoners, who were sometimes sold as slaves to be used as forced labor but were most often sacrificed in large numbers to Aztec deities like Huitzilopochli, the god of war.

Conflicts within the Aztec Empire hastened its demise. With the help of the Tlaxcalans and other Aztec enemies, the Spaniards (whose numbers never exceeded 600) finally defeated the last Aztec emperor, Cuauhtemoc, in 1521. This signaled the formal end of what had been a great, although autocratic, civilization. When the capital had been stripped of its gold and silver, Cortés ordered the temples burned and the city of Tenochtitlán razed. As a way of legitimizing European rule, orders were given to have Mexico City built on the ruins of the old city. It can be argued, however, that the hierarchical power configurations, brutality of those who ruled, and political patriarchy were part of the legacy that did survive and that they left indelible marks on subsequent society and the polities that emerged in the centuries that followed.

The Incas. The third great pre-Columbian civilization in the Americas at the time of the conquest was the Incan Empire. The Incas date their early development back to the 1200s but did not begin to expand into an empire until the middle of the fifteenth century. This expansion was led by a series of extremely capable rulers. Outstanding among these was Pachacuti Inca Yupanqui (ruler from the late 1400s to 1525), who many consider to be one of the great rulers and conquerors in the annals of history. The empire was centered in the Andes Mountains around the valley of Cuzco in southern Peru and eventually extended from what is now Colombia's southern border for 2250 miles through Ecuador, Peru, and Bolivia into northern Chile and northwest Argentina. At its zenith in the early 1500s, it was tied together by an excellent system of often narrow stone roads, which facilitated communication and troop movement. A system of relay runners could carry messages at the rate of some 150 miles a day. The llama was used as a pack animal, but the wheel was not part of their technology. There was no written language, and history and events were kept by official memorizers. Also employed was the *kipu*, a memory device composed of a handle with cords of different colors attached to it. Knots were tied in the different color strands at different lengths to signify quantity and events.

The land was intensively tilled, and terraces were built in the highlands to improve and expand the fields. The cultivation of a variety of different types of potato (which originated in the Andes) was highly perfected, as was the cultivation of corn. The common people primarily ate potatoes and corn. The latter crop was also collected by the rulers as a form of tribute. A portion of the grain harvest was given to the state to be kept in state storehouses. It was distributed to the elderly, the infirm, and the widowed or to villages in times of famine or natural disaster. Coca leaves (which are still used today), beans, amaranth, and other crops were also grown.

The state was more developed than other pre-Columbian civilizations and ruled by a semidivine hereditary king called the *Inca*. Power was centralized in his hands, and he was assisted by other members of the royal family, the nobility, and the royal administrators, who were responsible for running the far-flung empire. A lesser nobility also existed. The artisans and agriculturists were on the bottom of the social pyramid and lived in humble, adobe-sided, thatched roof huts with simple furnishings. Priests and public officials also received grain from the storehouses, as did those pressed into public labor. The state owned or administered most of the society and could require unpaid labor on roads, other public works, or the land of the *ruler* or estate holders. Writers like the Peruvian indigenist José Carlos Mariátegui have characterized this as a form of state socialism. Even today, there is still a strong communal heritage in the Indian villages in the Andes.

Some have also noted the importance of the collection of tribute in this system and have further suggested that, as was the case in the Aztec Empire, the tradition of tribute made it very easy for the Spaniards to also extract tribute from the indigenous population.

The Incan Empire was administratively divided into four parts, with each part subdivided into provinces. The basic unit was the *ayllu*, which was organized around the extended family. Villages were formed by a collection of *ayllus*, and a grouping of these was ruled over by a *curaca*, or ethnic lord.

Like their Mayan and Aztec counterparts, the Incas had a developed theological system. They had a pantheon of gods beginning with Viracocha, the creator, and Inti, the sun god. Also included was Tumi, the god invoked in human sacrifice. They gave special attention to events like the summer solstice, which occasioned great ceremony and feasting. This is still a major festival in the Peruvian highlands.

The Incas excelled in pottery and weaving and had the proficiency to open the skull in a form of brain surgery. Their architecture was impressive and marked by their ability to move huge stones (on wooden rollers) that weighed tons and then carefully cut and fit them together without mortar. The Cuzco fortress of Sacsahuaman is an excellent example of this. In metallurgy they were quite proficient in the production of gold, silver, and copper; and they even made some of their tools from bronze. They did not, however, utilize iron.

Less Centralized Societies. There were many other less centralized native civilizations as well. These societies were based on hunting, gathering, and agriculture. When they did grow foods, they often practiced slash-and-burn agriculture. Their social organization was much more decentralized than that of the Aztecs, Incas, or Maya. Carib (the origin of the word *Caribbean*), Taíno, and other Arawak peoples populated Antilles islands like Hispaniola, Cuba, and Puerto Rico and were the first to have contact with the Spanish explorers. At the time of Colombus' arrival, there were Arawak settlements extending from Florida to the Amazon basin. Also of importance were the Taínos, who were a native people found in Puerto Rico, Cuba, Hispaniola, and elsewhere in the Caribbean. Their treatment by the Europeans and susceptibility to disease caused them to virtually disappear during the first generation after the conquest.

Other less politically centralized groups fared better. The Araucanians of Chile and Argentina offered such spirited and sustained resistance to the European invaders that they were not completely conquered until 1883. Similarly, the Apaches of northern Mexico battled on until the last decades of the nineteenth century.

The Conquest

The first clash of European and native American civilizations occurred when the Spanish explorers and *conquistadores* consolidated their power in the Caribbean in the 1490s and early 1500s. Santo Domingo and later Havana in particular had become major staging areas for expeditions to other areas. Native people in the

Caribbean were rapidly subjugated, and the conquerors looked elsewhere for gold and glory. By the second decade of the sixteenth century, rumors of a rich civilization in central Mexico reached the new colonial rulers in the Caribbean.

Like many of the *conquistadores*, Hernán Cortés was a poor noble, or *hidalgo*, who came to the New World to make his fortune. Commissioned by the colonial authorities to explore the Mexican gulf coast, he led an expedition of 600 men from Cuba to Mexico in 1519. Violating orders established by the governor of Cuba, Cortés landed on the coast and soon made allies with local tribes that had been forced into tributary status by the Aztecs. He was given a resourceful native woman by one of the chiefs. Malinche (Marina), or "la Malinche" as she was called by subsequent generations, became Cortés' translator, advisor, and eventually mistress. Because of this collaboration, she has often been equated with the betrayal of Latin American culture and autonomy and is sometimes seen as a symbol of selling out to outside interests. Others note that a more complex reading of her life reveals her to be a woman trying to survive in a complex time in which both indigenous and European societies cemented relationships through the use of native women.

Cortés sent some of his force back to Cuba for more proper authorization and reinforcements and left other men installed in the newly formed municipality of Vera Cruz on the coast. He then ordered his ships burned and directed his main force toward the Aztec capital. They were greatly aided not only by their horses (which were unknown to the natives), diseases, steel swords, steel armor, guns, and cannons but also by an Aztec myth. Cortés was coming in the year that was foretold for the return of the deposed plumed serpent king Quetzalcóatl. The Spanish leader was seen by the Aztec ruler Moctezuma II as Quetzalcóatl returning to claim his throne, and his arrival was not resisted, although Aztec resistance did spring up once the avaricious nature of the Spaniards became evident and the indecisive Moctezuma was replaced by more aggressive rulers.

Christopher Columbus landed in Central America in 1502 on his fourth voyage to the Americas. After Vasco Nùñez de Balboa crossed the isthmus and discovered the Pacific Ocean in 1513, settlements were set up on the Caribbean side of Panama. They were later used as transit points between the two oceans. On the Pacific coast, Panama City was not founded until 1519. As expeditions went north from Panama into what is now Costa Rica and Nicaragua, no large, centralized civilizations were encountered and the indigenous groups were soon subjugated. By the second decade of the sixteenth century, Cortés was sending expeditions south from Mexico. By this time, the Maya in Central America were not highly organized in city-states, although there were heavily populated areas in Guatemala. Guatemala City, founded in 1524, eventually became the administrative center for the part of Central America north of Panama. From the time of the earliest European arrivals, there were rivalries among different groups and leaders and a great deal of conflict. Indeed, within 2 years of the founding of the cities of Granada and León in present-day Nicaragua, the two centers were engaged in a conflict that might be best described as a civil war. This pattern of behavior has persisted in most of the Central American isthmus to the present.

After reports of the riches of the empire to the south had reached the Spanish settlement in Panama, considerable interest in conquest developed. After going back to Spain for special authorization to colonize the great civilization in South America, Francisco Pizarro sailed from Panama with a band of some 200 *conquistadores*. They landed on the Peruvian coast in 1532. The Incan Empire was then at the height of its territorial expansion and encompassed more than 10 million people. However, it was engaged in civil war. The last *Inca* Huayna Capac had died without naming his successor, and his two sons, Huáscar and Atahualpa, were both competing for the throne. Atahualpa had just captured Huáscar as the Spaniards arrived, but many followers of the latter were still ready to continue the conflict. Pizarro arranged a meeting with the victor in Cajamarca but used the occasion to capture Atahualpa and slaughter many of his surprised followers. Atahualpa ordered the execution of Huáscar lest he mobilize his supporters and soon offered his Spanish captors a surprising ransom to gain his freedom. Realizing the Spaniards' obsession with gold, he offered to buy his freedom by filling the room where he was kept with gold and silver to the height of his raised arm. As pack trains of llamas were bringing the ransom from the far corners of the empire, Atahualpa's cruel captors nonetheless executed him by garrote. From there, Pizarro and his men went on to capture and loot the Incan capital Cuzco, despite the heroic resistance led by the new *Inca*, Manco Copac. By 1535 the empire was, for all intents and purposes, under Spanish control.

How Could They Do It?

One question remains unresolved: How could a few hundred Spaniards conquer empires of millions? One reason would surely be the indomitable Spanish spirit forged in the crucible of Iberian culture, where for centuries men had symbolically pitted themselves against huge bulls and reveled in the seemingly impossible victory. It is difficult to explain all the reasons for the ease of the conquest, but authors like Benjamin Keen note some of the following:

1. The Spaniards and Portuguese had honed their fighting and tactical skills in the 700-year reconquest of the Iberian peninsula from the Moors.
2. The Spaniards came outfitted as the soldiers of the great power of the time and enjoyed the latest in military armament and technology: steel swords and armor from foundries like those in Toledo, guns and cannons, horses, cavalries, and huge attack dogs. The Amero-Indian armies had neither steel nor guns and had never seen horses at all. Further, their notion of war was more limited, and their tactics were generally more ritualistic and emphasized advance warning of attack and capturing the enemy so as to increase the pool of sacrificial victims. The Europeans focused on swift, sure victory and dispensed with their enemies quickly.
3. As suggested earlier, the diseases that the Europeans brought wiped out whole native populations and greatly debilitated the native armies.
4. The Indian peoples often first saw the Spaniards as gods or demigods and were initially reluctant to destroy them.
5. The three most highly advanced indigenous civilizations had become quite sedentary over the years and would not think of fleeing their agricultural land to regroup elsewhere.

6. The hierarchical and often cruel nature of the political leadership in the native civilizations had accustomed the common people to authoritarian decision making and arbitrary acts from above and had conditioned the common people not to rebel against the current leaders or those who wielded power. The Spaniards were at least initially perceived as just one more ruling group that had taken over.

Early Colony

The conquest was a joint endeavor between the crown and private entrepreneurs. The conquistador leader was expected to equip his band with the necessary arms and supplies or find financial backers who would. In turn, he and his mates had a royal license to hunt treasure and native peoples who had not embraced Christianity, for their own profit. The only requirement was that they pay the royal fifth, or *quinto real* to the crown. Much of the nature of the early colony was dictated by the conditions of the conquest. The Spaniards came for gold, glory, and God and competed fiercely for the former. Many were poor noblemen or *hidalgos*, but most came from more humble origins. The wealth from looted native cities and civilizations was shared among the members of the conquering military bands. *Encomiendas* and titles were handed out later but usually just to the captains and leaders. Cortés, for instance, proved to be as successful in business as he was in conquest. He amassed a series of large and very profitable holdings in Mexico and proved very apt in his business dealings.

However, only a few of the *conquistadores* achieved the fortunes they desired, and many remained disappointed and bitter. After the initial years of the conquest, more and more Spaniards came in search of fortune at a time when there were few additional native civilizations to loot. In Peru, much of the early sixteenth century was spent in fighting, assassination, and intrigue among the conqueror Francisco Pizarro, his brother, and other Spaniards. Treachery and betrayal were common. The native peoples were often completely brutalized in the plundering of their societies and were at best seen by most as instruments of lucre and occasionally lust: slaves to capture and sell, laborers to exploit, owners of land or property to be seized, women to be used. The colonialists often rose in rebellion when reforms were attempted.

The Spaniards conquered an area forty times the size of Spain. They and the Portuguese had the power and the audacity to enslave the better part of the population on two continents. They did not come as equals but as forceful conquerors. It was their belief that they were morally superior, possessed of the true faith (which was to be imposed more than practiced), and presented with the opportunity of their lives for fame and wealth. The nature of the colony was foretold by Columbus' action on the island of Hispaniola during his second voyage. Anxious to prove the economic viability of the lands he had found, he began to force the natives to bring him a tribute of gold dust. When they refused and rebelled against their would-be masters, Columbus gave the orders to have large numbers of the locals captured and held. As a way of continuing to extract value from the natives, he sent several hundred to Europe as slaves. To placate the gold-starved settlers on the island, he distributed most of the remaining prisoners to them as a form of bounty. As was to be the case throughout the region, the original Americans would be enslaved out-right or divided among the European settlers who took their land and then forced them to contribute their labor to the new European enterprise. The original inhab-itants of Hispaniola declined rapidly because of disease and the harsh treatment handed out by the Europeans. From several hundred thousand inhabitants on His-paniola at the time of Columbus' arrival, only some 29,000 were alive two decades later. By the mid-1500s, hardly any natives were left.

Ironically, the original *conquistadores* proved to be an endangered group as well. They were soon removed from power and replaced by direct representatives of the king whose loyalty to the crown was unquestioned. In this and other areas, Euro-pean institutions began to replace the military structures and unbridled civilian power that marked the conquest. Thus, the Iberian colonial bureaucracy began to replace the arbitrary rapaciousness of the conquerors.

ESTABLISHING A NEW SOCIAL STRUCTURE: THE *CASTAS*

Spanish legislation created a complicated system of social classification consisting of the *castas*, defined by descent and color. On the top were the recently immigrated white Spaniards, the peninsular whites; below them were the descendants of the white colonists, called white *criollos*; after them came the brown people, the *pardos* or *mestizos*, who consisted of people with mixed ancestry. As time went on, the ranks of the lower and middle classes were bolstered by *mestizos, mulattos*, and *zambos*. The social pyramid that resulted from the conquest and the colonization consisted of a small group of powerful and usually wealthy Europeans or their descendants on top; a large number of natives and, soon, African slaves on the bottom; and a few Spanish artisans, soldiers, or small merchants as a wisp of a middle class.

The society that the Europeans brought with them from the Iberian peninsula was feudal in nature. Land tenure and many of the social institutions of the colony were more feudal than modern. The early colony still labored under the medieval philosophical doctrine of scholasticism. Thus, considerable time was spent debating the true nature of the Indian population and the comparability of their souls with those of the Europeans. Moral argument and ethical debate were, however, rarely a match for the immense influence of a powerful person in the New World. Like the *grand seigneur* in Spain or Portugal, he (rarely she) was the unchallenged master of his domain. His will could be imposed in high and low places. Judges would listen, and peons, his to use as he saw fit, had very few practical rights (as contrasted to often extensive but unrealized legal rights).

WOMEN AND POWER

Few European women came in the earliest years of the colony. Those who did were subject to the strict traditional mores of the Iberian peninsula. However, women unprotected by both class (upper) and race (white) might well be available to the person of power to *coger* (generally meaning "to grab or seize," although in parts of Latin America it came to mean "to have sexual relations"). Thus, lower-class women of color were often at the disposal of men of lighter caste and higher class. In mostly Indian Bolivia, for instance, many *latifundistas*, or large landowners, were able to exercise the *derecho de pernada* (the sexual right to women on their estate) well into the twentieth century. Most upper-class women were strongly subordinated to male members of the family. There are, however, cases of a few women running large estates and even participating in colonial administration. There are more cases of women being the owners of record for huge amounts of land or other forms of wealth. Many of these inherited their wealth and prestige from a husband or father. In more general transgender terms, their power and strength were respected (although not necessarily liked or even accepted whenever an opportunity for noncompliance or rebellion presented itself). In that women were socialized to be meek, they were at a distinct disadvantage. Further, domination in many forms was omnipresent, and it colored the colony and subsequent social and political relations in Latin America in gender relations, politics, and many other areas.

LABOR

Persons of importance in Spain and Portugal did not engage in manual labor, in large part because they were nobles or aspired to be like them. This attitude was carried over into the American colonies and permeated the societies with a disdain for manual labor that is perhaps most poignantly manifest in the low wages and lack of respect such labor still engenders and the hesitancy to engage in it carried by most members of the upper class and many in the middle class. The initial abundance of free Indian labor heightened this characteristic, as did the subsequent importation of large numbers of African slaves. Over time these labor pools were augmented by the progeny of often illicit unions of Europeans and Amero-Indians (*mestizos*) and Europeans and Africans (*mulattos*).

Symbolic of the exploitative use of Amero-Indian labor and land was the *encomienda* (*sesmaria* in Brazil). The *encomienda* originated in a Spanish practice of granting jurisdiction over lands and peoples captured from the Moors to one of the warriors who led the reconquest. In Spanish and Portuguese America, it came to be the assignment of a group of native people to a conquistador or other colonist. He would oversee them and the land on which they lived and be responsible for their proper Christianization. They in turn were to serve him with their labor and by paying him tribute. This form of forced semi–slave labor was often supplemented with the labor of Indian slaves. The Dominicans and church officials like Bishop Bartolomé de las Casas championed Indian rights and endeavored to stop some of the worst practices against the indigenous population. In 1512, the crown responded with the Laws of Burgos to outlaw some of the worst abuses of the Native Americans and make Indian slavery illegal. In 1549, the *encomendero's* right to demand labor from his *tributarios* was also outlawed. Both practices did, however, continue well beyond these dates in some areas.

After the decline of the *encomienda*, land, mine, and *obraje* (textile workshop) owners were forced to rely on the *repartimiento* for their free labor. The *repartimiento* was the practice of requiring the Indian population to provide a set amount of free labor to the landowners, the owners of the mines, the workshop or *obraje* operators, or the state for public works. In Peru, where the *repartimiento* was known by the old Incan term *mita*, as much as 6 months to a year of service could be required from each male every 7 years. The Indians were often horribly exploited (thousands died at mines like Potosí, in what is now Bolivia), even though they did receive a token wage. As historian Benjamin Keen observes, "the repartimiento like the enco-mienda was a disguised form of slavery." Indeed, there were harsh penalties for those who avoided service and for community leaders who could not provide the required quotas of laborers.

SLAVERY AND OTHER FORMS OF ORGANIZATION

As is the case in the United States, Latin America is still feeling the effects of slavery. It is not possible to understand society or working conditions in Brazil, Cuba, Haiti, the Dominican Republic, or the other Latin American societies without understand-ing the lasting effects of this institution. As suggested by the popularity of a Brazilian *telenovela* (soap opera) bearing her name, Brazilian society is still reverberating from the adoration a rich Brazilian miner showered on Xica da Silva, the mulatto slave woman he called his "African queen." Yet, one of the worst aspects of the process of colonization was enslavement. The Eurocentrism and racism of the European colo-nizers initially allowed them to see the native peoples as non-Christian pagans who were inferior and, like the rest of what they found, there to be used by the colonizers. Slavery existed in Europe, North Africa, and the Middle East from long before the conquest. From this, the practice of enslaving native people spread to the Americas. In the initial years of the colony, raiding parties were sent out to find slaves to be used for forced labor. Thus, thousands of the original inhabitants of the Americas were enslaved in the first century of colonization. As the native population was rap-idly depleted and as more laws to protect the indigenous population were passed and sometimes enforced by the crown, landowners needed to look elsewhere for exploitable labor. The outlawing of Indian slavery accelerated this process.

As with other areas, slavery was also an institution in Africa, but it was tied to specific functions. It was, for instance, a way of punishing incorrigible criminals in societies that had mores against drawing blood from their own clansmen. Slavery became a recognized institution in Middle Eastern Muslim societies. So it was that there was a growing slave trade in Arab lands and from northern African societies that were conquered by them. Slave traders were soon penetrating farther south into Africa from the area around the Sudan and elsewhere. The proximity of the market for African slaves in the Middle East and North Africa helped to establish the slave trade as an international activity.

Seeking a route to the Far East that did not have to pass through the Muslim-controlled Middle East, the Portuguese began to penetrate farther and farther south on Africa's west coast. Spurred on by advances in navigation that were supported by Prince Henry the Navigator after 1450, they eventually circumnavigated the African continent to establish sea routes to the Indies. As they did this, Portuguese settle-ments were established all along the African coast and trade was begun. Soon, the Portuguese took over islands off the Atlantic coast (Madeira, Cape Verde Islands). Later, they colonized several of the areas where they had settlements (Angola, Guinea Bissau, and Mozambique).

Stimulated by the strong market for sugar in Europe, Arabs had begun the cul-tivation of sugar in North Africa. Slave labor was used to supply the intense labor needed in the sugarcane cutting and milling process. When the Portuguese decided to cultivate sugar in their Atlantic Islands, they copied the Arab use of slave labor.

The Portuguese then began to use their outposts in western and southern Africa to capture or buy slaves. When the Portuguese took the cultivation of sugar to their colony in Brazil in the 1500s, they also installed the plantation system based on slave labor. As the Dutch, English, and French adopted this crop in their Caribbean possessions, they too relied on a system of slave labor. On arriving in the Americas, the European colonists were faced with tremendous expanses of land available to them. It soon became clear that they needed to find crops and the labor to cultivate them if they were to turn their new possessions into paying propositions. In northern Brazil and the Caribbean, native slavery failed, and the native peoples would not otherwise provide the abundant labor needed. The superutilization of native peoples and their understandable dislike for the European system combined with factors like their rapid depletion by European-born diseases (particularly in the Caribbean) and their ability to flee farther into the interior in Brazil to minimize the number of available workers. This ensured that the Europeans' voracious appetite for cheap and easily exploitable labor could not be satisfied by the local supply in these areas. The use of indentured servants was also to become part of colonial life, but this source of cheap labor also proved insufficient for the demand. Nor did the well-to-do European landowning elite have any intention of farming the land themselves. They were much more prone to use the labor of others to accumulate their wealth and finance trips to London, Madrid, or Lisbon.

Slaves, then, had initially been acquired by Portuguese and Arab raiding parties and traders. Later, the Portuguese used their trade connections, outposts, and a series of slave forts to buy more and more slaves for the growing market in the Americas. During the first century of the colony, they enjoyed a monopoly on the importation of slaves in the Spanish colonies and Brazil. In this way, the transatlantic slave trade was begun. As the trade in humans grew, England and other countries also engaged in the lucrative business. The triangular trade took guns, rum, metal tools, and whiskey to Africa, where these were traded for slaves. Those who survived the horrendous Middle Passage were in turn sold in the slave markets in Havana and elsewhere and the ships loaded with tobacco, rum, and indigo for the trip back to Europe. From here the journey began anew. More than 7 million souls were brought to the Portuguese and Spanish colonies in this way.

The African diaspora had a major demographic and cultural impact on all areas of Latin America and the Caribbean, from Mexico to the Bahamas, Martinique, Grenada, Guatemala, Cuba, and Brazil. The arrival of African slaves to the Americas started roughly in 1502. African slaves were imported to substitute for the rapidly diminishing indigenous population. These first groups of slaves came from the slave markets of Spain. The slave markets in Seville, while relatively small, were the most active in Europe during this time. With colonization of the Americas, the demand for slave labor increased dramatically. Europeans were looking to satisfy their labor demands in the New World. After 1519, slaves were taken directly from Africa by European slave ships. The transatlantic slave trade dates from 1519 to 1867; by 1530, the Spanish crown had authorized the spread of slavery to Puerto Rico, Cuba, and Jamaica.

Law and Slavery. Spanish law legitimized the practice and ownership of other persons in the Caribbean and Latin America. The foundation of Spanish jurisprudence acknowledged the legality of the institution of slavery even while declaring it contrary to natural law. These laws protected enslaved persons from serious abuse by their masters and gave them the right to marry, inherit property, and be manumitted. Spanish slave law was developed from Roman slave codes. The French had no slave laws on the books, so they eventually enacted the Code Noir, a 1685 compilation designed to regulate slavery in the French Caribbean. Like Spanish law, the Code Noir accorded the slaves basic rights such as marriage, manumission, and judicial recourse in the case of mistreatment. The British had no tradition of slavery in their land and had no elaborated slave codes to define relations between slave and master. This left the English slaveholders in the Caribbean to their own devices. They developed slave codes that essentially gave all of the power to the slave masters.

Comparative Slave Thesis. In the areas of the New World where there were more carefully elaborated slave codes and laws, as in the Spanish colonies, one theory holds that the nature of slavery was more humane or less dehumanizing. The slave—according to the argument—had a legal personality and was recognized by the law. Thus, slaves could learn to read and even buy their freedom. Along with the process of *miscegenation*—the mixing of the races—some scholars believe that the Spanish slave codes created a far different life for slaves.

In contrast to the Spanish-speaking Caribbean, the English had no elaborated slave codes and had to make them up as they went along. Thus, in British slave codes, slaves were not recognized as persons but as property. They were accorded no rights: slaves were strictly forbidden to learn how to read or write and to own property. Moreover, miscegenation was less frequent.

Nonetheless, the massive degradation and exploitation of millions of human beings uprooted from their homes in Africa combined with the treatment of the Native American population imbued the Spanish and Portuguese colonies with a deep-seated racism, institutionalized callousness toward laborers (particularly when they were of color), and a proclivity toward (often brutal) exploitation that remains today.

Not all exploited the indigenous or African population with the same degree of harshness. The settlements that the Jesuits set up in Paraguay and elsewhere were notable exceptions, although they too enforced cultural assimilation of native peoples like the Guaraní. The Spanish and Portuguese crowns did not take kindly to the independent power of the Jesuits in these or other matters. Further, many of the powerful in the colonies resisted and sharply criticized the protective role progressive sectors in the Catholic Church played in regard to Indian rights. The *encomendero* turned priest and Indian advocate Bishop Bartolomé de las Casas was repeatedly rebuked and threatened. Bishop Antonio Valdivieso was threatened and eventually assassinated for his pro-native stances in the area that is now Nicaragua. The Spanish crown did eventually decree minimal protection for indigenous peoples starting with the Law of Burgos (1512) and outlawed practices like Indian slavery. Compliance took much longer. Nor was the more humane treatment by the Jesuits always accepted. They were expelled from the colonies by the Portuguese in 1757 and the Spanish in 1767. African slavery continued into the nineteenth century in the remaining Spanish colonies in the Caribbean and until 1888 in Brazil. The status of enslaved or horribly exploited Africans did not attract the attention of enlightened

Church officials. Even de las Casas recommended the use of African slave labor to free the indigenous people from slavery. Further, given the power and prerogative of local notables and their influence on local public officials, many of the worst practices toward the natives and former slaves continued on well after being outlawed. One could draw parallels between these practices and the way sectors of the old elite in the American South were able to exploit and deny fundamental rights to former slaves and their descendants in rural areas of Mississippi and Louisiana.

The Indian and African slaves and laborers were, it seemed, to be used and exploited (at times to the point of extinction) to achieve the production necessary to enrich the European owners and to funnel wealth and products back to the metropolitan centers of power and wealth in Europe. As pointed out by many observers, the conditions in the mines, workshops, and farms were often horrendous. They were reflective of the callousness of many of the powerful to the condition and suffering of those more lowly than they.

Production, Trade, and Extraction of Riches

The native gold and silver were quickly expropriated and sent back to Spain in fleets of galleons. The crown always got its *quinto real*. After the existing riches in gold, silver, and gems were depleted by the first conquerors, the Spanish administration began to foster the establishment of durable production of mercantile goods and the introduction of trade in Indian societies that had not yet begun to exchange their products for money. Of primary interest to the mercantilist leadership were precious metals, such as gold and silver; pearls; and precious stones. Where these were not found, the colonial leadership sought to grow commercial goods such as dyes, sugar cane, tobacco, and cocoa. Soon after the conquest, they discovered rich silver mines in Mexico and in Potosí Mountain in the Andes in Upper Peru (Bolivia). The extraction of silver and gold in Mexico and Peru stimulated the colonizers' keen interest in the lands of the former Aztec and Incan Empires. In the regions surroundings these centers, the production of food and other necessary supplies began to determine how the land was used. In Chile, the land was used to produce wheat for Spanish bread; in northern Argentina, the land was used to breed cattle, horses, and mules for work in the mines and for hides to make leather. The beef was dried and salted to make *charqui*, jerked meat.

Tremendous amounts of wealth were removed from the colonies in the form of preexisting gold and silver. Next, the conquerors turned to mining, often expending thousands of Indian lives each year to extract the precious metal (as suggested earlier, mining at Potosí is reputed to have consumed as many as 8 million native lives over three centuries). Between 1531 and 1600, over 33 million pounds of silver were exported back to Spain. By the last quarter of the sixteenth century, silver bullion accounted for about 90 percent of Latin American exports. Some three-fifths came from mines in what is now Peru and Bolivia. The silver mine at Potosí was legendary. The town attracted so many fortune seekers that it was the largest city in Latin America (population 160,000) at the beginning of the seventeenth century.

The silver was extracted by the miners and shipped to Spain in different ways. First, the crown took the *quinto real* of gross production. The other 80 percent stayed in the hands of the mine owners and was used to pay the workforce and for materials, animals for transportation, food, and luxury products for the rich miners. Here, the merchants who worked in the colony itself dominated, as did those who had the exclusive rights to export goods from Spain to the American possessions. This latter group principally resided in the center of Spanish colonial administration in Spain, Seville. Furthermore, the Spanish crown levied taxes on all imported goods. The capacity of the Spanish state to add more, higher taxes on colonial commerce was astonishing. The consequence was that the goods became very expensive because of the excessive taxation imposed by Spain's colonial monopoly.

As a way of ensuring increased consumption of such imported goods, the *repartimiento de mercancias* was introduced as a way to tax native Americans who were not or were only marginally incorporated in the market economy. Under this system, the *corregidor* or other local official was able to oblige each household in his charge to buy some Western merchandise at a substantial (and usually highly inflated) price. The colonial official became the monopoly supplier to a captive market.

The high taxes on all imported and exported goods caused considerable discontent among the *criollo* producers and merchants in the colonies, and they were soon ready to evade them by trading with unauthorized merchants from other countries. Their trade was principally with Dutch, British, and French *contrabandistas*. The whole of colonial history is characterized by the efforts of the Spanish authorities to eliminate smuggling by patrolling the coasts, controlling the accounts of the merchants, or forming monopolistic companies such as Guipuzcoana in Venezuela. These efforts never enjoyed much success because the smuggled goods were much cheaper than those coming from Spain.

The Church

The Catholic Church was a major political institution in the colony and was in charge of (Catholic) Christianization and education. It was in charge of the spiritual conquest of the Americas. It acted as an agent for the crown, incorporating native peoples into the European world and European economy through participation in and payment for baptism and other rites and the still popular street processions celebrating Church holy days and the lives of favorite saints and local madonnas. The Church's power was exercised in concert with the state and utilized to extend European control and influence. Its autonomy was mitigated by the fact that in 1508 Pope Julius II granted the Spanish monarch the *patronato real*—the right to nominate all church officials, collect tithes, and found churches and monasteries in the Spanish Americas. This allowed the state a great deal of control over the Church and helped to fuse the two. Nonetheless, the Church did engage in a variety of different activities, amassed considerable wealth, and was often the largest landowner in different regions of the colony.

The cultural and political evolution of Spanish America was also influenced by an instrument employed to purify the Catholic faith. The Spanish Inquisition persecuted alleged heretics (mostly Jewish and Muslim converts) and was in large part responsible for the mass exodus of non-Christians from Spain in the late fifteenth and sixteenth centuries. In 1569, the institution of the Inquisition began in Latin America in Lima and Mexico City. It was charged with investigating signs of heresy. Later, it spread to other Spanish (but not Portuguese) possessions and became a license to search out any deviant or different thinking or innovation. Although indigenous people were exempted from the Inquisition after the 1570s and its victims were relatively few in number, it did have the effect of enforcing a certain heterodoxy in thought and suppressing an unfettered spirit of inquiry. Some have even seen it as the forerunner of the infamous secret police employed by Latin American dictatorships and military governments. Others speculate that the lax enforcement of the Inquisition in the Portuguese territories helps to account for the less constrained approach to thinking and social and business relations that developed in Brazil. The Museum of the Inquisition in downtown Lima attests to the chilling nature of the interrogation and brutality of the instruments of torture employed to induce confessions in Spanish America.

Colonial State Organization

Political power was highly concentrated in colonial governmental structures as well. A *virrey*, or viceking (viceroy), headed the colonial administration, ruling as the king's representative in his designated area. The region was first divided into the Spanish viceroyalties of Nueva España (Mexico, Central America, and the Caribbean) and Lima (all the Andean countries, present-day Panama, Argentina, Paraguay, and Uruguay) and the Portuguese viceroyalty of Brazil. Later, the viceroyalties of New Granada (present-day Venezuela, Colombia, and Ecuador) and Río de la Plata (present-day Argentina, Uruguay, and Paraguay) were separated. Unlike the English colonies in North America, there were no representative assemblies in Latin America. Laws and decrees came from the Iberian monarchs or the Council of the Indies in Seville, Spain, and were implemented by colonial authorities from Spain and Portugal. Communication was slow, imprecise, and greatly filtered by the interests of the powerful. The colonists often felt that they were living under orders or laws imposed from afar that did not respond to their needs. This led to one of the most famous dictums during the colony—*Obedezco pero no cumplo*, "I obey but I do not comply." In other words, I will yield to your orders and authority, but you will be hard-pressed to make me carry them out. The colonial elite that emerged amassed considerable wealth and power. They were all too willing to employ both to frustrate laws or decrees they found objectionable or impractical. The large landowners in Brazil were perhaps the most independent, a tradition that continues to the present. In Spanish and Portuguese America, laws like those that protected the native peoples were often unenforceable because of the concerted power of local elites. There was also a fault line between the newly arrived colonists from Spain and Portugal, the *peninsulares*, and the sons and daughters of the earlier arrivals from the Iberian peninsula, the *criollos*. The *criollos* resented the fact that the best positions in the colonial administration and the Church went to the *peninsulares* even though they had just stepped off the boat and did not have the *criollos'* history, family, or wealth in the Americas.

Governmental Organization

The viceroy was indeed the king's representative and could truly rule. Executive, military, and some legislative powers were combined in such a way as to establish the cultural model of the all-powerful executive that has permeated Latin American political (and business) culture to the present day. Captains general were appointed to rule over smaller and usually more distant divisions of the viceroyalties and governed in much the same way. Thus, the captain general of Guatemala ruled Central America (excluding present-day Panama) from his headquarters in Guatemala City but was ostensibly subordinate to the viceroy of New Spain in Mexico City. The captains general in colonial Brazil were given even greater power over their domains and enjoyed greater autonomy from the crown and the viceroy.

The viceroyalties of New Spain and Peru were further subdivided into *audiencias*, or advisory councils, that were presided over by judge-presidents and composed of appointed judges, or *oidores*. They were established in Santo Domingo, Mexico City, Panama, Lima, Guatemala, Guadalajara, Santa Fe, La Plata, Buenos Aires, Quito, Santiago, Cuzco, and Caracas. Beneath the *audiencias* were the governors and at the local level, the notoriously corrupt *corregidores* and mayors (*alcaldes*). At the higher levels of government, the judicial, legislative, and executive functions were mixed, with the viceroys generally also in charge of the military. Functions and powers often overlapped in a system that was designed to encourage mutual suspicion, spying, the checking of a potential rival's power, and thus the supremacy of the power of the crown. The *cabildo*, or town council (*câmara* in Brazil), was one of the few political structures with any degree of popular participation or democracy. Many councils were all or partly elected and were truly representative of the population. Many others were dominated by powerful and often corrupt political appointees. Offices were, however, frequently sold, and corruption and intense exploitation of the native population were all too often the norm. The official who did not use his office to accumulate a fortune to take back to the Iberian Peninsula might well be considered the exception.

The Bourbon Reforms

Conditions did improve somewhat after the late eighteenth-century Bourbon reforms, but many of the worst practices had by then become ingrained and segments of the population were already chafing under the colonial yoke. This helped lead to the uprisings in the central Andes led by Túpac Amaru in 1780 and Tupac Katari in 1781, and the revolt of the *comuneros* in New Granada (1781). These uprisings helped set the stage for the independence movement.

Historical Time Line in the Americas

40,000 B.C.E.–8000 B.C.E. Migration of Asian people to North America across the Bering Strait

1500 B.C.E.–1000 C.E. Mayan civilization develops in the Yucatan Peninsula, Guatemala, and parts of Honduras and El Salvador

1150 B.C.E.–500 C.E.   Olmec culture flourishes in Mesoamerica

1000   Incan culture emerges in the Cuzco Valley of South America

1200   The Aztecs arrive in the central plateau of Mexico

1466   The Aztec emperor, Moctezuma Xocoyotzín, is born in Mexico

1492   Christopher Columbus arrives at what he called San Salvador Island in the Caribbean and encounters Native American culture

1494   Treaty of Tordesillas is signed by Spain and Portugal, establishing a line of demarcation from pole to pole 370 leagues west of the Cape Verde Islands; Spain receives the right to colonize all territory to the west of that line; Portugal colonizes lands to the east

1500   Pedro Alvares Cabral arrives in Brazil and claims it for Portugal

1508   In Hispaniola, the first sugar mill is constructed

1509   Pope Julius II authorizes the Spanish Catholic monarchs to propagate the Catholic Church in the Americas; *patronato real* gives power to crown to appoint Church officials

1510   Two-hundred and fifty slaves are imported to the Americas to work in the gold mines in Hispaniola

1512   The Laws of Burgos are promulgated to protect the Native Americans from the worst ravages of Spanish conquest

1516   Bartolomé de las Casas is named the official protector of the Indians

1519   Hernán Cortés marches into Tenochtitlán and takes Moctezuma prisoner

1521   Spaniards complete conquest of the Aztec Empire

1521   Conquistador Gil González de Avila converts 30,000 Indians to Christianity in the area called Nicaragua and sends some 500,000 as slaves to other parts of the Spanish Empire

1524   Council of the Indies is established by King Charles V (Holy Roman Emperor Charles V)

1532   Francisco Pizarro invades the Incan Empire, captures and executes Emperor Atahualpa, and conquers the Incas

1538   The first university in the Americas is established: St. Thomas Aquinas in the city of Santo Domingo

1541   Francisco de Orellana discovers the headwaters of the Amazon River in what is now Ecuador

1542   The New Laws of the Indies are issued by Spain, officially eliminating the *encomienda*

1551   In Mexico and Lima, new universities are created

1554   Araucan Indian chief Caupolican, allied with Chief Lautaro, defeats Spaniards, kills Pedro de Valdivia, and defeats the forces of Francisco de Villagrá of Chile

1739–1780s   Bourbon Reforms

1767   King Charles III expels the Jesuits from the Spanish Empire

1780   Incan descendant Túpac Amaru leads a 2-year rebellion against authorities on behalf of the Indians

1781   Tupac Katari leads rebellion in what is now Bolivia and besieges La Paz in 1881

1781   *Comunero* revolt in New Granada

Bibliography

Adelman, Jeremy. *Colonial Legacies: The Problem of Persistence in Latin American History.* New York: Routledge, 1999.

Bakewell, Peter. *A History of Latin American Empires and Sequels, 1450–1930.* Oxford: Blackwell Publishers, 1997.

Burkholder, Mark A., and Lyman L. Johnson. *Colonial Latin America.* 5th ed. New York: Oxford University Press, 2004.

Conniff, Michael, and Thomas Davis. *Africans in the Americas: A History of the Black Diaspora.* New York: St. Martin's Press, 1994.

Davis, Darien, ed. *Slavery and Beyond: The African Impact on Latin America and the Caribbean* (Jaguar Books on Latin America, 5). Wilmington, DE: Scholarly Resources, 1995.

Fagan, Brian. *Kingdoms of Gold, Kingdoms of Jade: The Americas Before Columbus*. London: Thames and Hudson, 1991.

Keen, Benjamin. *A History of Latin America*. 7th ed. Boston: Houghton Mifflin, 2004.

Kicza, John E., ed. *The Indian in Latin American History: Resistance, Resilience and Acculturation*. Wilmington, DE: Scholarly Resources, 1993.

Leon-Portilla, Miguel, ed. *The Broken Spears: The Aztec Account of the Conquest of Mexico*. Translated by Lysander Kemp. Boston: Beacon Press, 1992.

Newson, Linda. "The Latin American Colonial Experience." In *Latin American Development: Geographical Perspectives*. 2nd ed. Edited by David Preston. Harlow, UK: Longman, 1996.

Ohaegbulam, Festus U. *Toward an Understanding of the African Experience from Historical and Contemporary Perspectives*. Lunham, MD: University Press of America, 1990.

Rosenberg, Mark B., A. Douglas Kincaid, and Kathleen Logan, eds. *Americas, An Anthology*. New York: Oxford University Press, 1992.

Schele, Linda, and David Freidel. *A Forest of Kings: The Untold Story of the Ancient Maya*. New York: William Morrow, 1990.

Smith, Carol. *Guatemalan Indians and the State: 1540 to 1988*. Austin: University of Texas Press, 1990.

Soustelle, Jacques. *Daily Life of the Aztecs, on the Eve of the Spanish Conquest*. Stanford, CA: Stanford University Press, 1970.

Stavig, Ward. *The World of Túpac Amaru: Conflict, Community, and Identity in Colonial Peru*. Lincoln: University of Nebraska Press, 1999.

FILMS AND VIDEOS

The Buried Mirror. Reflections of Spain in the New World. Part Two: The Conflict of the Gods. United States, 1991. Video version of Carlos Fuentes' insightful commentary on the indigenous world conquered by Spain and the transposition of the new belief system.

The Mission. United States, 1986. An excellent feature-length film starring Robert De Niro; graphically depicts the colonization process among indigenous peoples above the Iguassú Falls in southern Brazil.

Popol Vuh. United States, 1991. An animated video that portrays the creation myth of the Mayas.

Prayer of Viracocha. United States. A beautifully animated indigenous lament to the Incan god Viracocha at the time of the conquest.

Quetzalcóatl. United States, 1951. A vision of the Mesoamerican winged serpent god.

The Spanish Conquest of Mexico. United States, 1999. Tells the story of how the Aztec empire was conquered.

Sword and Cross. United States, 1991. Tells the story of the conquest.

Xica. Brazil, 1976. The embellished story of Xica da Silva.

THREE

Democracy, Dictators, and *Tío* Sam

A Historical Overview from Independence to the Present Day

Independence

The independence movements that created most of the nation-states that currently make up Latin America developed during the first 25 years of the nineteenth century as the result of events occurring in both Europe and Latin America. Haiti became an independent republic in 1804, and most of the other Latin American states achieved their independence by the early 1820s. The local elites succeeded in transferring political power into their own hands outside of the control of Madrid or Lisbon. However, the underlying systems of social and economic power inherited from the colonial era remained largely intact. Further, the authoritarian tradition inherited from Spanish and Portuguese colonialism was very much in place and would plague Latin America into the twenty-first century. There was a continual and generally unresolved tension between authoritarian rule learned from years of heavy-handed, top–down colonial (and often precolonial) practice, on the one hand, and the democratic ideals and inspiration that the independence movements chose to rely on to explain and set up the state structures in the independent nations, on the other. Nonetheless, the end of direct colonialism did initiate a nation-building process that would eventually modernize governmental structures and bring Latin America closer to the world economic system. The political change also produced a legitimacy crisis that led to nearly a century of political struggle and the eventual hegemony of liberalism. These more profound changes for the Americas began in the last 25 years of the nineteenth century, when the region's long-standing social and economic structures were challenged by the arrival of the Industrial Revolution and market capitalism. These forces eventually weakened the traditional elites and laid the groundwork for the political struggles of the twentieth century.

To better understand the independence movements of the early nineteenth century in Latin America, it is necessary to look to Europe. By the beginning of the eighteenth century, the Spanish Empire was already well into a decline that proved to be permanent. However, as was suggested in the last chapter, the Bourbon monarchs of Spain, whose family had assumed the crown in 1713, had embarked on a series of political and economic reforms in their American colonies that they hoped would solidify that rule. In reality, these reforms contributed to the eventual triumph of the independence movements. Inspired by Enlightenment political and economic thought, the Bourbons sought to reform the existing overlapping systems of authority by centralizing political power. They created new administrative units in New Granada (1717) and Buenos Aires (1776). More importantly, Charles III, who ruled from 1759 to 1788, established a new administrative system that resulted in the appointment of local governors by the crown in Madrid. These rulers, called "intendants," were almost all Spanish-born rather than American *criollos*. This approach marginally solidified the hold of the monarchy over the colonies but brought the crown into more direct conflict with the local *criollo* elites, who had prospered under the previous system of less intrusive rule from Madrid. In one significant example, the monarchy sharply reduced *criollo* control of the administrative and court system, which it had originally established in the late seventeenth century by purchasing judgeships. Charles III also strengthened his hand by taking greater control of the Church. In his boldest move, he expelled the Jesuits from all Spanish colonies in 1767. Charles saw the Jesuits as an independent power base, so he removed them and profited from the sale of their lands. The Spanish crown also engaged in economic reform that freed the various ports of the empire to trade with other ports in Spanish America and in Spain itself. Illegal trade had long flourished on the forbidden routes, with most of the profits staying within the Americas; but now the Spanish crown was gaining a greater share of the wealth through the collection of customs duties. These economic reforms resulted in a more prosperous colonial economy, where new ports such as Buenos Aires flourished; but their most important long-term effect was the resentment generated among *criollos*, who saw the moves as a plot to undermine their status and power. This resentment, more than any other factor, fueled the independence movements of the early nineteenth century.

Ironically, another reform instituted by the Spanish crown unwittingly aided the cause of American independence. During the eighteenth century, the monarchy had authorized the creation of colonial militias as a protection against feared British and French invasions; by 1800, 80 percent of the soldiers serving in Spanish America were American-born. A military career was one of the few remaining avenues of advancement for socially ambitious *criollos*. These forces provided the core of the local forces that would later fight for independence.

THE FRENCH REVOLUTION, LOCAL UPRISINGS, AND INDEPENDENCE

Events in Europe determined the timing of the independence movement. The French Revolution of 1789 launched ideas of freedom and equality throughout the French Empire, and cries of *liberté, égalité,* and *fraternité* fell on receptive ears among the slave population in Haiti. In 1791, a slave uprising was led by Toussaint L'Ouverture, an extremely able, self-educated freed slave. After a series of successful battles against opposition forces that included a formidable contingent of Napoleon's army in 1802, the popular forces triumphed. Haiti gained its independence from France in 1804 and thus became the first independent Latin American nation. In other parts of Latin America, a few, like the Afro-Venezuelan José Leonardo Chirinos, even spoke of proclaiming a republic of the "law of the French" in 1795. Meanwhile, the Spanish monarchy had tried to save its Bourbon counterparts during the French Revolution in 1789; but having failed that, Spain allied itself with Napoleon Bonaparte in 1796. However, in 1808, Napoleon turned on his Spanish allies and occupied Madrid, placing his brother Joseph on the Spanish throne. This act by Napoleon was the catalyst for rebellion in Spain and the Americas that would eventually lead to independence for most of Spanish America. Some historians do argue, however, that the resistance of indigenous peoples in the latter part of the eighteenth century was the real catalyst. As noted in the last chapter, in 1780, Túpac Amaru II, claiming lineage from the ancient Incan Empire, led a revolt that mobilized more than 80,000 mostly indigenous fighters and lasted for 2 years in southern Peru and Bolivia before it was defeated by the Spanish army. The struggle was joined by Tupac Katari in Upper Peru (now Bolivia) in 1881. There was also a popular revolt of the *comuneros* in New Granada in 1781. These movements are important in the history of indigenous struggles and popular uprisings but may be better understood outside the context of the independence movements. With radical demands for land reform and indigenous rights, the political thrust of these movements was not supported by the *criollo* independence leaders of the early nineteenth century. In fact, the Peruvian rebellions and the later rebellion in Mexico led by Father Hidalgo in 1810 frightened the *criollos* into making common cause with the Spanish-born elites and delayed independence in both Mexico and Peru. It also meant that, outside of Haiti, rebellions against colonial rule by the masses (who were predominantly people of color) did not triumph.

The *criollos*, born in America, increasingly longed to wrest political power from the *peninsulares*. In the late eighteenth century, the *criollos* began to look outward for guidance, increasingly to France. As a result, the French Revolution had more impact than the American Revolution. As suggested earlier, the most dramatic example of the influence in Latin America was in Haiti. Of course, the majority of creoles were not Jacobin revolutionaries. They wanted to reform the local political systems to give themselves power, but they were in no way interested in revolution or in giving all the power to the common people. Napoleon's invasion of Spain in 1808 provided that opportunity.

In the wake of the Napoleonic invasion, the Spanish king, Ferdinand VII, was imprisoned and the Braganzas, Portugal's royal family, escaped to Rio de Janeiro. The Brazilians received their royal family warmly and celebrated their extended stay in Rio de Janeiro. In contrast, the initial instincts of Spanish Americans were to pledge loyalty to Ferdinand; but fairly quickly, the creole elites began to realize their own power, and by 1810 the creoles had moved from tentative autonomy to open declarations of independence. However, despite the fortuitous circumstances for independence, the events that followed did not easily lead to independence for most of Latin America during the ensuing 25 years. Nor did the newly formed United States Republic assist in the struggles for independence.

ARGENTINA, 1806–1810

One of the earliest examples of the capacity of resistance by the local population came in Buenos Aires. In 1806, the British occupied the city, forcing the viceroy to flee to Córdoba. The British, however, were driven out by a locally organized citizens' army, which also successfully defended against a counterattack in 1807. This local action independent of Madrid set a powerful example for future actions. The viceroyalty of Buenos Aires was also able to negotiate a better deal in the arena of free trade after the expulsion of the British forces. Ironically, it involved the desire of the local commercial elite to trade directly with the British, who provided the most promising market for their growing production of hides and salted beef. In 1809, Spain granted Buenos Aires limited freedom of trade with nations allied to Spain or neutral in the Napoleonic Wars. This agreement helped to strengthen the self-confidence of the local elites.

Early Drive for Independence in Hispanic America

The first phase of the Spanish American independence movements occurred between 1810 and 1814. In 1810, Napoleon's forces completed their victory over the Bourbons and established a liberal constitution for Spain; but in 1814, Ferdinand VII returned to the Spanish throne and annulled the liberal constitution of 1812. In 1810, Argentine local elites came together to create a provisional government of the provinces of the Río de la Plata. Prior to their declaration of independence of 1816, these local elites pledged their allegiance to Ferdinand VII; but the pattern of local initiative, first shown in the rebellions against the British, was institutionalized.

Venezuela was the scene of a movement similar to that in Buenos Aires. In Caracas, a local council expelled the Spanish governors and organized a new government under Ferdinand VII. The best-known of the leaders was Simón Bolívar. Born into a wealthy Caracas family and tutored by the great Latin American liberal thinker Simón Rodríguez, Bolívar was educated in Spain and came in contact with the ideas of the Enlightenment (especially Rousseau and romanticism). In 1805, he committed himself to the independence of his homeland. In 1811, the local Caracas authorities, under his influence, declared Venezuela's independence. After an initial series of military defeats, the exiled Bolívar returned to Venezuela and defeated the Spanish army in a series of exceptional military victories, earning him the title "The Liberator" (*El Libertador*).

In the provinces of New Spain (Mexico), this time period also saw exceptional developments. By 1810 a group of *criollos*, including priest Miguel Hidalgo, began plotting to seize authority in the name of Ferdinand. When the plot was discovered by the Spanish authorities, Hidalgo led a popular uprising centered in the village of Dolores, thus the famous *grito de Dolores*. A powerful response came not from the local elites but rather from the impoverished *mestizos* and indigenous people. Uniting under the banner of the long-adored dark-skinned Virgin of Guadalupe, they comprised a fighting force of 50,000. In a decision whose motivation has been debated ever since, Hidalgo turned away from a probable victory over the Spanish authorities in Mexico City and moved to the north. In 1811, his army was defeated near Guadalajara, leading to his capture and execution.

Following Hidalgo's death, leadership of the independence forces was taken by José María Morelos, another priest even more strongly committed to radical social reform, including the end of slavery. A republican, Morelos believed that the whole population should participate in political affairs. In 1813, the Congress of Chilpancingo declared Mexico's independence from Spain and decreed that slavery should be abolished. The congress' liberal constitution of 1814 created a system of indirect elections and a powerful legislature. However, it was never enacted because Morelos' guerrilla army did not control enough territory to seriously threaten Spanish authority.

In 1814, Napoleon's defeat restored Ferdinand VII to power in Spain. The colonial authorities used this fortuitous event—along with military reinforcements—to regain control in the face of the developing independence movements. Ferdinand annulled the liberal Spanish constitution of 1812 and reestablished himself as an absolute ruler. The king's return divided *criollo* leaders, with many concluding that there was no reason to continue their rebellions. By 1816, with the exception of Buenos Aires, Spanish rule had been reestablished throughout the empire. In Venezuela, even the victorious Bolívar saw his support significantly reduced; he was forced into exile on the English island of Jamaica. The independence movement in New Spain also suffered serious setbacks. In 1815, Morelos was captured, tried, and executed as the Spanish military commanders regained the upper hand and blocked implementation of the liberal constitution that had been enacted the previous year. Only the government in Río de la Plata survived the reconquest. It struggled to survive and had not yet become a full-blown independence movement.

The Spanish reconquest was short-lived. In 1816, Bolívar returned to Venezuela from his exile on Jamaica and launched a new campaign for the independence of his country. His new ally was José Antonio Páez, the leader of the *llaneros* (cowboys) who had fought alongside the royalists during the previous struggles. In 1819, Bolívar mounted an army of 4000 and succeeded in defeating the Spanish and their royalist collaborators. Meanwhile in the south, José de San Martín initiated a significant military campaign. San Martín, the son of a Spanish military officer, entered the service at age 11. In 1812, he offered his services to the junta in Buenos Aires. Over the next 5 years, he developed the rebel forces into an army and then led 5000 soldiers across the Andes in a surprise attack on the loyalist forces in Chile. The Spaniards were defeated in the battle of Chacabuco, and San Martín entered Santiago triumphantly. San Martín's next target was the liberation of Peru; in 1820, he prepared for the attack on Lima, the capital of the viceroyalty. He faced a city where monarchist sentiment was quite strong. Both the *criollos* and the *peninsulares* favored the continuation of Ferdinand's rule. Wary of a defeat, San Martín withheld his attack. At that point, decisive events in Spain again intervened. Ferdinand reversed his political course and abruptly embraced the previously annulled Spanish liberal constitution of 1812. Monarchists throughout Spanish America were shocked by the turnabout, which abolished the Inquisition, thus unacceptably weakening the power of the Church. The changes in Spain suddenly altered the climate for independence in both Lima and Mexico City, where the monarchists held sway. The monarchists now viewed independence as a means of preserving the status quo, which would uphold traditional values and social codes. As a result of this sudden change of perspective, in 1821 the municipal council of Lima invited San Martín to enter the city; on July 28, he formally proclaimed the independence of Peru. Meanwhile in the north, Bolívar, after defeating the Spanish forces in New Granada, attempted to create a new state of Gran Colombia, uniting Venezuela, New Granada, and Ecuador under republican principles. This effort received little support, so Bolívar moved south, hoping to confront and defeat more of the royalist forces as he sought to achieve his vision of a united continent independent of colonial control and organized along republican principles.

Antonio José de Sucre was sent by Bolívar to liberate Ecuador. Sucre led the combined Ecuadorian, Colombian, and Venezuelan forces against the Spanish and finally defeated them in the battle of Pichincha in 1822. In Ecuador, Bolívar met with San Martín and declared that they were "the two greatest men in America." Personal and political differences, however, precluded the consummation of an alliance. Bolívar rejected San Martín's proposal for a monarchy in Peru and San Martín's offer for Bolívar to serve under his command. Further, Bolívar's plans for the union of Gran Colombia were rejected by San Martín. Disillusioned and unwilling to split the revolutionary forces, San Martín soon after resigned his post and retired to France, where he died in 1850. However, even San Martín's departure did not slow the independence movement. In late 1823, Bolívar's forces confronted the large Spanish force that had retreated inland from Lima; and a year later, the royalists were defeated decisively at the battle of Ayachucho, effectively ending three centuries of Spanish rule in the Americas. In 1825, Bolívar entered Upper Peru to press the idea that the two Perus should form a single nation. The leaders of Upper Peru, however, having already struck an independent course, declared their own republic and named it Bolivia in honor of Bolívar. Over the next 5 years Bolívar tried unsuccessfully to promote his idea of political union. His ideas were resisted by the local elites, including some of his own lieutenants, who feared the reinstatement of centralized control. In 1826, Bolívar tried to implement his vision of a united Spanish America by convening the Congress of Panama. His efforts were not successful, and in 1830, the Liberator died a bitter man who failed to achieve a united Latin America and saw many of his democratic dreams languish. Toward the end of his life he concluded that he and the other independence leaders "had plowed the sea."

Simultaneous to these events in South America, the conservative independence movement went forward in Mexico. The royal government was disintegrating; Agustín de Iturbide, the creole commander of the army in Mexico, seized the moment to declare Mexican independence with little bloodshed on September 28, 1821. Only the Spanish garrison in Veracruz held out against Iturbide's proclamation. It was a conservative revolt that even many Spaniards supported. The new regime was marked by three conservative principles: constitutional monarchy, official Catholicism, and equality of *peninsulares* and *criollos*. Iturbide had himself proclaimed emperor only when "no suitable European monarch could be found." Central America, with its traditional strong ties to Mexico, followed suit and declared its independence from Spain in 1821. In 1822, the Central American landowners, fearing liberal dominance in Spain, transferred their loyalty to royalist Mexico. However, the Mexican monarchy lasted only 2 years. In 1823, when Iturbide abdicated, the modern-day Central American states from Guatemala to Costa Rica became the Independent United Provinces of Central America. With the independence of Mexico and Central America, Spanish control in the Western Hemisphere was reduced to Cuba and Puerto Rico.

Brazilian Independence

Brazilian independence was achieved in a manner very different from that of Spanish America. The differences were rooted in the character of the Brazilian state and economy and in the special role played by Britain in the context of the Napoleonic Wars. When the Napoleonic army invaded Portugal in 1807, the entire royal family was able to flee to Brazil with the assistance of the British navy. The royal family ended Portugal's commercial monopoly by opening Brazil's ports. Soon after 1810, Britain gained privileged access to Brazil through low tariffs, a commitment to the gradual end of the African slave trade, and extraterritorial privileges for British citizens living in Brazil.

When Napoleon was decisively defeated, the Portuguese monarchy was free to return to Lisbon; initially, they did not, and instead Dom João proclaimed Brazil to be a coequal kingdom with the same rank as Portugal. Dom João, however, did eventually return to Lisbon and left his son Dom Pedro behind with the prerogative to declare Brazil independent. The new king declared independence on September 7, 1822, with the full support of the Brazilian elites and with only token resistance from a few Portuguese garrisons. In sharp contrast to much of Spanish America, independence was achieved in Brazil without significant bloodshed and without the development of a strong military caste. The nation also remained united despite some small-scale regional revolts. Furthermore, Brazil did not see a strong republican/monarchist split because the overwhelming majority of the local elite sided with monarchism. Brazilian sugar barons were dependent on the slave trade and thus on the monarchy, which lasted only a year beyond the abolition of slavery in 1888.

Early Years of Independence

Thus, the Latin American nations became independent of European rule. It was, however, a much longer struggle to liberate themselves from their inherited political and cultural traditions. Foremost among these was the authoritarian proclivity that was strongly ingrained in political culture. For instance, Bolívar, the great Liberator, frustrated with regionalism and the assertion of political autonomy by various leaders in the Republic of Gran Colombia, often forsook formal democracy and reverted to dictatorial rule in order to hold the republic together. Much of the early history of the republics was filled with such local and national *caudillos*—by men on white horses. An even more telling example is that of Dr. Francia. Soon after independence in Paraguay, the then-leader of the country, Dr. José Gaspar Rodríguez de Francia, proclaimed himself dictator in perpetuity. His rule from 1816 to 1840 set a pattern for extended dictatorial rule that would continue to plague Paraguay until 1989. This and similar traditions of extended authoritarian rule continued to haunt many other Latin American countries through the nineteenth and twentieth centuries. Indeed, authoritarian rule would predominate in Paraguay, Bolivia, and Haiti through the nineteenth and twentieth centuries. The military-style leaders would dominate the period up until the 1850s in most countries, including Mexico, Argentina, and Peru. The seeds of democracy had been planted, but the early years of republican history seemed to justify Bolívar's previously noted conclusion the "we have plowed the sea."

The Aftermath of Independence and the Monroe Doctrine

The aftermath of independence was a difficult time for most of Latin America. The newly independent nations faced terrible obstacles as they sought to move forward economically, politically, and socially. The consolidation of national rule was even more difficult than in the United States, which in light of its defeat by Great Britain in the War of 1812, limited its initial contacts with Latin America and formulated the still controversial Monroe Doctrine in 1823. Enunciated by John Quincy Adams, it was primarily designed to preclude continued European interference in independent Latin America and stop any reimposition of colonial rule in the hemisphere. Within the Latin American nations, it was a considerable struggle to establish national control and move beyond the regionalism that was so strong in most of the nations. Further, politics were generally dominated by the upper-class landowning elite, whose concept of democracy was quite limited. With the primary exception of Brazil, the new leaders took over power in the context of the physical devastation brought by the wars for independence. Devastation was particularly heavy in Mexico and Venezuela, but everywhere the burden of supporting the large armies of liberation was significant. Economic activity was also greatly affected by the continuous wars. Trade had almost ceased during the period. Trade with Spain ceased, of course; but inter-American trade was also adversely affected. Communication almost completely collapsed among the new countries. The economies of the newly independent countries also faced challenges related to their very nature. Based almost exclusively on mining and agriculture, the colonies had been marginally integrated into the world economy before independence; but they now faced new challenges not based on their previous colonial commitments. The failure to achieve political unity meant that each new country faced the challenge of creating its own national economy. There were also regional differences; Mexico had a fairly well-developed national economy, but most of the other countries did not. As countries sought to develop themselves, they often faced internal divisions as well as interference from outside political and economic influences. Most new regimes lacked the financial assets even to equip a national army, let alone embark on significant national economic development. Mechanisms for tax collection and other standard methods of revenue collection were simply not sophisticated enough to meet the new nations' considerable needs. As a result, many countries, including Mexico and Argentina, turned to loans from foreign banks as a way out of their crises. Foreign governments, especially Britain, eagerly provided money in hopes of significant returns. These loans, made more than 150 years ago, began a dependence on external finance and external actors that has persisted to the present day.

The era of free trade was also launched during this time period, as Latin America slowly adapted itself to the world economy. Exports to the United States and Europe began to increase—nitrates from Chile, hides and salted beef from Argentina, sugar from Cuba, and sugar from Brazil. The growth in exports was also accompanied by a corresponding rise in manufactured imports, especially textiles. Latin American artisans and small producers were often driven out of business in the exchange. This time also saw the arrival of a small number of foreign merchants who took up key positions in the fields of shipping, insurance, and banking. The pattern of losing out to foreign competitors was primarily the result of the technological superiority of the Europeans, but the local elites exacerbated the problem with misguided political choices. The traditional landowning elites first ensured that their holdings were secure and then retreated to the security of their *haciendas* and *fazendas*, not particularly concerned about maximizing production or contributing to the economic modernization of their countries. Political power was left largely in the hands of military men who had become *caudillos*, among them Juan Manuel de Rosas, the governor of Buenos Aires province; Antonio López de Santa Anna, the president of Mexico; and a lieutenant of Bolívar, José Antonio Páez. These military governments, without significant streams of revenue, were vulnerable to being overthrown and incapable of sustaining local economic growth. Some leaders recognized the dangers inherent in a weak central state, so in many countries conflict developed between locally based power brokers and the centralizers. These struggles were to be the forerunners of later battles for political power between Conservatives and Liberals.

One group negatively affected by independence was the indigenous peoples. They had not been a consistent force for elite-led independence and therefore were not seen by the new governments as important allies. As a result, they lost whatever protections they may have had under colonial administrations. Their land became increasingly vulnerable to takeover and their condition, even more impoverished.

Enter the United States

By the mid-nineteenth century the United States, often motivated by the doctrine of Manifest Destiny, began to expand its economic and political power into Latin America. Cornelius Vanderbilt established a a transisthmus transportation route through Nicaragua. U.S. nationals flocked to the Mexican territory of Texas and soon pushed for independence from Mexico. Subsequent tensions with Mexico under Santa Ana's rule led to broader conflicts and the Mexican-American War of 1846–1848. Further, this conflict reestablished a pattern of foreign intervention in Latin America and cost Mexico nearly half of its national territory.

1850–1880

The second stage of Latin America's integration into the world economy occurred between 1850 and 1880. National unification became the political theme as local *caudillo* rulers were slowly supplanted by national leaders, who began to construct the apparatus of the modern state. Liberal reform leaders like Benito Juárez in

Mexico, Domingo Sarmiento in Argentina, and Justo Rufino Barrios in Guatemala appeared.

As Latin American nations were ever more integrated into the commercialized world economy, liberal political (and economic) reforms and modernization that began in the 1850s continued. The epic Argentine struggle between the rural *gaucho* and remaining Indians, on the one hand, and the Europeanized *porteño* (port) elite from Buenos Aires, on the other, was indicative of this trend. The 1853 defeat of the *gaucho* dictator Juan Manuel de Rosas by reformist forces ushered in a new regime that opted for the "civilizing" influence of the port city over the rural land owners, the *estanciaros*. The government and economy were modernized, and massive European immigration (mostly from Italy) began. European capital, science, and technology were interjected into the development process. Liberal reforms set the stage for the emergence of other sectors in Argentine society. The meat-packing and grain-exporting industries gradually facilitated the emergence of an industrial proletariat and the beginning of a middle class. Argentina became ever more closely tied to England through the sale of its beef and the influx of British investment.

Meanwhile, peasants were beginning to feel the squeeze as their countries were further incorporated into the world market. Economic pressures and social upheaval fomented political restructuring as well. As a result, the region began to witness the emergence of reformist parties like the Radical Civic Union in Argentina, which held sway for most of the second and third decades of the twentieth century.

Periods of democratic rule began to appear, and political participation and the franchise were slowly widened beyond the elite to include common people in most countries. The transformation was in part driven by the slow rise of Latin America's export trade and the need to have a national infrastructure to support such trade. This era saw the beginning of efforts by national governments to transform long-standing land tenure arrangements that were dominated by largely unproductive *latifundios* and government land. This was the era of liberal ascendency almost everywhere in Latin America. During this period, there were significant efforts to undermine Church authority and establish secular, public education. Liberal ideas also made their way into the prison system and even military organizations. All of these Liberal reforms and this nation building occurred in the context of the penetration of North American and European capital.

To transport the region's coffee, sugar, nitrates, and other primary products to Europe and elsewhere, there was a strong need to replace the region's antiquated transportation system with new roads, canals, railroads, and docks. The traditional landowning elites had no need for infrastructure development to prosper, so they had not built it and were indifferent to its construction. The impetus for such development came primarily from abroad. European industrialization created a great thirst for everything from foodstuffs to fertilizers to metals. The developing European industries also sought out new markets for their manufactured goods. These twin European needs laid the groundwork for the next phase of Latin American development. Latin American countries willing to do business with Europe gained rising political power and wealth that challenged the traditional elites. However, the character of this economic arrangement—Latin American primary goods traded for European finished goods—established the pattern of Latin America's role in the world economy that persists to this day. The countries saw very little growth of domestic industry as European producers of machinery, weapons, and other light manufactured goods often blocked the development of indigenous industries. Competing with European entrepreneurs would have been difficult given their head start in technology; nor were Latin American governments of the time inclined to set up tariff barriers to spur local development. Generally, they were more than happy to welcome unrestricted foreign trade in return for their share of the profits. The era of 1850–1880 was one of laying the groundwork for even more dramatic changes that would occur in the last 20 years of the nineteenth century.

1880–1910

The needs of European industrialization that had been developing slowly throughout the nineteenth century came to a head after 1880. The demands for food by Europe's industrial workers and for raw materials to fuel factories were insatiable. Several key Latin American countries were transformed by these demands. Argentina became a great producer of beef, wool, and wheat. Brazil and El Salvador became the world's primary producers of coffee, satisfying Europe's newfound addiction, with Peru, Mexico, and Cuba supplying the sugar. Mexico provided Europe and North America with a variety of raw materials, including hemp, copper, and zinc. Thus, the pattern established in earlier decades of Latin American countries producing primary goods in exchange for European manufactured goods was deepened.

European countries also invested in Latin America. During this period Britain was by far the dominant investor, with almost two-thirds of the total investment by 1913. Railroads and mining were the two key sectors into which Europeans and North Americans placed their money. American investment also began to increase dramatically after 1900. Only modest amounts of Latin American capital went into these sectors, so the pattern of economic control by foreign powers became well established. Thus, Latin American prosperity became increasingly tied to the health of the European and North American economies. It also meant that most of the key decisions about the economic direction of Latin America were not being made in Rio de Janeiro or Buenos Aires but rather in New York, London, and Paris.

The new economic reality was justified and validated by the growing predominance of liberal ideology in most parts of Latin America. Free trade political liberals who favored less centralized state rule formed liberal parties, while traditional agricultural interests and pro-Church conservatives formed conservative parties. Local political leaders and their foreign counterparts extolled the virtues of free trade and open borders. It was viewed as simply "unnatural" to stand in the way of the economic and social progress that such arrangements were supposed to bring. Even the traditional landed elites in large measure cooperated in the modernization process, providing generous concessions to foreign companies while relying on traditional labor practices. To local governments it seemed only logical to collect some revenue from commercial trade, which during colonial times had flourished illegally outside their control. Of course, it was only a tiny slice (less than 5 percent) of the populations that benefited from these free trade agreements. Local elites, who viewed the native populations as significantly inferior, excluded them systematically from national political life. Democracy developed slowly. Where elections were held in Latin America in the nineteenth century, fewer than 10 percent of the population was eligible to vote. Most of the countries were organized as republics, but it was in form only. Political participation was limited to segments of the elite, and democracy was weak.

Elitist domination of politics persisted through the end of the nineteenth century but in a different form. The dominance of the local *caudillo* was over. National governments were now dominant, epitomized in the Porfirio Díaz regime in Mexico, 1876–1880 and 1884–1911. In some ways, leaders like Díaz were mirror images of the local *caudillo*. Usually military men, they were no longer doing the bidding of a local *hacienda* owner. Instead, they were representing the interests of commercial farmers and merchants whose economic success was predicated on foreign trade and a national infrastructure. To achieve the national power they needed, local authorities had to be put in line, a process that was consummated in Argentina and Mexico during this period. All such national regimes had a law-and-order focus designed to achieve political stability and therefore attract foreign investment.

The turn of the twentieth century saw the beginning of the consolidation of the modern nation-state in Latin America. As suggested earlier, this process had begun with Liberal reforms in Mexico under Benito Juárez in the 1850s and by Bartolomé Mitre and Domingo Faustino Sarmiento (1862–1874) in Argentina. In each country, the consolidation of power by newly emerging commercial elites was tied to increasing trade with the industrialized world. This movement of power away from more traditionally oriented elites would continue in the region through the 1940s.

Late nineteenth-century Brazil and Mexico saw the strong influence of developmental thought associated with Auguste Comte's philosophical positivism. Indeed, it was positivism that inspired the modernization of the Brazilian state and the foundation of the Brazilian Republic in 1889. Thus, the new elites in both of these countries began to rely on science and technology and tried to organize their societies to conform to the scientific law of progress. Following the advice of his positivist scientific advisors, or *científicos*, Díaz consolidated the commercial integration of Mexico into the world economy and was responsible for the massive foreign investment and improved infrastructure that characterized his rule. As with elite-run regimes in virtually all Latin American countries save Argentina, these new regimes did little to enfranchise the peasant and laboring masses economically (or politically). Indeed, the economic conditions of the common people had changed little since independence, and conditions that favored the emergence of a substantial middle class developed at a slow pace.

Early U.S. Involvement: *Tío* Sam and the Gringos

As a young republic suspicious of European ambitions for the region, the United States enunciated the Monroe Doctrine, mentioned earlier, in 1823 as a way to foreclose continuing intervention by the European powers in the hemisphere. From the earliest years, U.S.–Latin American relations were made more difficult by a commonly held view that U.S politicians and U.S. citizens were politically and economically, if not morally, more developed than the sister republics and their citizens to the south. Indeed, questions were at times raised as to Latin Americans' fitness for stable government. By the mid-nineteenth century, some in the United States had designs on parts of Latin America. In this context, the Mexican-American War (1846–1848) marked the beginning of a period of more direct U.S. involvement. Indeed, the term *gringo* is reputed to have been a by-product of the war. As the story goes, it resulted from a group of Mexicans overhearing the U.S. soldiers singing a song of the time that repeated the phrase "green grows." Thus, the Mexicans began to refer to the Americans as "green grows" or *gringos*. Needless to say, after losing the war and half of their territory, the Mexicans did not always think well of their *gringo* neighbors. The way the term spread and the slightly pejorative connotation usually attached suggested that Latin Americans would not always value the involvement of their North American neighbor. However, *Tío* Sam maintained economic and political interest in the region. By the last decade of the century, the **Pan-American Union** was formed (1890) as a mechanism to facilitate commercial and other interactions between the United States and the Latin American states. The nineteenth century ended with U.S. involvement in Cuba (1898). The twentieth century would see increasing U.S. intervention in Latin American affairs as the United States aided the residents of Panama to become independent from Colombia in 1903 and then constructed a canal there. Although no longer interested in Nicaragua as the preferred location for a transoceanic canal, U.S. involvement continued with a Marine incursion in 1909. The Mexican Revolution prompted renewed involvement in Mexico, such as the naval bombardment of Vera Cruz in 1914. Theodore Roosevelt's "**big stick**" became legendary in the Caribbean basin, as did "**gunboat diplomacy**." As financial interests intensified, these more primitive instruments of U.S. policy were replaced by "**dollar diplomacy**." Nonetheless, numerous interventions and heavy-handed diplomacy became common. The Marines were not only in Nicaragua again (1912–1925 and 1926–1933) but also in Haiti (1916–1934) and the Dominican Republic (1916–1922). As witness to—and participant in—such actions, U.S. Marine Corps Major General Smedley Butler noted that

> I spent thirty-three years . . . being a high-class muscleman for Big Business, for Wall Street and the bankers. In short, I was a racketeer for capitalism . . . I helped purify Nicaragua for the international banking house of Brown Brothers in 1909–1912. I helped make Mexico and especially Tampico safe for American oil interests in 1916. I helped make Haiti and Cuba a decent place for National City [Bank] boys to collect revenues in. I helped in the rape of half a dozen Central American republics for the benefit of Wall Street.

The Good Neighbor Policy under Franklin Delano Roosevelt and the need for allies and bases during World War II made for more cordial relations and much less outright intervention until the early 1950s and the onset of the Cold War.

Post-1910

By 1910, Latin America was being integrated ever more strongly into the world capitalist economy, assigned the role of peripheral producer of primary goods and consumer of industrialized goods from the developed nations at the center of the system. Further, there was increasing investment in plantations like those that grew sugar in Cuba or bananas in Central America and mines in countries like Mexico (silver), Chile (copper), and Bolivia (tin). Likewise, British and American financial capital sought even more investment opportunities in the expanding Latin American economies. The Great Depression temporarily halted the integration of Latin America into the international capitalist economic system, but the pace of integration continued and quickened in the second half of the century.

As we suggest in the chapter on economics (Chapter 7), increased demand for the export commodities and increasing imports helped commercialize Latin American economies. Import substitution industrialization (ISI) further changed the face of Latin America, as did the subsequent phase of export-led growth and the growing production and export of manufactured goods. The 1970s saw Latin American countries borrow more and more capital from outside the region, greatly increasing their external debts in the process. Debt and debt repayment remained a poignant problem into the twenty-first century. The last decades of the twentieth century witnessed the transformation of the region from what at the beginning of the century was a rural area where wealthy landowners and poor peasants or rural laborers predominated to a modern, urbanized area where three-quarters of the people lived in cities. By the turn of the twenty-first century, the largest class in most countries was the urban working class, which included a growing informal sector. Likewise, a significant middle class had developed and cut its political teeth. As these new classes were joined by new segments of the upper class tied to industrialization and commercialization and the increased involvement of multinational corporations and foreign investors, new political forces were mobilized and new political coalitions developed.

THE MEXICAN REVOLUTION

These and other factors led to the development of the first great revolutionary movement of the twentieth century, the Mexican Revolution. The dominance of traditional landowners, the Church, and the Díaz dictatorship kept developing social and political forces in check for many years. However, the struggle for change finally erupted in 1910 and spread throughout the society. The mostly rural masses soon mobilized with cries of *"pan y tierra"* (bread and land) and participated full force in the many revolutionary armies that fought for the next 7 years under such generals as Pancho Villa and Emiliano Zapata. It was indeed a revolution won by *los de abajo*, those from below, to use Mariano Azuela's term. The radical constitution of 1917 manifested many of the new ideas of the revolutionaries, set the stage for the development of modern Mexico, and infected the rest of Latin America with new ideas and expectations. Hereafter, land reform, legislation protecting workers, secular education, reduction of the power of foreign investors, and the Church's power and influence—as well as the ability to break with overly European models in favor of those that recognized the culture, history, and ethnicity of the masses—began to filter through Latin America. They soon combined with ideas from the second great revolution of the twentieth century (in Russia in 1917) to stimulate the development of new, more progressive social movements and political parties that would endeavor to forge a very different Latin American reality. The rest of the twentieth century witnessed myriad struggles between the conservative political and economic forces and mobilized classes and coalitions advocating significant reformist or revolutionary change.

Forces favoring reform and revolution would hereafter battle conservative forces and those tied to the existent system. After the Russian Revolution and subsequent spread of more radical forms of socialism and Marxism, these struggles would often become more class-oriented and often quite bloody as the dominant classes fought tooth and nail to preserve their status and privilege.

DEMOCRATIC REFORMISM IN URUGUAY

The modern reformist era arrived in Uruguay at the turn of the century. Like Argentina, Uruguay had an urban working class and the beginning of a middle class whose interests were quite different from those of the traditional landholders. The dynamic leader of the liberal Colorado party, José Batlle y Ordóñez, chose his 1903 election as president to enact a series of extensive economic and political reforms that would turn Uruguay into a modern social democracy and welfare state by the 1920s. Further, in a fascinating experiment with less autocratic forms of rule, Uruguay was even governed by a *colegiado,* or collective presidency (where power was shared among members of a presidential council and the titular head of state rotated), from 1917 to 1933 and from 1951 to 1967. Thus, from 1903 until 1973, Uruguay was regarded as the Switzerland of Latin America and as an example of just how democracy and enlightened social democratic-style rule could triumph in a Latin American state.

Later, conditions changed in Uruguay, and the threat of even greater popular mobilizations and the threat to the domestic upper class and foreign capitalists posed by the often popular Tupamaro guerrillas mobilized conservative forces against further change. Thus, even in democratic Uruguay, the rising tide of bureaucratic authoritarian military governments in the 1970s undermined their hard-won democratic political culture and the working- and middle-class benefits and liberties that had been achieved. This experiment with reformist democracy and a fully developed welfare state was cut short when the military staged a coup in 1973. The military controlled the country for the next 12 years. Full democratic rule was not restored until 1985; but the *colegiado* was no longer employed, and the working and middle classes were forced to accept government cutbacks and other structural adjustments. More recently, a progressive coalition, the *Frente Amplio,* has become a major power contender. Dr. Tabaré Vázquez led an even broader leftist electoral coalition, the Frente Amplio Encuentro Progresista Nueva Mayoria, to a first-round electoral victory in October of 2004. The Tupamaro guerrilla group turned political party (Movimiento de Liberación Nacional-Tupamaros) was a member of the winning coalition, which also carried a legislative majority in both houses. The leftist victory was initially seen as a clear repudiation of neoliberal policies and an assertion of popular control.

DEMOCRACY AND DICTATORSHIP IN ARGENTINA

It was suggested earlier that in the nineteenth century Argentina evolved from the gaucho dictatorship of Juan Manuel de Rosas to the reformist civilian rule of presidents like Domingo Sarmiento. By the turn of the century, Argentine beef and wheat were flooding into Europe and British investment was pouring into Argentina. The South American nation was developing rapidly and had a higher per capita income than several European nations. It soon spawned a proletariat and a nascent middle class. These groups became the base for a newly formed, European-inspired Radical

Party, which promised to bring enlightened democratic rule to Argentina. Before Argentina could experience sustained economic or political development, the Great Depression dashed hope for continued economic development, and the weakening of the Radical Party and a subsequent coup d'état in 1930 plunged the nation back into a military dictatorship.

After oligarchy-inspired conservative rule in most of the 1930s and early 1940s, a group of officers again intervened to take over the government in 1943. The junta they formed was eventually dominated by Colonel Juan Domingo Perón, who was later able to consolidate his power with the help of Eva Duarte and successfully ran for president in the 1946 elections. Peronism, as his political movement came to be called, became the dominant political party and political movement in Argentina. Peronism displaced the Socialist Party as the party of the masses and remained the largest political party for the rest of the twentieth century. Juan Perón was a dynamic, charismatic, and often dictatorial leader who was famous for his mass rallies and ties to the Argentine labor movement. Eva Perón became the darling of the masses and greatly bolstered the Peronist project. She died in 1952 and Juan Perón was ousted from power in 1955, yet their influence would linger; when again allowed to run for president in 1973, Juan Perón was reelected, with his then wife María Isabel Martínez Perón as his vice president. He died the next year, and Isabel Perón became the first female president in Latin America, only to be overthrown by a military coup in 1976.

From 1955 to 1966, Argentina was characterized by frequent alternation between military regimes and weak democratic governments. The country was industrializing and engaging in successful policies of import substitution, but it continued to be plagued by high inflation and a growing foreign debt. Strikes, labor actions, and guerrilla warfare challenged the oligarchy and the government. The military ruled outright from 1966 to 1973 and instituted a brutal "dirty war" against leftists and other political enemies from 1976 to 1983. After the military government initiated and lost the Falkland Islands War in 1982, elections brought a return to civilian government in 1983. Although initially threatened by barracks revolts and plagued by economic difficulties that allowed rightist Peronist President Menem to impose unpopular austerity measures, democracy continued through the rest of the century. His replacement, Fernando de la Rua, was forced from office because of an economic meltdown in 2001 and early 2002. Mass mobilizations, economic chaos, and massive street demonstrations continued until the third congressionally appointed president (Eduardo Duhalde) was able to stabilize the situation and hold presidential elections in 2003. Nestor Kirchner, a leftist Peronist who voiced strong opposition to the neoliberal policies advocated by the International Monetary Fund (IMF), won the presidency. Economic conditions had finally stabilized by 2005 as Kirchner developed policies that contested much of the advice of international financial institutions and neoliberal economists.

AUTHORITARIANISM, APRISMO, MARXISMO, AND DEMOCRACY IN PERU

Peru's defeat in the War of the Pacific (1879–1883) caused a national reexamination that began the consolidation of the modern nation-state and unleashed new social and political forces. Critical writers like Manuel González Prada spawned the radical reformist movements that eventually led to state centralization and consolidation under subsequent presidents and radical political movements like Victor Raúl Haya de la Torre's Alianza Popular Revolucionaria Americana (American Popular Revolutionary Alliance, APRA) and José Carlos Mariátegui's Peruvian Socialist Party (later the Peruvian Communist Party).

Haya de la Torre, heavily influenced by the Mexican as well as the Russian Revolutions, came to believe in a necessary political, economic, and social restructuring of all of Latin America. He founded APRA while visiting Mexico in 1924 and began a lifelong struggle to found political movements that would enfranchise the masses, promote land reform, improve the treatment of indigenous Americans, and resist the dominance of the United States. This movement led to the formation of APRA in Peru (which was kept from power by conservative and then reformist military forces until Alan García's presidency in 1985) and similar political movements in other countries. These movements represented the aspirations of the toiling masses—particularly indigenous peoples—and many sectors of the emerging middle class. The groups were often characterized as national revolutionary parties even though they were generally more reformist than revolutionary by the time they came to power. They came to be dominant parties in Venezuela (Acción Democrática, founded by Rómulo Betancourt), Costa Rica (Liberación Nacional, founded by José Figueres), Bolivia (Movimiento Nacionalista Revolucionario [National Revolutionary Movement, MNR], founded by Víctor Paz Estenssoro), Puerto Rico (Popular Democratic Party [PDP], founded by Luis Muñoz Marín), and the Dominican Republic (Partido Revolucionario, founded by Juan Bosch).

Coming from a more modest background than the aristocratic Haya de la Torre and more specifically focused on the Indian peasants and rural laborers, miners, and the small urban proletariat, the self-educated Mariátegui was heavily influenced by his reading of Manuel González Prada and about the indigenist movement in Peru, Marxist literature, Lenin and the Russian Revolution, and the Mexican Revolution. He supported indigenous rights and the workers' movement in Peru and went on to found the Peruvian Socialist Party, which soon affiliated with the Communist International. In so doing he stimulated the development of a Marxist–Leninist movement in Peru and gave impetus to revolutionary struggle in Peru and elsewhere. Indeed, he argued for a Latin American socialism that was "neither copy nor imitation" of any other; but his early demise in 1930 and strong criticism from the Soviet-controlled Communist International limited his influence for many years. Marxists in Peru and Latin America rarely followed his independent stance, and communist parties were generally subordinate to European influences and Soviet control. Not until the last decades of the twentieth-century was Mariátegui's open brand of Marxism fully appreciated by a broad spectrum of the Latin American left.

Substantial structural change did not come to Peru through a socialist movement or through APRA; rather, it arrived with a reformist military takeover in 1968 that maintained power until 1980. Thus, it was the military—not reformist or radical civilian politicians—that instituted a comprehensive system of land reform in Peru (although they did not set up sufficient financial mechanisms to empower poor peasants and agricultural workers who were the beneficiaries of this reform) and addressed the conditions of the workers. Previously, Peru's political history had been marked by dictators like Augusto Leguía (1919–1930) and Manuel Prado (1949 and 1956–1962) and by intermittent periods of democracy.

There was a return to democratically elected governments after 1980, but the struggle against severe economic conditions for the masses and the rise of the guerrilla group Sendero Luminoso stretched the democratic institutions beyond their limits. By the mid-1990s, events such as the 1992 *auto-glope* (self-coup) of elected president Alberto Fujimori had greatly diminished the practice of democracy. This trend was continued with the 2000 fraudulent reelection of Fujimori for a constitutionally prohibited third term, though he was forced from office in 2001 and new elections were held. By 2004, elected successor President Alejandro Toledo, who was accused of favoritism and corruption, insisted on following neoliberal policies that became increasingly unpopular. His support was so small (measured in single digits in opinion polls) that some wondered if he would even be able to finish his term. Indeed, 2005 began with an armed uprising demanding his ouster (see section on Peru in Chapter 9).

DEMOCRACY, SOCIALISM, INTERVENTION, AND DICTATORSHIP IN CHILE

Political reform came to Chile earlier. It began with the formation of a parliamentary republic (1891–1924) and came to include a proletariat and a nascent middle class. The predominance of copper mines owned by foreign corporations sparked the formation of a strong socialist-oriented union movement, and the large number of socialist immigrants helped create a socialist political movement in Chile. Like Mariátegui in Peru, labor leader Luis Emilio Recabarren championed a Marxist party in Chile. Building on the newly developing political forces unleashed by a nitrate boom, the parliamentary republic, and the development of copper mining, Chile continued to evolve, experiencing a short-lived socialist republic under Marmaduke Grove in the early 1930s.

Along with more traditional parties, a substantial socialist movement developed. As its support among the miners and urban working class and sectors of the middle class grew, it was challenged by a strong, reformist Christian Democratic Party that had also created a union movement. The Christian Democrats headed off the leftist challenge, mobilized workers, and, with support from the United States and their Christian Democratic allies in Europe, won two important elections in the 1960s and went on to establish themselves as a major reformist party. Even greater structural change began when the Socialist Party, in coalition with the Communist and Radical Parties, finally achieved power in 1970 with the election of Salvador Allende as president. This was a clear triumph of the popular classes.

Up to this point Chile, like Uruguay and Costa Rica after 1948, was considered a nation where the seeds of democracy had taken root and flowered. Indeed, many thought that the thoroughgoing socialist restructuring proposed by Allende might actually be carried out by peaceful, constitutional means. Some significant progress was made during the first years of Allende's Popular Unity government from 1970 to 1973, but Chilean society became increasingly polarized. The United

States and conservative sectors in Chile made every effort to destabilize the newly elected government. U.S. military aid to the Chilean military was, interestingly, continued, even though all other aid was cut. Finally, Chilean democracy was shattered by a brutal United States–supported and Central Intelligence Agency (CIA)– sponsored military coup in September 1973. The workers had lost. The coup displaced all progressive forces and instituted a repressive military regime run by Augusto Pinochet that lasted until 1990. Thousands were murdered by the state security forces. A return to free market economics was one of the primary goals of the military dictatorship. As the country came to terms with the brutality of the military dictatorship in the post-Pinochet period, three democratic elections were held and a socialist once again became president in 2000. From 1990 on, civilian presidents helped to soften aspects of the rather austere neoliberal economic policies. On the whole, the country was considered to have developed a thriving economy based on neoliberal principles. Indeed, the George W. Bush administration's plan to privatize Social Security was beholden to a similar plan implemented in Chile, even though in Chile it soon became fraught with problems and many of the privatized pension funds left their participants with very little indeed (see Chapter 16).

U.S. Policy and the Cold War

The end of World War II set the stage for the Cold War, and Latin America became one of the theaters of operation. Fearing communist influence in Guatemala (and because of complaints by the United Fruit Company), the U.S. CIA planned and executed a coup that overthrew the constitutionally elected government in 1954. This became a model for often heavy-handed meddling in the internal politics of Latin American nations by the United States. The specter of world communism facilitated a retreat from the Good Neighbor Policy to one premised on the assumption that Latin American sovereignty could be subordinate to the fight against communism, if not U.S. policy interests generally. As will be detailed below, there were a series of subsequent interventions in sovereign Latin American states. Further, throughout the Cold War period, the U.S. military, the State Department, and other U.S. agencies also worked closely with Latin American militaries to train them in counterinsurgency and national security policy to resist Marxist guerrillas and other real and imagined threats from the left. More positive policy instruments such as the Alliance for Progress and U.S. aid were also used to try to remedy the economic and social conditions that might breed communism and instability.

Cuba, Colonialism, and Communism

Much of the inspiration for the democratic attempt at a constitutional socialist revolution in Chile was derived from the Cuban example as well as from Chile's own socialist and democratic tradition. Indeed, the event after the Mexican Revolution that inspired the most attempts at radical change in Latin America was the revolution that took place in Cuba in 1959. As it evolved toward a socialist path that eventually embraced Marxism–Leninism, Cuba became a model for radical change throughout the region.

Cuba, like Mexico, was an example of change delayed. Even independence had come late to Cuba; Cuban patriots lost the Ten Years War (1868–1878), and slavery was not abolished until 1886. Spanish colonial rule endured until 1898, and independence was not achieved until 1902 (and then only under U.S. tutelage). The system that ensued was dominated by sugar plantations and sugar refineries (*centrales*) that were increasingly owned or controlled by U.S. businesses as American investment capital flooded into the island in the first decades of the twentieth century. A Cuban upper class centered in sugar production also developed, while the masses were generally relegated to positions as cane workers and *guajiros* (peasants). Poverty and seasonal unemployment characterized rural agricultural labor, as did de facto subordination of people of color. A monocrop economy and dependent nation par excellence, Cuba became closely tied to the United States for sugar sales and the importation of finished goods. Indeed, it was often suggested that the American ambassador to Havana was nothing less than a proconsul.

By the 1920s Cuba had already experienced its first dictatorship (Gerardo Machado, 1924–1933). A second coup was led by a noncommissioned officer, Sergeant Fulgencio Batista, in 1934. Batista maintained good relations with the United States and, promoted to colonel, was elected to the presidency in 1940 as a reformer. In 1952, he executed another coup and established what became a brutal and unpopular dictatorship, which was eventually overthrown by Fidel Castro's 26th of July movement. Supported by peasants and agricultural workers, segments of the Cuban upper class, and many from the middle class that had emerged in Havana, the revolutionaries took power in 1959 and went about reforming the country, basing many of their ideas on the reformist constitution of 1940. The guerrilla war that put them in power became immortalized in fellow guerrilla leader Ernesto "Che" Guevara's manual on guerrilla fighting, *Guerrilla Warfare*.

The examples of the Cuban Revolution and of forming guerrilla groups to wrest power from dominant elites were of immediate interest to the Latin American left. The Cuban Revolution became Marxist after the United States organized the Bay of Pigs invasion in 1961 and, thus, also became an example of the revolutionary transformation of a Latin American society. The notion of overthrowing the status quo with a band of guerrilla fighters and addressing the economic and social injustices and foreign control that had characterized the region was widely acclaimed by progressive forces. A variety of Fidelista guerrilla groups were organized throughout Latin America and set about emulating the Cuban example and fighting their way down from the hills into the corridors of power in the nations' capitals. Guerrilla movements like the Frente Sandinista de Liberación Nacional (FSLN) in Nicaragua, the Armed Forces of National Liberation (FALN) in Venezuela, the Revolutionary Armed Forces of Colombia (FARC), and the Movement of the Revolutionary Left (MIR) in Peru and Chile began to operate from Mexico and Guatemala in the north to Argentina and Chile in the south. Radical change and socialist revolution through violent struggle were now added to the political mix. The revolutions were not led or fomented by Latin American Soviet-oriented communist parties, which generally had very limited success, frequently criticized the young Fidelista revolutionaries, and often did not support the movements. Cuba became the revolutionaries' mecca and source for moral and sometimes material support. The radical regime continued in power into the twenty-first century (see Chapters 10 and 13 for additional material).

EARLIER ATTEMPTS AT CHANGE: BOLIVIA AND COLOMBIA

Before the Cuban Revolution, other less radical attempts at change had been made in Latin America in the post–World War II period. The MNR in Bolivia was inspired by the philosophy and example of the Peru-based APRA and the Mexican Revolution. Led by Víctor Paz Estenssora, National Revolutionary Movement (MNR) radicals had led the strongly indigenous and heavily unionized radical tin miners, indigenous peasants, and middle-class supporters to seize power in 1952. They soon nationalized the tin mines and engaged in a major agrarian reform that distributed large amounts of land to impoverished peasants. Difficult economic conditions and the hostility of the United States made it difficult to maintain the reformist project. The experiment was cut short in 1964 when the vice president took power through a military coup. A series of military governments followed, but the masses mobilized once again in late 2003 to force the U.S.-linked president to resign. The mostly indigenous masses and their social and political movements again mobilized in 2005 to force the former vice president and now president to resign to pave the way for the new elections in December 2005. Indeed broad indigenous support facilitated the election of Evo Morales as president (see Chapter 20 on Bolivia).

The movement to enfranchise the masses in Colombia was manifest in the figure of progressive Liberal politician Jorge Gaitán. He represented the progressive wing of the Liberal Party and promised better conditions for the labor movement and for peasants. Before he could mobilize support for such badly needed reforms, he was assassinated in Bogotá in April 1948. Those committed to change took to the streets, and days of violent rioting followed. Known as the *Bogotazo*, the violent actions in the capital soon spread throughout the country, where bands of Liberals attacked Conservatives, whom they believed had denied them the change they so badly needed. Soon, the entire country was caught up in a decade of fighting known as *La Violencia*. It was finally ended by the formation of the National Front, a common front based on a political pact between the elites in the Conservative and Liberal Parties whereby they agreed to share power among the mainstream elements of the two parties. A clear example of politics by pact among the elite, the agreement lasted until the early 1970s.

In the meantime, those desiring more fundamental change gravitated to a variety of guerrilla groups that began to operate in Colombia from the 1960s onward. Many of these gained such power that they were able to negotiate special agreements with the government; one of the original and surviving guerrilla groups, the Fuerzas Armadas Revolucionarias de Colombia (FARC), even managed to negotiate a temporary cease-fire with the Colombian government that gave them control over part of Colombian territory. They and other guerrilla groups had been greatly strengthened in the 1990s by agreements with several Colombian drug cartels that guaranteed protection and economic well-being for the peasants in their areas and gave the cartels certain protection from the armed forces as long as they paid their taxes to the guerrilla organization. By 2000, the eroding power and legitimacy of the government and the growing strength of FARC and the Ejército de Liberación Nacional (ELN) suggested that change in Colombia could still come through a revolutionary take-over. This and the continuing power of the drug cartels prompted the United States to greatly increase military, antidrug, and economic aid to Colombia in 2000. The U.S. War on Drugs and the continued existence of FARC prompted the Clinton Administration to create Plan Colombia, the multibillion-dollar plan to eradicate coca fields and stop the production of illegal drugs in Colombia. Conflict continued, but by 2007 the level of U.S. funding for Plan Colombia was being reduced despite President Alvaro Uribe's hard line with guerrilla groups and his close cooperation with the United States (see Chapter 18 for additional information on Colombia).

BRAZIL, U.S. FOREIGN POLICY AND THE NATIONAL SECURITY STATE

Like Cuba, change and social restructuring came late to Brazil. From independence in 1822 until 1889, Brazil was an empire under the control of emperors from the Portuguese royal family. Brazil did not see the consolidation of the modern nation-state until Getúlio Vargas' takeover of the federal government in the revolution of 1930 and his subsequent establishment of the "new state" in 1936. Vargas and his personal style of populism dominated Brazilian politics until his suicide in 1954. Through the efforts of many progressive political movements, change again occurred in the late 1950s. Juscelino Kubitschek was elected in 1955 by promising to move the country forward. His dynamic approach to government action and the founding of the new capital of Brasília helped heighten expectations for a brighter future.

After 1960, the United States became increasingly concerned with political mobilization of the masses and political movements that might, as had occurred in Cuba, become radicalized as they struggled to break away from the stultifying economic and social structures that had condemned the vast majority of Latin Americans to poverty and suffering. U.S. policy toward Latin America in the 1960s was twofold: foment gradual change and restructuring through the Alliance for Progress and related activities (this would undermine the political base of more revolutionary movements) and support the development of counterinsurgency and the national security states to fight and defeat the radical guerrilla movements that did appear. To the latter end, military training in places like the School of the Americas in the Panama Canal Zone and aid to Latin American militaries were greatly increased. Soldiers and lower-level officers were trained in counterinsurgency tactics. Command officers were imbued with a version of the national security doctrine that suggested that the Latin American governments and especially the military were responsible for protecting the nation and state from the threat posed by guerrillas, leftist political movements, and communism. Since many Latin American military leaders already thought of themselves as guardians of the nation, this training—which was replicated and emphasized in national war colleges—served as a further impetus to intervene when there was danger of uncontrollable popular mobilization or unchecked guerrilla activity. In 1965, U.S. President Lyndon Johnson even enunciated the Johnson Doctrine (a corollary to the Monroe Doctrine) to explain the need of the United States to intervene in its sister republics to stop the spread of communism.

The shadow of the Cuban Revolution, peasant mobilization, worker militancy, and domestic radicals who might opt for violent revolution—all seen through the lens of national security doctrine—convinced the Brazilian military and conservative forces that they were facing a revolutionary situation. The United States had already expressed concern and was communicating with the military and sympathetic politicians. A military coup was staged in 1964, and a long period of authoritarian military rule was initiated.

The military regime that took power did not, however, stabilize the situation and then hold elections, as was often the case when military juntas took over. Rather, it usurped power from civilian politicians, closing congress, arresting some leftist leaders, banning traditional political parties, and generally arguing that the Brazilian military could develop the country much better than the civilian politicians could. The peasant mobilization and worker militancy that helped spark the popular movement were suppressed, as were radical groups. There would be no revolution in Brazil. Instead, a long period of military rule (lasting until 1985) was initiated, and the military took it upon itself to guide Brazil in achieving its *grandeza* (greatness) by developing along more conservative, state-directed capitalist lines. Large *fazendas* were continued, foreign capital was invited in, the government went into joint business ventures with multinational corporations, the Amazon was thrown open for development, and indigenous people were seen as expendable in the rapid developmental process that ensued. Growth and development were expected; socioeconomic restructuring and income redistribution were unacceptable. This long-term economically and politically involved military rule and the resultant national security state designed to stop political or social revolutions like that which occurred in Cuba came to be called *bureaucratic authoritarianism*. Brazil was the prototype (see Chapter 14 on Brazil). After Brazil's return to democracy in 1985, new power contenders like the Workers' Party (PT) appeared.

The Cold War and Change

THE DOMINICAN CASE

In early 1965, political instability and the possibility of the mobilization of the Dominican masses by Juan Bosch and his APRA-style Dominican Revolutionary Party raised the specter of a reformist party taking power but, like the 26th of July Movement in Cuba, then becoming radicalized as it endeavored to effect change in An economy heavy with U.S. investment. Red flags went up in the White House and the Pentagon, and in April 1965 25,000 Marines were dispatched to Santo Domingo to restore order and staunch any leftist threat. No more Cubas would be tolerated. Conservative rule was restored and continued into the 1980s. More progressive leaders such as Leonel Fernández (PLD, 1996–2000 and 2004–2008) charted a new course in the 1990s and after. With the signing of the Central American Free Trade Agreement (CAFTA) and the inclusion of the Dominican Republic, the island nation was drawn even more strongly into the U.S. sphere of influence.

CENTRAL AMERICA AND U.S. HEGEMONY

The quest for change in Central America came more slowly. American involvement in the region dated from William Walker's intervention in Nicaragua in the 1850s.

American investment grew through the latter part of the nineteenth century and all during the twentieth.

The case of U.S.–Nicaraguan relations will be discussed below. Other attempts were also made to transform the traditional reality of Central America. For instance, from 1944 to 1954, reformist forces in Guatemala attempted to consolidate a modern nation-state and make economic and social reforms that would economically and politically empower the peasants, banana workers, and majority indigenous population for the first time. However, the new government soon found itself in a heated dispute with the Boston-based United Fruit Company, which had very strong ties to the U.S. government. Before the land reform program could be completed, the Revolution of 1944 was overthrown by a CIA-organized military coup in 1954. A virtual civil war erupted in the 1960s as Cuba-inspired guerrillas tried unsuccessfully to overthrow the military and conservative forces. The struggle continued into the 1990s and claimed some 200,000 Guatemalan lives (see Chapter 11).

In El Salvador, a small oligarchy reigned as fourteen families ruled and used brutal repression to maintain their virtual monopoly on wealth and power (as in the Matanza of 1932). The families frequently used their military allies to maintain an unjust status quo. Military rule predominated in the 1960s and 1970s, and pressure for change grew by 1979. Rather than allow needed land and other reforms, the rulers once again opted for repression. This led to strong civilian opposition and the eventual formation of the Farabundo Martí Front for National Liberation (FMLN). A civil war developed in the 1980s as a coalition of reformers and revolutionaries battled the military and the U.S.-backed civilian government. More than 70,000 lives were lost in the civil war in El Salvador; the United States supplied more than $5 billion in military and economic aid to stop the revolution. Peace was finally negotiated in the 1990s, and the FMLN was transformed into a major political party, although the U.S-backed Alianza Republicana Nacionalista (ARENA, National Republican Alliance) party consistently won the presidency and most though certainly not all other offices through 2007 (see section on El Salvador in Chapter 10). El Salvador and Guatemala were not able to escape the consequences of the lack of socioeconomic reform or the culture of violence that the brutal civil wars had engendered. Brutal gangs (*maras*) developed. M S or M S 13 (the Mara Salvatrucha) and M 18 were reputed to have as many as 100,000 members in Central America by 2008 and could not be controlled by the governments in El Salvador, Guatemala, and Honduras. El Salvador and Guatemala were two of the most violent societies in the world. The homicide rate for El Salvador alone was 55 per 100,000 (as compared to 5.7 in the United States). There were 10 homicides a day in a total population of 6.8 million. By the beginning of 2008, the *maras'* organizations extended through the three countries and reached back into the United States.

Events were different in Costa Rica. The victory of José Figueres and his National Liberation forces in the Costa Rican civil war of 1948 and the subsequent establishment of a modern social democratic state in the 1950s marked the only example of progressive change to endure in the region. Figueres' strong ties to the United States and his American wife helped facilitate the success of the Costa Rican experiment, which turned into a two-party dominant democracy that valued honest elections

Farmers and ox cart in rural Costa Rica. *(Photo by Patrice Olsen)*

and electoral competition. The country opted for a European-style social democracy that achieved high levels of education, health care, and sanitation.

COUNTERINSURGENCY, HEGEMONY, AND U.S. INTERVENTION

As mentioned earlier, the Cold War and the socialist turn of the Cuban Revolution encouraged the United States to suppress progressive political movements throughout the second half of the twentieth century, lest they lead to communism or Cuba-like revolutions. This often buttressed the most conservative forces and the status quo at the expense of much-needed reforms. Indeed, it sometimes served to kill hope for those who tried to effect change. U.S. policy makers encouraged their military and civilian allies in Latin America to think in terms of the national security state. Thus, the United States sponsored counterinsurgency training for Latin American militaries at the School of the Americas in the Panama Canal Zone and at U.S. military bases such as Fort Bragg, North Carolina. Since the U.S. intervention in Guatemala in 1954, there has been significant U.S. military or political involvement in Cuba (Bay of Pigs, 1961), the Dominican Republic (Marines in Santo Domingo, 1965), Chile (destabilization and overthrow of Allende, 1973), Jamaica (destabilization of Manley government, 1980), El Salvador (continued political and military involvement, 1980–1992), Nicaragua (U.S.-inspired Contra War, 1981–1990), Grenada (military invasion, 1982), Panama (military invasion, 1989), and Colombia (aid and military advisors, 2000 on). Thus, reform, revolution, and change often had to be played against a backdrop of real or potential involvement by the United States. As civil wars and guerrilla movements wound

NOTES ON NICARAGUAN–U.S. RELATIONS: A CAUTIONARY TALE

As a way of understanding what many consider the hegemonic relations that the United States has with Latin America, a brief look at how relations between Nicaragua and the United States have developed is offered below.

Nicaragua has seen many manifestations of the hegemonic influence of the United States. The United States not only waged a massive covert action against the small Central American state for almost a decade but also intervened to influence the outcome of the 1990 election. More subtle forms of intervention have extended through the late 1990s and into the twenty-first century as neoliberalism and globalization were strongly advocated. Other forms of intervention began nearly 150 years ago when a group of Nicaraguan Liberals mistakenly invited a band of U.S. mercenaries to aid them in their ongoing struggle with the Conservatives. The result was unique among Latin American nations because a U.S. citizen (William Walker) was able to force his way into the presidential palace and the nation's presidency. Nicaragua had become a transit corridor for Americans wishing to take advantage of the gold rush boom on the west coast of the United States. It was seriously considered as a location for a canal to connect the Atlantic and Pacific Oceans. Indeed, Nicaragua has been tied to U.S. power since the 1850s and is still struggling to assert its sovereign independence.

Nicaraguan and Central American relations with the United States were once more fraternal. Contacts between the United States and the region were at first sparse but sometimes based on the Jeffersonian concept of relations among equal, sister republics. Indeed, in the first half of the nineteenth century, the United States was still a struggling young republic that had not yet consolidated its power or position in the world. It fought and lost its last anticolonial war against the British in 1812. However, by the middle of the nineteenth century, the nature of international relations in the hemisphere began to change. American power was first projected south in the Mexican-American War of 1846–1848, which resulted in the annexation of half of Mexico's territory by the United States. Commercial penetration also increased. This projection of power from Washington was soon manifest in Nicaragua. Cornelius Vanderbilt developed financial interests when he set up a stagecoach and steamship line to carry passengers across the Central American isthmus after the California gold rush in 1849. Soon thereafter, the American filibuster William Walker took over Nicaragua in 1855 and even had himself declared president after he stipulated that English was to be the official language. Later, the post-Civil War industrialization and economic expansion of the United States began to redefine the economic interests of the northern state. It would no longer be primarily a producer and exporter of raw materials like its sister republics to the south. Rather, it was becoming an industrialized creditor nation that started to search out new markets for its industrial products, additional sources of raw materials, and new locations to invest its growing capital. By the turn of the century, relations began to reflect the hegemonic position that the United States was establishing in the Caribbean basin, if not Latin America more generally. From 1903 through the 1990s, Central America witnessed a diverse variety of hegemonic initiatives by the United States: Marine occupations, gunboat diplomacy, dollar diplomacy and financial penetration, Roosevelt's Good Neighbor Policy, anticommunism, the Alliance for Progress, covert intervention, and direct occupation by U.S. troops, as most recently occurred in Panama in 1989.

Nicaragua started to consolidate its power as a nation-state under the presidency of José Santos Zelaya (1893–1909). The Liberal president soon introduced reforms that alarmed the Conservative forces and threatened the interests of U.S. capital. As Zelaya faced increasing internal and external pressure, his rule became more dictatorial. The United States did not hesitate to show its displeasure and even went so far as to land Marines in the Atlantic coast city of Bluefields in 1909. Zelaya was forced from power in that same year. U.S. intervention increased over the next years as Marines were again landed in 1912 to prop up the U.S.-installed puppet regime of Adolfo Díaz. They stayed until 1925 and suppressed several nationalist uprisings, like that begun by nationalist hero Benjamín Zeledón in 1912.

In 1925, a new Liberal uprising against a Conservative coup and the U.S.-inspired reinstallation of Adolfo Díaz as president developed. The Marines once again intervened. Sandinista namesake Augusto César Sandino returned from Mexico in 1926 to head one of the liberal bands and continue the struggle after the other Liberal generals accepted a U.S.-brokered peace. The Marines stayed on to fight the strongly nationalist movement headed by Sandino and based primarily on segments of the popular classes who grasped the nationalist, anti-imperialist nature of the struggle. The first Sandinistas fought the Marines and a U.S.-organized Nicaraguan National Guard to a stalemate. The negotiated settlement of 1933 was, however, betrayed by the Guard and its sycophant leader Anastasio Somoza García. Somoza parleyed his close ties to the United States and his position as leader of the National Guard to become the most powerful leader in the country and had himself elected president in 1936. He and his sons would rule Nicaragua until militarily defeated by the Frente Sandinista de Liberación Nacional (FSLN) in July of 1979. Always a great friend of the United States, Somoza opened the country to U.S. investment and encouraged companies like United Fruit and Standard Fruit to increase their business operations in Nicaragua. The leadership in Washington became accustomed to what they perceived as a subservient government in Managua. Indeed, the training for the Bay of Pigs invasion of Cuba was done in Nicaragua. Thereafter, the Somozas were vociferous in their anticommunist declarations.

To understand the specifics of the Nicaraguan case, it is necessary to follow the development of the country since the Sandinista takeover in 1979. Under the Sandinistas, Nicaragua was one of the countries that insisted on maintaining its national sovereignty in economic and political matters and argued for a new international economic order. The Sandinistas endeavored to remove the nation from the hegemonic control of the United States. It became a member of the Nonaligned Movement and pursued a very independent foreign policy. Its ties to the nonaligned movements and its economic relations with a variety of countries including Cuba, the Soviet Union, and Eastern Europe allowed it a certain amount of economic flexibility. However, when Ronald Reagan was elected president of the United States in 1980, he began a policy of bringing pressure to bear on Nicaragua. This included an economic embargo and low-intensity warfare that utilized CIA-organized counterrevolutionaries who came to be called *contras*. Indeed, the Contra War cost some 30,000 Nicaraguan lives and devastated the Nicaraguan economy. In 1990, casualties and material damages inflicted by the *contras*, external pressure, Sandinista errors, and the dynamics of internal Nicaraguan politics combined to cause the electoral defeat of the Sandinistas and the election of Violeta Chamorro to the Nicaraguan presidency. Yet, the electoral victory of anti-Somoza martyr Pedro Joaquín Chamorro's widow was in large part engineered by the United States, which in turn left the new government beholden to Washington and consequently with much less autonomy.

In Nicaragua, Guatemala, and El Salvador, the United States had mobilized considerable resources to make sure that the revolutionary forces would be defeated. Through
U.S. military involvement and the Central American peace process championed by
Costa Rican president Oscar Arias and other regional leaders, the struggle was moved
from military to political and electoral means. By the early 1990s, the independent,
radical thrust of political movements in all of these countries had been greatly reduced
and no radicals were in control of their respective nations. Official relations were once
again cordial with the United States, which expressed great satisfaction that (U.S.-
style) democracy had been restored in Nicaragua and Central America. By the end of
the 1990s, democratization was in full bloom and political struggle in these nations
had been channeled into less violent avenues that were more easily influenced by the
United States. Nicaragua's new subservience to U.S. policy suggested that it would
vigorously implement neoliberal economic policies. As it did, its economy worsened
even more; and by the end of the 1990s, it suffered massive unemployment and was
the second poorest country in the hemisphere (see Chapter 19 on Nicaragua for more
recent events).

down in the 1990s, the United States continued to exert strong pressure on the
internal politics of Latin American countries. The end of the Cold War and the new
international order, however, made for less violent—but no less forceful—forms of
economically focused intervention.

THE POST-COLD WAR PERIOD AND U.S. HEGEMONY

The 1991 demise of the Soviet Union, the main socialist rival to the ascending
hegemony of the United States, and the resultant difficulties for Cuba and the
Cuban revolutionary model meant that neither communism nor Cuba was perceived as an immediate threat in Latin America. This, in turn, relaxed the emphasis on the national security state and counterinsurgency in Latin America. Further,
the end of bureaucratic authoritarian regimes by the early 1990s signaled a return
to greater formal democracy. The triumph of capitalism in Eastern Europe further
stimulated the process of free-market capitalist globalization. In Latin America,
nationalist economic policies that protected and promoted import substitution
industrialization and the growth of national businesses were rapidly abandoned
in favor of free markets, free trade, and the free flow of investment capital. Latin
America now seemed to be a safe place for international capital to do business. By
2000, Colombia was the only country to have any significant radical groups contesting power through the use of force and challenging the new Pax Americana.
Throughout the region, increasing pressure came from international financial
institutions like the International Monetary Fund (IMF) to globalize and set aside
policies that would directly transfer benefits, income, or wealth to the still-suffer-
ing masses of Latin Americans. The new focus was not on socioeconomic change,
restructuring, or income redistribution; rather, it was on capitalist growth that
would—Latin Americans were told—benefit all. Those suspicious of the continuing intervention of the United States believed that Marine uniforms and guns may

well have given way to business suits and IMF portfolios. Others felt that Latin American nations might now finally be able to compete in the international economic arena on more equal ground because the globalization of their economies would force them to modernize and become more competitive. By 2008, this later view was not widely shared.

Venezuela: Dictatorship, Democracy, and the Post-Cold War Bolivarian Republic

The combination of neoliberal-inspired economic policy, continued impoverishment of the masses, and shoddy statesmanship created conditions that generated a movement led by a progressive army officer in the country where Simón Bolívar had started the struggle for independence in South America. In 1810, Bolívar and the junta in Caracas struggled to establish democracy in Caracas and the rest of what is now Venezuela and Colombia. Yet, the march toward democracy was not always easy in Bolívar's homeland. The Venezuelan nation saw its share of dictators in the remaining years of the nineteenth century and experienced a long period of dictatorial rule in the first part of the twentieth century. Indeed, the dictatorship of Juan Vicente Gómez (1908–1935) is one of the most notorious in Latin American history. Before Gómez, Venezuela almost experienced another wave of European intervention. At the turn of the century, several European states, led by Germany, wanted to take over the customs operations of the nation to get funds to repay debts owed by Venezuela. This plan was frustrated by the U.S. invocation of the Monroe Doctrine, but even so, Germany, England, and Italy did engage in a naval bombardment of Puerto Cabezas in 1903. These economic problems were resolved with the beginning of petroleum production under the Gómez dictatorship.

Modern democracy came to Venezuela with the APRA-inspired Acción Democrática takeover in 1945 and the election of civilian president Rómulo Gallegos in 1947. But he too was overthrown by another coup in 1948. From 1952 to 1958 Venezuela suffered the military dictatorship of Marcos Pérez Jiménez. Led by Rómulo Betancourt, Acción Democrática instituted an open democracy, political competition (mostly with the Christian Democratic COPEI Party) that lasted until 1998. A founding member of the Organization of Petroleum Exporting Countries (OPEC), Venezuela was able to build a governmental and physical infrastructure from its increasing petroleum revenues. Although many lived well, the proceeds from petroleum production were concentrated in the middle and upper classes and a few well-paid unionized petroleum workers. The vast majority continued to live in poverty despite the petroleum bonanza. Strong civilian government and a stable two-party system did, however, develop. This system suffered its first challenge when major riots broke out after IMF-inspired austerity measures were met with massive rioting by the poor in Caracas in 1989. The inability of the governments and increasing corruption led to two serious coup attempts by reformist military officers in 1992 and the eventual emergence of one of the coup leaders as a challenger to the old political system. After serving 2 years in prison, Hugo Chávez assembled an opposition movement (Fifth Republic Movement) and successfully ran for the presidency in December 1998. He defeated the candidates fielded by the two main parties and swept many of his supporters into office throughout the nation. The two long dominant parties lost legitimacy in the face of the traditional system's breakdown and Chávez's promises to confront neoliberalism and the conditions that were keeping the masses in poverty. Further, he charged the old political structures with corruption and of only benefiting the elite. He spoke of the need for structural change and made favorable references to the achievements of the Cuban Revolution and Fidel Castro after his visit to the island. In 2000, Chávez managed to have a much revised constitutional system passed in a national plebiscite and to again hold elections at all levels to legitimize his mandate. He won 60% of the vote. The newly restructured state was dubbed the "Bolivarian Republic of Venezuela." His power was threatened by a coup attempt in 2002 and a popular referendum to remove him from office in 2004. Neither was successful, and *Chavismo* was still solidly in control in 2008, though Chávez was not able to secure a majority for all the constitutional reforms he championed (see Chapter 17 on Venezuela).

GROWTH, PERSISTENT POVERTY, AND IMMIGRATION TO THE UNITED STATES

As was the case in Venezuela, by 2005 most Latin American economies experienced some economic growth but maintained a wide gap between upper-class beneficiaries of globalization and the still-prevalent misery of the masses. In many cases, income distribution even widened. However, a few countries, such as Costa Rica and Chile after 1990, developed sufficient social welfare programs to at least soften the savage capitalism that globalization had unleashed in Latin America. It remains to be seen if this new direction in economic policy will engender sufficient benefits to satisfy the masses, if the people will mobilize behind new political leaders and political movements that challenge the status quo and promise greater economic equality, or if they will just leave if they can. By 2005 there was an upsurge in popular movements and leftist leaders had taken power in Argentina, Brazil, Uruguay, and Venezuela. Radical popular movements had displaced less progressive politics in Bolivia and Ecuador and leftist presidents were elected in both Andean nations. For a while a leftist was the leading candidate for the 2006 election in Mexico but was narrowly defeated at the polls. Alternatively, Latin American immigration into the United States was increasingly adopted by others as a survival strategy, and the number of legal and illegal immigrants crossing U.S. borders continued to surge. Indeed, remittances sent home by Latin Americans working in the United States became a major source of income in many countries like Mexico and the Dominican Republic. This also began to change the population dynamics and politics on both sides of the U.S. border. People and thus labor—like capital—became ever more fluid and able to flow past borders. Indeed, there were many dimensions to the globalization process in the twenty-first century in the Americas and fences, walls, or increased border patrols could not even begin to stop it. It should also be noted that there was increased migration within the region as well, especially to economic centers such as southern Brazil, Argentina, and Costa Rica.

TABLE 3. Remittances to Latin American and Caribbean Countries, 2006

Country	Amount (Millions of Dollars)
Argentina	850
Belize	93
Bolivia	1,030
Brazil	7,373
Colombia	4,200
Costa Rica	520
Cuba	N/A
Dominican Republic	2,900
Ecuador	2,900
El Salvador	3,316
Guatemala	3,610
Guyana	270
Haiti	1,650
Honduras	2,359
Jamaica	1,770
Mexico	23,053
Nicaragua	950
Panama	292
Peru	2,869
Trinidad & Tobago	110
Uruguay	115
Venezuela	300

Note: These figures represent total remittances rather than those only from the United States, although the United States accounts for 75 percent of the total.

Source: http://www.iadb.org/mif/remesas_map.cfm?language=english&parid=5&item1d=2, 2006.

TABLE 4. Immigrants in the United States by Region and Country of Birth, 1996–2006

Region and Country of Birth	Legal Immigrants			Estimated Illegal Immigrants Residing in the United States	
	1996	2000	2005	1990	2006
North America	340,428	344,805	345,575	2,789,000	8,400,000
Mexico	163,556	173,919	161,445	2,040,000	6,570,000
Caribbean	84250*	88,198	91,378	X	X
Antigua-Barbuda	406	431	440	X	X
Bahamas	767	768	698	X	X
Barbados	1,041	783	846	4,000	5,000^
Cuba	26,438	20,831	36,261	2,000	7,000^
Dominica	797	96	198	3,000	4,000^
Dominican Republic	39,599	17,536	27,504	91,000	91,000^

(continued)

TABLE 4.   Immigrants in the United States by Region and Country of Birth, 1996–2006
Continued

Region and Country of Birth	Legal Immigrants			Estimated Illegal Immigrants Residing in the United States	
	1996	2000	2005	1990	2006
Grenada	785	655	840	X	X
Haiti	18,383	22,364	14,529	67,000	76,000^
Jamaica	19,084	16,000	18,346	37,000	41,000^
Trinidad and Tobago	7,331	6,660	6,568	23,000	34,000^
Central America	60331*	66,443	52,636	X	X
Belize	785	760	876	10,000	8,000^
Costa Rica	1,502	1,344	2,278	5,000	17,000^
El Salvador	17,902	22,578	21,359	298,000	510,000
Guatemala	8,762	9,970	16,825	118,000	430,000
Honduras	5,866	5,939	7,012	42,000	280,000
Nicaragua	6,901	24,029	3,305	50,000	21,000^
Panama	2,559	843	1,815	7,000	11,000^
South America	61,744	56,074	103,143	185,000	1,000,000
Argentina	2,450	2,331	7,081	7,000	15,000^
Bolivia	1,913	1,772	2,197	8,000	13,000^
Brazil	5,888	6,959	16,664	20,000	210,000
Chile	1,706	1,712	2,404	6,000	17,000^
Colombia	14,275	14,498	25,571	51,000	141,000^
Ecuador	8,319	7,685	11,608	37,000	108,000^
Guyana	9,489	5,746	9,318	13,000	22,000^
Paraguay	615	342	516	X	X
Peru	12,869	9,613	15,676	27,000	61,000^
Suriname	211	257	300	X	X
Uruguay	539	430	1,154	2,000	2,000^
Venezuela	3,465	4,716	10,645	10,000	34,000^

* From the year 2000 instead of 1996; data not available for 1996.^ From the year 2000 instead of 2006; DHS does not provide a comprehensive breakdown of illegal immigration in 2006. X = Data not available. D = Data withheld to limit disclosure.

Sources: 2005 Yearbook of Immigration Statistics, Table 2 and Table 3. Office of Immigration Statistics in the Department of Homeland Security, Nov. 2006. Located on the Internet at http://www.dhs.gov/xlibrary/assets/statistics/yearbook/2005/OIS_2005_Yearbook.pdf.
Estimates of the Unauthorized Immigrant Population Residing in the United States: January 2006, December, 2007. Department of Homeland Security. Located on the Internet at http://www.dhs.gov/xlibrary/assets/statistics/publications/ill_pe_2006.pdf

Nineteenth-Century Time Line

1804   Following mass slave rebellion led by Toussaint L'Ouverture, Haiti becomes the first independent republic in Latin America

1807   Napoleon Bonaparte invades Spain and Portugal; Ferdinand VII imprisoned and forced from Spanish throne, and Napoleon names his brother as successor; in the Americas, creoles begin plotting the independence of their Spanish American countries; the Portuguese court escapes and, with the British navy's help, flees to Brazil

1810 Mexico declares independence from Spain under the leadership of Father Miguel Hidalgo

1811 Venezuela declares its independence by forming a junta that expels the Spanish governor

1813 Father José María Morelos revives the Mexican independence movement; José de San Martín and the Army of the Andes liberate Argentina

1816 The United Provinces of the Río de la Plata declare their independence

1817 Chile is liberated by Bernardo O'Higgins; Spain outlaws the slave trade in all of its provinces to the north of the equator

1819 The United States buys Florida for $5 million

1821 On July 28, San Martín proclaims Peru independent; Dom Pedro defies summons of Cortés by remaining in Brazil, creating the only durable monarchy in Latin American history; Stephen F. Austin and other settlers move into Texas; Mexico and Central America gain independence

1822 Agustín de Iturbide is crowned emperor of Mexico

1823 The Central American Federation is established; the Monroe Doctrine is announced by U.S. President James Monroe; Peru passes its constitution

1824 The defeat of the Spanish army in Ayachucho, Peru, marks the end of Spanish rule in the Americas

1825 Bolivia gains its independence

1825–1828 War between Brazil and United Provinces of the Río de la Plata (present-day Argentina); the peace treaty created the independent state of Uruguay

1826 Congress of American Republics held in Panama; independence leaders sign concordats with the Vatican making Catholicism the state religion

1830 In Chile, beginning of the Conservative Republic; the Conservative Party holds power for 30 years

1835 Texans revolt

1836 Texans declare independence from Mexico

1845 U.S. Congress annexes Texas

1846 War between the United States and Mexico begins

1848 The Treaty of Guadalupe Hidalgo brings end to war between United States and Mexico; the United States gains approximately half of Mexico's territory

1855 U.S. citizen William Walker and former troops from the Mexican-American War invade Nicaragua; Walker declares himself president and holds power until 1857

1857 In Mexico, the Laws of Reform are promulgated by Benito Juárez

1864 Maximilian given Mexican throne by Napoleon III

1867 President Juárez expels the French and marches into Mexico City

1868–1878 Ten Years War; nationalist Cubans lose fight for independence from Spain

1871 Chilean constitution is changed, disallowing consecutive presidential terms; Brazil passes "law of the free womb"—all children born to Brazilian slaves are considered free; also in Brazil, ex-Liberals found the Republican Party

1876–1880, 1884–1911 General Porfirio Díaz rules over Mexico

1879–1883 War of the Pacific between Chile, Peru, and Bolivia; Bolivia loses land access to sea

1886 Slavery ends in Cuba

1887 In Chile, the Democratic Party is founded

1888 Brazil passes "golden law," which frees all slaves without compensation

1889 On November 16, Brazil is declared a republic as Emperor Dom Pedro II and his family leave in exile

1890 Increasing commercial relations between United States and Latin America and formation of the Pan-American Union

Contemporary Time Line

1910–1917 Mexican Revolution

1911 Madero elected president of Mexico

1912 Universal male suffrage granted in Argentina; U.S. military intervenes in Nicaragua; U.S. troops stay until 1925

1913 Madero killed

1914 Panama Canal opens

1915–1934 United States occupies Haiti

1916–1922 U.S. Marines occupy Dominican Republic

1916 Hipólito Yrigoyen, leader of the Unión Cívica Radical (UCR, or Radicals), elected president of Argentina; workers' compensation laws passed in Chile

1917 Chile passes employer liability laws; Venustiano Carranza assumes presidency in Mexico; a new constitution is written; U.S. military intervenes in Cuba; Puerto Rico is legally annexed to the United States; Puerto Ricans given U.S. citizenship

1919 Chile passes retirement system for railway workers in the same year that 100,000 workers march past presidential palace; Emiliano Zapata murdered

1922 Communist Party formed in Brazil; oil found in Venezuela

1924 Military junta in Chile; Alianza Popular Revolucionaria Americana (APRA) formed by Victor Raúl Haya de la Torre

1926 Augusto César Sandino returns to Nicaragua to fight with liberals; begins guerrilla war against newly occupying U.S. forces

1926–1929 Mexican Church suspends worship, protesting state harassment; many priests and civilians killed in the Cristero rebellion

1926 Democratic party founded in São Paulo, Brazil

1929 Ecuador is the first Latin American country to grant suffrage to women

1930 On September 6, the military of Argentina overthrows the Yrigoyen government; October coup in Brazil; Getúlio Vargas takes over government

1932 Brazil and Uruguay grant suffrage to women; Chaco War between Bolivia and Paraguay; Paraguay gains more territory; uprising in El Salvador is brutally repressed in *la Matanza*

1933 U.S. troops leave Nicaragua; Anastasio Somoza begins to take power; U.S. president Franklin Roosevelt announces Good Neighbor Policy

1934 Lázaro Cárdenas becomes president of Mexico; during his term he redistributes 44 million acres of land to landless Mexicans; Sandino murdered in Nicaragua

1938 Mexican oil industry nationalized under Cárdenas

1939 El Salvador grants suffrage to women

1943 Juan Perón and other military officers take over in Argentina

1944 Democratic revolution in Guatemala

1945 Modern democratic era begins in Venezuela with takeover by APRA-inspired Acción Democrática, led by Rómulo Betancourt; Guatemala and Panama grant suffrage to women

1946 Juan Perón elected president of Argentina; Eva "Evita" Duarte Perón becomes first lady

1947 Argentina and Venezuela grant women suffrage

1948   José Figueres and APRA-inspired Liberación Nacional Party lead reformist revolution in Costa Rica and establish modern democratic social welfare state; Costa Rican army banned by its new constitution; *Bogotazo* in Colombia; *La Violencia* begins

1949   Chile and Costa Rica grant women suffrage

1952   Evita Perón dies of cancer; Fulgencio Batista takes direct power in Cuba; Puerto Rico becomes a commonwealth of the United States; Marcos Pérez Jiménez stages coup in Venezuela, initiating a dictatorship that lasts until 1958; Bolivia grants women suffrage; Bolivian revolution led by Movimiento Nacionalista Revolucionario (MNR) and Víctor Paz Estenssoro

1954   Alfredo Stroessner takes over as president of Paraguay and rules until 1989; in Guatemala, CIA-organized coup deposes constitutional President Jacobo Arbenz and begins three decades of often brutal military rule; United Fruit regains land nationalized in land reform program during 1944 revolution

1955   Juan Perón ousted from power by the military and goes into exile; Honduras, Nicaragua, and Peru grant women suffrage

1956   Juscelino Kubitschek de Oliveira inaugurated president of Brazil; construction of Brasília begins

1957   François "Papa Doc" Duvalier elected president of Haiti; Colombia grants women suffrage

1958   Dictator Pérez Jiménez ousted in Venezuela; Acción Démocratica's Rómulo Betancourt elected president, beginning modern democratic era

1959   Batista flees Cuba; Fidel Castro and the 26th of July Movement take power

1960   Construction of Brasília completed

1961   Paraguay is the last Latin American country to grant suffrage to women; the United States organizes unsuccessful Bay of Pigs invasion by Cuban exiles

1962–1965   The Second Vatican Council (Vatican II) commits the Church to work for human rights, justice, and freedom

1962   Peronists again allowed to run for office in Argentina; Cuban Missile Crisis; Jamaica gains independence from Britain

1963   Rural unionization legalized in Brazil; peasant leagues grow

1964   Eduardo Frei Montalva elected president of Chile; military coup in Brazil; bureaucratic authoritarian military stays in power until 1985

1965   U.S. Marines invade the Dominican Republic

1966   Brazil's government unveils Operation Amazonia, a plan to develop the Amazon basin

1967   Ernesto "Che" Guevara dies in Bolivia

1968   October 2 student massacre in Tlatelolco, Mexico City; meeting of Latin American bishops in Medellín, Colombia adopts a "preferential option for the poor" under the influence of liberation theology; reformist military leaders take over in Peru under Juan Velasco Alvarado

1970   Salvador Allende elected president of Chile; he is the first freely elected Marxist president in Latin America; the Communist Party of Peru– Sendero Luminoso (PCP-SL)—emerges after an ideological split in Peru's Communist Party; origins of the group can be traced to a study group formed in the early 1960s by Professor Abimael Guzmán Reynoso at the University of San Cristóbal de Huamanga; Sendero Luminoso, the Shining Path, later takes the form of a revolutionary movement

1971   Haitian president "Papa Doc" Duvalier dies; his son, Jean-Claude "Baby Doc" Duvalier, takes control; U.S. Peace Corps accused of sterilizing Indian women without their knowledge, expelled from Bolivia

1973 Juan Perón reelected president of Argentina; his wife Isabel becomes vice president; Salvador Allende dies in a September 11 military coup in Chile; General Augusto Pinochet initiates a brutal military dictatorship that rules until 1990

1974 Juan Perón dies; Isabel Perón becomes first female president of a Latin American country

1975 UN Conference on Women held in Mexico City, kicking off the Decade for Women; Cuba passes law requiring men and women to share responsibilities for housework and childrearing

1976 Argentine military ousts Isabel Perón; General Jorge Rafael Videla takes power, and the "dirty war" begins; the Mothers of the Disappeared begin to hold weekly vigils challenging the military government's human rights abuses

1978 John Paul II becomes pope; the Catholic Church becomes more conservative; conservative Church leaders begin to attempt to eliminate liberation theology

1979 Somoza regime collapses; the Frente Sandinista de Liberación Nacional (FSLN), or Sandinista National Liberation Front, takes power

1980 Archbishop Oscar Romero of San Salvador assassinated; four American church women murdered by Salvadoran military; Farabundo Martí National Liberation Front (FMLN) formed in El Salvador

1981 United States inspires contras to war against Nicaraguan government; 30,000 die before 1990

1982 Falklands/Malvinas War begins between Argentina and Britain; Brazil elects first freely elected governors since 1965; General Efrain Rios Montt becomes Latin America's first evangelical dictator in Guatemala and embarks on a brutal counterinsurgency that often targets entire Indian communities

1983 U.S. Marines land in Grenada

1985 Brazil elects Tancredo Neves as first freely elected president; the night of his inauguration he has surgery and never recovers; Vice President José Sarney becomes president

1986 "Baby Doc" Duvalier flees Haiti

1988 Amidst well-documented charges of election fraud, Institutional Revolutionary Party (PRI) candidate Carlos Salinas defeats Cuauhtémoc Cárdenas and Party of the Democratic Revolution (PRD) to gain presidency of Mexico

1989 Carlos Menem elected president of Argentina; Patricio Aylwin elected president of Chile, the first elected president of Chile since Allende took power; Pinochet maintains his position as commander-in-chief of the Chilean armed forces and as senator for life; in Brazil, Fernando Collor de Mello elected president, defeating Workers' Party (PT) leader Luiz Inácio "Lula" da Silva; U.S. troops invade Panama to oust Manuel Noriega; six Jesuit priests assassinated in El Salvador by U.S.-trained troops after the FMLN overruns much of San Salvador; announcement of austerity package in Venezuela causes riots, in which 276 die

1990 Alberto Fujimori elected president of Peru; stays in office until 2001; President Salinas of Mexico announces his intent to negotiate the North American Free Trade Agreement (NAFTA) with the United States; Jean-Bertrand Aristide elected president of Haiti; a military coup prevents him from taking power; Violeta Barrios de Chamorro elected president of Nicaragua, defeating FSLN candidate Daniel Ortega

1991 Jorge Serrano of Guatemala becomes Latin America's first elected evangelical president

1992 In Brazil, Collor is impeached and Vice President Itamar Franco becomes president; Fujimori closes congress in an *auto-golpe*, or self-coup; leader of the Sendero Luminoso Abimael Guzmán captured; World Summit on the Environment and Development held in Rio de Janeiro; guerrilla war ends in El Salvador; two military coup attempts occur in Venezuela

1993 Eduardo Frei Ruiz-Tagle (son of the president 1964–1970) elected president of Chile; Carlos Andrés Pérez forced to step down in Venezuela

1994 Fernando Henrique Cardoso elected president of Brazil; NAFTA goes into effect on January 1; Zapatista National Liberation Army revolts in Chiapas; Ernesto Zedillo elected president of Mexico after first PRI candidate is assassinated; United States occupies Haiti; Aristide assumes presidency

1995 Menem reelected president of Argentina; Fujimori reelected president of Peru; new quota in Argentina making sure that one in four congresspeople are women; *Mercosur*, or Southern Cone Common Market is founded, including Argentina, Brazil, Uruguay, and Paraguay, later joined by Bolivia and Chile

1998 Pinochet loses post as commander-in-chief of Chilean armed forces; Cardoso reelected president of Brazil, once again defeating Lula; former coup leader Hugo Chávez elected president of Venezuela, ending domination by two traditional parties, Acción Democrática and the Social Christian Party (COPEI)

1999 Mireya Moscoso elected first female president of Panama; Plan Colombia initiated

2000 Socialist Ricardo Lagos elected president of Chile as the Concertación candidate; Confederation of Indigenous Nationalities of Ecuador (CONAIE) and military officers briefly take over congress in Ecuador; Fujimori reelected in Peru after forcing constitutional changes allowing him to run for a third term; opposition candidate Vicente Fox elected president of Mexico, breaking seven decades of presidential domination by the PRI; in Venezuela, president Hugo Chávez reelected for 6-year term under new constitution

2001 Argentina experiences severe economic and political crisis; President Fernando de la Rua resigns; Alejandro Toledo elected president in Peru after Fujimori forced out of office

2002 Workers' Party candidate Luiz Inácio "Lula" da Silva elected to presidency of Brazil on fourth run; attempted coup in Venezuela reversed by massive street demonstration supporting President Hugo Chávez; hardline Alvaro Uribe elected president of Colombia

2003 Massive mobilization by *cocaleros,* indigenous peoples, unions, and others force Bolivian President Gonzalo Sánchez de Lozada from office; Argentina elects leftist Peronist Néstor Kirchner as president

2004 Dr. Tabaré Vázquez of leftist Broad Front wins presidency in Uruguay; Venezuelan president Hugo Chávez registers strong support in referendum on his rule

2005 Ecuadoran president Lucio Gutiérrez is forced from office by popular mobilizations; Bolivian president Carlos Mesa also forced to resign and former Cocalero leader Evo Morales elected as first indigenous president of Bolivia later in the year

2006 Lula and Worker's Party government survive scandal to win second presidential term in Brazil; left-leaning Rafael Correa elected president of Ecuador; Alvaro Uribe continues hard line on negotiating with guerrillas and is reelected president of Colombia; Sandinista leader and former president Daniel Ortega is again elected president in Nicaragua; in a hard-fought campaign in Mexico, P.A.N. candidate Felipe Calderón wins presidential election by razor-thin margin; Leftist PRD candidate Miguel López Obrador contests vote and vows parallel government; Hugo Chávez reelected president of Venezuela with 62 percent of vote; Michelle Bachelet elected first female president of Chile

2007 Evo Morales continues reforms in Bolivia and asserts nation's right to own and control all natural gas; Hugo Chávez asserts socialist nature of Venezuelan regime and continues strong leader style while confronting George Bush and increasing hostile U.S. foreign policy; Nobel prize winner Rigoberta Menchú makes poor showing in Guatemalan presidential election, which is won by Alvaro Colom; Néster Kirschner decides not to run for a second presidential term in Argentina in favor of his wife Christina Fernández Kirschner, who wins vote to become first woman elected to the presidency

Bibliography

Azuela, Mariano. *The Underdogs (Los de abajo)*. New York: Penguin, 1962.

Beezley, William H., and Judith Ewell, eds. *The Human Tradition in Latin America*. Wilmington, DE: Scholarly Resources, 1997.

Bethell, Leslie, ed. *The Cambridge History of Latin America*. Vols. IV and V. Cambridge: Cambridge University Press, 1986.

Blum, William. *Killing Hope: U.S. Military and CIA Interventions since World War II*. Monroe, ME: Common Courage Press, 1995.

Bulmer-Thomas, Victor. *The Economic History of Latin America since Independence*. New York: Cambridge University Press, 1994.

Butler, Smedley D. *War is a Racket*. Los Angeles: Feral House, 2003.

Burns, E. Bradford. *Latin America, A Concise Interpretive History*. 6th ed. Englewood Cliffs, NJ: Prentice Hall, 1994.

Cortés Conde, Roberto, and Shane J. Hunt, eds. *The Latin American Economies: Growth and the Export Sector, 1880–1930*. New York: Holmes and Meier, 1985.

Galeano, Eduardo. *Open Veins of Latin America: Five Centuries of the Pillage of a Continent*. New York: Monthly Review Press, 1997.

———. *We Say No: Chronicles 1963–1991*. New York: W. W. Norton, 1992.

Keen, Benjamin. *A History of Latin America: Independence to the Present*. 7th ed. Boston: Houghton Mifflin, 2004.

LaFeber, Walter. *Inevitable Revolutions*. 2nd ed. New York: W. W. Norton, 1992.

Langley, Lester. *The Americas in the Age of Revolution 1750–1850*. New Haven, CT: Yale University Press, 1996.

Leo Grande, William. *Our Own Back Yard: The United States in Central America, 1977–1992*. Chapel Hill: University of North Carolina Press, 1998.

Lynch, John. *The Spanish-American Revolutions 1806–1826*. New York: W. W. Norton, 1986.

Macauley, Neil. *The Emergence of Latin America in the Nineteenth Century*. New York: Oxford University Press, 1988.

McSherry, J. Patrice. *Predatory States: Operation Condor and Covert War in Latin America*. Lanham, MD: Rowman and Littlefield, 2005.

Oliva Campos, Carlos, and Gary Prevost, eds. *The Bush Doctrine and Latin America*. New York: Palgrave, 2007.

Rodríquez, O. Jaime E. *The Independence of Spanish America*. Cambridge: Cambridge University Press, 1998.

Russell-Wood, A. J. R. *From Colony to Nation: Essays on the Independence of Brazil*. Baltimore, MD: Johns Hopkins University Press, 1975.

Schoultz, Lars. *Beneath the United States: A History of U.S. Policy Toward Latin America*. Cambridge, MA: Harvard University Press, 1998.

Skidmore, Thomas E., and Peter H. Smith. *Modern Latin America*. 6th ed. New York: Oxford University Press, 2005.

Smith, Peter H. *Talons of the Eagle: Dynamics of U.S.–Latin American Relations*. 2nd ed. New York: Oxford University Press, 2008.

Vanden, Harry E. "Nicaraguan Foreign Relations." In *Revolution and Counterrevolution in Nicaragua: 1979 Through 1989*. Edited by Thomas Walker. Boulder, CO: Westview Press, 1991.

———. "State Policy and the Cult of Terror in Central America." In *Contemporary Research on Terrorism*. Edited by Paul Wilkinson and A.M. Stewart. Aberdeen, UK: Aberdeen University Press, 1987.

———. "Terrorism, Law and State Policy in Central America: The Eighties." *New Political Science* no. 18/19 (fall/winter 1990): 55–73.

Vanden, Harry E., and Thomas Walker. "U.S.–Nicaraguan Relations." In *The Central American Crisis*. 2nd ed. Edited by Kenneth M. Coleman and George C. Herring. Wilmington, DE: Scholarly Resources, 1991.

FILMS AND VIDEOS

The Battle of Chile. Chile, 1976.
Evita. United States, 1997.
Missing. United States, 1982.
The Official Story. Argentina, 1985.
Que Viva Mexico. Russia/USSR, 1931.
Reed: Mexico Insurgente. Mexico, 1971.
Romero. United States, 1989.
State of Siege. France, 1973.

WEBSITES

www.presidencia.gov.bo/ Presidential website in Bolivia.
www.presidencia.gov.ve/ Presidential website in Venezuela.

FOUR

THE OTHER AMERICANS

Details of the Spanish and Portuguese colonization of Latin America were provided in earlier chapters in this volume. The purpose of this chapter is to explore the contemporary consequences of that conquest on the indigenous peoples of the Americas who lived in the region prior to 1492 and to examine the fate of the more than 10 million Africans who were brought to the Caribbean and Latin America as slaves.

In 1992, the 500th anniversary of the first voyage of Columbus provided renewed focus on the current conditions of those segments of Latin American society who have been often ignored and marginalized by governments and scholars alike. It is estimated that more than 40 million indigenous people are alive today. Indigenous people constitute clear majorities in Guatemala and Bolivia, close to half of the population in Peru and Ecuador, and a substantial minority in countries such as Mexico, Brazil, El Salvador, Nicaragua, and Colombia. In the 1980s, conflict and then negotiation between the revolutionary government of Nicaragua and the peoples of the Atlantic Coast focused international attention on the region's indigenous people. In recent years, indigenous people have become more politically active in both Latin America and worldwide. In 1990, a nationwide indigenous uprising paralyzed Ecuador. A decade later, the national indigenous group the Confederation of Indigenous Nationalities of Ecuador (CONAIE) was one of the primary political actors in a government takeover that forced out President Jamil Mahuad. In 1994, an indigenous-based guerrilla movement, the Zapatistas, drew international attention to the southern Mexican state of Chiapas. In many countries, indigenous movements have been in the forefront of struggles over the control of natural resources and the environment and have begun to move from a position of marginalization to one of centrality in Latin American society.

In 1492, Spain turned westward in search of wealth and empire. That same year the Spanish monarchy had recovered Granada from the Moors, the culmination of a struggle that had lasted seven centuries. It was an era of reconquest for Spain, undertaken in the context of its Christian vision. Queen Isabella became the patroness of the Inquisition, which was designed to root out all alien religions (Judaism, Islam, and so forth) in Spain. Pope Alexander VI, who was Spanish, ordained Isabella the master of the New World. Three years after the discovery, Columbus directed a military campaign against the native population in Hispaniola. His cavalry decimated the native inhabitants, and more than 500 were shipped to Spain and sold as slaves. Most died within a few years. Throughout the conquest of the Americas, each military action began with the Indians being read a long narrative (in Spanish, without an interpreter) exhorting them to join the Catholic faith and threatening them with death or slavery if they did not comply. The brutality of the proselytization notwithstanding, in many ways the religious arguments were only a cover for the primarily commercial basis of the conquest.

The newly powerful Spanish government had decided to establish its own direct links to the east, hoping to bypass the independent traders who up until that time had monopolized the trade there for spices and tropical plants. The voyages also sought precious metals. All of Europe needed silver. The existing sources in central Europe had largely been exhausted. In the Renaissance era, gold and silver were becoming the basis of a new economic system, mercantilism. Those nations that had supplies of these precious metals could dominate the Western world. Despite that, most of the expeditions that came to the Americas in search of wealth were not sponsored by governments (Columbus and Magellan were the exceptions) but by the *conquistadores* themselves or by businessmen who backed them. The *conquistadores* did indeed find gold and silver in large quantities; but in order to mine it, they needed local labor. That drive for labor produced what Eduardo Galeano has called the "Antillean holocaust":

> The Carribean island populations were totally exterminated in the gold mines, in the deadly task of sifting auriferous sands with their bodies half submerged in water or in breaking up the ground beyond the point of exhaustion, doubled up over the heavy cultivating tools brought from Spain. Many natives of Haiti anticipated the fate imposed by their white oppressors: they killed their children and committed mass suicide.

The civilizations confronted by the Spaniards in Mexico and Peru were large and prosperous ones. The Aztec capital Tenochtitlán (present-day Mexico City), with 300,000 people, was then five times larger than Madrid and double the population of Seville, Spain's largest city. Tenochtitlán had an advanced sanitation system and engaged in sophisticated agricultural techniques in the marshland around the city. It was a majestic city dominated by the Templo Major, its most sacred site.

When the conqueror Pizarro arrived in South America, the Incan Empire was at its height, spreading over the area of what is now Peru, Bolivia, and Ecuador and including parts of Colombia and Chile. The third great civilization was that of the Maya, who inhabited the Yucatan Peninsula of Mexico and south into Guatemala. The Maya were skilled astronomers and mathematicians who had developed the concept of the number zero.

Despite their high level of civic and scientific development, the indigenous people in the Americas were defeated by a variety of factors that favored the

European invaders. The European military commanders were also quite skillful at exploiting divisions among the indigenous people. In Mexico, Cortés allied with the Tlaxcalans against Moctezuma and the Aztecs of Tenochtitlán. Pizarro also succeeded in exploiting family disputes among the Incas to foster his advantage in Peru.

The brutality of their conquest was unlimited. They took the gold and melted it into bars for shipment to Spain. Sacred temples and other public places were simply destroyed. Later, in Mexico City, the Spanish would build their metropolitan cathedral and government buildings on the foundations of the primary religious and political buildings of the old Aztec capital, as if to symbolize the total subjugation of the original inhabitants. Pizarro's forces in Peru did the same, sacking the Temple of the Sun in Cuzco, the capital of the Incan Empire.

The Europeans also brought with them diseases not found in the Americas—smallpox, tetanus, leprosy, and yellow fever. Smallpox, the first to appear, had devastating consequences. The indigenous people had no defenses against these plagues and died in overwhelming numbers. As much as half of the existing population may have died as a result of the first contact.

As suggested in Chapter 2, the scope of the genocide against the indigenous people of the Americas is staggering. There were probably upward of 70 million people living in the Americas when the Europeans arrived, between 30 and 40 million in Mexico alone. By the middle of the seventeenth century, that number had been reduced to 3.5 million. In some countries, such as Cuba, the native population had been completely exterminated, while in one region of Peru, where there had been more than 2 million people, only about 4000 families survived. Over the course of three centuries, silver production at Potosí consumed 8 million lives.

In addition to such dramatic loss of life through forced labor, the mining system indirectly destroyed the farming system. Forced to work in the mines or as virtual slaves on crown lands, indigenous people were forced to neglect their own cultivated lands. In the Incan Empire, the Spanish conquest resulted in the abandonment of the large, sophisticated farms that had grown corn, peanuts, yucca, and sweet potato. The irrigation systems that had been built over centuries were neglected, and the land reverted to desert, a condition that persists today.

European Justification

While millions of indigenous people perished, Europeans engaged in marginalized debates over the legal status of their victims. The Spanish court in the sixteenth century acknowledged in principle their legal rights and entitlement to dignity. Various religious leaders spoke out against the inhumane treatment that the native people received, but these legal statements and religious proclamations ultimately had no meaning because the exploitation of indigenous labor was essential to the functioning of the colonial system. In 1601, Philip III formally banned forced labor in the mines but in a secret decree allowed it to go forward; his successors, Philip IV and Charles II, continued the exploitation.

The ideological justifications for the exploitation of the indigenous people were many and varied. Political and religious leaders often characterized the native people as "naturally wicked" and viewed their back-breaking work in the mines as retribution for prior transgressions. Many religious leaders offered the opinion that as a race indigenous people lacked a soul and therefore could not be "saved" by the Church in the traditional sense. Many Church leaders never accepted Pope Paul III's declaration of 1537 that the indigenous people were "true men." Others viewed them as natural beasts of burden, better suited for much of the region's manual labor than its four-legged creatures. The Spanish and Portuguese colonizers were not alone in consigning the indigenous to a subhuman status. Some European intellectuals of the Enlightenment, such as Voltaire and Montesquieu, refused to recognize them as equals.

The indigenous population of the Americas, though conquered and defeated by the Spanish and Portuguese during the sixteenth century, continued its resistance on an ongoing basis. Probably the most dramatic example of that resistance occurred in Peru near the end of the eighteenth century. At that time, Spanish pressures and demands on the Peruvian Indians increased considerably. In particular, under the *repartimiento de mercancias* the natives had to purchase goods from the Spanish traders whether or not the items were useful. Locals were often unable to pay for these purchases and, as a result, were forced from their villages to earn money in mines or on *haciendas,* neglecting their own productive enterprises. During this time, the Spanish rulers also sought to dramatically increase silver production at Potosí and did so with harsh forced labor programs. These conditions fostered a strong desire among the indigenous population to return to the glories of the Incan Empire of three centuries earlier. Their aspirations led to the great revolt of 1780–1781. These dramatic events had many forerunners; 128 rebellions took place in the Andean area between 1730 and 1780. From 1742 to 1755, a native leader, Juan Santos, waged partisan warfare against the Spaniards. The memory of his exploits was still alive when the revolt of José Gabriel Condorcanqui erupted. A well-educated, wealthy *mestizo* descendant of Incan kings, Condorcanqui took the name of the last head of the neo-Incan state and became Túpac Amaru II. His actions began with an ambush of a hated local Spanish commander; by early 1781, the southern highlands of Peru were in full revolt. The objective of Amaru's revolt was the establishment of an independent Peruvian state that would be essentially European in its political and social organization. His vision was that caste distinctions would disappear and that the *criollos* would live in harmony with Indians, blacks, and *mestizos.* The Catholic Church was to remain the state church. However, the Indian peasantry who responded to his call for revolt had clearly more radical goals, no less than total inversion of the existing social order and a return to an idealized Incan Empire where the humble peasant would be dominant. The peasants exacted their revenge on all those viewed as European, including the Church hierarchy and its priests. These actions frustrated Amaru's strategy of forming a common proindependence front of all social and racial groups. Some Indian leaders, fearing the radical direction of the revolt, threw their support to the Spaniards. Despite some initial successes, the rebel movement soon suffered a complete rout. Amaru, members of his family, and his leading captains were captured and brutally executed in Cuzco. While the most spectacular indigenous rebellion of that era, it was not unique. The revolt of the *comuneros* in New Granada in 1781–1782 had its origin in intolerable economic conditions. Unlike the Peruvian upheaval, it was more clearly limited in its aims. Its organization and its effort to form a common front of all colonial groups with grievances against Spanish authority were advances over Amaru's rebellion. A central committee elected by thousands of peasants and artisans directed the insurrection, which carried out an assault on Bogotá. Negotiations followed the rebellion, and an apparent agreement reached in June 1781 satisfied virtually all of the rebels' demands. However, the Spanish commissioners secretly voided the deal and, following the demobilization of the rebel army, regained control by crushing the leadership of the *Comuneros*.

The exploitation of the indigenous population did not end with Spanish and Portuguese colonial rule. The continuing oppression was never more graphic than in Bolivia, which always had one of the highest percentages of indigenous people. Well into the twentieth century, *pongos*, or domestic servants, were being offered for hire as virtual slaves. As they had in colonial times, the locals acted as beasts of burden for the equivalent of a few pennies. Throughout much of the continent, they continued to be marginalized, driven from the little good land they had been able to maintain during colonial times. In the latter part of the nineteenth century, and the early part of the twentieth century, the dramatic expansion of commercial farming fell heavily on those indigenous communities that had survived the earlier genocide of the mining operations.

TABLE 5. How Many Native People?

	Estimated Population	% of Total Population
Mexico	32,610,267	30.0%
Peru	12,903,641	45.0%
Guatemala	5,154,885	40.5%
Bolivia	5,015,534	55.0%
United States	3,613,679	1.2%
Ecuador	3,438,920	25.0%
Brazil	1,710,096	0.9%
Argentina	1,209,058	3.0%
Canada	667,803	2.0%
Honduras	523,863	7.0%
Chile	488,542	3.0%
Panama	453,904	14.0%
Colombia	443,796	1.0%
Venezuela	390,353	1.5%
Nicaragua	283,768	5.0%
Paraguay	166,727	2.5%
El Salvador	69,481	1.0%
Guyana	53,837	7.0%
Belize	49,162	16.7%
Costa Rica	41,339	1.0%
Suriname	9,416	2.0%
Total	69,298,071	12.6%

Source: CIA World Factbook, https://www.cia.gov/library/publications/the-world-factbook/index.html, 2007.

The Role of Sugar and Slavery

Gold and silver were the primary targets of the conquest, but on his second voyage Columbus brought sugarcane roots from the Canary Islands and planted them in what is now the Dominican Republic, where they grew quite rapidly. Sugar was already a prized product in Europe because it was grown and refined in only a few places (Sicily, Madeira, and the Cape Verde Islands). Over the next three centuries, it would become the most important agricultural product shipped from the Western Hemisphere to Europe. Cane was planted in northeast Brazil and then in most of the Caribbean colonies—Barbados, Jamaica, Haiti, Santo Domingo, Guadeloupe, Cuba, and Puerto Rico. In the places where it was developed, the sugar industry quickly became dependent on the importation of slaves from western Africa. This industry became central to the development of significant parts of Latin America and left a legacy of environmental destruction and racism that still influences the region.

This is not to say that all slave systems in the Caribbean and elsewhere were based on the sugar plantation. Also, not all black people in the Americas are descendants of slaves, and not all slaves worked on sugar plantations. An important exception is the role slaves played in the extraction of gold in Brazil, which will be discussed later. However, it was the development of the sugar plantations of Brazil and the Caribbean in the seventeenth century that provided the impetus for the massive importation of Africans throughout the Americas. A full-blown transatlantic slave trade began after 1518 when Charles I of Spain authorized the direct commercial transfer of Africans to his possessions in the New World. It took some time for slavery to develop as we would come to know it, but it is estimated that eventually the slave trade moved more than 10 million Africans into various parts of the Americas between 1518 and 1870. Of those 10–11 million, more than 4 million wound up in the Caribbean islands. Brazil was the only area of the Americas to receive more slaves than did the Caribbean, with more than 5 million. The North American colonies received fewer than 1 million. Brazil was the first place where a slave society was established in the Americas, and it was the last country in the Western Hemisphere to abolish slavery, doing so only in 1888, 2 years after it was ended in Cuba and 23 years after it came to an end in the United States.

The contemporary condition of northeast Brazil is a testament to the destructive power of the sugar industry. From the beginning of Portuguese colonization early in the sixteenth century, Brazil was the world's largest producer of sugar; initially in the Spanish colonies, it was only a secondary activity. Brazil would remain the largest producer of sugar for over 150 years; from early on, it required the importation of African slaves because of scarce local labor and the large-scale loss of life among the native population. The sugar industry was labor-intensive, needing thousands of workers to prepare the ground and plant, harvest, grind, and refine the cane. Ironically, although the Portuguese crown initiated the colonization of northeast Brazil, Dutch entrepreneurs actually dominated the sugar industry, including participation in the slave trade. In 1630, the Dutch West India Company conquered northeast Brazil and took direct control of sugar production. From there the sugar production facilities were exported to the British in Barbados. Eventually, sharp competition developed between the two regions, with the Caribbean island eventually winning out as the Brazilian land began to deteriorate. The land was left permanently scarred by the 150 years of sugar monoculture. It had been a vast and fertile area when the colonists arrived, but the agricultural methods used were not sustainable. Fire was used to clear the land, and as a result considerable flora and fauna were permanently destroyed. The condition of life for the African slaves who worked on the plantations was horrendous. No food was grown; all had to be imported, along with luxury goods, by the owners of the plantations. In this way, the plantation workers were totally dependent on the landowners. The result was chronic malnutrition and misery for most of the population. The current legacy of the sugar monoculture is that northeast Brazil is one of the most underdeveloped regions of the Americas, inhabited by more than 30 million people who are primarily the descendants of African slaves brought there more than four centuries ago. Sugar remains an important crop for the region, but today less than 20 percent of the land is used for sugar production; much of the rest is simply unusable because of environmental degradation. Other regions of Brazil have gone on to produce more sugar. As a result, this once fertile region must import food from other parts of Brazil, and more than half of the people in the region live below the poverty line.

Northeast Brazil is not the only region to be permanently scarred by the production of sugar and the slavery that accompanied it. The islands of the Caribbean have suffered much the same fate. The Spanish had originally grown sugarcane in Cuba and Santo Domingo but on a relatively small scale. Barbados under Dutch entrepreneurship became the first great sugar experiment in the Caribbean, beginning in 1641. In just 25 years, Barbados had 800 plantations and over 80,000 slaves. The island's previously diverse agricultural production was slowly destroyed as virtually all good land was given over to sugar production. However, before long, the island's ecology was destroyed and its sugar production was no longer competitive, leaving behind a destitute people. From Barbados, sugar production shifted northward to Jamaica, where by 1700 there were ten times as many slaves as white inhabitants; by the middle of the eighteenth century, its land had also become depleted. In the second half of the eighteenth century, sugar production shifted to Haiti, where more than 25,000 slaves per year were being imported to increase the size of the industry to meet growing European demand. Haiti soon ceased to be the center of Caribbean sugar production, not as the result of an ecological disaster but rather as the result of revolution.

Revolution erupted in Haiti in 1791, and over the course of the next 12 years the sugar economy of the island was devastated. The rebellious slaves eventually succeeded in driving out the French army in 1803 and establishing Haiti as an independent nation. However, independence had high costs, including an embargo by both the United States and France. Although Haiti eventually won its recognized independence from France in 1825, the island's economy was devastated by continual attacks by French expeditionary forces and because of a large cash indemnity paid upon recognition of independence. As a result, Haiti ceased to be at the center of sugar production; that focus shifted northward to Cuba.

After the Haitian rebellion and subsequent reduction in production, the price of sugar in Europe doubled; and after 1806, Cuba began to sharply increase its production. Sugar production had begun its shift toward Cuba in 1762 when the British briefly took control of Havana. To expand the sugar industry, the British dramatically increased the number of slaves brought into Cuba. During the 11-month British occupation, Cuba's economy turned toward sugar. Previously vibrant Cuban production of fruit, beef, and light manufactured goods was largely set aside for the growth of the sugar industry. This period also saw the destruction of Cuba's forests and the beginning of the process of degrading the fertility of Cuban soil. Following the Haitian revolution, Cuban sugar production was also given a boost when Haitian sugar producers fled with their slaves to set up production in eastern Cuba. The doubling of the capacity of the Cuban sugar industry after 1806 also required the continued importation of slaves over the ensuing decades even as the slave trade was gaining more and more international condemnation. More than 1 million Africans were brought to Cuba as slaves and in the process transformed the face of Cuban society forever. Today, close to 50 percent of the Cuban population is of African heritage.

Resistance to Slavery

Similar to the long history of indigenous resistance to colonialism, Africans who survived the voyage and were sold into slavery did not willingly accept their fate. *Marronage* (flight from slavery) was a recorded fact almost from the first days that Africans were brought to the island of Hispaniola. Indigenous people and slaves fled into the inaccessible mountains of the interior, sustaining a condition of liberation and keeping alive a sense of independent identity. In 1514, on the island of Puerto Rico, two Taíno/Arawak chiefs and their people allied with Africans against the representatives of the Spanish crown. A second uprising occurred 17 years later when the enslaved black population rose up against its oppressors. In 1522, an uprising in Santo Domingo began with the revolt of forty sugar mill workers. Although these uprisings were eventually defeated and no full-scale rebellion would succeed prior to 1803, marronage was common throughout the Americas where large numbers of African slaves were concentrated. As Michel Laguerre observed, "Wherever there were slaves, there were also maroons. . . . [L]iving in free camps or on the fringes of port cities, they were a model for the slaves to imitate, embodying the desires of most of the slaves. What the slaves used to say in Sotto Voce on the plantations, they were able to say aloud in the maroon settlements." These maroon communities were common through four centuries of slavery in the Americas. Known by a variety of names (*palenques, quilombos, mocombos, cumbes, ladeiras,* or *mambíses*), these communities ranged from tiny, ephemeral groupings to powerful states encompassing thousands of members and surviving for generations or even centuries. Such maroon communities were generally well organized. They had political and military organization and were not, as is sometimes said, groups of wild, runaway, disorganized blacks. Some of these maroon communities were so powerful that they were able to negotiate treaties with European powers. These free and independent communities forged autonomous societies and protected their freedom and liberty. They rejected any outside domination.

In some places throughout the Americas, these communities still exist, often maintaining their cultural heritage and bearing living witness to the earliest days of

African presence in the Americas. One of the best examples of such a community are the maroons of the Cockpit Country of northwestern Jamaica, who trace their roots back to the sixteenth century and have survived as a community to the present day. Today, their early leaders are recognized as national heroes by the Jamaican government. The maroons of Jamaica are probably the best-known group in North America, but many other similar communities exist throughout the Americas. San Basilio de Palenque near Cartagena, Colombia, is a surviving example. There, the inhabitants of the ex-maroon community speak Palenquero, a dialect that fuses Spanish and elements of several West African (Bantu) languages. Most black people of the Pacific lowlands of Panama, Colombia, and Ecuador do not see themselves as so directly connected to Africa. They lay full claim to their own homeland—the coastal section of this tropical rain forest. They are similar in outlook to maroons in the interior of Suriname and French Guiana, who maintain their distinct cultural heritage.

In Brazil, fugitive slaves organized the black kingdom of Palmares in the northeast and throughout the seventeenth century successfully resisted military expeditions of both the Dutch and the Portuguese. The independent kingdom of Palmares was organized as a state, similar to many that existed in Africa in the seventeenth century. Encompassing an area one-third the size of Portugal, it boasted a diversified agriculture of corn, sweet potatoes, beans, bananas, and other foods. Land was held in common, and no money was circulated. The ruling chief was elected from the ranks of the tribe and organized a defense of the territory that successfully protected it for several decades. When the Portuguese finally conquered Palmares in 1690s, it required an army of several thousand, the largest colonial army of the time. Ten thousand former slaves fought to defend the kingdom in the final battle, but they were defeated by superior firepower.

The slave trade, which left its lasting legacy on the Americas, was driven in large measure by the profits it generated in Europe. Britain is probably the best example of that profiteering. Queen Elizabeth I was reportedly opposed to the slave trade on moral grounds when the first English slave traders landed in Britain, but she quickly changed her perspective when shown the financial benefits that could flow from the trade. Once its lucrative nature was clear, the British moved quickly to overcome the Dutch dominance of the early trade. A key factor in the success of the British was the concession of the trade monopoly granted to them by the weakened Spanish. The South Sea Company, with significant investment from Britain's most powerful families, including the royal court, was the chief beneficiary of the monopoly. The impact of the slave trade on Britain's economy was significant. Traffic in slaves made Bristol Britain's second most important city and helped make Liverpool the world's most important port. Ships left Britain for Africa with cargoes of weapons, cloth, rum, and glass, which served as payment for the slaves who were obtained in West Africa and then shipped to the Americas. The African chiefs who cooperated in the slave trade used the weapons and the liquor to embark on new slave-hunting expeditions. Conditions on the ships were horrific, and often as many as half of the people on board died during the voyage. Many died of disease, while others committed suicide by refusing to eat or throwing themselves overboard. Those who survived the voyage but were too weak to impress buyers were simply left on the docks to die. The healthy survivors were sold at public auction.

Despite the losses at sea, the trade was highly lucrative as the ships sailed back to Britain with rich cargoes of sugar, cotton, coffee, and cocoa. Liverpool slave merchants were making more than £1 million in profits per year, and there was considerable spinoff to the rest of the economy. Liverpool's dockyards were improved considerably to handle the increased commerce. Banks in Britain's largest cities prospered through the trade. Lloyd's of London became a dominant force in the insurance industry, covering slaves, ships, and plantations. Almost 200,000 textile workers labored in Manchester to provide needed products for the Americas, while workers in Birmingham and Sheffield made muskets and knives. Although initially dominated by the Portuguese, it was the slave trade that positioned Britain to be the dominant world power by the end of the eighteenth century. At the start of the nineteenth century, Britain turned against slavery, not primarily out of any newfound moral revulsion but through a calculation that its growing industrial production needed wage earners throughout the world to buy its products.

The British were by no means alone as a nation that participated in the slave trade. Equally important were the Portuguese, who supplied the millions of Africans necessary for the exploitation of their primary colony, Brazil. In addition to providing slaves for the sugar industry, the Portuguese developed gold extraction in Brazil using slave labor. From 1700 onward the region of Minas Gerais in central Brazil was the focal point of the extraction. For more than a century, gold flowed out of the region, with Portuguese and British slave traders gaining massive profits. The region itself was left destitute, a condition that persists today for the descendants of those slaves who worked the mines. Subsistence farming replaced the mines and, as in northeast Brazil, became, in Galeano's words, "the Kingdom of *fazendas*."

Concept of Race

Race must be understood as a socially constructed, not biologically determined, concept. According to Michael Hanchard, race in Latin America determines status, class, and political power. In this respect, race relations are power relations. Being black in Brazil generally signifies having a lower standard of living and less access to health care and education than whites have, but in the minds of many it also signifies criminality, licentiousness, and other negative attributes considered to be related to African peoples. It follows, then, that the meaning and interpretation of racial categories are always subject to revision, change, and negotiation. Most importantly, racial constructs are dynamic and fluid insofar as racial groups are not categorized in isolation but in relation to other groups who have their own attendant values of class, status, and power. The concepts of blackness and race have long been controversial in Latin America, and only in recent years have scholars and political activists for black and indigenous rights begun to create a dialogue that can shed light on the issues. The term *black* is an adjective derived from Latin, meaning in a literal sense "sooted, smoked black from flame." In practical terms, in Latin America, it has been defined as being "not white" and as having a connection to Africa. As in North America, blackness can equally be the target of unrelenting racism or the basis of deeply held religious and aesthetic attachment to a heritage of struggle, survival, and achievement. The dominant, lighter-skinned ruling elites of Latin America historically have viewed the population of African descent with a mixture of fear and hatred. The blacks who lived free in isolated areas such as the Cauca Valley of Colombia have been the targets of campaigns of fear, labeling them as subhuman beasts who had brought a "primitive" culture with them from Africa. Such historical labeling meant that these groups in Colombia were marginalized from national political life.

The racism of the dominant classes of the Americas comes through in the historical treatment of the greatest of Latin America's heros, Simón Bolívar. In the wars of liberation led by Bolívar between 1813 and 1822, black troops from revolutionary Haiti helped overthrow colonial governments in the territory that became the Republic of Gran Colombia. The liberation of these territories helped foster an era of black consciousness among the indigenous black communities. It has often been speculated that Bolívar may have had black ancestors, but this idea has generally been rejected in Colombia and Venezuela by white and *mestizo* biographers who were clearly uneasy about the implications of such a possibility.

Race is a powerful ideological concept in contemporary times throughout the Americas. There are two competing concepts that vie for recognition. *Mestizaje* is the ideology of racial mixture and assimilation, which is the adopted perspective of most of the political elites of the region. *Négritude,* on the other hand, is a concept that celebrates the positive features of blackness. At the national government level only in Haiti is *négritude* the explicit national ideology. In most countries where there is a significant population of African heritage, the concept of *négritude* has been both the basis of societal discrimination and a symbol of racial pride for the oppressed. Of course, such pride is often seen by the dominant political culture to be a threat to the sovereignty and territoriality of the nation.

When reviewing their own history and social movements, black social activist and movement leaders in Latin America inevitably raise the comparison with the U.S. Civil Rights movement and state with deep regret that black Latin America never had an equivalent movement. However, black-based social movements over the years have gained momentum and are now challenging centuries of domination. For example, black social movements are gaining strength in Brazil, Colombia, Ecuador, Venezuela, Uruguay, Nicaragua, Costa Rica, Honduras, and other Latin American countries (see Dixon 1996). These movements are fighting for social inclusion and development, equality before the law, human rights protections, and democratic reform.

Black organizations in Brazil are some of the best organized and politically developed in the region. The black movements in Brazil are not monolithic and are quite diverse in scope, practice, and philosophy. Like all social movements, there are basic points of convergence and divergence. However, most of the progressive black movements agree that racism is an obstacle to Afro-Brazilian progress. One of the most powerful examples of a movement that has promoted black liberation is Brazil's black consciousness movement, a loosely linked network of nearly 600 organizations that has the goal of preserving ethnic heritage and fighting against the discrimination and poverty of contemporary Brazil. The groups are not united by a single ideology, and they pursue their campaign against racism using a variety of methods. Some organizations focus almost exclusively on culture,

TABLE 6. How Many Afro-Latin Americans?

Country/Year	Estimated Population	% of Total Population
Brazil (1995)	74,833,200	45.0%
Colombia (1995)	8,500,000	24.3%
Venezuela (1995)	7,950,000	37.7%
Haiti (1999)	7,653,200	95.0%
Cuba (1995)	5,050,000	48.0%
Mexico (1995)	4,737,000	5.3%
Dominican Republic (1995)	3,293,500	50.5%
Jamaica (1970)	2,455,213	96.7%
Peru (1995)	1,800,000	7.8%
Puerto Rico (1995)	1,600,000	43.4%
Panama (1995)	1,075,000	43.0%
Ecuador (1995)	836,500	7.5%
Trinidad and Tobago (1980)	733,164	57.1%
Nicaragua (1995)	493,000	11.5%
Guyana (1980)	355,240	41.5%
Barbados (1980)	253,260	94.5%
Honduras (1995)	196,000	3.5%
Bolivia (1995)	158,000	2.0%
Paraguay (1995)	156,000	3.5%
Santa Lucia (1980)	142,228	95.1%
San Vicente & Grenadines (1980)	110,285	95.9%
Belize (1995)	102,000	52.0%
Granada (1980)	88,815	95.5%
Costa Rica (1995)	66,000	2.0%
Suriname (year unknown)	62,400	15.0%
Antigua and Barbuda (1970)	60,300	89.0%
St. Kitts and Nevis (1980)	40,016	97.6%
Uruguay (1995)	38,000	1.0%

Note: Table accounts for both black and mixed-race population.

Source: CIA World Factbook, https://www.cia.gov/library/publications/the-world-factbook/index.html, 2007.

believing that the rediscovery of African roots can transform the consciousness of Brazil's black population. Other groups, such as the São Paulo–based Unified Black Movement (MNU), are politically focused, arguing that racism must be combated through changes in political, social, and economic structures. The groups have demonstrated against police violence and have fought in the courts for the enforcement of existing laws against discrimination in the workplace. During the writing of Brazil's constitution in the 1980s, MNU was instrumental in convening the National Convention of Blacks for the Constitution. The grassroots debates of this initiative, together with the efforts of Carlos Alberto de Oliveira and Benedita da Silva, two black congresspeople elected in 1986, resulted in the inclusion of a constitutional amendment that outlawed racial discrimination. The activity of the black consciousness movement has also forced the traditional Brazilian political parties to react with statements against racism and to make commitments to include blacks among their lists of political candidates and appointments to public office. These efforts have borne some fruit with the appointment of a number of blacks to key positions by the centrist Brazilian Democratic Movement Party (PMDB), but there are only a handful of black deputies in the national legislature. Pressure on the political elites has helped break down the long-held elite-generated myth that Brazil is a "racial democracy."

However, the black movement is currently far from the mass political phenomenon that it aspires to be. Part of the limitation of the movement is its narrow social base. Black consciousness groups are composed primarily of professionals, intellectuals, and upwardly mobile students. The movement is relatively small in total numbers, with probably 25,000 sympathizers out of an Afro-Brazilian population of some 70 million. Despite these limitations, the movement does represent an important contribution to the cause of racial justice in the continent's largest country. The recent use of quotas to ensure adequate Afro-Brazilian admissions to universities was one gain achieved by the Black movements. Afro-Colombians have also struggled for equality and have modestly succeeded in raising consciousness of their separateness from the majority of the Colombian nation.

Contemporary Struggle of the Indigenous People

The history of exploitation of the indigenous people at the time of the conquest and the century that followed is generally not disputed. Rather, it is the history that follows that is controversial. Even those who have sympathy and understanding for the oppression of the indigenous people have tended to avoid a systematic understanding of its contemporary reality. There has been a common perception that Native American cultures are primarily relics of the past, doomed to be abandoned as modernity spread to the deepest regions of rural Latin America. To the degree that indigenous cultures survived, it would be as rural, isolated communities clinging to traditional ways of life. Although such communities exist, they make up only a tiny fraction of the approximately 70 million native peoples who live in the Americas today. Because the stereotype of the isolated rural community is not actually the norm, our understanding of the issues and needs of this population must change.

The indigenous people who survived the conquest recovered their numbers slowly but steadily. Contrary to the predictions of assimilative policies, native peoples have remained demographically stable; bilingualism has increased without the disappearance of native languages. The native peoples have not been defeated or eliminated. Indigenous peoples still live in nearly all of the regions where they lived in the eighteenth century. They have expanded into new territories and established a presence in urban, industrialized society that challenges the stereotypical image of indigenous peasants. Indigenous squatters are prominent throughout the major cities of the continent.

ECUADOR

One of the strongest contemporary movements of indigenous peoples is CONAIE. A nationwide organization that has sought to represent the native peoples of Ecuador, who make up between 37 and 40 percent of the population—the fourth largest percentage of indigenous people in the hemisphere—CONAIE initially reached prominence in June 1994, when it sponsored a strike that shut down the country for 2 weeks. The target of the protest was the Agrarian Development Law, approved by the Ecuadorian congress, which called for the elimination of communal lands in favor of agricultural enterprises. The 1994 protests in Ecuador also demonstrated the ability of the indigenous movement to link up successfully with other nonindigenous social and political movements. Commerce was brought to a halt throughout Ecuador when CONAIE set up road blocks and boycotted marketplaces. Trade unions joined in the action by calling a general strike and stopped the delivery of goods into the cities. In parts of the Amazon, indigenous communities took over oil wells to protest the privatization of Petroecuador, the state-owned oil company.

CONAIE succeeded in getting a broad range of organizations to unite behind its own progressive agrarian reform proposal, which called for the modernization of communal agriculture but not through the government's plan of commercialization. Rather, CONAIE's proposal called for government support for sustainable, community-based projects that emphasized production for domestic consumption rather than foreign export. CONAIE also proposed the use of environmentally sound farming techniques. At the heart of their counterproposals was the idea that organized groups of civil society in the countryside would play a central role in implementing the new law.

The protests and counterproposal met stiff resistance from the government of Sixto Durán Ballen, which viewed the Agrarian Development Law to be at the center of its broader package of neoliberal reforms. The government declared a state of emergency and put the armed forces in charge of dealing with the protests. The armed forces arrested protest leaders and violently suppressed street demonstrations. The army occupied many indigenous communities, destroying homes and crops. However, the repression was not fully successful at stopping the protest movement. The government was forced to negotiate with CONAIE and ultimately to make modifications in the agrarian reform law that limited its potentially worst features. However, probably the most important result of the 1994 protests was the recognition that the indigenous movement is a significant actor in contemporary Ecuadorian politics. CONAIE and the indigenous people as a whole achieved this position through their mobilizations, successful linking with nonindigenous groups, and dynamic formation of political demands.

Provincial and regional indigenous organizations were created in the 1970s. In 1980, the Confederation of Indigenous Nationalities of the Ecuadorian Amazon (CONFENAIE) was founded to represent the indigenous population of the Oriente, an important step toward a national organization. In the highlands, indigenous organizations dated back to the founding of the Ecuadorian Indigenous Federation (FEI) in the 1940s. CONAIE was established in 1986 to form a single, national organization. In the 1970s and 1980s, the organizations tended to have a local focus; but in the 1990s, the movement adopted a broader agenda, the right to self-determination, the right to cultural identity and language, and the right to economic development within the framework of indigenous values and traditions. Land became the focal point for the indigenous movement in Ecuador. It has also been the issue on which it has connected most successfully with nonindigenous groups.

Indeed, land was the focal point of CONAIE's first national actions in 1990. After weeks of organizing and stagnated discussions with the national government, CONAIE orchestrated an uprising that paralyzed the country for a week. The protests ended when the government agreed to national-level negotiations with CONAIE. While not succeeding in most of its demands, CONAIE did win the right to name the national director of bilingual education programs and the granting of some significant tracts of land to indigenous organizations. These mobilizations laid the groundwork for the larger and more powerful actions of 1994. However, the demand for more equitable distribution of land faces a long and difficult road. According to 1994 data, in the highlands 1.6 percent of the farms occupy 43 percent of the land, while on the coast 3.9 percent of the farms occupy 55 percent of the land. Communal lands are acknowledged and theoretically defended in the Ecuadorian constitution, but they represent only 4 percent of the land in the highlands.

In January 2000, CONAIE organized several thousand indigenous people to protest the government's handling of an economic crisis and to call on the president, Jamil Mahuad, to resign. Working with cooperative members of the military, the protesters occupied the national parliament and declared a new government headed by a three-person junta including indigenous leader Antonio Vargas. However, their victory was short-lived. Under pressure from the United States and the Organization of American States (OAS), the military withdrew from the junta and conceded the presidency to Mahuad's vice president Gustavo Noboa. CONAIE was defeated in the short term in its efforts at radical reform, but its considerable power was made dramatically evident to the country's traditional rulers. In 2002, support from CONAIE was crucial to the success of the presidential campaign of populist Lucio Gutiérrez. Gutiérrez swept to victory promising to challenge the neoliberal orthodoxy and appointing indigenous representatives to government positions. However, by 2004 Gutiérrez had betrayed his promises and CONAIE was back in the streets as a leading opposition force. In April 2005, CONAIE was part of a broad coalition of opposition forces that drove Gutiérrez from office following an ill-fated scheme to overhaul the nation's court system to his benefit. With strong support from CONAIE and other indigenous groups, progressive candidate Rafael Correa won the presidency in a landslide victory in 2006 and is moving forward with major constitutional reform that has the potential to deliver tangible gains to Ecuador's indigenous groups.

BRAZIL

In Brazil, the issue that most marks the indigenous struggle is the contest for land. Land is the subsistence base of indigenous groups, whether they are hunters and gatherers in the Amazon or small farmers in the northeast. It is the issue that unites Brazil's 206 indigenous societies.

Brazil's indigenous people are only 0.2 percent of the national population, speaking 170 languages, with legal rights to about 11 percent of the national territory. Much of the indigenous land is rich in natural resources. Nearly 99 percent of indigenous land is in the Amazon region, occupying more than 18 percent of the region, but little more than half of the indigenous population lives there. In the other densely populated parts of the country, almost half of the indigenous population lives on less than 2 percent of the indigenous land.

The current struggle over land is not a new one. Expropriation of indigenous lands and decimation of the indigenous population have usually paralleled the drive by Europeans for a particular raw material, whether it be timber, gold, sugar, or rubber. A contemporary case of the devastation of an indigenous group occurred with the isolated Canoe and Mequens peoples in the Amazonian state of Rondô-nia. Fewer than fifteen people from these two groups have survived. Over the last decade, ranchers in the region may well have killed most of the two groups and destroyed their livelihood to make way for cattle pasture. There is evidence of some fifty-three still isolated groups, probably small remnants of larger groups that moved in response to the Brazilian government's massive resettlement programs. The administration of President José Sarney (1985–1990) was especially aggressive in moving forward with Amazonian development projects. The army's Northern Tributaries Project, begun in 1987, had as its goals the reduction of indigenous land areas and the subsequent opening up of large new areas for both farming and mining. As a result, between 1987 and 1990 the Yanomami's 23.5-million-acre territory was reduced by 70 percent and divided into nineteen different unconnected parcels of land. The Yanomami people were devastated by the activity of almost 50,000 freelance gold diggers. The gold diggers drove 9000 Yanomami from their lands, and 15 percent of the population died from diseases introduced by the gold miners. Mercury contamination downriver and mercury vapors released into the atmosphere had serious environmental consequences. Protests at the 1992 Earth Summit led to the creation of land reserves by the governments of both Brazil and Venezuela. Despite the newly created reserves, conflict between the gold miners and the Yanomami continued. In 1993, many Yanomami were massacred in an attack by the miners and with no effective intervention by the Brazilian government. The 1988 Brazilian constitution contained progressive provisions for environmental protection and indigenous people's rights, but the reality was that they were generally not implemented. Powerful private economic interests moved forward with their projects, often buying off government officials with large bribes. The government itself moved forward with environmentally questionable projects such as the planned Paraná-Paraguay River seaway.

However, sole focus on these devastated and isolated groups would miss an important part of the story. In the last 30 years, the indigenous people have begun to change their situation through political organization. The demographic decline reached its low point in the mid-1970s, and the population has risen ever since. The first complete indigenous census, in 1990, counted about 235,000 indigenous people. By the year 2000, the number had grown to 300,000. Between 1990 and 1995, the area of indigenous land with complete legal documentation increased more than fourfold.

The most recent drive of the Brazilian government into the indigenous lands in the Amazon region was initiated in the 1940s but took on full force in the 1960s and 1970s. The military government that came to power in 1964 was motivated by an almost messianic desire to conquer these supposedly undeveloped lands so that Brazil could take its place among the world's most important countries. As a result, the Brazilian government conceived and executed the development of an infrastructure (roads, dams, and hydroelectric stations) that preceded the actual economic development of the region.

Because the concept of privately held land was largely nonexistent in the Amazon region, it was necessary for the government to step up mechanisms for the demarcation of land based on private ownership. Private investors were willing to enter the region only after such procedures had been established. From the beginning, the approach of the Brazilian government toward the indigenous groups was to limit their land ownership to relatively small areas so that their ambitious development plans could proceed on the rest. In 1967, the Brazilian government created the National Indian Foundation (FUNAI) as the agency responsible for indigenous people and their land. While it had not been the intent of the government to create a rallying point, FUNAI has become exactly that. For 40 years its headquarters in Brasília has been the focal point for indigenous groups rallying to register land claims and to forestall the projects of the developers. Using FUNAI as a target, indigenous groups developed their own organizations in the 1970s with the assistance of the wider society. The first organizations came from within the church community— the Indigenist Missionary Council (CIMI), the indigenous rights organization of the Catholic Church, and the Ecumenical Center for Documentation and Information (CEDI). Indigenous groups took a large step forward in 1978 with the formation of the first national organization, the Union of Indigenous Nations (UNI). The UNI was able to make important links both domestically and internationally. In the late 1970s and early 1980s, during the height of the movement against the military dictatorship, indigenous groups were able to make links with students and intellectuals. As a result, the issue of indigenous land rights made it to the agenda of the broad movement for the restoration of political democracy.

At the same time, the Brazilian indigenous movement also made important links in the international community, most especially with the environmental community. During the 1980s, there developed among environmentalists internationally a significant consciousness of the destruction of the Amazon rain forest. In developing international attention about the problem in Brazil, groups like Greenpeace and the World Wildlife Fund made common cause with Brazil's indigenous groups. Both sets of groups began to speak the same language—sustainable development. Both indigenous peoples and environmentalists argued that the rain forest was not a wilderness to simply be preserved but rather an area that was inhabited and contained important resources for the world that the people who currently lived there could provide—medicines, rubber, foodstuffs. The activists argued that the kind of development being projected and carried out by the Brazilian government—primarily slash-and-burn agriculture—was inappropriate for the fragile character of the land. They pointed to vast tracts of land that had been exploited in the 1960s and 1970s and were now worthless semidesert. Considerable international attention was also brought to the region by the work of Francisco "Chico" Alves Mendes, leader of the National Council of Rubber Tappers, who was assassinated in 1988 after his organization, the Alliance of the Peoples of the Forest, organized to block further dam construction and defend the environment. Internationally, consciousness has clearly developed on this and related environmental issues and has placed significant pressure on the Brazilian government since the mid-1980s. However, this has not stopped the government from moving forward with its development plans. Often, the government has successfully created a nationalist backlash against international pressure by characterizing it as a form of neocolonialism. However, in 2007 a potentially important development occurred when President Luiz Inácio da Silva announced an agreement with several indigenous groups acknowledging their autonomy and claim to resources.

MEXICO

On January 1, 1994, a rebellion led by the Zapatista National Liberation Army (EZLN) began in the state of Chiapas in southern Mexico. This rebellion, more than any other indigenous political action in the 1990s, captured the attention of scholars and political activists alike. On that day, within a few hours after the takeover of San Cristóbal de las Casas, computer screens around the world sparked with news of the uprising. The Zapatista uprising was the world's first online rebellion as the EZLN communicated its cause directly and electronically. The indigenous explosion in Chiapas, in which several hundred people lost their lives in 12 days of fighting, was only the beginning. Ten years later, the government continued to renege on accords it had signed recognizing indigenous rights and culture and federal troops still occupied the indigenous parts of the state, though the rebels forged ahead with autonomous structures of local government.

The EZLN had its origins in indigenous and peasant organizing initiatives of the 1970s, which began to link up with leftist political organizers arriving in the Lacandón Jungle of Chiapas from other parts of Mexico. A combination of growing repression and the impact of neoliberal policies in the early 1980s radicalized some of these groups, leading them to join in an armed movement initially known as the National Liberation Forces (FLN), the precursor of the EZLN, which burst on the scene as the North American Free Trade Agreement (NAFTA) went into effect. The roots of their rebellion ran very deep. The indigenous people of Chiapas, mostly Mayan, have labored under conditions of semislavery and servitude for centuries. The state is the principal source of the nation's coffee, and just over 100 people (0.16 percent of all coffee farmers) control 12 percent of all coffee lands. The large coffee farms have the best land, most of the credit, and the best infrastructure. Even more important are the cattle lands. Some 6000 families hold more than 3 million hectares of pastureland, equivalent to nearly half the territory of all Chiapas rural landholdings. Many of these vast cattle ranches were created through violent seizures of community and national land. The current struggles here date back to the early period of this century when the local oligarchs resisted any attempt at land reform. The program of Institutional Revolutionary Party (PRI) President Lázaro Cárdenas, which distributed millions of acres of land elsewhere in Mexico in the 1930s, lagged in its implementation in Chiapas. In 1974, the local elites harshly repressed indigenous efforts at political organizing for land reform. The massive repression of the 1970s was followed by a more selective repression, consisting of the assassination of several peasant leaders. The peasants responded by creating networks of self-defense, but the authoritarian PRI governors responded with harsh tactics. The state repression was carried out by a combination of the federal army, state and local police forces, and so-called white guards—hired security forces at the service of the big landowners. PRI leaders deliberately provoked conflicts among peasants, between peasants and small proprietors, and between PRI village leaders and opponents of the regime. The local PRI leadership operated through a loose organization known as the "Chiapas Family." The family was made up primarily of big ranchers, owners of coffee farms, and lumber barons who controlled local elected offices. The control was enhanced by the cooption of local indigenous leaders, many of whom were bilingual teachers. Operating through PRI-dominated organizations like the National Peasant Confederation (CNC), the local leaders were given economic advantages that were passed on to their closest supporters in the communities. This divide-and-conquer strategy led to many violent confrontations in the period of the Zapatista uprising.

Despite the historic dominance of the region politically and economically by the PRI and its supporters, an independent civil society began to develop after 1975. Organizers from the outside participated, including liberation theology–inspired Catholic clergy and members of Mexican leftist parties. Two grassroots organizations formed in the 1970s exist today, the Regional Association of Collective Interest Union of Ejido Unions (ARIC-UU) and the Emiliano Zapata Peasant Organization (OCEZ). The organizations use a variety of tactics, including direct action, to press their grievances against the Mexican government. A new phase in the impact of civil society began on October 12, 1992, with a demonstration in San Cristóbal de las Casas to commemorate the 500th anniversary of indigenous resistance to the European conquest. Thousands of people from different ethnic groups took over the colonial capital and destroyed the statue of conquistador Diego de Mazariegos. The event foreshadowed the EZLN uprising a little more than 1 year later.

A fundamental catalyst for the 1994 uprising was the reform of Article 27 of the Mexican constitution announced by President Carlos Salinas de Gortari in 1992. This reform, for the first time since the programs of Cárdenas, halted land redistribution and permitted the sale of communal lands that up until that time had been protected. For the peasants of Chiapas, this meant the end of agrarian reform, which up to that point had been slow and arbitrary but was now effectively dead. The peasants felt that they could no longer turn to the government as a mediator in land disputes. For the landowners, the reform was a green light to end once and for all the peasant resistance to their plans for greater commercialization of agriculture in the region. Government troops first confronted a column of Zapatistas in May 1993, but the Salinas government, in the midst of an intense effort to win support for NAFTA, did not wish to tarnish its image by acknowledging the existence of a significant armed challenge within its borders. It was in that context of political change and resistance that the Zapatistas burst onto the scene.

From the beginning of their appearance, it was clear that the EZLN insurgency, made up of several thousand indigenous people and their "support base" communities throughout the highlands and the jungle, was a different kind of political movement from the traditional guerrilla armies that preceded them in Mexico and Central America. From the beginning they were a civil resistance organization seeking reformist goals using revolutionary tactics. The EZLN never claimed as a goal the overthrow of the Mexican state. Rather, it called for the immediate resignation of Salinas, subsequent fall elections, and the expansion of peaceful, popular political participation. From the beginning its actions were the catalyst for generalized civil resistance throughout Chiapas.

Within 1 month of the launching of the Zapatistas' war, the National Mediation Commission (CONAI) headed by Bishop Samuel Ruiz brokered a cease-fire between the warring parties and began negotiations that continued on and off until June 1998, when Bishop Ruiz resigned from CONAI and the commission dissolved, charging the government with pursuing a path of war rather than peace. The Mexican Congress formed the Commission for Concord and Pacification (COCOPA) in January 1995 to continue negotiations with the Zapatistas while a cease-fire was in place. The government broke the truce in February 1995 with an army offensive that unsuccessfully attempted to capture the Zapatista leaders. The 1995 offensive was made possible by a massive deployment of 60,000 Mexican soldiers into the region. The army, with U.S., Argentine, and Chilean advisors, employed counterinsurgency tactics honed during Latin America's guerrilla wars of the previous three decades. Between 1996 and 2007, the United States provided over $440 million in military and police aid to Mexico, including helicopters that can be used in counterinsurgency operations. The Mexican army cooperated on its southern border with the Guatemalan army, well trained in counterinsurgency warfare. During its February 1995 offensive, the army destroyed the basic resources of a number of villages suspected of collaborating with the Zapatistas. The offensive forced the EZLN to retreat into more remote areas, but the Mexican government was not able to destroy the EZLN, in part because of the presence of many international human rights observers in the area and the mounting of large demonstrations on behalf of the EZLN in Mexico City. Unable to destroy the EZLN militarily, the government returned to negotiations; and in February 1996, the government and the EZLN signed accords on the rights of indigenous communities. The San Andrés Accords included two key demands of the EZLN, official recognition of the rights of indigenous communities to choose their own leadership and to control the natural resources in their territory. However, in reality the Mexican government did not implement these measures. The primary point of conflict centered around the autonomous municipal councils created by the Zapatistas since 1994. The Zapatistas claimed the right to local self-governance under Article 39 of the Mexican Constitution, which gave people "the inalienable right to alter or modify the form of their government," and the International Labor Organization's Convention 169 (ratified by the Mexican government in 1991), which gave indigenous peoples control over their habitats. In scores of communities, local councils were elected only to be denied recognition by the Mexican government, which continued to recognize local government structures dominated by politicians from the major parties. As a result, many villages split into progovernment and pro-EZLN factions. Despite the lack of official recognition, these autonomous municipal councils no longer recognize the official judicial system and have established alternative methods of conflict resolution. They have also set up community development projects, such as community corn and coffee fields and vegetable gardens. These alternative institutions have gained some financial backing from international nongovernmental organizations in sympathy with the Zapatistas.

The end of the 1990s saw a dramatic increase in violence in the Chiapas region, much of it carried out by paramilitary organizations with links to the government. The most horrific incident occurred on December 22, 1997, when forty-five residents of the Tzotzil indigenous town of Acteal (including thirty-six women and children) were killed in an attack on their chapel by a heavily armed paramilitary gang. It has been reported that one group, the Anti-Zapatista Indigenous Revolutionary Movement (MIRA), received $1250 a month from the PRI-led state government. From April through June 1998, the government launched a series of joint military/police invasions (often coordinated with paramilitaries) which dismantled the Zapatista autonomous municipalities of Ricardo Flores Magón, Tierra y Libertad, and San Juan de la Libertad and raids on Zapatista communities such as Unión Progreso, where eight indigenous residents were taken away by public security forces and their mutilated bodies later returned.

When this militarization provoked the dissolution of CONAI in 1998 and the collapse of negotiations, the Zapatistas launched a national "consultation" in which nearly 3 million Mexicans participated, expressing support for compromise legislation drafted by COCOPA to implement the San Andrés Accords on indigenous rights. Hopes for implementing legislation were briefly raised by the 2000 election of President Vicente Fox from the opposition National Action Party (PAN), who had boasted during the campaign that he would solve the Chiapas problem "in 15 minutes." Later that year, Pablo Salazar was elected state governor on an "Alliance for Chiapas" coalition ticket of anti-PRI parties, and the Zapatistas announced three conditions for resuming peace talks: (1) fulfillment of the San Andrés accords approving the COCOPA law, (2) freeing all Zapatista prisoners, and (3) closing seven (out of 259) military bases in areas of major Zapatista influence. In response, the government closed four bases and released a few dozen out of about 100 prisoners and Fox presented an indigenous law to Congress but backpedaled from the COCOPA version. The Zapatistas then took their case directly to the public and to Congress, organizing a caravan from Chiapas to Mexico City in February–March 2001 that included 23 indigenous EZLN commanders plus Subcommander Marcos. The caravan culminated in one of the largest gatherings in Mexico City's zócalo (main plaza) in modern history, and a historic address to the Congress by ski-masked Commander Esther. However, after the Zapatistas returned to Chiapas, Congress passed an indigenous law that gutted the key provisions of the San Andrés accords and the COCOPA law. The sham legislation was rejected by the congresses of all six Mexican states with the largest proportion of indigenous populations and denounced by indigenous and human rights organizations, which filed 329 constitutional challenges in the Supreme Court. Nevertheless, it was entered into law in August and upheld by the Supreme Court in September 2001.

The struggle for recognition of indigenous rights and for participatory democracy continued. On January 1, 2003, 20,000 indigenous people marched in San Cristóbal to demand revision of the indigenous rights law and the EZLN broke a 2-year silence to condemn the three major parties for betraying the spirit of the San Andrés Accords. Meanwhile, in late 2002, government agencies and paramilitaries began a new escalation of violence against Zapatista support communities in the Montes Azules Biosphere Reserve near the Guatemalan border. This region was coveted by transnationals for its potential hydroelectric and biodiversity resources, in the wake of President Fox's multibillion-dollar Plan Puebla Panama (PPP), which would turn all of southern Mexico and Central America into a giant free-trade zone. Grassroots organizations in Chiapas joined their counterparts in Central America in cross-border networks to resist the PPP. Meanwhile, the Zapatistas continued their patient construction of autonomous government from the bottom up, announcing in July 2003 that their five *Aguascalientes* resistance centers in Chiapas would be renamed *Caracoles* and would be the seats of a new regional structure of "Good Governance Councils" (*Juntas de Buen Gobierno*). Each junta became a regional rebel government, incorporating rotating delegates from some 30 Zapatista rebel autonomous municipalities.

In June 2005 the EZLN issued the "Sixth Declaration of the Lacandón Jungle," inaugurating a national initiative called "The Other Campaign" to link progressive struggles across Mexico. Subcommander Marcos headed the first phase of the campaign in early 2006 as "Delegate Zero." The tour was temporarily halted following massive government repression of some allied organizations in San Salvador Atenco (near Mexico City) in May 2006. After a disputed presidential election in July 2006 in which conservative PAN candidate Felipe Calderón claimed victory, the government appeared to shift to more militarized responses to social movements. Federal forces were deployed against protesters in Oaxaca in November 2006, and in September 2007 the EZLN announced the suspension of the second phase of the Other Campaign (scheduled for south/central Mexico from October–December) due to escalating paramilitary attacks on Zapatista communities. In October 2007 a caravan carrying Marcos and other Zapatista leaders was detained at one of the growing number of roadblocks across Mexico as they traveled to an encounter of indigenous peoples in Vícam, Sonora, highlighting the escalating government threat against the movement.

With or without official recognition from the state, the Zapatista movement continues to represent innovative forms of resistance to the dictates of global capital and oppressive government. As a result, the region is likely to remain a focal point of indigenous resistance that will be modeled elsewhere in the Western Hemisphere.

Conclusion

As Latin America enters the twenty-first century, its image as a continent populated only by Spanish- and Portuguese-speaking *mestizos* is gone forever. The indigenous peoples of the region and the descendants of the African slaves have clearly asserted their claim to a role in the future of the region. No longer forgotten and marginalized, these groups will likely grow in their political and social roles in the coming years.

Bibliography

Andrews, George Reid. *Afro-Latin America 1800–2000*. New York: Oxford University Press, 2004.
Applebaum, Nancy. *Race and Nation in Modern Latin America*. Chapel Hill: University of North Carolina Press, 2003.

Benjamin, Medea, and Maisa Mendonça. *Benedita da Silva. An Afro-Brazilian Woman's Story of Politics and Love*. Oakland, CA: Food First, 1997.

Conniff, Michael, and Thomas Davis. *Africans in the Americas: A History of the Black Diaspora*. New York: St. Martin's Press, 1994.

Cook, Noble David. *Born to Die: Disease and New World Conquest, 1492–1650*. Cambridge: Cambridge University Press, 1998.

Davis, Darien, ed. *Slavery and Beyond: The African Impact on Latin America and the Caribbean* (Jaguar Books on Latin America, 5). Wilmington, DE: Scholarly Resources, 1995.

Díaz Polanco, Héctor. *Indigenous Peoples in Latin America*. Boulder, CO: Westview Press, 1997.

Dixon, Kwame. "Race, Class and National Identity in Ecuador: Afro-Ecuadoreans and the Struggle for Human Rights." Ph.D. diss., Clark Atlanta University, 1996.

Freyre, Gilberto. *The Masters and the Slaves, A Study in the Development of Brazilian Civilization*. Berkeley: University of California Press, 1986.

Galeano, Eduardo. *Open Veins of Latin America*. New York: Monthly Review Press, 1972.

Graham, Richard, ed. *The Idea of Race in Latin America, 1870–1940*. Austin: University of Texas Press, 1990.

Hanchard, Michael. *Orpheus and Power: The Movimento Negro of Rio de Janeiro and São Paulo, Brazil, 1945–1988*. Princeton, NJ: Princeton University Press, 1994.

Hemming, John. *Amazon Frontier: The Defeat of the Brazilian Indians*. London: Macmillan, 1987.

Kicza, John E., ed. *The Indian in Latin American History: Resistance, Resilience and Acculturation*. Wilmington, DE: Scholarly Resources, 1993.

Klein, Herbert. *Slavery in Latin America and the Caribbean*. New York: Oxford University Press, 1986.

Menchú, Rigoberta. *I Rigoberta Menchú: An Indian Woman in Guatemala*. Edited by Elizabeth Burgos-Debray. London: Verso, 1984.

Morner, Magnus. *Race Mixtures in the History of Latin America*. Boston: Little, Brown, 1967.

Olson, James. *The Indians of Central and South America: An Ethnohistorical Dictionary*. Westport, CT: Greenwood Press, 1991.

Price, Richard, ed. *Maroon Societies*. Baltimore: Johns Hopkins University Press, 1986.

Selverston-Scher, Melina. *Ethnopolitics in Ecuador: Indigenous Rights and the Strengthening of Democracy*. Coral Gables, FL: North-South Center Press, 2001.

Smith, Carol. *Guatemalan Indians and the State: 1540 to 1988*. Austin: University of Texas Press, 1990.

Twine, France. *Racism in a Racial Democracy: The Maintenance of White Supremacy in Brazil*. New Brunswick, NJ: Rutgers University Press, 1998.

Urban, Greg, and Joel Sherzer, eds. *Nation-States and Indians in Latin America*. Austin: University of Texas Press, 1991.

Wade, Peter. *Blackness and Racial Mixture: The Dynamics of Racial Identity in Colombia*. Baltimore: Johns Hopkins University Press, 1993.

Wearne, Philip. *Return of the Indian: Conquest and Revival in the Americas*. London: Latin American Bureau, 1996.

FILMS AND VIDEOS

Blood of the Condor. Bolivia, 1969.
How Tasty Was My Little Frenchman. Brazil, 1973.
Quilombo. Brazil, 1984.

FIVE

SOCIETY, FAMILY, AND GENDER

The social milieu in Latin America is a fascinating, complex, and often magical reality that frequently seems to defy description. Societies in the region were forged over five centuries from a multitude of diverse, dynamic influences. Foremost among these are the European values and social institutions the colonists brought with them. To these are added those of the preexisting native societies as well as those of the African cultures carried to the Americas by enslaved western and southern Africans. They have blended in different ways to form societal characteristics that have evolved over the centuries and are manifest in a fascinating array of different forms in each country. They have been molded and modified by land tenure, subsequent immigration, trade and commercialization, industrialization, intervention, the modern media, and, now, globalization. There are, however, some constants that will help us understand this reality.

To gain some insight into Latin American society, we can look at how competition among groups and individuals is carried out on the playing field. We need to see how the game is played. Sports are often an excellent reflection of culture—by understanding athletic interactions, we can often better understand other forms of societal relation.

Like politics, *futbol* (soccer) is an area of great passion in most Latin American countries. *Futbol* unifies regions, classes, racial groupings, and even gender in ways few other activities can. When the national team is competing for World Cup standing, it provides a focus, a commonality, and a sense of community much more strongly than most other activities, save a real or possible foreign military threat. World Cup victories are also used by governments to bolster their legitimacy.

Regional and team rivalries also exist. Fans show their spirit and team allegiance by wearing team colors, driving with team banners flowing, and engaging in rhythmic chants through the course of the game. Passions run so high that the field and the players are protected by high barbed wire fences and water-filled moats. In 1969, passions exploded after a game at a regional World Cup match between El

Salvador and Honduras; the event became the spark that ignited long-standing tensions to create the so-called Soccer War.

Like football and basketball in the United States, hockey in Canada, and soccer in Great Britain and continental Europe, *futbol* has provided a way out of slums and poverty. *Futbol* further offers one of the few ways to transcend classism and the omnipresent barriers to socioeconomic mobility. To carry the analogy further, it could be argued that the soccer field is one of the few places in society where one is not excluded from play or at least handicapped by class, color, or lack of connections to the powerful.

Traditionally, soccer was a male domain and there were few opportunities for young women to learn or play the game, although women were welcome to watch, cheer, and support the men who played. Only in recent years has the internationalization of women's sports begun to change this; the Brazilian women's soccer team made it to the 1999 World Cup semifinals before being defeated by the U.S. women's team and in 2007 reached the finals before falling to Germany.

Venezuelan President Hugo Chávez playing the pitcher in a baseball game. (*Ministry of Information, Venezuela*)

These analogies are equally valid for baseball in those societies where the ongoing (usually military) presence of baseball-playing North American men has made the U.S. pastime the primary national sport: Cuba, Nicaragua, Panama, and the Dominican Republic. U.S. and Canadian oil technicians introduced baseball in Venezuela, where both baseball and *futbol* are played. The ease of baseball assimilation suggests not only the strong U.S. cultural influence but also the instant enthusiasm displayed by Latin Americans when they too could compete on a level playing field with occupying military forces or technologically sophisticated foreign workers. Their success is brought home by the presence of growing numbers of Latin American players in the U.S. major leagues. This was underscored when Dominican-born Sammy Sosa of the Chicago Cubs engaged in a dramatic duel for the home run record with Mark McGuire in the 1998 baseball season. Male success notwithstanding, at present women are not often invited to play baseball, nor are women's softball teams yet popular.

The popularity of the ball game dates back to indigenous civilizations in Mexico and Central America, although the current version of soccer was brought from Europe. Hotly contested matches were played for as long as days, and the winners could enjoy great success as bestowed by the wealthy and powerful. The losers were, however, often killed or sacrificed.

Like the losers of ball games in pre-Columbian times, those in Latin American society who cannot win the wealth–status–power game (the poor) suffer from powerlessness and repression and are frequently sacrificed to poverty, exploitation, humiliation, malnutrition, and occasionally torture and death. Their blood, it could be argued, flows to satisfy the new—now globalized—gods of the day. Why do the poor lose so often? Culture defines much of the playing field and most of the rules of the game. Latin American culture is quite distinct from that in the United States, Canada, Great Britain, or Australia. The sections that follow discuss some of the key aspects of Latin American culture.

From classical Mayan times to the present, the rules of the game have been dictated by those with power and wealth. This began with the Incan and Aztec emperors, Mayan kings, and aristocrats and priests—those who ruled. After the conquest, new hierarchies and dominant classes developed. Society in colonial times could be described as a sharply pointed upper-class pyramid seated on a broad base of indigenous and African peoples (see Figure 1). The small European elite enjoyed wealth, status, privilege, and power—they became the new ruling class. Even European artisans enjoyed a status well above virtually all of the indigenous masses. The exceptions to these classifications would be the *mestizo* sons and daughters of the Spanish and Portuguese elite and native women (who sometimes came from pre-Columbian royal families). Also in this category would be the mulatto children of Portuguese colonists and Africans in Brazil. However, the African and indigenous masses enjoyed neither wealth nor privilege and could exercise little power—they were the lower class. As the subaltern, those who were subjected to elite power, they most commonly led lives characterized by economic deprivation and exploitation.

This basic structure set the tone for Latin American society. A few continued to have it all, while the darker masses suffered the vicissitudes of poverty and powerlessness. With few exceptions, the elite upper class, or *oligarchy* as it is sometimes

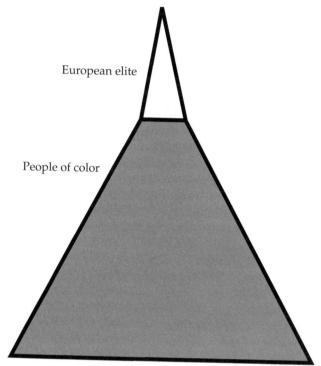

FIGURE 1: Colonial Latin American society.

called, still makes the rules of the game and dominates the lives of the many. Lighter generally rules darker, and male typically dominates female. At the beginning of the twenty-first century, those living in poverty accounted for between 40 and 60 percent of the population in most Latin American countries. Even by the rather optimistic statistics used by the regions' governments, some 40 percent still lived in poverty as of the mid-1990s. Indeed, in 1999, the newly elected populist president of Venezuela, Hugo Chávez, spoke of the 80 percent of Venezuelans who lived in poverty. Conversely, the wealthy and the superwealthy—the upper class—live very well indeed. For instance, it is estimated that the wealthiest 10 percent of the population receives close to 50 percent of the income, while the bottom half of society receives only about 4 percent of the income. The richest 20 percent of the Brazilian population receives an income that is thirty-two times the income received by the poorest 20 percent. Official statistics for urban households show much the same pattern (see Table 7).

The inequitable distribution of wealth and power continues to plague Latin American societies. In pre-Columbian times, it was the Aztec, Mayan, and Incan royalty and nobility and, later, the *conquistadores*, viceroys, *encomenderos*, and *latifundistas* who ran the game. Still later, power was monopolized by the rural landowners (the *hacendados*, *estanciaros*, and *fazendeiros*), *caudillos*, and Church leaders. By the twentieth century, it was not only the wealthy—the oligarchy—but also the

TABLE 7. Distribution of Income in Urban Households, by Quintile (Percentages)*

Country	Year	Quintile 1 (Poorest)		Quintile 2	Quintile 3	Quintile 4	Quintile 5 (Richest)	
		Decile 1	Decile 2				Decile 9	Decile 10
Argentina	1990[†]	1.5	2.6	8.2	12.6	20.1	15.6	39.3
	1999[§]	1.2	2.3	7.3	11.7	19.1	15.6	42.9
	2005	1.1	2.4	7.8	12.3	19.3	15.5	41.7
Bolivia	1989	0.9	2.3	7.4	11.6	19.5	16.5	41.8
	1999	1.3	2.6	8.1	12.5	20.0	16.7	38.9
	2002	1.2	2.3	7.1	10.9	18.1	15.1	45.4
Brazil	1990	0.8	1.6	5.6	9.7	17.5	16.4	48.5
	1999	0.7	1.6	5.4	9.2	16.2	15.3	51.5
	2005	0.9	1.8	5.9	9.9	16.8	15.0	49.8
Chile	1990	1.3	2.4	7.2	11.2	18.4	15.9	43.7
	2000	1.2	2.3	7.0	10.9	17.7	15.3	45.7
	2003	1.3	2.4	7.2	11.2	17.9	15.0	44.9
Colombia	1991	1.6	2.9	8.6	12.8	20.2	16.0	38.0
	1999	0.8	1.8	5.9	9.5	15.9	14.1	51.9
	2005	0.9	2.0	6.4	10.3	17.2	15.0	48.3
Costa Rica	1990	1.4	3.3	10.1	15.4	22.8	16.4	30.6
	1999	1.5	3.0	9.0	14.0	22.3	17.1	33.2
	2005	1.5	2.9	9.0	13.8	21.8	17.0	34.1
Ecuador	1990	1.7	3.1	9.1	13.7	20.6	15.9	36.0
	1999	1.2	2.6	7.7	11.8	19.1	15.7	41.9
	2005	1.3	2.5	7.9	12.3	19.7	16.1	40.3
El Salvador	1995	1.6	3.1	9.2	13.6	20.4	15.3	36.8
	1999	1.5	2.9	8.9	13.8	21.5	16.6	34.8
	2004	1.5	3.0	9.1	14.1	21.6	16.4	34.2
Guatemala	1989	0.8	2.0	6.7	11.4	19.2	16.0	43.8
	1998	1.6	2.6	7.9	11.8	18.2	14.3	43.5
	2002	1.2	2.3	7.5	12.1	19.7	16.2	41.1
Honduras	1990	1.1	2.1	6.7	10.8	18.6	16.5	44.3
	1999	1.2	2.4	7.9	12.4	20.3	16.3	39.4
	2003	1.1	2.3	7.4	12.1	20.1	16.0	41.0
Mexico	1989	1.5	2.7	7.8	11.6	17.9	14.6	43.9
	1998	1.8	2.8	8.2	11.9	18.8	15.1	41.5
	2005	1.9	2.9	8.5	12.3	18.8	14.9	40.8
Nicaragua	1993	0.6	2.2	7.1	11.9	19.5	15.4	43.2
	1998	0.9	2.2	7.3	11.6	19.1	14.9	44.1
	2001	1.0	2.2	7.1	11.2	18.2	14.2	46.0
Panama	1991	0.8	2.1	7.0	11.5	20.1	16.9	41.6
	1999	1.1	2.3	7.2	11.8	19.6	16.5	41.4
	2005	1.2	2.5	7.9	12.7	21.1	17.4	37.2
Paraguay	1990	2.0	3.3	9.3	13.6	20.9	16.6	34.4
	2005	1.5	2.7	8.1	12.4	20.0	15.5	39.8
Peru	1997	1.7	3.0	8.7	12.9	19.9	15.8	38.1
	1999	1.6	2.8	8.2	12.2	18.3	15.0	42.0
	2003	1.8	3.3	9.3	13.6	20.3	15.6	36.1

(continued)

TABLE 7.   Distribution of Income in Urban Households, by Quintile (Percentages)*
Continued

| Country | Year | Quintile 1 (Poorest) | | Quintile 2 | Quintile 3 | Quintile 4 | Quintile 5 (Richest) | |
		Decile 1	Decile 2				Decile 9	Decile 10
Dominican	1997	1.4	2.6	8.2	12.4	19.3	15.3	40.7
Republic	2000	0.7	2.1	7.0	11.7	19.5	16.3	42.7
	2005	0.8	1.8	6.2	10.9	19.7	17.2	43.5
Uruguay	1990	1.9	3.2	9.4	13.7	20.0	15.0	36.9
	1999	1.8	3.1	9.6	14.3	21.5	16.2	33.5
	2005	1.8	3.0	9.2	14.0	21.2	16.3	34.5
Venezuela	1990	1.5	2.9	9.0	13.7	21.3	16.4	35.2
	1997**	1.8	3.2	9.7	14.4	21.4	16.8	32.8
	1999**	1.2	3.2	10.1	15.3	22.5	16.4	31.4

*Ordered according to per capita income.
**National total.
†Refers to metropolitan areas.
§Twenty-eight urban agglomerations.

Source: ECLAC/CEPAL, *Statistical Yearbook for Latin America and the Caribbean.* Santiago, Chile: United Nations 2002, Table 50, pp. 62–63.

military leaders, dictators, and civilian politicians who frequently shared and held absolute power on a recurring basis, using their political–military power to consolidate their place in the upper class. They were joined by emerging commercial, financial, and industrialist elites and by multinational corporations and their foreign managers. Power, like wealth, remained concentrated—often absolutely. Indeed, some observers suggest that a requisite for belonging to the ruling class is to know, to have, and to exercise power. This was not only true with the hierarchical native civilizations but has been so since colonial times, when a small European elite allocated resources for larger societies whose majorities were made up of indigenous, African, *mestizo*, and mulatto majorities. For the sake of simplicity, one could argue that up to 1950 most of Latin America, outside of a few major cities like Buenos Aires, was comprised of an upper class including *hacienda-, fazenda-, plantation-,* or mine-owning *patrónes* and a lower class including peasant or rural laborer *peones,* or plantation or mine workers. Indeed, much of the basic social–political structures of Latin America hearken back to the traditional large estate, plantation, or mine run by European or mostly European owners who commanded absolute or near absolute power over the masses of people of color toiling on their property. In this hierarchical, authoritarian system, the peasants, laborers, servants, and even overseers were strongly subordinated to the *patrón.* The difference in power, wealth, and status was extraordinary. The basic structure of the system was most often brutal for those on the bottom. Most struggled on in grinding poverty; a few fled to the interior like the runaway slaves (maroons); and occasionally there were local rebellions. In what became a classic part of Latin American society, some decided that they could best survive and maximize their lot by formalizing their position in a classical patron–client relationship. In this way, they made their well-being in large part a function of the paternalism of the *patrón* and his family. In return for their loyalty and support, the power and influence of the *patrón* would, they hoped, be employed to protect and promote them. Leaving the area and enlisting in reform or revolutionary movements were less frequently exercised options.

Yet, there have been changes. The advent of urbanization, industrialization, and the diffusion of advanced technology, as seen in the proliferation of televisions, cellular phones, computers, and cars, has stimulated the growth of new groups. There were hardly any members of the middle class through the nineteenth century in Latin America, yet their numbers have increased drastically in recent decades. They now account for as much as a quarter of the population in many countries and have lifestyles that are not totally unlike their North American or European counterparts. Further, the middle class has the added advantage of access to very affordable domestic help. Limited employment horizons for lower-class women and men, low wages, and a tradition of subordination make domestic help plentiful and affordable for most middle- and all upper-class households. Industrialization, *maquiladora*-style assembly plants, and a growing demand for services have burgeoned throughout the region, stimulating demand for middle-class positions in the clerical, supervisory, and technical fields. The social pyramid is now a little flatter and might look more like Figure 2.

As the new century begins, the vast majority of Latin Americans are urban workers of different types and peasants. As Latin America has industrialized in recent years, the number of industrial workers has skyrocketed and the number of peasants has fallen. Indeed, Karl Marx's vision of a large, brutally exploited, poorly

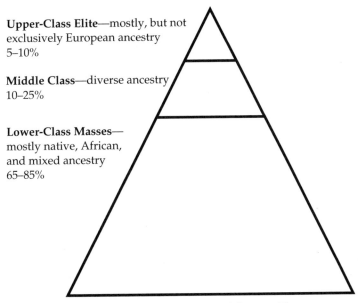

Upper-Class Elite—mostly, but not exclusively European ancestry 5–10%

Middle Class—diverse ancestry 10–25%

Lower-Class Masses—mostly native, African, and mixed ancestry 65–85%

FIGURE 2:   Latin American social pyramid.

treated proletariat driven from the land and unable to change its lot without total revolution could be coming to pass in Latin America in the twenty-first century. Unlike the nineteenth-century Europe of Marx, in most of Latin America, neither reformers nor the labor movement have been able to change the working conditions of most workers to any appreciable extent. Many still work for less than U.S. $5 a day (the minimum wage was less than $4 a day in Mexico in 2007), and few make more than $10. The boss is still very much the authoritarian figure; the workers are very much subordinate.

This domination of the many by the few has not changed as more women enter the formal workforce. In Brazil, 56 percent of women are employed in the formal sector; in Mexico, the figure is 40 percent (see Table 8). If informal sectors (street vendors and in-home producers) are added, the figures would be 72 percent for Brazil and 62 percent for Mexico. Women are thought to be less apt to resist management decisions—or to strike—and more willing to work for lower wages. Further, the proclivity of predominantly male management to hire female workers in the *maquiladoras* has also helped reinforce authoritarian control systems and feminize some of the worst worker poverty. It has also exposed a new generation of younger Latin American women to new forms of patriarchy and sexual harassment that are outside of the protective familial and community contexts in which they were raised.

As the new millennium begins, the conditions in which most Latin Americans live are very difficult indeed. Although literacy rates have improved, educational levels are still low, and basic indicators like infant mortality reflect a great deal of suffering (see Table 1). Out of every 1000 live births in Bolivia, seventy-five infants die in their first year of life. In Haiti, eighty-seven of every 1000 children die in their first year. Cuba, Costa Rica, and Chile are the only Spanish-, Portuguese-, or French-speaking countries in the hemisphere to have an infant mortality rate lower than 10 per 1000 live births. Elsewhere in Latin America, thousands of children live on the streets and must struggle to survive each day. More than 7 million children live on the streets in Brazil alone. Large numbers die of neglect, disease, or outright murder each year; and many are eliminated as nuisances by merchant-paid death squads or off-duty police.

As can be seen in Table 8, many who have dwellings do not even have water in their homes and fewer still have sewer services. Conditions are hard for the masses. Caloric intake and the availability of protein (see Table 9) are low among many, and malnutrition is a severe problem for the poorer sectors in most Latin American countries. Cuba is one of the few countries to radically improve such conditions. Even there, as late as 1950, 30–40 percent of the general population and 60 percent of the rural population were undernourished. Twenty years after the revolution, malnutrition had been lowered to 5 percent, although it began to grow again in the 1990s as a result of the decrease in Soviet and Eastern European trade and aid and the stiffening of the U.S. trade embargo to include food and medicines.

Health care for most Latin Americans is poor. The public hospitals that serve the great majority are generally of very low quality outside of a few countries such as Cuba and Costa Rica (see Table 9). Good health care is usually in short supply and rationed by wealth and power. The combination of lack of health care, poor

TABLE 8. Population and Social Conditions

	***Estimated Total Population (Thousands) (2007)	***Annual Population Growth Rate (%) (2007)	***Life Expectancy at Birth (Years) (2007)	**Population with Access to Drinking Water Services (%) (2005)	~Population with Access to Drinking Water Services (%) (Urban) (2003)	Population with Access to Drinking Water Services (%) (Rural) (2005)	**Population with Access to Sewage Disposal Services (%) (2005)	>Female Economically Active Rate (%)
Argentina	39,531	1.0	75.3	94	98.6	...	82	43***
Bolivia	9,525	1.8	65.6	85	86.9	33.6	45	60^
Brazil	191,791	1.3	72.4	89	89.2	26.8	75	56***
Chile	16,635	1.0	78.6	95	99	45.2	92	38>
Colombia	46,156	1.3	72.9	92	98.1	64	86	49>
Costa Rica	4,468	1.5	78.8	97	99.5	96.7	92	40>
Cuba	11,268	0.0	78.3	91	...	...	98	38>
Dominican Republic	9,760	1.5	72.2	93	83.1	...	57	53**
Ecuador	13,341	1.1	75	86	88.4	...	72	54***
El Salvador	6,857	1.4	71.9	82	73.6	31.7	63	44>
Guatemala	13,354	2.5	70.3	95	93.8	62.2	61	42**
Haiti	9,598	1.6	60.9	71	...	63.7	34	51
Honduras	7,106	1.9	70.2	90	90.6	63.7	68	39>
Nicaragua	5,603	1.3	72.9	81	83.5	26.4	66	47^
Panama	3,343	1.6	75.5	91	...	...	72	47>
Paraguay	6,127	1.8	71.8	83	61.4	32.7	78	54^
Peru	27,903	1.2	71.4	81	80.2	...	62	50>
Puerto Rico	3,991	0.5	78.7	...	...	...	...	37>
Uruguay	3,340	0.3	76.4	98	97.8	...	94	49***
Venezuela	27,657	1.7	73.7	83	...	...	68	55**
NAFTA countries								
Canada	32,300	1.0	80.2	100	...	99.2	100	62>
Mexico	103,100	1.0	75.4	91	95.2*	76	77	40>

(*continued*)

TABLE 8. Population and Social Conditions *Continued*

	***Estimated Total Population (Thousands) (2007)	***Annual Population Growth Rate (%) (2007)	***Life Expectancy at Birth (Years) (2007)	**Population with Access to Drinking Water Services (%) (2005)	~Population with Access to Drinking Water Services (%) (Urban) (2003)	Population with Access to Drinking Water Services (%) (Rural) (2005)	**Population with Access to Sewage Disposal Services (%) (2005)	>Female Economically Active Rate (%)
United States	296,400	1.0	77.7	100	... *2005	100	100	59> *2000 ^2001 **2002 ***2003 >2004 ~2005

... Data not available

Sources: *World Bank, World Development Indicators, 2005, http://web.worldbank.org/WBSITE/EXTERNAL/DATASTATISTICS/0,,contentMDK:20535285~menuPK:1192694~pagePK:64133150~piPK:64133175~theSitePK:239419,00.html

**Pan American Health Organization, Health Analysis and Information Systems Area. Regional Core Health Data Initiative; Technical Health Information System. Washington DC, 2005. http://www.paho.org/English/SHA/coredata/tabulator/newTabulator.htm

***Pan American Health Organization, Basic Indicators 2007. http://www.paho.org/english/dd/ais/BI_2007_ENG.pdf

>Statistics and Indicators on women and men. U.N. Statistical Division. December 17, 2007. http://unstats.un.org/unsd/demographic/products/indwm/tab5a.htm

~Statistical Yearbook for Latin America and the Caribbean, 2004, p. 117.

~Statistical Yearbook for Latin America and the Caribbean 2006, p. 71.

TABLE 9. Nutrition and Health Care

	*Availability of Calories Per Day (Kcal Per Capita) (2005)	***Availability of Protein Per Person Per Day (grams) (2001–2003)	*Physicians Per 10,000 Population (2005)	% of Births Attended by Trained Personnel	^Number of Deaths Due to AIDS (2005)	**Public Expenditure on Health as a Proportion of GDP (%)
Argentina	2985	94	33.4	99.1 (2005)	4300	4.4 (2004)
Bolivia	2128	57	7.6	64.2 (2006)	<500	1.4 (2004)
Brazil	3244	83	16.1	96.8 (2004)	14000	2.4 (2003)
Chile	3079	80	9.3	99.6 (2005)	<500	2.8 (2005)
Colombia	2745	60	12.7	96.9 (2005)	8200	4.7 (1995)
Costa Rica	2618	71	20.0	94.3 (2006)	<100	4.1 (2005)
Cuba	3547	78	63.4	99.9 (2006)	<500	6.9 (2005)
Dominican Republic	2673	49	20.0	95.5 (2006)	6700	1.6 (2005)
Ecuador	2770	57	14.4	80.0 (2005)	1600	0.9 (2000)
El Salvador	2680	67	12.6	43.9^^ (2005)	2500	3.4 (2005)
Guatemala	2239	56	9.7	31.4 (2004)	2700	1.0 (2002)
Haiti	1945	47	2.5 (1999)	26.1 (2005–06)	16000	1.3 (1990)
Honduras	2435	57	8.7 (1999)	66.9 (2001–05)	3700	2.5 (2002)
Nicaragua	2402	62	16.4	79.7 (2005)	<500	4.3 (2002)
Panama	2681	64	13.8	91.1 (2005)	<1000	4.1 (2005)
Paraguay	3101	69	6.0	85.9 (2004)	<500	2.3 (2004)
Peru	2411	67	10.0	71.1 (2004)	5600	1.2 (2005)
Puerto Rico	…	…	17.5 (1999)	99.8 (2005)	<500	…
Uruguay	3066	86	39.0	99.5 (2005)	<500	2.8 (2003)
Venezuela	2509	62	20.0	95.0 (2005)	6100	1.7 (2004)
NAFTA countries						
Canada	3486	106	19.1	100.0 (2004–05)	<1000	6.9 (2003)*
Mexico	3117	91	10.4	93.7 (2006)	6200	3.0 (2005)
United States	3637	114	22.5	99.5 (2004)	16000	6.3 (2003) *from PAHO

Sources: *Pan-American Health Organization. Basic Indicators 2007. http://www.paho.org/english/dd/ais/BI_2007_ENG.pdf.

** Statistical yearbook of Latin America and the Caribbean, 2006. p. 70.
*** United Nations Food and Agriculture Organization (FAO). 2005-2006 FAO Statistical Yearbook. D.1 Consumption: http://www.fao.org/statistics/yearbook/vol_1_1/xls/d01.xls
^ World Health Organization. Global Online Database. http://www.who.int/globalatlas/includeFiles/generalIncludeFiles/listInstances.asp

sanitation, and malnutrition fed a major cholera epidemic that appeared in Peru in the early 1990s and then spread throughout the region. As with wealth, health care is also very poorly distributed in the region. The bulk of the best physicians and medical facilities are for the wealthy and the middle class and are concentrated in the capitals and largest cities. Many—particularly in rural areas—do not have access to modern health care at all and either simply suffer or die or seek relief from practitioners of folk or traditional medicine. Yet, the medical care provided for the upper classes in exclusive private clinics is often quite good, although many prefer to go to the United States for specialized treatment.

Conditions for the upper class rival or exceed upper-class lifestyles in industrialized, northern nations; conditions for the masses in areas like Brazil's northeast, Haiti, much of Bolivia, and Nicaragua rival those of the poor in less developed nations in Africa and parts of the Indian subcontinent. It could well be argued that this inequality of wealth and disparity of power and influence are Latin America's greatest curses and are at the root of many of the developmental, social, criminal, and thus political problems that continue to plague the region. Yet, if varied social strata have very different economic realities, cultural similarities and interconnecting social relations tie them together into national societies that share many characteristics, as well as a few differences. To fully understand the complexity of these relations, one needs to understand the nature and importance of the family and gender roles in Latin American society.

Family and Gender Roles

Throughout Latin America the family is of fundamental importance. The family and family ties are the basis of identity and orientation to the greater society and political system. Much of one's life revolves around the family, and young people (especially, but not exclusively, women) usually stay with the family at least until they marry, even if this does not occur until their late twenties or later. Unmarried daughters often stay in the family house and, according to some traditions—as depicted in the Mexican film *Like Water for Chocolate*—are to stay and care for their parents in their old age. Government and private pension systems are often unreliable in Latin America. Children, in fact, may be the main or only pension system that aging parents have.

Personal ties and relationships form the basis for much of Latin American society and politics, and these begin with the family. If the world outside the family unit is often perceived as hostile and dangerous, the world within is seen as safe and secure. It is a given that family members help and protect each other, and in Latin America the traditional family has been large. Most early social interaction occurs within the sphere of the extended family, which includes not only father, mother, and children but also grandparents, aunts, uncles, and first and second cousins on both sides. As beautifully depicted in novels like *One Hundred Years of Solitude* by Gabriel García Márquez and *House of the Spirits* by Isabel Allende, three or even four generations often live in the same household. Nor has the nuclear family been small. Families of eight to ten children were not uncommon in rural areas; now, three or four children are still common and double that number are still seen, although less so in urban areas. Treasured, doted upon, and highly valued, children generally receive special attention from all adults. Cultural values and the adamant stand of the Catholic Church against artificial means of contraception and abortion have combined with traditional practices of measuring women's and men's worth by how many children they have to maintain large families. Yet, as Latin America becomes increasingly urbanized (about 75 percent), financial pressures and the increasing need for a second income have begun to reduce family size, but not necessarily the importance of the family unit.

Patriarchy is strong in Latin America and is even manifest in the old Roman term *patria potestas* (powerful patriarch). Frequently found in Latin American constitutions and legal codes, it means that the father is all-powerful in the family and in family matters. The term preceded *pater familias* in Roman times and originally meant that the father had unrivalled authority in the family and even held life-and-death power over other family members. Property for the family was most commonly held in the elder male's name (although there have been significant exceptions since colonial times), and women often had to go through fathers or brothers to exercise property-owning rights. Today, fathers and husbands enjoy a great deal of power in the Latin American family. Male prerogative often seems unbounded. While the woman is expected to come to the marriage pure and virgin and to protect the family honor by remaining above reproach, it is expected that the male has considerable sexual experience before marriage. Further, any extramarital affairs he might have are considered by the general society to be something that men do and typically not sufficient to jeopardize the marriage or to besmirch the family's reputation or honor. Mistresses are maintained, often openly, and the tradition of the *casa chica* (the little house or second household) continues. Wealthy and not so wealthy men often maintain an entire second family in a second household, acknowledge their children, and give them their name. Eva (Evita) Duarte Perón was the product of such a union. Even today one still hears of well-known public figures being seen with their mistresses, but the dual standard suggests a very different code of behavior for married women. For instance, in rural areas of Brazil and elsewhere in the region, a husband who comes upon his wife in bed with another man and shoots them dead may argue that his actions were necessary to protect family honor. Many a judge and jury have found this sufficient grounds for acquittal. In a similar vein, daughters are carefully guarded and protected by their fathers and brothers.

Men in general and male heads of household in particular have a great deal of power and prerogative in Latin American society. Most Latin Americans are socialized into households where a strong man ostensibly rules (strong women often head single-parent households or use indirect, yet no less effective, means of control in two-parent families). Thus, effective political action in the greater society is often equated with the strong, dominant, uncompromising ruling style that most Latin American patriarchs display. The traditional expectation for the Latin American politician, or *político*, is that he exhibit characteristics most often identified with the strong, dominant male—the *macho*. Strength and resolve are valued; weakness and an overly conciliatory orientation are not. Indeed, when a country is passing through a time of crisis, one can frequently hear the oft-repeated opinion that what is needed is a *mano dura*, a strong hand, and someone with the maleness to exercise it. Yet, in family and politics alike, the leader is expected to have a great deal of grace and style and not to be crude or coarse—at least until driven to it. Even so, the heavy-handed use of power may be grudgingly accepted if it is clear that the leader is intent on and competent enough to impose his will.

Machismo, or maleness, is very much a part of Latin American culture and clearly defines traditional male–female relations. In the 2000 presidential election in Mexico, the successful opposition candidate, Vicente Fox, frequently asserted his macho image in the campaign and even impugned the masculinity of his less force-ful Institutional Revolutionary Party (PRI) opponent. In its worst forms, machismo rationalizes total male dominance and even domestic violence. In its less violent form, it frequently robs women of their confidence and independence by socializing them to believe they need a male to protect them, do things for them, provide for them economically, and guide them in their daily lives and development. From an early age, the socialization of male children is much different from that of female children. Males are taught to be assertive and their aggressiveness is tolerated, if not encouraged, while female children are most often taught to not cause a commotion, not challenge authority frontally, and at least appear to be submissive.

Also of importance is *marianismo*, the glorification of the traditional female role. The term comes from the cult of the pure Virgin Mary (María)–like woman, who is expected to be the bastion of family honor, the submissive woman, and long-suf-fering family anchor. Yet, even in the traditional family, the woman often skillfully employs her role as mistress of her own home in childrearing, social engagements, and religion to guide and even manipulate the ostensibly dominant male.

It has further been suggested that Latin American women traditionally have been limited to the private space of the house and family while the public space out-side the home was the sole preserve of the male. Traditionally, the woman's place was in the home with the children. She was to support her spouse in his endeavors in external public space. While this was generally true, it should be noted that Latin American women have sometimes used their traditional roles to penetrate public space. Thus, a very competent, ambitious Mexican noblewoman of the seventeenth century joined a convent and became Sor Juana Inés de la Cruz so that she could pursue her studies and be free to write some of the best (and most passionate) poetry and prose of the colonial era. Yet, the fact that she felt obliged to take this path sug-gests how limited the options were for education and public expression for women. Indeed, the Latin American universities started as seminaries and excluded women for many years. Only toward the middle of the twentieth century was it possible for women to pursue university education in large numbers, and most were concen-trated in traditionally female fields like education, nursing, and social work.

Women have been controlled and inhibited. Courting—particularly for women of some status—was often supervised by the omnipresent chaperone in the form of a grandmother, aunt, or other female relative. Women were often expected to stay in the home and not work outside, while men were to go forth in the outside world to gain bread and fortune. Later, when it was more permissible for women to work outside the home, many occupations were closed and remuneration was markedly inferior to that of men. Nor has it been easy for women to occupy posi-tions of authority or supervise large numbers of men. In the political sphere, those women who did aspire to public position often used their upper-class position or ties to a famous father or husband to gain access (as was the case for Violeta Chamorro in Nicaragua). Talented women like Eva Perón or President Mireya Moscoso of Panama sometimes traded on their husband's position to acquire visibility and power in their own right. Aside from a few such famous personages, competent *políticas* were, however, all too often assigned "female" posts, such as minister of education or minister of social welfare (see Table 10). With the election of Michelle Bachelet as President in Chile and Cristina Fernández de Kirchner to the same office in Argentina, it could be argued that women are taking a much more active role in national politics. The fact tht Bachelet had been Latin America's first female minister of defense, was not married to the father of her third child, and was an agnostic suggested that women could be much less constrained by traditional roles—even when in public office.

Many have observed that some of the most assertive political actions by women have come from their traditional, private roles as mothers or wives. This was seen

TABLE 10. Women in National Government

| | Women Occupying Parliamentary Seats (Number) | | | |
| | Monocameral or Lower Chamber | | | Upper Chamber |
Country	1999	2004	2007	Last Election
Argentina	28	34	90	31
Bolivia	12	19	22	1
Brazil	6	9	45	10
Chile	11	13	18	2
Colombia	12	12	14	12
Costa Rica	19	35	22	N/A
Cuba	28	36	219	N/A
Dominican Republic	16	17	35	1
Ecuador	17	16	25	N/A
El Salvador	17	11	14	N/A
Guatemala	13	8	13	N/A
Haiti	4	4	4	4
Honduras	9	6	30	N/A
Mexico	17	23	113	22
Nicaragua	10	21	17	N/A
Panama	N/A	17	13	N/A
Paraguay	3	10	8	4
Peru	11	18	35	N/A
Uruguay	7	N/A	11	3
Venezuela	13	10	31	N/A

Sources: UN. *The World's Women: Trends and Statistics,* 2000; UN, Human Development Report, 2000, table 31 as cited in the *Statistical Abstract of Latin America,* 38. Los Angeles: UCLA Latin American Center Publications, 2002, table 600, p. 174.

*U.N. Statistics Division. Statistics and Indicators on Women and Men. December 17, 2007. http://unstats. un.org/unsd/demographic/products/indwm/tab6a.htm

Violeta Chamorro, campaigning in her successful bid for the Nicaraguan presidency in 1990. Note her white dress and hair and motherly outstretched arms. (*Photo by Bill Gentile/ CORBIS*)

in the weekly protests begun by the Mothers of the Disappeared during the dirty war in Argentina in the late 1970s and early 1980s. The Madres de la Plaza de Mayo, as they came to be known, became politically active as they sought to find and, if possible, save their children and other family members. They marched every week in the Plaza de Mayo in the center of Buenos Aires, carrying pictures of their disappeared relatives. In Chile, women publicized the disappearance and murder of their family members by sewing together *ampilleras*—quilts that told the stories of their loved ones. When Violeta Chamorro emerged as a presidential candidate and then president in Nicaragua in 1990, she did so as the wife of a martyred hero in the struggle against the dictator Somoza and as the reconciling mother who could unite her politically divided children and the Nicaraguan nation itself. She arrived at her culminating political rally in Managua symbolically dressed all in white, white hair flowing, riding in the white "pope mobile" that John Paul II had used on his historic visit to Nicaragua a few years before.

The Nicaraguan figure of Sandinista guerrilla Comandante Dora María Téllez, however, suggests the emergence of more independent and directly public roles for women. Women comprised some 33 percent of the Sandinista combatants, and women like Téllez and Mónica Baltodano were Sandinista *comandantes* in the struggle against the Somoza dictatorship. Many of their stories are told in *Sandino's Daughters* by Margaret Randal. The situation was similar among the insurgents in the civil war in El Salvador. As underlined by these examples, the emergence of other prominent female politicians such as 1998 Venezuelan presidential candidate and then governor Irene Saez, and statistics on the percent of economically active women (Table 8), the traditional role of the woman in Latin America is rapidly being redefined. This process is being moved forward by the following:

- Women who work outside the home.
- Women who exercise more independence by having their own apartments and entering into a relation with a *compañero*, exploring the full dimension of their sexuality.
- Revolutionary women like guerrilla *comandantes* in El Salvador and Nicaragua and the third of the Sandinista combatants who were women.
- The emerging figure of *La Presidenta*. With the election of Michelle Bachelet in Chile in 2006, Cristina Fernández de Kirchner in Argentina in 2007, and Mireya Moscoso in Panama in 1999, Latin America witnessed the election of four female presidents (Violeta Chamorro in Nicaragua was the first). Elected as vice president, Isabel Perón also served as president of Argentina for more than a year after husband Juan Perón died in office. Before this, three other Latin American women served as unelected chief executives in Bolivia, Haiti, and Ecuador for shorter periods.
- Radical feminists who challenge many vestiges of machismo and maintain a coherent line through their creative work, writing, magazines, journals, organizing, and personal example.
- Stronger national women's movements such as the Association of Nicaraguan Women Louisa Amanda Espinosa (AMNLAE) began under Sandinista rule.
- The new generation of young women who politely but persistently decide not to be bound by the same constraints that restricted the occupational and relational horizons of their mothers and grandmothers.

There is growing participation by women in education, the professions, government, and business (see Table 11). Gender roles are rapidly and radically being redefined. Feminism and women's movements have grown substantially in recent decades. There are a variety of women's organizations and feminist publications in Mexico, Argentina, Chile, Brazil, and the other larger countries. Strong women's movements can also be found in Nicaragua, Costa Rica, as well as Cuba. Women's groups are also active in the smaller countries and in cities and intellectual centers throughout the region. It should, however, be noted that feminism in Latin America is well rooted in Latin American culture and can be quite distinct from North American or European feminism. Thus, most Latin American feminists would define the female role as eventually including a role as spouse or *compañera* and mother. Attitudes on abortion—but not birth control—can also be quite divergent from those held by most feminists in the United States. Indeed, as the new century begins, Latin American women are seeking and gaining empowerment in a variety of ways that they define on their own terms.

Class, Gender, Race, and Mobility

Even though women are gaining power at an ever increasing rate, their mobility is still limited. Cuba is one of the Latin American countries with the highest degree of equality. Socialist Cuba legislated equality some years ago and even passed the

TABLE 11. Women in High-Level and Decision-Making Occupations

Country	Legislators, Senior Officials, and Managers (%)	Share of Women in the Adult Labor Force (%)
Argentina	33 (2003)	43 (2003)
Bolivia	36 (2000)	46 (2001)
Brazil	34 (2004)	43 (2003)
Chile	25 (2005)	36 (2004)
Colombia	38 (2000)	42 (2004)
Costa Rica	25 (2005)	35 (2004)
Cuba	34 (2004)	36 (2004)
Dominican Republic	32 (2005)	42 (2002)
Ecuador	35 (2005)	41 (2003)
El Salvador	33 (2004)	40 (2004)
Guatemala	...	36 (2002)
Haiti	...	...
Honduras	41 (2005)	34 (2004)
Mexico	29 (2005)	36 (2004)
Nicaragua	...	45 (2001)
Panama	43 (2005)	37 (2004)
Paraguay	...	39 (2001)
Peru	34 (2005)	38 (2004)
Uruguay	40 (2005)	45 (2003)
Venezuela	27 (2002)	40 (2002)

... = No data.

Sources: http://unstats.un.org/unsd/demographic/products/indwm/tab5d.htm, http://unstats.un.org/unsd/demographic/products/indwm/tab5a.htm

Cuban Family Code in 1975. It requires men and women to share household tasks and childrearing equally. In a trend that is beginning to spread throughout the region, women can enter most career paths and most professions. Although conditions for women in Cuba are very good in comparison to most Latin American countries, their mobility is limited. Although thousands belong to the ruling Communist Party in Cuba, their representation is less than equal in the party congresses. As one moves upward to the Central Committee and higher levels of government, the representation of women diminishes even further. Women generally experience greater equality at the lower levels: the higher women go in the political and party structure, the greater the barriers to their upward mobility. This is even more the case in most other Latin American countries. In countries where capitalism is dominant, women have generally found it very difficult to obtain management positions and even more so to rise to positions of power or prominence. Positions in the government bureaucracy or educational institutions have been easier to obtain. Not surprisingly, gender is frequently a barrier to upward mobility even in Cuba and Costa Rica (which has also passed progressive legislation guaranteeing legal equality), not to mention other more traditional areas of Latin America. Latin American nations are now beginning to pass legislation requiring a minimum percentage of women on party lists for the legislatures. But gender is not the only impediment to

Two Zapatista guards at entrance to EZLN encampment in Chiapas, 1996. As with other mass and revolutionary organizations in Latin America, more and more women are participating in all aspects of activity. (*Photo by H. Vanden*)

equality or upward mobility. Racism and a rigid class structure pose equally formidable barriers.

The class system in most of Latin America is fairly rigid, and it is very difficult for most to experience much upward mobility. As was suggested in the discussion of Amero-Indian and African peoples in Chapter 4, race has also remained a barrier to acceptance and mobility. There have been examples of successful indigenous Latin Americans, such as Benito Juárez of Mexico, who ascended to the presidency of the republic without ever repudiating his native heritage. More commonly, native peoples have had to assimilate to some extent to occupy positions of responsibility outside their native communities. Even in countries like Guatemala and Bolivia, which are inhabited predominantly by native peoples, Hispanicizing family names, the predominant use of Spanish, and adoption of Western dress are generally necessary for upward mobility. Indeed, many native people feel obliged to pass as *mestizos* (*ladinos* in Guatemala). The election of Evo Morales as the first indigenous president in Bolivia (55 percent indigenous) is indicative of both the historic inclusion of indigenous people and the sea change that is underway. Yet, as suggested by the testimony of Domitila Barrios de Chungara (*Let Me Speak*) in Bolivia and Rigoberta Menchú (*I Rigoberta*) in Guatemala, indigenous peoples are still second-class citizens, particularly when they come from the working class. When they are also female, they suffer even more discrimination.

The lot of Afro-Latins has also been fraught with difficulty. Racial discrimination in Latin America was never as institutionalized as it was in the United States, but it nonetheless existed. Slavery continued in many countries until the second half of the nineteenth century. When it ended, black Latin Americans emerged from slavery into societies where official segregation was not legislated but was practiced in more subtle forms. Some observers have noted that most of the governments of Latin America have espoused a philosophy of racial democracy but have simultaneously instituted a social order that in large part excluded their African populations from many key aspects of national life. As suggested by the eloquent testimony of Brazilian congresswoman Benedita da Silva, in *Benedita da Silva*, lower-class origins and being female make the struggle of people of color even more difficult. Afro-Latin women have made a significant contribution to the women's movement in Latin America and have played a key role in social transformation. There is, however, a paucity of literature and research in this area.

Black women—like indigenous women—are at the bottom of the social pyramid in Latin America. Afro-Latin women have had to form their own organizations in order to address issues of specific concern. Indeed, many black women in Latin America complain that mainstream white organizations do not understand the intersection of race and gender. For many black women's organizations, this nexus provides a much-needed framework of understanding. Field research by Kwame Dixon suggests that in the human rights area, this framework allows researchers to see the racial and gender bases for many rights violations. For instance, as a result of the war in Colombia, displaced persons tend to be disproportionately female and Afro-Colombian or indigenous. This suggests the intersection of multiple forms of discrimination. There are also distinct forms of discrimination that occur against a person when gender and race or ethnicity intersect. That is, women who are black or indigenous are more apt to suffer discrimination than either a white woman or a black or indigenous man.

As noted in Chapter 4, there is, however, growing black consciousness and movements in several countries to pass legislation prohibiting racial discrimination. Currently, black women's organizations are developing frameworks that incorporate race, class, and gender. Within the black community in Brazil, one finds several groups that also focus on gender inequality. Among these are the Geledés Instituto da Mulher Negra and the Centro de Referencia da Mulher Negra in Bahia.

Initial colonial society set up a rigid system in which classism and elitism in many forms were pervasive. Even today, one is still often judged by her or his birth and family name. Indeed, the Iberian tradition of using the paternal as well as the maternal maiden name is still in practice; for example, in Hispanic Latin America, José Sánchez López is the son of his father Sánchez and his mother, whose father's name is López (in Brazil both names may also be used, but the mother's family name appears first). Thus, mobility and entrance to social circles or employment opportunities are often defined more by who one is in terms of class, race, and gender and the circles in which one's family travels than by one's actual accomplishments and abilities. Indeed, it may take a generation or two for a family to gain access to social institutions like the Club Nacional in Peru, even if they have achieved economic or artistic success in their time. This process may take even longer in some countries if a person is primarily of indigenous or African ancestry. Some have even suggested that a process of whitening by wealth, great success (e.g., Pelé in Brazil), or substantial power (e.g., Batista in Cuba or Somoza in Nicaragua) must occur first. Indeed, many of the competent professionals who immigrate to the United States do so because they find that they have a much better chance of being hired or accepted for their actual accomplishments and demonstrated abilities rather than being pre-judged by class, race, gender, or family. In this and other areas, cultural norms and mores strongly precondition perceptions.

CLASSISM CHALLENGED: MASS ORGANIZATIONS

Movements bubbled up in the nineteenth and twentieth centuries, such as those that resulted in major peasant uprisings in El Salvador in 1832 and—assisted by Faribundo Martí and the Salvadoran Communist Party—1932. Thus, there is a long and well-developed tradition of popular uprisings and resistance movements. In more recent times, these have coalesced in mass movements and nongovernmental organizations that take advantage of the increased political space that new regimes and democratization have provided to assert their strength and push for their objec-tives. Latin American women's and feminist movements are but one example of this. Likewise, there are urban slum-dweller movements such as those in Mexico City and movements of rural workers such as the Landless Movement (Sem Terra) in Brazil. The reemergence of indigenous people's movements, such as the Confed-eration of Indigenous Nationalities of Ecuador (CONAIE) in Ecuador, and the many indigenous movements in Bolivia are also of particular significance. Indeed, Alva-rez, Dagnino, and Escobar argue that social movements are revitalizing civil society in their important *Cultures of Politics, Politics of Culture, Revisioning of Latin American Social Movements*. (See section on social movements in Chapter 10.)

Homosexuality and Transgenderism

Another area that is undergoing challenge concerns traditional views about homo-sexuality. Although often not discussed openly, homosexuality has been part of Latin America since precolombian times. Today, a growing awareness has allowed customs regarding gender, sexuality, and the family to be challenged by homosexu-ality and transgenderism. In this and other areas of Latin American culture and society, it is necessary to put aside preconceived notions and fixed labels coming from societies outside the region to understand the phenomena. Because most pre-colonial history was lost, destroyed, or interpreted through the eyes of the con-quistadors, there are few accurate records of how indigenous societies prior to the conquest dealt with the issue. From the evidence that does exist, it appears that both Aztec and Mayan civilizations focused mostly on male–male sex acts and inter-preted them through an honor–shame paradigm. In the systemization, there was a clear difference between the active and passive roles in intercourse: The active role stood for the masculine characteristics of strength and virility, whereas the passive role resembled the weakness and frailty of women. These discourses of penetration were frequently evoked in a number of ways to symbolize power and domination. Finally, in a slightly different understanding, sodomy signified the mentoring rela-tionship involved in the transfer of knowledge and power through blood and semen from community elders to coming-of-age noble young. This understanding, called the *age-stratified model*, is similar to how ancient Greek civilization conceptualized sexuality. Indigenous groups in the Andean region conceptualized homosexuality and transgenderism quite differently. As opposed to focusing on the act of penetration as a means for domination, the Incans celebrated individuals, both male-bodied and female-bodied, who deviated from gender and sexual norms, often designating them as having a *third gender*. The term *two-spirited* has also recently been coined to explain these individuals, with its origin emanating from the belief that two-spirited persons did not just have one spirit living within them but two—a male and a female. Consequently, they were revered as enlightened and blessed individuals, often occupying very prestigious social roles within the tribes, such as chiefs and shamans.

The conquistadors from the Iberian Peninsula brought with them their own ideas about gender and sexual deviance, and much more is known about their thoughts on the subject compared to indigenous groups. Over time their ideas slowly overtook indigenous views and formed the basis of the social stigma and legal persecution that came to dominate the region for centuries. Two separate, and sometimes contradictory, strains of thought are of particular importance: the views of the Catholic Church and Mediterranean ideas of masculinity.

Catholicism was central to both the Spanish and Portuguese Empires at the beginning of the 1500s and as such, Church teachings played a significant role in how gender and sexual transgressions were considered. The official position of the Church was that sex for any purpose other than procreation was lustful, therefore violating the Sixth Commandment. Sodomy, or *pecado contra natura*, then was a sin, whether man–man, woman–woman, or man–woman. Homosexuality was understood as a behavior, not as a person with a distinct identity.

Even though Church doctrine influenced the state's actions on homosexuality, the same gendered ideas of masculinity that form the basis of machismo also significantly influenced how colonial Latin American societies thought about gender and sexuality. Homosexuality was understood according to a *gender-stratified model*, whereby one's identity is strongly influenced by the "sexual function" one performs. The central characters of Manuel Puig's famous novel *Kiss of the Spider Woman*, about two prisoners locked away during the last military dictatorship in Argentina, epitomize this divide. Under this model, there was no homosexual group consciousness as no distinctive homosexual identity existed.

As Latin American countries achieved independence from Spain and Portugal, they fashioned their constitutions and laws after the Napoleonic code, removing most explicit prohibitions against sodomy. In Argentina, for example, Article 19 of the 1853 Constitution states: "Private activities that do not affect public order and morality and do not harm other people are reserved to the judgment of God and off-limits to the authority of magistrates." However, this does not mean that homosexuality was by any means more socially accepted. Similar to the social structuring in the United States at the time, inherent in this system was an implicit agreement that homosexuality would be tolerated in private as long as it was never openly discussed or visible in any way in public. Most countries had vague laws against vagrancy, public decency, and cross-dressing that were used at the discretion of police to enforce this public–private divide. This social and legal system came to dominate the region for centuries.

However, over the past few decades, globalization has helped bring along another paradigm shift in thinking about homosexuality in Latin America as the Western industrialized world's *gay/egalitarian model* is slowly replacing the gender-stratified model. Whereas before identity was based on the gendered notion of one's sexual role (activo or pasivo), this new understanding instead links one's identity to his or her object of sexual choice (male or female). The political implications of this are profound: both activos and pasivos now share a collective homosexual identity.

With this new understanding taking hold, modern homosexuality in Latin America has two characteristics that are of fundamental importance to how it has developed socially and politically. First, because attraction to members of the same sex is not necessarily an outwardly visible characteristic, gays and lesbians exert some power in controlling who knows. Strategically, this can be important, as homosexuals can hide their sexuality to avoid discrimination. Second, homosexuality is not a condition shared with members of one's core social group, the family, and therefore one can never be certain of their reaction on disclosure. Because the family plays such a fundamental role in social life in Latin America, it can be very dangerous for lesbians and gays to "come out": They not only risk losing their primary social unit, but their economic base as well. This has led to what is understood as a public–private divide for most homosexuals, forcing them to live two separate lives: a public life revolving around their family and another private life where they engage in homosexual relationships. Also, because young adults typically live with their parents until they are married, it has prevented gay barrios from forming in most large Latin America cities, impeding the ability for gay communities to form. Homosexuality under this arrangement was tolerated as long as these boundaries stayed intact.

However, over the past several decades, two things have generally worn down this barrier. First, the emergence of AIDS (SIDA) in the 1980s forced a number of people to come out of the closet. Many people who formerly were able to compartmentalize their dual lives became visibly sick and could no longer hide it from their families. Also, as many gays and lesbians witnessed members of their private homosexual world begin to die en masse, it helped solidify group solidarity, as those affected sought ways to slow the spread of the epidemic and treat those who were sick. As organizations began to organize around issues like HIV, visibility became one of their primary political tactics.

Second, social movement organizations representing sexual and gender minorities began to appear in most Latin American countries starting in the 1970s. In South America, many groups began to form as repression eased with the end of the military dictatorships and the reemergence of democracy. In what was once a mostly underground phenomenon that was rarely discussed in public and not organized politically, this nascent movement has only recently begun publicly challenging social mores and entering public policy debates. This was all made possible because the new gay/egalitarian model created an identity from which to petition for rights and protections.

Many of the first organizations had very revolutionary philosophies, calling for radical social change. However, the Left in Latin America did not initially welcome them with open arms, following the doctrine of the Communist parties of the Soviet

Union and China that homosexuality was merely bourgeoisie decadence that went beyond the clearly demarcated lines of class. Because the gay rights movement was of multiclass composition, there was always the fear that its interests really did not align that clearly with the working class. Over time, leftist organizations continued to discriminate against homosexuals and transgender persons. Indeed, socialist Cuba after the revolution was repressive to homosexuals in the 1960s and 1970s as exemplified in the film *Before Night Falls*. In more recent years some parts of the Left have changed their views. Homosexuals were allowed to play fairly active roles in the Sandinista revolution in Nicaragua, and recently the Cuban government has moderated its position significantly.

Over the past several decades, the homosexual and transgender movements that have appeared have not necessarily stayed together as cohesive units. In many countries, groups representing lesbians and transgender persons have splintered off from traditionally male-dominated organizations. Although gay men, lesbian women, and transgender persons all share stigma and repression from society at large, and are often the victims of violent acts, the problems they face are in many cases very different. Many of the political concerns for gay men, for instance, revolve around AIDS activism and sodomy laws. However, because HIV transmission sexually between two women is nearly nonexistent and most sodomy laws that do exist tend to punish only male–male sodomy, these are not the most pressing issues for lesbians. On the other hand, lesbians typically have felt more solidarity with the feminist movement and women's rights organizations. Their main concerns have typically focused on the same social restrictions and discrimination that heterosexual women also face. Finally, transgender persons have their own concerns. Typically, they are the demographic group hardest hit by HIV, but they also tend to face some of the greatest discrimination and violence as they are less able to hide their stigma than gays and lesbians.

Regardless of these fissures, homosexual and transgender organizations have made fairly steady progress in recent years. Political activism is growing: Sao Paulo, Brazil, is now home to the world's largest pride celebration, which in 2007 attracted more than 3.5 million people. Also, attitudes have warmed on the subject and the movements have secured some impressive legal victories thought impossible only a decade ago. Politically, a few issues have dominated the agendas of most gay rights organizations: decriminalizing sodomy/homosexuality, passing nondiscrimination protections, securing additional funding and protections for persons with HIV, and more recently getting the state to recognize same-sex partnerships.

Because rates of violence and other forms of discrimination against homosexuals and transgender persons are still high in most parts of Latin America, gay rights groups have also directed their attention to fight these problems. For example, even though Brazil has the reputation of being a country where "anything goes" because of its widely flamboyant Carnival, it is actually home to some of the most savage violence against homosexuals and lesbians. Rates of violence are also especially high in several Central American countries. As a result, many countries in South and Central America (some at the local and some at the national level) have enacted some types of ordinances making it a crime to discriminate based on sexual orientation, gender identity, or both. Finally, many gay and lesbian organizations have made HIV activism one of their top priorities. Brazil notably stands out, as it has provided HIV medication universally and free of charge since 1996 and has fought to obtain the rights to produce low-cost generic antiviral drugs to treat HIV.

Same-sex partner recognition has become a new issue for most gay and lesbian organizations, and it has slowly moved its way up the agenda. Initially, lesbian and gay organizations began pushing for relationship recognition in a piecemeal fashion—first seeking health care benefits, inheritance rights, access to partner's pensions, and so on. More recently, however, they have been pushing for broader social recognition in the form of state-sanctioned unions. The city legislature of Buenos Aires (an autonomous federal district) was the first to pass legislation recognizing these relationships in December 2002. Two years later the province of Rio Grande do Sul in Brazil followed suit, but in this case did so because of a judicial ruling, not legislative action. In Mexico, Mexico City and the province of Coahuila became the next in 2006 and 2007. Many countries such as Argentina, Brazil, Chile, Columbia, Costa Rica, Ecuador, and Uruguay have debated civil union bills at the national level, but at the time of this writing none have yet passed. There are also indications that same-sex marriage may also soon take on greater political significance, as the first bill to recognize relationships at this level was introduced to the national legislature in Argentina in 2007.

The main opposition today to the homosexuality and transgenderism still comes from religious conservatives repeating many of the same arguments used centuries before. However, in some South American countries, the Catholic Church has lost some of its political effectiveness. In places such as Argentina and Chile, the Church's reputation was tarnished during the 1960s and 1970s as it was seen as being too complicit in human rights abuses at the hands of the military dictatorships. Because of this, it has had to carefully walk the fine line between arguing against homosexuality but not against human rights. In addition, clergy abuse scandals have also plagued the Church in some parts of Latin America, in some ways severely crippling their moral authority. However, the recent rise in Protestantism presents a unique challenge to gays and lesbians, as many of these denominations are more vehemently antihomosexual than Catholicism is today.

As Latin America becomes more urban and educated and as egalitarian values are championed by women, indigenous organizations, Afro-Latins, landless workers, neighborhood organizations, gays and lesbians, and many others, the nature and structure of Latin American society will continue to change, and many of the old barriers will be challenged, if not overcome.

Bibliography

Alvarez, Sonia E., Evelina Dagnino, and Arturo Escobar. *Cultures of Politics/Politics of Culture: Revisioning Latin American Social Movements.* Boulder, CO: Westview Press, 1998.

Balderston, Daniel, and Donna J. Guy. 1997. *Sex and Sexuality in Latin America.* New York: New York University Press.

Barrios de Chungara, Domitila, with Moema Viezzer. *Let Me Speak! Testimony of Domitila, a Woman of the Bolivian Mines.* New York: Monthly Review, 1978.

Benjamin, Medea, and Maisa Mendoca, *Benedita da Silva, an Afro-Brazilian Woman's Story of Politics and Love.* Oakland, CA: Food First, 1997.

Bose, Christine E., and Edna Acosta-Belén, eds. *Women in the Latin American Development Process*. Philadelphia: Temple University Press, 1995.

Bouvard, Margarite Guzman. *Revolutionizing Motherhood: The Mothers of the Plaza de Mayo*. Wilmington, DE: Scholarly Resources, 1994.

Caipora Women's Group. *Women in Brazil*. New York: Monthly Review Press, 1993.

Craske, Nikki. *Women and Politics in Latin America*. Piscataway, NJ: Rutgers University Press, 1999.

Cubit, Tessa. *Latin American Society*. 2nd ed. Harlow, UK: Longman, 1995.

Dore, Elizabeth, ed. *Gender Politics in Latin America: Debate in Theory and Practice*. New York: Monthly Review Press, 1998.

Dore, Elizabeth, and Maxine Molyneux, eds. *Hidden Histories of Gender and the State in Latin America*. Durham, NC: Duke University Press, 2000.

Eckstein, Susan, ed. *Power and Protest: Latin American Social Movements*. Berkeley: University of California Press, 1989.

French, William, and Katherine Elaine Bliss, eds. *Gender, Sexuality and Power in Latin American Since Independence*. Lanham, MD: Rowman and Littlefield, 2006.

Grandin, Greg. *The Blood of Guatemala: A History of Race and Nation*. Durham, NC: Duke University Press, 2000.

Hanchard, Michael, ed. *Racial Politics in Contemporary Brazil*. Durham, NC: Duke University Press, 1999.

Hillman, Richard S., ed. *Understanding Contemporary Latin America*. Boulder, CO: Lynne Reinner, 1997.

Horswell, Michael J. *Decolonizing the Sodomite: Queer Tropes of Sexuality in Colonial Andean Culture*. Austin: University of Texas Press, 2005.

Imaz, José Luis de. *Los Que Mandan* [Those Who Rule]. Translated by Carlos A. Astiz. Albany: State University of New York Press, 1970.

Janvry, Alain de. *The Agrarian Question and Reformism in Latin America*. Baltimore: Johns Hopkins University Press, 1988.

Jesus, Carolina María de. *Britita's Diary: The Childhood Memories of Carolina María de Jesus*. Armonk, NY: M. E. Sharp, 1998.

Kampwirth, Karen. *Women and Guerrilla Movements*. State College, PA: Penn State University Press, 2002.

Kulick, Don. *Travesti: Sex, Gender, and Culture among Brazilian Transgendered Prostitutes*. Chicago: University of Chicago Press, 1998.

Kuppers, Gaby, ed. *Compañeras: Voices from the Latin American Women's Movement*. London: Latin American Bureau, 1994.

Levine, Daniel, ed. *Constructing Culture and Power in Latin America*. Ann Arbor: University of Michigan Press, 1993.

Minority Rights Group. *No Longer Invisible: Afro-Latins Today*. London: Minority Rights Group Publications, 1995.

Murray, Stephen O. *Latin American Male Homosexualities*. Albuquerque: University of New Mexico Press, 1995.

Randal, Margaret. *Sandino's Daughters*. New Brunswick, NJ: Rutgers University, 1995.

Sigal, Peter Herman. *Infamous Desire: Male Homosexuality in Colonial Latin America*. Chicago: University of Chicago Press, 2003.

Stahler-Sholk, Richard, Harry E. Vanden, and Glen Kuecker, eds., *Latin American Social Movements in the Twenty-First Century, Resistence, Power and Democracy*. Lanham, MD: Rowman and Littlefield, 2008.

Stephen, Lynn. *Women and Social Movements in Latin America*. Austin: University of Texas Press, 1997.

Thiesenhusen, William C. *Searching for Agrarian Reform in Latin America*. Boston: Unwin Hyman, 1989.

Trexler, Richard C. *Sex and Conquest: Gendered Violence, Political Order, and the European Conquest of the Americas*. Ithaca, NY: Cornell University Press, 1995.

Windance Twine, Francis. *Racism in a Racial Democracy: The Maintenance of White Supremacy in Brazil*. New Brunswick, NJ: Rutgers University Press, 1998.

FILMS AND VIDEOS

Before Night Falls. United States, 2000.
Black Orpheus. Brazil, 1958.
Blossoms of Fire. Mexico, 2000.

Eles ñao usam Black Tie. Brazil, 1980.
Buenos Días Compañeras/Women in Cuba. Cuba, 1974.
Burnt Money. Argentina, 2000.
Central Station. Brazil, 1998.
Details of a Duel: A Question of Honor. Chile/Cuba, 1988.
Doña Herlinda and Her Son. Mexico, 1985.
The Double Day. United States, 1975.
In Women's Hands (Americas Series). United States, 1993.
Like Water for Chocolate. Mexico, 1992.
Los Olvidados. Mexico, 1950.
Mexican Bus Ride. Mexico, 1951.
Mirrors of the Heart (Americas Series). United States, 1993.
Place without Limits. Mexico, 1978.
Portrait of Teresa. Cuba, 1979.
Shoot to Kill. Venezuela, 1990.
Strawberry and Chocolate. Cuba, 1994.
We're All Stars. Peru, 1993.

WEBSITES

www.casarosada.gov.ar President's office in Argentina.
www.presidencia.cl President's office in Chile.

SIX

RELIGION IN LATIN AMERICA

Treatments of contemporary Latin American politics often pay relatively little attention to the role of religion. Such an omission is a serious one because from the era of the great Meso-American civilizations to the present time spiritual factors have had a great impact on the political scene. This chapter will explore that evolution over time. The Roman Catholic Church will be a major focus but not to the exclusion of other religions, especially the rapid rise of evangelical Protestantism in the last 25 years.

The primary perception of the religious character of Latin America is Roman Catholic. For nearly five centuries the Catholic Church had a virtual monopoly on religious life. During that time, religious and political authorities were tightly bound together. The North American concept of separation of church and state was not known in Latin America until almost the twentieth century. Today's reality in Latin America is somewhat different, although close to 70 percent of the population still identify themselves as Roman Catholic. During the last 25 years, the most important development in Latin American religiosity has been the exponential growth of evangelical Protestantism. In 1970, only 2–3 percent of the population in most Latin American countries were evangelical; today, that number has reached close to 15 percent. The last 40 years have also witnessed significant turmoil within the Catholic Church. Following the historic second Vatican Council in the early 1960s, the region's bishops began meeting regularly; in 1968, at a meeting in Medellín, Colombia, they issued a groundbreaking document that seemed to commit the Church to a much greater role in promoting social justice. If the Medellín document had been fully implemented, it would have marked a dramatic reversal of the historical role played by the Catholic Church as the ally of the wealthy and powerful. However, the promise of Medellín to stand with the poor brought resistance from the more conservative clergy in both Latin America and Rome, leaving a divided Church that has been vulnerable to inroads from Protestantism. It is also inaccurate to view the totality of Latin American religion as falling within the scope of Protestantism and

Catholicism. A variety of spiritist cults and movements also continue to exist in the region, many with their roots in the large number of slaves brought to the Western Hemisphere from Africa in the sixteenth through the nineteenth centuries. In many cases, the indigenous peoples of the Americas have also maintained a spiritual identity independent of Western religions.

Historically, religion and politics have been deeply intertwined in Latin America. This interconnection began with the role the Roman Catholic Church played in the military conquests of the Spanish and Portuguese in the fifteenth and sixteenth centuries. Church authorities came ashore with the *conquistadores* in search of souls to convert and provided ideological justification for the military conquests and for monarchical rule. Ultimately, the Church was rewarded for this role with vast amounts of wealth and power. The Church set up parallel institutions to the royal administration. It was granted significant tracts of land from which it generated wealth and was given free reign to develop the region's educational system.

TABLE 12.   Religious Affiliation in Latin America

Country	Roman Catholic	Protestant	Hindu	Muslim	Jewish	Other	Non-Believers/ No Affiliation
Argentina	70%	8%		2%	less than 1%	1%	18%
Belize	58%	26%				10%	6%
Bolivia	95%	2%				3%	
Brazil	76%	19%				5%	
Chile	77%	13%					10%
Colombia	95%	1%				4%	
Costa Rica	76%	15%				3%	6%
Cuba	20%	2%				33%	45%
Dominican Republic	68%	11%					21%
Ecuador	90%	9%				1%	
El Salvador	57%	18%				2%	23%
Guatemala	60%	39%				1%	
Haiti	80%	14%					6%
Honduras	60%	29%				11%	
Jamaica	4%	74%				10%	12%
Mexico	89%	4%				3%	4%
Nicaragua	73%	16%				2%	9%
Panama	82%	10%				5%	3%
Paraguay	95%	2%				3%	
Peru	89%	7%				3%	1%
Suriname	23%	21%	27%	20%		6%	3%
Trinidad and Tobago	29%	31%	24%	6%			
Uruguay	52%	16%			2%	3%	27%
Venezuela	75%	18%		less than 1%	less than 1%	6%	

Source: World Religions and Cultures. Retrieved from www.wrc.lingnet.org.

The relationship between religion and politics is a complex one. Strong religious communities help set the value structure of a society by stating what is important in life. In doing so, religious values help frame what the citizenry expects out of their lives and therefore, on one level, what they may expect from government authorities. For example, traditional Roman Catholic teaching, which emphasized the glories of eternal salvation rather than the material pleasures of one's current life, seemed to dampen the expectations of the citizenry and therefore reduce the pressure on the political authorities to provide a good life in the here and now. Catholic theology rooted in Thomas Aquinas also provided a direct justification for monarchy and elite rule. All humans were deemed to be born in original sin, and it was only through God's grace that some people were better suited to rule than others. The essence of politics was then to elevate such people to power so that they could be responsible to God's will, not to the will of the people. This reasoning was used to justify the Spanish and Portuguese monarchies. It was only in the eighteenth and nineteenth centuries that ideas began to develop in the church teaching that provide justification for democratic thinking. Religious authorities can also play a more direct role in politics by influencing their followers to support a particular political leader or party. In recent times, Argentina and Chile have shown contrasting examples of Church policy. In Argentina, the Catholic hierarchy actively supported the two military regimes that ruled between 1966 and 1983. Such support was important in a country where military rule had earlier been supplanted by constitutional parliamentary governance. In contrast, the Catholic hierarchy became an outspoken critic of the Chilean military regime during the 1980s. That opposition helped pave the way for the defeat of a military-sponsored referendum in 1988 and the return to civilian rule in 1990. Despite these contrasting examples, historically most interventions by the Church have been to support the status quo.

The question of separation of church and state has long been a contentious one, with the establishment of such a principle being slow to arrive in Latin America in comparison with the United States. As elsewhere, the impetus for such a separation came from those who sought independence in spiritual matters from an overbearing government that gave favors only to persons from a particular religion. In Latin America, the challenge to the tight relationship between church and state came from the Liberal political movements of the nineteenth century. In response, the Church closely allied itself with the Conservatives in an attempt to maintain its historically privileged position. When Liberal regimes came to power, the Church was usually *disestablished*, meaning that the hierarchy lost its direct control over political matters. The dates of disestablishment range from the initial case of Colombia in 1848 to Mexico in 1857 and Brazil in 1889. Unlike the Liberal establishment in the United States, which granted freedom of religion and then largely stayed out of church affairs, the Latin American Liberals granted official freedom of worship but then sought to interfere in the affairs of the Church by attempting to compel priests to marry and reorganize diocesan boundaries. By 1910, virtually all of the Latin American countries, with the exception of Colombia, which reversed its disestablishment from 1886 until 1930, had granted formal religious liberty. As a result, the Catholic hierarchy ended its sole association with the Conservatives and broadened its relations to include the Liberal elites with whom they had fought so bitterly. The terms of their dealings with the state were now different, lacking the legal and financial privileges of the previous centuries.

In the early twentieth century, the Catholic Church also faced for the first time a significant thrust of Protestant missionary work into the region. However, the Catholics retained a strong position based on their large following and the rootedness of their ideas in the popular culture. Also, as the fierce anticlericism of the nineteenth century began to fade, the Church, without official representation in government, began to regain its political influence with the elites as newer, more powerful challenges from revolutionary movements united Liberal and Conservative elites. The Church concentrated its political efforts on protecting its own position in society by pushing for mandatory religious education and public funding of its organizations and projects. The new tactic of accommodating both Liberal and Conservative elites and even the populist leaders in Brazil and Argentina actually succeeded in winning back some privileges previously lost and in guaranteeing the Church a prominent societal position through education and public festivals.

Today, Roman Catholicism remains the dominant religion of Latin America, but it is facing an increasing challenge from both evangelical Protestantism and the overall secularization of society. In several countries, Protestants may surpass Catholics in numbers of adherents if the current trends continue. Philip Berryman has observed that because of the relatively low percentage of Catholics attending mass regularly, the number of churchgoing Protestants may be roughly equal to that of Catholics. As Protestantism grows, the political implications of this development are unclear. Many of the evangelical movements are closely connected with right-wing political movements based in the United States, but overall the evangelical movement is quite pluralistic and represents a liberalizing trend in comparison to the most conservative forces within the Catholic Church. In this chapter, we analyze all of the religious movements in greater depth, with an emphasis on their relationship to politics.

Indigenous Religious Practice

Any discussion of religion in Latin America must begin with a discussion of the spiritual practices of the indigenous peoples who lived in the Americas prior to the conquest. What are the traditional spirits of the indigenous people? Jean Schobinger argues that indigenous religious practice as it evolved to the time of the conquest was significantly different from that of European religious tradition. He argues that indigenous religion was intuitive, open to nature, and communitarian, and tended to see everything visible as a symbol of something greater on which the people depended. This religious tradition was seen as contrasting with the more individualistic thrust of European religion. Religious rites became more sophisticated over time, and practices were passed from one generation to the next and from one civilization to the next. Several high points are worth noting. The classic Mayan period from 300 to 900 C.E. in what is today southern Mexico and Guatemala was governed by a priestly elite who was inspired by deities. The civilization was sophisticated in that there was both an official religion of the upper classes and a popular spiritualism. This spiritual divergence may help us to understand the painful nature of the encounter between the two civilizations.

Anthropological research on the indigenous civilizations of the Americas demonstrates a broad evolution of religious and spiritual practices. Our knowledge of these activities comes primarily from wall art and carvings that survived to the twentieth century, when the majority of research was done. The pattern that can be observed is one of a growing religiosity of the lower classes. The spiritual life was constructed around both official ceremonies or feast days and series of myths and stories that framed a worldview.

Mayan religious life was centered around the magnificent stepped pyramids, which symbolically reached toward the cosmic world. Their worldview was embodied in the story of the Popol Vuh, whose basic idea was that there had been four ages previous to the one in which they were living. Each previous one had been brought to a cataclysmic end by gods dissatisfied with the imperfections of humans. Life was focused on activities and rites designed to convince the gods not to bring their civilization to an abrupt end. The ceremonies were elaborate and preceded by strict fasts. Sacrifices played an important part, but in the classic Mayan period human sacrifice was not involved. That practice emerged only later; it originated in Mexico with the Toltecs and was then adopted by Mayans under their influence.

The arrival of the Spanish and Portuguese conquerors had a devastating impact on the spiritual life of the indigenous civilizations, especially the ones that were at the height of their development in the sixteenth century, the Aztecs and the Incas. The conquerors often destroyed the public religious buildings and, through the missionaries who accompanied them, forcibly converted the local population to Catholicism. Perhaps the most blatant example of this was in the capital of the Aztecs, Tenochitlán, where the Spanish conquerors constructed the Catholic metropolitan cathedral on top of the foundations of the destroyed Templo Mayor of the Aztecs, destroying the official and public form of indigenous religion. Indigenous leaders were subjugated and, with them, the ability to conduct the festivals that had dominated their religious practice. This approach by the conquerors led to two parallel phenomena, the maintenance of indigenous religious beliefs through popular culture and the quiet practice of indigenous religions in former Mayan lands and Bolivia, and the adoption of European religious forms as a way to maintain traditional practices in the face of a superior power.

Colonial Catholic Church

From its first appearance in the New World, the Catholic Church was an essential element in the conquest and colonization of the native peoples by Spain and Portugal. From the beginning, it held a privileged position with considerable economic and political power. It provided ideological justification for the subjugation of the native peoples encountered by the conquerors. As a reward for its role, the Church was granted significant landholdings and a central role in the new colonial societies as the primary provider of education. The Church viewed the natives as people who could be converted to the faith, thus augmenting the Church's ranks worldwide. The Church had no respect whatsoever for the existing spiritual beliefs of the native peoples. For example, when the Spanish conquered Tenochtitlán, the capital of the Aztecs, they destroyed the chief temple and constructed the metropolitan cathedral of Mexico City directly on top of its foundations. This aggressive and intolerant Catholicism reflected that era when the Spanish monarchy defeated the Moors in southern Spain and expelled the Jews. The early sixteenth century was also marked by Catholicism's vigorous reaction to the Protestant Reformation. The Church's stature was further enhanced when Pope Alexander VI in 1494 adjudicated the division of the continent between Spain and Portugal and conferred on their monarchies the right and duty of propagating the Catholic faith. The model of social order the Iberian conquerors brought was that of "Christendom." Ironically, this model arrived in Latin America just as it was beginning to unravel in Europe. Berryman has called the Latin American form "colonial Christendom." Under this system of patronage, the Spanish and Portuguese monarchs exercised full administrative control over the churches in their territories. This set the stage for struggles over church–state relations during the independence period when the new leaders assumed that their governments would retain the administrative powers previously held by the monarchies.

In many ways, the role played by the Catholic Church in Latin America was simply an extension of the role that it had played in Europe. After its first four centuries of existence as a movement that struggled to survive in the face of hostile opponents, the Church succeeded in gaining recognition from the political and economic elites who allowed it to carry out its spiritual mission without significant interference from government authorities. It protected its position by endorsing governments and social systems that were willing to further Catholic values and protect Church interests. The Church always had an ambivalent view toward secular life. It tended to view the difficult human existence of the majority of the people as a burden to be endured in the hopes of a glorious afterlife. Secular authorities were viewed with a skeptical eye, but as long as they permitted the Church authorities to carry out their pastoral mission, the Church leaders gave their backing to the political and economic leaders.

The Latin American Catholic Church adopted this model and applied it throughout the New World, but it is important to note that from the beginning of the Church's presence in Latin America there were missionaries who protested the cruelty of the conquest. The most famous is Dominican priest Bartolomé de las Casas, who came to Hispaniola in 1502. Although he initially held Indian slaves, las Casas experienced a conversion and spent the remainder of his life arguing that the indigenous people should be treated with respect and won over to Catholicism with the power of the gospel rather than the force of arms. He wrote in *In Defense of the Indians*, "With what swords and cannons did Christ arm his disciples when he sent them to preach the gospel. Devastating provinces and exterminating natives or putting them to flight, is this freely sharing the faith?" Many Dominican bishops followed las Casas in the defense of the Indians. The tradition continued in the late twentieth century with Church leaders like Bishop Samuel Ruiz defending indigenous peasant interests in Chiapas. The primary motivation for such actions may well be moral, but they are also aimed at preventing the government from interfering with the Church's efforts to increase the size of its ranks.

The Church in Modern Latin America

In the first 25 years of the nineteenth century, Latin America broke away from Spain and Portugal. The independence movement and its aftermath created a crisis for the Catholic Church. Most of the bishops sided with the Spanish crown, and popes made pronouncements against independence in 1816 and 1823. Some clerics, including Mexican priests Hidalgo and Morales, were leaders of the independence movement; but for the most part, the Church found itself on the losing side of the political change. The Vatican only began to recognize the new states in 1831, and in many countries the clergy left, leaving some dioceses vacant. Those clerics who remained in most cases allied themselves with the newly created conservative parties, who pledged to support the historic role of the Church in Latin American society. In societies where the Conservatives held sway, the Church was able to prosper, albeit in a more limited way. However, in those countries where the Liberals came to power, the Church faced new laws that enabled the government to confiscate their lands. In the eyes of the Liberals, the Church represented an obstacle to their vision of progress and development. The nineteenth century also saw the rise of Freemasonry in Latin America as a challenge to the dominance of the Church in secular matters. As a result of attacks from the Liberals and Freemasons, the Catholic Church was thrown into crisis in much of Latin America in the nineteenth century. The Church came to rely on a steady flow of priests from Europe as it could not recruit enough clergy from within the region. Even today Catholic clergy are primarily foreign in many Latin American countries, including Guatemala, Venezuela, and Bolivia.

The Catholic Church entered the twentieth century in considerable disarray, weakened by attacks from Liberal governments and facing an increasingly aggressive Protestant challenge. The Protestant missionaries began arriving in the last decades of the nineteenth century and often received favorable treatment from the Liberal governments, who saw them as a useful tool in breaking the hold of the Catholic Church. Inroads in Catholic dominance did occur, but most Latin Americans continued to view themselves as Catholic. In the early twentieth century, the Catholic hierarchy initiated changes in response to the challenges it faced. The Church embraced new values as it sought to maintain its hold on a population that was also undergoing significant change. Religious freedom was embraced, and there was a limited recognition of the principle of separation of church and state. The latter was limited because Catholic schools continued to receive government subsidies and Catholic teaching was promoted in public schools. The Church also embraced the concept of social justice as it sought to relate the gospel to people's actual living circumstances on this earth as opposed to being concerned only with heavenly salvation. Church leaders also began to speak out on a variety of universal issues, such as freedom, equality, and women's rights. This era was marked by serious efforts to combat what the Church saw as alien influences on its traditional followers. The Church created organizations like Catholic Action to resist the influence of liberalism, Masonry, and Marxism. Catholic Action especially targeted university students and middle-class youth, who were seen as the likely future leaders.

The Vatican originally developed Catholic Action to combat socialism among working-class Europeans, but Pope Pius XI saw benefits in the Latin American incarnation. The organization was firmly rooted in such early social encyclicals as Rerum Novarum, but its success in Latin America was limited because the sectors to which it was targeted were so much smaller than in western Europe. One exception to this pattern was in Chile, where the efforts of Catholic Action contributed to the formation of the Christian Democratic Party as a centrist alternative between the Conservatives and the Socialists and Communists.

The Church also organized competing unions or "workers' circles" to directly compete with socialist- and communist-led unions, which were gaining significant influence in the Latin American working class. Anthony Gill, an expert on the Roman Catholic Church in Latin America, points out that the turn to organizing workers did not represent a significant ideological shift for the Church because it was limited to those places and groups that were being seriously courted by socialist ideologies. In this period, the rural poor were largely ignored. In another break with tradition, the Church hierarchy also sanctioned a much greater role for laypeople. These changes occurred very slowly over the early decades of the century, but the pace of change accelerated in the 1950s and 1960s as the Latin American Church increasingly shaped its teaching and practice of Catholicism to the particular conditions of Latin America.

The first plenary meeting of the Latin American Bishops' Conference (CELAM) occurred in 1955 in Rio de Janeiro. This conference would become influential in shaping the direction of the Church over the remainder of the century. The Latin American Church had been moving closer to greater acceptance of a role in social change and social justice, but the Second Vatican Council in Rome (1962–1965) accelerated the process. The documents produced by the council committed the Church to oppose governments that restricted religious or political freedoms and to acknowledge the significance of working for social justice in a variety of settings. During the early 1960s, the Catholic Church became involved in various movements that sought agrarian reform, expanded voting rights, and greater government spending on health and education. The Church also became the direct vehicle for improving people's lives through health training, literacy programs, and production cooperatives. Such programs contributed to a wider movement for nonviolent, reformist-oriented change.

In addition to promoting social justice, Vatican II articulated a more collegial model for the bishops. Rather than simply being subordinates of the pope, bishops came to be seen as peers who needed to work together to address concerns in their particular geographical area. Although the Vatican Council was an important turning point, socially conscious activity by the Church predated it in some places. In Brazil in the late 1950s, the Catholic hierarchy united with the government of reformer Juscelino Kubitschek to oppose the country's landowning oligarchy. The Church was instrumental in the formation of a development agency for northeast Brazil. Kubitschek used the Christian language of social justice to justify his reforms. It was in this era that Paulo Freire, a Catholic educator in the northeast, developed a new method for teaching literacy. Catholic Action movements of students and workers organized in many places to promote a progressive agenda. The activities of Catholic Action led to discussion of the need for political action to change the basic structural inequalities that were limiting the effects of reform and social work. Before these discussions were fully consummated, the 1964 Brazilian military coup occurred, placing the Church and its activists in a more defensive mode and setting the stage for its next important contribution to Latin American political life. During the 1950s, bishops in Chile became involved in programs of land reform, literacy, and rural cooperatives. These efforts went beyond the Church's traditional social work and, as a result, brought the Church into conflict with the traditional elites.

A New Political Role

From the 1960s through the 1980s, the Catholic Church became a focal point in many areas of resistance to military rule. In Brazil after the military coup of 1964, the Catholic hierarchy broke from its traditional role of absolute defender of the status quo. This stance in Brazil contrasted with the role that the Catholic Church had played during the Cuban Revolution. The Church had stood with the Batista dictatorship to the end, and few Catholic activists had been involved in the revolutionary movement. After the 26th of July movement took power, the Church became the focal point of resistance to the new government and suffered significant repression, including the expulsion of foreign priests, which further debilitated an already weak Cuban Church. As a result of the Cuban Revolution, the Latin American hierarchy saw the potential danger to the future of the Church in an uncompromising stand toward revolution and radical reform. In societies under dictatorial rule, like Brazil, the Church was just about the only institution that could provide a haven against the overwhelming power of the state. Aided by the Church's organizational and financial resources, local parishes were able to provide material and legal assistance for those who were repressed. Agencies established by the Church monitored human rights violations and provided lawyers for those accused of political crimes. The Church also set up programs that distributed food and clothing to the families of those who were imprisoned, and upon release from jail political prisoners received aid from the Church in the form of counseling and employment assistance.

In many countries, Catholic clerics and laypeople became part of nonviolent resistance movements that argued for the restoration of civilian rule. Catholic leaders not only criticized specific military governments but also rejected authoritarianism as a method of rule, a significant break from the past. In the context of that ferment, CELAM met in Medellín, Colombia, in 1968. The conference came on the heels of the historic Second Vatican Council, which had turned the Church to a social justice vision and encouraged the regional conferences of bishops to look more closely at the specific challenges of their areas. The Latin American bishops picked up this challenge and in the process produced a document that has influenced the Church's work ever since. In 1967, Pope Paul VI's encyclical On the Development of Peoples focused on Third-World development issues, containing a mild rebuke of the existing international economic order. Soon after the pope's encyclical, groups of bishops and priests began to lay out a program for Latin America in advance of the conference. A group of eighteen bishops, half from Brazil, went beyond the pope's statement while also drawing heavily upon it. They wrote approvingly of both revolution and socialism. In Argentina, Peru, Colombia, and Mexico, new groups of priests formed to press a progressive agenda as the gap between the rhetoric of the Vatican Council and the reality of everyday life in Latin America became more obvious. They raised fundamental questions about the wealth of the Church, its historic support for the status quo, and the need for political action to achieve change. These groups did not speak for anywhere near a majority of the clergy, but their ideas shook up the complacency of the Church and dominated the discussion leading into the conference.

The task of those at CELAM was to apply the work of the Second Vatican Council to Latin America, but they met at a particularly significant moment in the history of the struggle for social change. The year had been one of dramatic developments—students had occupied universities in the United States, factory workers and students had united in France, Mexican police had repressed student demonstrations, and the Soviet invasion of Czechoslovakia had ended the drive for reform in that country. Combined with the force of Pope Paul's encyclical, these events pushed the bishops to produce a philosophy and plan of action that would be more progressive than its conservative past and probably more radical than most were actually prepared to carry out in practice. The documents emerging from the conference were striking in that such topics as justice, peace, and education received greater attention than did the traditionally dominant topics of pastoral work and Church structures.

At the most basic level, the bishops called for Catholics to be involved in the transformation of society. "Institutionalized violence" in the form of poverty, repression, and underdevelopment was decried and categorized as "sin." Such a categorization represented a significant expansion of the concept beyond its traditional meaning of individual transgression. They called for "sweeping, bold, urgent, and profoundly renovating changes." Revolutionaries were presented in a very positive light and not tainted with an identification with violence. The Church made a number of commitments that included the defense of human rights and the sharing of the conditions of the poor. The conference also raised the idea of neighborhood-based, lay-led ecclesial communities that would soon begin springing up all over Latin America. The term *liberation* was used often and placed primarily in human rather than spiritual terms. However, the bishops stopped short of endorsing the right of the oppressed to fight for their rights. Some feared being labeled as condoning violence, while others remained committed in a principled way to nonviolence. The conference came to grips with the realization that a new Catholic theology needed to emerge from the Latin American condition. Theology was no longer viewed as universal and could not simply be imported from Europe or North America. A key figure in the development of liberation theology, as it came to be called, was Peruvian theologian Gustavo Gutiérrez. Gutiérrez had first used the term *liberation theology* shortly before Medellín, and soon afterward Gutiérrez and Brazilian theologian Hugo Assmann published full-length books on the subject. From the early 1960s, Catholic theologians had begun to discuss the necessity of developing a specific Latin American theology, but they were slow to break with the long-standing tradition of a universal theology. Ultimately, the pressure of events resulted in the breakthrough works of Gutiérrez and Assmann. For decades Catholicism had struggled to be relevant to the modern world, but with liberation theology it sought to find in Christianity guidance in the struggle for change. As Berryman states, "It is a critique of how social structures treat the poor and how Christians and the church itself operate."

As Gill points out, a key element of liberation theology is the reliance on Marxist methodology. The theologians based their understanding of Latin American poverty on dependence theory, a perspective that views poverty and oppression in the Third World as a direct consequence of the world capitalist economy dominated by Western Europe and the United States. Some theologians, such as Ernesto Cardenal of Nicaragua, also embraced the Marxist idea of class struggle and from that justified participation in revolutionary movements. In the wake of the 1968 conference, Catholic clergy and laypeople throughout Latin America increasingly took up the Church's call for greater attention to matters of social justice and political involvement. Thousands of Catholic nuns and priests moved out of traditional convents and religious houses and into poor neighborhoods, where they shared the difficult living conditions of the poor. Part of the motivation was to make the Church more relevant to its majority poor constituency. Traditionally, the Church had devoted a great proportion of its time and resources to the middle and upper classes and had sustained itself in significant measure through the tuition payments it received to educate the sons and daughters of the wealthy. The move to the poor neighborhoods was seen by those who did it as a means to better carry out their religious vocation. Although the moves did involve some personal hardship, the nuns and priests who engaged in this new form of pastoral work were freer than their counterparts who remained in traditional roles as parish priests and educators.

Most of the clergy who went into the poor neighborhoods adopted the educational approach of Brazilian educator Paulo Freire, called *concientización* (consciousness-raising), detailed in his classic work *Pedagogy of the Oppressed*. Rather than imparting their wisdom to the people in the neighborhoods, the clergy saw their role as drawing out conclusions through group reflection. These discussions were often carried out in what became known as ecclesial base communities, meetings in homes to read and discuss the Scriptures with the purpose of drawing conclusions about their relevance to everyday life. Those leading the discussion, religious or lay, urged people to search for the underlying causes of their poor situation. In rural areas, these discussions would often move from immediate problems to matters such as land ownership and class structures. Similar developments occurred in urban settings, where people would seek to understand the root cause of poor sanitation or poor public transportation in their neighborhoods. More often than not, the consciousness-raising led to the formation of groups that had a variety of purposes—soup kitchens, peasant associations, cooperatives, and so forth. Some were primarily self-helping in their focus, while others were oriented more toward political action. Self-help activities included programs to teach job skills or to serve as Alcoholics Anonymous centers. In Brazil, the groups formed an important core of the resistance to military rule at a time in the 1970s when few other outlets for political opposition existed. Political activities ranged from voter registration to serving as centers for revolutionary organizing in Nicaragua and El Salvador.

Impact of Liberation Theology

The impact of liberation theology and the work of nuns, priests, and laypeople in advancing an agenda for social change was considerable, but it never succeeded in fully transforming the historic role of the Church as a bastion of the status quo in Latin America. Within 5 years of the historic conference at Medellín, conservative Latin American bishops, especially in Brazil and Mexico, began a systematic counterattack against liberation theology. As the first step in their strategy, they took control of CELAM, the very organization that had initiated the progressive changes. Their counterattack was not initially a frontal assault. For example, no attempt was made to repeal the documents that were passed in Colombia. However, the conservatives were given a large lift with the ascension of Pope John Paul II in 1978. John Paul had been archbishop of Kraków, Poland, and a staunch anti-communist. It was natural that he would side strongly with those in the Latin American Church who saw themselves as working against the influences of Marxism within the Church. The papacy's assault on liberation theology proceeded on many fronts during the 1980s. In 1984, the Vatican issued a document that strongly criticized liberation theology; in the same time period, Rome was successful in marginalizing the influential Brazilian theologian Leonardo Boff. The revolutionary government in Nicaragua, which contained several priests sympathetic to liberation theology, was singled out for harsh criticism during a papal visit in 1983. Those priests in the Nicaraguan government were prevented from carrying out their religious duties. However, the papacy's strongest move against liberation theology may have been its appointment of new bishops who would hold steadfastly to Rome's conservative stance. Archbishop Helder Camera of Recife, Brazil, one of the region's harshest critics of military rule and a strong proponent of the strategy of working with the poor, was replaced by a conservative, who moved almost immediately to reverse the fruits of Camera's work. In Cuernavaca, Mexico, there was a high concentration of Christian base communities as a result of the work of Bishop Sergio Mendez Arceo; but when he retired in the late 1980s the Vatican appointed a conservative to replace him and the grassroots work suffered. Overall, the counterattack of the conservative forces in the Church was directly related to the growing strength of the left and the high stakes that were involved. In Brazil, the Workers' Party (PT) was on the verge of winning the national presidency in the late 1980s, and only a united front of all the conservative forces succeeded in defeating their candidate, Luiz Inacio da Silva, in the 1989 election. In Central America throughout the 1980s, revolutionary forces were on the upswing in Nicaragua, El Salvador, and Guatemala. The revolutionary shock waves were felt as far north as Mexico. In that context, the papacy weighed in on the side of the anticommunist forces, a decision that dovetailed with the foreign policy initiatives of the United States. Progressive Church forces came to be seen as part of a revolutionary upsurge that had to be suppressed.

The diminishing impact of liberation theology in the 1990s cannot be blamed exclusively on the counterattack by the Vatican. Part of the failure of liberation theology to fully transform the Church lies within the movement itself. Liberation theology never really succeeded in becoming a mass movement within the Church. Fewer than 10 percent of the nuns and priests actually moved into communities to work directly with the poor. CEBs did arise in significant numbers in some select places, such as in Brazil during the military government in the 1970s; but they never came close to their goal of transforming the manner in which the Church functioned. In Brazil, close to 100,000 CEBs developed by the mid-1980s, but that accounted for only about 2.5 percent of the Catholic population. Significant lay leadership was involved in the CEBs, but most remained dependent on the leadership of clergy, which limited the CEBs' ability to grow into a mass movement. However, one very positive result of the work of the CEBs was a significant increase in the proportion of women in leadership roles in comparison to the past. The CEBs also gave the Catholic Church a significant presence in working-class neighborhoods that had been previously ignored. The decline of liberation theology, acknowledged by Gutiérez in 1994, was also the result of a changing political climate. Born in the era of 1960s revolutionary idealism, liberation theology has declined with the assault on the progressive agenda marked by the collapse of East European socialism and the defeat of the Sandinista revolutionary project in Nicaragua. These setbacks led many within the progressive Church community to scale back their short-term expectations for dramatic social change and to work for more reformist goals within the existing system. The restoration of democratic systems throughout the region in the 1980s facilitated this change in strategy.

The horizons of the reformers may have been limited by world events and their own shortcomings, but their political legacy has not been unimportant. In several key situations in the 1980s, progressive Roman Catholic bishops played an important political role as mediators. In El Salvador, Archbishop Arturo Rivera y Damas, who assumed the leadership of the Church after the military assassinated outspoken Archbishop Oscar Romero, made numerous attempts to bring an end to that country's devastating civil war. The military initially rejected such appeals as treason, but the archbishop's efforts eventually contributed to the 1992 peace agreement. The Guatemalan bishops played a similar role against the wishes of the military to help broker the eventual agreement in that country that ended a 40-year civil war in 1997. Chilean bishops were also instrumental in bringing about a negotiated end to the Pinochet regime. In the conflict in Chiapas in the 1990s, Bishop Samuel Ruiz played an important role as a mediator between the Mexican government and the Zapatistas. During the 1970s and 1980s, scores of human rights monitoring organizations were formed in the region, often with the protection and funding of the Church. Under different political circumstances, most of these organizations are now independent of the Church, but their work continues; they represent an important legacy of the movement for liberation theology.

Pentecostalism

The most important development in the Latin American religious sector in the last 20 years is the remarkable growth of Pentecostalism. Less than 20 years ago, the groups made up no more than 2–3 percent of the population, but today they have reached the significant level of 15 percent continentwide, with a much greater presence in countries such as Guatemala. It also should be pointed out that a focus on absolute numbers is misleading because in comparison to those who identify themselves as Catholic, the Evangelicals tend to be more active in church life. Pentecostal churches were founded mostly in the early part of the twentieth century. They are often connected to Charles Parham's spiritual revival in Topeka, Kansas, in 1901 and a subsequent revival in Los Angeles in 1906. From those revivals came churches such as the Assemblies of God, the Church of God, and the Church of God in Christ.

It is important to not place any single label on the Pentecostal churches, which are quite diverse in both their religious and political practices. Some, such as the Universal Church and the Deus e Amor Church, are not built around fixed church structures but instead draw followers to tents and warehouses where the emphasis is on singing and spiritual healing. Their services are dramatic, with considerable moaning, screaming, and crawling on hands and knees. The object of the services is to drive out the demons that have "infected" the members. These churches also have a considerable presence on the radio, with hundreds of hours of programming in countries such as Brazil. The Universal Church tends to draw a middle-class constituency, while the Deus e Amor Church followers are overwhelmingly poor. The largest single Pentecostal group in Latin America is the Assemblies of God, who have 8–12 million followers and 35,000 churches in Brazil alone. In contrast to lack of institutionalism in the previously discussed Evangelicals, the Assemblies of God, with their origins in North America, are highly organized and have considerable financial resources. Although the majority of their members are very poor, their relative wealth belies their North American ties.

Evangelical Movement

Berryman has attributed the appeal of the Pentecostals to a simple message of love and prayer that provides community and a sense of self-respect. Another basis of the success of the movement among the region's poorest citizens is that most Evangelical ministers come from the same social class as their congregants. In contrast, most Catholic priests, even those who espouse liberation theology, come from middle- and upper-class backgrounds. It is also very difficult to characterize the political impact of the Evangelical movement. Unquestionably, some churches, such as the Word of God movement in Guatemala, have directly promoted right-wing politics through the born-again leader José Efraín Ríos Montt, who carried out massive repression in the early 1980s. Later Jorge Serrano based his Guatemalan presidential campaign on Evangelical votes, and Alberto Fujimori reached out to Evangelicals in his 1990 run for the presidency in Peru. Evangelical representatives are an important voting bloc in the Brazilian congress. However, beyond these examples, the Evangelicals have not really developed anything close to a clear, coherent political message. Not all Evangelicals are politically conservative. The Brazilian PT has many Evangelicals within its ranks, including one of its congressional leaders, Benedita da Silva, an active member of the Assemblies of God. Many Pentecostals consciously reject any significant involvement in politics.

African-Inspired Religions

After indigenous religion, Catholicism, and Prostestantism, the fourth religious tradition in Latin America is that of African-inspired religion. This religious trend is present to some degree throughout the continent but is especially prevalent in countries such as Cuba, Haiti, and Brazil, where millions of slaves were imported from West Africa. The Africans brought their spiritual beliefs with them and have maintained them for more than three centuries in the face of efforts by both political and religious authorities to marginalize them. In some instances the well-developed

Yoruba religion was transferred to the New World without significant modification (Santaría in Cuba and Puerto Rica and Condomblé in Brazil). In other instances, the African beliefs have commingled with Catholic and Protestant spirituality to form a hybrid. Generally speaking, those practicing these religious traditions believe that the dead continue to live and communicate with the world through a variety of means. They believe that these spirits influence the manner in which the living exist, sometimes for good and other times for evil. A series of deities or *Orishas* are also prominent in the Yoruba-based religions.

One of the strongest movements is the **Voodoo** of Haiti, which developed among the slave population and was influential in the abolitionist and independence movements at the end of the eighteenth century. It also would later become a tool of the Duvalier dictatorships from the 1950s to the 1980s. Voodoo spirits are called *loas*, and the objective of the religion is to connect the living with the *loas*. The spirits' help is sought to cure ailments and to provide advice for solving daily problems. Priests, called *hougans*, facilitate the connection between the spiritual world and the followers of voodoo. The priests have an authority that can be based on either their charisma or the patrimony of a local political or military leader.

Following an instrumental role in achieving Haitian independence in 1804, the voodoo movement was largely driven underground for the next 150 years at the behest of the country's white and Catholic elite. However, a strong underground network of priests and their followers was constructed in Haiti's poorest communities, and the religious beliefs were passed on from generation to generation. Then, in the late 1950s, these local voodoo organizations became the power base for the political movement of François Duvalier, who won the 1957 elections and later established a harsh dictatorial rule that was eventually passed on to his son. The feared Tonton Macoute militias organized by Duvalier for use against his political foes came from his voodoo power base. The younger Duvalier was driven from power in the mid-1980s, but voodoo retains a strong spiritual following in contemporary Haiti without, however, the politicization that it had during the Duvalier period.

A less known but equally important African-based movement called **Santería** has a very important presence in contemporary Cuba and Puerto Rico and is part of the changes occurring in socialist Cuba. Like voodoo, Santería has its origins in the African slaves brought to Cuba to harvest sugarcane. Santería came from the Yoruba people of what is today Nigeria. Like voodoo, Santería provided a link to their African past and some respite from the brutality of slavery. As in Haiti, the bonds of the Santería communities helped pave the way for independence and abolitionist movements that developed in the latter part of the nineteenth century in Cuba. However, in contrast to voodoo, Santería, out of an instinct for survival in strongly Catholic Cuba, often linked its rituals and spirits to those of the Roman Catholic Church. The key figures of the Catholic Church, such as Jesus and various saints, were masked as Yoruba deities or *Orishas*. The *Santerístas* also timed their main festivals according to those of the Catholic Church, such as Easter and Christmas. Such accommodation simply reflected the relationship of forces that existed in Cuba and Puerto Rico during the long years of Spanish and Catholic rule. However, it was a very successful accommodation because it allowed the spiritual beliefs of the Afro-Cuban population to survive into the twentieth century. The movement went into decline with the advent of the revolutionary government in Cuba in 1959

Shrine to the Black Virgin in Regla, outskirts of Havana. Type and placement of candles also suggest the shrine is worshipped by practitioners of Santería, who frequent the church along with the Catholic parishioners. *(Photo by Patrice Olsen)*

but underwent a revival in the 1990s with the more tolerant attitude toward religion by the government. The Cuban Catholic Church has even complained that the Santería movement is the favored religion of the current government. Santería is also practiced in the United States, where there are heavy concentrations of Cubans and Puerto Ricans.

Brazil is another country where African-based religious movements have a significant following. There are two major variants in the country. **Umbanda** shares the practice with Santería of pairing its deities with those of the Catholic Church. Similar to voodoo and Santería, Umbanda's followers seek advice from the spirits on problems of everyday life. There are many Umbanda centers, especially in Rio de Janeiro, which holds full schedules of cultural activities alongside exercise programs and social services. The intermediaries between the people and the spirits, called *mediums,* often obtain a large personal following. Even more akin to Santería is **Candomblé**, also brought by slaves from the Yoruba region of West Africa. Like Santería, it sometimes links its deities or *Orishás* with those of the Catholic religion. **Candomblé** generally appeals more to the poor. The spirits are also less connected to practical advice and more to pageants of dancing and eating. The movements in Brazil have probably been less directly political than similar movements in Haiti and Cuba, but they can be credited with helping the poor maintain their cultural identity in the face of the dominant white and Catholic culture.

Judaism

Any discussion of religion in Latin America should make mention of the region's Jews. They are not large in number, probably under 500,000 in the region as a whole, with the largest communities in Argentina (240,000), Brazil (100,000), and Mexico (35,000). Most Jews who live in Latin America came as part of nineteenth- and twentieth-century immigration, but they have faced persistent anti-Semitism and marginalization that dates to the time of the conquest.

By the fifteenth century, Jews had lived in Spain for 1000 years. Always a minority, the Jews were often caught in the battle between Catholicism and Islam and manipulated by both. Over the 1000 years, periods of great Jewish contribution to Spanish life alternated with periods of persecution and forced conversion. Their situation worsened after 1391 when pogroms broke out, first in Seville and then throughout Spain. In 1492, the Spanish crown expelled the Jews from Spain and soon established a series of laws that excluded all Jews, even those who had converted to Catholicism, from Spanish public life. Anyone who had any Jewish or Moorish "blood" was excluded from positions in the professions, the Church, the military, and the government. This indelible labeling of those with Jewish ancestry, converted or not, led to the widespread labeling of Jews as a "race," a perspective that was imported to Latin America and continues to the present time.

The exclusion of Jews from Spain was extended to Spanish lands in the Americas. In her first instruction to the governor of Hispaniola, Queen Isabella forbade Jews and "new Christians" (as the converts were called) from settling in the Indies. This legal prohibition continued throughout Spanish rule into the nineteenth century. Many new Christians and some Jews did succeed in settling in the Indies by subverting the law. However, the local missionaries laid the groundwork for long-term anti-Semitism among the native population. Jews were singled out as the tormentors and killers of Christ. Primary among the charges leveled against Jews was subversion. Popular opinion blamed converted Jews for the Dutch defeat of the Portuguese in Brazil in 1630. It was alleged that the new Christians assisted the invaders because they hoped to reestablish Judaism under more tolerant Dutch rule. The stereotype of Jews as subversives persists in Argentina, the country with the largest Jewish population. The generals who carried out Argentina's dirty war in the 1970s attacked Jews as subversives and Marxists. Their most famous target was the Jewish journalist Jacobo Timmerman, but the campaign revived anti-Semitism in contemporary Latin America.

Conclusion

As the twenty-first century began in Latin America, the impact of religion on society was more complex than ever before. The absolute hold of Catholicism on the region is now part of history, and despite the Church's attempts to remake itself in the last 30 years, there will likely be no return to its former dominance. Protestantism has made great strides in recent years, especially with the rapid growth of Evangelical sects. However, it should be remembered that these groups claim the allegiance of fewer than one in five Latin Americans. The political impact of the rapid growth of Protestantism is difficult to measure. Some groups are avowedly conservative in their political thrust, but most discourage social activism in their theology. Although generally critical of liberation theology, the Evangelicals have largely failed to develop their own strategy for confronting the region's ongoing social ills. That failure may yet derail the long-term growth of the Evangelical movement.

It would seem that the work of liberation theology begun in the 1960s has run its course in the current dominant political climate in the region, but that does not mean that its future impact will be marginal. The Catholic Church's commitment to social justice seems to have been firmly established. Pope John Paul's visit to Mexico in early 1999 underscored this fact. Twenty years earlier, on his first visit to Mexico, he spoke harshly of liberation theology and emphasized his opposition to communism of any kind. That message inevitably bolstered the status quo and by implication was procapitalist. On the 1999 visit, the pope's message was strikingly different. In reference to the contemporary emphasis on neoliberalism and free markets, he said "The human race is facing forms of slavery which are new and more subtle than those of the past." The pope called on both governments and international organizations to carry out plans aimed at Third-World debt relief and wealth redistribution. Some have called this perspective "post–liberation theology." The long-term impact of the Vatican's new emphasis is yet to be seen. It will likely take a new generation of theologians and Church activists to fully articulate a new vision of social change. The diversity of views within the Protestant sector definitely leaves the field open for a theological alliance that could bridge the two different traditions.

Bibliography

Berryman, Philip. *Stubborn Hope: Religion, Politics, and Revolution in Central America*. Mary Knoll, NY: Orbis Books, 1994.

——. *Religion in the Megacity: Catholic and Protestant Portraits from Latin America*. Mary Knoll, NY: Orbis Books, 1996.

Betances, Emelio. *The Catholic Church and Power Politics in Latin America*. Lanham, MD: Rowman and Littlefield, 2007.

Cleary, Edward, and Hannah Stewart-Gambino. *Power, Politics, and Pentecostals in Latin America*. Boulder, CO: Westview Press, 1997.

Davis, Darien. *Beyond Slavery: The Multilayered Legacy of Africans in Latin America and the Caribbean*. Lanham, MD: Rowman and Littlefield, 2006.

Efunde, Agun. *Los Secretos de la Santería*. Miami, FL: Ediciones Cubamerica, 1983.

Fleet, Michael, and Brian Smith. *The Catholic Church and Democratization in Latin America: Twentieth-Century Chile and Peru*. Notre Dame, IN: University of Notre Dame Press, 1996.

Freire, Paulo. *Pedagogy of The Oppressed*. New York: Herder and Herder, 1970.

Gill, Anthony. *Rendering unto Caesar: The Catholic Church and the State in Latin America*. Chicago: University of Chicago Press, 1997.

Hess, David. *Samba in the Night: Spiritism in Brazil.* New York: Columbia University Press, 1994.

Languerre, Michael S. *Voodoo and Politics in Haiti.* New York: St. Martin's Press, 1989.

Levine, Daniel. *Popular Voices in Latin American Catholicism.* Princeton, NJ: Princeton University Press, 1992.

Martin, David. *Tongues of Fire: The Explosion of Protestantism in Latin America.* London: Basil Blackwell, 1990.

Peterson, Vasquez. *Christianity, Social Change, and Globalization in the Americas.* Piscataway, NJ: Rutgers University Press, 2001.

Stevens-Arroyo, Anthony M., and Andrés I. Pérez y Mena. *Enigmatic Powers: Syncretism with African and Indigeneous Peoples' Religions among Latinos.* New York: Bildner Center for Western Hemispheric Studies, 1995.

FILMS AND VIDEOS

Americas 6, Miracles Are Not Enough. United States, 1993.

From Faith to Action in Brazil. United States, 1984.

Onward Christian Soldiers. United States, 1985.

Remembering Romero. United States, 1992.

THE POLITICAL ECONOMY OF LATIN AMERICA

On Economics and Political Economy

In Latin America, one cannot fully understand the political game without understanding its economic underpinnings. The initial encounter between the Old World and the Americas resulted from Iberian desire for the economic advantage gained from new trade routes to the East Indies. From the onset, the Americas were an economic enterprise for European colonizers; subsequently, local elites have used the region for their gain. Since the conquest, the economic good of the masses has frequently been sacrificed for the enrichment of foreign and domestic interests. Political power and economic power have generally reinforced each other in Latin America. Those with the wealth have written the political rules. Thus, an understanding of the economics of the region enriches our understanding of its politics and vice versa.

We note that the discipline of economics studies the allocation of scarce resources—how goods and services are produced, distributed, and consumed. It has its immediate origins in the eighteenth century in works such as Adam Smith's *An Inquiry into the Nature and Causes of the Wealth of Nations* (1776). In more recent times, economists—like political scientists—often have tried to separate the study of politics and economics. Yet, this was not the original intent of Smith, his fellow political economist David Ricardo, or a subsequent student of political economy, Karl Marx. Indeed, if we go back to the original writings of Adam Smith and David Ricardo, we find that they preferred the concept of "political economy" because such an approach took into account the complexity and unity of political and economic phenomena.

Modern students of political economy thus believe that an approach that encompasses both politics and economics is much more effective in studying how scarce resources are allocated and how political values and political power affect that allocation. Given the considerable concentration and interconnection of economic and political power in Latin America, a more comprehensive approach would seem in order.

When Adam Smith was writing in the late 1700s, the dominant economic system for Great Britain, Spain, Portugal, and the American colonies was *mercantilism*, in which the state implemented a policy of increasing exports and acquiring bullion and raw materials through carefully restricted commerce. This was a politically directed policy that used state control of trade and colonization. The government exercised considerable control by regulating production, directing foreign trade and tariffs, and exploiting commerce, particularly with a European nation's colonies. Thus, Smith and Ricardo realized the fundamental role of the state and the political power that defined the policy-making process. Indeed, they hoped to induce the state to exert less control over economic interactions. As the discipline of economics evolved over the years, the difficulty in understanding economic phenomena led some commentators to refer to economics as the "dismal science." Yet, by looking at economics and politics jointly and taking into consideration historical context and sociological factors, a more comprehensive approach to understanding resource and power allocation in different nations can be achieved. This is very much the case in Latin America. Such an approach will be employed in this text.

The Latin American Economy

As in the rest of the world, economies in the Americas began as small, local spheres that were isolated from events outside their valley, village, or small region. As time and productive forces progressed, this initial isolation slowly began to break down in many regions. Civilizations such as the Olmec in eastern Mexico (1500–400 B.C.E.), the early Maya (1500 B.C.E.–900 C.E.), and the Mochica (400–1000 C.E.) in northern Peru appeared and began to tie the hitherto isolated population clusters together. As the Aztec and Incan Empires grew, trade and commerce over much wider regions developed. Such economic intercourse was, however, limited to regions and did not extend far beyond the actual political entities. Latin America's integration into the world economy only began when the Europeans arrived. However, even after centuries, one could still find isolated villages and valleys that were only marginally integrated into the world economy. During colonial times and well into the twentieth century, haciendas were often near self-contained economic units with minimal contact with the outside, save the sale of one or two cash crops for national consumption or export to Europe or North America. Indeed, a few native Amazonian groups such as the Yanomami were only being integrated into the world economy as the twentieth century ended.

A substantial sector of agriculture made up of Native American and other subsistence farmers who used the bulk of their production to feed themselves and their families was only slowly integrated into the international system. These farmers' growing need for goods that they could not produce themselves led to their gradual integration into the national and international economy as they sold small amounts of a cash crop, handicraft, or their labor to landowners, plantations, or tourist enterprises. Yet, as the sad history of the Yanomami in recent times suggests, integration into the international economic system did not necessarily benefit those who were losing their isolation. Indeed, as their consumption and nutritional patterns changed, they were more likely to suffer from malnutrition.

Latin America was integrated into the world economy after 1500. Due to improvements in navigation and seafaring, Portugal and Spain established world trade routes that circumnavigated Africa and eventually came to include the Americas. From Columbus' second voyage on, the Americas were used to extract wealth for European powers—beginning with gold and silver bullion and slaves. As suggested previously, a pattern was soon established whereby land, people, and resources were used to benefit nations outside the region and for the advantage of the local European or mostly European elite, rather than the native masses. As gold and silver stocks were eventually depleted, new crops and minerals were found to export to Europe and other industrializing areas such as the United States. Indigo, cacao, brazilwood, and sugar were exported in colonial times, as were rubber, nitrates, copper, and tin in the nineteenth century and coffee, grains, beef, bananas, and petroleum in the twentieth century.

As time passed, Western and Western-trained economists came to believe in the economic doctrine of *comparative advantage*, whereby a country that is especially well endowed by climate, resources, soil, or labor can produce a product comparatively better and more efficiently than any other. Coffee exports from Colombia are an example. By specializing in the production of that product and trading it in the international market for products that other countries could produce better and more cheaply because of their comparative advantage, the producing country can maximize revenues in world trade. That is, Colombia currently produces coffee cheaply and uses the money from the sales of the coffee to buy, for example, computers and stereos from Japan, where these products are produced best and most cheaply. This view holds that it would be expensive, inefficient, and all but impossible for Japan to produce coffee and difficult and costly for Colombia to produce stereos and computers. Both countries, it is argued, gain when they specialize in the production of one or a few products that they are best able to produce. After World War II, the Latin American experience with international trade and the pioneering work of the Economic Commission for Latin America (ECLA) challenged this view. However, before this view is explored, a more thorough explanation of the production and export of commodities will be offered.

After 1500, Latin America became tied to the Western economic system that had become the basis for the international economic system in two distinct ways: first, products were exported according to the demands of the market and development in Europe and, second, the region became an outlet for European products. Much like the old South in the United States, most of the local economy revolved around the production of one crop and most of the infrastructure was geared to getting that commodity to ports where it could be loaded on boats and shipped (see Table 13). As cotton was king in the antebellum South, so sugar was king in northern Brazil, Cuba, the Dominican Republic, Haiti, and much of the rest of the Caribbean. Coffee and bananas became the prime export crop in Central America and Colombia. Economies also revolved around the extraction and export of minerals: copper in Chile, tin in Bolivia, and oil in Venezuela. Luxury goods for the landowning elite or for mine owners came from the advanced industrialized areas, as did the tools and most of the finished products that could not be made by the local blacksmith or carpenter. There are even tales of Brazilian planters sending their shirts to Europe

TABLE 13. Major Exports of Latin American Nations, 2003, 2004, and 2005 (More Than Two Commodities When Closely Ranked)

Country	Commodity	% of Total Exports		
		2003	2004	2005
Argentina	Oil seed cake and meal and other vegetable oil residues	11.2	10.7	9.7
	Petroleum products	7.3	7.7	6.9
	Soya beans	6.2	5.0	5.7
	Soya bean oil	7.0	6.8	5.6
	Crude petroleum	7.7	6.5	6.2
Bolivia	Natural gas	23.3	27.7	35.2
	Oil seed cake and meal and other vegetable oil residues	13.1	11.8	7.5
	Ores and concentrates of zinc	7.4	6.7	7.1
	Crude petroleum	5.7	7.6	11.1
Brazil	Iron ore and concentrates	4.7	4.9	6.2
	Soya beans	5.9	5.6	4.5
	Petroleum products	3.8	3.3	4.1
Chile	Refined copper including remelted	22.3	27.1	26.3
	Ores and concentrates of copper	12.0	16.0	15.7
Colombia	Crude petroleum	18.9	17.9	19.0
	Coal	10.6	10.6	11.5
Costa Rica	Thermionic valves and tubes, transistors, etc.	...	4.5	12.2
	Parts of office machinery	23.7	15.1	10.2
	Medical instruments	8.0	8.0	7.5
	Fresh bananas including plantains	9.7	9.3	7.3
Cuba	...	...	...	...
Dominican Republic	...	...	...	...
Ecuador	Crude petroleum	38.1	50.3	53.4
	Fresh bananas including plantains	17.7	13.2	10.7
El Salvador	Coffee, green or roasted	8.4	8.4	9.9
	Medicines	4.7	4.8	4.8
	Articles of artificial plastic materials	3.2	3.6	4.6
	Raw sugar, beet and cane	3.7	2.5	4.0
Guatemala	Coffee, green or roasted	11.4	11.2	13.8
	Fresh bananas including plantains	9.0	8.5	7.7
	Sugar (raw beet and cane)	8.1	6.4	7.0
Haiti	...	...	...	...
Honduras	Coffee, green or roasted	13.8	16.0	17.5
	Insulated wire and cable	4.9	8.9	9.3
	Crustacea and molluscs, fresh, chilled, salted dried	10.3	7.9	7.7
	Fresh bananas including plantains	8.5	8.7	7.2
Mexico	Petroleum (crude)	10.2	11.3	13.2
	Passenger motor cars, other than buses	7.2	6.3	6.3
Nicaragua	Coffee, green or roasted	14.2	17.4	15.1
	Meat of bovine animals, fresh,chilled, salted, dried	13.9	15.2	14.4
	Crustacea and molluscs, fresh, chilled, salted dried	12.1	8.2	7.0

(continued)

TABLE 13.   Major Exports of Latin American Nations, 2003, 2004, and 2005 (More Than Two Commodities When Closely Ranked) *Continued*

Country	Commodity	% of Total Exports		
		2003	2004	2005
Panama	Fish, fresh, chilled or frozen	35.9	35.5	32.3
	Other fresh fruit	6.0	8.0	12.3
	Fresh bananas including plantains	13.2	12.2	10.0
	Crustacea and molluscs, fresh, chilled, salted dried	9.0	8.4	9.4
Paraguay	Soybeans	41.6	35.6	31.3
	Meat of bovine animals, fresh,chilled, salted, dried	4.8	9.7	16.0
	Oil seed cake and meal and other vegetable oil residues	10.4	10.8	7.6
Peru	Gold, non-monetary, unwrought, semi-manufactured or dust	23.1	18.6	17.1
	Refined copper including remelted	9.1	10.5	10.7
	Ores and concentrates of copper	4.8	9.1	8.4
Uruguay	Meat of bovine animals, fresh,chilled, salted, dried	16.3	20.5	21.6
	Leather of other bovine cattle and equine leather	10.1	8.0	7.1
Venezuela	Crude petroleum	81	57.6	64.6
	Petroleum products	...	23.9	20.7

... data not available

Source: Statistical Yearbook for Latin America and the Caribbean, 2006, pg. 196–217, located at: http://www.eclac. org/cgi-in/getProd.asp?xml=/publicaciones/xml/4/28074/P28074.xml&xsl=/deype/tpl-i/p9f.xsl&base=/ tpl-i/top-bottom.xsl

for proper cleaning and pressing. During colonial times, manufacturing was often outlawed (in 1785 all manufacturing was prohibited in Brazil) and was usually discouraged. Thus, most of the finished products came from outside. Indeed, such practice was consistent with the free trade concepts of specialization and comparative advantage. There was very little industry in Latin America until well into the twentieth century—after World War II in most countries—and very little interregional trade existed within countries or among them, given the external orientation of the infrastructure.

A new group of merchants sprung up as part of these trade patterns. The *comprador class* made their living from selling finished goods that were imported from the outside. From importer to wholesaler to distributor to merchant, each made a considerable markup on each product sold. This tendency toward high markup was also passed on to the local merchants and was even greater among those who transported the products to remote areas where choice was very limited. The idea of mass retailing to reduce unit cost came slowly and late to Latin America. The state also charged high import taxes on imported goods, particularly if they were classified as luxuries. Monopoly was not uncommon, and personal and political ties helped secure import licenses, exclusive rights, and favorable terms. The little manufacturing that existed was usually protected by power and privilege and was not forced to compete directly with foreign products. The quality of products was often well below that of similar products on the world market.

Agrarian Production

Until the second half of the twentieth century, most of Latin America was agrarian. Traditional landed estates (*latifundios, haciendas, fazendas*) produced crops such as cotton, cattle, sugar, or coffee. Their feudal-like origins in the Iberian peninsula often meant very traditional forms of production as well as social relations. Workers were subordinated to the *patrón* (landlord) and his family, paid poorly, generally treated miserably, and often held in debt peonage through the monopolistic sale of necessary goods at high prices at the estate store. Armed guards and control over the roads into and out of the estate were—and sometimes still are—used to further control the labor force. The original landed estates were not overly efficient, relying principally on abundant land and inexpensive labor. The earnings from the sale of cash crops were generally used more to support the upper-class lifestyle of the family than for capital improvements on the estate. The owners often spent a considerable amount of their time in their city home in the regional or national capital or in Europe and thus were absentee landowners. The more abundant small farmers, or *minifundistas*, had very little land and thus had to use very labor-intensive forms of cultivation. Nor did they have capital or credit to invest in their land. The abundance of land (often left fallow or otherwise unused) in the hands of the landed elite and the paucity of land for the *campesinos* (farmers or tenant farmers) and rural landless laborers have perpetuated the disparity of income derived from the original distribution of land and power. Of equal importance, these inequities fueled demands for land reform, economic restructuring, and occasionally revolution. In more recent times, small farmers had to increasingly turn to paid labor outside their own land (usually for large landowners or commercial farms or plantations) to survive. Pressured by debt and intense poverty, they often sell what little land they have, become rural laborers, or move to urban areas.

As the national economies developed, regions and often whole nations became what is referred to as *monoculture* or *monocrop economies*—dedicated to the production of one crop or commodity (see Table 11). As late as 1985, more than 50 percent of Colombia's official export earnings were derived from the sale of coffee on the international market. In El Salvador, the focus on coffee was even greater—67 percent. Mexico also derived some 67 percent of its export earnings from the sale of one commodity—petroleum. In Venezuela, that figure was more than 84 percent for the same product. Chile derived 46 percent of its export earnings from the sale of copper. Reliance on one export commodity was even higher in previous decades. For instance, in 1958, the Bolivian economy centered around the production of tin; 58 percent of its export earnings derived from the sale of that commodity. Since the latter part of the nineteenth century, coffee and bananas have been big in Central America. By the middle of the twentieth century in Honduras, more than 50 percent of export earnings were derived from bananas (31 percent) and coffee (23 percent). Nor do radical political transformations necessarily change the basic production of a nation. In the last 100 years, Cuba has changed from a Spanish colony to a capitalist country closely linked to and dependent on the U.S. economy to a socialist state closely tied to the economies of the Soviet Union and its Eastern European allies to a socialist state going it alone. Only in the 1990s did Cuba's dependence on sugar

Traditional, labor-intensive agricultural methods are still used in much of Latin America, as suggested by this toiling farm worker in Rancho Ancihuácuaro, Michoacán, Mexico, 1987. *(Photo by Devra Weber)*

change dramatically. In the 1920s, roughly 75 percent of Cuba's exports were sugar. That number had grown to 83 percent in 1958 on the eve of the revolution. Thirty years of a revolutionary government that sought to diversify the country's economy saw a decline to only 79 percent as Cuba assumed the role of sugar producer to the East European socialist countries at above–world market prices. Only in the 1990s with the collapse of the Soviet Union has Cuba's dependence on sugar decreased dramatically. By 1997, sugar fell to just 47 percent of Cuba's export earnings. The dramatic drop was brought about by sharply reduced sugar production and prices and the marked increase in the role of tourism in the Cuban economy. However, the impact of centuries of monocrop dependence on sugar production places great burdens on the Cuban government as it is forced to close sugar production facilities and retrain workers for other occupations.

Foreign Investment and Enclave Production

Mining and sugar and banana plantations have often been dominated by foreign investment as they are much more capital-intensive and strongly employ U.S. and Canadian concepts of business efficiency. Initially, these foreign corporations created types of *enclaves*, where the company, upper-level management, and even middle-level management were all foreign and often lived in a special compound fenced off from local inhabitants. Tools, explosives, fertilizers, and other elements in the productive process were shipped into the country and taken directly to the mine or plantation. Products were shipped directly out of the country—often on foreign-owned railroads—and profits were sent back to corporate headquarters in New York, Boston, or London. More local people and products were eventually incorporated into local production, but ownership, upper-level management, and the end source for profit remission (the countries where the profits ended up) remained foreign. An example would be a company known to much of North America, Chiquita Banana. United Brands (formerly United Fruit Company) started as a Boston-based company founded by a New England sea captain in the 1880s. It grew to become a huge producer and exporter of bananas and one of the largest multinational corporations (MNCs) operating in Central America. It conducted operations in Guatemala, Honduras, Nicaragua, Costa Rica, and Panama and came to exercise considerable power over local governments, particularly in Honduras and Guatemala. Union movements sometimes challenged United's treatment of the workers, and bitter strikes and repression often ensued, as was the case in Guatemala and Costa Rica in the 1930s. The Central Intelligence Agency (CIA)–organized coup against the constitutional government in Guatemala in 1954 was directly related to United Fruit's pressure on the U.S. government to stop the expropriation of its unused land by the reformist Arbenz government.

Dependency and Underdevelopment

The problems with monocrop or near monocrop are twofold. By making the entire economy dependent on one primary product, the nation's economic health becomes heavily tied to the fortunes of that product in the international market. Boom periods are often followed by devastating busts. Coffee trees planted during a time of high coffee prices often mature a few years later when the coffee price is depressed. When their beans are sold on the international market, the excess supply only depresses coffee prices further. A dip of a few cents in the international price for coffee—or sugar or copper—can mean a recession or worse in the national economy. For instance, copper prices fell to 5 cents a pound during the Depression and rose steadily in the 1940s, only to fall 4 cents a pound in 1950. When this occurs, the resultant worsening economic conditions often stimulate unrest and have contributed to the downfall of many presidents and other political leaders in Latin America.

Attempts to organize producers into international cartels or producers' associations have generally had only the most minimal effect on the stabilization or maintenance of commodity prices. Attempts have been made to organize international associations of coffee producers to maintain the price of coffee. In the early 1960s,

THE CROP THAT COULD

Since Latin America was brought into the international system as a producer of primary products, the region has sought a product that could demand a good price on the world market and that its farmers could produce using traditional methods without making huge investments. In this way, small and large farmers could easily grow the crop and earn a good living from its sale. They needed a crop that would hold its value in the markets in the north and could be turned into a finished product in the south with minimal investments in equipment and technology. To date, the only major crop to fill that bill has been coca. Unlike any other commodity, cocaine's manufacture, transport, and distribution in the north is controlled by Latin America–based business organizations (cartels) that bring most of the profits back to their home countries. Further, the coca leaves from which cocaine is made have been part of traditional indigenous culture for more than 1000 years and are thought to have special spiritual and medicinal qualities by large parts of the populations of Peru, Bolivia, and Ecuador. In these Andean nations, chewing the coca leaf is legal and common among indigenous peoples in the highlands. The leaves are also used to make tea or moistened and applied directly to heal sore or swollen eyes. Thus, it is difficult for the local population to conceive of many of the pernicious effects of the highly refined extract of the coca leaves—cocaine.

It is estimated by the U.S. Drug Enforcement Agency (DEA) that drug trafficking in the United States is more than a $200 billion business each year. A great deal of this figure results from the sale of powdered or crack cocaine. South America exports some 600 metric tons of cocaine each year. As with other products from the region, the primary markets are the United States, Canada, and Western Europe. Using a minimal U.S. street value price of $14,500 per kilo, this would mean that sales of South American cocaine earn $8.7 billion a year. A great deal of this goes back to Latin America. For instance, it is estimated that Colombia alone exports 555 metric tons of cocaine each year (165 metric tons made from 101,000 metric tons of Colombian coca leaves, 390 metric tons made from Peruvian and Bolivian leaves). Using the street value price, this would mean that cocaine exports for Colombia account for some $8.05 billion per year. If only half of that amount stayed in the country, that would be more than $4 billion. The official figure for all goods and services exported from Colombia was $18.0 billion in 2003 (drug sales are not reported and thus not part of official figures). About half of this resulted from the sale of coffee. Using these figures, one could deduce that the revenue for the export sale of cocaine could be as much as half that for the sale of Colombian coffee.

Unlike the production of most other Latin American products, all who work in production are relatively well paid, from the peasant who grows the leaves to the pilot who flies it into the United States. It is only as the finished product begins to be consumed in the producing countries that the full extent of the hazard becomes known. Nor do many in the producing countries see the negative effect on tourism and investment or the damage done to legitimate businesses that are crowded out of the market by enterprises that sell on a very low or negative profit margin to launder huge amounts of money.

Efforts by the U.S. government to eradicate Latin America's most lucrative export commodity have been less than successful for the above reasons and because many local and national police officers usually make less than $200 per month and are hard put to make ends meet. One way to increase income has been to accept payments for not reporting traffic or other violations or for simply looking the other way. Commanders and military officers make relatively modest salaries, as do most judges. Governmental officials and politicians seem particularly susceptible to bribes and campaign donations. Even former Colombian

President Samper was accused of taking a large campaign donation from a drug cartel. The corruption has also spread into transshipment points in Central America, the Caribbean, and especially Mexico. In that country, drug-induced corruption has spread widely. Many police officers, upper-level officials, military officers, and governmental officials have been indicted for accepting bribes. In 1988, Mexico's drug czar was removed from office and indicted for being on a Mexican cartel's payroll. Throughout these countries, the amounts of money available to bribe or otherwise induce local and national officials to ignore certain activities or give intelligence on impending government actions is many times more than most officials make in a year, if not a lifetime. The temptation is too great for many; and for those who will not be bought, there are always other ways. Indeed, many police and other public officials are given a choice: *plata o plomo* (money or lead). Others are assassinated outright, as occurred on a massive scale in Mexico in 2008.

the International Coffee Agreement was signed and, later, the International Coffee Organization was established. Production quotas were assigned to all producing members in an effort to control the supply of coffee and thus the price. However, in part because of the resistance of African nations, who preferred to set their own production quotas, these efforts failed; and coffee continues to be subject to market fluctuations. The Organization of Petroleum Exporting Countries (OPEC), of which Venezuela was a founding member, was for many years the only producers' association that was able to influence the price of its product. Yet, by the late 1990s, petroleum prices had fallen significantly. These falling prices helped put considerable strain on the long-dominant Democratic Action and Independent Political Electoral Organizing Committee (COPEI) parties in Venezuela. As Venezuelan petroleum prices fell to a low of less than $10 per barrel at the end of 1998 (from a high of $35 a barrel in the early 1980s), the presidential election campaigns of candidates from these parties wilted in the face of the newly organized Patriotic Pole coalition formed to back Hugo Chávez. Both parties even abandoned their candidates in the last 2 weeks of the electoral campaign to back the candidate of the newly formed Project Venezuela movement. However, the opposition candidate and political outsider could not be stopped. Former coup leader Chávez won with 57 percent of the vote. Fortunately for his administration, prices for oil again rose to $30 a barrel by the second half of 2000, a result of the new OPEC agreement. However, it was not yet clear how long the OPEC agreement could sustain higher prices. Since 2001, driven in part by increased global demand, especially from China, world oil prices have soared, reaching $50 per barrel in 2005 and over $125 per barrel in 2008. This provided an economic base for many domestic and international programs launched by President Hugo Chávez.

Many national leaders and thinkers have wondered why Latin America has remained less developed than its neighbor to the north, the United States. Most Latin American nations have abundant resources and sufficient land. Gradually, national leaders and scholars have learned the same bitter lessons that U.S., Canadian, and many European farmers have found to be all too true: if unprotected by government price controls, prices for primary products fluctuate greatly and rise very slowly. Like the farmers, Latin Americans have produced more and more at ever greater efficiency but have received comparatively less and less for it—while paying increasing prices for cars, machinery, and other finished goods from industrial, more developed national and international centers.

Raúl Prebisch and the ECLA

Such an economic understanding by the Latin Americans was stimulated greatly by the pioneering work of ECLA and its director, Raúl Prebisch. Prebisch, an Argentine-born and -educated economist, had previously held high-level economic positions in the Argentine government. In the late 1940s, he gathered a team of Latin American economists at the Santiago, Chile, headquarters of ECLA. He and his fellow economists made extensive studies of the prices for primary products exported by Latin America and compared them to those of the finished goods that were imported. Their studies indicated that the relationship between these product prices, or the terms of trade, were unfavorable to Latin America. Posited as the now-famous *Prebisch thesis*, the theory argued that there is a structural tendency for Latin American terms of trade to deteriorate over time because of the concentration of exports in primary commodities. As suggested by Figure 3, over time the price for finished goods rises much faster than the price for primary goods.

These findings, which were initially considered controversial by Western economists from industrialized nations, called into question the argument for specialization in the production of any one primary product in the international market. Interestingly, later studies by the Economic Commission for Africa of the United Nations Economic and Social Council found that the terms of trade for African primary exports vis-à-vis finished imports from Europe and the United States

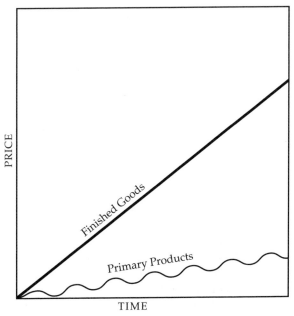

FIGURE 3: Finished goods and primary products graph.

were also unfavorable to Africa. ECLA's findings were one of the principal reasons that the organization so strongly advocated import substitution industrialization (ISI) for Latin America.

Dependency Theory

ECLA's work and the Prebisch thesis were fascinating examples of how Latin American economists working from a perspective grounded in their own reality could see how their relationship with the industrialized center (Europe and United States) was less than satisfactory. This gave great impetus not only to new economic policy direction in the Latin American nations but also to the development of a whole new way to view Latin American development—*dependency theory*. The ECLA studies were symbolic of the post–World War II decolonization process and the subsequent willingness to assign negative consequences to the relations imposed by actual or formal colonial masters on the development of native peoples. This also represented a significant break with metropolitan theorists and economists who saw underdevelopment as inherent to Latin America and other Third-World nations and caused primarily by economic, social, or cultural patterns that had developed within those societies.

The late 1940s also provided alternative explanations for the lack of development in Latin America, Africa, and Asia. Basing their understanding in large part on V. I. Lenin's classic Marxist work *Imperialism, the Highest Stage of Capitalism* (1916), scholars familiar with this Marxist analysis argued that the colonies were used as places to invest surplus capital and sell goods from the colonizing countries and as sources of cheap raw materials and cheap labor. Indeed, according to this view, the high return on investment and low prices paid for raw materials and labor meant that value was extracted from the colonized countries and exported to the developed countries, where it further fueled their development. It was further argued that such surplus value was the difference between what was paid and what it would have cost if fair value had been paid at the industrial center. As with the initial taking of gold bullion in the colonial era, this extracted wealth helped continue the impoverishment of the colonized country and made the colonial country rich.

This thesis was updated by African leader and intellectual Kwame Nkrumah. The first president of Ghana and intellectual author of Pan-Africanism argued that imperialism had taken on a new but equally pernicious form—neocolonialism. In his work *Neocolonialism, the Last Stage of Imperialism* (1965), Nkrumah argued that former colonizers now controlled their former colonies and other former colonies by less direct means. They established economic spheres of influence, pound or franc areas where the former colonial currency and its financial sector dominated; dominated the area by investment and a foreign economic presence; and bought the same raw materials at the same prices and sold the same finished goods. Further, the former colonizers were aided in this endeavor by native politicians and pro-Western elements of the native bourgeoisie, who often did the bidding of the former colonial masters and generally helped maintain their neocolonial dominance in the face of any radical reformers or revolutionaries who attempted to change the subordinate nature of this relationship. Latin American intellectual Eduardo Galeano labeled this group "the commission bourgeoisie." Foreign aid and missionaries were but more subtle means of continuing neocolonial control. Political and economic control was exercised in a more indirect way than under direct colonialism, but the effect was very similar for the native people. The title of a book by Guyanese intellectual Walter Rodney is most evocative of this view, *How Europe Underdeveloped Africa*. Such views clearly helped shape the intellectual climate in the Americas. Also of note was Paul Baran's seminal work, *The Political Economy of Growth*.

Other advocates of dependency theory argued that Latin America was maintained in a neocolonial state under the tutelage of the United States and European powers. Given that the Latin American nations had been independent much longer than the African states, the mechanisms of control were different and often more subtle. Thus, one finds more discussion of cultural imperialism in Latin America. It is often asserted that economic relations, foreign aid and diplomacy, and the media and other forms of control were employed to keep Latin America subordinate. Neocolonialism was thus manifest throughout Latin American society, as could be seen in U.S. movies, television series, religious evangelization, the spread of Western consumption patterns, the canonization of Mickey Mouse and Donald Duck, and the mass pilgrimage to Miami and Florida's Disney World by Latin America's elites and many from the middle class.

Andre Gunder Frank's *Capitalism and Underdevelopment in Latin America* brought dependency theory to the fore. As suggested earlier, Frank and other dependency theorists argued that the relationship between the developing area (satellite or periphery) and the developed area (center or metropol) was one of dependence. Thus, the *dependentistas* argued that underdevelopment in Latin America resulted from the region being brought into the capitalist system to satisfy the economic needs of the metropolitan powers. Decisions as to when and where to develop mines, plantations, or infrastructure were made according to the requirements of the metropolitan powers, not the Latin American nations. From colonial times on, economic decisions responded more to the needs of the industrializing center than to the needs of the agrarian periphery. Over time, the national economic systems in Latin America thus became dependent on the production and export of primary products to Europe and the United States (the industrialized center or metropol). The economic and political elites that emerged also became tied to this system and dependent on it for their well-being. Although they did not accumulate as much wealth per product unit as did their counterparts in the metropolitan nations, they were able to exploit the native labor force and take advantage of the abundant access to cheap land and minerals to accumulate their wealth. As more foreign corporations arrived to exploit these factors of production themselves, the national upper class often worked with or for them and became even more closely tied to the economic interests of the center.

It is argued, then, that the economic development and even the political autonomy of Latin American nations became dependent on the outside forces of the metropolitan powers. They did not possess full independence and, hence, were dependent on and subordinate to outside forces. Latin American underdevelopment was thus a result of the exploitation and control of forces outside the region. As Latin America had been incorporated into the international capitalist system, it had lost its wealth and autonomy. The plundering of the gold and silver of the region was symbolic of how the capitalist system had served the interests of the Latin American nations. Indeed, capitalism and economic penetration by the metropolitan capitalist powers were responsible for a great deal of Latin American underdevelopment. Frank and others argued that even the feudalistic *latifundios* had been incorporated into the international system and were part of the worldwide spread of capitalism. Latin America's problems thus resulted from the nature of capitalism itself and the way it subordinated classes in nations and even developing nations themselves. Some further expanded this concept to argue that the capital cities in the region acted as metropolitan areas that extracted value from the peripheral countryside.

The dependency perspective also contradicted what had become a common view about Latin American economies. The *dual-economy* view held that the economies were divided into two sectors. One was comprised of near-feudal social and economic relations on the *latifundio* and in landowner–sharecropper relations and subsistence agriculture; the other was centered in the modern export sector that tended to employ modern capitalist practices. Each national economy was divided in two, one traditional and feudal-like and the other modern and capitalist. The *dependistas* saw only one economy well integrated into the world capitalist system. Frank and the early dependency writers thus focused on external linkages and the international capitalist system in particular to explain Latin underdevelopment.

There were, however, later dependency writers who enriched this perspective by also looking more closely at the specific historical, social, and economic configurations of nations such as Brazil and Argentina. They examined such internal factors as class and intraclass competition to further explain the complex phenomenon of development in the region. Foremost among these was Brazilian social scientist Fernando Henrique Cardoso, who, together with Chilean sociologist Enzo Faletto, wrote *Dependency and Development in Latin America* in 1971. The more subtle analysis of internal class formations and historical development patterns and the role of multinational corporations made this one of the most useful analyses of the Latin American reality.

Import Substitution Industrialization

As these new perspectives stimulated a rethinking of how development should be pursued, policies began to change more rapidly. ECLA recommended ISI as a way to reduce the importation of finished goods. From the 1930s on, several of the larger nations had begun to focus on what became known as *inward-looking development*, reasoning that the path to development was through developing internal economic capacity, including industrial capacity, while continuing to export primary products. ECLA now recommended strongly that internal industrialization be pursued. This would mean that less of the foreign exchange earned through the sale of primary products would be expended on finished goods and more capital would stay in the country. In this way, the negative effects of the terms of trade would be minimized. Latin American domestic manufacturing was officially and continually encouraged. A growing number of new industries began to produce for the domestic market. Sporadic industrialization had occurred in some of the large countries, such as Mexico, Argentina, and Brazil—particularly during World Wars I and II and even the Depression, when Latin America was cut off from its external supplies of finished goods. This time, however, ISI became official policy and was pursued vigorously through increasing domestic manufacturing. Domestic entrepreneurs were encouraged to set up new industries and expand old ones, and MNCs were invited to set up plants to supply the domestic market. Even car companies set up assembly plants, as was the case with Volkswagen in Mexico and Brazil and Fiat in Argentina. Chrysler also began assembling cars in Latin America and was joined by Toyota in the 1970s. Panasonic, Motorola, and other electronics companies began to manufacture in Latin America, as did most of the major pharmaceutical companies and even food processors like Nabisco and Nestlé.

Attempts were made to control the national content of the components used in the finished product, the percent of nationals in middle- and upper-level management, and the amount of profit that could be remitted to the home office of the MNC each year. These attempts to assert national sovereignty met with varying success and were often skillfully circumvented by sophisticated multinationals. From the late 1940s on, Mexico required that 51 percent of all companies doing business in Mexico be owned by Mexican nationals or Mexican corporations (the dropping of this provision after the North American Free Trade Agreement [NAFTA] caused some controversy in Mexico). There was some nationalization of foreign corporations by Latin American governments (Bolivian tin mines after 1954, foreign assets in Cuba after 1960, copper mines in Chile in the 1960s and 1970s, and the International Petroleum Company in Peru in 1968), but the general trend was for more and more foreign investment to flock to the region. This wave of investment was particularly strong after military coups in Brazil in 1964 and Chile in 1973. Manufacturing and MNCs became part of the economic panorama in Latin America. Smaller and relatively less developed nations such as Guatemala, El Salvador, Costa Rica, and even Honduras experienced increases in manufacturing and the arrival of MNCs that produced finished products. The formation of the Central American Common Market in 1959 attracted new manufacturing plants, as was the case with Firestone in Costa Rica and Van Heusen shirts in Honduras. The trend was also encouraged by U.S. government policies beginning with the Alliance for Progress programs after 1961.

Export Orientation

Industrial production was initially destined for internal national markets or those of neighboring nations who had entered into an agreement such as the Central American Common Market (1960), the Latin American Free Trade Association (1960), or the Andean Pact (1967). This was a great stimulus for the industrialization of Latin America; for example, Mexico and Brazil further developed their own steel and automobile industries. The nature of production also changed. Domestic manufactured products became more similar to those manufactured for Western consumer taste. Gradually, as the domestic demand for manufactures faltered, Latin American nations began to take on an externally oriented perspective. Hereafter, manufacturing and crop diversification would be done with an eye toward external sales as well as the domestic market.

The influx of international capital, more sophisticated technology, and the opening up of internal markets made for more and better manufactured goods. The entrance of the MNCs drove some local producers out of business, and others were forced to upgrade the quality of their products. Of those local producers who survived, many soon realized that they too could enter the global market with their more sophisticated products. Nor were the products limited to those produced by sophisticated MNCs and high-technology national producers. Other domestic industries also grew: weaving and handcraft in Guatemala, wine in Chile, shoes in Brazil. Indeed, the Brazilian shoe industry eventually became one of the largest producers of footwear on the world market. As another way of gaining more foreign exchange, many countries encouraged the production of nontraditional exports, not only producing more finished goods that could be exported but also diversifying production of primary products. Such was the case in Colombia, where a vigorous export industry in flowers developed. As this process occurred over the 1960s, 1970s, and 1980s, Latin America became more integrated into the international economic system, primarily through ties to industrialized capitalist nations—the United States, Western Europe, and later Japan.

The transformation of Latin American economies can be seen in the following:

- More extensive use of capital-intensive technology.
- Increased training in manufacturing-related engineering and for those who employed and replicated technology in capital-intensive techniques used in advanced industrial nations. Many engineering students were sent to the United States or Europe and brought back advanced capital-intensive technology with them.
- Lack of development of appropriate technology that could take advantage of Latin America's abundant and inexpensive labor supply.
- The spread of Western-style consumerism to the upper, middle, and lower classes.
- State intervention to encourage and protect export-oriented domestic industries and sometimes to nationalize them or, as in the case of Brazil, to set up key industries such as aircraft production.
- The growth of middle sectors who worked in management and technologically sophisticated aspects of production (e.g., engineers, skilled technicians, accountants).
- The growth of an industrial proletariat.

Increasing Foreign Debt and the Debt Crisis

Newer plants created in Latin America were often copies or near copies of standard plants from a particular MNC, although often using the less advanced technology and relatively outdated standards that operated in the developed world, where capital was plentiful and labor was expensive. The employment created for such plants was modest, but the investment in new machinery and patented processes was not. This type of production used up local sources of capital quickly. Thus, even as there were more goods to export, it became necessary to borrow money from abroad to satisfy these capital needs. The growing demand for Western consumer goods also meant that more and more products were being imported to keep consumers satisfied. This also used up scarce foreign exchange. These two processes and the acquisition of expensive military hardware by countries like Peru, Chile, Brazil, and Argentina meant that more external borrowing was necessary to compensate for the net outflows of funds. This caused what came to be called "debt-led growth." The result of this outward-directed orientation and debt-led growth was that the external indebtedness of Latin American nations began to grow. Brazil is a prime example of this.

Prior to 1970, most of the Latin American external debt was owed to individual states or to multilateral lending institutions such as the Inter-American Development Bank. Interest rates were minimal. The petroleum crisis of 1973–1974 changed this. First, it meant that those Latin American nations that were net importers of petroleum were forced to use more of their foreign exchange to pay for the hydrocarbons they imported. Second, it meant that petroleum-producing countries began to amass significant foreign exchange surpluses and needed to find places to invest these funds. Most of these petrodollars ended up in Western banks, which soon had more than ample funds for lending but, because of the stagnation in developed countries, could not find borrowers in those countries. Large banks like Chase Manhattan and Bank of America began to make large loans readily available to private and public borrowers in Latin America. These factors combined to radically increase the external debt in Latin America, which jumped from less than $30 billion in 1970 to more than $230 billion in 1980. By the beginning of the 1980s, debt service payments alone were some $18 billion per year. Drops in commodity prices and world recessions in the 1980s did not improve this picture. Economic growth slowed in most countries and shrank in a few. Indeed, the 1980s were referred to as the "lost decade" because growth rates were so abysmal in most of Latin America, for many countries only 1 or 2 percent per year. A few countries even experienced negative growth rates.

Mexico and Brazil experienced high levels of economic growth in the 1960s and 1970s; each had periods of economic growth during this time that were referred to as economic "miracles." Both, however, continued to borrow from abroad. This situation was aggravated by OPEC-induced increases in petroleum prices in the 1970s and early 1980s. The Latin American nations' indebtedness grew, and both Mexico and Brazil acquired external debts in excess of $110 billion (see Table 14). By 1982, Mexico declared that it could not meet all the loan payments that were due. This caused considerable concern in the international investment community. Large banks in the United States were particularly concerned and sought relief from the Reagan administration. After some discussion, the U.S. government tendered an emergency loan package to Mexico to stop it from defaulting. Other countries came close to defaulting as well; Peru, under the Alan García presidency, even declared a moratorium on repaying its external debt. The prospect of widespread default created near panic among many large banks in the United States and Europe since many of them had made very high percentages of their loans (mostly unsecured) to Latin American public and private institutions. Since a large portion of their capital had been loaned out and could not be called back, they were, in bankers' language, "overexposed." There was also talk of the Latin American nations joining together

TABLE 14.   Total Disbursed External Debt, 2000, 2002, 2005

Country	Amount (Millions of Dollars)		
	2000	2002	2005
Argentina	155,015.0	156,747.8	113,518.30
Bolivia	4,460.3	4,399.6	4,941.60
Brazil	216,921.0	210,711.0	169,450.00
Chile	37,177.0	40,504.0	45,014.00
Colombia	36,130.4	37,328.6	38,350.20
Costa Rica	3,150.6	3,280.6	3,625.80
Cuba	10,961.3	10,900.0	...
Dominican Republic	3,681.9	4,536.0	6,755.70
Ecuador	13,216.3	16,236.3	17,237.00
El Salvador	2,831.0	3,987.0	4,976.00
Guatemala	2,644.0	3,119.0	3,723.30
Guyana	1,193.2	1,246.7	1,094.10
Haiti	1,170.3	1,211.9	1,344.90
Honduras	4,710.8	4,922.4	5,082.30
Jamaica	3,375.0	4,348.0	5,371.80
Mexico	178,651.9	134,978.8	127,089.40
Nicaragua	6,659.9	6,362.6	5,347.50
Panama	5,604.1	6,349.1	7,579.70
Paraguay	2,869.0	2,899.6	2,761.00
Peru	27,981.0	27,873.0	28,604.90
Trinidad and Tobago	1,680.0	1,549.0	1,281.00
Uruguay	8,894.9	10,547.8	11,440.90
Venezuela	36,437.0	35,460.0	47,233.00

...data not available.

Source: Statistical Yearbook for Latin America, 2006, pg. 286 located at *http://www.eclac.org/publicaciones/xml/4/ 28074/LCG2332B_2.pdf.*

and negotiating terms of debt repayment or even refusing to pay altogether. Despite official encouragement from Cuba and Fidel Castro, this movement never materialized. Instead, Western nations and international financial institutions such as the International Monetary Fund (IMF) and the World Bank were instrumental in renegotiating more favorable repayment packages, reducing interest rates, and even formulating debt-for-nature agreements, where debt is forgiven if environmental protection is guaranteed for parts of the national territory.

As the Latin American nations became even more dependent on external sources to solve their financial problems, the role of international financial institutions such as the IMF, the World Bank, and the Inter-American Development Bank became ever stronger. This was also true for the role of the Agency for International Development (AID) of the U.S. Department of State. In addition to the growing importance of AID, the United States and its Western capitalist allies were able to exercise a tremendous amount of control over decision making in these international bodies. Further, pursuant to the victory of the conservative economic policy embodied in Thatcherism in the United Kingdom and the Reagan revolution in the United States, the policies advocated by AID and the international financial institutions became ever more conservative. Indeed, the free market free trade ideas of Milton Friedman and the Chicago School soon began to appear as policy recommendations.

Structural Adjustment and the Move to Neoliberalism

As conditions for continued borrowing, international financial institutions began to first suggest and then insist on economic structural adjustments to the national economies. Indeed, more and more of the loans were conditional on such adjustments. It was argued that the Latin American nations must take the bitter pill of austerity through these structural adjustments. Government costs and inflation had to be reduced through such measures as fiscal reform, monetary restraint, cutting back jobs and services in the public sector, and stopping government subsidies for basic goods or petroleum. Likewise, wages were to be held down as a way of checking inflation and keeping wage costs at bay in the ever more important export industries. Orthodox economic thought became more widely accepted, and the ISI advocated by ECLA fell from favor.

As Eastern European socialism weakened and then began to disappear in the late 1980s and as the Soviet Union's breakup moved the world from the Cold War and a strong bipolar system to one dominated by Western capitalism and the United States, economic policy recommendations became ever more dominated by the orthodox capitalist economic thinking advocated by the conservative governments in power in the United States and United Kingdom. Keynesian economics and its advocacy of state intervention in the market economy and deficit spending to stimulate business activity was no longer in favor. Rather, the free market and free trade ideas championed by economists like Milton Friedman became popular. Indeed, the conservative economic thought of opponents of state intervention and planning, such as Friederich A. von Hayek, became influential. By the early 1990s, such thought was dominant in the IMF, the World Bank, the Inter-American Development Bank, and AID. Since the headquarters of all of these organizations are located in Washington, D.C., this thinking became referred to as the "Washington Consensus."

Neoliberalism

In Latin America, this type of economic policy was characterized as "neoliberalism" because it seemed to be a new version of the classical eighteenth- century economic liberalism of Adam Smith and other earlier economic liberals. Classical economic liberals believe that the magic hand of the market, not government control or trade barriers, should regulate the economy. Indeed, political liberalism in nineteenth-century Latin America included a belief in increasing commerce through free trade.

Globalization

Other factors were at work as well. The success that a variety of MNCs, such as Nike, had with moving all or part of their production to plants they established

---

KEY COMPONENTS OF NEOLIBERALISM AND THE WASHINGTON CONSENSUS

1. Radically reducing government size and spending by cutting back on government jobs and programs—especially social programs.
2. Fiscal and monetary reform.
3. Minimizing government regulation in economic matters (deregulation).
4. Liberalizing commerce through the reduction and eventual elimination of all tariff barriers and trade restrictions.
5. Opening up the national economy to foreign investment and allowing the free flow of capital.
6. Privatization of government-owned corporations, industries, agencies, and utilities.
7. Eliminating government subsidies for essential consumer goods, such as bread or tortillas and petroleum products.

---

in Asia became widely known. More and more assembly plants, or *maquiladoras*, were established first just across the U.S. border in northern Mexico, then spread throughout the Caribbean basin and into some South American countries, such as Ecuador. Electronic components, the unsewn pieces of cloth that make up clothing, and other unassembled parts in other industries were manufactured in the United States, Japan, Western Europe, and even Taiwan and assembled in Latin America in an ever growing number of *maquiladoras*. Regular manufacturing for export production was also encouraged, and multinationals came to Latin America in increasing numbers to take advantage of low wages, lax labor and environmental protection, minimal regulation and taxation, and generally sympathetic governments. Free trade zones were also set up, where companies could be completely free of any governmental regulation. The process of neoliberal globalization, it was argued, would be beneficial for all; thus, all were expected to expedite its implementation.

As the world became increasingly subject to economic globalization, capital and production plants became ever more fluid, moving freely from one country to another according to who offered the most favorable terms. The new wisdom was for each nation to produce everything it could as efficiently as possible and to export as much of it as possible to maximize export earnings. This allowed the nation to keep up with external debt payments, pay for an expanding number and amount of imports, and hopefully have some foreign exchange earnings left over to add to foreign exchange reserves. The national borders were to be open to imports so that national consumers could get the lowest prices on the goods they consumed. If some national industries could not compete with the increased number and variety of imported goods then so be it. They should be closed and capital and labor should be shifted to those industries that could compete and export their goods.

Privatization and Neoliberalism

The new mantra was Globalize, Globalize, Globalize; and in Latin America it was combined with the specifically neoliberal mantra of Privatize, Privatize, Privatize. As suggested earlier, mines had been nationalized in Bolivia and Chile, and considerable state-owned industry existed in Brazil and elsewhere. Most of the states owned all or part of the national telephone and telecommunication companies, and many had autonomous state-owned agencies, such as the Peruvian national fishing company PescaPeru. In Mexico, all aspects of petroleum production had been nationalized since 1936; the resulting state-owned enterprise, Pemex, is one of the largest national companies. It was also thought that it might be possible to privatize some governmental infrastructure, such as new highways. Thus, much new superhighway construction in countries like Brazil and Mexico was financed by private capital and/or run by private companies through their direct administration of the roadways and collection of tolls.

The movement toward privatization was especially strong in Latin America because state-owned entities had generally been little more efficient than the government bureaucracies themselves. Often, they had been subject to cronyism, bloated employment practices to accommodate payback for political or personal support, and corruption. Thus, one could easily wait up to 2 years for the installation of a phone line (unless phone company employees were "motivated" through monetary inducements) or suffer frequent loss of electricity or water service.

As Latin American nations returned to international lending agencies (the IMF in particular) for additional short- and long-term loans, they found that the imposed neoliberal conditions (conditionality) included the privatization of major public enterprises, such as the telephone companies. They were to be sold or auctioned off, and a substantial part of the proceeds were to be used to pay off part of the external debt. This led to increasing pressure on the political leaders to sell off these enterprises (usually to foreign corporations or consortia) to meet the conditions of the loans. However, utility rates were generally very low for consumers, and thousands of jobs were at stake. Not surprisingly, there were substantial popular and political mobilizations, union strikes, and job actions to resist the sales. The mobilization to protest the privatization of the water company in Cochabamba, Bolivia was one of the most notable. Nonetheless, many of these entities were partially or wholly sold off, frequently at bargain prices. The lucrative entities that made good profits attracted considerable investment interest and sold rapidly, whereas those that lost money and were government liabilities went begging for buyers. This in turn led to the perception on the part of some that decisions were once again being made because of foreign influence and for the benefit of foreign corporations, not the national populace. As will be discussed later, these and other factors led to growing political discontent and new political mobilizations. Despite popular resistance concerning such privatizations, Latin America soon became a place where MNCs could go to reduce their production costs. By the early twenty-first century, more and more manufacturing jobs from the United States were moving to Latin America.

Regional Integration, NAFTA, and the Globalization Process

In 1826, Simón Bolívar convened the Congress of Panama to foster the uniting of Spanish America into one political–economic entity. He dreamed of a united Latin America to rival the growing power of the United States in North America, but his proposal failed. Others had visions of unity in Central America. From 1824 to 1840, the Central American states that were part of the Captaincy General of Guatemala in colonial times (Guatemala, El Salvador, Honduras, Nicaragua, and Costa Rica) were united in the Central American Federation. However, the Central Americans could not remain united. Their shattered dreams of unity lay dormant until after the Europeans began a process of regional economic integration out of the ashes of World War II. The beginnings of a united Europe and the creation of the European Common Market in 1957 proved to be a catalyst for Latin American efforts at economic integration.

Encouraged by the ECLA and the United States, the Central American Common Market was formed in 1960. Its common tariff walls were to encourage import substitution and internally oriented economic growth within the region. Promoted more by Latin American initiative, the Latin American Free Trade Association was also founded in 1960, and the Andean Pact (1967) was forged with the same expectations. However, internal political pressure and vested national economic interests made it difficult to reduce tariffs among the respective member nations. None of these pacts had any appreciable success. The next stage in regional integration was not forged until the era of globalization.

In 1989, President George H. Bush launched the Enterprise for the Americas Initiative. This plan envisioned a common area of economic cooperation for the Americas extending from the frozen north in Canada to Tierra del Fuego in southern South America. All the Americas would move toward one gigantic economic zone that could easily rival a united Europe. Unlike the European Union, however, no attempt would be made to gradually integrate while ensuring that all member states had similar costs of production and approximately the same labor and political rights. Under this plan, Canada and the United States would combine with their less powerful sister republics in the south on the assumption that free trade and increased commerce could cure all ills and benefit all member nations. The first concrete action in this process developed among the United States, Mexico, and Canada. **NAFTA** was signed in 1992 and went into effect on January 1, 1994, following ratification by the legislatures of the three governments. Building on a bilateral U.S.–Canadian agreement initiated in 1989, NAFTA created one of the two largest trading blocs in the world, with a population of 370 million and a combined economic production of $6 trillion, a worthy rival to the European Union. NAFTA also removed most restrictions on cross-border investment and allowed the free flow of goods and services. All tariffs on goods traded among the three were to be eliminated by 2005. The agreement was vigorously pursued by the Salinas administration in Mexico in the hope that increased investment in Mexico and a greater North American market for its products would stimulate the Mexican economy and create jobs for the millions of unemployed and underemployed Mexicans. In contrast, the U.S. labor movement feared that thousands of jobs would head south, where wage rates were approximately one-tenth of what they were in the United States and labor rights and safety regulations were minimal. The movement convinced presidential candidate Bill Clinton to oppose the agreement in the 1992 election campaign. However, once in office, President Clinton bowed to pressure from large U.S. corporations that wanted to set up more factories and retail stores in Mexico and investment firms and business interests that saw lucrative investment opportunities. Clinton led a difficult but successful battle for ratification of the agreement that had been negotiated by President Bush. After the agreement went into effect, many more U.S. firms moved their plants to Mexico to set up regular factories and *maquiladoras*. They took thousands of jobs with them, although some new jobs were created in the United States to supply the now open Mexican market. There was, however, a net loss of U.S. jobs. Ford, General Motors, and Chrysler set up factories in Mexico to manufacture cars for Mexico, the United States, and Canada that were not only put together locally but also made mostly from parts manufactured in Mexico, including the engines and transmissions.

In Mexico, many small- and medium-sized industries and businesses were not able to compete with their larger U.S. or Canadian counterparts and went bankrupt. Mexican agriculture in general and corn farmers, more specifically, were especially hard hit as they were unable to compete with heavily subsidized U.S. agriculture. These and related events caused considerable political turmoil in all three countries. In Mexico, they led to charges that the Mexican elite was selling out the country to U.S. corporate interests, especially since most of the jobs created were at or around the minimum wage of less than U.S. $4 per day. Many in both Canada and the United States feared that their political leaders entered into an agreement that will be more a net exporter of jobs than a bonanza for the common people. As with the general process of globalization and the implementation of neoliberal reforms elsewhere, the benefits of growth have been distributed very unevenly (see Table 15). As labor, political groups, and mass organizations have mobilized against the negative effects of many of these changes in a variety of countries, including Venezuela, Ecuador, Costa Rica, Nicaragua, Argentina, and Brazil, political leaders have felt internal pressure against neoliberal changes while still being pressured by the international financial institutions and the United States to make them.

Buoyed by the successful implementation of NAFTA at the beginning of 1994, the Clinton administration promoted and hosted the Summit of the Americas in Miami in December 1994. Attended by thirty-four heads of state, with the conspicuous absence of Fidel Castro, it was the first such hemispheric gathering since 1967. The 1994 meeting represented an assurance from the United States to Latin America that it would not be neglected in the twenty-first century. The primary achievement of the meeting was to create a framework of negotiations for the creation of a hemisphere-wide customs union, the Free Trade Area of the Americas (**FTAA**) by 2005.

Clinton's statement that the gathering was "a watershed in the history of the continent" was overblown. As a first step, Chile was to be integrated quickly into NAFTA, then Clinton—with renewed "fast-track" negotiating authority from the U.S. Congress—would lay the groundwork for the FTAA. In the years since the Miami summit, the prospects for hemispheric economic integration have dimmed. President Clinton failed to get renewed negotiating authority. As a result, Chile's entry into NAFTA was not secured. It should also be noted that the same type of concentration of income in the hands of the economic elite that has characterized Latin America also began to be noticed in the United States (see Table 15).

Difficulties for the FTAA project and the expansion of NAFTA began at the end of 1994. At that time, the Mexican peso had to be sharply devalued and was rescued

TABLE 15.   U.S. Income Inequality: Household Shares of Aggregate Income by Fifths of the Income Distribution: 1967–2005. Is neoliberalism concentrating income in the U.S. ?

| Year | Fifths | | | | | |
	Lowest	Second	Middle	Fourth	Highest	Top 5 Percent
2005	3.4	8.6	14.6	23.0	50.4	n/a
2004	3.4	8.7	14.7	23.2	50.1	n/a
2003	3.4	8.7	14.8	23.4	49.8	n/a
2002	3.5	8.8	14.8	23.3	49.7	n/a
2001	3.5	8.7	14.6	23.0	50.1	22.4
2000*	3.6	8.9	14.8	23.0	49.8	22.1
1999	3.6	8.9	14.9	23.2	49.4	21.5
1998	3.6	9.0	15.0	23.2	49.2	21.4
1997	3.6	8.9	15.0	23.2	49.4	21.7
1996	3.7	9.0	15.1	23.3	49.0	21.4
1995	3.7	9.1	15.2	23.3	48.7	21.0
1994	3.6	8.9	15.0	23.4	49.1	21.2
1993	3.6	9.0	15.1	23.5	48.9	21.0
1992	3.8	9.4	15.8	24.2	46.9	18.6
1991	3.8	9.6	15.9	24.2	46.5	18.1
1990	3.9	9.6	15.9	24.0	46.6	18.6
1989	3.8	9.5	15.8	24.0	46.8	18.9
1988	3.8	9.5	16.0	24.3	46.3	18.3
1987	3.8	9.6	16.1	24.3	46.2	18.2
1986	3.9	9.7	16.2	24.5	45.7	17.5
1985	4.0	9.7	16.3	24.6	45.3	17.0
1984	4.1	9.9	16.5	24.7	44.9	16.5
1983	4.1	10.0	16.5	24.7	44.7	16.4
1982	4.1	10.1	16.6	24.7	44.5	16.2
1981	4.2	10.2	16.8	25.0	43.8	15.6
1980	4.3	10.3	16.9	24.9	43.7	15.8
1979	4.2	10.3	16.9	24.7	44.0	16.4
1978	4.3	10.3	16.9	24.8	43.7	16.2
1977	4.4	10.3	17.0	24.8	43.6	16.1
1976	4.4	10.4	17.1	24.8	43.3	16.0
1975	4.4	10.5	17.1	24.8	43.2	15.9
1974	4.4	10.6	17.1	24.7	43.1	15.9
1973	4.2	10.5	17.1	24.6	43.6	16.6
1972	4.1	10.5	17.1	24.5	43.9	17.0
1971	4.1	10.6	17.3	24.5	43.5	16.7
1970	4.1	10.8	17.4	24.5	43.3	16.6
1969	4.1	10.9	17.5	24.5	43.0	16.6
1968	4.2	11.1	17.5	24.4	42.8	16.6
1967	4.0	10.8	17.3	24.2	43.8	17.5

*After the implementation of a 28,000-household sample expansion.

Source: http://www.census.gov/hhes/www/income/histinc/p60no231_tablea3.pdf

from disaster only by a multibillion-dollar bailout from the IMF spearheaded by the United States. The bailout stabilized NAFTA, but it undercut political support within the U.S. Congress for making new trade agreements and potential commitments for further financial bailouts. As a result, an anti-FTAA coalition developed in the U.S. Congress with support in both major parties; this coalition succeeded in both 1997 and 1998 in blocking attempts by FTAA supporters to grant renewed fast-track negotiating authority to the president. Without such authority, foreign governments became unwilling to negotiate agreements with the United States for fear that they will be significantly altered by the U.S. Congress. Until a U.S. president regained this authority, progress toward the FTAA was unlikely. In 2001, President George W. Bush recommitted to the FTAA project and began the process of lobbying Congress for the renewed fast-track authority. Bush, aided by the events of September 11, 2001, regained fast-track authority in 2002. 2003 was to be the breakthrough year for completing the treaty along the line of the U.S. vision. However, renewed Latin American skepticism, fueled by the election of Lula in Brazil in 2002 and Kirchner in Argentina in 2003, derailed U.S. plans. Meeting in the Argentine capital in October 2003, the two leaders formulated the Buenos Aires Consensus as an alternative to the Washington Consensus. This Argentine–Brazilian skepticism about the FTAA as projected by the United States doomed the project to failure. The November 2003 FTAA meeting in Miami went ahead as scheduled, and countries meeting there did not officially end the idea, but rather talked of a scaled-back treaty, a so-called FTAA Lite. In reality, no further FTAA meetings have been held and efforts at regional integration have moved along several parallel lines, reflecting the political differences in the hemisphere.

Following the defeat of the FTAA, the United States moved to implement an alternative strategy based on the Central American Free Trade Agreement (**CAFTA**) and selected bilateral agreements with willing Latin-American countries. Since 2003 that U.S. strategy has seen some success. Negotiations for CAFTA were completed in late 2003, and the pact was eventually approved by most Central American governments and the U.S. Congress in 2006. The final piece of the CAFTA puzzle came into place in October 2007 with its approval by a narrow margin in a Costa Rican referendum. Thus Costa Rica joined Nicaragua, Guatemala, and El Salvador in the pact. In theory, the agreement will boost trade and investment among the countries involved, including more access to U.S. markets for the Central American countries and CAFTA's other member, the Dominican Republic. Its critics are skeptical, pointing out that NAFTA, structured along similar lines as CAFTA, has hurt the Latin American side, especially farmers. CAFTA was signed by the Central American countries without any significant reductions in U.S. agricultural subsidies, a key sticking point for Argentina and Brazil in the FTAA negotiations. Ultimately, the Central American countries, long more dependent on the United States in comparison to the larger countries of South America, felt compelled to sign on, hoping that less foreign investment might be shifted to Asia than would have been the case without CAFTA.

The United States also aggressively pursued bilateral agreements with sympathetic neoliberal governments in Peru, Ecuador, Colombia, and Panama. With all but Ecuador, the United States succeeded in crafting agreements along the lines of the 2004 U.S.–Chile agreement. Negotiations with Ecuador broke down when the neoliberal Lucio Gutierrez was forced from office by mass demonstrations in 2005 and eventually replaced by Rafael Correa, a clear anti-neoliberal. The other three agreements were stalled in the U.S. Congress following the Democratic takeover after the 2006 midterm elections. However, the U.S. neoliberal trade agenda scored an important victory when the U.S.–Peru agreement was passed in late 2007, following the inclusion of significant labor and environmental clauses. The fate of the agreements with Panama and Colombia were uncertain as 2008 began. The strategy of the United States to pursue neoliberal trade deals remains largely intact with bipartisan support in the United States, but the main factor in the new century has been a growing reluctance in Latin America to accept the U.S.-driven plans.

As the FTAA was going down to defeat, the pace of Latin American efforts at regional integration independent of the United States began to take different forms, primarily under the leadership of Hugo Chávez, the Venezuelan president. Of course, **MERCOSUR,** the Common Market of the South, formed in 1994 by Argentina, Brazil, Paraguay, and Uruguay (Bolivia and Chile became associate members), has always been the most vibrant project, built around the two largest economies of Latin America and formed at the time of neoliberal optimism. It remains an important project that has expanded trade and investment in a modest way among its members over its nearly 20-year existence. Venezuela requested membership in 2006 and Chávez has spoken of the need to reform its neoliberal character, but at this point little has changed and ongoing trade issues between Brazil and Argentina challenge its future. In addition, the smaller countries of Uruguay and Paraguay have complained that the agreement does not work well for them and have explored the possibilities of bilateral agreements with the United States, steps that have been sharply criticized by Argentina and Brazil. In any case, a dynamic future for MERCOSUR is uncertain.

Bolstered by its strong oil and gas revenues in recent years, the Venezuelan government has embarked on a bold path of challenging U.S. dominance in the region through government-to-government direct financial aid and through its support for two multilateral projects, the **Bank of the South** and the Bolivarian Alternative (**ALBA**). In 2007 alone Venezuela pledged close to $10 billion in aid to Latin American governments, three times the amount given by the United States. These are unprecedented amounts for a Latin American country and have the potential to fundamentally change the dynamic of political influence in the region. The most dramatic example of Venezuelan assistance has been to Argentina. Saddled with billions of debt to the IMF and wishing to free itself from the neoliberal constraints of the fund's conditionality programs, Argentina and president Nestor Kirchener turned to Chávez for help and Venezuela responded by purchasing more than $5 billion of Argentina's IMF debt, allowing them to repay the IMF and walk away from the IMF-imposed neoliberal policies. The independence from the IMF has proven to be a boon to the Argentinean economy and to the recovery of its social indicators. Other significant government-to-government aid has gone to Bolivia, Ecuador, and Nicaragua following the election of progressive presidents in those countries in 2005 and 2006.

Venezuela has also taken the lead in the creation in late 2007 of the Bank of the South, a project designed to sideline the role in Latin America of the U.S.-dominated

Interamerican Development Bank, World Bank, and IMF. With seven initial members (Argentina, Brazil, Bolivia, Ecuador, Paraguay, Uruguay, and Venezuela) the bank has an initial capital base of $7 billion and is designed to give member states access to loans for emergency situations and to develop programs for social services. The bank, with its headquarters in Caracas, began functioning in November 2007 and represents another potential challenge to U.S. hegemony in the region.

A very different project under Venezuelan and Cuban leadership is the Bolivarian Alternative (ALBA). Launched in 2005, initially as a project of bilateral cooperation between Cuba and Venezuela, it has now been broadened to include Bolivia, Ecuador, and Nicaragua following the change of the political landscape in those countries. Presenting itself as an alternative to the neoliberal model of the FTAA, ALBA involves the exchange of services, primarily in the fields of education and health care. Cuba contributes its human resources, cultivated over the long years of the Cuban revolution in the form of teachers and medical personnel who do extended service in the other member countries of ALBA. In return, energy-poor Cuba receives oil and gas from the energy-rich members of the group, Venezuela and Bolivia. The current economic value of the exchange is dwarfed by the size of Venezuela's other aid programs but it has the potential to change the social dynamics in the impoverished countries that are participating. The exchange is especially important for Venezuela as Chávez seeks to deliver on his promises to improve the daily life of poor Venezuelans.

Economic Legacy

Neoliberalism, the structural adjustments of the 1990s, and the globalization process generally did have a considerable effect on the Latin American economies. They generally recovered from the lost decade of the 1980s and began to experience growth in the early and mid-1990s, although growth did begin to slow in many economies by decade's end. Another clear area of success was the reduction of inflation to single-digit figures in most of Latin America. This was particularly noteworthy in Brazil and Argentina, which had both experienced inflation in excess of 1000% per year in past decades (see Table 16). Real wage rates for the vast majority of workers did not, however, improve. Unemployment remained a severe problem in most countries, and growing numbers of workers were forced to go into the informal sector to survive. Indeed, the number of those selling all manner of fruits, vegetables, clothing, household products, and auto products on the streets and at traffic lights in larger cities all over Latin America increased exponentially. A new type of dual economy may be developing where the working class is forced to buy its necessities in the markets and on the streets, where quality and prices are lower, while the upper and upper middle classes go to supermarkets, specialty shops, and the growing number of malls to make their purchases. The lower segments of the middle class may frequent all of these places depending on their precise need, income that month, and interest in being seen in the right place. More consumer goods of better quality are available at better prices, but many cannot begin to afford them. Poverty and misery continue and have increased in some countries. Income and wealth have become even more concentrated in the hands of the wealthy few, although the spread continues to the middle class. Many argue that the social costs of this form of development are too high. This consensus is spreading as far as the international financial institutions themselves, as suggested by the title of a recent book by the InterAmerican Development Bank, *Facing Up to Inequality in Latin America, Economic and Social Progress in Latin America, 1998–99 Report.* Even the World Bank has begun to insist that loan packages contain programs specifically designed to improve living conditions for the masses and mitigate some of the worst aspects of the reforms. It remains to be seen, however, if such concerns are sufficient to prompt a reevaluation of the neoliberal model by the international financial institutions that are advocating it.

The economic scene is changing radically in Latin America. One sees major stock exchanges in São Paulo, Mexico City, Lima, Santiago, and Buenos Aires; more and more manufactured goods or key components are being made in the region; and modern aspects of Western consumption such as computers, cable TV, mass retail stores, and the omnipresent auto are inundating national societies. Brazil is already the ninth largest economy in the world, and more and more products on the world market come from Brazil and other countries in the region. Although conditions for the masses in Mexico are still bleak, Mexico is generating more and more millionaires and now counts some of the wealthiest people in the world among its population. On an international scale, Brazilian managers are among the very best paid. Yet, globalization and the neoliberal reforms imposed on Latin America have only added to the highly inequitable distribution of wealth and income that have historically characterized the region.

Twenty-First-Century Prospects

Fueled in part by higher commodity prices for the region's primary exports (beef, oil, corn, soybeans, coffee, etc.) the major economies have generally been growing in the early years of the new century with annual growth rates between 5 and 10 percent. This newfound macroeconomic economic prosperity, coming in the wake of almost two decades of economic stagnation, finds democratic governments in power throughout the hemisphere and their historically influential militaries largely consigned to the barracks. With the exception of a few countries such as Colombia and Peru, left of center governments are in power, having been placed there by electorates who grew weary of the unfulfilled promises of Latin America's neoliberal governments in the 1990s (headed by Menem in Argentina and Cardoso in Brazil). This new political leadership, headed by Kirchner in Argentina and Lula in Brazil, stopped the U.S.-inspired FTAA dead in its tracks by 2003. That reversal was stunning as it had been unamiously endorsed by the Latin American presidents present at the 1994 Miami summit.

The FTAA is dead as a comprehensive U.S.-driven political and economic strategy for Latin Ameica but as discussed earlier in the chapter a comprehensive alternative strategy has not emerged. Chávez offers a socialist vision backed up by currently high oil and gas prices, but as his December 2007 referendum defeat showed, universal endorsement of his radical vision is not always present, even in his home country of Venezuela. Other political visions emanating from Brazil

TABLE 16. Latin American Inflation (Average Annual Change in Consumer Price Index)

	1900s	1910s	1920s	1930s	1940s	1950s	1960s	1970s	1980s*	1990–95	1996*	1997*	1998*	1999*	2000*	2001*	2002*
Argentina	3.0	7.0	-3.0	0.0	36.0	31.0	21.0	142.0	437.6	43.0	0.2	0.5	0.7	-1.2	-0.9	-1.1	25.9
Bolivia	—	—	—	—	17.0	69.0	6.0	20.0	222.7	12.0	12.6	4.7	7.9	2.2	4.6	1.6	1.7
Brazil	-2.0	7.0	3.0	2.0	13.0	21.0	45.0	37.0	330.2	1,270.0	15.4	6.1	3.7	4.9	6.2	6.8	8.5
Chile	8.0	6.0	2.0	7.0	18.0	38.0	27.0	175.0	20.3	19.0	7.6	5.9	5.1	3.3	3.8	3.6	2.5
Colombia	20.0	12.0	2.0	4.0	13.0	7.0	12.0	21.0	23.7	25.0	20.8	18.5	18.7	10.9	9.2	8.0	6.3
Costa Rica	—	—	—	—	10.0	2.0	2.0	11.0	25.6	19.0	17.5	13.3	11.6	10.0	11.0	11.3	9.2
Cuba	2.0	4.0	-2.0	-1.0	10.0	1.0	N/A	N/A	N/A	N/A	—	—	—	—	—	—	—
Dominican Republic	—	—	—	—	10.0	1.0	2.0	11.0	26.0	16.0	5.4	8.3	4.8	6.5	7.8	8.8	5.3
Ecuador	—	—	—	—	15.0	2.0	4.0	13.0	36.4	40.0	24.4	30.6	40.8	52.2	96.1	37.7	12.5
El Salvador	—	—	—	—	10.0	3.0	1.0	11.0	19.0	13.0	9.8	4.5	2.5	0.5	2.3	3.8	1.8
Guatemala	—	—	—	—	11.0	1.0	1.0	10.0	13.9	16.0	11.1	9.2	6.6	5.2	6.0	7.3	8.1
Haiti	—	—	—	—	—	0.0	3.0	12.0	6.7	19.0	18.3	16.4	10.6	8.7	13.7	14.2	9.9
Honduras	—	—	—	—	6.0	2.0	2.0	8.0	7.8	21.0	23.8	20.2	13.7	11.6	11.1	9.7	7.7
Mexico	7.0	62.0	-2.0	2.0	11.0	8.0	3.0	17.0	65.1	12.0	34.4	20.6	15.9	16.6	9.5	6.4	5.1
Nicaragua	—	—	—	—	15.0	5.0	4.0	14.0	618.8	749.0	11.6	9.2	13.0	11.2	11.6	7.4	4.0
Panama	—	—	—	—	6.0	1.0	1.0	7.0	1.8	1.0	1.3	1.2	0.6	1.3	1.4	0.3	1.1
Paraguay	—	—	—	—	25.0	33.0	3.0	13.0	21.7	17.0	9.8	7.0	11.6	6.8	9.0	7.3	10.5
Peru	—	11.0	-2.0	1.0	15.0	8.0	9.0	32.0	332.1	113.0	11.5	8.5	7.3	3.5	3.8	2.0	0.2
Uruguay	—	—	—	1.0	5.0	17.0	48.0	59.0	60.6	62.0	28.3	19.8	10.8	2.6	4.8	4.4	13.9
Venezuela	3.0	7.0	-4.0	-3.0	8.0	2.0	1.0	9.0	23.3	45.0	99.9	50.1	35.7	23.6	15.7	12.5	22.4

*ECLAC/CEPAL, *Statistical Yearbook for Latin America and the Caribbean.* Santiago, Chile: United Nations, 2003, table 76, pp. 80–81.

Sources: Thorp, Rosemary. *Progress, Poverty and Exclusion: An Economic History of Latin America in the 20th Century.* Baltimore: Johns Hopkins University Press, 1998, p. 332.

and Argentina seem to fall back toward older models of protectionism, akin to ISI. Although politically popular at home, especially in Argentina, they do not resonate well in the global economy of the twenty-first century. The reality is that the economics of Latin America face major challenges from their industrial competitors in Asia, who are generally better positioned in manufacturing in the new century. Brazil and Argentina have signed long-term trade deals to provide agricultural commodities to China. These agreements can be lucrative in the short term but over the long haul they may only serve to place Latin America even longer where it has been for centuries, the relatively impoverished region providing the more developed world, now including China, with its needed raw materials and foodstuffs. In the process Latin America will remain vulnerable to the inevitable swings of commodity prices, as dependent as ever, and without long-term solutions to its deep-seated history of poverty and inequality. To avoid that fate, Latin American governments must craft policies that use the current positive position in the world economy to diversify their own economies beyond commodity production while systematically working to reduce absolute poverty and make significant investments in health care and education.

Bibliography

Baran, Paul A. *The Political Economy of Growth.* New York: Monthly Review Press, 1957.

Berry, Albert, ed. *Poverty, Economic Reform, and Income Distribution in Latin America.* London: Lynne Reinner, 1998.

Blumer-Thomas, Victor. *The Economic History of Latin America since Independence.* Cambridge: Cambridge University Press, 1994.

Cardoso, Eliana, and Ann Helweg. *Latin America's Economy: Diversity, Trends, and Conflicts.* Cambridge, MA: MIT Press, 1995.

Cardoso, Fernando Henrique, and Enzo Faletto. *Dependency and Development in Latin America.* Berkley: University of California Press, 1979. [First published as *Dependencia y desarrollo en América Latina,* 1971.]

Chilcote, Ronald. *Development in Theory and Practice: Latin American Perspectives.* Lanham, MD: Rowman and Littlefield, 2003.

Drug Enforcement Agency. Data supplied by DEA Statistical Unit, Dr. Mark M. Eiler, Director, and *Major Coca & Opium Producing Nations, Cultivation and Production Estimates, 1994–98.* Washington, DC: Inter-Agency Narcotics Control Reports, 1999.

ECLA. *Study of Inter-American Trade.* New York: United Nations, 1956.

———. *Towards a Dynamic Development Policy for Latin America.* New York: United Nations, 1963.

Frank, Andre Gunder. *Capitalism and Underdevelopment in Latin America.* New York: Monthly Review Press, 1967.

Franko, Patrice. *The Puzzle of Latin American Economic Development,* 3rd ed. Lanham, MD: Rowman and Littlefield, 2007.

Handelman, Howard, and Werner Baer. *Paying the Costs of Austerity in Latin America.* Boulder, CO: Westview Press, 1989.

Jameson, Kenneth P., and Charles Wilber, eds. *The Political Economy of Development and Underdevelopment,* 6th ed. New York: McGraw-Hill, 1996.

Lenin, V.I. *Imperialism, The Highest Stage of Capitalism.* New York: International Publishers, 1979.

Nkrumah, Kwame. *Neo-Colonialism, The Last Stage of Imperialism.* London: Nelson, 1965.

Rodney, Walter. *How Europe Underdeveloped Africa.* Washington, DC: Howard University Press, 1981.

Salvucci, Richard J. *Latin America and the World Economy, Dependency and Beyond.* Lexington, MA: D. C. Heath and Company, 1996.

Smith, William C., and Roberto Patricio Korzeniewicz, eds. *Politics, Social Change, and Economic Restructuring in Latin America*. Miami, FL: North-South Center Press, 1997.

Tucker, Richard. *Insatiable Appetite: The United States and the Ecological Destruction of the Tropical World*. Lanham, MD: Rowman and Littlefield, 2007.

United Nations Human Development Program. *Human Development, 1999*. New York: Oxford University Press, 1999.

Veltmeyer, Henry, James Petras, and Steve Vieux. *Neoliberalism and Class Conflict in Latin America, a Comparative Perspective on the Political Economy of Structural Adjustment*. New York: St. Martin's Press, 1997.

Films and Videos

Unless otherwise noted, all films are available from the Filmmakers Library, New York.

Amazonia: The Road to the End of the Forest. Canada, 1990.

The Battle of the Titans. Denmark, 1993.

Coffee: A Sack Full of Power. United States, 1991.

Deadly Embrace, Nicaragua, the World Bank and the International Monetary Fund. United States, 1996. (Available through Ashley Eames, Wentworth, NH, 03282.)

The Debt Crisis. United States, 1989.

Lines of Blood—The Drug War in Colombia. United States, 1992.

Mama Coca. United States, 1991.

Traffic. United States, 2000.

Website

www.eclac.org.cl Economic Commission for Latin America. The Political Economy of Latin America.

EIGHT

DEMOCRACY AND AUTHORITARIANISM

Latin American Political Culture

To better understand the very unique context in which politics are conducted in Latin America, it is necessary to understand not only general aspects of Latin American society, economics, and culture but also those specific beliefs and views that affect how Latin Americans see, judge, and participate in politics. *Political culture* develops in a society over a period of time. The concept helps us focus on the political beliefs and values that are embedded in a particular culture. Developed through the study of comparative politics, *political culture* is defined as those attitudes and beliefs that affect the way we think about, engage in, and evaluate politics and political events. Thus, the strong-man rule and authoritarian decision making that is so common in Latin America might be totally unacceptable in Great Britain, Canada, or the United States, where moderation, compromise, and consensus are more highly valued. Conversely, the political vacillation for which U.S. President Bill Clinton became famous would be little tolerated in a Latin American president, even though his personal indiscretions might.

The nature of politics in Latin America developed over many centuries, with the most remote origins in the pre-Columbian hierarchical and authoritarian rule that characterized the governing process among the Aztecs, Mayans, Incas, and other highly structured indigenous groups. There were, however, more participatory practices among less centralized indigenous groups and at lower levels in the far-flung Incan Empire. The communally based *ayllu* would be an example of the latter and one that has recently helped to engender community-based participatory politics in indigenous Andean areas where this unit existed. To this was added the authoritarian, hierarchical, and often dictatorial forms of governing that were brought from the Iberian Peninsula and developed in the colonial and early republican era. Of particular note is the *absolutist tradition* (from the absolute monarchies in the Iberian Peninsula) that became manifest in the Americas in the unchecked power of the viceroy and other governmental leaders in the colonies and the fusion of political and military power in the hands of the viceroy or captain general. Similarly, the seignorial *latifundista* enjoyed almost virtually unchecked power on his estate, if not in the area in which it was located. All of these factors made for a tradition and thus a political culture that was generally far from democratic.

Authoritarian Legacy and Weak Democratic Tradition

For the vast majority of Latin American countries that gained their independence in the early nineteenth century, this authoritarian tradition weighed heavily and was further strengthened by the dictatorial practices of the leaders of the independence movement as they took the reigns of power in the newly independent nations and by the less statesmanlike dictators who all too often followed. One is here reminded of authoritarian *libertadores* like Simón Bolívar and dictators like Juan Manuel de Rosas in Argentina and Antonio López de Santa Anna in Mexico.

As Latin America developed, there was little experience with democracy during the colonial period. There were no legislatures or popular representative bodies where the people could make their views known or participate in governing, above the municipal level. This level was the exception. For instance, in many areas, the town council, or *cabildo*, did allow some degree of participation and democracy in many—but not all—municipalities. Many indigenous villages also exercised some degree of democracy in decision-making practices. The general lack of experience with democracy led one astute student of Latin America, Mario Hernández Sánchez-Barba, to observe that the democratic constitutions patterned on the United States and France that were enacted in Latin America during the early nineteenth-century independence struggles were attempts to impose a democratic framework on a very authoritarian reality. Although the new Latin American nations were launched as democracies with constitutional structures similar to those of the United States and the French Republic, democratic experience and a democratic political culture lagged far behind. It was perhaps a little like introducing cricket and cricket rules to players who have never seen the game and have been playing soccer all their lives. Although some countries took to the new game faster than others, all underwent a long period of assimilation that included periods of play much more like the old game. Some even suggest that in times of crisis the players still revert to the old (authoritarian) patterns of play. As was suggested in Chapter 3, nineteenth- and twentieth-century Latin American history saw ongoing pendulum swings between periods of democratic and authoritarian rule. Indeed, it might be argued that Latin American political culture in most countries is characterized by a nominal commitment to the practice of democracy and a deep-seated reverence for authoritarian rulers with the strength to govern effectively. On the other hand, after 1950 in Costa Rica and, to a lesser degree, Venezuela and Colombia from the late 1950s on, the commitment to democracy and democratic means has been much more pervasive. This was also the case in Uruguay and Chile before they were beset by long periods of bureaucratic authoritarianism in the 1970s and 1980s, when the military ruled.

Individualism

In addition to authoritarianism, individualism is strong in Latin American political culture. The individual does not like to be subordinated by government or other powerful political forces and often will only accept such control when there is sufficient power to sustain it. When power weakens or countervailing power can be invoked, rebellion often follows and the will of another group or individual may become dominant. Political leaders also sometimes individualize their rule. Power is used by the individual ruler and oftentimes for the individual benefit of the ruler or by or for the group to which the ruler belongs. Equally, power is wielded by small groups, such as the fourteen families in El Salvador or socioeconomic or political elites, and monopolized for their benefit. A commonly held view among many is that, like the colonial rulers, those who hold power will use it in ways that will directly benefit them or their political or socioeconomic group and that this will be done at the expense of the general population. This may result in special projects for home regions or political or business friends or, at times, outright corruption and individual enrichment. Nor do such actions buttress the belief that government benefits all the people equally or that special interests or elites do not rule.

Democracy and Authoritarianism

Discussing elite politics and the roots of democracy in *Building Democracy in Latin America,* John Peeler observes that the royal absolutism that so heavily influenced the authoritarian tradition became dominant only in the fifteenth century and that it was resisted at the elite level by the medieval tradition of the *fueros,* or special privilidges extended to religious personnel and the nobility. Thus, the idea of special rights and privileges for favored groups and their ability to resist even the strong control of the state became entrenched in Latin America as well. The local elite often displayed and used its own autonomy to resist state authority, as suggested by the oft-quoted phrase "obedezco pero no cumplo" (I obey but do not comply). This has continued to the present day and helps to explain why civilian and military elites are often loath to submit to governmental rule. Indeed, they often see themselves as immune from, jurisdiction—not controlled by the law. Impunity in such situations is common.

Democratization

Democratization has grown slowly in most of Latin America. Although the process has accelerated dramatically since the end of military rule in the 1980s and 1990s, it started in the early nineteenth century with elitist or aristocratic democracies where power was held in few hands. Gradually, it evolved and incorporated more participants as literacy levels rose, property requirements were abolished, slavery ended, women were afforded the franchise, and lower-class groups mobilized. The democratic ideals continue to inspire and suggest how the republics should function. The persistence of such ideals has helped to shape political culture. In *Democracy in Developing Countries: Latin America,* Larry Diamond notes that elitist democracies helped to get important players involved and invested in the democracy, which in turn allowed for participation, to which others could aspire. The elitist model of democracy was gradually popularized as new groups began to participate effectively in the political systems. Diamond further argues that the constitutional, liberal, and democratic idea delegitimized the authoritarian use of power but ultimately did not radically change the elitist proclivity of the system.

In his seminal work, *Democracy in Latin America*, George Philip is clear as to the persistence of the authoritarian as well as democratic beliefs. He acknowledges the variation in the region but sees predemocratic patterns of political behavior surviving democratization. Nor does he see the broad institutional changes that have usually preceded democratization and democratic consolidation taking place in most of Latin America. There is positive institutional change in some countries, but throughout the region authoritarian legacies have survived even the most recent transition to democracy in the 1980s and 1990s. Even more critically, he observes that the bureaucracy remains patrimonialist, law enforcement is weak, and public opinion is often ready to support open law breaking by political leaders. Thus, the conflicting values that leaders and the public have about democracy versus authoritarian rule have not allowed for the consolidation of democracy in most of Latin America. Earlier in the work he cites a respected poll taken in Chile in 2001 to the effect that only 45% of those sampled thought democracy was preferable to any other kind of government, while 11% agreed that in "certain circumstances an authoritarian government can be preferable to a democratic one." Other polls have shown similar results elsewhere in Latin America.

Politicians and the public have often shown themselves quite willing to support extra-constitutional uses and assumptions of power at critical times. Venezuela has one of the strongest democratic traditions in Latin America. But, even in democratic Venezuela, there was considerable support for the 1992 coup attempt by Hugo Chávez to overthrow the widely discredited Carlos Andrés Pérez government. The polarization of attitudes that transpired after Chávez was elected president and began to transform the state was also very strong. Indeed, the partisanship became so intense that there was also significant support for the short-lived coup that temporarily displaced President Chávez from power in 2002. Nor were most Chávez supporters overly concerned with the leader's tendency to concentrate more power in the presidency or his attempts to extend the presidential term in office. (See Chapter 17 on Venezuela for a fuller discussion.)

The Conflict Society

Societies and the proponents of political systems in nations like Great Britain often pride themselves on the high degree of consensus on fundamental values and the rules of the game. Others, like politicians in Lebanon and the former Yugoslavia, are divided into factions that have very different views of what the society—or even the nation—is or should be and were widely divergent ideas of how to achieve their political objectives in that national political system. There is also a willingness to resolve these issues through the concerted use of organized violence and forms of warfare and to engage in human rights violations of those who challenge their power.

As Latin America developed, different historical epochs added new terms of conflict. Thus, to the struggles of the nineteenth-century Liberals and Conservatives was added the conflict between those advocating radical restructuring on the lines of the Mexican Revolution, such as Alianza Popular Revolucionaria Americana (APRA) in Peru, or total, comprehensive revolution based on the Cuban process that began in 1959. After 1960 and the radicalization of the Cuban Revolution, leftists and leftist insurgencies challenged mainstream parties in charge of governments and right-wing military groups. Thus, ideological values were often polarized between those advocating a political agenda inspired by socialism or leftist nationalism and those advocating a political agenda based on different conservative ideologies or U.S.-style anticommunism and the national security state. The wide gap between these positions and the lack of consensus on common objectives (and sometimes the rules of the game) made for a political culture that in most instances was not consensual (Costa Rica since 1948 is one notable exception). As suggested by the title of Kalman Silvert's well-respected work *The Conflict Society,* Latin American society and political culture have strong conflictual elements. Indeed, conflict is often taken to the extreme. Like a high-stakes poker game, there is a willingness on the part of many to take their political struggle to the wall. Politics is seen as a winner-take-all game, and losing often means losing power and thus being forced to fold and cash in one's chips. Players gamble with the power chips they have to win the game. The pot is not to be split. There are winners and losers. Power is to be used to the maximum. In the last hands of the game, push may come to shove—and that means one plays all one's power chips. This may mean buying votes, closing polling places where the opposition is strong, mobilizing friendly army garrisons, or executing a full-blown coup d'état. In such situations, there is frequently a resort to violence or the threat of violence. The willingness at times to take the political struggle to such intense and passionate levels means that violence is regularly employed through intimidation, repression, assassination, rebellion, guerrilla warfare, coups, or even civil war. The authoritarian military regimes in Chile and Argentina were even willing to engage in massive torture, murder, and other human rights violations to make sure that leftist groups would be kept from power. Alternatively, the Shining Path guerrillas in Peru executed a brutal campaign to overthrow the Peruvian government in the late 1980s and early 1990s that included frequent assassination and massive car and truck bombs. Much of the political conflict in Colombia has been played out in violent confrontations between Liberal and Conservative bands in the late 1940s and 1950s (*la Violencia*) and between guerrilla groups like the Fuerzas Armadas Revolucionarias de Colombia (FARC) and the Ejército de Liberación Nacional (ELN) and the government from the early 1960s to the present day. The last few years have seen the interjection of extremely violent paramilitaries begun by wealthy landowners or businessmen and sometimes tied to elements of the Colombian military. They operate extralegally and are notable for their brutality and human rights violations (see Chapter 18).

Other key elements of Latin American political culture include some of the following.

ELITISM

Elites have dominated Latin America since the Mayan monarch and nobles ran the Mayan states in preclassical times. As suggested earlier, there have been a variety of economic, political, and social elites. Early democratization after independence was also controlled by these same elites. Similarly, there are intellectual elites, cultural elites, and even elites that dominate leftist parties and guerrilla movements. The conscious or unconscious belief that an elite should lead, decide, dictate, or otherwise rule has greatly buttressed authoritarian practices in politics and many other areas of society.

PERSONALISM

As suggested in Chapter 5, personal relations are fundamental in Latin America. In societies where trust comes hard, one wants to deal with only those with whom one has "confianza"—trust. Further, since the time of the early *hidalgos* (less-well-off noblemen) and upper-class representatives of the crown, a charming personal veneer has been deemed necessary for successful civil relations. A charismatic manner and personal warmth are thus highly valued commodities that are prerequisites for higher-level positions. Men physically embrace each other if they are friends or close business associates (the *abrazo/abraço*), and opposite-sex and female–female greetings in the same circles include a kiss on one cheek (Hispanic America) or both cheeks (most of Brazil and French Latin America). For new introductions and less-well-known acquaintances, one *always* shakes hands when one is introduced or enters a room and when one departs. The more grace and charm a person displays, the higher his or her presumed social status.

Such is equally the case in politics. *Personalismo* is a valued commodity among politicians. Much of their popularity and following may well be based on their personal charm and warmth. A leader is expected to be able to inspire a personal commitment from his or her following, and this is done in large part through his or her *personalismo*. In this context, the term takes on a meaning closer to *charisma* and has defined some of the region's most successful political leaders: Victor Raúl Haya de la Torre of Peru's APRA, Juan Domingo Perón of Argentina, or Fidel Castro of Cuba. Each of these leaders was capable of exuding an immense personal charm in virtually all social contacts, be it a private meeting with an individual or small group or a speech to an assembled throng of thousands. Fidel Castro became known for his ability to hold an audience's attention in speeches that lasted hours.

STRONG-MAN RULE: *CAUDILLO, CACIQUE,* AND *CORONEL*

We have established that political leadership in Latin America has often tended to be authoritarian, with the political leader exercising a great deal of power and control. Military dictators who can employ the force and power to maintain their position are tolerated or at least endured until time passes or they can be overthrown. Brutal rulers such as Augusto Pinochet (the military dictator in Chile from 1973 until 1990) have not always had the *personalismo* of most civilian politicians. Pinochet simply relied on overwhelming force. Since before the conquest, the tradition of the strong local leader became well established. The *cacique* came to mean a local indigenous leader who could be best described as a political boss. In his local community and among his own people, his power base was strong, but it diminished rapidly as he moved away from it. After colonial rule was put in place, other strong men developed. The *caudillo* initially was a regional political leader or boss who might exercise absolute or near-absolute power in his region. Often a local landowner or other local notable, he usually had an independent base for economic–political power. As time went on, the *caudillo* and *caudillismo* also came to refer to strong, if rather authoritarian, national political leaders such as Juan Perón of Argentina. In the rural areas of traditional Brazil, the large landowners, or *fazendeiros*, were often given the rank of colonel in the state militia. This also came to be an honorific title given to a powerful local notable. Like the colonels in the postbellum American South, *coronéis* were, and sometimes still are, powerful political players in much of rural Brazil. It would be difficult to understand politics in rural Brazil without referring to *coronelismo* or realizing the power and impunity of the *coronel*.

CUARTEL, CUARTELAZO, GOLPE DE ESTADO, AND THE JUNTA

Political culture in Latin America is also influenced by the tendency of the military to leave their barracks, or *cuartel*, to intervene in the political process, the *cuartelazo*. Indeed, when the government is indecisive, ineffective, or overly corrupt or leans too far to the left, many civilians call on the military to intervene. Military intervention has been an ongoing phenomenon in most Latin American countries. With few exceptions, such as Costa Rica since the 1948 revolution and the subsequent abolition of the armed forces, and Mexico since the 1920s, the militaries have engaged in *golpismo*. They believe themselves to be defenders of the constitution, upholders of national honor, or defenders against subversion, corruption, or tyranny. The Latin American militaries have staged some 250 coups d'état, or *golpes de estado*, since most of the nations became independent in the early part of the nineteenth century. After the successful *golpe*, the dominant military coup makers, or *golpistas*, typically set up a military *junta* to rule until civilian government is restored. Most commonly, the *junta* is comprised of upper-level officers from the army, navy, and air force. The period of rule can range from the time it takes to elect or appoint a new civilian president (usually a few months) to more than a decade, as was the case in Brazil (1964–1985) and Chile (1973–1990). This latter type of extended military governance came to be what Guillermo O'Donnell called "bureaucratic authoritarianism." It was used to refer to the extended period of military rule where the military actively ran the bureaucratic governmental apparatus. Such bureaucratic authoritarianism characterized many of the governments in South America during the 1960s (beginning with the coup in Brazil in 1964), 1970s, and 1980s. Nations under such rule included not only Brazil, Chile, and Argentina but also Bolivia and Uruguay. A progressive Nasserite (a nationalist military government patterned after that led by Gamal Abdel Nasser in Egypt from 1952 to 1970) ruled Peru from 1968 to 1980. A conservative form of extended military rule characterized Guatemala from 1954 until 1985, and the military dominated politics well into the 1990s. In Paraguay, a traditional military *caudillo*, General Alfredo Stroessner, ruled from 1954 to 1989. Since democratization has intensified and has butressed continuing civilian rule in the 1990s, the tendency toward military intervention and *golpes de estado* has diminished. It should be noted, however, that a *golpe* was executed against Hugo Chávez in 2002 and the new government was readily accepted by the Bush administration, which may have had some role in facilitating it. This time, however, the coup was not accepted by the pro-Chávez masses and younger military officers who mobilized to force the end of the coup and Chávez's return to power.

With the return to democracy and greater focus on civil society, democratic (and authoritarian) attitudes are being explored and charted by a number of opinion polls and survey research organizations. Of particular interest are the regionwide surveys done by Latin Barometer (Latinobarómetro.org). Newer works on *Democracy in Latin America* (both titles begin with this phrase) by George Philip and Peter H. Smith also explore democratic attitudes in some depth.

OTHER *POLÍTICOS*

Professional politicians are *políticos*. In fact, all those who engage in politics could be described as *políticos*, or *políticas* if they are women. One does not, however, need to be authoritarian to qualify. Different countries have different political cultures. In Brazil, the tradition of the *chefe político* emerged. It came to have special meaning and refers to a *político* with special powers and attributes who could best be described in English as a political boss. The figure of the political boss also exists in Spanish-speaking America and could be referred to as a *jefe político*, although the connotation of power might not be quite so strong. The *caudillo* would be more powerful, if even less likely to abide by the rule of law.

CORPORATISM

Another aspect of Latin American society that strongly influences the political system is corporatism. The concept dates back to the medieval Iberian Peninsula when society was conceived organically. The whole society was divided into different bodies (*corpus*) or corporations according to specific function or profession. The identification of individuals is oftentimes stronger to their particular body than to the nation. Church officials highly identify with the Catholic Church and display intense loyalty to it. Military officers in particular frequently display more loyalty to their military institutions than to civilian government or national civilian leaders. Thus, military officers often remain more loyal to their service branch, if not the military more generally, than to the government or civil society. Such feelings facilitate coups and narrow interpretations of the public interest.

PATRON–CLIENT, CLIENTELISM, AND OTHER SPECIAL RELATIONS

As was suggested earlier, there is often great disparity in power and prerogative in Latin America. Those who do not have power seek protection from those who do. Thus, alliances between the powerful and the not-so-powerful are often made. Indeed, this practice began on the large landed estates between the *patrón* and the *peon*, his humble employee. As with patrons and their supporters and followers elsewhere, this type of relationship spread throughout the society. The *patron–client relationship* refers to the special ties of personal loyalty and commitment that connect a powerful person with those below him. The *patrón* will look after his followers and personally intervene to make sure they are well treated or to assist them in a time of trouble, even paying for medical treatment for a family member from personal funds. As the *patrón* rises or falls, his retainers rise or fall with him. The followers give unswerving support to their leader and can always be counted on because of their personal loyalty. The practice is common in politics and the governmental bureaucracy, as well as society more generally. It has characterized many political movements as well. Indeed, it has been suggested that many Latin American political parties are personal parties grouped around the party leader. Many observers have also noted the existence of personal factions or groups within parties and government—public administration in particular is often rife with these personal groupings. Taken one step further, this can lead to *clientelismo,* which is the practice of filling governmental positions with one's friends and associates to the exclusion of other, often better-qualified job candidates.

COMPADRES AND COMADRES EVERYWHERE

Another important social relationship that spills over into business and politics is that of the *compadre* and the *comadre,* the godparents of one's children. Given the traditional importance of the Church, it is not surprising that those who stand with the parents at the christening of their child should play an important role in the life not only of the child but also of the parents. The *compadre* or *comadre* is someone with whom one's relationship has been cemented. Like a blood relative, they generally are people who can be trusted. *Compadres* protect each other, as do *comadres.* They can gain access or special favors and can always count on one's help. If amenable, a person of a higher social status, like the *patrón,* may be chosen as a *compadre* or *comadre,* thus creating a special tie to the *patrón* for the whole family. The terms can also mean a close friend who can be counted on.

CAMARILLAS AND OTHER SMALL GROUPS

Personal or professional networks are always significant. The importance of the small group, or *grupito,* cannot be underestimated. The *camarilla,* or clique, is pervasive in Mexican society and politics. In the political context, it specifically refers to a self-promoting political group that maximizes the power and position of its members through concerted collective action. In Brazil, friends, political allies, or associates often form a *panelinha* so that they can do business with each other or be assured of contacts through people they know they can trust.

Finally, finesse and the ability to improvise are greatly valued. One hopes to move things along with the same deftness that world-famous soccer player Pelé moved the ball down the field. Indeed, the Brazilians have a special word for such adroitness, *jeito.* To give a *jeito* is to finesse something, to manage it, to make things happen.

Conclusion

The conduct of politics in Latin America is a complex process that occurs in a reality far different from that found in the United States, Canada, Great Britain, or elsewhere. In political and social interactions, all the factors we have discussed—and many others—come into play. Ultimately, power rules; but it is exercised through the culturally based concepts, rules, and techniques that define the power game in Latin America. Further, the nuanced nature of the role these factors play is often the deciding factor in many key political and other events. Their importance in business or economics cannot be underestimated; in the game of politics, their comprehension is essential.

Bibliography

Almond, Gabriel, and Sidney Verba, eds. *The Civic Culture Revisited*. Newbury Park, CA: Sage Publications, 1989.

Almond, Gabriel, G. Binghum Powell, Kaarne Strøm, and Russell J. Dalton. *Comparative Politics Today*. 8th ed., New York: Pearson/Longman, 2004.

Avritzer, Leonardo. *Democracy and the Public Space in Latin America*. Princeton, NJ: Princeton University Press, 2002.

Camp, Roderic Ai, ed. *Democracy in Latin America, Patterns and Cycles* (Jaguar Books on Latin America, 10). Wilmington, DE: Scholarly Resources, 1996.

Diamond, Larry, Jonathan Hartlyn, Juan J. Linz, and Seymoul Martin Lipset, eds. *Democracy in Developing Countries: Latin America*. 2nd ed. Boulder, CO: Lynne Rienner, 1999.

O'Donnell, Guillermo. *Modernization and Bureaucratic Authoritarianism*. 2nd ed. Berkeley: Institute of International Studies, University of California, 1979.

Peeler, John. *Building Democracy in Latin America*. 2nd ed. Boulder: Lynne Rienner, 2004.

Philip, George. *Democracy in Latin America: Surveying Conflict and Crisis*. Cambridge/Oxford: Polity Press/Blackwell, 2003.

Smith, Peter H. *Democracy in Latin America: Political Change in Comparative Perspective*. New York: Oxford University Press, 2005.

Silvert, Kalman. *The Conflict Society: Reaction and Revolution in Latin America*. New York: American Universities Field Staff, 1966.

Touraine, Alain. *What Is Democracy?* Translated by David Macey. Boulder, CO: Westview Press, 1997.

Tulchin, Joseph S., with Bernice Romero, eds. *The Consolidation of Democracy in Latin America*. Boulder, CO: Lynne Rienner, 1995.

FILMS AND VIDEOS

Details of a Duel: A Question of Honor. Chile/Cuba, 1988.

Evita. United States, 1997.

Missing. United States, 1983.

State of Siege. United States, 1982.

WEBSITES

Latinobarómeter.org An excellent source for recent survey research on Latin American political attitudes.

NINE

POLITICS, POWER, INSTITUTIONS, AND ACTORS

Power moves politics in Latin America, and naked power often rules. As we suggested in Chapters 5, 7, and 8, politics in Latin America has to do with powerful political and economic actors. Powerful *políticos* (and the occasional *política*) have dominated most Latin American societies since classical Mayan and Aztec times. Dictators such as Santa Anna in Mexico, Juan Perón in Argentina, and Anastasio Somoza in Nicaragua have ruled absolutely. Oligarchies such as the dominant fourteen families in El Salvador have dominated politics and brutally suppressed those who challenged them. Military juntas have monopolized power, cancelled elections, imprisoned and sometimes eliminated the opposition, and ruled for decades. The military and other groups have ignored constitutions and seized power forcefully, as when the Chilean military bombed the presidential palace to overthrow Salvador Allende in 1973. Also, power can come from the mobilized masses, demonstrations, or general strikes that force a government out of office or a dictator to resign. There have been more than 200 extraconstitutional assumptions of power in Latin America since the republics became independent. Indeed, it has been the constellation of power and not constitutional constraints that has conditioned the conduct of politics during most of Latin American history. It is the powerful individual, group, institution, or party that most often rules. Only those who know how to use power can be serious players.

Yet, as Latin American societies have become more complex, those who rule do so through the apparatus of the state and its interaction with political parties, political movements, individuals, and interest groups. Those who aspire to power must take over the apparatus of the state and use it to rule. This can be done by a coup d'état, a fraudulent election, a political agreement among political and/or economic elites to share power, or a relatively honest election with some real political competition. However the state apparatus is taken over, any discussion of the nature of political systems in Latin America must begin with a realization of the greater role that has been traditionally assigned to the state, particularly compared to classical models of liberalism. John Locke and other classical liberal thinkers believed that the best government was that which governed least. They were reacting to that absolutist configuration of the state that monarchies like Spain used to rule domestically and over their colonies in the sixteenth, seventeenth, and eighteenth centuries. Yet, it was precisely this absolutist state that served as the model for Latin American rule. Its use and misuse in Latin America have been quite different from the way the liberal state developed in Great Britain and the United States.

When the Latin American nations gained their independence in the early nineteenth century, there was a serious struggle over the political forms that would be adopted by the newly independent nations. During the colonial period, the region experienced different forms of authoritarian rule and state absolutism. The traditional elites who retained power, now independent from Madrid and Lisbon, had little, if any, democratic experience. Indeed, since the conception of the state that was projected from Madrid or Lisbon was absolutist during the colony, the elites had to find informal, noninstitutional (and not institutionalized), more personalistic ways to assert their authority and adapt to local conditions. There was almost no experience with institutionalized representative or popular democracy. The regional assemblies that were found in North America were absent in Latin America. Democracy was little practiced. The postindependence rulers were short on practical democratic models. Indeed, after independence, several countries experimented with monarchical and/or dictatorial rule.

The constitutional structures of the newly independent states were nominally democratic and modeled on the liberal constitutions of France, the United States, and the Spanish liberal constitution of 1812. Yet, political practice and political culture tended to be authoritarian and absolutist, even for committed democrats like Simón Bolívar. Gradually, new groups emerged and democratic practice engendered more democratic and less absolutist attitudes, although the latter have persisted to the present day. A strange hybrid resulted. Most countries adopted a republican, democratic form of government; but in reality, traditional authoritarian patterns were most often employed by the elites and suffrage was very limited initially. In the century and a half after independence, suffrage was gradually expanded, but there was frequent reversion to authoritarian politics and elitist, if not dictatorial, rule. As suggested in Chapter 8, much of the course of Latin American history has been an alternation between the authoritarian tendencies that were acquired during colonial and even pre-colonial times and the democratic ideas and ideals that were interjected at the time of independence. Democracy has been gaining ground in recent years, but reversions to authoritarian rule are frequent and decision-making practices continue to reflect the authoritarian aspects of the political culture. In his seminal work on Latin American democracy, George Philip observes that predemocratic patterns of political behavior (institutional, organizational, and cultural) have frequently survived democratization. Thus in the region "authoritarian legacies have survived the democratic transition. The bureaucracy remains patrimonialist, law enforcement is weak and public opinion will often support open law breaking by political leaders." He goes on to observe that there is more to succesful democracy than holding elections. Both he and Peter Smith frequently refer to unconsolidated democracy in Latin America.

Constitutions

Jurisprudence is a highly developed art in Latin America. Legal documents are beautifully written and comprehensive. Latin American constitutions are no exceptions. They tend to be long, detailed, flowery documents with a large number of articles (the Mexican constitution of 1917 has well over 100 articles) covering a great many specific situations. As such, they frequently need to be modified or replaced. Based on code law, they are not open to case-based interpretation, as is the case with Anglo-Saxon case law. Nor is legal precedent part of the judicial system. Constitutions have historically been more a norm to strive toward than a strict basis for the rule of law. Presidential power and prerogative are often more important than specific constitutional provisions or prohibitions.

Like the idealism of Don Quijote that permeates the culture, Latin American constitutions represent an ideal to which those who govern and are governed aspire. There have been times and places in Latin American history where the constitutions have been carefully followed (Costa Rica from 1950 to the present, Uruguay and Chile in the 1960s), but they are frequently subordinated to the power of the strong executive, dictator, or military junta. Those who rule have and use power and are less likely to be constrained by the constitution or other legal codes, although they may pay lip service to them. Like U.S. President Franklin Delano Roosevelt in the 1930s, they are more likely to find ways to massage the courts and the constitution to achieve desired policy results. The political tradition in most of Latin America is of strong-man rule and the subordination of law and the courts to the executive and other powerful political and economic actors. The concept of the rule of law and protection of the individual against the arbitrary power of the state (through government) that classical liberals from Hobbes on have espoused is not well developed in most of Latin America, although the process of democratization has begun to tentatively incorporate some liberal concepts of human rights and procedural protections. On the whole, though, power and the powerful have generally ruled. Historically, protection for specific groups often came from *fueros* or *amparos*, which protected specific rights—or privileges—for designated groups (rather than as a constitutional right that protected all).

Only in recent decades have supreme courts become apt at delimiting presidents' interpretations of what is permissible under the constitution. It should be noted, however, that the process of democratization based on Western concepts of classical liberal democracy that has recently spread through the region has strengthened democratic aspects of political culture in all countries where it is practiced and has begun to place a greater emphasis on the subordination of power and the powerful to the law. Nonetheless, practice is often contradictory. In 2000, the Chilean Supreme Court stripped former President Augusto Pinochet of his congressional immunity so that he could be tried for human rights violations committed during his brutal dictatorship—as had been the case earlier for a former general who ruled Argentina during the dirty war—but Peruvian president Alberto Fujimori was inaugurated for his third term after fraudulent elections were held when he forced the Peruvian Supreme Court to exempt him from a constitutional prohibition against third terms. He was later forced from office by political pressure that developed from an evolving corruption scandal and tried and convicted on his return to Peru in 2007. It is of interest to note that although President Hugo Chávez enjoys broad popular support, he could not quite muster the majority needed to remove presidential term limits from the constitution in a closely contested referendum in 2007 (49 percent in favor, 51 percent opposed).

Like the constitution in the United States, Latin American constitutions almost universally created three branches of government: executive, legislative, and judicial. However, very rarely are they coequal, even in the constitutions. Two realities common to Latin American systems are a granting of greater power to the executive branch over the legislative branch and a general lack of significant judicial review. Further, while most Latin American constitutions contain a significant listing of human, civil, and political rights, they also include provisions whereby the executive can suspend those rights in an emergency or time of crisis.

STATE OF SIEGE

A state of siege (*estado de sitio*) or state of emergency (*estado de emergencia*) may be invoked by most Latin American presidents (usually with the consent of the legislature) for a given period of time, normally ranging from 30 to 90 days. It allows the president to suspend most constitutional guarantees, such as freedom of speech and assembly as well as habeas corpus, and to legislate by decree. After the initial period runs out, it may be renewed. This has often been an avenue by which presidents acquired dictatorial powers. Latin American constitutions are also often contradictory on the question of the military, asserting in one place the primacy of civilian rule but in another granting the military a special responsibility for protecting national sovereignty and maintaining domestic order.

CODE LAW

The legal systems in Latin America are based on code law. Most analysts of Latin American constitutions and laws stress that the systems are based not on the flexible notions of British common law but rather on strict interpretation of extensive legal codes. Rather than building on a series of case law decisions, Latin American law is deductive. This code-based law has its origin in Roman law, Catholic traditions, and especially the Napoleonic Code. Much of the code law in place was inspird by the Napoleonic Code, which was promulgated in France in 1804, became the basis for the French Civil Code, and was copied across Continental Europe and in the state of Louisiana in the United States. The influence of Roman traditions can be traced to the long Roman domination of the Iberian Peninsula, which left more than just its language. This tradition emphasized the importance of a comprehensive, written law that is applicable everywhere, in contrast to the medieval traditions of law on which the English system is based, with its emphasis on limits. What was clearly missing from the Iberian ideas of law transported to the New World were the notions of social contract developed in the English ideas of Hobbes and Locke, which laid the groundwork for the idea of a rule of law based on the consent of the governed.

CORPORATISM

John Peeler argues that another feature of Latin American constitutionalism drawn from earlier traditions is corporatism. In contrast to the more individualist ideas of the social contract, the Iberian tradition is more corporatist, with a great emphasis on the sociability of humans and their collectivity. Latin American constitutions are more likely to acknowledge the legitimacy of the interests of collective groups than of individuals. It is therefore interesting that in contemporary Latin American politics the struggle is often over which groups should have their interests acknowledged. For example, some of the constitutions (Argentina, Brazil, Colombia, and Mexico) specifically acknowledge the rights of indigenous groups, children, senior citizens, workers, women, and so on (see Tables 17 and 18 on women's political rights).

TABLE 17. Women's Constitutional Guarantees

Country	Legal Text	Statement of Equality
Argentina	Political constitution of 1994	All inhabitants are equal before the law. No privileges of blood or birth are recognized, nor personal exceptions nor titles of nobility.
Bolivia	Political constitution of 1967	All human beings enjoy guarantees and rights regardless of race, gender, language, religion, or any other form of discrimination. Men and women are equal in rights and obligations.
Brazil	Federal constitution of 1988 and state constitutions of 1989	Men and women are equal in rights and obligations.
Chile	Political constitution of 1980	All are born free and equal in dignity and rights.
Colombia	Political constitution of 1991	All people enjoy the same rights, without discrimination based on gender or other reasons.
Costa Rica*	Political constitution of 1949	All are equal before the law and cannot commit any discrimination contrary to human dignity.
Cuba	Political constitution of 1976	Women enjoy the same rights as men.
Dominican Republic	Political constitution of 1966	Does not expressly relate the equality of rights between women and men.
Ecuador	Political constitution of 1979	Women have the same rights and opportunities as men.
El Salvador	Political constitution of 1983	All people are equal before the law.
Guatemala	Political constitution of 1985	Men and women have the same opportunities and responsibilities.
Honduras	Political constitution of 1965	All Hondurans are equal. Any discrimination based on gender is prohibited.
Mexico	Political constitution of 1917	Men and women are equal before the law.
Nicaragua	Political constitution of 1987	All people are equal. Discrimination based on birth, race, nationality, origin, or other factors is prohibited.
Panama	Political constitution of 1972	There are no personal exceptions or privileges, nor discrimination by reason of gender, race, social class, religion, or political beliefs.

(continued)

TABLE 17. Women's Constitutional Guarantees *Continued*

Country	Legal Text	Statement of Equality
Paraguay	Political constitution of 1992	Men and women have equal rights. The state should concern itself with making equality a reality and with facilitating the participation of women in all arenas of national life.
Peru	Political constitution of 1993	No one should be discriminated against for reasons of origin, gender, race, language, religion, or other.
Uruguay	Political constitution of 1967	All people are equal before the law.
Venezuela	Political constitution of 1961	Discrimination based on gender, race, creed, or social condition is prohibited.

*The constitution of Costa Rica establishes that mothers, children, and the elderly enjoy special protection by the state.

Source: Statistical Abstract of Latin America, Vol. 35. Los Angeles: UCLA Latin American Center Publications, 1999.

TABLE 18. Women's Political Rights

Country	Year Right to Vote Granted	Right to Be Chosen through Popular Election	Year CEDAW* Ratified
Argentina	1947	Since 1991, candidate lists for popular elections must include women in a minimum of 30% of elected positions.	—
Bolivia	1952	Same for men and women.	1980
Brazil	1932	Same for men and women.	1984
Chile	1949	Same for men and women.	1989
Colombia	1954	Same for men and women.	1981
Costa Rica	1949	Same for men and women.	1984
Cuba	1934	Same for men and women.	—
Dominican Republic	1942	Same for men and women.	1982
Ecuador	1929	Same for men and women. The law establishes the obligatory inclusion of 25% of women on candidate lists in multiperson elections.	1981
El Salvador	1950	Same for men and women.	1981
Guatemala	1945	Same for men and women.	1982
Honduras	1955	Same for men and women.	1983
Mexico	1953	Same for men and women.	—
Nicaragua	1955	Same for men and women.	—
Panama	1946	Same for men and women.	1981
Paraguay	1961	Same for men and women.	1986
Peru	1955	Same for men and women.	1981
Uruguay	1932	Same for men and women.	1981
Venezuela	1947	Same for men and women.	1982

*Convention on the Elimination of All Forms of Discrimination Against Women, adopted by the United Nations in 1979.

Source: Mujeres Latinoamericanas en Cifras, 1995, pp. 138–139, as cited in *Statistical Abstract of Latin America*, Vol. 35. Los Angeles: UCLA, 1999.

Institutions

THE PRESIDENT

Latin American republics are based on the strong presidential form of government. Chile did experiment with parliamentary government around the turn of the twentieth century but has since employed presidential rule. Like France, Haiti does have both a president and a prime minister, but most power resides with the president, who appoints the prime minister. The single most distinctive political feature of Latin American rule is the power of the executive. Contemporary Latin American presidential power is deeply rooted in the autocratic traditions of the colonial period. Presidential power in the twentieth century has many different underpinnings that are post-colonial, including populist and revolutionary mobilizations, but the continuity with the past is strong. Also, the contemporary Latin American president wears many hats: chief executive, commander-in-chief, head of state, and head of party, to name a few. Multiple powers are not unique to Latin American presidents, just as U.S. and French presidents share similar multiple roles. In Latin America, these multiple roles only further strengthen an already strong presidency, especially because of the president's ability to invoke broad emergency powers. Even during the last decade, when democratic rule predominated in the region, ruling presidents have occasionally assumed dictatorial power, the most dramatic case being Peruvian president Alberto Fujimori's *autogolpe* of 1992. Latin American presidents often tend to continue in office—*continualismo*. This is often how elected presidents have evolved into dictators. As a way of curbing this aspect of presidential power, many Latin American constitutions, including those of Peru and Argentina, limit the time in office to two terms. The Mexican constitution of 1917 goes one step further, limiting the president to one 6-year term. Several other states also limit the president to one term. Others, like Costa Rica, specify that if a president serves more than one term in office, the terms cannot be consecutive.

The president is also the personification of the state, as manifest in the presidential sash worn on formal occasions. His or her figure commands a great deal of respect and authority. Some observers place considerable emphasis on the role of the Latin American president as the national *patrón*, replacing the local landowners and *caudillos* of the past, arguing that the president is the symbol of the national society, seen as being responsible for the well-being of the country. Consistent with the classic definition of personalistic politics, the president is seen as being responsible for the allocation of resources through presidential favors and patronage. Another side of this practice is that such a personification of power may lead to corruption; it is not unusual for Latin American presidents to leave the office considerably richer than when they arrived.

LEGISLATURE

As opposed to the parliamentary system of government, where the legislature is the dominant branch of the political system, or the government of the United States, where the legislature is coequal, in Latin America the legislative branch is seen as clearly subservient, often acting as an advisory body to the executive or occasionally as a rubber stamp. Most of the legislatures in Latin America are bicameral,

Sample ballot from the 1998 presidential election in Venezuela. Thirty-six different parties competed, but Fifth Republic Movement candidate Hugo Chávez easily won the election with close to 60 percent of the vote.

with a chamber of deputies or chamber of representatives and a senate. However, almost all Central American states (not including Belize) follow the model of the Central American Federation and have unicameral legislatures, usually called "legislative" or "national assemblies." Venezuela and Cuba are also now unicameral. The legislatures' budgets are relatively small and their staff support, minimal. In many states, the legislators may have to share a secretary and basic office equipment. The committee system is neither strong nor well developed, nor have Latin American legislatures usually retained the ability to veto acts of the executive or to initiate programs. They have served more modest goals of providing a locus for the political opposition and special interests or for refining laws for implementation. It is too early to definitively declare a new trend for Latin American legislatures, but with the region's wide reestablishment of democratic rule in the 1990s, legislatures in some countries have begun to assert their power and independence. Most significantly, in 1992 and 1993, legislatures in Brazil and Venezuela removed sitting presidents from office on the basis of official corruption while reasserting their prerogatives in countries such as Mexico, Argentina, Chile, and Uruguay. Such actions were virtually unprecedented. The Costa Rica Legislative Assembly has remained strong during past decades.

Legislators are most commonly elected to 4-year terms for the lower house or unicameral legislatures and 4- or 6-year terms for the upper house. Legislators are usually elected from single-member constituencies, although there has been some experimentation with forms of proportional representation in countries such as Chile. The legislative sessions have historically been short and have been known to last as little as a month. Legislative debate is often acrimonious, with walkouts, protests, and sharp denunciations. Compromise and consensus are often in short supply.

As a form of protection against abuse or coercion by the powerful, Latin American legislators enjoy a special right—immunity from arrest or prosecution while the legislature is in session.

COURTS

The organization of the legal system in Latin America is not unlike that of the United States, with a supreme court, appeals courts, and local courts. Judges are generally appointed, although the national legislatures may be involved through nomination or approval of presidential nomination or, in the case of Costa Rica, in the election of supreme court justices. Supreme court justices are not, however, appointed for life, as in the United States. Rather, they serve for a fixed term and must have their term renewed by appointment or election. A tradition of a strong, independent judiciary is not well developed in Latin America. From the supreme court down, the judiciary has tended to be susceptible to political pressure from the executive or other powerful groups. Further, certain crimes, such as terrorism or actions by military officers, may not be within the purview of civilian courts. Rather, such cases are referred to special military courts. In recent times, Latin American courts, although still weak, have begun to seek more effective ways of attacking official corruption and protecting individual rights. Symptomatic of this trend is the increasing use of *amparo*. The writ of *amparo* allows the individual to protect his or her rights by making a special appeal to the judicial system. It is one way the individual can protect himself or herself from the power of the state.

GOVERNMENT STRUCTURE AND LOCAL GOVERNMENT

Most Latin American states are unitary, meaning that there are no state-level governmental organizations with autonomous power or independence. The only federal states are Mexico, Brazil, Argentina, and Venezuela. The other nations are divided into provinces or departments. Traditionally the national government usually appoints prefects or other administrative heads to rule over them. The process of decentralization has allowed for the elections of prefects or governors in many of the unitary states in more recent years. Municipalities exist at the lowest levels and may elect their mayors and councils (although the national government may appoint some council members as well). The organization of the four federal systems is similar to that in the United States, with elected state governors and legislatures and municipalities at the lowest level. Further, any discussion of the relative weights of central and local authorities in Latin American political systems must recognize a certain evolution over time. During the colonial period, the monarchies were largely ineffective at controlling the interiors of their vast empires. Local authorities were generally appointed by the crown, but after appointment they largely functioned in an autonomous way. In rural Latin America prior to the middle of the nineteenth century, local landowners and *caudillos* were the de facto rulers. Later, the process of nation building in the last half of the nineteenth century focused primarily around the communication system—roads, rail, and so on. These systems allowed central governments to extend their authority over the hinterlands, thus replacing the rule of the *caudillos*. As a way of centralizing power, most Latin American countries adopted unitary governmental structures with national/local relations similar to that of France, with almost all authority flowing from the top down—from the central government to local authorities. The local *caudillos* were eventually supplanted as national armies and bureaucracies were created late in the nineteenth century. Rudimentary systems of national taxation were established, although no formal authority to raise taxes was given to local authorities (this general lack of revenue-generating authority poses a major problem for local governments today, which most commonly must rely on funding from the national government).

CENTRALIZATION AND DECENTRALIZATION

This pattern of centralization was the clear intent of most national rulers in the nineteenth century, but three countertrends of the twentieth century must be mentioned lest one be left with the impression that Latin American politics has been marked only by centralized rule. First, four countries have adopted federal systems that have devolved some powers to the states—Brazil, Argentina, Venezuela, and Mexico. (Much of the autonomy of the states in Brazil and Argentina was, however, undermined by the long periods of bureaucratic authoritarianism in the 1960s, 1970s, and early 1980s.) Second, the sheer remoteness of some regions in countries like Brazil, Mexico, Argentina, and Colombia has significantly slowed down the integration process, although much of this regional remoteness has disappeared in the last 25 years. Finally, local leaders ranging from revolutionary chiefs and guerrilla leaders to drug traffickers and entrenched large landowners have often used the remoteness of their zones of activity to maintain relative independence from the central government. That combination is probably most evident today in Colombia. Recent years have seen significant initiatives across the region to decentralize government. They have met with some success and have opened the way for local governments to tax and raise some of their own revenues. This has made for significant reform and renovation in some municipalities.

Electoral Tribunals

In that their electoral systems have at times been highly susceptible to influence and manipulation, many Latin American nations have established a separate branch of government to oversee elections. Called "supreme electoral councils" or "supreme electoral tribunals," these independent bodies are charged with overseeing the electoral process and guaranteeing honest elections. They have separate budgets and are not under the control of any other branch of government. In countries like Costa Rica, they have become quite strong and independent and have helped ensure electoral integrity. In other instances, they too proved to be vulnerable to powerful influences. As democracy continues to develop in the post-1990s period, their existence is a very positive factor in maintaining honest elections and open political competition.

The Bureaucracy

Political scientists have long acknowledged the importance of another part of government—the administrative sector, or bureaucracy. Bureaucracies in Latin America have tended to be large, poorly paid and administered, and unmotivated. Staffing is often done as a form of political favor to supporters of winning candidates or ministerial or agency appointees (one form of quid pro quo in a patron–client relationship). Professionalism and motivation are low, and the susceptibility to corruption or being suborned is often great. Indeed, the bribe, or *mordida* ("little bite in the hand"), is frequent in Mexico and most other countries. Corruption and favoritism often permeate the bureaucracies and feed negative perceptions of government in the general population. Bureaucratic appointments are not always made on the basis of clear standards. Costa Rica is the only Latin American country to have a professional civil service system. Elsewhere, each ministry or agency may have its own recruitment criteria and job classification system, with no general standardization or means of doing cross-agency comparisons. Nor are programs or university training in public administration widespread. Government offices are often open only in the mornings or until 1:00 or 2:00 P.M., and many workers have other jobs in the afternoons. In most cases, resources are very scarce. Similarly, phones go unanswered, lines are frequently long, service is poor, and the ability to have a request processed or a problem resolved is minimal. One frequently hears stories of requests simply not being processed until an extra inducement is added to the application. A sense of professionalism based on high levels of training, adequate compensation, and good morale is hard to find among public employees.

Knowledge of the bureaucratic sector is absolutely crucial to an understanding of Latin American politics. The implementation of government policy and programs is totally dependent on different segments of the bureaucracy. Bureaucratic functioning needs to be understood because many casual observers of the region are unfamiliar with the extensive role of government entities in the economy. In reality, most of the large Southern Cone countries, in pursuit of national development in the twentieth century, established significant state sectors to control everything from steel mills to coffee plantations. As in a socialist system, state employees set wages, prices, and production quotas. In the case of Argentina under Perón, a government corporation Institute Argentino de Promoción del Intercambio (IAPI) was established to purchase all agricultural products from the farmers and then to sell them on the international market with all proceeds going to the government. In some instances, more than 50 percent of the gross national product (GNP) was generated in the public sector. Such large-scale government intervention in the economy allowed many governments to establish significant social welfare programs in education, health, and social services, each with its own administrative bureaucracy. These large bureaucracies provided central governments with vast amounts of patronage that could be used to reward friends and co-opt opposition groups. The bureaucracies generally have lacked significant legislative oversight and, in many cases, have been both highly inefficient and corrupt, allowing both bureaucrats and those who appoint them to become wealthy. The nature and efficiency of these organizations have helped to legitimize neoliberal characterizations of a bloated, inefficient government apparatus that needed to be downsized. In the last two decades, however, processes of privatization and downsizing of the state have resulted in a significant decline in the size and role of the bureaucracy in most of Latin America and in the loss of thousands of jobs.

NEW DIRECTIONS: DEMOCRACY AND DEMOCRATIZATION

As Latin America enters the twenty-first century, important questions are being asked about the direction of the region's political systems. The history of the region, as discussed in Chapters 2 and 3, saw the emergence of a wide range of governments: monarchies, rule by a *caudillo* or strong man, civilian and military dictatorships, oligarchic democracies, parliamentary democracies, populist–corporatist regimes, and, in the case of Cuba, a communist-led state. It is difficult to generalize about the location of the different types of regime except to say that the parliamentary or Westminster-style governments developed only in countries such as Belize and Jamaica, which were formerly under British rule. Monarchical rule had some presence in the immediate post-independence period in the Latin countries, but by the latter part of the nineteenth century, the trend toward republican forms of rule, albeit with limited suffrage and strong elite rule, was well established. However, for most of the twentieth century, the trend toward democracy in the major countries of the region was blunted by a series of countertrends. The most pervasive was the short-circuiting of democratic rule by powerful leaders, both civilian and military. Mexico is a good example of this pattern. After initial flirtation with monarchical rule in the 1820s, republicanism flourished in the middle of the nineteenth century under Benito Juárez as a system was established with limited suffrage and regular elections. However, in the late 1870s, this trend was blocked by the emergence of a classic *caudillo*, Porfirio Díaz, who gained power by legitimate electoral means only

Anti-Vicente Fox demonstration, Mexico City, 2000 election. *(Photo by Patrice Olsen)*

to terminate the process and be continuously reelected through fraud and repression. He ruled for over 30 years, being defeated and driven from office in only 1910 by the powerful forces of the Mexican Revolution. After years of turmoil in the wake of the revolution, Mexico returned to a form of democratic rule with a federal republic in the 1930s. However, Mexican democracy was limited over the ensuing decades by a form of populist and corporatist rule that maintained the same political party, the Institutional Revolutionary Party (PRI), in power through a combination of popular mobilization, clientelism, repression, and voting fraud.

However, the Mexican PRI is not the only twentieth-century example of limitations on democracy that have occurred from regimes operating on a populist and corporatist model. Such regimes have mobilized popular support behind the government from the masses, especially the urban dwellers and working class, by attacking the traditional elites and promising significant increases in the standard of living for the majority classes. The classic examples of such regimes are those of Getúlio Vargas in Brazil and Juan Perón in Argentina. It would be unfair to classify these regimes as simply a continuation of the Latin American trend of strong-man rule, although there clearly was an element of that in them. However, they often did operate within an electoral framework and did bring about significant democratic reforms in the areas of social welfare and education. At the same time, limitations on civil liberties and political opposition prevent the placing of such governments completely under the banner of democracy. Venezuelan president Hugo Chávez has managed to mobilize popular support under a strong presidency but has done so by remaining in the general confines of a democratic system. That fact was underscored when he accepted the defeat of a 2007 referendum that would have significantly expanded his power.

Yet, populist or corporatist rule has not been the primary impediment to democratic rule in Latin America in the last 100 years; that has come from the military. In virtually every country of the region, with the exception of the British colonies that became independent in the last 40 years, the military has assumed dictatorial powers, short-circuiting democratic rule for shorter or longer periods of time. The most recent strong intervention of the military into the region's political systems came in the 1960s and 1970s in prominent countries in South America and the almost continual dominance over the last half-century of military regimes in most of Central America (except Costa Rica).

In the late 1950s, many analysts of Latin America were arguing that the era of tyrannical rule was coming to an end. They pointed to long-standing democratic regimes in countries such as Chile and Uruguay and to emerging democracies in Venezuela, Brazil, and Argentina. However, these predictions proved to be short-lived. A military coup in Brazil in 1964 that would begin 21 years of dictatorship started a process that would be repeated in Argentina (1966 and 1976), Peru (1968), Uruguay, and Chile (both 1973). In addition, efforts at achieving political democracy in El Salvador, where the military had ruled for decades, came to an abrupt end in 1972 when the military blocked the election of Christian Democrat José Napoleon Duarte. As the 1970s came to an end, the great majority of Latin American countries were under military dictatorships. The 1980s were dubbed the "lost decade" in Latin America because of dramatic economic declines and rampant social problems. Military rule came to an end throughout the region, in large measure because the military governments had proven themselves incapable of dealing with economic and social woes. In the first years of the twenty-first century, no country in Latin America was under military rule, the last regime falling in Haiti in 1995 under the threat of a U.S. invasion.

It is generally acknowledged that five countries in Latin America stand out for the length and stability of their democratic experiences—Chile, Uruguay, Costa Rica, Colombia, and Venezuela. However, only Costa Rica has not suffered a serious setback or rupture of democratic rule in the period since 1948. What these countries generally have in common is that at some point in their history the economic and political elites found a way to act cooperatively for the purpose of staving off more radical demands for political and economic restructuring. In fact, when democratic rule broke down, as it did in Chile and Uruguay in 1973, it was because the elites came to the conclusion that revolutionary forces could not be contained by constitutional means.

Liberal democratic regimes were established in Uruguay and Chile between 1918 and 1932; Costa Rica established its regime in 1948. Colombia and Venezuela came close to establishing democratic rule in the late 1940s but only fully succeeded a decade later. Peeler argues that the key to the establishment of democracy was an agreement among the competing elites on the process of expanding political participation. He argues by counterexample that the failure to achieve such an agreement in Argentina after Perón's fall in 1955, marked by the continued exclusion of the Peronists, doomed the democratic process in that country.

All five countries conducted elections in the nineteenth century, but these elections were not the principal means of changing governments. Once in power through elections, individuals or parties regularly manipulated the system to maintain themselves in office, often forcing their opponents to turn to force to remove them. If elections were not a sufficient condition for democracy in the nineteenth century, how did that change in these five countries in the twentieth century? Chile may provide the best example. In the nineteenth century, Chile did enjoy a high level of political stability, interrupted only by a civil war in 1891. The basis of the stability was the political domination of an agro-export oligarchy that ruled through a series of limited-suffrage elections. By the 1930s, Chile had developed a clear tripartite system of Liberals, Conservatives, and Radicals. Although some parties would change, this tripartite division has persisted to the present. Key to the system is a center party that often holds the presidency—the Liberal Party until 1912, the Radical Party from 1938 to 1952, and the Christian Democrats from 1958 to 1973 and again from 1990 to 2000.

Chile has had the most openly class-divided politics of any country in the region in the twentieth century. It is argued that the traditional Liberal/Conservative alliance ruled until 1920 and then regained power during Pinochet's military rule. Otherwise, in the twentieth century, the oligarchy has protected its interests not by direct rule of its political party but rather by maneuvering within Chile's tripartite system and using the checks and balances established in the 1925 constitution, which was not fully implemented until 1932. Such checks continue today through the Chilean senate, whose appointed Conservative faction acts as a check on radical action by the governing center–left administration. Various center and center–left governments ruled during the unbroken 41 years of democratic rule between 1932 and 1973. These governments promoted a series of reforms supporting labor union organization and the creation of an extensive social welfare system. However, they never attacked the serious interests of the traditional oligarchy. There were never any actions to enfranchise rural workers or to redistribute rural property. In fact, the traditional landowners actually gained the cooperation of several reform governments in their efforts to directly obstruct the organization of the rural workers. A variety of constitutional means, including 6-year presidential terms with no reelection, a congress chosen on proportional representation, and judges insulated from direct political control, served to deny any sector the possibility of centralizing power and implementing their full agenda. In essence, it was a guarantee for the traditional oligarchy that their fundamental economic power would not be challenged. In return, the oligarchy supported the democratic system and did not turn to the military to defend their interests. The limitation of this system as a guarantor of democracy was demonstrated in 1973 when the oligarchy supported a military coup out of the fear that Popular Unity President Salvador Allende had set in motion political forces that could ultimately lead to the expropriation of their wealth. Democracy was reestablished only in 1990 when the oligarchy was convinced that the radical left was in full retreat and that power could again be placed in a trusted center party, the Christian Democrats, which had successfully mediated class interests prior to Allende's rule. The Chilean example demonstrates that democratic rule in Latin America in the twentieth century has been based on cooperation among elites. Only when the traditional oligarchy has been willing to support democracy have there been long periods of rule without military intervention to protect their wealth and property. This also suggests the importance of the idea of **"pacted democracy,"** whereby the political elites make varied agreements to share power or alternate rule for a given period, and thus discourage and exclude new political leaders or political movements from challenging their power. Whether this pattern will persist in the twenty-first century remains to be seen.

Political Actors

Powerful actors dominate the political game in Latin America. We would agree with the definition of these players offered by Gary Wynia: "any individual or group that tries to gain public office or influence those who do." In Latin America, as elsewhere in the world, the list of such actors is a long one—landowners, businesspeople, peasants, industrial workers, civil servants, and military officers, to name just a few. However, these labels are not sufficient to fully understand the different groups or their interaction. It is important to analyze each and to ascertain the role of each within the Latin American context. Wynia also makes some important observations about Latin American politics in comparison to other parts of the world. For instance, he notes that Latin America's political systems are not replicas of those in North America and Western Europe. They have more varied rules, and there is often not as much consensus among the political actors. Further, many interest groups are not as strong or well financed as in the United States or Europe.

We have previously discussed individual actors like dictators and the strong president; next, we turn to groups. Looking at each group, we need to ask, Who are the people involved, and from what social class, region, or ethnic group do they come? It is also necessary to ask what, if anything, they want from the political process and when and how they hope to get it. We must also realize that there may be groups that largely wish to be left alone by the political process. However, by and large we will focus on groups that seek to utilize the political process to their advantage. Another important variable to be studied is the resources that are available to each group—those that can be utilized to influence the political process. Resources can range from sheer numbers and the ability to mobilize them, organizational cohesion, and dedication to wealth and strategic presence in the economy to the capacity to engage in violent activity.

TRADITIONAL LARGE LANDOWNERS: *LATIFUNDISTAS*

In all of the countries of Latin America, with the exception of Costa Rica and Paraguay, the Spanish and Portuguese monarchies granted lands to a group of landowners during colonialization. Initially, the monarchies had primarily been interested in the extraction of gold and silver from the Americas, but as time passed the grant of royal lands for the cultivation of foodstuffs became more the norm for their penetration into the new world. These plantations took on some of the forms of the feudalism of medieval Europe. The local populations were forced to work on the land as virtual slaves. The workers were not paid in wages but rather lived on the *latifundio*, *hacienda*, or *fazenda* and were given a small piece of land to grow their own food in return for their free labor on the *patrón's* land. The *hacendados* and *fazendeiros* came to be the dominant class of the colonial period, both politically and economically. They were generally not interested in any significant involvement in the central national government or the distant monarchy in Lisbon or Madrid. All that they needed was the loyalty of local politicians and a local police force that could be called in case of worker unrest.

At the time of independence early in the nineteenth century, this group, made up of *criollo* descendants of the early European settlers, eventually took the lead in breaking ties with Spain and Portugal, taking advantage of the relative weakness of those governments at the time. In the years since independence, this once-dominant class has seen its political and economic power eroded throughout the region. In countries such as Mexico, Bolivia, and Cuba, dramatic twentieth-century revolutions almost eliminated this class altogether. In most countries, over the last century, the large landowners slowly lost political power to the emerging commercial farmers and industrial elites. Beginning in the latter part of the nineteenth century, land ownership and cultivation practices began to change, bringing forward a new class of commercial entrepreneurs who ran their landowning operations as businesses. In some instances, the traditional large landowners transformed themselves into commercial farmers; but in the majority of cases, their lands were eroded by land reform and the cultivation of new land by the commercial farmers reduced their political and economic influence. Changes in the rules of politics over time also cut into their power; but as long as dictatorship and military rule prevailed, the playing field favored the elites, especially the traditional landowners. Later, as republican forms of government emerged in the nineteenth century with greater and greater extension of suffrage, the influence of this group began to erode. However, this erosion of influence has been a slow one because of the enormity of the power once held. In countries where the large landholders continued to dominate the economic landscape, such as El Salvador, they have wielded significant political power to the present time. *Fazendeiros* still have tremendous power in much of rural Brazil, as do their commercial counterparts.

Business and Industrial Elites

While it is correct that rural elites held a dominant position politically and economically in most of Latin America well into the twentieth century, wealth has never been monopolized by them. Beginning in colonial times, businesspeople who engaged in a wide range of commercial enterprises, from trading to banking, have been a part of the political scene. The turning point for the industrial elites came with the Great Depression of 1929. The Depression devastated the region economically, but it also opened the door to entrepreneurs producing goods that were no longer being supplied by depressed European economies. Many of the emerging entrepreneurs in countries like Brazil, Argentina, and Venezuela were new immigrants who generated considerable wealth within one generation. In these large countries, the manufacturing sector began to grow and eventually contributed a greater share of national wealth than agriculture did. The process of becoming more economically independent from Europe was further enhanced by the isolation generated by World War II. As their contribution to national wealth grew, industrial entrepreneurs sought and gained important concessions from the national governments. Unlike the rural elites, who largely favored the import of foreign finished goods without any significant tariff protection, the burgeoning industrialists sought to have their growing industries protected from foreign competition. In addition to government subsidies, the industrial entrepreneurs sought government support for the subordination of organized labor. For obvious reasons, the entrepreneurs generally did not want the interference with their management prerogatives or profits that labor unions generally attempt. Industrialists have had only mixed success in this arena. While military dictatorships like those in Chile, Brazil, and Argentina in the 1970s and 1980s repressed the labor movement, other governments have been less willing to blunt the power of the unions because of their ability to deliver votes, engage in demonstrations, and disrupt the economy.

All members of the business elite do not have the same economic interests or policy agendas. Some elements of the commercial elite have been more engaged in buying and selling traditional primary goods and importing and distributing finished goods. Their interest in import substitution industrialization (ISI) was thus muted. Further, smaller national industries and banks were often at odds with those interests that allied themselves with multinational corporations (MNCs) engaging in manufacturing and finance. The specific financial interests of each group defined their political position. Such elites, since they are few in number, generally did not seek to influence the government through the traditional political process; rather, they served on government boards and commissions or appealed directly to government officials. In many instances, these entrepreneurs sought to bribe government officials for favors for their individual firms. Such bribes were often an accepted part of the political process; however, when such payments came to light, as in Brazil in the 1990s, officials were indicted or forced to resign, as was the case with President Fernando Collor de Mello. Industrialists also sought and gained such overt favoritism as easy credit, export subsidies, and government purchase of only domestically produced manufactured goods. Although some businesspeople espoused the ideology of free trade, very few were actually prepared to go without government subsidies. Until the 1980s this protectionist mantra generated by the ISI model was largely accepted without question by the governments of the large countries of the region—Mexico, Brazil, and Argentina. This perspective was bolstered by the ideas of economist Raúl Prebisch and Economic Commission for Latin America (ECLA). However, the revival of the free trade ideology under the banner of neoliberalism resulted in some profound changes. Begun under the Chilean dictatorship of Augusto Pinochet in the 1970s and 1980s, neoliberal ideas took hold in Argentina, Brazil, and elsewhere in the 1990s. As a result, tariff walls have been lowered and government subsidies of industry have been reduced. New competition from North American, Asian, and European entrepreneurs has weakened the economic and political position of many of the local industrial elites or has forced them to become associated with foreign investors. Commercial business elites may be able to adapt to the new sources of supply, but they may also be challenged by foreign chains like Wal-Mart.

THE MIDDLE OR INTERMEDIATE SECTORS

This is an important and pivotal group in the Latin American political scene. We use the term *intermediate sector* to distinguish it from the concept of middle class, which is prominent in the analysis of North America and Europe. Unlike the middle classes in these countries, which gained prominence and stature through economic activity following the Industrial Revolution and industrialization, Latin American intermediate sectors were primarily professional functionaries such as government bureaucrats, doctors, lawyers, shopkeepers, managers, accountants, middle-level military officers, and some teachers. This group has expanded with urbanization and industrialization and is marked by a relatively high level of education and centrality to the functioning of modern society. Their numbers, small until Latin America began to industrialize and urbanize, have grown significantly in recent years. In comparison to the middle classes of Europe and North America, they generally developed less class consciousness and have remained a diverse and fragmented community. Their diversity and specific interests have at times made them forces for change, as was the case with their support for the reformist Radical party in Argentina during the twentieth century. At other times, they have not been a force for societal change, being largely dependent on the landed and industrial elites that dominated. Most sought to emulate the lifestyle and consumption patterns of upper classes rather than to supplant them, and they have definitely been much less entrepreneurial than their counterparts in the north.

The relationship of the intermediate sectors to the political process has been an interesting one. Not surprisingly, what they have demanded from the political system are resources that further the position of their group—government funds for education, industry, and communication infrastructure. They can move into or out of a particular political camp depending on how well they think their goals can be achieved. They have not been universally consistent in their support of any particular form of government. However, in the twentieth century, more often than not the intermediate sectors have been strong supporters of political reform and multiparty democratic systems. In those situations where these movements have come to the fore, they have clearly favored the expansion of the franchise and the development of defined civil liberties. The intermediate sectors can be connected directly to the development and prosperity of such political parties as the Radicals in Argentina and the Colorados in Uruguay. However, their support for democracy has not been unflagging. The Mexican middle sectors have always given strong support to the one-party domination of the PRI, and in the 1960s and 1970s the middle sectors generally supported the military regimes of Chile, Brazil, and Argentina. Generally, they fear radical or revolutionary movements because the success of such movements might herald the end of their hard-won standard of living. They are horrified by the prospect of slipping into the poverty of the masses. Their ambivalence is partially the result of the resources they bring to the table. In most Latin American countries, this sector has not been large enough to act as a definitive voting bloc, although this is changing in some countries. Instead, they bring to the political process their organizing skills and their central position as cogs in the government, industrial, and business/financial bureaucracy. Such positions lead them to be more comfortable in bargaining with the elites than in mobilizing the masses to achieve their political ends.

ORGANIZED LABOR

Labor organizing began in Latin America in the 1890s but had relatively little success in its early years. Much as in the United States, it was hampered by divisions among immigrant workers, who often spoke different languages, and by opposition from government authorities, allied with entrepreneurial elites in their implacable opposition to workers' organizations of any kind. The workers' movement may have seemed even more threatening in Latin America than in the United States as it was led almost entirely by political radicals espousing either socialist or anarchist ideas for the complete reorganization of society and the expropriation of the property of the ruling circles. In Argentina, the labor movement organized hundreds of thousands of workers in response to the abysmal working conditions of the time. However, the strong influence of labor was broken by severe repression early in 1919. Hundreds of workers were killed by the police and the army, and the militant leadership was broken. A similar situation occurred in Brazil during the same time period as socialist and anarchist labor leaders were jailed and deported.

Regionwide there was little successful union organizing in the 1920s. Only in the 1930s did labor begin to become a large enough force in the most industrializing countries to become a significant political factor. During the 1930s, significant labor struggles emerged again in Brazil, Argentina, Colombia, El Salvador, Bolivia, and Venezuela. However, even as labor succeeded in organizing many workplaces, the owners of industry and their representatives in government refused to recognize the legitimacy of their organizations or to grant them a significant political role. One exception was Mexico, where the regime of Lázaro Cárdenas (1934–1940) included the labor movement as part of a wider populist strategy aimed at further transformation of Mexican society in the wake of the 1910 revolution. The labor movement has had significant influence to the present time within the PRI. Argentina is also an interesting case of labor influence. By 1943, Argentine labor had recovered from the earlier repression to organize 500,000 workers into its ranks. After initial attempts by the military to repress the movement, Colonel Juan Perón emerged to harness the power of the labor movement behind his nationalist and populist political program. With the support of the labor movement, Perón easily won the 1946 presidential election despite active opposition by the United States. Perón responded by delivering tangible benefits to Argentina's working class over the following decade in the form of higher wages and significant government spending on health care and education. Perón was removed in a 1955 military coup, but the party he created has retained significant labor union support to the present time. In other countries, unions have been allied with other parties.

In contemporary Latin America, the labor movement has many resources at its disposal. While the labor movement does not represent all of the working class, but rather its aristocracy, in a democratic context it has the ability to mobilize considerable votes for its candidates. Yet, women and racial minorities are often underrepresented in leadership positions (see Table 19). Between elections, organized labor exercises important economic influence through strategic control of industrial enterprises. Strikes in industries such as transportation, banking, and mining can have great leverage in a society. In extraordinary situations, the labor movement can also be a catalyst for a more far-reaching general strike or even an armed insurrection. Most labor unions are organized into national labor federations, like the General Federation of Labor or General Confederation of Labor, and are affiliated with the Communist, Socialist, or Christian Democratic Parties or with strong nationalist parties like the PRI in Mexico or the Peronists in Argentina. A few unions have been

TABLE 19. Women on the Main Executive Boards of Nationwide Unions, Selected Years, 1983–1994

Country	Year	Both Sexes	Women N	Women %	Level	Organization
Argentina	1994	24	0	0	National Directing Council	General Confederation of Labor (CGR)
Bolivia	1994	37	1	2.7	Executive Committee	Central Union of Bolivian Workers (COB)
Brazil*	1991	25	2	8.0	National Executive	Unified Central Union of Workers (CUT)
Chile	1992	59	5	8.5	National Direction	Unitary Central Union of Workers (CUT)
Cuba	1990	17	4	23.5	XVI Congress Secretariat	Central Union of Cuban Workers (CTIC)
Dominican Republic[†]	1991	11	2	18.2	Executive Bureau	Unitary Central Union of Workers (CUT)
Mexico	1991	47	2	4.3	National Direction	Confederation of Mexican Workers (CTM)
Nicaragua[‡]	1993	12	3	25.0	National Direction	National Confederation of Workers (CNT)
Paraguay[§]	1990	15	1	6.7	National Direction	Unified Central Union of Workers (CUT)
Peru[¶]	1983	41	1	2.4	National Direction	General Central Union of Peruvian Workers (CGTP)
Uruguay	1993	17	3	17.6	Executive Secretariat	Intersyndical Plenary of Workers National Convention of Workers (PIT-CNT)
Venezuela	1990	17	1	5.9	Executive Committee	Confederation of Venezuelan Workers (CTV)

*The main trade union.
[†]There are several other trade unions in the country.
[‡]Trade union with the longest history.
[§]Trade union with the most members.
[¶]Corresponding to the strongest trade union.

Source: Social Watch. *The Starting Point,* 1996, p. 41, as cited in *Statistical Abstract of Latin America,* Vol. 38. Los Angeles: UCLA Latin American Center Publications, 2002, table 606, p. 178.

formed with the help of the U.S. American Federation of Labor/Congress of Industrial Organizations (AFL/CIO) and are heavily influenced by the less political U.S. labor model.

Rural Poor

The rural poor have often received considerable attention from scholars, but historically this group has been the most marginalized from political power. First of all, it is necessary to state that this group is not homogeneous and that its role in Latin American society has evolved over time as the result of both land reform programs and economic transformation. The term *campesino* has been used to label those low-income agricultural producers who have some attachment to the land in rural Latin America. *Rural laborers* comprise another group made up of landless agricultural workers. In many ways, the basic conditions of their lives have changed very little over the course of several centuries. The great majority of both groups have lived in dire poverty, barely earning enough for their survival and reproduction, with little chance for advancement. Most people born as *campesinos* or rural laborers died in the same social situation and passed that legacy on to their children and grandchildren. While having common characteristics, it is also important to see the significant differences between various groups of the poor based on their different circumstances of employment.

The first group is known as *colonos*. They work on the large plantations described earlier as the *haciendas* and *fazendas*. Whether they are tenant farmers or sharecroppers, they are all too often bound to the plantation by generations of debt. This group is generally not paid in wages but allowed a small plot of land to grow food for their sustenance and provided the other basic necessities of life by the owner of the plantation in return for labor. In the best of situations, this group can be said to be protected from the greatest uncertainties of harsh rural life by the *patrón*. As one might expect, their political position is especially precarious. Since they are wholly dependent on the *patrón*, they have often been either marginalized from politics or manipulated by the *patrón*'s dictates. In the context of democratic elections, *colonos, campesinos,* or rural laborers can be coerced into voting for the chosen political candidates of the estate owner. Because of its numbers, this group could be a significant political force. However, because they were traditionally isolated from one another on different estates and in different villages, their organizing power was often muted. Organizing efforts were often resisted with force by local owners and their allies among the police and judiciary. Currently, better opportunities for exchange of information and interaction are offered by the expanding modern communication infrastructure, but the forced commercialization of farming is rapidly forcing this group either off the land and into the cities or to become landless rural laborers.

The second important group is the rural wage laborers, who have become increasingly dominant through the economic transformation of Latin America in the twentieth century. These are the workers on Latin America's commercial farms and plantations who are hired first to plant and then later to harvest the region's primary cash export crops: cotton, coffee, sugarcane, and bananas. Many wage laborers may own small plots of land but are forced to sell their labor to supplement their income in order to survive. In many places, they are migrants because they often have to travel great distances to find enough work to survive throughout the year. North Americans are somewhat familiar with this class of Latin Americans because many work each year, both legally and illegally, in the agricultural fields of the United States. Like the *colonos*, this group is largely marginalized from the Latin American political process. The combination of their constant travel and precarious economic situation makes it difficult for them to become involved in politics, either as voters or as protestors; but there are important exceptions. Banana workers in Honduras, Costa Rica, Panama, and Guatemala have been very political at times, with involvement in both elections and protest actions. In recent times, many rural labors have joined the Landless Movement (Movimento dos Trabalhadores Rurais Sem Terra) in Brazil and have begun to exert greater political pressure. Likewise, much of the organizational base of the Zapatistas in Mexico and the Confederation of Indigenous Nationalities of Ecuador (CONAIE) is rural.

The third group are the subsistence farmers, the *minifundistas* and *microfundistas*. As was pointed out earlier, there may be overlap between the last two categories because many subsistence farmers supplement their income with wage labor. The land that they occupy, sometimes with legal title and sometimes as squatters, is usually less than ten acres. The crops are grown largely without mechanization or fertilizers because the use of either is out of the financial reach of the cultivator. In good times, the farmer grows enough for the family to survive and sells a small surplus at a local market. If there is crop failure due to storms or drought, there may not be a surplus and the family is driven toward the wage labor/migrant situation. In difficult economic times, the small farmer is also vulnerable to foreclosure if money is owed. This category of existence is generally preferred to that of wage labor, but it faces pressures from many directions. Proponents of land reform programs have often viewed this group's level of economic production as marginal and inefficient, so they have been targeted for elimination, with the hope that their labor can become available for the more efficient larger farms. Others have argued that giving them more land, irrigation, agricultural credit, and technical assistance would resolve much of rural poverty and increase the efficiency of production.

The rural poor have definite grievances to pursue with the political authorities. The *colonos* generally want the opportunity to improve their own lives and those of their children, usually by gaining the opportunity to work their own land. The wage workers want higher wages but are generally frustrated with the government's unwillingness to help them. Those who own small farms seek credit and technical support from the government and protection from their creditors.

For most of Latin American history, the rural poor were not in a strong position to pursue their grievances, divided as they were by both geography and differing interests. However, the twentieth century has seen a significant change in their political importance. In Mexico and Venezuela, mass political parties succeeded in organizing the rural poor into the political process as voters behind a clear political agenda. They have been even more important in revolutionary movements, playing a key role in such movements in Cuba, Bolivia, El Salvador, Guatemala, Peru, Colombia, and Nicaragua. In addition, the growth of grassroots movements such as the Peasants League and Landless Movement in Brazil (MST) and the peasant unions and other organizations in Bolivia underscore their growing political importance.

THE MILITARY

The armed forces must definitely be treated as a singularly important group in the political history of Latin America, although that prominence needs to be tempered by the fact that as Latin America enters the twenty-first century, for the first time in its modern history, no country is under military rule. Such a situation represents a stark contrast to the 1970s and 1980s, when more than half of the region's governments were military-led. However, a strong process of democratization beginning in the mid-1980s brought civilian governments to power across the region, led by Peru in 1980, Argentina in 1983, Brazil in 1985, and Chile in 1989. Today, the discussion of the role of the military in much of Latin America revolves around its role as a significant bureaucratic interest group. Acceptance of the legitimacy of civilian rule and the subordination of the military to civilian political rule has seemingly become the norm in much of Latin America. Yet, the military still holds veto power in countries such as Guatemala and is still able to operate with impunity in some aspects of civil society. The military remains an active force in contemporary politics, and its current position flows from its long-standing power.

Since World War II and with the strong backing of the government of the United States, Latin American militaries have been competent, professional organizations with considerable modern weaponry. Not surprisingly, the region's largest country, Brazil, has the largest armed forces, with close to 300,000 soldiers in uniform. Brazil spends over $3 billion a year maintaining its forces, which include an aircraft carrier and more than 200 combat aircraft. Other countries that have maintained significant military forces in recent years include Mexico, Argentina, Chile, and Cuba. (Cuba significantly reduced its forces in the 1990s after maintaining close to 50,000 soldiers in Africa, with Soviet help, during the 1970s and 1980s.) Yet, the primary role of most militaries in Latin America has been the maintenance of internal order. However, the size and sophistication of military forces are not in reality the prime determinants of political influence in Latin America or elsewhere. Throughout the twentieth century, the U.S. and British militaries have been powerful forces but have never challenged control by civilian authority. In contrast, relatively weak and small military establishments in Latin America have usurped civilian authority and sought to dominate the political process.

The involvement of the Latin American military in politics has its roots in the military nature of the conquest and early settlement, the class character of the military families throughout the course of Latin American history, and other factors. Over the course of Spanish and Portuguese colonial rule, the military officer corps were deeply intertwined with political rulers and the landowning elites. They were often one and the same as leading military people also controlled large tracts of land. If the military leaders did not happen in a given instance to own significant land, they acted as an important ally against any forces that sought to challenge the landed oligarchy. As a result, the military entered the age of democratic reforms in the twentieth century in a position deeply suspicious of forces that would have curtailed the political and economic power of the old political and economic elites through democratic political means. With few exceptions, the political stance of the military as an enemy of democracy and reform was well established entering the twentieth century. Understanding the military in the twentieth century and especially in the last 50 years becomes a more complex problem. During that time the class character of military officers has changed considerably as fewer of the children of the military continued the family tradition and as the modern, more professional militaries often became an important avenue of social mobility for those who aspired to become members of the middle class or to improve their relative standing in it.

The education system for military officers has long been an important determinant of their orientation toward politics. Military leaders have maintained their system of officer corps education independent of and isolated from the civilian education system. Traditionally, most military education focuses on technical warfare training with little time devoted to the humanities or the social sciences. The Centro de Altos Estudios Militares (CAEM) in Peru, which trained the Nasserite military officers who formed the reformist government of Juan Velasco Alvarado (1968–1975), is an exception; likewise, the training at the National War College (Escola Superior de Guerra) of Brazil viewed strategy as involving some degree of social involvement. Yet, in all military schools, to the degree that matters of history and society are treated, the ideological content very often views the military as the only institution of society that is unambiguously dedicated to the nation's welfare. All civilian politicians are treated with some suspicion, especially those of a center or left persuasion. However, certain interest groups, especially labor unions, are viewed as detrimental to the national interest. At least until recently, there has been little or no shift in this approach to education, which has definitely contributed to the military's willingness to carry out coups against civilian governments.

If military education has provided an ideological justification for certain forms of military intervention, then their disciplined and hierarchical forms of organization provided both the ability to carry out the overthrow of civilian governments and the ability to place themselves at the head of government bureaucracies previously headed by civilians. Military leaders in the 1960s and 1970s in countries such as Brazil argued that their hierarchical forms of organization could bring new levels of efficiency to government bureaucracies previously plagued by bad organization and chaos. This type of military government came to be termed *bureaucratic authoritarianism*. In general, claims that the military could be more effective rulers than civilians proved untrue and contributed to the downfall of military governments in the latter part of the 1980s. It is unclear just how readily the military can exercise its power in the current democratized period in Latin America. Yet, they still have the power to replace a government if they choose to mobilize.

GOVERNMENT BUREAUCRATS

Some have suggested that government bureaucrats should not be treated as distinct and separate actors within the Latin American political process because they simply carry out the wishes of whatever political leaders are in power. However, this view is insufficient for Latin America or most any other region of the world. The key factor in understanding the significant power of government bureaucrats is that while elected politicians serve distinct terms and military leaders can be driven from power at any time, the great majority of bureaucrats stay in their positions for lengthy time periods. In Latin America, government bureaucrats have wielded considerable power because of the post–World War II trend of large-scale government involvement in the ownership of important economic enterprises—banks, airlines, oil refineries, railroads, steel plantations, and many more—leading to the emergence of the nation of "technocrats" who played important political roles, particularly during the authoritarian periods in the 1960s and 1970s, in countries like Brazil, Argentina, Chile, and Uruguay. Privatizations within the last decade have reduced the government's role in countries like Argentina and Brazil, but public ownership remains formidable. A recent acknowledgment of the power of one segment of bureaucracy came in Venezuela where in 1999 elected populist President Hugo Chávez spoke of the need to trim the size of the giant bureaucracy of the state-run oil company PDVSA (Petróleos de Venezuela). Chávez acknowledged the power of its bureaucracy, calling it a "government within a government." Other presidents have talked of reducing the size of the bureaucracy at all levels.

This sector has engaged in a significant amount of self-promotion to boost its importance. In contrast to military officers, who stake their right to political office on their duty to country and their organizational skill, government bureaucrats advertise their skill as technocrats who can rise above the squabbling or corruption that may plague elected leaders. Increasingly, many Latin American technocrats are trained at foreign universities in Britain, France, and the United States. Oftentimes they return to their homelands with strong beliefs that their newfound technical skills have given them the right to a say in the political and economic direction of their nation, not just as administrators. In Mexico, the previous four presidents came from the ranks of these *técnicos*.

Government bureaucrats, like those in other sectors, may well be motivated by selfless and patriotic concerns; but those who manage government institutions share many interests. First, they desire to continue their influence over public policy. Second, they seek to administer their agencies with as little interference as possible. Third, they enjoy the power and, in some instances, the wealth that comes from providing goods and services that those in the private sector need.

The means to achieve these ends are fairly well known. The reality is that elected officials are dependent on administrators to carry out their economic and political development plans. If an administrator disagrees with a particular policy initiative, he or she definitely has the ability to sabotage its implementation. While such sabotage may need to be subtle to succeed, the elected officials usually lack the legal authority to remove recalcitrant officials from their posts. It is not yet clear whether the trend toward smaller government bureaucracies promoted by neoliberal reformers in the 1990s will significantly reduce the power of this sector. Ultimately, the sector may well turn out to be an insurmountable barrier to the full implementation of privatization plans or other government reforms. Likewise, oversized bureaucracies have become a fiscal problem that fuels inflation.

POLITICAL PARTIES

The role of political parties is evolving in Latin America. Wynia argues that political parties have traditionally played at least three separate and distinct roles in Latin American society. Like political parties in the United States and Western Europe, they participate in elections with the aim of gaining state power. In a few countries, like Costa Rica and Venezuela, political parties have played this role for decades, almost exclusively concentrating their energies on winning periodic contests for power. In countries where elections have been the norm, Ronald McDonald and J. Mark Rubl argue that parties tend to serve four functions: political recruitment, political communication, social control, and government organization and policy making. However, until the 1990s this role was sporadic in many countries, either because there were no elections, only military rule, or because their role was limited by the lack of constitutional norms. Beyond elections, there are two other roles for political parties, that of conspirators and the creation of political monopoly.

The category of conspirator describes those parties that do not accept the results of elections or operate in the absence of regular elections. These parties generally operate in the extraparliamentary arena, often turning to the use of force to gain power. Such parties could be coming from a variety of political positions, but most often they are movements that have been denied power through legitimate channels and turn to armed struggle to achieve their goals. Classic examples of this form of political activity occurred in Cuba, when activists in the Orthodox Party, denied the opportunity of gaining power through the 1952 elections because of Fulgencio Batista's cancellation of those elections, formed an armed organization (the 26th of July Movement) that challenged Batista and eventually defeated him.

Parties creating a political monopoly are those that seek to remain in power on a permanent basis. Latin America has two excellent contemporary examples of this type of political movement, the Cuban Communist Party (CCP) and the Mexican PRI. Both have been very successful in their efforts but have used different methods. The Cuban communists have succeeded in part through the establishment of formal rules of the game whereby the constitution enshrines the CCP as the country's only legal party, through its legitimacy as the party of the 1959 revolution, and through its social achievements. The PRI dominated the Mexican political scene for over 70 years, keeping the presidency up to the year 2000, when it finally suffered its first defeat in a presidential election. The party constructed a system where opposition parties competed for power but were limited in their real opportunities for victory by a series of PRI policies, including patronage, co-optation, voter fraud, and occasionally repression. Both movements were born in revolutionary conflict and maintained power in part by presenting themselves as the party of the revolution and as the only political force capable of moving forward the ideals of their revolutions. The success of such movements is not easy and is usually dependent on some measure of popular support together with the support of the military, although in both Mexico and Cuba the military remained subordinated to civilian politics and heavily influenced by the dominant party.

Latin American political parties emerged in the nineteenth century when most of the region's nations adopted republican forms of government with limited suffrage. Two primary political currents emerged during this time period, the Liberals and the Conservatives. The latter were drawn primarily from the traditional rural elites of the *latifundio* system, who primarily sought from the government a preservation of the economic and political patterns that were established during the colonial period. The Liberals represented the emerging modern upper classes of the nineteenth century, the owners of commercial agriculture and other newly founded activities. The Liberals wanted the government to undertake a more active role in breaking up traditional landowning patterns, separating church from state, and promoting foreign commerce. Latin American liberals were not as committed to the political side of liberalism with its emphasis on constitutional rule and freedom of thought. Elections in Latin America were largely an elite matter throughout the nineteenth century, involving only about 5 percent of the adult male population. These parties engaged in electoral contests but also were often the basis for armed conflict as both sides often refused to recognize the results and turned to violence to achieve their political ends.

Representative of elite dominance and patriarchy, women and minorities still struggle for adequate representation in party leadership positions (see Table 20). Internal decision making is frequently authoritarian and often based on *personalismo*.

TABLE 20. Women in National Directive Bodies of Selected Political Parties, Selected Years, 1990–1994

Country	Year	Party	Both Sexes	Women N	Women %
Argentina	1990	Radical Civic Union	24	0	0
Bolivia	1991	Movement of the Revolutionary Left	9	1	11.1
		Free Bolivian Movement	16	1	6.3
		National Democratic Action	13	2	15.4
Brazil	1991	Workers' Party	82	5	6.1
		Liberal Front	121	2	1.7
		Social Democratic Party	121	2	1.7
		Labor Democrats	119	11	9.2
		Brazilian Democratic Movement	121	4	3.3
		Brazilian Social Democratic Party	121	8	6.6
Chile	1991	Christian Democratic Party	40	5	12.5
		Socialist Party	19	4	21.1
		Party for Democracy	20	5	25
		Independent Democratic Union	26	2	7.7
		National Renovation	15	2	13.3
Colombia	1993	Liberal Party	3	1	33.3
		Democratic Alliance, M-19	5	1	20
Costa Rica	1990	Christian Social Unity	17	1	5.9
		National Liberation	25	3	12
Cuba	1991	Cuban Communist Party	25	3	12
Dominican Republic	1993	Christian Social Reform Party	39	10	25.6
		Dominican Revolutionary Party	297	30	10.1
		Dominican Communist Party	22	1	4.5
		Dominican Workers' Party	27	1	3.7
El Salvador	1993	ARENA	15	1	6.7
		Christian Democratic Party	40	3	7.5
		National Democratic Union	10	4	40
		National Revolutionary Movement	9	1	11.1
		Farabundo Martí Front for National Liberation	50	7	14
Mexico	1992	Institutional Revolutionary Party	34	4	11.8
		National Action Party	28	5	17.9
		Democratic Revolution Party	32	7	21.9
Nicaragua*	1994	Sandinista National Liberation Front	27	6	22.2
		Social Christian Party	58	12	20.7
		Liberal Independent Party	121	20	16.5
		Communist Party of Nicaragua	103	15	14.6

(continued)

TABLE 20. Women in National Directive Bodies of Selected Political Parties, Selected Years, 1990–1994 *Continued*

Country	Year	Party	Both Sexes	Women N	%
Panama	1991	Christian Democratic Party	4	1	25
		Authentic Liberal Party	14	0	0
		National Republican Liberal Movement	31	4	12.9
		Panamanian Party	9	1	11.1
		Labor Party	5	0	0
		Democratic Revolution Party	5	0	0
Paraguay	1994	National Republican Association	72	6	8.3
		Radical Authentic Liberal Party	46	5	11.1
		Febrerista Revolutionary Party	30	6	20
		National Encounter	38	5	13.2
Peru	1990	Peruvian Aprista Party	4	1	25
		United Left	6	0	0
		National Front of Rural Workers	20	3	15
		Change 90 Now Majority	5	0	0
Venezuela	1992	Democratic Action	33	7	21.2
		Christian Social Party	35	3	8.6
		Socialist Movement	34	4	11.8

*Regional Directive Council.

Source: Social Watch. *The Starting Point*, 1996, p. 40, as cited in *Statistical Abstract of Latin America*, Vol. 38. Los Angeles: UCLA Latin American Center Publications, 2002, table 605, p. 177.

Traditional Parties. As pressure for increased suffrage succeeded in widening the electoral base and new immigrant groups swelled the Latin American population in the early part of the twentieth century, two distinct patterns of political party loyalty developed: the **Liberals and the Conservatives**. They have persisted to the present day. In some countries, Colombia and Honduras being the best examples, the Liberal and Conservative Parties, despite being elite-driven, succeeded in gaining electoral support from the newly enfranchised rural and urban masses. The liberals stood for political and economic liberalism (thus greater political rights and the curtailment of church power on the one hand and free trade and free markets on the other). The conservatives stood for official religion, centralized government, and state-regulated trade and commerce. This political division basically continued throughout the twentieth century, leaving these countries with essentially two-party systems unchanged over time. The Liberals and Conservatives who succeeded in transforming themselves did so by a variety of means. *Hacienda*-owning Conservatives, using the strong bonds of the patron–client relationship, have often been able to secure the support of their *colonos* through a combination of reward and punishment. Wage-paying commercial farmers associated with the Liberals may not have had as direct control of their employees, but many did succeed in convincing rural workers that their self-interest lay with support for the Liberal cause. Both parties succeeded in gaining strong familial loyalty to their movements, a connection that has now been passed on through multiple generations.

TABLE 21. Participation of Women in Government, 1994

Country	Ministers	Under-Secretaries	Provincial or Departmental Governors	Local Officers	Senators	Deputies	Single-House Congress	Supreme Court	Court of Appeals	Judges
Argentina	0.0	9.8	0.0	3.6	4.2	13.2	—	0.0	15.3	29.9
Bolivia	0.0	5.4	—	10	3.7	7.7	—	0.0	—	—
Brazil	3.7	—	3.7	2.4	6.2	7.4	—	0.0	—	—
Chile	14.3	7.1	9.8	7.2	6.4	7.5	—	0.0	20.2	45.8
Colombia	13.3	13	3.7	5.6	4.9	11.5	—	0.0	7.7	49.3
Costa Rica	9.5	26.3	71.4	0.0	—	—	15.8	9.1	30.1	45.7
Cuba	2.6	9.4	0.0	5.3	—	—	22.8	39.3	14.3	43.8
Dominican Republic	14.3	12.9	28	4.9	0.0	11.7	—	0.0	30.7	35.4
Ecuador	0.0	7.9	11.1	3.1	—	—	5.6	0.0	4.0	11.7
El Salvador	10	8.8	—	11.1	—	—	10.7	13.3	0	14.7
Guatemala	23.1	12.5	—	1.2	—	—	7.5	11.1	11.5	11.7
Honduras	7.7	29.4	11.1	12.7	—	—	7	11.1	11.1	63.5
Mexico	17.6	—	3.2	2.9	11.8	13.8	18.5	19.2	1.5	34.7
Nicaragua	10	10.3	—	9.8	—	—	9	11.1	25	46.2
Panama	16.7	0	22.2	9	—	—	—	22.2	26.3	40.7
Paraguay	9.1	8.3	0	4.9	11.1	2.5	—	0	9	12.8
Peru	13.3	20	—	6.2	6.7	5.6	—	8.3	20.1	17.5
Uruguay	7.7	7.7	0	15.8	6.5	7.1	—	0	16.3	52.8
Venezuela	8.3	0	4.5	6.3	6.1	6.5	—	26.7	30	53

Source: Social Watch. *The Starting Point;* 1996, p. 24, as cited in *Statistical Abstract of Latin America,* Vol. 35. Los Angeles: UCLA Latin American Center Publications, 1999.

However, the cases where Liberals and Conservatives succeeded in transforming themselves into broad-based electoral machines were the exception. In some cases, such as in Chile, Liberals and Conservatives were forced to unite (Chile's National Party) to be able to confront new challenges to elite domination. In the majority of countries, the traditional parties rebuffed the demands of the newly emergent groups with the result that new, **European-inspired political parties** emerged on the scene after 1900. The most interesting were the Chilean Radical Party, the Argentine Radical Civic Union, and the Uruguayan Colorado Party. Modeled after the French Radical Party, these movements stood for suffrage, expanding public education and other government services, and the protection of workers' rights from the power of oligarchies, both urban and rural. Radical politicians succeeded in getting themselves elected in all three countries, drawing primarily on an immigrant and urban constituency, including the emerging proletariat and intermediate (middle) sectors. The Radicals generally did greater damage to the Liberals, who in some ways had attempted to appeal to the same constituency. As the Radicals eclipsed the Liberals, in some countries it turned the primary electoral battlefield into one of Radicals against Conservatives. In some instances, the elite former supporters of the Liberals turned to the Conservatives to form an oligarchic alliance. The heyday of the Radicals was relatively short-lived, although the Argentine party has undergone a rebirth in the last 15 years. The Radical parties faced increased pressure in the 1930s and, unable to deal with the economic challenges of the Great Depression, either were overthrown by the military representing the traditional oligarchy or faced increasing pressure from both populist and socialist movements. They are still important political actors in Argentina and Chile, and the Colorados won the presidential election in 2000 in Uruguay. The Liberals have remained relatively strong in Colombia.

Nationalist Populist Parties. The 1930s and 1940s saw the emergence of populist parties in both Brazil and Argentina. Each was organized around a single charismatic leader, Getúlio Vargas in Brazil and Juan Perón in Argentina. The populist movement founded by Vargas did not outlive him, but a Peronist Party still plays an influential role in Argentine politics to this day. It is important to understand that the roots of Latin American populism were clearly different from those in the United States, where the movement was primarily a rural-based protest against the railroad monopolies. The success of Latin American populists in the 1930s and 1940s was with the growing urban industrial working class, whose needs were largely ignored by the dominant parties of the time—Conservatives, Liberals, and Radicals. Unlike the other political parties discussed here, the populists are harder to pin down as the movements were uniquely shaped by their leaders. As movements, they did not concentrate as much as the other parties on building organizational entities. Instead, they depended on the mobilizing power of the leaders themselves and, in the case of Perón, on his popular spouse, Eva. To underscore the centrality of personal rule, Vargas did not launch his populist movement's political party until he had been in power for almost 15 years.

The heterogeneous political philosophy of the populists concentrated its attacks on the old order, the traditional *latifundistas,* but also on the commercial elites that had come to the fore in the beginning of the century. The populists were not revolutionaries; rather, their philosophy was to gain a greater share of the national wealth for their supporters within the framework of capitalism. It was also a nationalistic philosophy that sought to achieve national development without significant involvement of foreign investors, a stance that angered the foreign powers who had long dominated the region and those who had hoped to capitalize on the new opportunities. They were also supporters of rapid industrialization and state intervention in the economy.

The populists saw themselves as the archenemies of the Socialist and Communist Parties that were seeking to appeal to the same constituency—urban industrial workers. However, unlike the Conservatives and Liberals, the populists believed that it was possible to defeat the prospect of revolution by creating government-sponsored worker organizations, which could yield worker discipline in return for better wages and working conditions.

Even before creating a populist movement, Vargas had linked Latin American populism with European fascism through his concept of the *Estado Novo* (new state), a corporatist idea that combined strong government involvement in economic activities with the organization of workers into government-controlled unions. In the case of Brazil, the *Estado Novo* meant a centralizing of political power against the interests of regional authorities who dominated the country's politics prior to 1930. Vargas organized the Brazilian Labor Party in 1945 as a mass organization when his opponents in the traditional oligarchy tried to drive him from power. The Labor Party proved to be an effective vehicle for Vargas, winning the presidency for him in both 1945 and 1950. However, his role as a ruler who sought to mediate the diverse interests of Brazilian society was a failure. Vargas was hounded into suicide in 1954 by his political enemies, especially the military. Successors of Vargas, such as Juscelino Kubitschek, sought to continue elements of the populist program; but the Brazilian Labor Party did not succeed in becoming a permanent feature of political life.

The populism of Juan Perón in Argentina had many similarities to that of Vargas, but there were also some differences. Perón also incorporated elements of Italian fascism, but, unlike Vargas, who first gained power and then later created a movement to sustain his power, Perón gained power through the transformation of the Argentine General Labor Confederation into his personal instrument and the incorporation of conservative, radical, and socialist groups into his political movement. When the military and the traditional oligarchy sought to block his ascendancy to the presidency by arresting him, Perón and his future wife, Eva, mobilized his forces to gain his release and pave the way for his victory in the 1946 presidential election. In power, Perón's strategy was similar to that of Vargas. He implemented programs that delivered social services and a higher standard of living to the urban workers while guaranteeing entrepreneurs labor peace through tight control of the unions. Like Vargas, his rule took on strongly nationalist tones, and policies of economic protectionism were implemented. The government took a strong hold on the economy, the most dramatic example being the creation of a government monopoly over agricultural commodity trading, a strategy that captured the considerable profits of this section entirely for the government. He also nationalized the railroads, airlines, public utilities, and financial system, among other strategic sectors. In typical populist fashion, Perón did not move in any way to redistribute rural land as a revolutionary would have done but, rather, to simply bring the rural elites under government control. Perón used the profits from this scheme to finance industrialization, social welfare programs, and the takeover of the country's utilities from foreign owners. Once the Peronist economic strategy began to fail in the early 1950s, Perón fell victim to the power of the old elites, who engineered a military coup in 1955 and sent him into exile.

However, unlike the populist movement of Vargas that largely ended when he fell from power, the Peronist Party remained strong, in part inspired by its leader in exile in Spain. Fearing their power, the military prevented the Peronists from competing in elections or nullified the results if they favored the Peronists throughout the 18 years of his exile. Only in 1973 did the military allow a Peronist candidate to run for president and Perón to return in a desperate attempt to stem a growing revolutionary tide. His party swept the elections of 1973, only to have him die a year later. The party continued under the leadership of Perón's third wife, Isabel, but the military ended that rule with a coup in 1976 and 7 years of subsequent dictatorial rule. However, the Peronist Party, retaining its working-class base and nostalgia for the golden days of the late 1940s and early 1950s, succeeded in winning back control of the political system in both 1989 and 1995 under the leadership of Carlos Menem. Ironically, Menem shifted the ideology of the party almost completely away from that of its founder, embracing widespread privatization, free markets, and large-scale foreign investment. As a result, other political movements began to erode the electoral base of the Peronists, calling into question their influence into the next century. Returning to its populist roots, the Peronists successfully ran Nestor Kirchner for the presidency in 2003. It has also been suggested that Alberto Fujimori represented a new type of right-wing populism in Peru. Likewise, some see Hugo Chávez as representative of a type of leftist nationalist populism that has come to dominate politics in Venezuela.

Reform Parties. Another type of political party that emerged during the same era as the populists was the democratic reform parties. Basically there are two types of reform party, secular and religious. The traits that they shared were based on a rejection of both the populists and the revolutionaries. The democratic reformers did not accept the tendency toward demagoguery and the use of strong-arm tactics against political opponents but did embrace the populist strategy of maintaining capitalist, free enterprise systems. The democratic reformers, while sharing some of the short-term desires for social justice with the Socialist and Communist Parties, obviously broke with them over the vision of a classless socialist society.

APRA Parties. The secular reform movement began with the American Popular Revolutionary Alliance (**APRA**), founded by Peruvian Victor Raúl Haya de la Torre while he was in Mexico in 1924. The party was inspired by a range of political ideas, including socialism, indigenism and anti-imperialism and was more radical in its early years. The charismatic Haya de la Torre led the party through the 1970s. Long persecuted and marginalized in Peruvian politics, APRA only achieved government power under Alan García for a brief period in the 1980s and again in 2006. The return to power has rejuvenated the party considerably. However, similar political movements inspired by Haya de la Torre in Venezuela and Costa Rica have enjoyed considerable long-term success. The Democratic Action Party (AD) of Venezuela first governed in the late 1940s and held the presidency of the country for most of the 40 years prior to the rise of Hugo Chávez. The National Liberation Party of Costa Rica has held the presidency of that country five times since its founding at the time of the Costa Rican civil war in 1948. Similar parties developed in Bolivia (MNR), the Dominican Republic (Partido Revolucionario), and Puerto Rico (Popular Democratic Party).

Christian Democratic Parties. Religious reformers are grouped in the Christian Democratic movement, which originated in Western Europe after World War II. Drawing heavily on Catholic thought, the Christian Democratic parties emerged as alternatives to the powerful Communist, Socialist, and Labor parties. The rise of Christian Democrats was especially important in Germany and Italy, where earlier procapitalist parties had been irredeemably tainted by their association with fascism. In the Latin American context, these parties emerged in countries where populism never took significant hold and as an alternative to the revolutionary parties. Latin American Christian Democrats came to embody very similar political programs to the secular reformists, embracing political democracy in opposition to military rule and a package of reform proposals, especially in the agrarian sector. In contrast to the secular parties, they drew their inspiration from progressive papal encyclicals and reform movements within the Church. Christian Democrats sought to organize throughout the region but ultimately have achieved full success only in Chile and Costa Rica and limited success in Venezuela and El Salvador. In Chile, the Christian Democrats first gained power in the 1960s as a middle ground between the Conservatives and the Socialist/Communist coalition that became Popular Unity (UP). Defeated by the latter in 1970 and then driven underground by the 1973 military coup, the Christian Democrats emerged in a postmilitary period in 1989 as the country's leading political force in association with the moderate socialists. The party won reelection in 1993 and is positioned for long-term influence with its centrist reform-oriented policies and Chile's relative economic stability. Christian Democratic parties elsewhere have been less successful. Only in two other countries have they enjoyed political power—two presidential terms in Venezuela in the 1970s (Social Christian Party, COPEI) and brief rule in El Salvador in the 1980s under José Napoleon Duarte at the height of the civil war as the recipient of considerable U.S. economic and military aid.

Left Reform Parties. A contemporary reform party that clearly bridges the religious and secular boundaries is the Brazilian Workers' Party (PT). The **PT** emerged in the late 1970s during the growth of opposition to the military dictatorship. From the beginning, the PT had both Marxist and Catholic leadership, the latter being drawn from the powerful ecclesial base communities. The most popular leader was the leader of the resurgent metalworkers union, Luiz Inácio da Silva, known simply as "Lula." The PT grew in strength rapidly despite many obstacles thrown in its way, including the jailing of Lula in 1981. With the return of electoral democracy in 1985, the PT established itself as a primary opposition party, supplanting older, more established left parties. In November 1988, the PT's Luiza Erundina de Souza was elected mayor of São Paulo, Brazil's largest city. The party also demonstrated its mobilization powers through massive industrial strikes in 1988 and 1989. In the

1989 presidential elections, Lula nearly won the presidency in a runoff election against Fernando Collor de Mello, whose well-financed campaign defeated the PT leader by a scant 6 percent. The PT, seeking a more centrist image, voted at its 1991 convention to affirm its commitment to a mixed economy and democracy while retaining socialist ideals. Delegates representing the party's 600,000 members also voted to grant women a minimum of 30 percent of leadership positions. Initially favored in the polls leading up to the 1994 elections, Lula eventually finished a distant second to the well-funded campaign of centrist Fernando Henrique Cardoso. He was defeated again when Cardoso was reelected in 1999. After moving toward the center and reassuring business interests, Lula finally won the presidency in 2002 and was easily reelected in 2006. The PT has succeeded in becoming the government party but does not hold a congressional majority. Similarly, the Revolutionary Democratic Party (**PRD**) in Mexico is also representative of this new brand of leftist party, as is the Frente Amplio in Uruguay, which won the presidency and a congressional majority in the 2004 elections.

Revolutionary Parties. The final group of parties to be discussed are the revolutionary parties. Revolutionary movements are discussed in far more detail in Chapter 10, but it is necessary to briefly discuss the revolutionary parties in the wider context of other political parties. Two different types of revolutionary party are usually acknowledged in the Latin American context, those whose origins are in Marxist thought and those whose roots are elsewhere. However, it is also necessary to note that not all parties that begin their existence as revolutionary ones remain so. We must also discuss in this context those original revolutionary parties that have become thoroughly reformist in their behavior.

Communist and socialist parties had their roots in the ideas and political activities of Karl Marx and Friedrich Engels in the last few decades of the nineteenth century in Europe. Initially, the Marxist movement was united, but the 1917 October Revolution in Russia was a turning point. Most European socialist parties had abandoned the possibility of revolution in favor of the achievement of socialism by parliamentary means, but the success of the first socialist revolution in Russia under the leadership of the Bolshevik Party inspired the creation of an alternative set of revolutionary parties, called "communist," that accepted the international leadership of the Soviet Union. Because Latin America industrialized considerably after Europe, the development of socialist or revolutionary parties along Marxist lines was slow to occur. However, during the 1920s and 1930s, these parties did begin to emerge, largely among intellectuals, students, and industrial workers. Overall, these parties did not fare particularly well in the region as they faced wholesale repression from the established governments and fierce competition to organize workers from both the Radicals and the populists. The primary exception was in Chile, where the Marxist parties succeeded in gaining a large following in the working class and entry into coalition governments during the 1930s.

By the 1950s the Socialist and Communist Parties had largely ceased to be revolutionary in orientation. Where possible, in countries such as Guatemala, they sought to work through the political process, working with non-Marxist reform parties to obtain programs for workers' rights and land reform. However, the conservatism of these Communist parties only served to open political space to their left, which was soon filled by a new generation of revolutionary parties inspired by the success of the 26th of July Movement in Cuba. Basing themselves on Marxist ideology and co-opting the old, reformist Cuban Communist Party, movement leaders were soon at the head of a new generation of revolutionary parties that came to include the Sandinista National Liberation Front (FSLN) in Nicaragua, the Farabundo Martí National Liberation Front (FMLN) in El Salvador, and the Revolutionary Armed Forces of Colombia (FARC).

The best example of a non-Marxist revolutionary party is the PRI of Mexico. Founded in 1929, 12 years after the triumph of the revolutionary forces over the traditional oligarchy, this party has been one of the most successful in the twentieth-century history of political parties. From its founding in the late 1920s, the PRI won every presidential election in the twentieth century and held an absolute majority in the national legislature until the most recent election in 1997. Some dispute whether the PRI was ever a revolutionary party, but during the rule of Lázaro Cárdenas (1934–1940), the party used tactics of mass mobilization of workers and peasants to secure the gains of the 1910 revolution in the face of continued oligarchic resistance. After the period of Cárdenas' rule, the party became more traditional, maintaining its power through a variety of means ranging from repression to voter fraud to co-optation to maintain its absolute domination of the Mexican political system. By the 1980s, most considered that it had lost any revolutionary orientation.

Common Characteristics. Despite their obvious ideological differences, McDonald and Rubl argue that Latin American political parties share some important characteristics, primarily elitism, factionalism, personalism, organizational weakness, and heterogeneous mass support. The elitism revolves around the centralization of decision making within a small core of (male and mostly European) party leaders who are usually drawn from the upper and middle classes. Some parties engage in a facade of democracy through the conduct of public primaries, but in reality decisions are retained by the core leadership. The latest party to follow this more transparent approach was the Mexican PRI with its first-ever presidential primary in 1999. New parties like the PT and PRD also display a greater degree of leadership diversity and internal democracy.

Factionalism has also been an enduring problem in Latin American parties. Such factionalism is often most associated with the left, but bitter splits among party leaders on both personal and ideological lines have been common across the political spectrum. Only in the case of the existence of a strong figure, such as Fidel Castro in the Cuban Communist Party, Juan Perón in the Peronist Party, or Haya de la Torre in the APRA movement was serious factionalism avoided. When the latter died, his party split into several warring factions.

McDonald and Rubl also argue that Latin American parties have tended to more often be organized around personalities than ideologies. The roots of personalism are deep in Latin American history from the era of the *caudillos*, but they have been sustained throughout the twentieth century despite the development of party ideologies and structures. Beyond the obvious examples of Vargas, Perón, and Castro, others abound, including former army officer Hugo Chávez in Venezuela. As party leaders, these personalities in some cases are willing to quickly change their party's position to ensure continuation in office. Identification with a single leader has often proven easier than connection to party symbols and doctrines, especially in the case of the less-educated populations.

Latin America does have some significant examples of well-organized parties—the Mexican PRI, APRA up to the 1980s, the Cuban Communist Party, Argentina's Radical Party, Uruguay's Colorado and Blanco Parties, and Venezuela's Democratic Action, but these are the exception rather than the rule. Most Latin American parties are more similar to the U.S. Democratic and Republican Parties, coming to life primarily at the time of election, lacking strong ties to grassroots movements, and without a large number of formal members. Some are sustained by a relatively high level of party identification among the voting public, but in general party identification is weak in Latin America compared to Western Europe and the United States.

Class characteristics do tend to carry some weight in Latin American party identification but less so than in Western Europe because of the relatively late development of labor unions. An obvious exception to this rule is the Brazilian PT, which has a very clear worker and peasant allegiance. However, more common in Latin American politics are parties like the Mexican PRI, the Uruguayan Colorados, the Chilean Christian Democrats, and the Argentine Peronists, whose long-running electoral success is based on the creation of a multiclass constituency. Another basis of party identification in Latin America is region. Regional party identification has its roots in the nineteenth century, when warring Liberal and Conservative Parties developed regional strongholds. Such patterns continue today in countries like Colombia, Uruguay, Honduras, Peru, and Mexico. In the latter, the National Action Party (PAN) has developed a power base in the states nearest the U.S. border, likely influenced by the tradition of the two-party system in its neighbor to the north.

As suggested in Chapter 10, mass organizations have also become important political actors as well and may be displacing some parties or revolutionary movements.

Conclusion

One of the most important issues facing Latin America today is whether or not democratic rule will continue. Can the large steps taken in the last 20 years be sustained? To do so would clearly represent a significant break with Latin America's past. The most daunting issue may be whether or not democratic governments can be maintained in the face of deep socioeconomic problems that will not be solved overnight. As was discussed more fully in Chapter 7, in the 1990s most democratically elected governments carried out programs of economic neoliberalism that sought to open the countries to imports and foreign direct investments. These programs had mixed results and as a result there has been a fundamental shift to the left in the last 10 years, beginning with the election in 1998 of Hugo Chávez in Venezuela. In Argentina, Bolivia, and Ecuador, citizens protesting neoliberal governments took to the streets and forced those governments to step down. In the new century the citizens of Chile, Argentina, Uruguay, Brazil, Ecuador, Venezuela, Nicaragua, and Guatemala elected either socialist or progressive governments. In addition, the neoliberal

TABLE 22. Overview of Latin American Electoral Systems

Country	Presidential System	Legislative System	Governors and Municipalities	General Electoral Information
Argentina	The president is elected for a four-year term with the possibility of one successive term. If none of the candidates receives 45% or more of the votes in the first round of voting, a second round is held.	Bicameral congress. The 257 deputies are elected for four-year terms and may be reelected. Half of the Chamber of Deputies is renewed every two years. The 72 senators are elected according to procedure established in local provincial constitutions. One-third of the Senate is renewed every two years.	Governors and local authorities are elected according to the 24 provincial constitutions.	In December of 1983, Argentina returned to a democracy and since then has had free and fair democratic elections. In April 1994, elections were held to form a constituent assembly. The assembly modified the 1853 constitution with several reforms, including reduction of the president's term—from six to four years, with the possibility of a second term—and the adoption of a second round of voting if no candidate receives 45% in the first round. In addition, the reforms abolished the electoral college system.
Bolivia	Beginning in 1997, the president was elected for a five-year term without the possibility of consecutive reelection. The president may run for office again after one term has passed. If no candidate receives a majority, the Congress chooses the president from among the top two candidates in oral, roll-call vote.	Bicameral congress. The 130 deputies and 27 senators are elected for five-year terms with the possibility of reelection.	Bolivia is divided into departments; there is one *prefecto* (governor) per department. The *prefectos* are elected for five-year terms and have general executive powers. Municipal councils and mayors are directly elected by the people to five-year terms.	Two successive congresses must pass the same bill in order to reform the constitution. Many reforms to the constitution were passed in August 1994: the voting age was lowered from 21 to 18 years and the terms of office for the president and both houses of congress were increased from four to five years. In April 1994, a "popular participation" law was passed that gave local governments more control over their communities. In December 1995, reforms were passed to give more power to *(continued)*

TABLE 22. Overview of Latin American Electoral Systems *Continued*

Country	Presidential System	Legislative System	Governors and Municipalities	General Electoral Information
				the governors of the departments. Evo Morales was elected president in a special December 2005 election following a nationwide general strike in June 2005 that forced the resignation of Carlos Mesa. Constitutional changes were debated for action in 2008.
Brazil	The president is elected for a four-year term with the possibility of reelection to one additonal term. If none of the candidates receives a majority in the first round of voting, a second round is held between the top two candidates, 20 days after the first round.	Bicameral congress. The 513 members of the Chamber of Deputies are elected from party lists for four-year terms and may be reelected. When elections are held, all of the 513 seats are up for election at the same time. The 81 senators are elected to serve eight-year terms and may be reelected. Two-thirds of the Senate is renewed at one time and four years later the remaining one-third is renewed. Members of both houses are elected by a system of proportional representation.	All state legislators and governors are elected for four-year terms. Mayors and city council authorities are directly elected for four-year terms.	In 1993, a popular referendum was held to choose among moving to a parliamentary system, returning to monarchy, or keeping the presidential system. A great majority of those people who voted supported the existing presidential system. In 1994, an amendment to the constitution reduced the term of the president from five to four years and added the possibility of Presidential re-election.

Chile	The president is elected for a four-year term with no possibility of reelection. If no candidate receives a majority of the votes, a second round of voting is held.	Bicameral congress. There are 120 members of the Chamber of Deputies. They are elected from party lists for four-year terms and may be reelected. There are 38 members of the Senate. The senators are elected for eight-year terms and may be reelected. Every four years half of the senate seats are renewed.	Chile is divided into regions with one *intendente* (governor) per region. *Intendentes* are appointed by the president for a six-year term and may be replaced at any time during their tenure. Municipal authorities are directly elected for four-year terms and appoint the mayors.	In October 1988, a plebiscite defeat ended Pinochet's military dictatorship. In July 1989, a referendum approved 64 reforms to the constitution. The measures increased the number of directly elected senators from 26 to 38, reduced the president's term from eight to six years and prohibited reelection of the president. In September 2005, several other constitutional changes went into force, including the elimination of appointed senatorial positions and senators for life, granting the President the authority to remove commanders-in-chief of the Armed Forces, and reducing the Presidential term from six to four years.
Colombia	The president is elected for a four-year term with the possibility of reelection. If none of the candidates receives a majority of votes in the first round of voting, a second round of voting is held.	Bicameral congress. The 166 members of the House of Representatives and the 102 members of the Senate are elected for four-year terms and may not be reelected to consecutive terms.	Governors are elected for three-year terms. Since 1988, mayors have been elected for two-year terms.	In July 1991, the new constitution was approved which granted rights to minorities and introduced many political reforms aimed at decentralizing authority. In May 1994, vice presidential elections were held for the first time. Indigenous peoples have been allotted two seats in the Senate. In 2005, the Constitution was changed to allow for presidential reelection. The following year, Alvaro Uribe Pérez was reelected president in only one round of voting.

(continued)

TABLE 22. Overview of Latin American Electoral Systems *Continued*

Country	Presidential System	Legislative System	Governors and Municipalities	General Electoral Information
Costa Rica	The president is elected for a four-year term with the possibility of reelection. If one candidate receives more than 40% of the vote, no second round voting is held.	Unicameral congress. The 57 members of the National Assembly are elected for four-years and may not be reelected for consecutive terms.	Governors are named by the president for four-year terms. Municipal authorities are elected for four-year terms.	Elections have been regular and democratic in Costa Rica since 1949.
Dominican Republic	The president is elected for a four-year term with the possibility of one consecutive reelection. If none of the candidates receives a majority of the votes, a second round of voting is held.	Bicameral congress. There are 178 members of the Chamber of Deputies and 32 members of Senate. All members of congress are elected for four-year terms and may be reelected.	The governors of the 31 provinces are appointed by the president. The *síndico* (mayor) of each province is elected. Both serve four-year terms.	In May 1994, the Dominican Central Electoral Board declared President Balaguer the winner in a contest international observers cited as plagued by "serious problems and irregularities" that may have affected its out come. PRD opposition) candidate Francisco Peña Gómez officially lost by only 22,000 votes. After lengthy negotiations between parties and candidates. Congress reduced President Balaguer's term to two years and prohibited the consecutive reelection of future presidents. The Dominican Republic has existed under three different constitutions since 1990. The most recent form was ratified in 2002. One of the most significant changes is the return of presidential reelection, which had been outlawed since 1994 due to President Balaguer's victory in a faulty electoral process.

Ecuador	The president is elected for a four-year term without the possibility of consecutive reelection. The president may run for office again after one term has passed. If no candidate receives a majority, a second round of voting is held.	Unicameral congress. The 100 deputies of the Chamber of National Representatives are elected by a system of proportional representation. The national deputies are elected for four-year terms at the national level and provincial deputies are elected for two-year terms at the provincial level. All deputies may be reelected.	Governors and municipal authorities are elected for four-year terms.	In May 1996, congressional elections were held and the Social Christian Party won a majority in congress. A party representing the indigenous groups in Ecuador also won six seats. Prior to 1995, two constitutional reforms passed that have influenced the election of the president. The first reform revokes a previous law, which required that candidates for political office must belong to a political party, now allowing independents to run for any office. The second reform allows the president to run for reelection after one term has passed.
El Salvador	The president is elected for a five-year term without the possibility of consecutive reelection. If none of the candidates receives a majority of the votes, a second round of voting is held.	Unicameral congress. The 84 members of the National Assembly are elected for three-year terms and may be reelected.	At the municipal level, local authorities are elected for three-year terms. Governors of departments are appointed by the president.	In 1994, national and international observers judged the elections as having been generally free, fair, and nonviolent despite some irregularities. The former guerrilla movement FMLN participated as a political party in the elections in alliance with reformist groups and it became the second-largest political group in congress; however, it did poorly in local elections. The National Republican Alliance (ARENA) won a landslide victory.
Guatemala	The president is elected for a four-year term without the possibility of reelection. If none of	Unicameral congress. The 158 members of congress are elected by proportional	Governors are appointed by the president. The duration of their terms is also decided by the president.	In 1993, former President Jorge Serrano was constitutionally deposed after he attempted to seize full power. As a result of the crisis congress elected Ramiro

(continued)

TABLE 22. Overview of Latin American Electoral Systems *Continued*

Country	Presidential System	Legislative System	Governors and Municipalities	General Electoral Information
	the candidates receives a majority of the votes, a second round of voting is held.	representation. The candidates are elected by a national and a departmental list procedure. Of the 158 candidates in the last election, 29 were elected from the national lists and 129 were elected from the departmental lists. Votes are cast separately for the national and departmental lists.	Mayors are directly elected for terms of four years.	de León Carpio to be president and finish out Serrano's term. In 1994, the president held congressional elections and presented a referendum of constitutional changes to the Guatemalan people. The level of voter participation in the referendum was extremely low, but the constitutional reforms were approved. These reforms reduced the president's term from five to four years and established the current list system in congress by population.
Honduras	The president is elected for a four-year term during one round of voting and may not be reelected.	Unicameral congress. The 128 members are elected for four-year terms and may be reelected. Members of congress are elected on a proportional basis, according to votes cast for the presidential candidate of their party.	Governors are appointed for four-year terms. Municipal authorities are elected for four-year terms.	November 2005 marked the seventh consecutive election of a civilian president since 1982, when Honduras returned to civilian rule. In January 1995, the police force came under the direction of the civil government while the technical judicial police (i.e., federal investigative police) came under the direction of the attorney general. In May 1995, an all-volunteer military was put in place that ended forced conscription. In addition to these changes, many judicial changes are also under way.

Mexico

The president is elected for a six-year term and may not be reelected. There is only one round of voting.

Bicameral congress. The 500 members of the Chamber of Deputies are directly elected for three years; 300 are elected from single-member constituencies and 200 chosen under a system of proportional representation. The majority party will hold no more than 300 seats. In 1994, a six-year period of transition began that culminated in the formation of a new system for electing senators in the year 2000. This new system guarantees that at least 25% of the seats in the Senate will belong to members of minority parties.

In the 2000 elections three senators were elected by direct vote in each state, and a fourth senator was allotted to the majority opposition party within the state.

Governors are elected for six-year terms according to the organization and calendar of each state. The constitution allows for the replacement of governors by reelection during the first two years of their terms and by presidential appointment after that time. Municipal authorities are elected for three-year terms. The mayor of the federal district was elected, not appointed, for the first time in 1997.

Until 2000, the official party, PRI, won every presidential election since 1929. Measures have been taken in Mexico to open up the electoral process to other political parties. In recent years, through the reforms to the Mexican congress in late 1993, as well as the creation of the autonomous Federal Electoral Institute (IFE) to oversee federal elections, opposition parties have steadily expanded their representation in the political system.

The 1994 elections were seen as critical because prior to the election the country was plagued by a series of crises, including the assassination of PRI presidential candidate Luis Donaldo Colosio. For the first time, the Mexican government asked the United Nations to train Mexican electoral monitors.

(continued)

TABLE 22. Overview of Latin American Electoral Systems *Continued*

Country	Presidential System	Legislative System	Governors and Municipalities	General Electoral Information
Nicaragua	The president is elected for a five-year term, and may not run for reelection. If none of the candidates receives 45% or more of the vote, a second round of voting will be held.	Unicameral congress. The 92 members of the National Assembly are elected for five-year terms by proportional representation and may be reelected.	The office of governor does not exist in Nicaragua except in the autonomous Atlantic and South Atlantic regions. Municipal authorities are elected for five-year terms.	In March 1994, congress reduced the future terms of the president, members of congress, and mayors from six years to five years. Congress has also prohibited the election of the president's close relatives.
Panama	The president is elected for a five-year term and may not be reelected for two terms after his or her first term. There is only one round of voting; the candidate who receives a plurality of the votes becomes president.	Unicameral congress. The 78 members of the National Assembly are elected for five-year terms.	Governors of the nine provinces are named by the president and may be removed at any time. Municipal authorities are elected by the people and serve five-year terms.	On May 8, 1994, Ernesto Pérez Balladares of the PRD defeated Mireya Moscoso, widow of former President Arnulfo Arias of the Arnulfista Party, and salsa singer Rubén Blades of the Papá Egoró Party. International observers found the elections to be free, fair, and nonviolent. Moscoso was elected in 1999.
Paraguay	The president is elected for a five-year term and may not be reelected. Only one round of voting is held.	Bicameral congress. The 80 deputies and 45 senators are elected for five-year terms and may be reelected.	Governors are elected for five-year terms. Municipal authorities are elected for five-year terms.	In February 1989, the overthrow of General Alfredo Stroessner initiated a transition to democracy in Paraguay. The elections of May 1993 were the first free and uncontested elections with an all-civilian slate of candidates since 1928. On June 20, 1992, a new constitution was approved that created the office of the vice president and prohibits the president and vice president from

(continued)

				succeeding themselves. The constitution also established an electoral tribunal headed by three ministers of electoral justice who must be confirmed by congress. Municipal authorities are now elected and no longer appointed by the president.
Peru	The president is elected for a five-year term and may be reelected for a consecutive five-year term. If no candidate receives a majority in the first round of voting, a second round is held.	Unicameral congress. The 120 members of Congress are elected for five-year terms and may be reelected.	Presidents of Peru's 25 autonomous regions are elected for a five-year term. Municipal authorities are elected for a five-year term.	In April 1992, President Fujimori dissolved congress and called for new congressional elections. The new 80-member congress served for two years and drafted a new constitution approved by a nationwide referendum in October 1993 by 52% of voters. The new constitution dissolved regional government and created a larger 120-member unicameral congress. The new constitution also permits the president to run for reelection. Since then, the Constitution has been amended to allow for regional governance.
Uruguay	The president is elected by a party list procedure for a five-year term without the possibility of consecutive reelection. The president may run for office again after one If no candidate recieves the majority in the first round, a second round is held.	Bicameral congress. The 99 deputies and 30 senators are elected by a system of proportional representation for five-year terms and may be reelected.	Governors and municipalities are elected for five-year terms.	Since the end of military rule in 1985 four presidents have been elected. In May 1996, the Senate voted on an amendment to the constitution that will change the process of electing the president by including a primary election. This change has not yet been approved.

TABLE 22. Overview of Latin American Electoral Systems *Continued*

Country	Presidential System	Legislative System	Governors and Municipalities	General Electoral Information
Venezuela	The president is elected for a six-year term by the people. The executive vice president is appointed by the president. There is no second round of election for president.	Unicameral Chamber of Deputies. The 167 seats are elected from the federal territories and various indigenous communities to five-year terms. They may be reelected to two additional terms.	Governors and municipal authorities are elected for a four-year term.	Venezuela has a long-standing history of democratic rule, which began in 1958. However, in 1992 there were two coup attempts and in 1993 President Carlos André Pérez was impeached. After Hugo Chávez was elected president in December of 1998, a Constituent Assembly was convened to draft a new constitution which established a unicameral Chamber of Deputies and a 6 year presidential term. Chávez won new election in 2000 and his supporters gained dominance in the Chamber of Deputies. In 2007, Chávez proposed two constitutional amendments: one to grant the president emergency powers and the other to abolish term limits but they were defeated.

Sources: Georgetown University and Organization of American States Political Database of the Americas, http://www.georgetown.edu/pdba/; Wilfried Derksen, "Elections around the World," http://www.agora.stm.it/elections/election.htm.

Calderón narrowly held on to power for the PAN in the face of a strong challenge from the reformist PRD candidate López Obrador in Mexico.

In recent elections the only avowedly right-wing candidate to prevail in a major country of the region was Alvaro Uribe of Colombia, aided by the ongoing civil war in his country. These elections are part of a trend where new movements and social actors, especially from the indigenous peoples of the region, have thrust themselves into power. These movements are taking advantage of the democratic openings of the last 20 years and in the process are raising the expectations of the poor masses. Many of the governments elected have yet to show that they are capable of meeting the high expectations of their people. In the past such a situation often invited the intervention of the military to restore order but that period of Latin American history may well be over. There is little appetite, even among the business and financial elites for a return to circumstances of widespread repression and denial of civil liberties. It is significant that in the cases of Argentina, Ecuador, and Bolivia where mass street demonstrations brought down governments in recent years there was no intervention by the military and eventually, following caretaker rule, new governments were elected and took power by constitutional rule.

Bibliography

Asturias, Miguel Angel. *El Señor Presidente*. New York : Atheneum, 1972.

Black, Jan Knippers, ed. *Latin America: Its Problems and Its Promise*. 4th ed. Boulder, CO: Westview Press, 2005.

Chávez, David, and Benjamin Goldfrank, eds. *The Left in the City: Participatory Local Governments in Latin America*. London: Latin American Bureau, 2004.

Cleary, Edward. *The Struggle for Human Rights in Latin America*. Westport, CT: Praeger, 1997.

Close, David, ed. *Legislatures and the New Democracies in Latin America*. Boulder, CO: Lynne Rienner, 1995.

Dominguez, Jorge. *Democratic Politics in Latin America and the Caribbean*. Baltimore: Johns Hopkins University Press, 1998.

Foweraker, Joe, Todd Landman, and Neil Harvey. *Governing Latin America*. Cambridge: Polity Press, 2004.

Liss, Sheldon. *Marxist Thought in Latin America*. Berkeley: University of California Press, 1984.

Loveman, Brian, and Thomas Davies, eds. *The Politics of Antipolitics: The Military in Latin America*. Wilmington, DE: Scholarly Resources, 1997.

Mainwaring, Scott. *Building Democratic Institutions: Party Systems in Latin America*. Stanford, CA: Stanford University Press, 1995.

Mainwaring, Scott. *Christian Democracy in Latin America*. Palo Alto, CA: Stanford University Press, 2003.

Malloy, James, and Mitchell Seligson, eds. *Authoritarians and Democrats: Regime Transition in Latin America*. Pittsburgh, PA: University of Pittsburgh Press, 1987.

McDonald, Ronald, and J. Mark Rubl. *Party Politics and Election in Latin America*. Boulder, CO: Westview Press, 1989.

Peeler, John. *Building Democracy in Latin America*. 2nd ed. Boulder, CO: Lynne Rienner, 2004.

Philip, George. *Democracy in Latin America: Surviving Conflict and Crisis?* Cambridge/Oxford: Polity Press/Blackwell, 2003.

Smith, Peter H. *Democracy in Latin America: Political Change in Comparative Perspective*. New York: Oxford University Press, 2005.

Tulchin, Joseph, ed. *The Consolidation of Democracy in Latin America*. Boulder, CO: Lynne Rienner, 1998.

Wiarda, Howard. *Dilemmas of Democracy in Latin America*. Lanham, MD: Rowman and Littlefield, 2006.

Wiarda, Howard, and Harvey Kline, eds. *Latin American Politics and Development*. 5th ed. Boulder, CO: Westview Press, 2000.

Wynia, Gary. *The Politics of Latin American Development*. 3rd ed. Cambridge: Cambridge University Press, 1990.

FILMS AND VIDEOS

Confessing to Laura. Colombia, 1990.
Death of a Bureaucrat. Cuba, 1966.
Death and the Maiden. United States, 1994.
Evita. United States, 1997.
Doña Barbara. Mexico, 1943.
Missing. United States, 1983.
La Paz. Bolivia, 1994.
The Seven Madmen (Los Siete Locos). Argentina, 1973.
State of Siege. United States, 1982.

TEN

STRUGGLING FOR CHANGE: REVOLUTION, SOCIAL AND POLITICAL MOVEMENTS IN LATIN AMERICA

Latin America has struggled with the need for fundamental change and socio-economic restructuring from the time that Tupac Amarú and Tupac Katari led uprisings in 1780 and 1781. Most acknowledge the severe inequality that exists throughout the region and very much believe it needs to be changed. The means of doing so are, however, hotly contested. The term *revolution* is employed to evoke the fundamental restructuring that is so much needed in Latin America. Revolutions are, then, much touted and the term is often used to describe any power realignment in Latin America. Nonetheless, it could be argued that thoroughgoing revolutions are much talked about but little done in the region. Even the struggle for independence was more of a change in political elites than a comprehensive restructuring of the social–economic–political structures that the term *revolution* implies. Yet, the vision of a total transformation of oppressive societal structures that revolution involves has continued to inspire political leaders in Latin America. Indeed, many have argued that only through such a revolution can long-standing problems such as massive poverty, inequality, and malnutrition be remedied. Thus, each new revolutionary attempt at thoroughgoing change has been met with utopian enthusiasm by supportive sociopolitical groupings: in Mexico from 1910 to 1917, in Guatemala from 1944 to 1954, in Bolivia from 1952 to 1964, in Cuba from 1959 on, in Nicaragua from 1979 to 1990, in El Salvador during the revolutionary struggle from 1980 to the peace accords in 1992, and in Venezuela from 1999 on. But contradictions emerged in these processes as well. The resort to authoritarian methods and the many internal and external difficulties in achieving such revolutionary visions often dampened much of the initial enthusiasm and occasioned many defections from the revolutionary process.

To many analysts, the defeat of the Sandinistas in the 1990 Nicaraguan elections, coming in the context of the collapse of the Communist Party–led governments in

Eastern Europe, marked the end of an era of radical revolution in Latin America that had begun with the triumph of the Cuban Revolution in 1959. Many of the same observers noted the flagging fortunes of the revolutionary movements in Guatemala and El Salvador in the early 1990s and predicted the early demise of Fidel Castro's government in Cuba. Others were far less certain that the era of revolution in Latin America had ended. Armed insurgencies intensified in Peru in the 1990s, reappeared in Mexico, and continued in Colombia. Further, in El Salvador and Nicaragua the revolutionary movements have not been destroyed. The Sandinsta National Liberation Front (FSLN) of Nicaragua and the Farabundo Martí National Liberation Front (FMLN) of El Salvador were still important political movements that could contest power in presidential elections and command an important bloc of votes in their national legislatures and local governments. Yet, such a position is far short of the revolutionary goals that each of them sought. By 2005, the dominant national economic and political elites, aided by a variety of direct and indirect actions by the United States, had been able to blunt the drive for revolutionary takeover outside of Colombia, even though the revolution was still in power in Cuba. Indeed, the struggle for revolutionary change has always been difficult in Latin America, given the forces that have been arrayed against it. By 2008, new political and social movements and the leaders they supported were once again invoking the need for fundamental change and challenging the neoliberal agenda. This was particularly true with Hugo Chávez in Venezuela and Evo Morales in Bolivia, where socialist revolutions were once again being discussed.

In recent years, many seeking change and social–economic restructuring have begun to harness their vision and creativity to mobilize in less violent but highly effective ways. For instance, many had despaired of popular rule in Bolivia after the demise of the Bolivian revolution led by the Movimiento Nacionalista Revolucionario (MNR) in 1952 and ended by a military coup in 1964. Recent years had even seen the country led by a U.S.–educated member of the elite who seemed only too happy to bow to U.S. policy in such areas as the eradication of coca leaves. Thus, it was all the more remarkable that Bolivian President Gonzalo Sánchez de Lozada was forced out of office by massive displays of popular power by social movements, community organizations, unions, and students in October 2003. A staunch advocate of globalization and neoliberal policies prescribed by international financial institutions like the International Monetary Fund (IMF) and World Bank, he was also symbolic of the upper-class, Western-oriented political elite that have governed Latin America in an authoritarian manner since the Spanish conquest in the early 1500s. His tormentors were equally symbolic of those the political class had long ruled and repressed. They were small farmers, indigenous peoples, workers, miners, students, and intellectuals who dared to challenge the status quo. In 2005 successor president Carlos Mesa was also forced from office by the same forces. Later that year Evo Morales was elected to the presidency with their support. This was not, however, the first time people had arisen in the Andean highlands. There had, for instance, been an uprising in 1780 under the leadership of Incan descendant Túpac Amaru. The 1960s had seen the formation of Marxist guerrilla groups in both Bolivia and Peru. Like most other attempts at radical change from Túpac Amaru on, such attempts had been repressed, first by the European forces and then by the national military or the dominant political elite. This occurred in the central part of Mexico in the early 1800s when the mostly Indian, mostly peasant masses answered the famous *grito de Dolores*—the cry for freedom and independence that rang out in 1810. There, a popular movement under the leadership of Miguel de Hidalgo began the struggle for popular control and Mexican independence. The movement was brutally repressed by the Spanish authorities, and Hidalgo and his successor, José María Morelos faced the same fate as Túpac Amaru: they were executed by the Spanish colonial authorities. The mass uprising was not successful. Rather, Mexican independence, like that in Bolivia and all of Latin America save Haiti, was won by *criollo* political elites who ruled in the name of the majorities but rarely for them.

Dissatisfaction with elite rule, exclusionary political projects, or policies that cause or perpetuate the economic or ethnic marginalization of the masses has continued in Latin America. There have been many other uprisings, like that led by Farabundo Martí in El Salvador in 1932. Indeed, it was the generalized dissatisfaction with Porfirio Díaz' political ruling class in *fin de siglo* Mexico that induced *los de abajo* (those on the bottom) to enroll in the various armies—and thus the revolutionary project—of the Mexican Revolution. Such dissatisfaction and its focus on the failure of the political elite have led to other less successful political rebellions as well. The *Bogotazo* and the ensuing violence in Colombia from 1948 to 1956, the Bolivian revolution in the early 1950s, the popular struggle in Guatemala from the 1960s to the 1990s, and the decade-long civil war in the 1980s in El Salvador are cases in point. Before the most current forms of radical political mobilization are examined, a more careful discussion of revolutions and revolutionary mobilizations must be undertaken.

It is necessary to review the development of previous movements, tracing the demise of the belief in violent revolution in Latin America to the ascendance of political democracy throughout the region to the temporary political dominance of the ideology of free enterprise embodied in the programs of structural adjustment and neoliberalism, and to the resurgency of more radical movements after 2000. As the new century began, prescriptions for revolutionary change needed to undergo some reexamination. The heady days that revolutionaries experienced in the late 1970s were clearly not in evidence, but radical movements, and new leadership were considering some of the same policies that they had advocated.

Cuba

The modern wave of revolutions in Latin America began in the Caribbean island of Cuba. That revolution, under the leadership of Fidel Castro and the 26th of July Movement (discussed in more detail in Chapter 13), was a watershed event in Latin American revolutionary history. Following the cancellation of the scheduled 1952 national elections by Fulgencio Batista, Castro and several dozen followers organized an attack on an army barracks in Santiago, hoping to incite a nationwide uprising against the dictatorship. That attack failed, but 3 years later it led to the formation of the movement, named for the date of the 1953 failed attack. Drawing in part on the earlier experiences of Augusto César Sandino in Nicaragua in the late 1920s, the Cuban revolutionary movement based itself in the isolated Sierra

Maestra mountains of eastern Cuba and sought to build a revolutionary army from
the ranks of the local peasants. Given the history of rebellion of that region, the
tactics proved successful as the rebel army flourished and eventually engaged in
several successful battles against the conscript army of the dictator Batista. Aided
by other revolutionary actions in Cuba's cities and the flagging support for Batista
both domestically and internationally, the 26th of July Movement succeeded in taking power on January 1, 1959. In the ensuing months, the revolutionary government, with the support of mass mobilizations of workers and peasants, transformed
Cuban society. The economy was placed largely in the hands of the state, and by
1961 Fidel Castro had committed Cuba to the socialist path of development, the first
country in the Western Hemisphere to do so. Given the popularity of Fidel Castro
and the other Cuban rebels, it is not surprising that there was soon a proliferation
of self-declared Marxist guerrilla groups through much of Latin America. This proliferation of the Fidelista theory of revolution through armed struggle (*foquismo*)
marked what Regis Debray termed the "revolution in the revolution" (a revolution
in the Marxist theory of revolution in Latin America).

 Although the subsequent wave of guerrilla activity in the region and the virtual
canonization of Ché Guevara helped free Latin American revolutionary thought
from the dogmatic, static orientation that had come to characterize it during Joseph
Stalin's rule in the Soviet Union, the unyielding emphasis on armed struggle effectively foreclosed a broader examination of the doctrine and the search for more
effective ways to mobilize the masses. This new vision of revolution effectively challenged the now bureaucratized orthodox communist parties, but it did not produce
any successful guerrilla movements in the 1960s or well into the 1970s. It did, however, spawn a series of urban and rural guerrilla movements across Latin America
and generated a great deal of literature by and about these new Marxist revolutionaries. The introduction of Maoism and Chinese-oriented communist parties in
countries such as Colombia and Brazil further stimulated the development of new
forms of radical Marxism. However, the subsequent growth in Marxist parties and
movements also provided an excellent rationale for the creation and implementation of the U.S.-inspired national security doctrine, counterinsurgency training,
and its concomitant strong anti-communism. The U.S.-inspired counterinsurgency
defeated most of the original guerrilla movements by the early 1970s. Most significantly, Ché Guevara was killed in Bolivia by U.S.-trained soldiers while fighting
with a Bolivian revolutionary group in 1967. Guerrilla groups did, however, manage to struggle on in Guatemala, Colombia, and Nicaragua.

Other Revolutionary Endeavors

By 1970, several innovative approaches to Marxist thought were emerging. In Peru,
Hugo Blanco was breathing new life into the Trotskyist movement through his work
with the highland peasants. In Chile, socialists and communists were contemplat-
ing the realization of a peaceful revolution under the leadership of constitutionally
elected socialist president Salvador Allende. The far left Movement of the Revolutionary Left (MIR) did, however, argue that rightist forces would never allow such
a transition. In Argentina, leftist theorists began to apply and adapt the theory to
their own specific reality. A radical brand of Marxist-inspired Peronism (or Peronist-

inspired Marxism) ensued and eventually led to a Marxist faction within Peronism (Juventud Peronista) and the formation of the radical Peronist Montonero guerrilla group. The Montoneros and the Revolutionary Army of the People (ERP) eventually confronted Argentina's military government in an intense struggle. In Uruguay, the Robin Hood–like Tupamaros hoped to foment a popular revolution. Although gains were made toward less dogmatic interpretations and in political education, the lingering emphasis on armed struggle over political education or organization eventually led to intense conflict and violent repression, which the left was ultimately unable to resist. Revolutionary and socialist movements were profoundly affected by the results of Allende's Popular Unity socialist experiment in Chile. Allende sought to make radical changes in Chilean society (land reform, wealth redistribution, increased political participation) within the parliamentary process. Some progress was made during the 3 years he was in power (1970–1973), but the reformist socialist experiment was largely thwarted by Allende's lack of majority control of the legislature. The entrenched power and opposition by the country's elites together with international isolation engineered by a hostile U.S. government disrupted the country's economy and set the stage for a military coup. Allende's rule came to a bloody end in September 1973 when the Chilean military stormed the presidential palace and killed Allende and thousands of his supporters. A military government under General Augusto Pinochet was established and held power for 17 years. The primary impact of the Chilean events was to convince most of the Latin American left that reform-oriented efforts at achieving socialism were fruitless. These views were also bolstered by the 1973 military coup in Uruguay and the subsequent coup in Argentina in 1976. By 1976 military rule had become the norm throughout the region, and the combination of dictatorial rule and unsolved social and economic problems spawned a series of revolutionary upsurges, which were strongest in Nicaragua, El Salvador, Colombia, and Peru. Each had its own characteristics and should be viewed individually, although there were many similarities.

Nicaragua

Nicaragua's leading revolutionary movement, the FSLN, was formed in 1961 and was directly inspired by the success of the Cuban Revolution. Its early leaders, Carlos Fonseca and Tomás Borge, abandoned the reformist-oriented Nicaraguan Socialist Party (PSN) to form the FSLN. With direct Cuban assistance, the FSLN sought to replicate the Cuban experience and that of their namesake, Augusto Sandino, by establishing a guerrilla army in the mountains of northern Nicaragua that could eventually challenge the power of the dictator Anastasio Somoza. Another element crucial to the revolutionary philosophy of the FSLN was its emphasis on will and the belief that to some degree revolution could be improvised. They turned to the writings of Sandino, José Carlos Mariátegui, and Italian Antonio Gramsci to craft a philosophy based on revolutionary action, the importance of the subjective factor in making revolution, and the role of ideology in motivating the masses.

In its early stages, the FSLN consisted of just twelve people, including Colonel Santos López, a veteran of Sandino's earlier struggle. Fonseca fought successfully for the inclusion of Sandino's name in the organizational label, but the lack of unanimity on this shows that a variety of revolutionary influences were at work in the early 1960s. Led by Fonseca, the small group studied Sandino's writings and tactics as they prepared for their first guerrilla campaigns in 1963. Those campaigns, like many other similar ones in Latin America at the time, were a failure. The new Sandinistas had failed to do what their namesake had done so well—mobilize the local populace on the side of the guerrillas through well-planned political and organizational activities coordinated with and part of the armed struggle. Over the ensuing years, the FSLN managed to survive by realizing its mistakes and broadening its political work to include neighborhood organizing in the poorest barrios of the capital, Managua. However, the National Guard of the Somoza dictatorship was a powerful force, and it exacted many defeats on the Sandinistas during the 1960s. The Sandinistas survived and slowly built their organization, especially by reaching out to progressive members of the Catholic Church who had been inspired by liberation theology. The FSLN was the first revolutionary organization in Latin America to welcome Christians within its ranks, a position that would bear considerable fruit in the late 1970s.

Between 1967 and 1974 the FSLN carried on what it termed "accumulation of forces" in silence, largely recruiting members in ones and twos and engaging in few armed actions. The silence was broken in a spectacular way with the December 1974 seizure of the home of a wealthy Somoza supporter. An FSLN commando unit held more than a dozen foreign diplomats and top Nicaraguan government officials for several days, finally forcing Somoza to release key Sandinista political prisoners, pay a large sum of money, and broadcast and publish FSLN communiques. This dramatic act reinserted the FSLN into the political scene at an important time. Popular sentiment against the dictatorship had been growing since it had greedily profited from the devastating 1972 earthquake that had further impoverished more Nicaraguans. However, even as the FSLN reemerged, its own divisions had become clear. By 1975 the organization had split into three tendencies on the basis of tactical differences. The Prolonged People's War group was basically Maoist in orientation. Their strategy and concrete work emphasized rural guerrilla warfare. Relatively isolated in the countryside, they were probably the slowest to realize that a revolutionary situation was developing in the country. The Proletarian tendency based itself in large measure on dependency theory and the traditional Marxist emphasis on the industrial working class. This tendency saw the Nicaraguan revolution as unfolding along more traditional lines as a confrontation between the bourgeoisie and the proletariat. Nicaragua's urban working class, small as it was, was seen as the main motor force of the coming revolution. Political work in the cities was emphasized, and this group also built a base among students. The Insurrectionist, or Tercerista, tendency was the last to emerge. In reality, it did not represent an entirely new approach; rather, it served primarily as a mediator between the two existing tendencies. The Terceristas (or "third force") did not draw a sharp distinction between a rural and an urban emphasis, seeing the need for action in both arenas. Its main and most controversial contribution was its alliance strategy. While not the first group in the FSLN to propose such an orientation, they were the first in the era of Somoza's decline to place it at the center of political work. There was also ample historical precedent for it in the strategies of both Sandino and the 26th of July Movement in Cuba. Both earlier movements incorporated heterogeneous elements while maintaining a revolutionary position. The Insurrectionists believed strongly that it was necessary to mobilize a broad-based coalition to overthrow the dictatorship while maintaining the organizational integrity of the FSLN.

The separation into tendencies did not mean the disintegration of the FSLN. Each current pursued its political work in its own sector, and as the crisis of the dictatorship deepened, all achieved successes. Efforts by the leaders to reestablish unity did not cease, although they were hampered by the imprisonment of key figures such as Borge and the death of Fonseca in combat in November 1976. The three tendencies finally began to converge in the upsurge of mass anti-dictatorship activity in late 1977 and early 1978 in the wake of the death of popular opposition newspaper editor Pedro Joaquín Chamorro. In 1978, the three tendencies collaborated to establish the National Patriotic Front (FPN), which created an anti-Somoza front encompassing trade unions, the Moscow-oriented Nicaraguan Socialist Party, student groups, and some small middle-class parties like the Popular Social Christians—all under FSLN hegemony.

In September 1978, the FSLN, led by the Terceristas, carried out an insurrection which, while not successful, laid the groundwork for the dictatorship's defeat. Drawing on the lessons learned from the September 1978 action and with the organization formally reunited in March 1979, the FSLN launched its final offensive in the late spring of 1979. Somoza's National Guard fought hard to defend the dictator, who desperately ordered the bombing of Sandinista strongholds in the cities; but in July 1979, Somoza fled the country and the FSLN assumed power at the head of a provisional revolutionary government. The success of the Sandinistas in defeating the dictatorship and embarking on the fundamental restructuring of Nicaraguan society was a watershed event for Latin America, a second potential socialist revolution. As described in detail in Chapter 19, the Nicaraguan Revolution did not fulfill its promises, but that did not change the significance of the events that unfolded at the end of the 1970s in one of the region's poorest countries. The reelection of FSLN leader Daniel Ortega as president in 2006 once again challenged U.S. influence and opened the possibility for change.

El Salvador

Nicaragua was not the only Central American nation convulsed by revolution in the 1970s and 1980s. Neighboring El Salvador witnessed a bloody confrontation between the military and revolutionaries that cost 75,000 lives between 1975 and 1992 and sent more than 500,000 Salvadorans into exile in the United States. The revolutionary period ended with a United Nations–brokered peace agreement that rewarded the revolutionary coalition, the FMLN, with a prominent role in Salvadoran politics as the country's primary political opposition group. The Salvadoran military, while still a major political force, stepped down from the controlling position that it had held for more than half a century.

It is not surprising that revolutionary forces came to the fore in El Salvador, for no Latin American country better fit the profile for revolutionary change. The events of the 1970s and 1980s followed directly from dramatic confrontations of the early 1930s and the 50 years of direct military rule that followed. By 1932 Salvador was the most class-polarized society in the region. In the latter part of the nineteenth century, El Salvador had become one of the world's largest coffee producers, meeting the ever-growing European demand with the development of ever-larger coffee plantations dominated by a few wealthy families. The coffee boom enriched a series of oligarchic families, who came to dominate Salvadoran society, while it further reduced the peasant population to seasonal labor and marginal lands. From 1907 to 1931, political power rested in the hands of a single family, the Meléndez clan. The peasantry who were driven off their communal lands during the latter half of the nineteenth century did not accept their fate passively and engaged in several uprisings, both armed and unarmed, from 1870 onward. The conflict between the ruling oligarchy, made up of coffee farmers, foreign investors, military officers, and Church leaders, and the landless peasants came to a head in 1930–1932. The Great Depression had further impoverished both the remaining small farmers and the plantation laborers as the price of coffee fell precipitously. The possibility of revolution developed very quickly. In 1930, a May Day demonstration in San Salvador against deteriorating economic conditions drew 80,000. Liberal reformer Arturo Araujo won the presidential election in 1931 with the support of students, workers, and peasants. The new government attempted to broaden the political spectrum by announcing that it would permit the newly formed Communist Party, under the leadership of Farabundo Martí, to participate in the 1931 municipal elections. However, the military, under the leadership of Maximiliano Hernández Martínez, seized power in December 1931; and the following month, Martí led a premature, mostly peasant rebellion that succeeded in murdering a few landlords and seizing control of some small towns, primarily in the northwestern part of the country.

The response of General Hernández to the uprising was swift and brutal. Known ever since as *La Matanza* ("The Massacre"), the joint actions of the military and oligarchy killed between 30,000 and 60,000 people, a huge toll in a nation of only 1.4 million. The repression was both selective and widespread. Using voter rolls, the military hunted down and killed virtually everyone affiliated with the Communist Party, including Martí. At the time, the military's actions took on the character of a race war as indigenous people were also singled out for attack.

La Matanza did not end resistance to the rule of the oligarchy, but it reduced it significantly for the next 40 years. A series of military leaders ruled the country into the 1960s without even the façade of democracy. In that decade, a reformist challenge to the military developed under the leadership of the Christian Democratic Party and José Napoleon Duarte. Duarte, educated in the United States and the spirit of Kennedy's Alliance for Progress, developed a strong following among intellectuals, students, and a growing middle sector. Duarte's reformist challenge ended with a probable victory in the 1972 presidential elections, but the military voided the results and continued in power. Duarte and other Christian Democratic leaders went into exile, but other, more radical leaders saw the military's actions as proof that the reformist path was not viable in El Salvador. This view was reinforced by the fact that the U.S. government did not intervene, even to promote its seeming prototype for a centrist reformer like Duarte against the Salvadoran generals. As guerrilla groups began to form in the rural areas of the country, other factors also promoted revolutionary prospects. By 1975 about 40 percent of the peasants had no land at all, compared to only 12 percent in 1960. The other surprising force for revolutionary change that developed in the latter half of the 1970s was the Roman Catholic Church. The combination of the reform-oriented ideas of the 1968 Medellín Conference of Latin American Bishops and the repression of the Salvadoran military against the Church itself propelled the clergy and its followers into a central role in the political opposition to the military. The leader of the Salvadoran Church, Archbishop Oscar Romero, was a conservative at the time of his leadership appointment; but the death of a close friend at the hands of the military combined with the growing polarization in the country led him to the unusual position of supporting the right of armed rebellion. In response, the military assassinated Archbishop Romero in 1980 in the midst of growing civil and revolutionary resistance to the military regime.

In 1980, most of the revolutionary guerrilla groups that had begun armed activities in the 1970s came together to form the FMLN. The two primary organizations in the FMLN were the ERP and the Armed Forces of Liberation (FAL). The ERP was founded in 1971 by Marxist and Christian forces that were motivated by the *foco* theory of revolution inspired by Ché Guevara. The FAL was the armed wing of the outlawed Communist Party that developed into a significant force only in the late 1970s. The primary significance of the FAL was that it was one of the few cases where a reformist-oriented Communist Party opted to participate in an armed struggle. Also important in the revolutionary equation was the Democratic Revolutionary Front (FDR), an umbrella alliance also founded in 1980 that encompassed all major popular organizations, labor groups, and community groups. From the beginning it served as the political arm of the FMLN and after 1982 was recognized internationally as a legitimate political force. The heart of the FDR was the People's Revolutionary Bloc (BPR), the largest of the popular organizations. It was formed in 1975 by diverse organizations of shantytown dwellers, workers, students, teachers, and practitioners of liberation theology. By the late 1970s, despite the severe repression of the military, the organizations of the BPR had succeeded in many places in the country in establishing alternative governing bodies.

Following the decisive triumph of the Sandinista revolutionaries in the summer of 1979, the possibility of revolution in El Salvador seemed very real. Popular mobilizations spread throughout the country. Factories were occupied in San Salvador, and 1980 was declared to be the "year of the liberation." Fearing a repetition of the Nicaraguan Revolution, a section of the Salvadoran elites and the government of the United States carried off a military coup designed to forestall the revolutionary process by appearing to instigate significant reform. On October 15, 1979, a new military junta took power, promising reform. The new government even encompassed figures from the left, including Social Democrat Guillermo Ungo and a minister of labor from the small Communist Party. The new junta promised to reform the security forces, institute land reform, and recognize trade unions. However, the political practice of the new government was far different from its rhetoric. Within a week of taking power, the government security forces broke up strikes, occupied rebellious towns, and killed more than 100 people. In January 1980, Ungo and the entire civilian cabinet quit their posts, acknowledging that the military was already making all key political and security decisions. Three weeks later, the military opened fire on a massive demonstration of 150,000. In March, Romero was assassinated, and the military attacked his funeral procession of 80,000. Thirty people were killed. By March 1980 it was clear to most political activists in El Salvador that open, legal political activity in opposition to the military was impossible. Many political moderates, including a sizeable part of the Christian Democrats, joined with the revolutionary left. This movement soon coalesced into the FDR and FMLN. Christian Democrat Duarte assumed leadership of the junta, claiming to be in the political center between left- and right-wing forces. In reality, Duarte was a figurehead who ruled on behalf of the traditional elites.

In January 1981, on the eve of President Ronald Reagan's inauguration, the FMLN launched an insurrection that was intended to take power. However, the Salvadoran military, with significant resupply by the United States, defeated the offensive and set the stage for a protracted armed conflict. The FMLN had hoped to gain victory before the Reagan administration took office. It gambled that the Carter administration would not resume aid to the Salvadoran government, which had been suspended 1 month earlier in the wake of the killing of four North American churchwomen by Salvadoran security forces. However, the FMLN's judgment proved to be wrong. Citing proof of Nicaraguan Sandinista support for FMLN rebels on January 17, 1981, President Carter authorized the shipment of $5 million of military equipment and twenty additional U.S. military personnel. Three months later, the U.S. ambassador in El Salvador at the time of the shipments, Robert White, revealed that there was no real evidence of Nicaraguan involvement but the announcement of the shipment had served its purpose. The Salvadoran military had been reassured that despite obvious human rights violations even against U.S. citizens, the government of the United States was fully committed to preventing a victory by the Salvadoran revolutionaries. There was not going to be another Nicaragua in Central America.

The civil war continued for 10 more years. The FMLN showed considerable resilience in the face of a concerted effort by the Salvadoran army and its U.S. backers to eliminate the guerrilla challenge. At the high point of assistance in the late 1980s, El Salvador was receiving close to $1 billion per year in U.S. aid, ranking behind only Israel and Egypt. Total U.S. aid during this period exceeded $5 billion. The FMLN was a substantial force, with several thousand soldiers in arms. It controlled more than one-third of Salvadoran territory and carried out regular attacks in all but two of the country's fourteen provinces. However, throughout the 1980s, the Salvadoran revolutionaries faced the dilemma that even if they could mount an insurrection that challenged the hold of the Salvadoran military, they faced the prospect of a massive U.S. intervention that would deny them the victory that they sought. As a result, from about 1982 onward, the FMLN argued that the only solution to the civil war would be a negotiated settlement. Sporadic negotiations did occur throughout the 1980s, but the political situation both inside and outside of El Salvador prevented a successful conclusion. To ensure continued support from a reluctant U.S. Congress, the Reagan administration pressed the Salvadorans to hold elections, even though it was clear that these could not be fully democratic in the context of the civil war. There was little freedom of the press, and no candidates of the left could participate without risking assassination by right-wing "death squads." With significant U.S. backing, Christian Democrat Duarte won the 1982 presidential election but was largely a figurehead. Throughout the 1980s, real political power lay with the Supreme Army Council and Roberto D'Aubuisson's ultra-right National Republican Alliance (ARENA), which controlled the Salvadoran legislature. Duarte was allowed by the military to remain in power as long as he permitted them free reign against the FMLN. Obviously, such an arrangement did not allow for any real dialogue or hope for a settlement between Duarte and the FMLN. In 1989, with Duarte dying of cancer and the Christian Democratic Party deeply divided, ARENA candidate Alfredo Christiani won the presidency, further entrenching the hold of the far right on Salvadoran politics. The new ARENA government vowed a rapid campaign to defeat the FMLN, but the latter responded in the fall of 1989 with a significant military offensive that reached all the way into the capital. These events served to underscore the fact that after a decade of fighting, the civil war was a stalemate with no end in sight.

However, regional and international events intervened to bring about a negotiated settlement within 2 years. The electoral defeat of the FSLN in Nicaragua in 1990 and the rapid changes in the Soviet Union and Eastern Europe between 1989 and 1991 weakened the position of the FMLN but also put pressure on the U.S. government and its Salvadoran allies to come to the bargaining table. Under United Nations auspices, brokered settlements moved forward in Cambodia, Angola, Mozambique, and Namibia, placing additional pressure on Central America. In 1990–1991, the FMLN made several concessions toward peace that went largely unreciprocated. In the March 1991 national legislative elections, the FMLN and its sympathizers fielded candidates. Despite significant pressure against the left and intimidation of voters, the left managed to win eight seats and ARENA was denied majority control. In November 1991, the FMLN declared a unilateral cease-fire that was to last until a peace agreement was signed. In January 1992, under mounting international pressure, the ARENA government signed an agreement with the FMLN. The agreement called for the removal of more than 100 military officers implicated in human rights violations during the civil war. The army was to be reduced by 50 percent, the National Intelligence Directorate dismantled, a new police force created to include members of the FMLN, 1980 agrarian reform completed, democratic elections held, and the FMLN disarmed in exchange for land and resettlement compensation for its troops and the right to become a political party.

This agreement was clearly far short of the thoroughgoing social revolution to which the FMLN had committed itself a decade earlier, but it did represent a partial victory for the revolutionaries and a setback for El Salvador's traditional oligarchy. Since the signing of the agreement, El Salvador has remained a contradictory nation. The traditional oligarchy has worked hard to undermine the agreement. The Christiani government was reluctant to purge high-ranking military officers and to disarm the notorious army and police units. In March 1993, a U.N.-appointed truth commission named sixty-two Salvadoran officers responsible for the worst massacres, tortures, and murders of the 12-year war and called for the immediate dismissal of forty of them. The U.S. Army School of the Americas had trained forty-seven of them. The officers were eventually dismissed but only after pressure from a united opposition within El Salvador and a temporary suspension of aid by the Clinton administration in 1993.

Elections held under the aegis of the accords, especially the first one in 1994, were marked by significant fraud emanating from the government and periodic armed attacks against candidates and supporters of the left. The Christiani government used its control of the Supreme Electoral Tribunal to prevent opposition voters from registering. Especially in the 1994 elections, this fraud definitely denied the FMLN several seats in the National Assembly and control of the local government in several cities. Despite these obstacles, the FMLN succeeded in creating political space for the left that was unprecedented in Salvadoran history. In the March 1997 national and municipal elections, the FMLN fared quite well. It won the mayoralty of San Salvador—the most important political office after the presidency—as well as other key departmental municipalities. Of the country's 262 municipalities, the FMLN governed fifty-three, covering 45 percent of the population. On the congressional front, the FMLN won twenty-seven out of eighty-four seats, just one fewer than ARENA, which was forced into a government coalition with other conservative parties. The FMLN achieved its success in local elections based on its work in the fourteen municipalities it controlled from the 1994 elections and the role it has played in the national legislature as an opponent of the government's unpopular economic policies. As a result of the 2003 elections, the FMLN emerged as the largest single party in the National Assembly, with thirty-one seats, three more than the ruling ARENA Party. In 2004, its presidential candidate, former guerrilla leader Schafik Handal, lost his bid for the presidency to the ARENA candidate Tony Saca, but the party maintained a strong presence in the country.

Guatemala

A discussion of revolution in Guatemala must encompass a long period of time and does not involve transcendent events like the Cuban Revolution of 1959 or the Sandinista Revolution of 1979. The high point of revolutionary forces in Guatemala may well have been in 1944, when an armed uprising succeeded in driving the long-time dictator General Jorge Ubico y Castañeda (1931–1944) from power. The movement against Ubico began with a student strike and escalated into a general strike that forced Ubico's resignation in June 1944. However, the resignation was a front for the continuation of Ubico's system, and it soon led to an armed rebellion of students, workers, and dissident army officers. The rebel movement won an easy victory and set up a junta government known as the "October Revolution." The rebellion paved the way for elections that brought Juan José Arévalo to power in 1945. Once in power the Arévalo government pursued a reformist strategy rather than a revolutionary one. There was unprecedented government spending on schools, hospitals, and housing; and workers were allowed to unionize and engage in collective bargaining. However, rural Guatemala, which held 90 percent of the country's population, was largely untouched by the reforms. Arévalo was followed in office by Jácobo Arbenz, who deepened his predecessor's reform program but maintained Guatemala fully within the framework of capitalism. In fact, in 1950, Arbenz declared that his primary intent was to make Guatemala "a modern capitalist country." His primary extension of Arévalo's reforms was to carry them to the rural sector by inaugurating a modest land reform that challenged the most blatant policies of the U.S.-owned United Fruit Company. Arbenz also legalized the Communist Party, a reform-oriented organization with significant influence among unionized workers. These reforms, although modest in character, were too much for the country's oligarchy and the government of the United States. In 1954, Arbenz was removed from power in a military coup strongly backed by the United States through the actions of the Central Intelligence Agency (CIA). The newly installed government of Castillo Armas cracked down on anyone suspected of revolutionary activity. This witch hunt succeeded in setting back the possibility of a Guatemalan revolution by many years. The military coup ushered in a 30,000-strong armed force that brutally repressed any opposition political movements over the ensuing 40 years. Peaceful forms of protest were routinely outlawed, and rural villages were often attacked by army patrols seeking to capture "subversives."

The revival of an armed resistance to the Guatemalan military began with the November 1960 revolt of army officers against President Miguel Ydígoras. The revolt was crushed when the United States sent Cuban exiles being trained for the ill-fated Bay of Pigs invasion. However, several rebel leaders escaped and established low-grade guerrilla warfare against the regime. One of the guerrillas' first leaders was Marco Antonio Yon Sosa, originally trained by the United States. Yon Sosa was killed in combat, but guerrillas who survived helped form the Guerrilla Army of the Poor (EGP) in 1972. Inspired by liberation theology, they built a base among the highland Indians, the first revolutionary movement to do so. By 1980 the EGP and other smaller groups had more than 5000 members. The growing strength of the rebel movement alarmed the Guatemalan oligarchy, and fierce repression was unleashed against the rural areas in the early 1980s. The military's strategy was to destroy the guerrillas' base of operations by terrorizing the civilian population.

During General Romeo Lucas García's rule (1978–1982), there were numerous massacres. With financial support from the U.S. government, the military evacuated Indians from the northern highland guerrilla strongholds in Quiche and Huehuetenango departments and organized them in "model villages," a strategy developed by the United States in Vietnam. The military offered the local population a stark choice: work with us and be housed and fed, or die. In 1982, Lucas García was replaced in a coup by General Efraín Ríos Montt, a "born-again" Christian. Montt declared a state of siege and dramatically increased the level of repression. On July 6, 1982, more than 300 Indian residents of Finca San Francisco in Huehuetenango were massacred outside of their local church. Between 1981 and 1983, it is estimated that 100,000 Indians in 440 villages lost their lives at the hands of government forces. More than 1 million people were displaced from their homes. The repression resulted in the growth of the revolutionary movement. In 1982, the four main guerrilla groups, headed by EGP, united to form the Guatemalan National Revolutionary Union (URNG). With stepped-up covert U.S. assistance, the Guatemalan military escalated its war against the guerrillas. Newer, more sophisticated weaponry, including helicopter gunships, forced the URNG into retreat by 1983, a move that the Guatemalan government falsely labeled as a defeat of the revolutionary forces. The revolutionary movement survived throughout the 1980s and was bolstered by the growth of strong social protest movements in Guatemala's cities led by labor unions and human rights organizations. In 1987, the labor organizations formed a coalition with the Group of Mutual Support (GAM, an organization of relatives of the victims of repression) and the Peasant Unity Committee (CUC) to demand improved wages, an accounting for the victims of the repression, and land distribution. These forces of civil society, viewed by the military as allies of the guerrilla movement, also faced harsh repression. Despite the repression, the civil society organizations survived and participated in the 1992 U.N.-brokered negotiations started between the URNG and the government and military. The negotiations occurred because the guerrillas, with their numbers reduced to less than 3000, realized that military victory was unlikely and the Guatemalan government was under pressure from the administration of George H. W. Bush to reduce emphasis on military aid programs and increase emphasis on consolidating a regional trading bloc. However, given the depths of Guatemala's repression and the reluctance of the oligarchy to accept cooperation with the revolutionaries, the peace settlement did not come easily. In 1993, President Jorge Antonio Serrano attempted to reimpose military rule and return to tactics of harsh repression. However, his coup attempt was reversed by a combination of street demonstrations and opposition from the Clinton administration. Serrano was replaced by Ramiro de León Carpio, the parliament's human rights adviser. His appointment put the stalled negotiations back on track, and a peace settlement was finally achieved on December 27, 1996, bringing an end to Central America's longest civil war. The peace agreement formally ended the civil war but did not end violent conflict in the country, nor did the settlement significantly address the long-standing social inequalities that have fueled the conflict. Most importantly, there was little change in the pattern of land tenure, with 65 percent of the country's arable land remaining in the hands of just 2.6 percent of the population. The peace agreements called for peaceful settlements of land claims and the return of thousands of displaced families, but the administration of President Alvaro Enrique Arzú Yrigoyen, with the support of the country's traditional oligarchy, did little to further those aspects of the accords. The former revolutionaries, the URNG, operating as part of the civil opposition, now use the courts and public protest to press their reform agenda; but at this time, the relationship of forces is against them.

Colombia

Another of Latin America's most important contemporary revolutionary movements is the Revolutionary Armed Forces of Colombia (FARC). In 2008, the FARC had a presence in more than 60 percent of Colombia's municipalities. Although under sharp attack from well-armed paramilitaries and the Colombian government, the FARC sustained itself for more than three decades and contributed significantly to that country's continuing political unrest. The origins of the FARC lie in the peasant struggles of more than a half-century ago. Facing harsh living and working conditions, the workers on coffee plantations began to organize around labor demands and broader political concerns. The movement was most active in central Colombia but faced brutal repression by the army. The peasants responded with armed self-defense groups as early as the 1940s. In 1948, a 10-year period known as *La Violencia* was sparked by the assassination of populist leader Jorge Gaitán. The Colombian Communist Party was very active in this time period and assisted in the organization of self-defense and guerrilla groups. With the triumph of the Cuban Revolution in 1959, the concept of self-defense began to be transformed into the idea of the pursuance of guerrilla warfare with the goal of achieving state power for the purpose of social revolution. It was in this political context that the FARC was founded in 1964.

The organization began among communities of displaced peasants who had settled uncultivated lands in the hope of fleeing the repression of the state. Those who were fleeing state violence traveled in large groups protected by armed self-defense units, a process known as "armed colonization." These settlements were strongly under the influence of the Communist Party. It was these communities that later became the base of the FARC. The nature of national politics in Colombia also contributed to the development of a revolutionary movement. Two political parties, the Liberals and Conservatives, totally monopolized political power and prevented the development of any role within the system for legal means of dissent. To move competition from more violent forms and share power through alternation, they signed a power-sharing agreement in 1956. This alliance, known as the National Front from 1958 to 1974, has dominated the Colombian political scene to the present. Until the implementation of a new constitution in 1991, these two parties ruled under a permanent state of siege designed to curtail virtually all social protest. By blocking almost all possibility of a democratic left, the state created conditions for the emergence of an opposition that was outside of the parliamentary framework.

The FARC was not the only revolutionary group to be founded in this context. The National Liberation Army (ELN) was formed in 1964, the Popular Liberation Army (EPL) in 1965, and the April 19th Movement (M-19) in 1973. Smaller urban groups were also formed in this time period. In its early years, the growth of the FARC was slow. By the late 1970s, it had established a marginal presence in the central and southern parts of the country; but in the early 1980s, the FARC grew rapidly as the result of a government crackdown on legal opposition. Up until that time it had operated primarily in the political arena but now began to more clearly articulate its role as a military vanguard. It acquired the organizational structure of an army and developed an autonomy from the Communist Party. By 1983, it had expanded its military activity to eighteen fronts.

The FARC was committed to fundamental societal transformation through the armed achievement of state power, but it also pursued a flexible tactical position. In 1983, the government of Belisario Betancur made a significant peace overture. Departing sharply from the political stance of his predecessors, Betancur acknowledged many of the socioeconomic demands of the FARC. A cease-fire was arranged, and the possibility of a political revolution of the conflict became real. In the context of the cease-fire, the FARC formed the Patriotic Union (UP), a political front in which the Communist Party played a significant role. The FARC was preparing for a possible electoral role but did not dismantle its military apparatus.

The possibility of a political settlement was scuttled by Betancur's opposition in the congress, which rejected the reforms proposed in the accords. The political opposition represented the traditional oligarchy and its allies in the military. When a new government under Virgilio Barco came to power in 1986, the government's overture to the armed opposition officially ended. It refused to recognize the demands of the opposition as legitimate and immediately launched harsh repression against the rebels and their supporters in civil society. During 1988 alone, close to 200 UP leaders were assassinated; and in a decade of repression, nearly 3000 UP members, including mayors, municipal council members, and senators, were killed, virtually eliminating the organization. Despite this repression, the FARC did not officially return to a stance of war until 1991, after the military occupied the town of Casa Verde, the home of the FARC leadership. Although brief peace talks were conducted in mid-1991, the war intensified from that time onward. A constitutional assembly convened in 1991, and the FARC blamed the government for missing an opportunity to incorporate the political opposition through that process.

As the decade of the 1990s wore on, the FARC and other armed rebel groups found themselves at the center of political unrest in the country. The central government in Bogotá was increasingly unable to govern the country effectively as it battled the increasing influence of both drug cartels and rebel political movements. Unable to control the country by normal means, the government turned to paramilitary organizations to deal with problems by sheer force. In essence, it privatized the war against the FARC and the ELN and in the process served to delegitimize the state. As a result, the 1990s saw great ongoing costs in terms of human lives and property. The weakness of the central government opened the door for the FARC to implement a strategy of undermining local ruling structures by its tactic of "armed oversight." By gathering detailed information on local government financing and spending, the guerrillas were able to both target and expose corrupt local officials while also steering some government revenues toward FARC-sponsored projects.

The ongoing crisis of agriculture also contributed to the growing strength of the FARC. As traditional agricultural production declined, the rebels built support among those sectors hardest hit by the decline. The FARC successfully attracted unemployed youth from the countryside into its ranks. As the peasants increasingly looked to coca production to make up for the decline in other production, the

The late Manuel Marulanda Velez, also known as "Tirofijo" (sure shot) in the mountains of Colombia. He had been the undisputed leader of the FARC, the oldest and largest guerilla movement in Latin America. (*Printed with permission of Diego Giudice/Archivolatino.com*)

FARC stepped forward with protection for those communities. Such actions helped finance the FARC's activities while also raising its political legitimacy among the poorest sectors. The support of the coca growers has contributed to the growing polarization of the society as the government has ignored the real socioeconomic issues and sought with the support of the U.S. government to place the rebels' activities within the militarized scope of the War on Drugs.

The relationship between the FARC and the political process has been more problematic. In 1996, in the midst of sharp conflict between the coca growers and the central government, the FARC organized a highly successful boycott of the municipal elections in the areas where its influence was strongest. In some cities, mayors were elected by as few as seven votes but prevented from taking office by popularly convened local councils. However, the ability of the guerrillas to protect those communities that defied the central government was limited. The government authorized campaigns of terror against these communities, carried out by private paramilitaries. Such growing polarization and the growing importance of the ELN make the prospect of a political settlement to Colombia's long-running insurgent rebellion unlikely in the near future. Heightened U.S. involvement through Plan Colombia further escalated the conflict. The election of hardline President Alvaro Uribe in 2002 dashed any immediate hopes of a negotiated settlement of the long-running civil war. Uribe ruled out negotiations with the FARC and, with the support of the United States through Plan Colombia, vowed to militarily destroy the guerrilla movement. In 2003, the government won some significant victories over the FARC, including targeted attacks on its leadership; but the FARC escalated its own tactics with increasingly bold terror attacks on wealthy Bogotá neighborhoods, including the bombing of the El Nogal club that killed 36 persons in February 2003. With the war continuing in stalemate, negotiations between the FARC and Colombia resumed in 2004 over ending the conflict and the prisoners held by both sides. Aided by the Venezualan and other Latin American governments, a dramatic prisoner release was negotiated in 2007, but the process was stimied after the Colombian armed forces raided a FARC camp just inside Ecuadoran territory and killed the FARC leader who was coordinating prisoner exchanges in 2008.

Peru

One of Latin America's most interesting revolutionary movements is Peru's *Sendero Luminoso* (Shining Path) *of José Carlos Mariátegui*. In the late 1980s and early 1990s, they were the most active rebels in Latin America and were seen as seriously challenging state power against an increasingly weak central government in Lima. A decade later, with most of its key leaders either in jail or dead, Shining Path was reduced to a marginal position in Peruvian politics. Its relative demise provided some interesting insight on revolution and revolutionary movements.

Shining Path was founded in 1980 by Abimael Guzmán, a philosophy professor at the university in Ayacucho. He had been doing preparatory work in the area for some years before. For the next 13 years, the Communist Party of Peru, known as Shining Path, was a central actor in Peruvian politics. Founded on the Maoist principle of a peasant-based revolution that would gain control of the countryside and eventually encircle and overwhelm the central government, Shining Path was quite successful in reaching out from its original student base to gain widespread influence among the indigenous people of the Ayacucho region, long ignored by the central government in Lima. The rebels burst onto the scene by assassinating local officials who refused to cooperate with their efforts and by seeking to create armed, liberated communities out of the reach of the central government. Their political strategy was fiercely sectarian, rejecting all other political movements as part of the status quo. Shining Path was willing to use violence against any reformist forces that refused to cooperate with its strategy—trade unionists, neighborhood organizers, other leftists, or priests and nuns engaged in community organizing. This harsh sectarianism eventually contributed to the movement's decline. Initially, the government's response was almost entirely counterproductive. In the 1980s, the government carried out a military occupation of the highlands region where Shining Path was based. The army's draconian actions did not succeed in defeating the revolutionaries in their strongholds, and popular reaction to the government repression actually helped to spread the revolution to other provinces. Between 1989 and 1992, Shining Path stepped up its armed activity in Lima and engaged in a highly effective car- and truck-bombing campaign, badly shaking the government's confidence. However, upon a thorough review of its earlier counterproductive repression, the government began to reformulate its counterinsurgency strategy. Playing on the divisions in the rural communities that were created by Shining Path's sectarian tactics, the government began to succeed in getting rural inhabitants to join government-backed armed self-defense groups. It was a testament to Shining Path's brutality that the government began to succeed despite its own previous brutality. Shining Path's war became one of *campesinos* against *campesinos*. Shining Path's base of support generally did not grow beyond the most marginalized people—students, teachers, and unemployed youth from the shantytowns. It became more a sect than a broad-based popular movement.

In 1992, through stepped-up intelligence activities, the police were able to arrest a number of key intermediate-level officials, weakening the organization's internal structures. This increased repression occurred in the framework of President Alberto Fujimori's auto-coup, or assumption of dictatorial powers, under the guise of fighting Shining Path. Fujimori's efforts culminated later in 1992 with the arrest of Guzmán. Soon after his capture, Guzmán called off the armed struggle and sought political dialogue with the government. However, in 1994, several key Shining Path leaders denounced Guzmán's call for negotiations and vowed to continue the armed struggle. Most of them were later arrested. Shining Path has not been completely destroyed, but as the decade ended it sought to remain politically relevant in the wake of its disunity and numerous defeats at the hands of the government. By 2005, it had been reduced to a few small bands operating in remote areas where the production of coca leaves and the related drug trade could help to finance its existence.

New Social Movements

In recent years, protest and resistance have taken on different forms. New types of mobilization are developing all over Latin America. Unlike radical revolutionary movements of the last few decades, these new movements do not employ or advocate the radical, revolutionary restructuring of the state through violent revolution. Rather, their primary focus is to contest power by working through civil society to modify the existing political system and pushing it to the limits to achieve needed and necessary change and restructuring. Although there have been some exceptions, like the initial Zapatista uprising of early January 1994 and the very brief participation of the Confederation of Indigenous Nationalities of Ecuador (CONAIE) in a would-be junta that held the Ecuadorian Congress building overnight in January 2000, they were short-lived and both movements quickly moved from trying to insert themselves as the regional or national rulers to negotiating power with existing national political elites (while at the same time trying to change the composition of the national political class).

These new political movements all contest power but do so in a political environment that is substantially different from what it has been historically. National-level political participation was quite limited at the time of independence. As suggested above, mass political movements like that led by Hidalgo failed, while those led by the less popularly oriented members of the *criollo* elite, like Iturbide, succeeded and set the stage for the elitist politics of the nineteenth and much of the twentieth centuries. The franchise—and concomitant political participation—were widened in the nineteenth and twentieth centuries. This in turn challenged the political elite to seek mechanisms to incorporate (if not manipulate) ever wider segments of the population. This eventually led to the emergence of mass-based parties, reformist and revolutionary parties, and populism as a means of incorporating the masses into a national project led by a political elite. Some reformist parties, like Liberación Nacional in Costa Rica and Acción Democrática in Venezuela, were able to bring about some economic and political structural change and incorporate wider sectors of the masses into national society and competitive two-party dominant political systems. A few populist projects, like Peronism in Argentina, were also able to achieve significant economic redistribution, break the oligarchy's economic domination, and incorporate the laboring masses and segments of the middle class into the (one party-dominant) party system, albeit under the somewhat demagogic leadership of Juan and Evita Perón. On the other hand, the Cuban Revolution challenged traditional elitist rule in a different way but left little space for the development of autonomous social movements, though it did respond to the needs of the masses and developed mechanism of *poder popular* that fomented active participation at the neighborhood and local levels. The widespread rebellion against Anastasio Somoza in Nicaragua helped to make it possible for the Sandinista revolution to take power and for the FSLN-led government to begin an economic, social, and political restructuring of the Nicaraguan nation. Indeed, as we noted in *Democracy and Socialism in Sandinista Nicaragua*, the strength and relative autonomy of many of the mass organizations in Nicaragua in the early 1980s were significant and helped to show that new organizational structures and political movements that supported them could radically change the way power was exercised in Latin America. Likewise, the strength and dynamism of neighborhood- and community-based movements that began to flower all over Latin America in the 1980s (even under repressive military regimes) redefined the parameters of political activism and suggested new repertoires of action for emerging social and political movements.

Hugo Chávez with the people. (*Ministry of Information, Venezuela*)

The systems of mass communication and related communication technology as well as easy, low-cost access to the internet have combined with higher levels of literacy, widened access to higher education, and much greater political freedom under the democratization process. The result has been a new wave of political and social movements that are often different in their organization and strategy and endeavor to articulate popular needs in new ways. This has occurred when ideas of grassroots democracy, popular participation, and even elements of liberation theology and Christian base community organization have been widely disseminated. Likewise, there is a growing belief that racial, gender, and economic equality should exist and that systems that perpetuate inequality need to be changed.

Ever since the *Caracazo* in Venezuela in 1989, there have been different forms of popular protest against austerity measures and elements of the conservative economic policies that came to be called "neoliberalism" in Latin America. These have been manifest in diverse forms: the Zapatista rebellion in Mexico in 1994; the neopopulist Movimiento V República led by Hugo Chávez in Venezuela from the late 1990s on; the national indigenous movement led by CONAIE in Ecuador, the growth of its related party Pachakutik, and the election of Rafael Correa; the Movement of Landless Rural Laborers (MST) in Brazil; the *Asambleas Barriales* and other protest organizations in Argentina; and the indigenous peasant unions and Cocaleros Federation and their linked political movement, the Movimiento al Socialismo (MAS) in Bolivia.

Argentine Manifestation

In Argentina, popular mobilizations, street demonstrations, strikes, and neighborhood *asembleas populares* (or *Asambleas Barriales*) shook the political system and the political class to the core at the end of 2001 and occasioned the resignation of elected president Fernando de la Rua, and the rapid replacement of three other appointed presidents (the vice president had already resigned). In early 2002, a declared anti-neoliberal Peronist president, Eduardo Duhalde, was voted into office by the Argentine Congress. The unresolved economic crisis, default on the foreign debt, and Duhalde's perceived need to make some concession to the IMF, other international financial institutions, and U.S. policy kept the population angry and mobilized. Demonstrations and protests continued through early 2003 as the Argentine nation grouped to find a political force capable of ending the crisis. There was so little confidence in traditional parties or politicians that one could frequently hear a popular refrain among many Argentinians—*Que se vayan todos!* (Throw them all out!). However, the limitations of this movement were shown when the Argentine people elected Nestor Kirchner, a more traditional politician from the Peronist Party, to be president in 2003. He promised to move away from neoliberalism and dictates from the IMF and other international financial institutions and return to the traditional nationalist positions of the Peronists.

The nature of the protest in Buenos Aires and other Argentine cities suggests the political sea change that is sweeping across Latin America. Governance is breaking down, and traditional political institutions are losing legitimacy as new movements surge to challenge traditional political leadership. In recent years, a great many of the masses—and some of the middle class—seem to be hit by a feeling that the much touted return to democracy, celebration of civil society, and incorporation in the globalization process have left them marginalized economically, if not politically as well. The reactions in Argentina, Mexico, Ecuador, Bolivia, Brazil, and Venezuela are strong and significant and, in varying ways, represent a new means of pressuring for much needed restructuring, not from above but by the common people. It is also quite possible that the democratization and celebration of civil society allow—some would say encourage—the political mobilization that is manifest in the widespread emergence of new social and political movements.

Dissatisfaction seems widespread. Selected abstention rates are indicative of growing disillusion with government and the political system. In elections in Argentina in 2001, some 41 percent of the voters abstained or cast annulled or blank ballots. The 1998 national elections in Brazil saw a similar phenomenon, with 40.1 percent of the electorate either abstaining or casting blank or annulled ballots. In the Mexican presidential election of 2000, the abstention rate alone was 36 percent.

As the continent democratizes, there is even greater discussion of the emergence of a new(er) political class. Such talk is, however, coupled to a growing consensus that the political class's new political enterprise is leaving behind the great majorities and effectively further marginalizing specific groups within those majorities. Such groups include indigenous people in southern Mexico and Ecuador, rural laborers and the poor generally in Brazil, the rural peasants and indigenous people in Bolivia, those who live in the slums and who have been left out of the diffusion of oil wealth in Venezuela, as well as large segments of the lower and middle classes in Argentina. Major organizations include the national indigenous group CONAIE in Ecuador, the Cocaleros Federation led by Evo Morales in Bolivia, and the MST in Brazil. Smaller groups include social movements like the Madres de la Plaza de Mayo in Argentina.

Chiapas: Regional Victory

In southern Mexico, local and community organizations began to resist the dire economic consequences engendered by globalization and globalized integration through free trade and the North American Free Trade Agreement (NAFTA). It is argued that similar forms of resistance have occurred throughout the hemisphere since the region was interjected into the international capitalist economic system. Yet, these previous struggles were more akin to traditional peasant or indigenous rebellions in that they did not spawn strong national or international links and as such were easily marginalized or defeated. Indeed, localized resistance had bubbled to the surface sporadically since the time of the conquest, if not before. This certainly had been the case in southern Mexico and the Yucatan. Perhaps stimulated by this tradition of rebellion, in the 1980s the indigenous rural population in Chiapas began to resist and organize against the traditional land inequity and the hardships that the commercialization of agriculture and Mexico's further integration into the global market structure caused them. Racial identity and unequal land distribution helped to solidify the movement and led to the formation of a social movement that eventually spawned the Zapatista Army of National Liberation (EZLN). Unlike some other groups, the Zapatistas were successful in linking their struggle to a growing continental indigenous identity and the disastrous effects of globalized free markets on local small farmers. Their ingenious use of the internet, the mountain or ski mask, public relations, marches, and mobilizations kept their cause before the Mexican nation and the international community. They were able to create a highly politicized movement with considerable regional power and national visibility. They were not, however, able to link their struggle to other large politicized social movements to form a national coalition. Nor were they able to mobilize their support behind a nationwide new political party or political movement (as was done in Ecuador and Brazil) that would be sympathetic to their demands once it achieved national power or that would at least ensure them adequate space in civil society to continue to mobilize support and pursue their demands (as would be done in Bolivia in 2003 and 2005).

Ecuador

Southern Mexico was not the only place where the effects of neoliberal policies and the globalization process generated innovative responses. Since Incan times, local indigenous communities have been marginalized from important decision-making processes in Ecuador. This practice was extended to virtually all indigenous people after the conquest and continued during the republic. Yet, by the 1990s, the traditional struggle for land, power, and some modicum of justice for the indigenous, mostly peasant masses was gradually transformed from a local, community-based one to a national one coordinated by CONAIE. CONAIE had become a national organization that was able to mobilize thousands of its people in land takeovers and marches. It connected different ethnic and regional groups and used modern means of communication to forge a national social movement. In the process, it became a major power contender that could challenge governmental action by the late 1990s. After the disastrous dollarization of the economy and imposition of other neoliberal economic policies by President Jamil Mahuad, CONAIE was able to mobilize tens of thousands of its constituents for a march on Quito that culminated in the taking of the congress building and—backed by a few progressive army officers and civilian politicians—the formation of a short-lived junta in January 2000. This was the first time indigenous people had governed substantial parts of Ecuador since the conquest. Their victory was, however, brief. Although some horizontal contacts with other organizations had been made, the CONAIE militants were not part of a broad-based national coalition that could retain power. With the support of the United States, the traditional political class was able to retake power and negotiate the exit of Mahuad by placing Vice-President Gustavo Noboa in power. Once mobilized, CONAIE, learning from the experience, initiated a national political strategy and even started an affiliated political party, Pachakutik in 1995. In the 2002 elections, they continued to cultivate their now highly politicized national social movement but were also able to field successful local and congressional political candidates. Eventually, they threw their support behind Lucio Gutiérrez, the army colonel who had been part of the short-lived junta in January 2000. Thus, they helped to elect Gutiérrez to the presidency, though their support was not unconditional. They maintained their autonomy but ensured that their demands would at least receive a hearing at the highest level and might even be received with some sympathy. This stance became important because, once in power, Gutiérrez moved away from his anti-neoliberal positions to the point of seeking a free trade agreement with the United States. CONAIE led the opposition against the turn in the president's politics, and in early 2005, he was forced from office amid large street protests. The support of CONAIE and other indigenous movements was fundamental for the 2006 election of left-leaning candidate Rafael Correa to the presidency, and his pursuit of a more progressive political agenda.

New Social Movements and New Politics: The MST

The radically different nature of these new social movements and the new politics can perhaps best be seen in the largest of the new social movements in Latin America, the MST in Brazil. Their ranks exceed 1 million, and on one occasion they were able to mobilize 100,000 people for a march on Brasília. In a pamphlet titled *Brazil Needs a Popular Project*, the organization calls for popular mobilizations, noting that "All the changes in the history of humanity only happened when the people were mobilized" and that, in Brazil, "all the social and political changes that happened were won when the people mobilized and struggled." Their political culture and decision-making processes break from the authoritarian tradition. The movement has been heavily influenced by liberation theology and the participatory democratic culture that is generated by the use and study of Paulo Freire's approach to self-taught, critical education.

The MST itself was formed as a response to long-standing economic, social, and political conditions in Brazil. Land, wealth, and power have been allocated in very unequal ways in Brazil since the conquest in the early 1500s. Land has remained highly concentrated, and as late as 1996, 1 percent of the landowners who owned farms of over 1000 hectares owned 45 percent of the land. Conversely, as of 2001, there were some 4.5 million landless rural workers in Brazil. Wealth has remained equally concentrated. In 2001, the Brazilian Institute of Government Statistics reported that the upper 10 percent of the population averaged an income that was nineteen times greater than that of the lowest 40 percent. The plantation agriculture that dominated the colonial period and the early republic became the standard for Brazilian society. The wealthy few owned the land, reaped the profits, and decided the political destiny of the many. Slavery was the institution that provided most of the labor on the early plantation system and, thus, set the nature of the relationship between the wealthy landowning elite and the disenfranchised masses who labored in the fields. Land has stayed in relatively few hands in Brazil, and agricultural laborers continue to be poorly paid and poorly treated. Further, after the commercialization and mechanization of agriculture that began in the 1970s, much of the existing rural labor force became superfluous. As this process continued, not only were rural laborers let go but sharecroppers were expelled from the land they had farmed and small farmers lost their land to larger family or commercial estates. This resulted in increases in rural unemployment and the number of rural landless families. Many were forced to migrate to the cities to swell the numbers of the urban poor, while others opted for the government-sponsored Amazon colonization program whereby they were transported to the Amazon region to cut down the rain forest and cultivate the land. Few found decent jobs in the city, and the poor soil of the former rain forest allowed for little sustained agriculture. As conditions deteriorated, the landless realized that they were fighting for their own existence as a group and, as such, were the authors of their own destiny. The origins of the organization go back to the bitter struggle to survive under the agricultural policies implemented by the military government. The landless in the southern Brazilian state of Rio Grande do Sul began to organize to demand land. Other landless people soon picked up their cry in the neighboring states of Paraná and Santa Catarina. They built on a long tradition of rural resistance and rebellion that extends back to the establishment of *palenques* or large inland settlements of runaway slaves and to the famous rebellion by the poor rural peasants of Canudos in the 1890s. In more recent times, it included the famous Peasant Leagues of Brazil's impoverished northeast in the 1950s and early 1960s and the "grass wars" in Rio Grande do Sul and the southern states in the 1970s. When the MST was founded in southern Brazil in 1984 as a response to rural poverty and lack of access to land, wealth, and power, similar conditions existed in many states. Indeed, there were landless workers and peasants throughout the nation. Thus, the MST soon spread from Rio Grande do Sul and Paraná in the south to states like Pernambuco in the northeast and Pará in the

Amazon region. It rapidly became a national organization with coordinated policies and strong local participation and decision making, with frequent state and national meetings based on direct representation. By 2001 there were active MST organizations in 23 of the 26 states.

This type of national organization had not been the case with the Zapatista movement because conditions and identity were much more locally rooted. Yet, in both cases, traditional politics and traditional political parties had proven unable and unwilling to address the deteriorating economic conditions of the marginalized groups who were suffering the negative effects of economic globalizaton. Their response was grassroots organization and the development of a new repertoire of actions that broke with old forms of political activity. Developing organization and group actions began to tie individual members together in a strongly forged group identity. The MST decided from the outset that it was to be an organization for the landless workers that would be run by the landless workers for their benefit as they defined it. They engaged in direct actions such as land takeovers from large estates and public lands, construction of black plastic-covered encampments along the side of the road to call attention to their demands for land, and marches and confrontations when necessary. They even occupied the family farm of President Fernando Henrique Cardoso to draw attention to his landowning interests and the consequent bias they attributed to him. They were at times brutally repressed, assassinated, and imprisoned; but they persevered, forcing land distribution to their members and others without land. Their ability to mobilize as many as 12,000 people for a single land takeover or 100,000 for a national march in 1997 suggested just how strong their organizational abilities were and how well they could communicate and coordinate at the national level. They also created a great deal of national support and helped to create a consensus that there was a national problem with land distribution and that some substantial reform was necessary. Struggles that were once local and isolated were now international and linked. The news media and growing international communications links, like cellular phones and especially electronic mail, greatly facilitated the globalization of struggle and of awareness of local struggles as well as support and solidarity for them. This and the dramatic actions like massive land takeovers by the MST also generated considerable support at the national level and helped to define what might have been considered a local problem as a national one that required national attention and national resources to remedy it.

The interaction between the MST and the Workers' Party (PT) is also instructive. Although relations between the two organizations are generally excellent at the local level, with overlapping affiliations, the national leaderships have remained separate and not always as cordial. The MST has maintained a militant line in regard to the need to take over unused land and assert its agenda, whereas much of the PT leadership has wanted to be more conciliatory. Thus, the landless backed and supported Luiz Inácio "Lula"da Silva and the PT in most local campaigns and the national campaign for the presidency. In this way, they helped to achieve significant regime change in Brazil, where Lula was elected with 61.27 percent of the vote in the second round of voting in 2002. Indeed, realizing the PT's historic challenge to neoliberal policies and elitist rule, the landless turned out heavily in the election to join some 80 percent of the registered voters who participated in the voting in both rounds. The Landless again supported Lula in the 2006 election, but were even more critical after major land reform initiatives failed to materialize in his second term. Once the elections were over, the MST did not press to be part of the government. Rather, they continued to press the government for a comprehensive land reform program and redistribution of the land and the wealth. There would be no return to politics as usual. The PT would press its "0 Hunger" program and other social and economic initiatives, and the MST would press the PT government for the structural reforms (e.g., comprehensive agrarian reform) that it considered necessary.

Conclusion

Political scientist Eric Selbin has suggested that, given Latin America's 500-year-old tradition of rebellion and revolution, we should be wary of dismissing the possibility of future revolutions there. An understanding of why revolution and serious study of it must remain integral to our study of Latin America is rooted in the fact that the recent growth of democratic political forms and economic restructuring have done relatively little to eliminate the social inequalities and political disenfranchisement that plagued Latin America in the twentieth century. The greater harbinger for the continued probability of revolutionary upsurges and movements for radical change in Latin America comes from the fact that as the region begins the new millennium more people live in poverty than was the case 20 years ago and the fact that the gap between the richest and poorest grows wider. Nearly half of the region's more than 580 million people are poor, an increase of more than 70 million in one decade. Most of the regimes that took power during Latin America's recent turn to democratic rule did not seem to make any significant progress in the arena of social justice, with the result that the neoliberal economic models triumphant at the start of the 1990s were increasingly being called into question. By 2008 politics were once again changing. There were myriad new social and political movements that were pressing hard for structural change and were democratizing the decision-making process if not the political culture itself. New leftist presidents had been elected throughout the region and many were beginning to implement projects for radical change. As U.S. President John F. Kennedy observed in the formulation of the Alliance for Progress, the stifling of reforms makes the violent struggle for change inevitable. Contemporary democratic regimes, as Selbin notes, rely far too often on pacts among elites (pacted democracy) and the marginalization of the indigenous population and masses generally. It would seem that social change will remain on the agenda in the twenty-first century in Latin America. It would also seem that new means of organizing for such change are being developed in communities and new social and political movements throughout the region. Yet, Latin America's ruling elites have rarely demonstrated great tolerance for such political opposition, and it is unclear whether that will change overnight. The social movements themselves, often with a single-issue focus, are not necessarily capable of articulating the broader vision for societal change that the region's social and political inequali-

Zapata lives! Legendary figures such as Mexican Revolutionary Emiliano Zapata inspire great admiration and emulation. After Zapata became the inspiration and namesake for the Zapatistas, pictures and Zapata decals like this one were freely circulated in Chiapas and other parts of Mexico.

ties demand. It remains to be seen if these new, highly politicized movements or new political parties, like Brazil's PT or Bolivia's MAS, will be able to remedy the region's problems through massive mobilizations and concerted political action. The extent to which they can achieve genuine change and socioeconomic restructuring will be key. If they cannot, then the next question to be asked is whether or not the traditional forms of revolution and rebellion will remain relevant or whether yet other forms of struggle will replace them.

Bibliography

Alvarez, Sonia, Evelina Dagnino, and Arturo Escobar, eds. *Cultures of Politics/Politics of Cultures: Revisioning Latin American Social Movements*. Boulder, CO: Westview Press, 1998.

Arnson, Cynthia. *Comparative Peace Processes in Latin America*. Palo Alto, CA: Stanford University Press, 1999.

Bradford, Sue, and Jan Rocha. *Cutting the Wire, the Story of the Landless Movement in Brazil*. London: Latin American Bureau, 2002.

Broad, Robin ed. *Global Backlash, Citizen Initiatives for a Just World Economy*. Lanham, MD: Rowman & Littlefield, 2002.

Colburn, Forrest. *The Vogue of Revolution in Poor Countries*. Princeton, NJ: Princeton University Press, 1994.

Debray, Regis. *Revolution in the Revolution?* New York: Grove Press, 1967.

della Porta, Donatella, and Sidney Tarrow, eds. *Transnational Protest and Global Activism*. Lanham, MD: Rowman & Littlefield, 2005.

Eckstein, Susan, ed. *Power and Protest: Latin American Social Movements*. Berkeley: University of California Press, 2001.

Ellner, Steve, and Daniel Hellinger. *Venezuelan Politics in the Chávez Era: Class, Polarization and Conflict*. Boulder, CO: Lynne Rienner, 2003.

Escobar, Arturo, and Sonia E. Alvarez. *The Making of Social Movements in Latin America: Identity, Strategy and Democracy*. Boulder, CO: Westview Press, 1992.

Hodges, Donald C. *The Latin American Revolution: Politics and Strategy from Apro-Marxism to Guevarism*. New York: William Morrow, 1974.

Kampwirth, Karen. *Women and Guerrilla Movements: Nicaragua, El Salvador, Chiapas, Cuba*. University Park: Pennsylvania State University Press, 2002.

Lefeber, Walter W. *Inevitable Revolutions: The United States in Central America*. 2nd ed. New York: Norton, 1994.

Liss, Sheldon. *Marxist Thought in Latin America*. Berkeley: University of California Press, 1984.

McClintock, Cynthia. *Revolutionary Movements in Latin America*. Washington, DC: United States Institute of Peace Press, 1998.

McLaren, Peter. *Che Guevara, Paulo Freire, and the Pedagogy of the Oppressed*. Blue Ridge Summitt, PA: Rowman & Littlefield, 2000.

Montgomery, Tommie Sue. *Revolution in El Salvador: From Civil Strife to Peace*. 2nd ed. Boulder, CO: Westview Press, 1995.

Palmer, David Scott. *Shining Path of Peru*. 2nd ed. New York: St. Martin's Press, 1992.

Selbin, Eric. *Modern Latin American Revolutions*. Boulder, CO: Westview Press, 1993.

Skocpol, Theda. *States and Social Revolution*. Cambridge: Cambridge University Press, 1979.

Stahler-Sholk, Richard, Harry E. Vanden, and Glen Kuecker, eds. Special issue: Globalizing Resistence: The New Politics of Social Movements in Latin America. *Latin American Perspectives*. Vol 34, No. 2, March 2007.

——. eds. *Latin American Social Movements in the Twenty-First Century: Resistance, Power and Democracy*. Lanham, MD: Rowman and Littlefield, 2008.

Stedile, João Pedro, and Bernardo Mançano Fernandes. *Brava Gente: a Trajetórai do MST e a Luta Pela Terra no Brasil*. São Paulo: Fundacão Perseo Abramo, 1999.

Vanden, Harry E. *Latin American Marxism: A Bibliography*. New York: Garland, 1991.

——. "New Political Movements, Governance and the Breakdown of Traditional Politics in Latin America." *International Journal of Public Administration* 27, no. 13–14 (2004).

——. "Globalization in a Time of Neoliberalism: Politicized Social Movements and the Latin American Response." *Journal of Developing Societies*.

Vanden, Harry E., and Gary Prevost. *Democracy and Socialism in Sandinista Nicaragua*. Boulder, CO: Lynne Rienner, 1993.

Wickham-Crowley, Timothy. *Guerrillas and Revolution in Latin America*. Princeton, NJ: Princeton University Press, 1992.

Wright, Angus, and Wendy Wolford. *To Inherit the Earth: The Landless Movement and the Struggle for a New Brazil*. Oakland, CA: Food First, 2003.

FILMS AND VIDEOS

Americas in Transition. United States, 1982.

El Salvador: Another Vietnam. United States, 1981.

Grass War! Peasant Struggle in Brazil. United States, 2001.

A Place Called Chiapas. Canada, 1998.

1932: Scars of Memory. United States, 2002. (The 1932 Matanza in El Salvador)

Raiz Forte/Strong Roots. Brazil, 2000.
Romero. United States, 1989.
Seven Dreams of Peace. United States, 1996.
Tupamaros. United States, 1996.
Ya Basta! The Battle Cry of the Forceless. United States, 1997.

WEBSITES

www.mst.br/ Landless Workers Movement in Brazil (MST).
conaie.nativeweb.org The Confederation of Indigenous Nationalities of Ecuador (CONAIE).

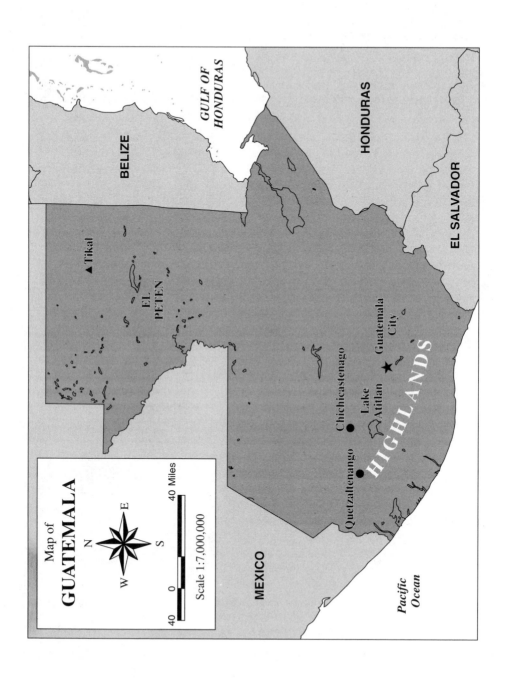

Map of
GUATEMALA

Scale 1:7,000,000

40   0   40 Miles

MEXICO

BELIZE

GULF OF
HONDURAS

▲Tikal

EL
PETEN

Quetzaltenango

Chichicastenago

Lake
Atitlan

Guatemala
City

HIGHLANDS

HONDURAS

EL SALVADOR

Pacific
Ocean

ELEVEN

GUATEMALA

Susanne Jonas

How is it possible that a country as small as Guatemala has taken on such grandiose and dramatic proportions in Latin America? Already in the mid-1960s, Uruguayan writer Eduardo Galeano referred to Guatemala as "the key to Latin America" and "a source of great lessons painfully learned." Beyond its dramatic, tortuous political history, Guatemala is distinguished by being one of the few Latin American countries with an indigenous majority of the population. During the second half of the twentieth century, Guatemala has also loomed large in the saga of United States–Latin America relations. Guatemala has suffered Latin America's longest and bloodiest Cold War civil war, lasting 36 years and leaving some 200,000 civilians dead or "disappeared." In the early years of the twenty-first century, Guatemala's peace process holds important lessons for the entire hemisphere.

Located just to the south of Mexico and slightly smaller than Tennessee (42,042 square miles), Guatemala is the most populous Central American country, its population having reached well over 11 million by 1999 and constituting over 30 percent of Central America's total. (It is worth noting that, by the end of the twentieth century, up to 10 percent of that population had migrated to the United States for political or economic reasons.) The diversity of its population, which is over 60 percent Mayan, is both a rich human/cultural resource and a source of the country's particularly turbulent history: the extreme polarization of Guatemala's social structure stems largely from the compounding of class divisions and exploitation with ethnic divisions and discrimination, which during some periods reached genocidal proportions.

The Mayan population (subdivided into twenty-two language groups) is dispersed today throughout almost all regions of Guatemala, but historically it was concentrated in the western highlands, or *altiplano,* which stretch from Mexico on the north into Honduras and El Salvador on the south. The highlands area, world famous for its spectacular beauty, contains a chain of volcanos, some of them sloping directly down into the also world-famous Lake Atitlán. The country's other major regions are the southern Pacific coastal lowlands, site of major agro-export plantations, and the large lowlands Petén area in the north, home to one of the continent's major tropical rain forests as well as the major Mayan ruins at Tikal. In the eastern half of the country, the Sierra de las Minas and Lake Izabal on the Rio Dulce lead to an Atlantic coastal lowland; this area has remained primarily *ladino* (*mestizo*), with Garifuna and Xinca indigenous populations on the Atlantic coast. Guatemala City, the capital, is located on a mesa surrounded by the central highlands.

About half of Guatemala's population is still rural, and 52 percent of its labor force is in the countryside (in part because of the scarcity of stable, permanent, full-time jobs in the cities). Guatemala City has come to concentrate 35 percent of the entire population, with Quetzaltenango at 11 percent (Los Angeles, California, has around 5 percent). The urban primacy of Guatemala City is even more striking in regard to political power and provision of social services.

Precolonial, Colonial, and Neocolonial History

Pre-Hispanic indigenous Guatemala was by no means "primitive"; what the Spanish conquerors found in 1524 was a complex, stratified, proto-class society torn by multiple social tensions. Despite these class divisions, the population was unified by a common belief system. The ruling elites were priests rather than warriors, which explains the predominance of temples in the Mayan ruins. Preconquest Mayan society had developed sophisticated technologies—more advanced and scientific in some areas (e.g., mathematics and astronomy) than those of Europe during the Middle Ages. By the sixteenth century, it was a society in transition; had it not been interrupted by the conquest, it might well have developed into a society as advanced as those in western Europe.

Despite the class divisions in pre-Hispanic Guatemala, at no time before the conquest did the Maya suffer the systematic material deprivation that has characterized Guatemala since 1524. Malnutrition, for example, was not a chronic condition of the population, as it is today. Prior to 1524, Guatemala was a primarily agricultural society in which land was cultivated both individually and communally to produce food and other necessities for the population itself, rather than for export to the world market, i.e., for consumption and profit by foreigners thousands of miles away. In this sense, underdevelopment as we know it today did not exist in Guatemala prior to 1524 but was the direct outcome of the conquest and Guatemala's integration into an expanding capitalist world economy.

The Spanish conquest itself, a violent clash of two socioeconomic systems and two cultures, forcibly integrated the Maya into "Western civilization": several million were killed immediately, and by 1650, an estimated two-thirds to six-sevenths of the indigenous population in Central America and Mexico had died, largely through disease epidemics. Following the military conquest, the colonization of Guatemala was carried out by Spanish state functionaries, Spanish settler planters and merchants, and the Catholic Church, which maintained a very close relation with the state.

The conquest and the subsequent three centuries of colonialism (1524–1821) integrated Guatemala into an expanding capitalist world market that determined the colony's production priorities and systematically channeled its surplus into the pockets of foreign ruling classes. This dependent relationship also left internal legacies that endured far longer than the colonial relation to Spain itself: agricultural monoexport (at the expense of food production, tying the ups and downs of the entire economy to the fortunes of export prices), concentration of landholding in the hands of a small minority, and various forms of unfree/forced indigenous labor as the underpinning of the entire socioeconomic structure. The overlap between the degrees of class and racial oppression was notable: unlike *indios,* as they were disparagingly called by the *criollo* (European) elites, and unlike African slave labor imported into areas where the indigenous populations had been exterminated, the *ladinos,* or mixed-origin populations, acquired greater freedom and social mobility and eventually formed the nuclei of the urban working and middle classes.

Independence from Spain in 1821 (led by the elites but supported by nearly all sectors of the population, each for its own reasons) brought little change in internal structures, although it initiated a diversification of Guatemala's external contacts. Spain's previous economic/commercial monopoly was replaced by British interests and (later in the nineteenth century) by German and U.S. interests. Within Guatemala, power alternated between Liberals and Conservatives from 1821 until the "Liberal revolution" of 1871. Both the Liberal and Conservative Parties were dominated by *criollo* elites, but they differed on issues such as the state's relation to the Catholic Church and the degree of centralization/federalism.

The 1871 triumph of the Liberals led by General Justo Rufino Barrios came in the wake of the rise of coffee as the dominant export. The land for the coffee estates, which required large concentrations of land and labor, came from the newly consolidated Liberal (anticlerical) state's confiscation of Catholic Church properties, once that Church had been disestablished, and from a major new wave of expropriations of indigenous communal lands. The Liberal revolution also saw the consolidation of the army as the principal labor mobilizer and enforcer; the army viewed its mission as maintaining "order" in the countryside. Ironically, the Liberal revolution, touted as a necessity for development, modernization, and "progress," proved far more costly than previous governments to the indigenous populations, which were now subjected to harsher forms of forced labor. Except for a brief democratic interlude in the early 1920s, Liberal military dictators ruled with an iron hand on behalf of the coffee oligarchy and foreign investors for over 70 years.

The other major change during the late nineteenth and early twentieth centuries was the expansion of U.S. private corporate interests into Guatemala and several other Central American countries. The most notable of the U.S. corporate investors in Guatemala, the United Fruit Company (UFCo), began monopolistic operations in banana production; UFCo became the largest landowner in Guatemala, writing its own contracts with the government and operating virtually unrestricted by any Guatemalan government regulations—functioning, in essence, as "a state within a state." UFCo also owned the only railroad and, hence, could dictate transportation prices. U.S. interests reinforced the interests of Guatemala's coffee growers: concentration of land ownership and coercion applied to the subjugated indigenous labor force.

This period also saw the rise of the United States as a world power and a great expansion of U.S. influence over internal Guatemalan political affairs, in alliance with the local landed oligarchy. This alliance was the key to the longevity of the Liberal dictatorships. Washington's support was crucial to the last of these dictators, Jorge Ubico, who ruled from 1931 to 1944. The Ubico regime contained social tensions, particularly after the world Depression left hundreds of thousands of rural workers unemployed during the 1930s, through top–down repression rather than reform. The model of the "pressure cooker" in Guatemala and other Central American nations contrasted sharply with the "safety valve" reforms and industrialization programs of the 1930s in larger Latin American countries such as Mexico, Chile, and Brazil. Although the purely repressive Central American model gave the appearance of guaranteeing stability, subsequent events revealed the fragility of that model.

The Revolution of 1944–1954 and the 1954 CIA Intervention

Under the weight of the economic and social crises caused by the world Depression of the 1930s, Guatemala's neocolonial order cracked in 1944, when a broad middle- and working-class coalition (including young army officers) overthrew the Ubico dictatorship. Thus was initiated the Revolution of 1944–1954, the only genuinely democratic experience in Guatemala's entire history. The two governments of Juan José Arévalo (1945–1950) and Jacobo Arbenz (1951–1954) for the first time guaranteed basic democratic liberties (including free elections and the formation of political opposition parties), abolished forced labor (which had been nearly universal for the indigenous population), granted minimum wages and basic organizing and bargaining rights for workers and peasants, and established basic institutions of social welfare. In addition, the Revolution modernized Guatemalan capitalism, undertaking agricultural diversification and industrialization programs, fomenting national enterprises, and regulating foreign investment to serve national priorities.

Most significant in this nationalist democratic revolution was Arbenz' far-reaching (but capitalist) agrarian reform of 1952, which distributed land to over 100,000 peasant families. The principle underlying the land reform was the government's expropriation of large tracts of land that were not being used by their owners, with compensation based on the value declared for tax purposes. The land would be used to produce, and the large numbers of landless would own enough land to have some disposable income; in short, the producers could become consumers, forming the basis for an internal market and reducing dependence on the world market. (This basic principle has always associated industrialization and modernization of the economy with labor guarantees and land reform.)

Coming on top of other nationalistic moves by Arbenz, the expropriation of unused land belonging to UFCo (the largest landowner in Guatemala, which had been using a mere 15 percent of its holdings) prompted an angry response from the U.S. government. (Not so coincidentally, John Foster Dulles, secretary of state beginning in 1953, and CIA director Allen Dulles had been major lawyers for UFCo.) More broadly, Washington feared the spread of the "example" of reform and popular mobilization from Guatemala to other Central American countries. The fact that the Guatemalan Revolution was occurring at the height of the Cold War enabled the United States to charge that Guatemala was serving as a "beachhead for Soviet expansion" in the Western Hemisphere (although in reality the Soviets were virtually uninvolved in Guatemala) and gave the Central Intelligence Agency (CIA) the justification it needed to plan the ouster of Arbenz.

After mid-1952, the CIA worked with Guatemalan rightist opposition forces (e.g., many of the large landowners, rightist politicians, and the Catholic Church) to organize the overthrow of the Arbenz government in June 1954 and install in its place a pro-United States counterrevolutionary regime led by (U.S.-chosen) Colonel Carlos Castillo Armas. In general, the "Liberation," as its Guatemalan supporters called it, marked the first major U.S. Cold War covert intervention in the Western Hemisphere and a turning point in U.S.–Latin American relations. Many elements of that CIA covert operation have subsequently been used against other leftist governments in Latin America—e.g., the Castro government in Cuba (1961), the Allende government in Chile (1973), and the Sandinista government in Nicaragua (1980s).

Aftermath: Chronic Crisis

The Castillo Armas regime immediately reversed the democratic and progressive legislation of the Revolution, including everything from the land reform and labor laws to literacy programs that were deemed "pro-communist indoctrination." All pro-Revolution organizations and political parties were declared illegal; under direct U.S. supervision, the government also unleashed a wide-ranging witch hunt and McCarthy-style repression campaign that cost the lives of some 8000 supporters of the Revolution and forced thousands of others into exile or hiding. The legacy of the Revolution and its violent termination was to compound the social polarization already characteristic of Guatemala, throwing the country into permanent crisis.

THE U.S. COVERT OPERATION IN GUATEMALA, 1954

- Sent a team of ambassadors to Central America instructed to collaborate with the ouster of Jacobo Arbenz; head of the team was John Peurifoy as ambassador to Guatemala, an extreme anticommunist with prior experience in defeating the rebels in the Greek civil war
- CIA chose Colonel Carlos Castillo Armas to be the Guatemalan pointman to lead the anti-Arbenz operation
- CIA fully trained, equipped, and funded the anti-Arbenz mercenary army (in Honduras) of Guatemalan rightists, led by Castillo Armas
- CIA carried out psychological warfare through clandestine "Radio Liberty" in Guatemala and through aerial propaganda leaflets dropped from planes
- Funded and worked with anti-Arbenz elements in the Guatemalan military leadership while neutralizing those loyal to Arbenz
- Maneuvered on the diplomatic front to get the Organization of American States to approve a resolution (March 1954) condemning Guatemala as posing a threat of "communist agression" against the entire hemisphere

- Imposed embargo on arms to Guatemala by all U.S. allies and subsequently used the shipment of (obsolete) arms from Czechoslovakia as a pretext for a final move against Arbenz
- Helped Castillo Armas' mercenary army "invade" Guatemala from Honduras on June 18, 1954; as soon as they were over the border, flew Castillo Armas (in Ambassador Peurifoy's private plane) to Guatemala City
- Simultaneously, CIA planes, manned by U.S. pilots, strafed and bombarded Guatemala City and other cities, to demoralize Arbenz and get him to resign (which he did on June 27)
- Despite having promised to allow prorevolution military officers to take charge following Arbenz' resignation, the United States double-crossed them and installed Castillo Armas in power
- Organized powerful lobby (largely United Fruit Company–orchestrated) in the U.S. Congress, media, and elsewhere to secure "consensus" in U.S. public opinion supporting the coup and to suppress criticism of the operation (this was the height of the McCarthy era in the United States)

(*Note:* Many members of the CIA team that organized the Guatemalan "liberation" went on to organize the Bay of Pigs invasion against Cuba [1961] and other covert operations.)

Nevertheless, even under the post-1954 counterrevolutionary order, history could not be reversed, since the same underlying structural dynamics and contradictions that had caused the Revolution continued to develop. The Guatemalan economy, like that of all Central America, enjoyed a 30-year period (1950–1980) of growth based on the expansion and diversification of agricultural exports to the world market; a minimal industrialization program during the 1960s and 1970s was carried out mainly by U.S. companies within the context of the Central American Common Market. However, even export-led growth generated turmoil because of the extreme inequities in resource and income distribution. To take the most telling indicator for Guatemala as an example, after the reversal of the land reform, 2 percent of the population controlled 67 percent of the arable land. In the 1970s, the diversification of agricultural exports brought significant new land expropriations from peasants and new concentrations of land tenure; the main beneficiaries were army generals using their control over the state apparatus to accumulate personal wealth. Thus, impoverishment stemming from land concentration intensified exponentially as Guatemala became virtually the only country in Latin America not to have sustained even minimal land reform.

At the social level, the diversification of the productive structure significantly modified Guatemala's traditional class structure and reshaped the ruling coalition between the army and economic elites, the latter being represented in a tightly knit umbrella organization, the Coordinating Committee of Agricultural, Commercial, Industrial, and Financial Associations (CACIF). Among other things, diversification of the ruling class meant incorporation of the upper ranks of military officers and a redefinition of the alliance between the army and the bourgeoisie (economic elites). Rather than "opening up" the class structure, these modifications only accentuated its overall polarization.

This billboard was at the entrance to Chichicastenango until after the signing of the Peace Accords at the end of 1996. It shows the degree of control by the army and the Civilian Self-Defense Patrols (PACs), misnamed "Comites Voluntarios," since there was nothing voluntary about them. *(Photo by S. Jonas)*

At the bottom of Guatemalan society, meanwhile, industrialization and agricultural diversification did not significantly expand the proletariat as a fully employed labor force. Rather, the countryside saw the growth of a semiproletariat: land-starved peasants from the highlands were forced to work on southern coastal plantations as seasonal migrant laborers during part of the year. In the cities, migrants from rural areas swelled the ranks of an underemployed informal proletariat. As a consequence, the "development" of the 1960s and 1970s actually left a decreasing proportion of the economically active population fully employed on a permanent basis. These tendencies were disastrously compounded during the 1980s, Latin America's "Lost Decade."

The profound changes in society after 1954 produced new generations of social movements (labor, peasant, indigenous, student, community, human rights)—first in the 1960s, then in the late 1970s, and (after they were destroyed in the late 1970s and early 1980s) again in the second half of the 1980s. In the absence of any serious attempt to meet the needs of the poor or the indigenous or to use the benefits of growth during the 1960s and 1970s to redistribute wealth, these movements continually exerted new pressures upon the state and the established social order. These pressures were contained by a level of repression at times unmatched anywhere else in Latin America; one generation after another of social movement leaders and activists, as well as moderate leftist political opposition leaders, was eliminated by the army and illegal paramilitary forces. Even systematic repression failed to stop the reemergence of popular movements in one or another form, although it severely restricted their functioning.

These massive social conflicts defined Guatemalan politics during the last four decades of the twentieth century. Within an overall framework of direct military rule, there was a civilian interlude under President Julio César Méndez Montenegro (1966–1970) and a more definitive return to civilian rule beginning in 1986; in both cases, the army dominated politics from behind the scenes. However, largely as a legacy of the experience of the 1944–1954 Revolution and its violent overthrow, hardline regimes, whether military or civilian, faced constant challenges. It was precisely the refusal to permit even moderate reformist political options that created the conditions for the growth of a revolutionary guerrilla movement attempting to repeat the experience of the 1959 Cuban Revolution. Quite literally, there was no alternative "within the system."

The first wave of guerrilla insurgency, during the 1960s, was centered in the eastern region, where the peasants were *ladino* rather than Mayan. Although small and without a base among the indigenous population, the insurgency of the Fuerzas Armadas Rebeldes (FAR) was contained only after a major counterinsurgency effort (1966–1968), organized, financed, and run directly by the United States along the lines of its operations in Vietnam. This was a turning point in Guatemala, with U.S. military advisers playing a decisive role in transforming the Guatemalan army (previously "weakened" in Washington's view by nationalist tendencies and inefficiency) into a modern, disciplined counterinsurgency army. The military grew to some 46,000 troops during the 1980s; it became known as the most brutal in Latin America—a literal "killing machine"—and during the 1970s and 1980s came to dominate the state directly.

The counterinsurgency state was institutionalized after 1970, when the head of the 1966–1968 army campaign, Colonel Carlos Arana Osorio (the "butcher of Zacapa"), used that victory to win the 1970 presidential election. Since the goal of this first "dirty war" had been to eradicate the civilian support base of the guerrillas, it cost the lives of over 8000 civilians. It was also within this context, in Guatemala, that Latin America first experienced the artifacts of counterinsurgency war: semiofficial death squads (based in the security forces and financed by economic elites, with such names as "White Hand" and "An Eye for an Eye") and "disappearances" of civilian opposition figures. Since that time, Guatemala has had more than 40,000 civilian disappearances, accounting for over 40 percent of the total for all Latin America. Thus ended the first phase of Guatemala's 36-year civil war, with the army's temporary victory by 1968 over FAR insurgents.

Insurgency and Counterinsurgency in the 1970s–1980s

As suggested earlier, the structural transformations of the 1960s–1980s caused Guatemala's Mayan populations to redefine their class identity. These same factors profoundly affected their self-conception and identities as indigenous. Economic growth followed by economic crisis broke down the objective barriers that had kept the Maya relatively isolated in the highlands. This was greatly intensified by the economic and political crises of the 1970s and 1980s, when growing numbers of

Maya were forced to migrate to the southern coast as seasonal laborers and to Guatemala City. These changes and displacements brought them into increased contact with the *ladino*, Spanish-speaking world. Rather than "ladinizing," or acculturating, them, however, these experiences reinforced their struggle to preserve their indigenous identity, although in new forms—as Guatemalan Jesuit priest/scholar/activist Ricardo Falla put it, to discover "new ways of being indigenous." These factors form the background for understanding why Guatemala's Mayan peoples became one of the powerful social forces driving the insurgency of the 1970s and 1980s.

In the countryside, structural contradictions—the crisis in subsistence agriculture compounded by a massive earthquake in 1976—uprooted and displaced thousands of indigenous peasants, causing them to redefine themselves in both class and cultural terms. As producers, they were being semiproletarianized as a seasonal migrant labor force on the plantations of the southern coast, meanwhile often losing even the tiny subsistence plots of land they had traditionally held in the highlands. The combination of their experiences of being evicted from their own lands and their experiences as a migrant semiproletariat radicalized large numbers of highlands Mayas. Even the more developmentalist influences were contradictory in that they raised hopes and expectations in the 1960s, only to dash them in the 1970s. The clearest examples of this dynamic were those peasants who received land from the government's colonization programs in the 1960s, only to have it taken away again in the 1970s, as powerful army officers grabbed profitable lands in colonization areas.

Culturally, highlands indigenous communities were being transformed and redefined throughout the 1960s and 1970s as they opened up to contact with the *ladino* world. Increased contact had the paradoxical effect of reinforcing their defense of their ethnic/cultural identity, and this became a factor in mobilizing their resistance to the *ladino* state. Politically, "reformist" parties such as the Christian Democrats came into indigenous communities, raising expectations of change—only to leave those hopes unfulfilled for most people. Meanwhile, Mayan organizations were defined by the government as "subversive" and excluded from "normal" political expression. Even their self-help organizations, formed in response to the devastating 1976 earthquake, were viewed as a threat.

Finally, increased army repression against indigenous communities had contradictory effects: rather than terrorizing the Mayas into passivity, by the late 1970s it stimulated some of them to take up arms as the only available means of self-defense against state violence. All of these contradictory experiences of the 1970s occurred in interaction with the transformation of grassroots organizations of the Catholic Church, the rise of Christian base communities, and the gradual emergence of a "Church of the Poor." These new religious currents became central to the radicalization of the Mayan highlands.

All of these strands were woven together by 1976–1978 in the emergence of the Comité de Unidad Campesina (CUC) as a national peasant organization, including both peasants and agricultural workers, both Mayas and poor *ladinos*, but led primarily by Mayas—by definition a "subversive" organization from the viewpoint of the ruling coalition. CUC came into the limelight after a major massacre at Panzós, Alta Verapaz, in 1978 and the 1980 massacre at the Spanish embassy, in which

Guatemalan security forces burned alive over three dozen indigenous protesters. Among the victims was Vicente Menchú, father of Rigoberta Menchú. In February 1980, CUC staged a massive strike of workers on the southern coast sugar and cotton plantations; from the viewpoint of landowners and the army, this strike was their worst nightmare come true.

Equally important in the growth of a politicized indigenous movement was a change in the stance of the revolutionary insurgents vis-à-vis the Mayan population, within the context of a broader reevaluation of strategy and organizational recomposition after the defeat of 1968. This involved a recognition of the failures of the *foco* strategy (see Chapter 10) of the 1960s as fundamentally militaristic and not rooted in a solid mass base. Even more serious, the insurgents had virtually ignored the indigenous population during the 1960s. By the time of their resurgence in the early 1970s, the three major organizations had generally come to understand some of these errors in their organizing strategies; two of them, Ejército Guerrillero de los Pobres (EGP) and Organización del Pueblo en Armas (ORPA), spent several years being educated by the indigenous population and organizing a political support base in the western highlands (and other areas) before renewing armed actions later in the 1970s.

In sum, veterans of the 1960s insurgency were able to reorganize and reinitiate their struggle in the early 1970s, this time in the western indigenous highlands and with Mayan communities becoming central participants. The active involvement of up to 500,000 Mayas in the uprising of the late 1970s and early 1980s was without precedent in Guatemala, indeed in the hemisphere. Coming in the wake of the 1979 Sandinista victory in Nicaragua and the outbreak of civil war in El Salvador, also in 1979, this remarkable "awakening" in the indigenous highlands provoked a revolutionary crisis, threatening the army's century-old domination over rural Guatemala.

The guerrilla military offensive reached its height in 1980–1981, gaining 6000–8000 armed fighters and 250,000–500,000 active collaborators and supporters and operating in most parts of the country. In the context of the Sandinista triumph in Nicaragua and the outbreak of civil war in El Salvador, (both in 1979), the new wave of armed struggle in Guatemala was taken very seriously by the ruling coalition as heralding a possible seizure of power by the insurgents. In early 1982, the various guerrilla organizations united in the Guatemalan National Revolutionary Unity (URNG), overcoming years of sectarian divisions.

Even as unity was proclaimed, however, and even as the revolutionary movement achieved its maximal expression during 1980 and 1981, a change in the balance of forces between the insurgents and the army began during the second half of 1981 as the army initiated an all-out "scorched-earth" counteroffensive. By the spring of 1982, the revolutionary movement had suffered serious losses to its infrastructure in the city, where security forces had previously, in 1978–1980, decimated the leadership and ranks of the unions and other popular movements and political opposition forces. In the highlands, the army unleashed a virtual holocaust upon the indigenous communities. Blinded by its own triumphalism, the URNG had in fact lost the initiative, and some of its fundamental weaknesses came to the surface. As a result of the URNG's weaknesses and of major changes within the ruling coalition, the army gained the upper hand and dealt decisive blows against the insurgents. For the next several years, the URNG was on the defensive; it did not recover a capacity to take new initiatives until the late 1980s.

A major reason for this second defeat of the guerrillas and the suffering inflicted on its supporters among the population was the failure to have anticipated the scorched-earth, genocidal war unleashed by the Guatemalan security forces in mid-1981; hence, tens of thousands of highlands Mayas were left unprepared to defend themselves. The statistics are staggering: from mid-1981 to 1983 alone, 440 villages were entirely wiped off the map and up to 150,000 civilians were killed or "disappeared." There were over 1 million displaced persons (1 million internal refugees, up to 200,000 refugees in Mexico). Accompanying these massive population displacements was the deliberate destruction of huge areas of the highlands (burning of forests, etc.), causing irreversible environmental devastation. The aim of these genocidal policies was not only to eliminate the guerrillas' popular support base but also to destroy the Mayan culture, identity, and communal structures.

The army carried out these goals in the first stage (1981–1983) through scorched-earth warfare and in the second stage (after 1983) through the imposition of coercive institutions throughout the countryside that were designed to consolidate military control over the population. Among these institutions were mandatory paramilitary "civilian self-defense patrols," or PACs (at one point involving 1 million peasants, one-quarter of the adult population); "development poles," rural forced resettlement camps where every aspect of people's lives was subject to direct army control; and militarization of the entire administrative apparatus of the country. These counterinsurgency institutions were legalized in the new constitution of 1985, which provided the juridical framework for civilian government in the late 1980s.

Transition to Restricted Civilian Rule

As discussed earlier, the beginning of revolutionary insurgency in Guatemala during the 1960s generated a counterinsurgent response on the part of the United States and the Guatemalan ruling coalition, which was institutionalized in state power after 1970. During the late 1970s, the ability of the military regimes to govern Guatemala deteriorated seriously as a consequence of relatively weakened internal cohesion within the ruling coalition and the lack of any consensual basis or societal legitimacy. The clearest examples were the openly fraudulent elections of 1974, 1978, and 1982. By 1982, these divisions were serious enough to spark recognition of the need for a change in the nature of military rule; to recover some modicum of legitimacy, at least among the ruling sectors; and to end Guatemala's international isolation as a pariah state and, hence, its restricted access to international financial assistance.

The shift is generally seen as beginning with the military coup of March 1982 (following the third successive electoral fraud), which brought to power the regime of General Efraín Ríos Montt. The Ríos Montt government (March 1982–August 1983) presided over the bloodiest era and the majority of the massacres. It was only after this most brutal phase of the counterinsurgency war had accomplished its goals under Ríos Montt that army leaders and their civilian allies, now under the military government of General Oscar Mejía Víctores (1983–1985), took concrete steps toward a return to civilian rule. They recognized that a facade of constitutional democracy was needed to overcome the contradictions of direct military dictatorship. This understanding was the background for the political process of 1983–1985, during which a constituent assembly was elected to write a new constitution containing basic guarantees of citizens' rights, at least on paper (alongside institutionalization of PACs, etc.). Finally, presidential elections were held in late 1985.

The 1985 presidential election, although free of fraud, was severely restricted and unrepresentative of large sectors of the population as only rightist and centrist parties that had reached agreement with the military were allowed to participate. Aside from the exclusion of the left, there were no real choices on substantive issues. Nevertheless, the election did permit nonmilitary candidates for the first time in 15 years; it was overwhelmingly won by Christian Democrat Vinicio Cerezo, the most progressive of the candidates. Cerezo's victory was greeted with high hopes for a real change from the many years of military dictatorship.

Despite these hopes and despite having come into power with a significant popular mandate, however, Cerezo chose not to fully use the space that he had—that is, not to wage the struggle that would have been needed to achieve a real transfer of power from the military to civilians. His government did very little to control the army or address the country's underlying social/economic problems; he accepted the army's priority of defeating popular and revolutionary forces, and this significantly limited the possibility for genuinely pluralistic politics or for ending the civil war. In this regard, the Cerezo period (1986–1990) turned out to be not so much a genuine "transition to democracy" as a necessary adjustment for trying to deal with Guatemala's multiple crises and reestablish minimal international credibility. It evolved into a civilian version of the counterinsurgency state, in some respects a continuation of what had been imposed in the late 1960s.

A second nonfraudulent election was held in 1990; it was viewed as significant insofar as it established the continuity of civilian rule, between Cerezo and newly elected Jorge Serrano. Nevertheless, abstention was extremely high, with only 30 percent of eligible voters participating; and once again, no leftist opposition parties were permitted. By 1990, however, there were new currents in the "informal" arena of Guatemalan civil society (outside the electoral process), and these began to undermine the foundations of the counterinsurgency state. One major expression of these currents was an emerging national consensus, articulated primarily in dialogues led by the Catholic Church, for an end to the civil war. Virtually all political sectors began to recognize that Guatemala could not be truly democratized until the civil war was ended through political negotiations (rather than a military victory by either side), until the country was demilitarized, and until underlying structural inequalities and ethnic discrimination were acknowledged and addressed.

Social Crisis and Reemergence of Social Movements

Structural social crisis—ironically, a product of macroeconomic growth during the 1970s—was compounded during the 1980s when the international capitalist crisis hit Central America (and all of Latin America) as severely as the Depression of the

1930s had. Among its principal manifestations were rising prices for all industrial imports (largely a consequence of the "oil shocks") coupled with falling prices for Central American exports. These crises left the Guatemalan economy suffering negative growth rates during the 1980s; both unemployment and inflation soared to unprecedented levels. As a result, purchasing power in 1989 was 22 percent of what it had been in 1972, and the overall poverty levels of 1980 jumped markedly during the late 1980s.

The central social characteristic of Guatemala during the 1980s (and into the 1990s) remained increasing concentration of wealth amid pervasive poverty. All of the Central American countries shared this characteristic, but Guatemalan poverty has been particularly extreme on several counts. First, the inequality of resource and income distribution has been greater, and no measures have been taken since the overthrow of Arbenz to alleviate it (i.e., there has been no land or tax reform). The second particularity of Guatemalan poverty has been the number of social indicators on which it ranks worst (illiteracy, physical quality of life, infant mortality). The third particularity is the ethnic component of poverty, with all statistics for the Mayan population being far worse than the national average. As elsewhere, there has also been a marked feminization of poverty, with increasing numbers of women becoming heads of household as well as low-wage workers (see details below).

These characteristics of extreme underdevelopment and inequality were not new to Guatemala, but a number of things did change dramatically during the 1980s. First, under the impact of the international crisis of the 1980s, all of Guatemala's economic and social problems were seriously aggravated. Even at the macroeconomic level, Guatemala lost over 15 years of growth during the 1980s, reversing the growth pattern of the previous 30 years. Second, after the mid-1980s, the government began to implement austerity policies more aggressively, culminating in the neoliberal structural adjustment measures of the late 1980s and early 1990s; these policies further aggravated the grave social crisis. Third, informalization of the urban economy left only slightly over one-third of the workforce fully and permanently employed.

This last indicator was among the important modifications in Guatemala's class structure during the 1980s, which left close to 90 percent of the population living below the official poverty line by the end of the decade (up from 79 percent in 1980); nearly three-quarters of the population lived in extreme poverty and were unable to afford a basic minimum diet. During the late 1980s, the impact of the economic and social crisis in regenerating social ferment among the poor proved greater than the ability of the counterinsurgency state to repress such ferment. Despite the reescalation of repression against labor and other popular movements, the constitution of this huge majority of the population that was united by being poor led to a slow rebuilding and reemergence of popular movements after the disasters of the early 1980s; a stream of austerity protests began even under the military government in 1985 and continued with surprising vigor.

Guatemala's new popular movements were the product not only of austerity measures but also of the country's multiple crises, including the many crises of uprooted populations. The war alone left over 10 percent of the population displaced. Natural disaster (the 1976 earthquake), war, and economic crisis during the late 1970s and 1980s brought significant migration to the capital, causing its population to double. Increasingly, the urban poor were indigenous, and more than half of the households came to be headed by women. A significant number of the new urban poor (250,000–500,000 people) lived in the city's massive shantytowns in precarious squatter settlements. The absence of basic social services (running water, sewage, electricity, transportation) sparked new community struggles that became as important as more traditional labor union struggles among organized sectors of the labor force. Residents of one such community protested by leaving the body of a child who had died from typhoid on the steps of the National Palace.

In the rural areas, meanwhile, hundreds of thousands of those displaced within the highlands or to the southern coast joined together with the landless already living there to form a national movement for land. The reconstituted popular movements of primarily rural Mayas also included human rights groups organized around demands that were openly political and directly related to the ongoing counterinsurgency war: for example, the Group of Mutual Support (GAM), an organization of wives and mothers of the disappeared and other human rights victims; the mainly indigenous widows' organization, the National Coordinating Committee of Guatemalan Widows (CONAVIGUA); the Council of Ethnic Communities "Everyone is Equal" (CERJ), founded to empower the highlands Mayas to resist service in the PACs; and the Council of Displaced Guatemalans (CONDEG), representing internal refugees. Many thousands of Mayas also defied army relocation and control programs by fleeing to remote mountain areas and forming permanent "Communities of People in Resistance" (CPRs), which began to gain formal recognition nationally and internationally in the early 1990s.

Among the main new characteristics of Guatemala's social movements in the late 1980s/early 1990s were the following. The first and most important was the centrality of the indigenous population and its double condition of exploitation and ethnic discrimination in both rural and urban settings. This was reflected in the rise of diverse movements and organizations fighting for a broad range of indigenous rights. These movements were bolstered by working with indigenous organizations throughout the Americas (the 1991 continental meeting was held in Guatemala) and by the awarding of the 1992 Nobel Peace Prize to Guatemalan Mayan and political opposition leader Rigoberta Menchú. The second novelty was the growing role of the Catholic Church alongside Guatemala's social movements. Liberation theology was a major influence throughout the 1970s and 1980s, and even after the appearance and rapid growth of evangelical Protestant groups during the 1980s (reaching up to one-third of the population), the Catholic Church remained a leading force in articulating the demands of the popular movements.

The third new element of the late 1980s and 1990s movements was the slowly emerging and increasingly visible protagonism of women. (By this time, women were also becoming more central to the labor force and as single heads of household.) Women had been excluded from traditional politics in Guatemala (voting as well as office holding), and their political activities had generally been very limited. Traditional political parties had excluded women from virtually all positions of political leadership. Only in the late 1980s did women begin to increase their participation in electoral (and nonelectoral) politics, although such participation remained limited by the traditional problems of discrimination and illiteracy. On the economic front, women began to organize in workplaces where they were over-represented (e.g., *maquiladora* industries, schools), although their presence in union leadership remained less visible. In their communities, by contrast, women became visible as the principal organizers of austerity protests in the 1980s and ongoing community mobilizations in the 1990s (e.g., for social services in shantytown neighborhoods). Women were also very prominent in human rights organizations such as GAM and indigenous human rights organizations such as CONAVIGUA, CERJ, and CONDEG. It was only in the 1990s, however, that Guatemalan women founded organizations designed explicitly to achieve their rights as women and began to demand equal participation for their organizations in broader coalitions.

In short, Guatemala experienced the gradual emergence of a bloc of popular and indigenous organizations. The notion of a "bloc" indicates that the social subject is not one class in the traditional sense but a combination of exploited and dominated sectors whose political expression is a coalition, or "front," of popular and indigenous movements; it incorporates conditions related to (ethnic) identity and (gender-based) reproduction as well as (class-based) exploitation. Guatemala's popular and Mayan organizations continued to suffer from many serious weaknesses—above all, continued vulnerability to the endless stream of kidnappings, disappearances, death threats, and assassinations. Their articulation as a social force was also hindered by continuing problems of disunity and inability to organize among the huge informal proletariat. Because repression forced them to operate semiclandestinely, their advances were often imperceptible. Nevertheless, their continued existence and growth was in itself a form of defiance of the counterinsurgency state.

By the late 1980s, the context for political action was also shaped by the resurgence of the URNG. Even having destroyed much of the URNG's social base in the highlands in the early 1980s, the army had been unable to inflict a "final" defeat upon the insurgent forces or to win the war definitively. Hence, the organizations of the URNG survived the holocaust; they remained the nuclei of future resistance even at their low point and gradually began to recover their ability to take initiatives, both militarily and politically. Nevertheless, their inability to resist the army's counteroffensive of the early 1980s combined with the "civilianization" of the counterinsurgency state in the mid-1980s required once again a profound reorganization and redefinition of strategy.

This redefinition became necessary, first, in response to the clear lesson of the early 1980s that "taking state power" through military victory over the counterinsurgency forces was a totally unthinkable objective—and that the cost of the second round of the war for the civilian population had been so high as to preclude a strategy based simply on continuing the war. Guatemala was one of the few countries in Latin America where the armed insurgent movement operated continuously since the 1960s. However, armed struggle is not what people choose; after 30 years of counterinsurgency war, particularly after the holocaust of the early 1980s, the URNG could not simply propose another decade of war. (In fact, the mid-1980s saw several splits within the organizations of the URNG, with dissidents arguing that the insurgents should have laid down their arms after the defeat of 1981–1983.)

Second, in view of the 1985 election and transition to civilian rule, that is, to a potentially legitimate government, the left had to find new ways of becoming a significant force in civil society. Hence, shortly after the 1985 election, the URNG began to propose dialogue/negotiations for a political settlement to the war. For the URNG, the emphasis on negotiations was part of several larger modifications of strategy: giving more weight to political aspects of the struggle while at the same time maintaining a military capacity, broadening its social and political alliances, slowly beginning to recognize the role of popular and indigenous sectors acting autonomously, and realizing the importance of an ideological pluralism that would allow the social movements to follow their own organizational dynamic. This was also a response to the growing protagonism, complexity, and plurality of interests in Guatemalan civil society.

To summarize, because of its profound contradictions, the Guatemalan counterinsurgency project could not be stabilized. First, it did not and could not win the battle for legitimacy, given its intrinsic brutality. Second, its basic premise, that the army had definitively won the war against the guerrilla insurgency, was disproven in practice, causing discontent and destabilization within the ruling coalition. Finally, this was combined with neoliberal economic policies designed to expand the economy solely through world market-oriented "nontraditional exports." Aside from intensifying social conflicts, these policies limited economic growth precisely because they did nothing to develop the internal market.

By the late 1980s, then, Guatemala was by no means in an insurrectionary situation or "ungovernable," but it was in a chronic social crisis. The counterinsurgency state made reformism by itself unviable by precluding partial solutions to the staggering problems of poverty and racism. Gradualist approaches to change simply were not permitted. However, faced with the deepening of these problems, important sectors of the population made continual efforts to organize in self-defense, as seen above. Meanwhile, the URNG was experiencing another resurgence; but even while continuing armed actions, its main strategic goal after 1986 was to pressure the government and army into negotiating a political settlement to the war.

For 4 years the Guatemalan government stubbornly insisted that the insurgents must "lay down their arms" and disarm unilaterally without negotiating any substantive issues. They maintained this stance even after the 1987 Central American Peace Accords negotiated (in Guatemala City) primarily to end the Contra War against the Sandinista government in Nicaragua but also to address the need for negotiated peace in El Salvador and Guatemala. Only several years later did Guatemalan army and government spokespeople finally acknowledge the significant upsurge in guerrilla actions. The implicit admission that the war could not be won militarily by either side created the conditions, for the first time beginning in 1990–1991, for serious discussions about ending the war.

Guatemala's Peace Process (1990–1996)

This section summarizes the saga of the Guatemalan peace process and the accords signed in December 1996. It is important to keep in mind that as recently as 1992–1993, hardliners among Guatemala's military and civilian elites were determined not to negotiate a settlement permitting a legal presence or political participation by the insurgent left or its allies, and they regarded virtually all of the organizations of civil society as the guerrillas' allies or "facades." Particularly after the signing of a negotiated peace in neighboring El Salvador in January 1992, the elites vowed "never" to tolerate such an outcome in Guatemala. The extraordinary story of how and why, from 1994 to 1996, the Guatemalan army and government found themselves involved in very much the same kind of process as the Salvadorans, with the United Nations as moderator and verifier of the process, is chronicled in detail elsewhere (Jonas 2000).

By 1990, considerable political pressure for peace had built up within Guatemala as well as internationally. During 1989, the National Reconciliation Commission (established by the 1987 Central American Peace Accords) sponsored a National Dialogue. Although boycotted by the army, the government, and the business elites, this Dialogue expressed a clear national consensus among all other sectors in favor of a substantive political settlement to the war. The dialogue process projected a series of URNG meetings with the political parties, "social sectors" (private enterprise, popular and religious movements), and finally with the government and the army. The 1990 sessions included a September meeting between the URNG and CACIF, an unthinkable event during the previous 30 years. Beyond the formal meetings, the dialogue process opened up spaces within a repressive context for public discussion of issues that had been undiscussable for decades; in this sense, it became an important avenue for beginning to democratize Guatemala.

In early 1991, the newly elected government of Jorge Serrano opened direct negotiations with the URNG. For the first time, top army officials agreed to participate in meetings to set the agenda and procedures for peace talks without demanding that the URNG first disarm, although they still hoped to win URNG demobilization in exchange for minimal, pro forma concessions. During the next year, there were agreements in principle on democratization and partial agreements on human rights. The precariousness of the process became evident when it stagnated in mid-1992 and moved toward total breakdown during the last months of Serrano's crisis-ridden government.

The entire peace process was derailed by the May 1993 "Serranazo," or attempted *auto-golpe*. Serrano's suspension of the constitution and dissolution of Congress in order to seize absolute control (initially but briefly supported by some factions of the army) unleashed a major political and constitutional crisis. After being repudiated by virtually all sectors of civil society and the international community, the Serranazo was resolved in June through the (most unexpected) ascendance of Human Rights Ombudsman Ramiro de León Carpio to the presidency. However, the peace process remained at a standstill during the rest of 1993. The new government, closely allied with the dominant wing of the army high command, presented unrealistic negotiation proposals that would have discarded previously signed agreements and, in essence, would have required the URNG to disarm without any substantive settlements. These proposals were widely rejected throughout Guatemalan society and were viewed as totally nonviable by the international community.

In January 1994, with these tactics having run their course, the negotiations were resumed, this time on a significantly different basis. During the 1991–1993 rounds,

Guatemala's peace talks had been moderated by Monsignor Rodolfo Quezada Toruño of the Catholic Bishops' Conference, with the United Nations in an observer role. As of January 1994, both sides agreed that the United Nations should become the moderator; this paved the way for significantly increased involvement by the international community, raising the stakes in the negotiations and giving the entire process a less reversible dynamic.

Furthermore, the January 1994 Framework Accord established a clear agenda and timetable. This accord also formalized a role for the broad-based multisector Assembly of Civil Society (ASC), which included virtually all organized sectors of civil society (even, for the first time, women's organizations) as well as the major political parties. Only the big business sectors represented in CACIF decided not to participate. Having gained new experience during the Serranazo, grassroots organizations had become increasingly vocal in demanding participation in the peace process. The ASC was also striking in the diversity or plurality of political/ideological positions represented within its ranks; unlike El Salvador's popular organizations in relation to the Farabundo Martí National Liberation Front (FMLN), the ASC was by no means a simple instrument of the URNG. As the main agreements were being hammered out, the ASC—after itself engaging in a fascinating process of consensus building among widely divergent positions—offered proposals to the negotiating parties on each issue. While not binding, their proposals had to be taken into account by the two parties, and the URNG adopted many of the ASC proposals as its own negotiating positions. The formation of the ASC also gave Guatemala's organized popular sectors their first sustained experience of participating in the political process and was the precursor to the eventual participation by many of those sectors in the 1995 election.

The breakthrough Human Rights Accord was signed in late March 1994, calling for the immediate establishment of international verification mechanisms to monitor human rights. After the mandated U.N. Verification Mission in Guatemala (MINUGUA) finally arrived in November 1994, its functioning on the ground throughout Guatemala created a political climate that was much more positive for ending systematic human rights violations (as well as mechanisms for denouncing such violations, an important change in a country previously dominated by fear). At the negotiating table, meanwhile, two new accords were signed in June 1994, on the Resettling of Displaced Populations (mainly Guatemalan refugees returning from Mexico) and a Truth Commission empowered to *esclarecer*, or shed light on, past human rights crimes, but without judicial powers and without naming the individuals responsible—which sparked fierce criticism from popular and human rights organizations.

The next item on the agenda, the Accord on the Identity and Rights of Indigenous Peoples, was the subject of negotiation for 9 months, until March 1995. The signing of this accord was a landmark achievement for a country whose population is 60 percent indigenous. This accord went far beyond antidiscrimination protections for Guatemala's indigenous majority to mandate a constitutional reform redefining Guatemala as a multiethnic, multicultural, and multilingual nation. If fully implemented, this agreement would require profound reforms in the country's educational, judicial, and political institutions. It laid the formal basis for a new entitlement of Guatemala's indigenous majority and established their right to make claims upon the state—all of which is a precondition for democracy and genuine pluralism in Guatemala. This accord together with independent initiatives by a variety of indigenous organizations also created a new context for social and political interactions and for a more democratic political culture. As an example of this new culture, after its signing, the residents of Sololá, a town in the heart of the conflict zone, decided to base the 1996 competition for the "Queen of Sololá," traditionally a beauty contest, on who could best explain the Accord on Indigenous Rights.

Nationally, the peace process was directly impacted by the dynamics of the campaign for the November 1995 general election and vice versa. The most important novelties of this electoral process were the URNG's early 1995 call, urging participation in the vote, and the formation of a left-of-center electoral front of popular and indigenous organizations (the "left flank" of the ASC), the New Guatemala Democratic Front (FDNG), to participate in the elections. In the November 1995 general elections, no presidential candidate received an absolute majority. The major surprise was the stronger-than-expected showing of the newly formed FDNG, which won six seats in congress; additionally, alliances between the FDNG and locally based indigenous "civic committees" (unaffiliated with the traditional political parties) won several important mayoralties, including Xelajú (Quetzaltenango), Guatemala's second largest city, half of whose residents are *ladino* and half indigenous. A January 1996 run-off for president pitted modernizing conservative Alvaro Arzú of the National Action Party (PAN) against a stand-in for the rightist former dictator Efraín Ríos Montt of the Guatemalon Republican Front (FRG), who opposed the peace process. Arzú won by a scant 2 percent margin.

Even before taking office, Arzú had already held several direct, secret meetings with the URNG. Shortly after taking office, Arzú immediately signaled his intention to bring the ongoing peace talks to a successful conclusion. Once the formal peace negotiations were reinitiated and following intensive consultations with the private sector, the Accord on Socio-Economic Issues was signed in May 1996—this time, finally, with CACIF support. The accord did not directly resolve Guatemala's most fundamental problems, such as grossly distorted land ownership and income distribution, widespread poverty, and un-/underemployment. However, it did commit the government to increase spending on health and education and to carry out a much-needed tax reform, the latter being the key to financing virtually all of the reforms from the peace accords and the minimum basis for any future change. Meanwhile, the most difficult issues of social justice were deferred to the future.

The crowning achievement of the peace process came in September 1996, with the signing of the Accord on Strengthening of Civilian Power and Role of the Armed Forces in a Democratic Society. This accord mandated constitutional reforms subordinating the army to civilian control and restricting the army's role to the sole function of external defense, a stark contrast to the army's past practices of involving itself in all areas of government. Most importantly, the accord created a new civilian police force to handle all internal security matters. The army's size (46,000) and budget were also to be reduced by one-third; the PACs and other counterinsurgency units were to be eliminated. This accord also contained important provisions for reforms of the corrupt and dysfunctional judicial system.

After a serious crisis in October 1996 that nearly derailed the entire process, the talks were resumed and operational accords were signed in December. These dealt with a definitive cease-fire, constitutional and electoral reforms, the legal reintegration of the URNG (entailing a partial amnesty for both the URNG and the army), and a timetable for fulfillment of all of the accords. Following the dramatic return of the URNG leadership to Guatemala on December 28, the historic Final Peace Accord was signed in Guatemala's National Palace on December 29, 1996, amid considerable national celebration and international attention. Thus ended the first phase of the peace process that the Guatemalan elites had vowed "never" to permit in Guatemala.

How did this "never" turn into acceptance? The United Nations played a role that no other mediating force could have played in facilitating agreements between the government and the URNG, making the peace process less reversible and beginning crucial measures of verification. In addition, six governments played an important supportive role as the "Group of Friends" of the peace process—the main "friends" being Mexico, Spain, Norway, and the United States. Within Guatemala, slowly but surely, despite fierce resistance and significant delays, the peace process acquired credibility. Even the recalcitrant army and CACIF could no longer afford to resist the process openly and found themselves having to defend their interests by participating in the negotiations. In short, none of the major Guatemalan players could afford to boycott the process.

Seen in its totality, the peace process was a great step forward for Guatemala's democratic development, although not for social justice. Rather than being imposed by victors upon vanquished, the negotiations represented a splitting of differences between radically opposed forces, with major concessions from both sides. In addition, most of the accords contained provisions for citizen participation in decision making, including *comisiones paritarias* (with equal representation from the government and indigenous organizations) and a host of other multisectoral commissions. Accord implementation also gave rise to a widespread practice of *consultas*, involving some (not all) policy makers in direct interchanges with citizens and social organizations, even outside the capital city (also a novelty). Finally, the accords provided innovative mechanisms, such as the Women's Forum, for training and participation by those who have never had such opportunities. (Although there was no accord on women's rights, several of the main accords contained provisions specifically designed to expand women's rights.)

Taken as a whole, the accords and the provision for U.N. verification of government compliance represented an *adios* to 42 years of painful Cold War history and provided the framework for institutionalizing political democracy. If fully implemented, the accords had the potential to open up an opportunity for significant transformations of Guatemalan society. However, even after the signing and initial implementation of some accords, the road remained full of mine fields: the efforts to fully implement the accords were bound to encounter very serious resistances from those who held power in the old system.

Postwar Guatemala (1997–2007)

By the early 2000s, 11 years after the signing of the final peace accords, it remained evident that the implementation phase of Guatemala's peace process was just as difficult and dangerous as the negotiations had been. Guatemala's "peace resisters" lost no time in sharpening their knives to defend the old order, taking every opportunity to challenge the substance and the continuity of the peace process. Just getting the entire complex of new laws and constitutional reforms through Congress sparked battles on many fronts. The Arzú government, which had taken such bold initiatives to finalize the peace negotiations, was much more timid—on many occasions, resistant—with regard to compliance with the accords. This became particularly evident in early 1998, when it pulled back from its commitment to carry out a reasonable tax reform that was to have been a long-range mechanism for internal financing of the peace accords. Meanwhile, the rise in common crime, a problem intrinsic to postwar situations around the world, provided a pretext for keeping the army involved in policing and other internal security matters, in violation of the demilitarization accord.

The most difficult moment for postwar Guatemala came in May 1999, with the referendum on constitutional reforms required to put into effect some of the most significant provisions of the accords on indigenous rights and on strengthening civilian power (limiting the functions of the army and making judicial reform). Although polls had shown ahead of time that the reforms were likely to be approved, a well-financed last-month blitzkrieg campaign by peace resisters (who urged a "No" vote, using blatantly racist arguments) succeeded in defeating the reforms—that is, in getting a 55 percent majority among the bare 18.5 percent of the electorate that voted. Clearly, the main winner of this vote was abstention, and the main loser was

---

PRESIDENTS/REGIMES SINCE 1930S

- Jorge Ubico (1931–1944) (military dictatorship)
- Juan José Arévalo (1945–1950) (freely elected)
- Jacobo Arbenz (1951–1954) (freely elected, overthrown)
- Col. Carlos Castillo Armas (1954–1957) (military coup)
- Gen. Miguel Ydígoras Fuentes (1958–1963) (military dictatorship)
- Col. Enrique Peralta Azurdia (1963–1966) (military coup and dictatorship)
- Julio César Méndez Montenegro (1966–1970) (freely elected) (Partido Revolucionario)
- Col. Carlos Arana Osorio (1970–1974) (elected, military dictatorship)
- Gen. Kjell Laugerud (1974–1978) (electoral fraud, military dictatorship)
- Gen. Romeo Lucas García (1978–1982) (electoral fraud, military dictatorship)
- Gen. Efraín Ríos Montt (1982–1983) (military coup and dictatorship)
- Gen. Oscar Mejía Víctores (1983–1985) (military coup and dictatorship)
- Vinicio Cerezo (1986–1990) (freely elected) (Democracia Cristiana Guatemalteca)
- Jorge Serrano (1991–1993) (freely elected, 1993 attempted *auto-golpe*) (Movimiento de Acción Solidarista)
- Ramiro de León Carpio (1993–1995) (appointed transition government)
- Alvaro Arzú (1996–1999) (freely elected) (Partido de Avanzada Nacional)
- Alfonso Portillo (2000–2003) (freely elected) (Frente Republicano Guatemalteco)
- Oscar Berger (2004–2007) (freely elected) (Gran Alianza Nacional)
- Alvaro Colom (2008–2011) (freely elected) (Unidad Nacional de la Esperanza)

the peace process itself. This political disaster raised a basic question as to whether Guatemala's fragile democracy could be consolidated. (For a detailed analysis, see Jonas 2000, chapter 8.)

The late 1999 general elections gave a strong victory to Alfonso Portillo, the presidential candidate of FRG, the party founded by ex-dictator Ríos Montt, one of the principal architects of the 1980s genocide. Politically, the FRG's victory resulted from an astute populist campaign by Portillo combined with a "punishment vote" against the Arzú government—primarily for the PAN's failure to take even the most basic measures to improve people's daily lives (socioeconomic situation and personal security), while maintaining the privileges of the rich. In this sense, it was a vote about people's most immediate concerns, not about the long-range structural issues addressed in the peace accords. Within the FRG delegation that was to dominate the new Congress were former army officials who had been key architects and henchmen of the scorched-earth dirty war of the 1980s—not to mention Ríos Montt himself, who was to preside over Congress.

At the same time as this contorted shift from a moderate rightist to an extreme rightist government, the election also featured a stronger than expected showing of the Alianza Nueva Nación (ANN), the leftist coalition constructed by the newly legalized URNG together with other progressive forces. Despite its scarce resources, internal divisions, and many other disadvantages, the ANN won 13 percent of the national vote and nine seats in Congress. Structurally, the participation of the left as the third force, albeit a very weak and splintered one, was a step toward normalizing Guatemalan politics; for the first time since 1954, all political/ideological tendencies were represented. The year 1999 was a high point for leftist electoral forces; in 2003 and 2007 elections, they declined significantly from 1999 (see below).

Furthermore, pro-peace forces in Guatemalan civil society—particularly Mayan and women's organizations—continued to pressure the government to honor and implement the peace accords. Although their efforts gained limited immediate results, they established for the first time the presence of counterhegemonic forces in a society where traditionally the only social sector to exercise any real power was the business elite (CACIF). Given the weakness of pro-peace forces within Guatemala, concerted international pressure—above all, a conditioning of international aid on compliance with the accords—remained a necessary complement to internal pro-peace efforts.

Despite these pressures for change, Guatemala's political and social institutions remained weak and dysfunctional (beyond the capacity to conduct fraud-free elections after 1985). A major legacy of the counterinsurgency state was the decades-long subordination of all state institutions to the army. Although this ongoing institutional weakness became clear with the 1993 Serranazo, its failure had been one of the first steps toward establishing, as a starting point, a strong defense of the constitutional order, an achievement that in Guatemala could never be taken for granted.

As late as the early 2000s, Guatemala's institutions were still unable to guarantee basic rights in practice. The peace process was a crucial mechanism for attempting to reform previously dysfunctional institutions. The accords mandated reform of the legislative and judicial branches, as well as the executive, and thorough reform of the electoral system. No less important than what the accords prescribed on

---

PRINCIPAL POLITICAL PARTIES REPRESENTED
IN CONGRESS AS OF EARLY 2000S

Gran Alianza Nacional (GANA)
Frente Republicano Guatemalteco (FRG)
Unidad Nacional de la Esperanza (UNE)
Partido de Avanzada Nacional (PAN)
Unidad Nacional Revolucionaria Guatemalteca (URNG)
Partido Unionista (PU)
Unión del Centro Nacional (UCN)
Patriota (PP)
Encuentro por Guatemala (EG—party of Rigoberta Menchúa)
*Comités Cívicos (Mayan organizations winning mayoral elections but no Congressional representatives)

*Parties Previously Important But Now in Decline,
Defunct, or Subsumed within Other Parties*

Democracia Cristiana Guatemalteca (DCG)
Movimiento de Liberación Nacional (MLN)
Partido Institucional Democrático (PID) (party of the army)
Partido Revolucionario (PR)
Frente Democrático Nueva Guatemala (FDNG)
Partido Socialista Democrático (PSD)
Alianza Nueva Nación (ANN)
Partido Guatemalteco de Trabajo (PGT) (Communist Party)

---

paper, the U.N. Verification Mission (MINUGUA), the U.N. Development Program, and other agencies of the United Nations and the international community invested substantial resources and energy for institutional strengthening programs. Among the most important focuses was creation of the new Civilian National Police force (independent of the army) and reform of the weak and corrupted justice system, which was characterized by pervasive impunity (nonpunishment of blatant crimes, including human rights crimes).

By the early 2000s, these efforts had yet to yield positive results. The most heinous peacetime crime was the April 1998 assassination of Bishop Juan Gerardi just 2 days after the Archbishop's Human Rights Office (which he had founded) released a report attributing 85 percent of the killings during the war to state security forces (the armed forces and PACs). The Gerardi assassination, along with other major assassinations and crimes from the 36-year war, remained unsolved and unpunished. The official Truth Commission (Historical Clarification Commission) established by the peace accords released a far-reaching report in February 1999, based on 9000 interviews; the report attributed 93 percent of the human rights crimes committed during the war to the army and its paramilitary units (vs. 3 percent to the URNG) and established that some actions and policies of the Guatemalan government during the 1980s constituted "acts of genocide." The report also sharply criticized the U.S.

GOVERNMENT INSTITUTIONS

Executive: President (elected every 4 years), cabinet, and armed forces (technically subordinated to the president as commander-in-chief but actually has functioned autonomously, including a host of subunits such as the presidential guard, military intelligence, etc.—all of which is slated by the peace accords to be radically changed)

Legislative: One-chamber Congress, with 158 members

Judicial System: Regular court system consists of sixty-five courts with jurisdictions for different regions of the country, appeals courts, and Supreme Court. Members of the Supreme Court are elected by Congress, and other court judges are nominated by the Supreme Court and approved by Congress. There is also an active Public Prosecutor's office. In addition, Guatemala has a Constitutional Court that has far-reaching powers in matters beyond traditional constitutional issues (e.g., new taxes).

The peace accords mandate thorough overhaul and reform of the judicial system, to eliminate ingrained problems of corruption and impunity, vulnerability to threats, incompetence, and so on. Additionally, the accords mandate incorporation of Mayan customary law (*derecho consuetudinario*) into the legal system. All of these reforms are under discussion, but most reforms have not yet been made.

Semi-Government Institutions: Supreme Electoral Tribunal, Constitutional Court (see above), Ombudsman for Human Rights

Local Government: Twenty-two departments, 330 municipalities; departmental governors appointed by the executive, municipal mayors elected

---

role in supporting the apparatus of terror for decades. However, implementation of the Truth Commission's follow-up recommendations would require new battles.

The Portillo government (2000–2003) remained under the sinister shadow of the party dominated by retired General Ríos Montt, and sent the incipient healing process into reverse gear. Instead of reparations to war victims, for example, this government initiated the payment of compensation to former members of the PACs, which were reconstituting themselves, although they had been identified by the Historical Clarification Commission and by virtually all human rights agencies as principal perpetrators of human rights crimes, and which were slated by the Peace Accords to be totally dissolved. The Portillo government was also notable for its total incompetence and unprecedented corruption in every sphere of public and private life.

The November 2003 election marked a significant step forward as voters decisively rejected the presidential candidacy of Ríos Montt; although he was temporarily unprotected from prosecution for crimes against humanity, this prosecution never occurred. After a December run-off election, the new government of the Grand National Alliance (GANA) that took office in January 2004 was led by conservative businessman Oscar Berger as president and progressive public servant Eduardo Stein as vice president. In theory, this new government had one last opportunity to return to the agenda of the Peace Accords and had promised to do so. Although it was heavily dominated by the business elites, a number of veteran human rights and Mayan activists joined this government, seeing for the first time an opportunity to move forward on Guatemala's healing, reconstruction, and social equity—or at least to make these goals central to the national agenda. Civil society organizations also had more space for articulating their demands. In short, the mood in early 2004 was one of cautious optimism, particularly in contrast to past decades.

The widespread raised hopes were being deflated already by the end of the first year (2004), and they continued to decline in subsequent years. The Berger government was less corrupt than its predecessor, but it was dominated by the interests of the business elite in CACIF. Social conflicts (e.g., over land) proliferated. The country was still marked by heavy remnants of the counterinsurgency apparatus: strong army influence in many spheres combined with a failure to purge or restructure the army, the reconstruction and coordinated actions of the ex-PAC networks (to which the government maintained Portillo's commitments for compensation), and the prominence of retired military officers in virtually every political party in Congress (except the small leftist parties). The executive branch remained beholden to clandestine "parallel powers" within public institutions, despite the creation of a new commission to investigate illegal and clandestine security forces and ongoing blatant human rights threats and crimes directed against social activists. Furthermore, institutionalized justice remained a distant goal in Guatemala as impunity reigned supreme and honest judges continued to be killed, threatened, or forced into exile.

Finally, another particular wave of human rights violations has been emerging, targeting women. This "feminicide" (meaning not simply female victims of generalized social violence, but the specific targeting of women—although without any single logic or profile) has been reflected in the brutal assassinations (often involving rape, torture, and bodily mutilation) of up to 3500 women between 2000 and 2007, with the numbers of reported cases increasing, and not counting unreported cases. Equally notable has been the indifference of governmental officials and institutions to this phenomenon, and a refusal to investigate specific cases. Once again, impunity remains the order of the day.

INTEREST GROUPS

By far the most powerful is the umbrella organization for big business, The Coordinating Committee of Agricultural, Commercial, Industrial, and Financial Associations (CACIF); labor unions and peasant federations have existed since the Revolution of 1944, but since the 1954 coup, they have been relatively weak. During the 1980s and 1990s, interest groups became organized in the following additional areas: human rights, both in general and with respect to indigenous concerns (reflecting the fact that the Mayan population was the main target of state repression); indigenous cultural, political, and economic issues; community organization, particularly in the urban shantytowns; student organization, at both the high school and university levels; women's rights, both as part of the broader popular movement and (more recently) for specifically women's issues; and small and medium businesses, as well as "guilds" of lawyers and other professionals. By far the most effective interest group activities during the 1990s were those undertaken in the broad cross-sector coalition, the Assembly of Civil Society, during the peace negotiations. Since the signing of the Peace Accords, the most effective organizing has been among Mayas and women.

Like the rest of Central America, Guatemala has been in the throes of neoliberal "reform," with all of its negative consequences for income distribution and social justice. The structural problems that had given rise to the 36-year war were further than ever from being resolved, poverty statistics were geometrically higher than in the 1950s and 1960s, and the official wisdom no longer even promised a "trickle-down" effect to eradicate poverty. Indeed, to mention just one example, while agrarian reform had been considered a "procommunist" idea during the Arbenz era in the 1950s, it has simply disappeared from the vocabulary of the new world order of the twenty-first century. Neoliberal economic policies emanating from Washington, combined with the ongoing refusal of Guatemala's own economic elites to pay taxes or redistribute land, have maintained extreme poverty, inequality, joblessness, and landlessness—and, in recent years, even such unprecedented phenomena as famine.

Given these massive socioeconomic problems, social violence of many different types has proliferated to alarming levels, especially in urban areas; this violence has been linked to drug trafficking, organized crime (in both cases, including elements within the national police and armed forces), gangs, and antigang vigilantes engaged in "social cleansing." Indeed, post-war social violence has largely replaced the massive political violence of the civil war years (although there are still many instances of political violence), maintaining "security" as a top concern of many Guatemalans. Rather than controlling social violence, state institutions (army and police) have been allegedly involved in perpetuating it through clandestine connections.

The other major consequence of these conditions, particularly the lack of decent jobs and social programs to guarantee decent living standards, has been a continuing stream of Guatemalan migration to the United States, which began in the late 1970s and the 1980s. But in this postwar era, the principal factors have shifted from political persecution as the primary cause to economic and social conditions and environmental disasters (most notably, Hurricane Stan in Fall 2005, a few short weeks after Hurricane Katrina in New Orleans). By 2007, at least 10 percent of all Guatemalans lived and worked in the United States, sending home remittances that have become a main pillar of the economy. U.S.-based Guatemalans have engaged in broad campaigns for their rights to legalization in the United States, even as Guatemala-based migrant rights organizations are holding their own government responsible for the socially inequitable development that forces so many people to migrate, insisting that migration should be a choice rather than a necessity.

The United States, as always, has retained a powerful influence over decision making in Guatemala. Particularly after September 11, 2001, U.S. foreign policy priorities have been centrally concerned with "anti-terrorism" and "security," with a stronger role for the Guatemalan army. Not surprisingly, Washington's obsession with "national security" matters since 2001 and its free trade agreement with Central America (CAFTA) that took effect in 2006, impacted the agendas of the Berger government.

Meanwhile, the U.N. mission, MINUGUA, which had been the principal external proponent and monitor of Peace Accord implementation, was phased out of Guatemala at the end of 2004. Despite this important change, other key agencies of the U.N. system in Guatemala—Guatemalan offices of the U.N. Development Program, the U.N. High Commissioners for Refugees and for Human Rights—remain very active in the country. But now the organizations and coalitions of Guatemalan civil society will have to strengthen and consolidate their efforts to pressure for compliance with the Peace Accords, demand justice for war victims, challenge the status quo, and advance proposals for alternative development and justice strategies.

The 2007 general election raised once again the issues of national priorities. The initial round of elections, held in September, with presidential candidates from numerous parties, was marked by the worst violence in decades, as well as some financing of almost all parties by drug traffickers and organized crime. The two main leftist forces, Rigoberta Menchú as presidential candidate and (separately) the URNG, gathered less than 6 percent of the vote, indicating a shallow social base. Both political and social movements on the Left remain relatively ineffective and extremely fragmented.

The run-off election, held November 4, pitted retired General Otto Pérez Molina (Partido Patriota) aginst Alvaro Colom Caballeros (Union Nacional de la Esperanza, UNE). Colom projected himself as a "social democrat," using the rhetoric of "hope." In contrast, Pérez Molina appealed to the quest for "security" among many Guatemalans, and campaigned on a platform of *mano dura* (heavy hand) or crackdown, defined so broadly as to potentially include many different "threats." Against general expectations that Pérez Molina would win, the victory went to Colom (53 percent vs. 47 percent). Election analysts emphasized that this was the first time that the electoral primacy of Guatemala City, where Pérez Molina won handily, was trumped by a strikingly unified vote in rural areas (20 out of 22 Departments), and particularly in Mayan areas—a strong rejection of military rule by a counterinsurgent from the 1980s. The disciplined vote for Colom and UNE, one of the few stable political parties in recent years, may also help explain why Menchú and the URNG did so poorly.

Yet there are various *lecturas* or readings of the outcome. Outside Guatemala, there has been a collective sigh of relief that the military option was rejected (although very narrowly) and that progressive forces will have at least some space to reorganize and renovate themselves and pressure the new government to return to the priorities of the peace agenda. Within Guatemala itself, however, among many analysts and social activists, the emphasis is less optimistic. While preventing the victory of a consolidated rightist force (the equivalent of ARENA in El Salvador), the new government is seen as arriving "conditioned" (limited) by commitments to the business elites and other conservatives (including some amongst his own supporters), hence possibly jeopardizing any serious agenda of "hope" or priorities of the peace accords.

By the end of 2007, then, post-war Guatemala has not yet achieved a lasting peace, and the ambitious peace agenda remains a "prize" that will be won only if enough Guatemalans pressure the incoming government to adopt that agenda. The wounds of the war are deep and the obstacles to peace are daunting. From the perspective of the fiftieth anniversary (in 2004) of the coup against Arbenz and with the United States casting a long "national security" shadow over Latin America (especially Central America), the long-lasting damage to Guatemala from the 1954 coup can be seen more clearly than ever. Nevertheless, there is a growing sense of entitlement among organized sectors of the population, and many Guatemalans, especially Mayas and women, are engaging in new forms of grassroots organizing. This may not guarantee social progress, but long range, it does represent rising expectations that cannot be stifled or reversed.

In sum, emerging from a war that cost over 200,000 civilian lives, Guatemala in the early twenty-first century remains very much a society in transition, with the outcome uncertain. Although the continuity of the constitutional and electoral order appears intact, virtually all other long-standing problems remain unresolved. The words of Salvadoran writer Roberto Turcios (in 1997) capture an essential dilemma of interpreting postwar transitions such as those of El Salvador and Guatemala: "Looking back over the past 25 years, you can see a gigantic leap forward; but looking ahead, what stands out is uncertainty."

Chronology

1524 Spanish conquest, beginning of colonial era
1821 Independence from Spain
1871 "Liberal reform" begins under presidency of General Justo Rufino Barrios, disestablishment of the Church
1901 United Fruit Company (UFCo) arrives in Guatemala
1931 Jorge Ubico takes over presidency
1944 Ubico overthrown in military coup, civilian–military uprising subsequently ousts military junta and begins Revolution of 1944–1954
1945 Juan José Arévalo elected president, new democratic constitution is promulgated
1947 New labor code establishes basic workers' rights
1949 Formation of Partido Guatemalteco de Trabajo (PGT, Communist Party), not legalized until 1951
1950 Jacobo Arbenz elected president
1952 Agrarian Reform Law passed
1954 (June) Arbenz overthrown in CIA-organized "Liberation"; Carlos Castillo Armas takes power
1957 Castillo Armas assassinated
1958 General Miguel Ydígoras Fuentes elected president
1959 Cuban Revolution
1960 (November) Major military uprising against Ydígoras suppressed, some participants take to the mountains
1962 Massive student and labor demonstrations, formation of Revolutionary Movement 13 of Noviembre (MR-13) and Rebel Armed Forces (FAR), and beginning of guerrilla insurgency
1963 Overthrow of Yidígoras in coup led by Colonel Enrique Peralta Azurdia to prevent 1963 elections
1966 Julio César Méndez Montenegro (Revolutionary Party) elected president
1966–1968 United States sends Green Berets, finances and directs counterinsurgency campaign led by Colonel Carlos Arana Osorio; founding of "The White Hand" ("MANO Blanca") and other death squads; by 1970, around 8000 unarmed civilians killed by security forces
1970 Arana elected president
1972 Entry of Ejército Guerrillero de los Pobres (EGP) guerrillas into Guatemala
1974 General Kjell Laugerud becomes president through electoral fraud

1975 Guerrilla activities resume

1976 (February) Massive earthquake, formation of National Committee of Trade Union Unity (CNUS), increased popular organizing

1977 Massive protest march by mine workers from Ixtahuacan to Guatemala City

1978 (March) General Romeo Lucas García becomes president through electoral fraud, (April) formation of Comité de Unidad Campesina (CUC), (May) massacre of Kekchi Indians at Panzós, United States bans arms sales to Guatemalan government

1979 (July) Sandinista victory in Nicaragua

1979 (September) Organización del Pueblo en Armas (ORPA) guerrillas launch first military operation

1980 (January) Government massacre and burning of the Spanish embassy, Spain breaks diplomatic relations, great increase in guerrilla activity in Mayan highlands

1981 Beginning of army counteroffensive, involving numerous massacres and destruction of over 400 Mayan villages by 1983

1982 (February) Formation of Guatemalan National Revolutionary Unity (URNG) by EGP, ORPA, FAR, and PGT Nucleus; (March) General Angel Aníbal Guevara "wins" presidency through fraudulent election, but discontented army officers led by Efraín Ríos Montt seize power in coup; Ríos Montt becomes president; counterinsurgency campaign escalates

1983 (January) United States resumes military sales to Guatemala; (August) General Oscar Mejía Víctores seizes power in military coup; counterinsurgency war continues

1984 Constituent assembly draws up new constitution

1985 Official U.S. economic and military aid resumed, formation of Group of Mutual Support (GAM), (December) Christian Democrat Vinicio Cerezo wins presidency in national election, takes office in January 1986

1987 (August) Esquipulas II, Central American Peace Accords signed in Guatemala; (September) Guatemalan army begins "year's end" counterinsurgency offensive

1988 (May) Abortive military coup attempt by rightist civilians and military officers

1989 (May) Another failed coup attempt

1990 Beginning of "dialogue" process of discussions between URNG and political and social sectors; (November) presidential election, first round; (December) massacre at Santiago Atitlán

1991 (January) Jorge Serrano wins runoff election; (April) beginning of government/URNG peace negotiations and establishing of agenda and procedures; (October) massive continental indigenous conference held in Guatemala, with march from Quetzaltenango to capital

1992 (October) Awarding of Nobel Peace Prize to Guatemalan Mayan and political opposition leader Rigoberta Menchú

1993 (May–June) Serrano attempts *auto-golpe,* or "Serranazo"; reversed/resolved by ascendance to presidency of Ramiro de León Carpio, former human rights ombudsman

1994 (January) Framework Accord signed, establishing United Nations as moderator of peace negotiations and formation of Assembly of Civil Society; (March) Human Rights Accord signed; (June) signing of accords on Resettlement of the Uprooted and Truth Commission (Historical Clarification Commission); (November) Arrival of MINUGUA, U.N. verification mission

1995 (March) Signing of Accord on the Identity and Rights of Indigenous Peoples; (March) eruption of scandal involving CIA-paid Guatemalan army officers in previous assassinations of U.S. citizen Michael Devine and guerrilla husband of U.S. lawyer Jennifer Harbury, Efraín Bámaca; (November–January 1996) in second round, Alvaro Arzú wins presidential election; first-time participation of center-leftist New Guatemala Democratic Front (FDNG) in election

1996 (January) New president Arzú takes office; (March) informal cease-fire between army and URNG; (May) signing of Accord on Socio-Economic Issues; (September) signing of Accord on Strengthening of Civilian Power and Role of Armed Forces in a Democratic Society; (December) operational accords signed (definitive cease-fire, constitutional and electoral reforms, reintegration of URNG, and timetable); (December 29) final Peace Accord signed in Guatemala City, ending 36-year civil war

1997 (January) International community (donor nations and agencies) pledges $1.9 billion to implement peace accords, conditioned on Guatemalan government compliance with accords

1998 (February) Government retreat on tax reform; (April) assassination of Auxiliary Bishop Juan Gerardi 2 days after release of major human rights report under his supervision; (October–November) Central America, including Guatemala, hit by devastating Hurricane Mitch

1999 (February) Historical Clarification Commission releases report on human rights crimes during the war; (March) U.S. President Clinton, in Guatemala, apologizes for U.S. role in Guatemalan counterinsurgency war; (May) constitutional reforms defeated in referendum; (November–December) in second round, Alfonso Portillo and Frente Republicano Guatemalteco (FRG, party of exdictator Ríos Montt) win election; first-time participation of (now legal) URNG in election as part of coalition Alianza Nueva Náción

2003 (November–December) In second round, Oscar Berger wins election; Ríos Montt decisively defeated, raising broad hopes for less corrupt and repressive government and more compliance with Peace Accords

2005 (March) Widespread demonstrations against Central American Free Trade Agreement (CAFTA) met by army/police violence

2006 (July) Central American Free Trade Agreement takes effect in Guatemala

2007 (September, November) General elections; in second round, self-denominated "social democrat" Alvaro Colom (Unidad Nacional de la Esperanza) narrowly wins election over Otto Pérez Molina (Partido Patriota)

Bibliography

This bibliography includes only references in English, although many of the best analyses written by Guatemalans are available only in Spanish; wherever possible, I am including translated works by Guatemalans and other Latin Americans. (Students who read Spanish should read, for example, the works of Edelberto Torres Rivas, Gabriel Aguilera, Ricardo Falla, and a host of Mayan analysts.) For reasons of space, this bibliography includes only books, not articles.

Adams, Richard. *Crucifixion by Power.* Austin: University of Texas Press, 1970.

Barry, Tom. *Inside Guatemala.* Albuquerque, NM: Inter-Hemispheric Education Resource Center, 1992.

Berger, Susan. *Guatemaltecas: The Women's Movement, 1986–2003.* Austin: University of Texas Press, 2006.

Carmack, Robert, ed. *Harvest of Violence.* Norman: University of Oklahoma Press, 1988.

Chase-Dunn, Christopher, Susanne Jonas, and Nelson Amaro, eds. *Globalization on the Ground: Post-Bellum Guatemalan Development and Democracy.* Boulder, CO: Rowman & Littlefield, 2001.

Falla, Ricardo. *Massacres of the Jungle.* Boulder, CO: Westview Press, 1994.

———. *Quiché Rebelde: Religious Conversion, Politics & Ethnic Identity,* Austin: University of Texas Press, 2001.

Galeano, Eduardo. *Guatemala: Occupied Country.* New York: Monthly Review Press, 1969.

Gleijeses, Piero. *Shattered Hope: The Guatemalan Revolution and the U.S.* Princeton, NJ: Princeton University Press, 1991.

Goldman, Francisco. *The Art of Political Murder: Who Killed the Bishop?* New York: Grove Press, 2007.

Grandin, Greg. *The Blood of Guatemala.* Durham, NC: Duke University Press, 2000.

——*The Last Colonial Massacre*. Chicago: University of Chicago Press, 2004.

Immerman, Richard. *The CIA in Guatemala*. Austin: University of Texas Press, 1982.

Jonas, Susanne. *The Battle for Guatemala: Rebels, Death Squads and U.S. Power*. Boulder, CO: Westview Press, 1991.

——. *Of Centaurs and Doves: Guatemala's Peace Process*. Boulder, CO: Westview Press, 2000.

Jonas, Susanne, and David Tobis, eds. *Guatemala*. Berkeley, CA: NACLA, 1974.

Manz, Beatriz. *Paradise in Ashes*. Berkeley: University of California Press, 2004.

Melville, Thomas. *Through a Glass Darkly*. XLibris Corporation, 2005.

Menchú, Rigoberta, with Elisabeth Burgos-Debray. *I . . . Rigoberta Menchú*. New York: Verso Press, 1980.

Nelson, Diane. *A Finger in the Wound*. Berkeley: University of California Press, 1999.

Payeras, Mario. *Days of the Jungle*. New York: Monthly Review Press, 1983.

Perera, Victor. *Unfinished Conquest: The Guatemalan Tragedy*. Berkeley: University of California Press, 1993.

Schirmer, Jennifer, *The Guatemalan Military Project*. Philadelphia: University of Pennsylvania Press, 1998.

Schlesinger, Stephen, and Stephen Kinzer. *Bitter Fruit*. New York: Doubleday and Anchor Books, 1983.

Smith, Carol, ed. *Guatemalan Indians and the State: 1540–1988*. Austin: University of Texas Press, 1990.

Warren, Kay. *Indigenous Movements and Their Critics: Pan-Mayanism and Ethnic Resurgence in Guatemala*. Princeton, NJ: Princeton University Press, 1998.

CENTRAL AMERICAN CONTEXT

Booth, John, Christine Wade, and Thomas Walker. *Understanding Central America*. Boulder, CO: Westview Press, 2006.

Dunkerley, James. *Power in the Isthmus*. New York: Verso Press, 1988.

LaFeber, Walter. *Inevitable Revolutions*. New York: Norton, 1984.

Pérez Brignoli, Hector. *A Brief History of Central America*. Berkeley: University of California Press, 1989.

Robinson, William. *Transnational Conflicts: Central America, Social Change and Globalization*. London: Verso Press, 2003.

Torres Rivas, Edelberto. *Repression and Resistance*. Boulder, CO: Westview Press, 1989.

Vilas, Carlos. *Between Earthquakes and Volcanoes: Market, State, and the Revolutions in Central America*. New York: Monthly Review Press, 1995.

Walker, Thomas and Ariel Arimony, eds. *Repression, Resistance, and Democratic Transition in Central America*. Wilmington, DE: Scholarly Resources, 2000.

LITERATURE, POETRY, AND PHOTOS

Arias, Arturo. *After the Bombs*. Translated by Asa Zatz. Willimantic, CT: Curbstone Press, 1990.

Asturias, Miguel Angel. *The President*. Translated by Frances Partridge. Prospect Heights, IL: Waveland Press, 1997.

Castillo, Otto René. *Let's Go*. Translated by Margaret Randall. Willimantic, CT: Curbstone Press, 1971.

Goldman, Francisco. *The Long Night of White Chickens*. New York: Atlantic Monthly Press, 1992.

Moller, Jonathan. *Our Culture Is Our Resistance*. New York: Powerhouse Books, 2004.

Montejo, Víctor. *Testimony: Death of a Guatemalan Village*. Translated by Victor Perera. Willimantic, CT: Curbstone Press, 1987.

Simon, Jean-Marie. *Guatemala: Eternal Spring, Eternal Tyranny*. New York: Norton, 1987 (photos).

Zimmerman, Marc. *Literature and Resistance in Guatemala*. Athens: Ohio University Center for International Studies, 1995.

FILMS AND VIDEOS

Devils Don't Dream. Guatemala, 1995.
Discovering Dominga, United States, 2003.
El Norte. United States/Guatemala, 1985.
Mayan Voices/American Lives. Guatemala, 1994.
Men with Guns. United States, 1997.
When the Mountains Tremble. Guatemala, 1983.
Border Stories. Mexico, 2001.

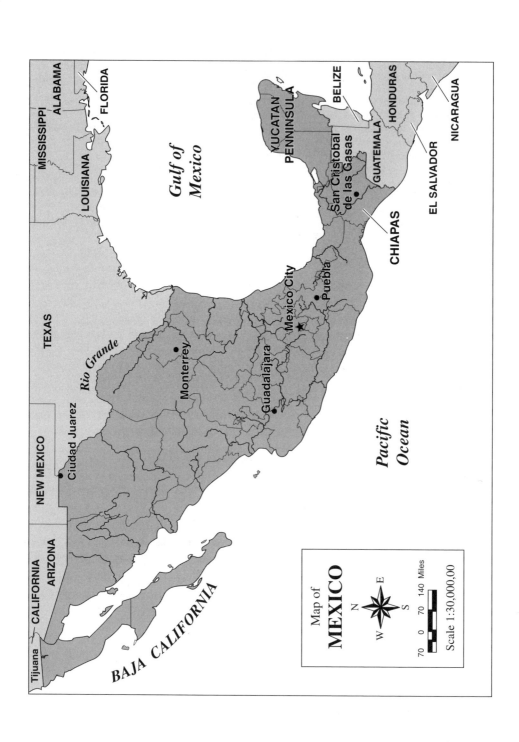

MEXICO

Nora Hamilton

Introduction

Mexico is a country of approximately 105 million people and 1,958,000 square kilometers, the second largest of Latin America in both population and size. Geographically part of North America, Mexico is characterized by a varied terrain, ranging from northern desert to temperate valleys in central Mexico, with tropical and semitropical zones in the east and southeast. Mountain ranges dissecting Mexico from north to south have made transportation and communication difficult for much of its history. Mexico is also part of the Pacific earthquake zone; in 1985, two severe earthquakes in Mexico City killed thousands of people and demolished a number of buildings.

Mexico's population grew rapidly during most of the twentieth century, although levels of growth were reduced from 2.8 percent per year in the 1970s to 1.8 percent in the 1990s. Its urban population is now over 75 percent of the total, up from 40 percent in 1950, with 30 percent of the total population in cities of over 1 million and over 20 million in greater Mexico City. The concentration of economic, political, and cultural life in Mexico City has been a major factor in its attraction of people from other parts of Mexico and has resulted in the attendant problems of pollution, overcrowding, traffic congestion, and shortages, including water and electricity. Other major cities include Monterrey, a northern industrial city, and Guadalajara, a more traditional colonial city of small and medium industries. Some decentralization has occurred in recent years with the growth of cities of the interior and particularly along the U.S. border.

Several factors have been important in shaping Mexico's history as well as its contemporary political, social, and economic life. First, it has a rich and varied cultural heritage, largely due to the substantial number of indigenous populations that inhabited the area for centuries prior to the arrival of the Spanish. Evidence of the artistic achievement and complexity of these pre-Columbian civilizations can be found at archaeological sites in various parts of Mexico and in Mexico's museums, especially the National Museum of Anthropology in Mexico City. As a result of the mixture of indigenous populations with the Spaniards, Mexico is today a predominantly *mestizo* country. However, some Mexicans claim pure European heritage, and there is a substantial minority of indigenous populations, approximately 15 percent of the total, chiefly in the southern and western regions. Mexico also has a small Afro-Mexican population, whose ancestors were brought in to work on plantations during the colonial period.

Second, Mexico has had a special, unequal, and often difficult relationship with the United States, in part due to geographic contiguity. Prior to the Mexican-American War in the mid-nineteenth century, Mexico extended into what is now the southwestern United States. Following the U.S. victory and its annexation of half

---

INDIGENOUS GROUPS

Although the Mexican population is predominantly *mestizo*, there is a large indigenous population, which has been variously estimated at from 10 to nearly 30 percent of the population, with most estimates at approximately 15 percent. The difficulty of ascertaining the exact number reflects the fact that indigenous designation is based less on race than on culture, with the acquisition of Western clothing and Spanish language often considered indicative of incorporation into the predominantly *mestizo* society (although this designation has been questioned by indigenous groups and some anthropologists). There are an estimated fifty-six different groups, among which the best known are the Yaqui in the northwest, Otomi in central Mexico, Mixtec and Zapotec in the south (particularly the state of Oaxaca), Tarascans in western Mexico, and various Mayan groups, among them the Mam, Tzotzil, and Tzeltal in the southeast.

The Mexican revolution led to a new emphasis on Mexico's indigenous past, evident in the works of Mexico's muralists in the 1920s and 1930s; but the policy of the post-revolutionary governments was based on the assumption that assimilation and cultural homogeneity were necessary for economic success. Indigenous groups in Mexico linked with indigenous movements in other parts of the Americas during the 1980s and succeeded in winning some concessions, including a reform of Article 4 of the Constitution to recognize the "pluricultural composition" of Mexico and to protect the languages and cultures of the indigenous people.

The Zapatistas, an indigenous revolutionary group based in the state of Chiapas, have given preeminence to indigenous rights, demanding political and cultural autonomy for Mexico's Indian nations. This was agreed upon in the 1996 Indigenous Rights and Culture (San Andrés) Accords, but the Zedillo administration resisted implementing them. The administration of Vicente Fox was initially more receptive to the Zapatista demands and sent the proposed reforms to Congress, but the version passed was considerably weakened and was rejected by the Zapatistas, who, with other indigenous communities have organized autonomous municipalities, some of which have come into conflict with official government representatives in local areas. In 2006, the Zapatistas rejected the electoral process and launched "the other campaign," traveling throughout the country and meeting with different social and grassroots organizations with the purpose of uniting them in the search for alternative forms of governance.

of Mexico's territory, Mexicans continued to live in the area, and their number has been substantially increased through Mexico–United States migration, facilitated by the 2000-mile border shared by the two countries. Although the threat of U.S. military intervention continued to be a real one until the 1930s, Mexico's current relationship with the United States is largely demographic and economic. Mexico is dependent on the United States for 80 to 90 percent of its exports, a relationship formalized in the North American Free Trade Agreement (NAFTA), which incorporates Canada, Mexico, and the United States. Other issues of concern between Mexico and the United States are Mexican migration, the treatment of Mexicans in the United States, and the War on Drugs. At the same time, Mexican immigration and settlement has had an important demographic, cultural, social, and political impact in the United States.

A third factor is the Mexican Revolution in the early part of the twentieth century, a cataclysmic event that resulted in the decimation of 10 percent of the population and has shaped Mexico's economic, political, and social life since that time. Although the goals of the various groups that fought in the revolution—democracy, land reform, social justice, and national sovereignty—have been only partially met, they constituted the prevailing ideology in twentieth-century Mexico, and the dominant political party during most of the century, the Institutional Revolutionary Party (PRI), based its legitimacy on its claim to represent these values.

The political structure emerging from the revolution has been an important element in Mexico's long-term political stability, a fourth factor distinguishing Mexico from most other countries of Latin America. Termed the "perfect dictatorship" by Peruvian writer Mario Vargas Llosa, Mexico's dominant party system combined authoritarian controls with flexibility in responding to its constituencies and was for the most part successful in neutralizing protests and dissident groups.

Mexico's political stability benefited from its economic growth between the 1940s and the 1970s. Mexico is one of the most industrialized countries of Latin America, and prior to the 1980s it was one of the most dynamic, with GDP growth rates averaging 6 percent annually (8 percent annually for industrial growth). Industrial expansion has been a factor in Mexico's urbanization and in the emergence of middle-income groups in a range of occupations, including small and medium farmers, business owners and industrialists, state workers, professionals, and upper levels of the working class.

Nevertheless, the benefits of growth have been unevenly distributed. In the agricultural sector, the relatively prosperous commercial farms of the northern states producing for export contrast dramatically with the impoverished *minifundia* and communal farms of southern Mexico, particularly in the southern states of Chiapas, Guerrero, and Oaxaca. Within the private sector as a whole, a small number of economic groups, consisting of industrial and commercial firms, banks, real estate companies, and other assets and controlled by a small number or networks of investors, have traditionally shared economic control with public sector firms and transnational corporations. Workers have been divided between those organized in corporate or independent unions, which have benefited at least to some extent by economic growth, and those in smaller firms or the informal sector, whose economic situation is much more precarious.

As in other Latin American countries, Mexico is undergoing rapid transformations in the economic and political spheres, which are having social and cultural repercussions. Economic globalization and the economic crisis of the 1980s have resulted in a rejection of old economic models and an acceptance of neoliberalism by Mexican policy makers. This new model is based on opening the economy to foreign trade and investment and the reduction of state intervention in the economy, a process institutionalized when Mexico joined NAFTA in 1994.

Economic crisis and the embrace of economic liberalism have in turn led to painful economic and social dislocations and adjustments due to loss of jobs, reduced wages, and the elimination of previous economic safeguards, in turn leading to new individual, household, and collective initiatives. Individuals and households rely increasingly on the informal sector and/or migration to the United States, and new forms of organization and mobilization have emerged, ranging from demonstrations by debtors to cross-border organizing among labor groups. On January 1, 1994, the day NAFTA went into effect, indigenous peasants in Chiapas staged a revolt targeting the new economic model as well as accumulated economic and political grievances at the local and regional levels. The worsening economic situation undermined one of the major pillars of PRI stability, leading to pressures for political reform and increased support for opposition parties.

International opening, internal economic changes, and social mobilization have in turn been factors in a process of democratization, involving increased opposition representation in municipal governments, in the national congress, and among individual state governors. A major milestone in this process was reached in 2000, when Mexicans elected opposition candidate Vicente Fox of the National Action Party (PAN) as president, ending the 71-year hegemony of the PRI. The subsequent victory of another PAN candidate, Felipe Calderon, in the 2006 presidential election was strongly contested, however, and left many Mexicans with the conviction that the democratic process still had far to go.

Historical Trajectory

EARLY HISTORY

Long before the coming of the Spaniards, the area that is now Mexico was the home of numerous different populations, ranging from nomadic hunting societies in the northern plains to complex civilizations that achieved high levels of artistic, scientific, and technological sophistication, notably in architecture, sculpture, mathematics, and astronomy. These civilizations were prominent in central and southern Mexico, particularly during the classic period (roughly 150–900 C.E.), when the major cities of Teotihuacán, Monte Albán, Palenque, and others were built and flourished.

The classic civilizations were succeeded by warrior groups. By the early fourteenth century, the Aztecs, a military group, had established a foothold in central Mexico, where they built their capital, Tenochtitlán. From here they conquered the neighboring populations and established an empire that extended from the Gulf of Mexico to the Pacific and from central Mexico into Guatemala. The Aztecs assimilated many of the religious beliefs and cultural practices of the populations they conquered, which were able to maintain their cultural autonomy. A hierarchical governing system was established through which the Aztecs collected tribute and commissioned labor from the subject populations.

The Spaniards, led by Hernán Cortés, arrived in Mexican territory in 1519 and by 1521 had completed the conquest of the Aztec Empire with the assistance of some of the subject populations. Because of the immense wealth of the capital city, Tenochtitlán, it became one of the two major centers of the Spanish Empire in the Americas, the Viceroyalty of New Spain. The colonial period was characterized by the struggle of the Spanish conquerors and their *criollo* descendants to extract the wealth of the colony, on the one hand, and to circumvent the political and economic restrictions of the Spanish crown, which was attempting to prevent the rise of a rival economic power in the colonies, on the other.

Three hundred years of Spanish colonialism had a profound effect in shaping Mexico's future. For the native populations and civilizations the effects were devastating: aside from loss through war, contact with the Spaniards brought diseases such as smallpox, which decimated much of the population; and many died through overwork in silver mines or on plantations. Many elements of pre-Columbian culture were destroyed or lost, among them the temple of Tenochtitlán, which was demolished and replaced by a cathedral.

The hierarchical system of the Aztecs was reinforced by the Spaniards with the addition of strong racial components. Initially, large areas were given to the Spanish conquerors in the form of *encomiendas*, a type of trust that gave the trustee the right

---

RELIGION

The Catholic Church has been a major force in Mexican history since the colonial period, although its role has been an ambiguous one. On the one hand, the official Church has been for the most part conservative, upholding authoritarian and hierarchical values, and has generally reinforced the status quo. On the other, individual members of the clergy and Catholic laity have actively defended the rights of downtrodden sectors, evident in the role of priests such as Miguel Hidalgo and José María Morelos in the early independence movements and more recently in the work of catechists influenced by liberation theology in areas such as Chiapas, where they have had a role in the organization of indigenous peasants since the 1970s. Prior to his retirement in 1999, Bishop Samuel Ruiz of San Cristóbal de las Casas worked tirelessly on behalf of the indigenous groups of Chiapas and played a leading role in efforts to mediate the conflict between the Zapatistas and the government.

Its economic and spiritual power and social and political conservatism made the Church a major target of reformist groups and governments. In the mid-nineteenth century, the Liberal government succeeded in undermining the economic power of the Church through the expropriation of its landholdings and encouraged Protestant missionaries to come to Mexico in an effort to counter its spiritual influence. In the early twentieth century, the revolutionary governments restricted its ideological role through the establishment of state control of education. Draconian measures against the Church in the 1920s resulted in the Cristero rebellion, which ended with an agreement curtailing state persecution of the Church in return for noninterference of the Church in politics, with the result that the political role of the Church was quite limited throughout most of the twentieth century.

Nevertheless, Catholicism has retained a considerable following; according to a 1989 poll, 92 percent of the population consider themselves Catholic. While the church tends to be socially conservative bishops and other members of the clergy have spoken out on political and social issues, including human rights violations, electoral fraud, and the gap between the wealthy and the poor. In 1991, the Salinas government proposed legislation that would reverse many constitutional restrictions on the Church, which was passed in 1992; and government representatives increasingly consult Church authorities on issues of mutual interest.

Approximately 5 percent of the Mexican population consider themselves Protestant. Evangelical movements have had a more limited role in Mexico than in some other Latin American countries but have been growing in recent years. Both Evangelical and main-stream Protestant groups have been particularly active in certain areas, such as eastern Chiapas, where they have introduced more democratic forms of religious practice and bro-ken down ethnic and gender barriers to participation. Friction between Catholics, Protes-tants, and Evangelical Christians has overlapped with political and social conflicts in the region; but the Zapatista movement incorporates members of all religious groups.

to collect tribute from the incorporated indigenous communities. As the mines were depleted, the Spaniards and *criollos* began to take over the lands of the indigenous communities and to force their inhabitants to work for them. The major strategy was a form of debt peonage, through which the Indians incurred debts from the landowners in order to pay tribute, which they were then forced to pay off by work-ing for the landowners, a form of servitude that was often passed on to succeeding generations.

As elsewhere in Latin America, the Catholic Church had an ambiguous role. Fol-lowing the conquest, several religious orders established houses in New Spain with the mission of converting the Indians to Christianity; while some were benevolent, if paternalistic, and attempted to modify the exploitative behavior of the Spaniards toward the Indians, others were extremely harsh. Ultimately, a form of Christianity emerged that incorporated elements of indigenous customs and rituals, including the Indian Virgin of Guadalupe and the celebration of the Day of the Dead. Many religious orders became wealthy owners of land, and the official Church became associated with the conservative elements of society, reinforcing the strict hierarchi-cal social order. There have been exceptions throughout Mexican history, however, of dedicated priests and some bishops who worked in the poor communities and sympathized with their needs and interests.

INDEPENDENCE AND THE MEXICAN REPUBLIC (1810–1910)

The initial independence movements in the early nineteenth century were in fact led by priests—Miguel Hidalgo, a creole, and José María Morelos, a *mestizo*—and incorporated Indian and *mestizo* peasants, mine workers, artisans, and unemployed as well as some of the lower clergy. These movements were oriented not only toward political independence but also toward the abolition of slavery and of tributes paid

by the Indians. The threat of social revolution frightened many of the *criollo* population as well as the Spaniards, who crushed the initial revolts. When independence
from Spain was eventually achieved in 1821 under General Agustín de Iturbide, it
left the existing social system intact. It is Hidalgo, however, who is remembered as
the father of Mexican independence and the date of his call to arms, September 16,
1810, that is commemorated as Mexico's Independence Day.

The legacy of the independence movement was a weak state and an oversized
military, resulting in several decades of anarchy characterized by internal and external wars, military coups, and economic devastation. Mexico was poorly prepared
to defend its borders or to prevent the westward expansion of the United States. In
1834, Texas seceded; and in the 1846–1848 Mexican-American War, Mexico lost most
of what is now the U.S. southwest.

Politically, power was contested by Conservatives, representing elite groups
who wanted a centralized state and the retention of the colonial socioeconomic hierarchy, and Liberals, representing a mostly urban middle class who opposed land
concentration, Church power, and monopoly control of trade. In 1855, the Liberals
came to power and under the leadership of Benito Juárez, a Zapotec Indian, passed
a series of laws and subsequently the constitution of 1857 to end the prerogatives of
the Church and the military. Catholicism was no longer the official religion; the prerogatives of military and ecclesiastical courts were eliminated; and corporate property, including not only that of the Church but also communal indigenous property,
was abolished, with peasants receiving individual titles. The government hoped
that the elimination of corporate property would result in an agrarian middle class
of family farms along the lines of the United States, but most of the land was eventually taken over by wealthy landowners, mine owners, and merchants.

This period, the *Reforma*, was interrupted by a Conservative revolt assisted by
the French, who took advantage of U.S. involvement in the Civil War to occupy
Mexico from 1863 to 1867, when they were finally defeated by the Liberals. However, a decade of intermittent war had left economic devastation, a weak central
state, and, despite the defeat of the Conservative army, an unruly military—this
time, the Liberal army. Ironically, it was only after another military revolt, led by a
Liberal general, Porfirio Díaz, and under the subsequent Díaz regime that the centralization of state power and conditions for political order and economic growth
were achieved.

Following his successful revolt, Díaz was elected president in 1876 and reelected
after an interim term in 1884, after which he held on to power, through largely fraudulent elections, until 1910. This period, subsequently known as the *Porfiriato*, was
characterized by the physical, economic, and political integration of the country, the
consolidation of the Mexican state, and economic growth through increased integration with the world economy. Railroad construction and the elimination of regional
tariffs opened up the national market, in the process eliminating a major power base
of regional generals and *caciques* and facilitating the centralization of state power.

Díaz sought to modernize Mexico on the basis of foreign investment and European immigration. Generous concessions were given to U.S. and European investors
in infrastructure, mining, agriculture, and petroleum. Mexican mineral and agricultural exports expanded dramatically, and manufacturing, based on light industries,

also grew. However, the benefits of economic growth were highly concentrated by foreign investors and a small number of domestic groups. Díaz' favoritism to foreigners irked domestic investors, and many were genuinely concerned at the growth of foreign, and particularly U.S., control of major sectors of the economy, including mineral resources, finance, and agriculture. The small industrial proletariat that worked in the railroads, mines, and manufacturing industries often received low wages for work in difficult and even harsh conditions and was subject to prohibitions against forming independent labor organizations.

The most exploited group was undoubtedly the rural sector, which included the majority of Mexico's population. The growth of Mexico's exports and domestic markets resulted in an expansion of agricultural production, often leading to landowner takeovers of the agricultural land of neighboring peasants and indigenous communities. Peasant revolts were ruthlessly crushed by guards hired by landowners or by federal troops. By the end of the *Porfiriato*, an estimated 97 percent of the rural population had no land. Labor conditions on the plantations and *haciendas* were often extremely harsh.

By the first decade of the twentieth century, there was a growing movement for democracy, including journalists and intellectuals demanding a return to the principles of nineteenth-century liberalism as well as regional elites—landowners, mine owners, bankers, and industrialists of the north and northwest—resentful of the concentration of political power by a small coterie around Díaz. The first group, which included the Flores Magón brothers, formed the Mexican Liberal Party and expanded their program to incorporate the rights of rural and urban workers, including the expropriation of unproductive land, land grants to rural workers, an 8-hour day, minimum wage, and other benefits. Linked to the International Workers of the World (IWW) and to anarchist movements in Mexico, the Mexican Liberal Party supported some of the major strike movements in the last decade of the Díaz regime.

The second group was composed of regional landowning, mining, industrial, and banking elites, who decided to contest the presidential elections of 1910. They formed the Anti-Reelectionist Party, with Francisco Madero as their presidential candidate, and campaigned under the slogan "Effective suffrage, no reelection." Díaz had Madero arrested but Madero escaped and fled to the United States, where he issued a call on Mexicans to take up arms against the discredited Díaz regime, a signal for uprisings in several states. Madero also obtained the assistance of a small group of peasant guerrillas under the leadership of Emiliano Zapata by promising a return of land usurped by landowners under Díaz.

THE MEXICAN REVOLUTION (1910–1934)

The revolt against Díaz succeeded in defeating the Porfirian army, and Madero easily won the subsequent elections. However, he failed to restore lands taken from the peasants in southern Mexico, which had the effect of turning Zapata and his followers against Madero and radicalizing their goals. With the Plan de Ayala, issued in 1911, Zapata expanded the call to return the land expropriated from peasant proprietors to incorporate demands for agrarian reform that would expropriate one-third of large landholdings and distribute them to landless workers.

Madero also failed to dismantle state institutions, notably the Porfirian army, led by General Victoriano Huerta. In 1913, Huerta, with the complicity of U.S.

Ambassador Henry Lane Wilson, carried out a coup against Madero. Madero was assassinated, members of Congress were arrested, and Huerta took control of the government.

This action reunited the heterogeneous forces that had opposed Díaz, who now attacked the counterrevolutionary government of Huerta. The Constitutionalist Army was formed under the leadership of Venustiano Carranza, a landowner from Coahuila; among his division leaders were Pancho Villa and Alvaro Obregón. In the rural central and southern regions, Zapata led the army of the south, incorporating peasants and rural workers from the *haciendas*. The revolutionary armies defeated Huerta in 1914.

With victory, however, the fragile unity of the revolutionary forces ended. While the leaders of the Constitutionalist Army wanted a return to democracy and national sovereignty, Zapata and Villa (who joined him) wanted more fundamental social reforms, particularly a redistribution of land, and distrusted the Constitutionalists. Unable to reach agreement, the revolutionary armies fought each other until the assassination of Zapata in 1919 and the defeat of Villa in 1920. By 1916, however, the Constitutionalists had gained control of the capital city and most of the country; Carranza became provisional president and called for a constitutional congress that would formalize the new regime.

To a remarkable degree, the constitution that emerged in 1917 reflected the heterogeneous goals of the different revolutionary groups. The Constitutionalists were themselves divided between the more conservative followers of Carranza and more radical groups who called for basic reforms, due to genuine sympathy with radical goals or pragmatic recognition that social peace could not be achieved without them. The constitution incorporated various provisions of the 1857 constitution, including a federal system with a separation of powers and no reelection; but it also called for an interventionist state that would in effect implement the goals of various revolutionary groups. It reinforced state control of education, eliminating Church-controlled education; called for national control over land and natural resources; enabled the state to expropriate and redistribute land in the public interest; and outlined extensive rights for labor, including an 8-hour day, a 40-hour week, and the right to organize and strike.

The years of violent revolution had resulted in the decimation of an estimated 10 percent of the population. The immediate postrevolutionary period was one of continued instability as various groups among the revolutionary leadership jockeyed for power. In the aftermath of the revolution, the revolutionary leadership confronted three basic challenges: to establish the institutions of an effective state and political system, to rebuild the economy and institute the basis for national economic control, and to establish the legitimacy of the new system by carrying out the political, social, and ideological principles incorporated in the new constitution.

This process pitted various groups against each other: the revolutionary leadership itself was in dispute as those who had established control over the central government were forced to defend their position against other military leaders ambitious for power. There were also confrontations between the Mexican government and foreign interests over issues involving subsoil rights and mining concessions; peasants and their supporters within the state opposed landowners and their advocates over the expropriation of land; and workers struggled against business groups (and both against the state) over labor rights and organization. The most serious conflict was the Cristero rebellion, a violent struggle resulting from government efforts to implement draconian anticlerical measures. The rebellion was instigated by the clergy and landowners but fought for the most part by peasants, particularly debt *peones* on the estates, whose religion was the basis of their way of life.

By 1930, the government had succeeded in consolidating the Mexican state, political power was concentrated in the central government, and the Cristero rebellion had been contained. The formation of a government party, the National Revolutionary Party (PNR), brought together different factions of the revolutionary leadership and provided for periodic changes in government leadership through regular elections without reelection. However, the electoral process was far from democratic. An opposition campaign for the presidency in 1929 was defeated with the help of stuffed ballot boxes and graveyard voters.

Social reforms had also been limited. A labor law was passed permitting workers to organize and even strike under certain circumstances, but it also instituted state control through the creation of tripartite federal labor boards giving the government final say in labor–management disputes. Agrarian reform had been intermittent and limited. Efforts to enforce legislation protecting national resources and subsoil rights was effectively resisted by foreign mining and petroleum companies backed by the U.S. government, including the threat of military force.

The limited reforms of this period can be in large part attributed to a conservative trend within the Mexican leadership, reflecting increased U.S. influence as well as rapprochement with prerevolutionary business elites. While the U.S. oil and mining companies had vociferously opposed Mexican efforts to limit concessions to foreign companies, calling for U.S. military intervention, the International Banking Commission, formed to negotiate with Mexico regarding its outstanding debts to European and U.S. banks, was more conciliatory. Negotiations over the debt and other outstanding issues also reinforced contacts between Mexican government officials and private bankers and their U.S. counterparts. Successive governments also collaborated with Mexican business groups to promote economic development and encourage foreign investment, particularly in manufacturing, and revolutionary generals and government officials took advantage of their position to acquire land or business ventures.

By the early 1930s, an informal alliance could be identified between members of the "revolutionary elite" of government officials and revolutionary generals, some of the larger Mexican business groups, and U.S. interests, united in the goal of limiting revolutionary change in the interest of protecting investment and property rights and promoting economic growth. At the same time, a potential alliance also existed among *agrarians* (progressive sectors of the government, including governors, who carried out land distribution programs and other reforms in their respective states) and members of the state bureaucracy who identified with peasant groups and workers in pushing for reform.

Lázaro Cárdenas and the Revolutionary Agenda (1934–1940)

The progressive sectors within the government party obtained control of the 1933 nominating convention and proposed a 6-year plan (influenced in part by the Soviet

5-year plan and Roosevelt's New Deal as well as the yet unfulfilled promises of the revolution) that set the parameters for the subsequent administration. Among other measures, it gave priority to agrarian reform and reinforced the concept of a strong state role in directing the economy, promoting union organization, and ensuring national control of natural resources. Their candidate was Lázaro Cárdenas, one of the agrarians who, as governor of Michoacán, had carried out a land reform program and promoted education.

Cárdenas' support for workers in labor conflicts led to a protracted showdown with more conservative political elites . The Cárdenas victory reinforced control by the progressive faction and consolidated labor support for Cárdenas, who continued to support workers in their conflicts with business groups and encouraged labor organizing, including the establishment of an independent labor confederation, the Confederation of Mexican Workers (CTM).

The Cárdenas government carried out an extensive agrarian reform, distributing land to individual peasants and to communities in the form of *ejidos*, owned by the villages, which could be farmed by individual peasant families or collectively. Land reform targeted not only traditional *haciendas* but also commercial estates, which were distributed to rural workers as collective *ejidos* and continued to be worked as an economic unit with the government providing credit and other inputs. The *ejidos* could not be bought, sold, or rented, in effect removing substantial amounts of land from the capital market—a measure that (in theory at least) would protect peasants from losing their land to landowners, as had occurred following the 1857 reform. Cárdenas also encouraged peasant organization, including formation of the National Peasant Confederation (CNC).

The Cárdenas government also took on the U.S.- and British-owned petroleum companies in a conflict that began when the petroleum workers' union attempted to obtain a collective contract and eventually went to the Mexican Supreme Court. It was the refusal of the companies to follow the ruling of the court that resulted in the government decision to expropriate and nationalize the companies. The move had significant internal and international repercussions: Britain broke off relations with Mexico, the United States suspended a silver purchase agreement with Mexico as well as negotiations for loans to Mexico, and the petroleum companies succeeded in having Mexican petroleum exports boycotted in the United States and major European markets. The move was very popular in Mexico, however, where it was seen as a blow for Mexican sovereignty against an industry that had not only exploited the workers but also consistently disregarded Mexican law.

Shortly after the expropriation and in the interest of consolidating his support, Cárdenas restructured the government party, changing its name to the Party of the Mexican Revolution (PRM) and creating four sectors: labor, incorporating the CTM as well as other confederations and independent unions; peasant, which would be dominated by the CNC; popular, which drew in different groups and organizations, including federations of teachers and state employees as well as organizations of women, students, professionals, and small farmers; and military, incorporating elected representatives from each military zone (this sector was subsequently dropped). Membership in the party would be based on membership in one of the organizations in the relevant sector. Ostensibly a mechanism for popular input into the party and government, including selection of party candidates for office, the party in fact became a mechanism for controlling the member organizations.

The reforms of the government aroused the opposition of powerful groups within the private sector and led to considerable anxiety among conservative groups within the party and government. A conservative opposition party, the National Action Party (PAN), was formed in 1939, incorporating pro-Church and pro-Hispanic groups opposed to Cárdenas' reforms and particularly "socialist" education. In the central and southern states where the Cristero movement had emerged in the 1920s, a new paramilitary group, the Sinarquistas, attacked peasants as well as rural teachers associated with land reforms and the "socialist" values of the revolution.

In the meantime, the pending war in Europe and U.S. fears of a two-front war with Germany and Japan led to U.S. efforts to ensure support and reinforce defenses in Latin America. The Cárdenas administration had pursued an independent foreign policy relative to the United States; it had taken the initiative to push for a nonintervention policy in the Americas at the Pan-American Conference in 1936 specifically aimed at preventing U.S. military involvement in the region. It had also supported the republicans in the Spanish Civil War, opened Mexico to Spanish exiles when the republicans lost, and provided refuge for Leon Trotsky when he was expelled from the Soviet Union. Nevertheless, the Cárdenas administration had maintained relatively good relations with the United States even through the petroleum conflict and was prepared to collaborate in mutual defense against fascism.

Thus, involvement in hemispheric defense and the need to appease business groups and foreign investors, as well as conservative groups within the government and party, in the interests of political and economic stability were factors in a shift in the government policy in the latter years of the Cárdenas administration. Strikes and other forms of labor protest were discouraged, and the progress of land distribution was slowed. A moderate, Manuel Avila Camacho, was selected as presidential candidate for the PRM and defeated an independent opposition candidate; as in the past, however, the government party used fraudulent means to ensure the victory of Avila Camacho.

In retrospect, the Cárdenas government succeeded to a greater extent than any of its predecessors (or successors) in implementing the social goals of the revolution. The agrarian reform provided land for a substantial number of peasants and was responsible for relative social peace in the countryside for several generations. More than any other government, it recognized the rights of labor and encouraged labor organization. The nationalization of Mexico's oil reserves asserted Mexico's sovereignty and established a precedent for the nationalization of other key economic sectors, generally through negotiated sale rather than expropriation. Mexico also continued to exercise independence in its foreign policy, albeit at a more symbolic level. Finally, the actions of the Cárdenas government affirmed the activist role of the state in social reform and economic development.

The 1920s and 1930s were a period of cultural foment and artistic creativity. It was during this period that Mexico's muralists, among them Diego Rivera, José Clemente Orozco, and David Alfaro Siqueiros, rejecting elitist notions of art and culture, produced their monumental murals in schools, hospitals, government buildings, and other public places. Writers such as Mariano Azuela (*Los de abajo/The*

Underdogs) also broke with European traditions in favor of a more direct, raw style that portrayed the brutal lives and exploitation of Mexico's poor. Painters such as Orozco as well as writers often portrayed not only the victimization of the poor by the wealthy or the Church but also the brutality and corruption of some of the revolution's leaders and government officials, themes that were later taken up by Carlos Fuentes (*The Death of Artemio Cruz*) and Juan Rulfo (*The Burning Plain*).

Economic Development and the "Perfect Dictatorship": 1940–1982

THE "MEXICAN MIRACLE"

Under the conservative presidents who followed Cárdenas, the focus of government programs shifted to economic development and particularly the promotion of industry. Agrarian reform was neglected, and party control over the member organizations of the labor and peasant sectors was tightened. In some cases, government or party officials removed democratically elected leaders of unions or other sectoral organizations if they threatened the status quo and imposed more compliant leaders.

Mexico's economic development was based on the import substitution industrialization (ISI) model followed by several Latin American countries, providing high levels of protection and tax relief for manufacturing industries oriented primarily to the domestic market. This model was partly the result of circumstances; the dramatic fall in exports of primary commodities during the Depression demonstrated the danger of excessive dependence on primary commodity export, while the cutbacks in manufacturing imports during World War II reinforced the validity of an industrialization strategy. A mixed economy evolved with substantial state involvement and an expanding public sector, which included strategic industries such as telecommunications, railroads, airlines, electric power, steel, mining, and, of course, petroleum and petrochemicals. Many services provided by public sector industries were subsidized to keep domestic industry costs low.

Foreign investment was encouraged, although subject to certain restrictions: areas such as petroleum, mining, and banking and finance were off limits to foreigners; foreign subsidiaries operating in Mexico were required to be at least 51 percent Mexican-owned (although this regulation was often weakly enforced); and performance requirements were established for certain industries, such as the automobile industry, which was required to obtain an increasing percentage of its inputs in Mexico and to achieve a balance of trade in the industry, increasing vehicle and parts exports to the level of auto-related imports.

In contrast to state promotion of industry, rural development, particularly of the small farm, peasant and *ejidal* sectors, was relatively neglected. Government promotion of agriculture tended to be concentrated on irrigation programs and technologies beneficial to large and middle-sized farms located in northern Mexico, most of them oriented to export. While agricultural exports did increase substantially during this period, food production for the domestic market stagnated, leading to increased dependence on food imports. Although several programs were instituted to help small farmers and improve domestic food production in the 1970s, their effectiveness was limited and most were discontinued with the economic crisis of the following decade.

The Mexican economy grew rapidly between 1940 and 1970 and more unevenly during the 1970s. Economic growth averaged 6 percent annually, and industrial growth increased at a rate of 8 percent annually. By the 1970s, Mexico, along with Brazil, was one of the most dynamic countries of Latin America and was recognized as a semideveloped industrial economy. However, economic growth was accompanied by growing inequality. Disparities were also evident within sectors. In agriculture, there was a striking contrast between the large and middle-sized commercial farms oriented to export, often highly mechanized and for the most part located in northern Mexico, and a large number of relatively poor *ejidos* and small peasant holdings in southern Mexico. In industry, a limited number of large firms controlled the majority of assets.

The economy was dominated by large state-owned firms, private domestic firms, and multinational corporations (MNCs). Firms of the public sector tended to be in infrastructure and strategic industries. MNCs were dominant in automobiles, electric machinery, and chemicals. Private domestic firms tended to be concentrated in consumer industries; many of these were part of economic groups, which combined banks, manufacturing industries, real estate agencies, construction firms, insurance companies, and other assets and were generally controlled by a small number of investors, often a few families, through interlocking ownership and directorates. The economic groups as well as the large state-owned firms had growing access to foreign capital and technology through joint ventures, loans, and technology transfers.

The economic groups, and to some extent the domestic private sector in general, tended to be divided between those dependent on close links with the state and those that were more independent. The former included small and middle-sized manufacturers, many of them organized in the National Chamber of Manufacturing Industry, as well as major economic groups in areas such as construction that benefited from state contracts. The latter included some middle-sized firms located outside the federal district as well as powerful economic groups in the city of Monterrey. The prototype for the independent business sector was the Garza Sada group, which began with a brewery established in the late nineteenth century; expanded into glass manufacturing, initially to make bottles for the brewery; subsequently into steel production; and later into chemicals and other industries. By the 1970s, there were four major groups, each with vertically integrated industries, banks, and other institutions and for the most part run by third-generation descendants of the original founders.

With the growth of the urban and industrial working class, divisions emerged between those able to secure a job in the larger unionized industries, particularly foreign or state-owned companies; those in small and medium-sized firms or shops; and those unable to obtain regular jobs, who became part of the growing informal sector. The first group, in party-controlled or independent unions, generally benefited from higher wages, job security, and in some cases additional benefits such as subsidized housing; but the second and particularly the third groups lacked job security and a dependable wage income.

The combination of industrial growth, centered in the major cities, particularly the federal district, and stagnation of the rural area was a factor in growing rural–urban migration and the massive growth in the population in and around Mexico City, putting a major strain on its resources. Squatter settlements were formed in the periphery of the city by new migrants as well as groups from crowded central city tenements. Some of these eventually became overcrowded satellite cities in their own right; the largest of these, Nezahualcóyotl, had 4 million inhabitants by the 1980s and is one of the largest cities in Mexico. The inability of industry to absorb many of these migrants was a major factor in the growth of the informal sector, which included skilled workers who contracted out their labor as well as street vendors and employees of small workshops that subcontracted with factories and other businesses.

This was also a period of substantial migration to the United States, encouraged by the *bracero* program, initiated during World War II, through which Mexican workers were contracted for specified periods of time to work in U.S. industry and agriculture. This led to a process of cyclical migration whereby Mexican workers, chiefly from the western states of Michoacán, Jalisco, Guanajuato, and Zacatecas, came to the United States as farm workers for part of the year, returning to their homes during the remaining months. By the 1950s, Mexican migrants were also working in industry and staying longer; some settled in the United States and brought their families.

POLITICAL POWER AND INTEREST GROUPS: MEXICO'S PERFECT DICTATORSHIP

Mexico's political system has been characterized as one of "flexible authoritarianism," its flexibility an important factor in its longevity and the political stability that Mexico enjoyed relative to other Latin American countries throughout much of the twentieth century. Political control was exercised through the government party, renamed the Institutional Revolutionary Party (PRI) in 1947, which was closely integrated with the state. Party membership was based on membership in labor, peasant, or other organizations, which in turn belonged to the labor, peasant, or popular sectors of the party. Through its corporate structure, the party was able to penetrate virtually all sectors of society.

Clientelistic relations linked party, state, and member organizations. Party and government officials provided favors in return for political support, such as voting for PRI candidates, participating in PRI-sponsored demonstrations, and working in political campaigns. Favors ranged from bribes (often used among peasant organizations in return for votes or participation in PRI rallies) to special institutional privileges, such as hospitals and medical insurance for state workers or subsidized housing programs for members of designated unions.

However, party–client relations went beyond political support. Corporate unions often controlled access to jobs, particularly in the state sector, and in some cases, such as the Oil Workers Union, workers "bought" their jobs. Street vendors paid a regular quota to political patrons for a particular space; the patrons in turn paid off officials above them. Bribes were also paid to the police to prevent harassment of various kinds. PRI leaders with connections to the informal sector took in an estimated $21 million monthly.

State control was centralized in the federal government and particularly the presidency. Despite constitutional checks and balances, the president (prior to 1997) controlled legislative as well as executive functions. Although governors and municipal officials were formally elected, the president often had a hand in their selection as well as their removal and/or replacement. With 85 percent of public funds, the federal government also exercised monetary control and could withhold funds from opposition or dissident state or local officials. At the same time, state governors and local officials could exercise considerable and even arbitrary power at the state and local levels, which was a particular problem in the southern rural states.

Access to high levels of government and the party ran along two parallel tracks. Career politicians, or *políticos*, rose through the party and/or electoral system, while highly trained specialists, or *técnicos*, often had careers in the federal bureaucracy. *Políticos* generally held party positions; elected offices, such as municipal officers, state governors, or members of the legislature; and certain cabinet posts, such as the interior (*gobernación*). *Técnicos* have been important in economic organizations such as the Banco de Mexico (central bank), development banks, and cabinet posts such as the treasury. Until the 1970s, the president had held an elected position in the past and had come from a political position, such as secretary of the interior.

Political success generally depended on membership in *camarillas*, cliques that form around individuals in a leadership position. At a given point, a political aspirant attaches himself or herself to the *camarilla* of a specific leader as a means of getting ahead. When the leader is elected or selected for a post in government, he or she brings his or her *camarilla* along to fill subordinate posts in the same bureaucracy. Family connections and education, especially at the university level, are important in the formation of *camarillas*. Until recently, the National Autonomous University of Mexico (UNAM), the major university in the country, and those in particular faculties such as law were important for political contacts. Beginning in the 1980s, education in private universities became more important, especially universities abroad, chiefly in the United States, such as Yale, Harvard, and the Massachusetts Institute of Technology (MIT).

An important element in the flexibility of Mexico's political system is the fact that the president could not succeed himself, although he generally chose his successor, in consultation with party and private sector leaders. This meant that aspiring politicians, by following one of the indicated trajectories and attaching themselves to a *camarilla*, could eventually aspire to a high-level government post. However, because of the turnover in top government positions with each new presidential election, high-level office could also be short-lived. One unfortunate consequence was that these positions were often seen as a one-time opportunity to ensure one's economic future through legal or nonlegal means, such as generous government contracts to family-owned companies or close business associates. Corruption reached unprecedented levels during the oil boom of the late 1970s when several members of the López Portillo government amassed billions of dollars through contracts with their own companies.

Opposition parties have existed throughout much of the postrevolutionary period, providing a veneer of political pluralism; but prior to the late 1980s, PRI control over the election process guaranteed that other candidates rarely achieved political office even at the lower levels of government. The most important opposition party before 1988 was PAN, a conservative, pro-Church, and generally pro-business party. There were also several left-wing parties, including the Mexican Communist Party, as well as a few parties that could be characterized as "loyal" opposition.

The government and the PRI were generally very skilled at co-opting opposition groups and neutralizing dissent, through tactics ranging from payoffs to limited reforms that responded to some opposition demands, a process that often succeeded in dividing the opposition. The revenues generated through Mexico's economic growth also enabled the government to expand services in areas such as health and education. Infant mortality declined from 91 per 1000 in 1960 to 35 per 1000 in 1993; most of the population has at least a sixth-grade education, and the percent of the relevant age group in secondary school increased from 11 percent in 1960 to 55 percent by the early 1990s. Increased economic resources also facilitated special services to the sectoral constituencies of the PRI.

For opposition and dissident groups that could not be co-opted, the government did not hesitate to use repression, particularly in rural areas, where assassinations were rarely publicized. Guerrilla movements that emerged in the 1950s and 1970s in southern Mexico were brutally repressed. However, the fact that repression was for the most part "hidden" enabled Mexico to retain the reputation of a relatively benign authoritarian regime throughout most of this period.

This changed with the student revolt in 1968, a series of protests of high school and university students that was met with escalating violence by police forces. On the evening of October 2, 1968, military forces fired into a demonstration of students and other dissidents gathered at Tlatelolco Plaza in Mexico City, killing an estimated 200–400 students and their supporters. Although the student movement was silenced, it raised awareness of the poverty and inequality accompanying Mexico's economic miracle and revealed the coercion and repression underlying the party's "perfect dictatorship."

THE "MIRACLE" UNRAVELS: 1970–1982

After 1968, the Mexican government confronted two challenges: to restore the legitimacy of the system, especially for groups left out of the Mexican miracle, and to cope with the stagnation and problems of the growth model. The government of Luis Echeverría (1970–1976) pursued a "democratic opening" in an effort to establish or reestablish dialogue with different groups. Political prisoners, including labor leaders arrested in the 1950s and student leaders arrested in 1968, were released, with some of the latter joining the government; the government also increased expenditures on health, housing, and social welfare.

On the economic front, Echeverría pursued a nationalist and statist agenda in an effort to stimulate the economy in the context of low savings and a slowdown in private investment. The government took control of a range of industries, and expanded investment in steel, chemicals, fertilizers, and heavy industry. The number of firms in the public sector increased from 277 to 845, and public investment increased from 37 to 51 percent of the total. Efforts to raise taxes to pay for increased investment were resisted by the private sector as well as groups within the government, but the government was able to take advantage of the increasing availability of foreign loans, raising the foreign debt from $280 million to $3 billion between 1970 and 1975.

MAJOR PARTIES, INTEREST GROUPS, AND OTHER ORGANIZATIONS: PARTIAL LISTING

	Membership in Chamber of Deputies			
Political Parties	1997	2000	2003	2006
Institutional Revolutionary Party (PRI)	239	208	222	106
National Action Party (PAN)	122	205	151	207
Democratic Revolutionary Party (PRD)	125	54	95	127
Ecological Green Party of Mexico (PVEM)	8	17	17	17
Labor Party (PT)	6	8	6	11
Party of Convergence for Democracy (PCD)	5	8	5	17
New Alliance Party				9
Social Democratic and Peasant Alternative				5
Independent				1
Total	500	500	496	500

Major Government Institutions

Chamber of Deputies (500 members)
Senate (128 members)
Supreme Court (11 members)
Armed Forces (181,356 members as of 2007)
Banco de Mexico (semiautonomous)
Instituto Federal Electoral (autonomous)
Comision Nacional de Derechos Humanos (CNDH)

Sectors of PRI and Major Affiliates

Labor Sector
Labor Congress (CT)
Confederation of Mexican Workers (CTM)
Peasant Sector
National Peasant Confederation (CNC)
Popular Sector
National Congress of Popular Organizations (CNOP)

Major Business Groups

Businessmen's Coordinating Council (CCE)
National Agriculture and Livestock Council (CNA)
Mexican Council of Businessmen (CMHN)
Mexican Employers Confederation (Coparmex)
Confederation of Chambers of Industry (Concamin)
Confederation of National Chambers of Commerce (Concanaco)
National Chamber of Manufacturing Industries (Canacintra)
Mexican Bankers Association (ABM)
Mexican Insurance Association (AMIS)

Mexican Association of Stock Investment Firms (AMIB)
Mexican Business Council for International Affairs (CEMAI)
National Council on Foreign Trade (CONACEX)
National Association of Mexican Importers and Exporters (ANIERM)

Labor Organizations

Corporate Sector

Congress of Labor (CT), umbrella organization
Confederation of Mexican Workers (CTM), member of CT
National Union of Teachers (SNTE)

Independent Organizations

National Union of Workers (UNT)
Authentic Labor Front (FAT), member of UNT
Union of Metal and Allied Industry Workers (STIMAHCS), affiliate of FAT
Union of Telephone Workers of the Republic of Mexico (STRM), member of UNT

Peasant Organizations

National Peasant Confederation (CNC), member of Peasant Sector of PRI
National Union of Autonomous Regional Peasant Organizations (UNORCA), independent
Permanent Agrarian Council (CAP)

Guerrilla/Revolutionary Organizations

Zapatista National Liberation Army (EZLN)
People's Revolutionary Army (ERP)

Other Organizations

El Barzón, debtors' organization
National Coordinating Committee of Urban Popular Movements (CONAMUP)
Civic Alliance, network of civic organizations
National Indigenous Congress
National Democratic Convention (CND)
National Women's Convention (CNM), member of CND
National Indigenous Convention (CNI), member of CND
Mexican Action Network Against Free Trade (RMALC)
Popular Assembly of the People of Oaxaca (APPO)

Nevertheless, the economic situation continued to deteriorate. Despite efforts to promote exports, the trade deficit tripled between 1970 and 1976. Dependence on loans and deficit spending led to growing inflation, which, combined with the negative trade balance, resulted in a 50 percent devaluation of the peso in 1976 (from 12.5 to 25 to the dollar), the first devaluation since 1954. Business sectors, concerned about increasing state intervention as well as inflation, began to withdraw investment and to export capital.

In the meantime, Echeverría's efforts to dialogue with different social groups were offset by his inability to cope with continuing social unrest. He initially supported a movement for democracy that emerged in several of the major unions, including electricians and automobile workers, in an effort to get rid of leaders imposed by the labor bureaucracy, but later backed down under pressures from corporate labor leaders. Police forces and hired thugs attacked student movements, and military forces crushed a guerrilla movement that emerged in southern Mexico.

Under Echeverría's successor, José López Portillo, the critical economic situation was temporarily relieved by an oil boom, the result of the discovery and development of Mexican petroleum in the southwestern part of the country and in the gulf region at a time of high and growing international oil prices. The government used the increased revenues from the growth of Mexico's oil exports as well as foreign loans attracted by Mexico's growth potential to expand oil production and petrochemical industries as well as other industries.

During the 3-year period between 1978 and 1981, the gross domestic product (GDP) increased by 8 percent annually; total investment, much of it foreign, jumped by 16.2 percent a year; and urban employment grew by 5.7 percent annually, with 4 million new jobs created in oil, public works, and industry. However, the net result was to make the economy even more vulnerable. The massive growth in oil exports ironically shifted what had become a diversified export sector, with manufactured goods constituting 47 percent of the total in 1976, to monoexports, with oil exports increasing from 15 to 75 percent of the total between 1976 and 1981. At the same time, the increase in oil exports was more than offset by imports of the new technology needed to develop oil reserves as well as necessary inputs for expanding industries and imports of consumer goods for the rapidly expanding domestic market. Increased loans necessitated by industrial expansion and the negative balance of trade increased the foreign debt to $86 billion by 1982.

High spending levels and the influx of foreign capital in turn resulted in an overheated economy and soaring inflation. The overvalued peso and fear of devaluation led to massive capital flight to banks in the United States and Switzerland and real estate investments in the United States and Europe.

Mexico's vulnerability became evident with the worldwide recession of the early 1980s, which led to a reduction of commodity prices, particularly oil, on the world market by 1981. At the same time, U.S. interest rates had increased from 6.5 percent to 16.7 percent between 1977 and 1981, a further factor in capital flight as well as the increased costs of servicing the debt. In August 1982, Mexico announced that it was unable to meet its debt obligations, portending the economic crisis that would engulf most countries of Latin America in the 1980s.

Because several major U.S. banks (such as Citibank and Bank of America) were heavily overextended in Latin America, default would have led to a crisis and possibly a collapse of the international banking system. Foreign creditors; the governments of the United States, Europe, and Japan; and the International Monetary

Fund (IMF) provided loans to Mexico and other debtor countries that attempted to stabilize their economies, instituting austerity programs that severely penalized the more vulnerable sectors of the population. The Mexican government immediately closed down 105 state firms and agencies, while many small and medium-sized private firms were forced to close or dismiss workers. In 1982 alone, 1 million Mexican workers lost their jobs.

Blaming the domestic banks for capital export and speculation, López Portillo nationalized the banking system, a move that was very popular among certain sectors, including small and middle-sized industries, since the large banks were seen as having monopoly privileges and focusing their lending on their own economic groups. However, the nationalization provoked the distrust and hostility of business groups, which became increasingly active politically during the 1980s and 1990s.

Economic Liberalization and Political Transition: 1982–2000

The last 25 years have been characterized by accelerated changes in Mexico's economic trajectory, which in turn have led to the creation of new social groups and changes in existing ones. While some sectors have been strengthened as a result of the new economic model, others have suffered severe dislocations, which have had economic, social, and ultimately political repercussions. In conjunction with changes in the international context, including the process of economic globalization, the demise of the Soviet bloc, and the transition from authoritarian to democratic regimes in Europe and particularly Latin America, these changes resulted in diluting PRI hegemony, strengthening opposition movements and parties, and a gradual, although convoluted, process of democratization.

Debt Negotiations, Austerity, and Restructuring: 1982–1988

The contours of the new economic system were not immediately evident. The initial priority was to stabilize the economy and to renegotiate external debt and obtain loans in order to maintain interest payments. Since debt repayment was the priority of foreign lenders, debt relief generally involved only sufficient funds to enable debtor countries to repay their debt, which as a result actually increased during most of the 1980s. At the same time, the austerity measures, involving the continued closing down of public agencies, the removal of price controls resulting in increased prices, and substantial declines in real wages, led to a deepening recession. Finally, renegotiations in 1989–1990 resulted in an agreement based on the Brady Plan (named for the U.S. treasury secretary), which reduced Mexico's external debt and provided some relief.

In the meantime, major international lending agencies such as the World Bank and the IMF, as well as U.S. government agencies, began to pressure for a more thoroughgoing economic restructuring in the direction of economic liberalization, or neoliberalism. Among other measures, the new model called for a reduction of the state role in the economy, including the privatization of public sector firms; trade liberalization and increased exports; an opening of the economy to foreign investment; and tax reform.

Other factors were also important in Mexico's economic transformation. The globalization of production and finance as well as dramatic technological developments led to a widespread perception by Mexican policy makers of the need for links with the world market. The policy makers themselves had changed: the *técnicos* were now a majority; President Miguel de la Madrid (1982–1988) and key members of his cabinet had received advanced degrees from major U.S. universities, and the architect of the new economic strategy, Secretary of Budget and Planning (and later president) Carlos Salinas de Gortari, had a Ph.D. in economics from Harvard. Several private sector groups, notably the more independent groups in the north, as well as a growing number of export-oriented firms in other cities had also been long-term advocates of a reduction of state economic intervention and an opening of foreign trade. Finally, de la Madrid and Salinas gave priority to attracting investment, especially foreign capital and Mexican flight capital from abroad, to promote Mexico's economic recovery.

In 1986, Mexico joined the General Agreement on Tariffs and Trade (GATT, now the World Trade Organization), thus committing itself to reduce tariffs and other barriers to trade. By December 1989, Mexico had moved beyond GATT requirements, decreasing its maximum tariff from 100 percent to 20 percent, and had reduced other import barriers. Manufactured exports were promoted, and automobile exports and *maquiladoras*, both predominantly foreign-owned, became particularly important. Auto exports increased from $81 million in 1982 to over $1 billion in 1988; and Ford, General Motors, and Chrysler, along with the government-owned PEMEX, constituted the four top exporters in 1991. The number of *maquiladoras* increased from 454 in 1975 to 1954 in 1992, employing nearly 500,000 people; employment was over 1,300,000 by 2000.

The economic crisis had a devastating effect on wages, which were reduced to half their precrisis levels during the 1980s. As elsewhere, economic restructuring also resulted in the "flexibilization" of labor, undermining the role of unions in the workplace and giving employers greater discretion in the hiring, firing, and placement of workers. The downsizing and closing of formal sector firms led to increased employment in the informal sector, and efforts of both employers and corporate party unions to eliminate independent unions further undermined the labor movement. Government control over union recognition and the legality of strikes has been used arbitrarily on behalf of employers, and in several cases labor activists have been fired and blacklisted. Union membership declined significantly. While there has been a rapid job increase in the *maquila* sector, these jobs are low-paying, with limited benefits, and are characterized by difficult working conditions and high turnover, making the *maquilas* difficult to organize.

Not surprisingly, migration to the United States also increased; according to the 1990 U.S. census, over half of the foreign-born Mexicans in the United States at that time had come in the preceding decade. The new migrants were also more heterogeneous in social composition and geographic origin, with an increasing number from urban and middle-class sectors and a substantial contingent from Mexico City, previously a center of attraction for rural migrants. There was also a growing number of migrants from the impoverished indigenous regions of southern Mexico and other rural areas.

At the same time, social movements and popular grassroots organizations, some of which had their roots in earlier organizing efforts, played an important role in representing the grievances of various population sectors.In September 1985, two devastating earthquakes in Mexico City and the inadequacy of government response galvanized a massive popular movement around issues ranging from housing for those who lost their homes to the need for democratic government. The women's movement also grew significantly during this period as more women entered the labor market and women's role in family and household survival strategies led to increasing activism. Women's committees were formed in several grassroots organizations in addition to organizations at the national level; their goals included giving women greater voice in existing organizations, empowerment and leadership training for women, and combatting patriarchy in its various forms.

Dissatisfaction with the new trajectory of the government also emerged within the PRI itself. In 1987, a group of dissidents formed the "democratic current" and campaigned unsuccessfully for the democratization of the internal nomination process for the 1988 presidential candidate. Several left the party and organized around an opposition candidate, Cuauhtémoc Cárdenas, son of Lázaro Cárdenas, who was also supported by a number of leftist and other small parties as well as some of the resurgent popular movements and grassroots organizations.

Cárdenas was a very popular candidate, drawing immense crowds wherever he campaigned. However, in an election characterized by spectacular fraud (including a computer breakdown during the vote-counting process), the PRI candidate, Carlos Salinas, was declared the victor with 50.7 percent of the vote; Cárdenas officially received 31.1 percent, and the candidate of PAN, Manuel Clouthier, 16.8 percent.

Super Barrio, symbol and protector of poor neighborhoods, and helper greet children in Mexico City, 2000. *(Photo by Patrice Olsen)*

Groups and parties supporting Cárdenas formed the Democratic Revolutionary Party (PRD), protesting the election fraud and calling for democratic reforms and a return to the principles of nationalism and social justice that they felt had been abandoned by the PRI government.

THE TRIUMPH OF THE TECHNOCRATS: 1988–1993

The denationalization of state-owned firms, which had begun gradually under de la Madrid, was accelerated in the early 1990s under Salinas. Between 1990 and 1992, the giant telecommunications firm TELMEX (Teléfonos de Mexico), the eighteen national-ized banks, mining companies, airlines, and other government assets were privatized or reprivatized, resulting in a one-time windfall for the state of $20 billion (used to pay off internal debt and for Pronasol, a government poverty relief program). Between 1982 and 1992, the number of state enterprises was reduced from 1155 to 232.

Mexico has also substantially reduced its restrictions on foreign capital. The 1994 Foreign Investment Law formalized reductions on domestic content require-ments and eliminated other performance criteria. Companies may be 100 percent foreign-owned, and areas previously off limits to foreign investment have gradu-ally been opened to minority foreign ownership. In the early 1990s, Salinas began negotiating with the United States and Canada to join NAFTA, an agreement that would eventually eliminate all trade barriers between the three countries, creating a single market and enhancing Mexico's attractiveness as an investment site, combin-ing cheap labor and direct access to the U.S. market. NAFTA was approved by the U.S. Congress in 1993 and went into effect on January 1, 1994.

Perhaps the most controversial initiative of the Salinas government was the Agrarian Law of 1992, which in effect reversed the agrarian reform, considered one

---

WOMEN

Like many Latin American countries, Mexico has traditionally been characterized by patriarchy, which often translates into fierce protectionism by men of their wives, sisters, and daughters. In extreme cases (notably in the countryside), the social life of women may be restricted to the private sphere of home and church. This syndrome is gradually breaking down under the pressures of industrialization, urbanization, and, increasingly, women's political organizing. The percentage of Mexico's labor force who were women grew from 18 percent in 1978 to 27 percent in 1993 and approximately one third in 2003, although many of these jobs are in Mexico's growing *maquiladora* sector, often character-ized by low wages, few benefits, and long hours.

Women's organizations are increasingly questioning existing gender relations. Women also constitute a large proportion of the leaders in nongovernmental organi-zations active in community organizing, civic action, and mobilization around human rights issues. In 1982, Rosario Ibarra de Piedra, a former housewife who became an activ-ist on behalf of political prisoners and the "disappeared" when her own son was arrested and disappeared in the 1970s, became the first woman to run for president of Mexico, as a candidate of the small Trotskyist Revolutionary Workers' Party. As this case demon-strates, women are frequently at the forefront of movements for reform, and they have played a significant role in the Zapatista movement in Chiapas.

Beginning in the López Portillo administration (1976–1982), an increasing number of women have been recruited into top administrative positions in the government. In the administration of Ernesto Zedillo (1994–2000), women held several cabinet-level positions, including Rosario Green, appointed to the important post of secretary of foreign relations in 1998. Women also hold electoral positions including state governor. Following the 1997 congressional elections, the Chamber of Deputies had eighty-five women (of a total of 500), or 17 percent of the total. This number declined in the 2000 elections but increased to 113—22.6 percent of the total—in 2003 and 116—23.2 percent—in 2006. Women control an increasing proportion (although still a minority) of positions in the national executive committees of the three major parties. The PRD and PRI have both pledged to increase the proportion of women in the executive committees to at least 30 percent of the total, and both parties have been headed by women in recent years.

In 2007 the PRD-dominated legislature of Mexico City passed a law decriminalizing abortion, the first such law in Mexico, and one of the few in Latin America.

of the pillars of Mexico's revolutionary legacy. Peasants are no longer able to petition for land, and the *ejidos*, which by law could not be sold or rented (although this did occur in practice), can now be divided among individual *ejiditarios*, permitting their sale to domestic or foreign corporations as well as the use of land as collateral for loans. The purpose was to promote agro-exports, either through joint ventures between agribusiness interests and former *ejiditarios* or through direct sale or rental of their land to agribusiness. However, few former *ejiditarios* have the necessary training and technological inputs for agro-export production, and in small farmer-agribusiness ventures, it is often the small farmer who bears the risks. Combined with NAFTA, which has undermined small peasant producers unable to compete with grain imports from the United States, the new agrarian law dealt a devastating blow to the small peasant and *ejidal* producer.

At the macroeconomic level, economic liberalization appeared to have been successful by the early 1990s. Following a downturn in 1986 (due to a sharp drop in oil prices), growth resumed, and exports increased from $16.8 billion to $70.3 billion by 1993. Furthermore, the composition of exports had shifted from primarily oil (75 percent) to 80 percent manufactured goods, especially automobiles, other vehicles, vehicle parts, and electronics and electrical machinery. By this time, inflation had also been reduced to single-digit numbers. Foreign investment, which reached a low point of $183 million in 1987, was up to $33.3 billion by 1993.

However, there were several danger signs. Most foreign investment—$28.9 billion—was in portfolio investment, attracted to the Mexican stock market and to the high interest rates of government treasury bonds. Imports increased even more rapidly than exports, resulting in an $18.5-billion deficit by 1994. High interest rates drew foreign capital but made loans prohibitively expensive for domestic businesses lacking access to foreign credit.

In the meantime, economic restructuring resulted in significant social transformation. In effect, both agriculture and industry are characterized by increasing complexity, with the emergence of new middle groups oriented to export, on the one hand, and increased polarization—the result of concentration or reconcentration of wealth, deteriorating conditions for many middle- and working-class groups, and increased poverty and destitution of poorer sectors—on the other.

The larger economic groups, temporarily weakened by the economic crisis and the 1982 bank nationalization, succeeded in reconstituting themselves with significant help from the government; and several new groups formed through buying firms very cheaply during the crisis of the 1980s. Both old and new groups subsequently benefited from the reprivatization of the banks and the privatization of other major firms such as the Cananea mining company, Azteca Television, and TELMEX.

The reconcentration of wealth and economic power in a small number of economic groups became evident in the growth in the number of Mexican billionaires identified in the annual reports of *Forbes* magazine: in 1994, Mexico had twenty-four billionaires, more than any other country with the exception of the United States, Germany, and Japan. The private sector, and particularly the large economic groups, have become more fully integrated with foreign and particularly U.S. corporations through joint ventures, marketing arrangements, franchises, and technical agreements, which now encompass virtually every sector of the economy.

Export promotion and trade liberalization did lead to the strengthening of some smaller firms, including subcontractors to larger manufacturing firms producing for export and to foreign (especially U.S.) manufacturers to produce specific brands, for example, in the apparel industry. However, trade liberalization has taken a toll on industries producing for the domestic market. Increased imports of consumer goods,

---

NORTH AMERICAN FREE TRADE AGREEMENT

The North American Free Trade Agreement (NAFTA), which was negotiated by the governments of Canada, Mexico, and the United States during the early 1990s and went into effect in 1994, calls for the elimination of tariffs and other barriers to trade between the three countries (for products meeting local content requirements) over a 15-year period, removes performance requirements for most investment, and protects intellectual property rights. For the Salinas government, it was a means to institutionalize, or "lock in," Mexico's new market model based on an opening to international trade and investment and to attract foreign investment to Mexico, where it would have access to the U.S. market at much lower labor costs.

One of the more controversial aspects of the negotiations was the secrecy that surrounded them. Efforts of Canadian, U.S., and Mexican labor, environmental, and human rights organizations and of cross-border alliances among them to promote the inclusion of regulations with respect to labor laws and environmental protection in the agreement were unsuccessful. The governments did agree to relatively weak side agreements addressing some of the issues, however. Labor unions have had some success in using the labor side agreement to challenge company practices contrary to the labor laws in the respective countries, as when companies in Mexico have tried to block the formation of unions or U.S. companies have violated the rights of migrant workers. But enforcement of environmental and especially labor agreements has been weak.

Because it has been embedded in a complex set of national policies and its implementation has been accompanied by dramatic changes resulting from the 1994 peso crisis and subsequent recovery, it is difficult to assess the effects of NAFTA. NAFTA does appear to have had a significant impact by increasing the level of foreign investment in Mexico and facilitating exports to the United States. Direct foreign investment between 1995 and 1999 was an estimated $54 billion, twice as much as in the previous 5 years. United States–Mexico trade has increased significantly, much of this intraindustry trade, and Mexico's total exports increased from $60.4 billion in 1994 to $136.7 billion in 1999 and $164.9 billion in 2003. However, as trade liberalizes, resulting in competition from low-cost imports, some small and medium-sized producers have been forced out of business. Small farmers producing corn for the domestic market have been particularly hard hit, forcing many to leave their farms and migrate to uncertain jobs in the cities or to the United States.

Because of its heavy dependence on the U.S., which is the market for 80 to 90 percent of its exports, the Mexican economy was severely affected by the recent U.S. recession. Mexico is also losing some of the initial advantages of NAFTA, as the United States expands its trade with other countries; China and other Asian countries, where wages are much lower, are also attracting some of the foreign investment that previously went to Mexico.

while offering benefits to consumers, forced many small and medium-sized businesses to close down, especially in such areas as textiles, clothing, shoes, and furniture; other businesses shifted from production to import. Both resulted in substantial job losses.

Although the new Salinas government gave priority to the continuation of economic reforms, the declining legitimacy of the PRI and the weakening of its labor and peasant base as well as the growing strength of the opposition demanded attention to political reform and party restructuring as well. During the Salinas administration, several laws were passed to reform the electoral process (e.g., through the appointment of neutral electoral officials to oversee the elections) and to permit greater participation by minority party representation. There were also efforts to weaken the sectoral bases of the PRI, but the corporate leaders fought changes, and their role in enforcing measures such as wage control and mobilizing electoral support diluted internal reforms.

To restructure the party base, Salinas continued a strategy begun by de la Madrid of encouraging individuals in business to participate in the party and become candidates for elections, and worked closely with the major business groups. The government also worked with PAN, many of whose members supported the government's economic program as well as its political reforms, and recognized PAN victories in several elections, including gubernatorial races. A't the same time, it attempted to neutralize the PRD, refusing to recognize its claims to electoral victories. Elections in some of the southern states, often controlled by the more corrupt and repressive PRI officials, also resulted in considerable violence, including the assassination of several PRD candidates and militants.

One of Salinas' most effective strategies in reviving support for the PRI was the National Solidarity Program, or PRONASOL, an antipoverty program that drew on resources from the privatization of major banks and industries to provide subsidized food for urban and rural neighborhoods as well as potable water, street paving, and other infrastructure for poor municipal communities. It also had a political agenda, targeting areas such as the state of Michoacán, where the PRD had significant support.

The Salinas government benefited from economic conditions in the early 1990s: growth rates were increasing after nearly a decade of declining and negative growth, the inflation rate was reduced, and foreign investment was growing. In 1990, negotiations began for Mexico's inclusion in NAFTA, which was presented to the people of Mexico as a highly beneficial arrangement that would result in increased jobs and broad economic improvements and would symbolize Mexico's incorporation into the "First World." The approval of the agreement by the U.S. Congress at the end of 1993 marked the culmination of Salinas' economic success, and his administration seemed to be headed to a triumphant conclusion.

ECONOMIC COLLAPSE, PARTIAL RECOVERY, AND THE RISE OF THE OPPOSITION: 1994–2000

The following year brought an end to illusions. It began with the revolt of indigenous peasants in the southern state of Chiapas organized in the Zapatista National Liberation Army (EZLN) on January 1, 1994, the day NAFTA went into effect. The causes were complex, but a central factor was the worsening economic conditions of the peasantry as a result of economic restructuring and a history of political repression by state and local government officials. The reversal of the agrarian reform and the threat posed by NAFTA to small peasant producers were additional factors in the uprising and its timing.

When the government sent troops to crush the revolt, repression by the government forces was broadly publicized, resulting in widespread national and international protest. Both the publicity and the reaction were in large part a consequence of Mexico's increased international visibility as a result of NAFTA negotiations as well as the emergence of grassroots human rights organizations throughout the country that had established links with international human rights movements.

The government ended the military assault and formed a commission to begin negotiations with the Zapatistas, a protracted process stalemated over disagreements about indigenous autonomy, the increased military presence in the region, and continued violations of human rights, including the assassinations of Zapatistas carried out by paramilitary forces linked to the PRI. At the same time, events in Chiapas and the communiques of the Zapatistas' charismatic spokesperson Subcomandante Marcos continued to be available to a large audience via newspapers, TV, and the internet; solidarity groups, human rights delegations, and international sympathizers visited the area in an effort to provide some protection to the population.

The uprising in Chiapas was followed in less than 3 months by the assassination of PRI presidential candidate Luis Donaldo Colosio on March 23, 1994. Although a young migrant worker was arrested, few believe he was acting alone; and suspicion fell on drug cartels, corrupt PRI officials opposed to political and economic reforms, and even high levels of government. In the meantime, several kidnappings of prominent businessmen heightened the sense of insecurity and crisis. Both foreign and domestic groups began withdrawing investment and exporting capital from Mexico.

The presidential elections took place in September. Ernesto Zedillo, another technocrat with a Ph.D. from Yale, had been selected by Salinas to replace Colosio; and he defeated both Cárdenas of the PRD and the PAN candidate in what most national and international observers considered relatively honest elections, despite some fraud, particularly in the rural areas. Electoral reforms enacted during the Salinas administration had increased the independence of the Federal Electoral Institute (responsible for overseeing the electoral process and the vote count), and the presence of grassroots observers throughout much of Mexico was a major factor in the honesty of the 1994 elections compared with those of the past.

Zedillo's victory could be attributed to a number of factors. The PRI's control of the government gave it greater access to campaign funds and media coverage; it also received large donations from major business interests. Neither of the two opposition parties ran an effective campaign, and the PRD had been further undermined by internal conflicts, differences regarding strategy, as well as deliberate efforts of the government and the PRI to neutralize its effectiveness. In addition, PRI hegemony guaranteed that neither of the two major opposition parties had much experience in governing; and it was probably felt by some voters that despite its problems, the PRI was the only party with sufficient experience for the difficult situation in which Mexico found itself.

The election was followed by another high-level assassination even before Zedillo came to office—this time, the secretary general of the PRI—in which members of the party and government were implicated. In the meantime, the hemorrhage of capital continued, with the result that foreign exchange reserves became dangerously low, confronting Zedillo with a major crisis shortly after he came to power. Zedillo attempted to float the peso, but instead it plummeted by 55 percent, immersing Mexico in another economic disaster just as it appeared to be recovering from the previous one. The devaluation of the peso on the international market revealed the precariousness of Mexico's earlier economic recovery. Far from joining advanced industrial countries, Mexico now confronted another severe economic crisis.

With the help of the Clinton administration, Zedillo secured $48.8 billion in foreign loans from the United States, the IMF, and other countries and international lending agencies. Zedillo instituted an austerity program, and Mexico's macroeconomic balance was quickly restored: after a negative growth of 5 percent in 1995, the economy grew by 5 percent in 1996 and by 7 percent in 1997. Inflation was reduced, and foreign investment again began to climb, with an increasing proportion in direct investment rather than the more volatile portfolio investment. Mexico's industrial growth reached 9 percent in 1997.

However, the combined costs of the crisis and the austerity program were again borne by the lower and middle sectors of the Mexican population, and income distribution again worsened. Real wages, which by 1993 had begun to recover to their 1980 levels, dropped substantially and in 2002 the median wage was half its 1990 level. An estimated 46 percent of the population was still in poverty and regional and sectoral contrasts between industrial cities and northern states, on the one hand, and poor rural states such as Chiapas, Guerrero, and Oaxaca, on the other, had widened. The government instituted an anti-poverty program aimed at improving health, nutrition, and education levels among the poor rural families, but insufficient resources limited its effectiveness.

The first years of the Zedillo administration were marked by increased demonstrations, marches, and other forms of protest. Sharp increases in interest rates charged by private banks led to a debtors' revolt under the impetus of El Barzón (its name denoting part of the yoke for oxen), a militant organization composed initially of farmers confronting the loss of their farms and subsequently expanding to include small business owners and middle-class consumers, which staged dramatic demonstrations throughout Mexico. In the countryside, peasants and *ejiditarios* carried out a series of land invasions; and in several instances, groups of peasants attacked freight trains or raided warehouses for grain and other food supplies. In the middle of 1996, a second guerrilla group, the People's Revolutionary Army (ERP), emerged in the southern state of Guerrero, which had been the scene of a massacre of seventeen *campesinos* by police forces the previous year.

Charges and revelations of corruption affected all levels of government and party as well as business groups, including Raúl Salinas, brother of the former president; ex-president Carlos Salinas, widely blamed for Mexico's economic problems, left the country for voluntary exile in Ireland. Mexico's role as the major cocaine route to the United States has been a further factor in corruption and violence. Lawyers and officials involved in prosecuting leaders of drug cartels as well as journalists exposing high-level corruption have been assassinated. In Juarez and other border cities, hundreds of young women, many of them maquiladora workers, have "disappeared" and been murdered. Human rights violations also include assassinations of members and leaders of political parties and social organizations. In December 1997, forty-five men, women, and children were massacred by paramilitary troops in Acteal, Chiapas.

Repeated economic setbacks and profound disillusion with the PRI resulted in increased support for the political opposition evident in several opposition victories in gubernatorial, municipal, and legislative elections. Initially, the PAN was the major beneficiary, winning several key states in 1995 and 1996. The PRD subsequently staged a comeback from its poor showing in the 1994 elections, partly the work of new party leader Andrés Manuel López Obrador. In the 1997 midterm elections, the PRI lost control of the legislative assembly to the opposition and PRD candidate Cuauhtémoc Cárdenas became the first elected mayor of Mexico City (a post previously appointed by the president and that the PRD has retained in the three subsequent elections).

Although the experience of opposition government has been mixed, both the PAN and the PRD have gained experience in governing at the state and municipal levels, as well as in the legislature, where the combined opposition was in the majority in the assembly as of 1997. Zedillo continued to recognize opposition victories and enacted further electoral reforms that among other measures provide government funding and media access to opposition parties, enabling them to compete more effectively with the PRI. In November 1999, the PRI held an open primary to select its presidential candidate for the first time, eliminating the practice of presidential selection of the candidate and thus an important source of presidential power.

Toward an Uncertain Future: 2000–2007

THE OPPOSITION IN POWER

In the July 2, 2000 presidential elections, PAN candidate Vicente Fox won a sweeping victory, obtaining 42.5 percent of the vote to 36.1 percent for Francisco Labastida of the PRI and 16.6 percent for PRD candidate Cuauhtemoc Cardenas. The election of an opposition candidate was widely seen as a milestone in Mexico's progress toward democracy, ending the PRI's 71-year monopoly on political power and signaling the shift from a hegemonic party system to a more pluralistic system with three major and several smaller parties vying for power.

But those hoping for substantial socioeconomic change were disappointed, as the Fox government continued the free-market policies of its predecessors. Fox proved ineffective in working with congress, however, where divisions within and among the three major parties blocked or weakened many of his proposed economic reforms. Moreover, the Fox government confronted changing international conditions, particularly in the United States. A projected agreement for U.S. immigration reform sought by Fox was delayed indefinitely as a result of the attacks on the World Trade Center and the Pentagon on September 11, 2001, and the resulting "war on terrorism," which has made conditions even more difficult for those trying to cross the border without documents. A recession in the United States in the early years of the decade reverberated in the Mexican economy, which grew at anemic rates during most years of the Fox administration, revealing Mexico's high level of dependence on the United States and vulnerability to conditions there. With the expansion of free trade agreements in the Americas and elsewhere, as well as the economic growth of China and other Asian countries, Mexico no longer enjoys the advantages of the early NAFTA years of cheap labor and privileged access to the U.S. market and faces stiff competition from other countries where labor is even cheaper. In 2003, China replaced Mexico as the second largest source of U.S. imports.

In the area of democracy and human rights, there were several high-profile initiatives, including the passage of a federal transparency law in 2002, the release of documents related to the 1968 Tlateloco massacre and the prosecution of high-level officials involved in the dirty war of the 1970s. The Fox government also expanded the anti-poverty program, changing its name to Oportunidades and extending it to poor urban families. In spite of its promising beginning, however, the Fox administration was a disappointment. A charismatic candidate, Fox was unable to deal effectively with the changing conditions and challenges confronting Mexico in the first years of the century.

THE CONTROVERSIAL ELECTIONS OF 2006

Whereas the 2000 elections demonstrated Mexico's progress toward democracy, those of 2006 demonstrated the limits of that democracy. The three major contenders were Felipe Calderon of PAN, Energy Secretary under President Fox; Roberto Madrazo, a former governor and president of PRI; and Andres Manuel Lopez Obrador, former PRD president and mayor of Mexico City. Madrazo's reputation for fraud and corruption and his unpopularity within his own party weakened his candidacy, and by early 2006 it was a race between Calderon and Lopez Obrador, with Lopez Obrador in the lead.

Even prior to the electoral campaign, the PAN and PRI joined forces to marginalize the PRD. In 2003, PAN and PRI excluded the PRD from the selection of councilors of the Federal Electoral Institute, previously decided by consensus among the three major parties, and their appointees were generally less qualified than the previous cohort, thus undermining the nonpartisan nature and prestige of the Institute.

Once it became evident that Lopez Obrador would be the PRD candidate the two parties attempted to disqualify the popular mayor by threatening impeachment for a minor violation, but withdrew the charges following massive demonstrations against the maneuver and international pressures. The PAN and the PRI also passed legislation, over PRD objections, highly favorable to the two major television networks, which in turn favored Calderon in electoral coverage.

During the campaign, PAN and business groups launched a series of negative ads accusing Lopez Obrador of being a demagogue and a danger to the country. This campaign was apparently successful, and together with some mistakes by the Lopez Obrador campaign, including failure to appear at one of two scheduled television debates, had reduced his lead by the day of the election. On July 2, Felipe Calderon was elected president by a slim majority of less than 1 percent. The results were contested by Lopez Obrador on grounds of fraud and illegal campaign practices of the opposition. He also called for several massive demonstrations, and on August 1 his followers occupied the Zocalo and the two major streets of Mexico City, erecting a tent city that lasted a month and a half. However, the electoral tribunal rejected charges of fraud, and while it admitted that the private sector campaign was illegal according to Mexican electoral law, it upheld the results, and Calderon was duly inaugurated.

The elections, which included legislative elections as well as the presidential elections, represented a decisive defeat for the PRI. Not only was its presidential candidate a distant third in the presidential race, but its representation in congress was reduced by half, putting it in third place, behind the PAN and the PRD, in the Chamber of Deputies. The PRI continues to have support at the local level, however, and retains the majority of state governors.

Analysts are divided regarding the new president, but most agree that after a little over a year in office Felipe Calderon has shown himself to be a more adroit and proactive executive than Fox. Although there is little doubt that he will continue the neoliberal agenda of his predecessors, he has negotiated successfully with both the PRI and PRD opposition in congress to pass a moderate fiscal reform that among other measures raises taxes on corporate income. As part of the agreement, all three parties supported a PRD demand for electoral reform, including a reform of the Federal Electoral Institute and the elimination of campaign expenditures on radio and television advertising, with the television stations required to provide free time.

Other measures have been more controversial. One of the president's first actions was to launch an anti-drug campaign that involved deployment of military forces to areas of drug activity in nine different states, the extradition of top drug cartel leaders to the United States for trial, and negotiations with the United States to implement an anti-drug program for surveillance and eradication of crops in drug-producing areas. Given the high levels of crime and insecurity linked to drug activity, this was a highly popular move, but critics have raised concerns about the militarization of the drug war, the potential corruption of the armed forces, and the resemblance of the proposed U.S.–Mexico anti-drug program to Plan Colombia, which experienced observers have denounced as counterproductive. Human rights activists in the United States and Mexico also complain of human rights violations, including rape and murder, by military forces in the areas in which they are deployed. Some analysts have charged that the government places protesters and opposition groups in the same category as drug cartels and terrorists, and treats them accordingly.

In the meantime, mobilization and protest by labor groups and grassroots organizations continue. In Oaxaca, demonstrations by the local teachers' union beginning in early 2006 for better wages and working conditions were supported by more than 300 local organizations concerned with such issues as indigenous rights and sustainable development, which formed the Popular Assembly of the Peoples of Oaxaca (APPO). Repression by the state and federal government left an estimated twenty dead, dozens injured, and more than 100 imprisoned, including three leaders of APPO who were invited to Mexico City to negotiate with the Minister of the Interior but were instead arrested and jailed. Teachers obtained their contracts, but APPO demands have escalated to include the resignation of the Oaxacan governor responsible for much of the violence against demonstrators.

Conclusion

The twentieth century was one of profound change for Mexico, from a poor, largely rural society with a few industrial enclaves, governed by a personalist dictatorship to a dynamic, relatively industrialized urban society with a large middle class and a modern state controlled for over 70 years by a hegemonic government party. By the end of the century, Mexico had begun the transition to a more democratic, pluralist political system.

However, this has also been a period of strong continuities. Economic growth and development increased the complexity of Mexico's social structure, but the gap between the wealthy and poor continues to be extreme. Foreign economic domination has been replaced by growing integration with the United States, which continues to exert a strong influence on Mexico's economy. NAFTA increased the attraction of Mexico for investments from Europe and Asia, but the United States remains the major source of foreign investment as well as the market for 90 percent of Mexico's exports.

In the late twentieth and early twenty-first centuries, globalization has taken not only economic but also social, cultural, and political forms, including the globalization of protest. In the case of Mexico, it is manifested in various forms that have increased the complexity of Mexico's relations to the United States. Mexican movements for social justice find support among international advocacy groups, labor unions, and other organizations, many of them U.S.-based, promoting human rights, environmental justice, gender equity, and indigenous rights, among other issues.

At the same time, Mexico is a major transit route to the United States for cocaine from Colombia, methamphetamine processed in Mexico from chemicals from companies in China and India, and heroin and marijuana cultivated in Mexico. The impact in Mexico has been devastating. Crime, much of it drug related, has increased. Battles between rival drug cartels for control of major transit routes to the United States have turned cities along the border into war zones. In 2006, more than 2000 people were killed in drug-related violence, which had already claimed more than 1000 lives between January and early May 2007. Judicial reforms have increased the autonomy of the judiciary, but they have not been able to effectively reduce corruption, abuse, and even complicity in the drug trade among local level officials.

Migration to the United States has continued even as the trajectory became increasingly difficult, dangerous, and costly as a result of more extensive border surveillance following 9/11, and U.S. hostility toward immigrants has grown. In addition to being the major source of U.S.-bound migrants, Mexico is also an important transit route for migrants from Central America and other parts of Latin America heading for the United States.

Migration has in turn had an important impact in transforming Mexico and Mexican–U.S. relations, most notably through the remittances sent by migrants that have become a mainstay of the Mexican economy as well as a significant source of foreign aid for poor Mexican families. Remittances, which totaled $23 billion in 2006, surpassed foreign investments and were second only to petroleum as a major source of foreign exchange. Hometown associations of migrants from particular Mexican communities also raise funds for schools, health clinics, street paving, and other civic projects in their hometowns; in some cases their donations are supplemented by contributions from local, state, and federal governments. Binational indigenous organizations support the rights of indigenous groups on both sides of the border, and a number of migrants participate actively in politics in their home communities as well as the United States.

The goals enshrined in Mexico's revolution and constitution for national sovereignty and social justice are still elusive. Economic inequality and the poverty of substantial sectors of the population, high levels of crime and official corruption, and the weakness of democratic institutions continue to present obstacles and challenges to authentic progress in Mexico. At the same time, like the Mexican revolution in the early twentieth century, the Chiapas revolt and the growing importance and visibility of social movements challenge the assumption that modernization can go forward without taking into account historic demands for social justice.

Chronology

150–900   Classic period of ancient Meso-American culture; rise of major cities including Teotihuacán, Palenque, Monte Albán

900   Decline of classic culture, rise of warrior tribes

1325   Building of Tenochtitlán, Aztec capital, now the center of Mexico City

1521   Conquest of Aztec Empire by Spaniards under Hernán Cortés

1521–1821   Spanish colonial period

1810–1815   Revolt against Spain led by priests Miguel Hidalgo and José Morales; put down by the Spanish but date (September 16) commemorated as Mexican independence day

1821   Mexican independence

1846–1848   Mexican-American War, culminating in Mexico's defeat; in the Treaty of Guadalupe Hidalgo, Mexico loses half its territory to the United States

1857   Beginning of the *Reforma*, Liberals come to power and a new constitution is adopted

1862   French intervention on behalf of Conservatives, who defeat the Liberal army

1864   Archduke Ferdinand Maximilian appointed by Napoleon III as emperor of Mexico

1867   Maximilian and the Conservatives are defeated by the Liberals under the leadership of Benito Juárez in 1867, the Liberal republic is reestablished

1876–1910   *Porfiriato*; coup carried out by General Porfirio Díaz, who controls power for the next 34 years

1910 Formation of the Anti-Reelectionist Party; revolt against Díaz, led by Francisco Madero; beginning of the Mexican Revolution

1911 Success of revolt with abdication of Díaz; Madero elected president

1913 Madero assassinated by Victoriano Huerta, who becomes president, dissolving congress; Constitutionalist Army formed under leadership of Venustiano Carranza; Army of the South under Emiliano Zapata and Constitutionalist Army battle Huerta

1914–1916 Huerta defeated; victorious forces meet at convention of Aguascalientes, but different parties are unable to come to agreement; there is a split between Constitutionalists and forces of Zapata and Pancho Villa, leading to conflict between the two sides; in 1915, Carranza gains control of Mexico City and, in 1916, calls a constitutional convention

1917 New constitution approved

1927–1929 Cristero rebellion: uprising of pro-Catholic groups, especially rural populations in central Mexico, against anticlerical provisions of the government

1929 Establishment of government party, National Revolutionary Party (PNR)

1934–1940 Lázaro Cárdenas president

1938 Expropriation of U.S.- and British-owned oil companies, which come under state control; government party restructured on corporate basis; name changed to Party of the Mexican Revolution (PRM); name changed to Institutional Revolutionary Party (PRI) in 1947

1939 Formation of National Action Party (PAN)

1940–1970 "Mexican Miracle"

1968 Student mobilization repressed when government agents and military surround student demonstration at Tlatelolco Plaza, firing into the crowd and killing an estimated 200–400 people

1982 Debt crisis, beginning of economic restructuring, nationalization of banks under José López Portillo

1988 Opposition candidacy of Cuauhtémoc Cárdenas in presidential election, formation of Party of the Democratic Revolution (PRD)

1988–1994 Salinas president; acceleration of process of economic restructuring, including privatization of government assets and negotiation of North American Free Trade Agreement (NAFTA) with Canada and the United States

1989 PAN wins gubernatorial election in Baja California, the first time an opposition candidate becomes a state governor

1994 (January 1) Uprising of Zapatista National Liberation Army (EZLN) in Chiapas; (March) assassination of PRI presidential candidate Luis Donaldo Colosio; (September) election of Ernesto Zedillo in relatively open elections; (December) foreign exchange crisis and peso devaluation, again plunging country into major recession

1996 Emergence of another guerrilla group, People's Revolutionary Army (ERP), in southern state of Guerrero

1997 Midterm elections, with Cárdenas becoming mayor of Mexico City, and loss of PRI control of Chamber of Deputies for the first time since the party was formed

1999 (November 7) First PRI primary in history; former interior minister and economist Francisco Labastida becomes presidential candidate

2000 (July 2) Vicente Fox, candidate of PAN, elected president, defeating PRI candidate Labastida and Cuauhtémoc Cárdenas of the PRD and ending 71 years of PRI dominance

2003 (July 6) Congressional and gubernatorial elections result in major PRI and PRD victories at the expense of PAN and reveal the growing importance of some of the smaller parties

2006 (July 2) Felipe Calderón of PAN wins narrow electoral victory over PRD candidate López Obrador in controversial presidential election

Bibliography

Bacon, David. *The Children of NAFTA: Labor Wars on the U.S.-Mexican Border*. Berkeley: University of California Press, 2005.

Bennett, Douglas C., and Kenneth E. Sharpe. *Transnational Corporations vs. the State: The Political Economy of the Mexican Auto Industry*. Princeton, NJ: Princeton University Press, 1985.

Bethell, Leslie, ed. *Mexico since Independence*. Cambridge: Cambridge University Press, 1991.

Camp, Roderic A. *Politics in Mexico: The Democratic Transformation*. 4th ed. New York: Oxford University Press, 2007.

———. *Entrepreneurs and Politics in Twentieth Century Mexico*. New York: Oxford University Press, 1989.

Centeno, Miguel Angel. *Democracy within Reason: Technocratic Revolution in Mexico*. 2nd ed. University Park: Pennsylvania State University Press, 1997.

Cockcroft, James D. *Mexico's Hope: An Encounter with Politics and History*. New York: Monthly Review Press, 1998.

Collier, George. *Basta! Land and the Zapatista Rebellion in Chiapas*. Rev. ed. Oakland, CA: Food First, 1999.

Collins, Ruth Berins. *The Contradictory Alliance: State–Labor Relations and Regime Change in Mexico*. Berkeley: International and Area Studies, University of California, 1992.

Cook, María Lorena, Kevin J. Middlebrook, and Juan Molinar Horcasitas, eds. *The Politics of Economic Restructuring: State–Society Relations and Regime Change in Mexico*. La Jolla: Center for U.S.–Mexican Studies, University of California, San Diego, 1994.

Cornelius, Wayne, Judith Gentleman, and Peter H. Smith, eds. *Mexico's Alternative Political Futures*. La Jolla: Center for U.S.–Mexican Studies, University of California, San Diego, 1989.

Cornelius, Wayne A., and David Myhre, eds. *The Transformation of Rural Mexico: Reforming the Ejido Sector*. La Jolla: Center for U.S.–Mexican Studies, University of California, San Diego, 1998.

Dresser, Denise. *Neopopulist Solutions to Neoliberal Problems: Mexico's National Solidarity Program*. La Jolla: Center for U.S.–Mexican Studies, University of California, San Diego, 1991.

Eckstein, Susan. *The Poverty of Revolution: The State and the Urban Poor in Mexico*. Princeton, NJ: Princeton University Press, 1988.

Foweraker, Joe, and Ann Craig, eds. *Popular Movements and Political Change in Mexico*. Boulder, CO: Lynne Rienner, 1991.

Fox, Jonathan, and Gaspar Rivera-Salgado, eds. *Indigenous Mexican Migrants in the United States*. La Jolla: Center for U.S.–Mexican Studies and Center for Comparative Immigration Studies, University of California, San Diego, 2004.

Fuentes, Carlos. *The Death of Artemio Cruz*. New York: Noonday Press, 1971.

Hamilton, Nora. *The Limits of State Autonomy: Post-Revolutionary Mexico*. Princeton, NJ: Princeton University Press, 1982.

Harvey, Neil. *The Chiapas Rebellion: The Struggle for Land and Democracy*. Durham, NC: Duke University Press, 1998.

Hellman, Judith Adler. *Mexican Lives*. New York: New Press, 1994.

Huber, Paul Lawrence. *Power from Experience: Urban Popular Movements in Late Twentieth Century Mexico*. University Park: Pennsylvania State University Press, 2004.

Knight, Alan. *The Mexican Revolution*. Vols. 1 and 2. Lincoln: University of Nebraska Press, 1986.

Lawson, Chappell H. *Mexico under Calderon: The First Hundred Days and the Challenges Ahead*. Los Angeles: Pacific Council on International Policy, April 2007.

Lustig, Nora. *Mexico: The Remaking of an Economy*. 2nd ed. Washington, DC: Brookings Institution, 1998.

MacLeod, Dag. *Downsizing the State: Privatization and the Limits of Neoliberal Reforms in Mexico*. University Park: Pennsylvania State University Press, 2004.

Massey, Douglas, Rafael Alarcon, Jorge Durand, and Humberto Gonzalez. *Return to Aztlan: The Social Process of International Migration from Western Mexico*. Berkeley: University of California Press, 1987.

Maxfield, Sylvia, *Governing Mexico: International Finance and Mexican Politics*. Ithaca: Cornell University Press, 1990.

Meyer, Lorenzo. *Mexico and the United States in the Oil Controversy: 1917–1942*. Austin: University of Texas Press, 1977.

Middlebrook, Kevin J. *The Paradox of Revolution: Labor, the State and Authoritarianism in Mexico*. Baltimore: Johns Hopkins University Press, 1995.

Middlebrook, Kevin J., and Eduardo Zepeda, ed. *Confronting Development: Assessing Mexico's Economic and Social Policies*. Palo Alto, CA: Stanford University Press, 2003.

Monsivais, Carlos. *Mexican Postcards*. London: Verso, 1997.

Otero, Gerardo, ed. *Neoliberalism Revisited: Economic Restructuring and Mexico's Political Future*. Boulder, CO: Westview Press, 1996.

Paz, Octavio. *The Labyrinth of Solitude: Life and Thought in Mexico*. New York: Grove Press, 1985.

Pozas, María de los Angeles. *Industrial Restructuring in Mexico: Corporate Adaptation, Technological Innovation, and Changing Patterns of Industrial Relations in Monterrey*. San Diego: Center for U.S.–Mexican Studies, University of California, 1993.

Randall, Laura, ed. *Changing Structure of Mexico: Political, Social and Economic Prospects*. London: M. E. Sharpe, 2006.

Rodriguez, Victoria E., ed. *Women's Participation in Mexican Political Life*. Boulder, CO: Westview Press, 1998.

Thacker, Strom C. *Big Business, the State, and Free Trade: Constructing Coalitions in Mexico*. Cambridge: Cambridge University Press, 2006.

Vaughan, Mary Kay. *Cultural Politics in Revolution: Teachers, Peasants and Schools in Mexico: 1930–1940*. Tucson: University of Arizona Press, 1997.

Williams, Heather L. *Social Movements and Economic Transition: Markets and Distributive Conflict in Mexico*. Cambridge: Cambridge University Press, 2001.

Wise, Carol, ed. *The Post-NAFTA Political Economy: Mexico and the Western Hemisphere*. University Park: Pennsylvania State University Press, 1998.

Wise, Timothy A., Hilda Salazar, and Laura Carlsen, eds. *Confronting Globalization: Economic Integration and Popular Resistance in Mexico*. Bloomfield, CT: Kumarian Press, 2003.

Womack, John, Jr. *Zapata and the Mexican Revolution*. New York: Vintage Books, 1968.

FILMS AND VIDEOS

The Five Suns: A Sacred History of Mexico. United States, 1996. A film by Patricia Amlen, University of California, Berkeley, Center for Media and Independent Learning.

The U.S.-Mexican War: 1846–1848. United States, Four-hour video. Paul Espinosa, Espinosa Productions.

The Sixth Section. United States, 2003. A documentary on Mexican immigrants in New York.

The Sixth Sun: Mayan Uprisings in Chiapas. United States, 1996. An excellent documentary on Chiapas uprising by Saul Landau.

Memorias de un Mexicano. Documentary with original film footage from the Porfiriato, the Mexican revolution, and the immediate post-revolutionary period. Available in video or DVD.

Letters from the Other Side. Film by Heather Courtney, which documents the causes of migration and its impact, focusing on the lives of four women whose sons and/or husbands have migrated to the United States.

Un poquito de tanto verdad. A documentary on the teachers' strike and organization of APPO in Oaxaca during 2006, focusing on use of media.

WEBSITES

http://ladb.unm.edu. Latin American Data Base, weekly summaries of major news sources.

http://www.library.cornell.edu/colldev/ladocshome.html Latin American Government Documents Project, includes texts of presidential messages, other documents, and content pages of Mexican journals.

http://www.lanic.utexas.edu University of Texas LANIC, major gateway to information on Mexico as well as other Latin American countries.

http://ags.inegi.gob.mx Instituto Nacional de Estadística Geográfica e Informática (INEGI), official statistical agency.

http: //www. ueinternational.org/Mexico_info/mlna.php. Mexican Labor News and Analysis, monthly analysis of labor issues and events.

http://www.wilsoncenter.org/index.cfm?topic id=5949&fuseaction=topics.home Mexican Institute of the Woodrow Wilson Center.

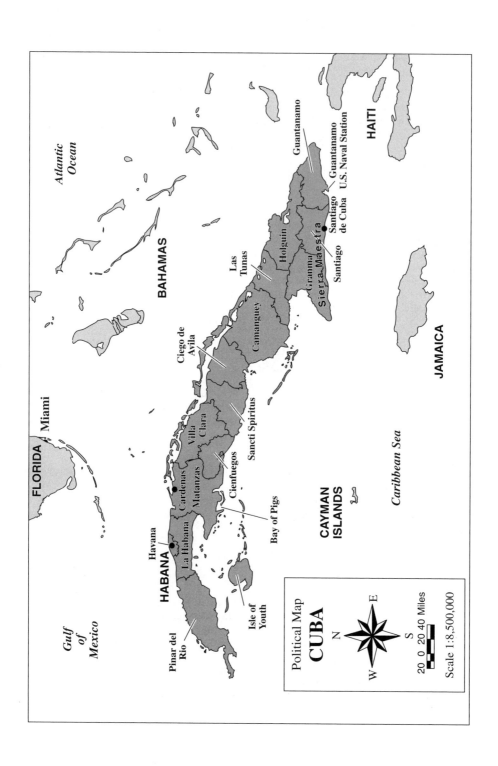

Political Map
CUBA

Scale 1:8,500,000

20 0 20 40 Miles

Gulf
of
Mexico

Atlantic
Ocean

FLORIDA

Miami

BAHAMAS

HABANA

Havana

La Habana

Cardenas

Matanzas

Pinar del
Rio

Cienfuegos

Villa
Clara

Sancti Spiritus

Bay of Pigs

Isle of
Youth

**CAYMAN
ISLANDS**

Ciego de
Avila

Camanguey

Las
Tunas

Holguin

Granma

Sierra Maestra

Santiago

Santiago
de Cuba

Guantanamo

Guantanamo
U.S. Naval Station

HAITI

Caribbean Sea

JAMAICA

THIRTEEN

CUBA

Gary Prevost

Introduction

Cuba is an archipelago of two main islands, Cuba and the Isle of Youth, and about 1600 keys and inlets. The total area of 42,803 square miles is nearly as large as Pennsylvania. Cuba lies just 90 miles south of Key West, Florida; flying time between Miami and Havana is just 45 minutes. Low hills and fertile valleys cover more than half of the country. Tropical forests and high mountains in the east, which sheltered the revolutionary movement in the 1950s, are contrasted with the prairies and western hills and valleys. Cuba's subtropical climate is warm and humid, with an average annual temperature of 75°F. The climate contributes to Cuba's attraction as a year-round tourist destination.

In 1959, Cuba began a social revolution under the leadership of the 26th of July Movement, named for the date in 1953 when movement leaders tried to overthrow the dictatorial regime of Fulgencio Batista with an ill-fated attack on the Moncada army barracks in Santiago, the country's second largest city. The movement, under the leadership of Fidel Castro and Ché Guevara, carried out profound changes in Cuban society, including the establishment of a socialist economic system. Today, the revolutionary movement that took control in 1959 is still in power despite a nearly 40-year economic blockade by the government of the United States and the collapse of Cuba's main trading partner, the Soviet Union. It is the character of Cuba's revolution and its success in resisting years of efforts by the United States to regain control of the island that have made Cuba far more prominent in world affairs than its small size would indicate.

Cuba's current population is 11.4 million, with an annual growth rate of less than 1 percent. More than 70 percent of the population live in urban areas, with the capital, Havana, having 2.5 million residents. Cubans of Spanish descent make up

37 percent of the population, while 12 percent have African ancestry and 50 percent are mulatto (mixed heritage of Spanish and African). There is a small community of persons of Asian heritage (less than 0.1 percent). More than half of all Cubans are under the age of 30—born and raised since 1959. Just over 1 million Cubans live in the United States, primarily in south Florida, where they have a major impact on political, social, and economic life. The core of this Cuban American community was roughly 150,000 middle- and upper-class Cubans who left between 1959 and 1961 during the dramatic changes brought on by the revolution. The community has been augmented through the years by tens of thousands of others who have migrated for both political and economic reasons. The government of the United States treats all refugees from Cuba who arrive on U.S. soil as political, a privilege extended to no other Latin American nation. Such a designation grants them the right to live and work in the United States.

Education is a priority in Cuban society, and the state provides free primary, secondary, technical, and higher education to all citizens. Cuba has an average of one teacher for every forty-five inhabitants, and the literacy rate of 96.4 percent is one of the highest in Latin America. Recent economic hard times have made for a shortage of supplies, but no children are without schooling. Cuba's health-care system has been a priority for the revolution and is a well-regarded model for the developing world, with more than 260 hospitals and 420 clinics. Family doctors are assigned to each community, and there is a doctor for every 260 Cubans. The average life expectancy is 77 years, and the infant mortality rate is 5.1per 1000—both the best in Latin America.

Women and Cuban citizens of African descent suffered from widespread discrimination prior to 1959, and the increased prominence of both groups in Cuban society is

Organic farm in Cuba. (*Photo by Patrice Olsen*)

one of the major achievements of the revolution, although racism and sexism are still prevalent factors in society. Racism is rooted in the importation of millions of slaves to Cuba to cultivate sugarcane from the eighteenth century onward. Prior to 1959, women worked outside the home only as domestic servants and prostitutes; but today, women have been integrated fully into the workplace and have equal access to education and equality before the law. Women also have much greater control over their lives through the widespread availability of contraceptives and abortion. As a result of the equal access to education at all levels since 1959, women now occupy prominent positions in almost all institutions of the society, especially in financial institutions, academia, and management of enterprises. The prominence of female leaders in society has continued to grow as the postrevolutionary generation assumes power. However, women remain underrepresented at the highest levels of the Communist Party, the country's only party, and in the government.

Racial discrimination was formally outlawed at the outset of the revolution, and long-standing customs that barred black Cubans from many public facilities were overcome. As the result of equal access to education, Afro-Cubans have risen to high places in the government, armed forces, education, and commerce. Recent years have seen a significant increase in the study and appreciation of the contributions made by persons of African heritage to the development of Cuba's distinctive culture. The links of this community to Africa were strengthened during the 1970s and 1980s when Cuba developed close political and military ties with the African nations of Angola and Ethiopia. However, racist attitudes still persist in the society; and although no formal statistics are available, black Cubans seem to make up a greater percentage of those at the bottom end of the economic ladder.

Cuba is a predominantly secular society, the result of both a relatively weak Catholic Church prior to 1959 and policies of the revolution. Among the believers, Catholicism is the dominant faith, although many people combine it with ideas of African origin in the religion Santería. Santería is probably the most widely practiced religion in the country, and in recent years it has benefited the most from a more tolerant attitude toward religion by the government. A number of Protestant churches also function, and there is a small and growing presence of the Evangelicals who have become important players in other parts of Latin America. At the time of the revolution in 1959, the Catholic Church sided with the Batista regime and many foreign priests, especially Spanish priests, were expelled from the country. While guaranteeing freedom of religious practice, the government actively discouraged religious participation for many years, barring believers from membership in the Communist Party and promotions in most areas of Cuban life until 1991. The changing role of religion in Cuban society was embodied in the visit of Pope John Paul II in January 1998. Church attendance and baptisms have risen significantly in recent years, but the number of practicing Catholics is still probably under 200,000.

History

Prior to the arrival of Columbus in 1492, Cuba was inhabited mainly by the indigenous Taíno, Siboney, and Guanahatabey people. In 1511, a Spanish colony was established and the indigenous were forced into slavery and wiped out, mostly by disease. As a result, contemporary Cuba, unlike much of Latin America, retains no indigenous subculture. In 1519, the Spanish governor of Cuba sent Hernán Cortés to conquer Mexico. Cuba became the last stop before Spain for ships delivering the riches of Spanish America and the Philippines. In 1762, Havana fell into British hands for a short period until it was returned to Spain in exchange for Florida the following year. Generally, the Spaniards had little interest in the island until the increased demand for sugar in Europe resulted in its selection for significant cultivation in the eighteenth century, when African slaves were brought to work on the plantations. By the nineteenth century, sugar production became the basis of the economy, a factor that has remained constant to the present day.

When Napoleon invaded the Iberian peninsula in 1807, Latin American nations began to use the occasion to gain independence; but Cuba remained Spanish, in significant measure because of the successful sugar industry and the close identification of the local elites with Madrid. However, Spanish control was resisted as three wars for independence were fought in the last decades of the century. The first, known as the Ten Years War, had an abolitionist component. It began in 1868 with the leadership of landowner Carlos Manuel de Céspedes, who freed his own slaves, and ended with minor Spanish concessions in 1878. Slavery was abolished 2 years later. A second inconclusive war lasted a year and ended in 1880. The final struggle began in 1895, led by Cuba's national hero, writer-poet José Martí, who was killed early in the war, and by General Antonio Maceo, an Afro-Cuban who had become a hero when he refused to accept the earlier peace agreement with the Spanish.

A Park (Parque de la Iglesia) in San Antonio de los Baños, Cuba. Bust of 1959 Cuban revolutionary hero Camilo Cienfuegos is seen against the background of a colonial-style church (La Iglesia Villa Ariguanado) built in 1826. *(Photo by Miguel Collazo)*

When the fight for independence seemed almost won, the U.S. battleship *Maine* blew up in Havana Harbor. The resulting war with the United States ended Spanish rule in 1898. Cuba expected immediate independence but instead gained only American occupation. Most European governments expected the United States, which had several times tried to buy Cuba in the middle of the nineteenth century, would annex the island along with Puerto Rico, Guam, and the Philippines; but Washington promised independence, primarily to avoid the payment of reparations to Spain.

The occupation government of General Leonard Wood began reordering Cuban life along the lines of North American society. The University of Havana was moved to a prominent location overlooking the city, other schools were organized, public health programs were initiated, and a presidential political system was installed, complete with checks and balances following the U.S. model. A capitol building, copied from the one in Washington, DC, completed the picture. Congress made the provision that an amendment to an appropriations bill introduced by Senator Orville H. Platt be incorporated in the Cuban constitution of 1901. The amendment limited Cuban sovereignty in fiscal and treaty-making matters and allowed the United States to intervene at any time to maintain a "government adequate for the protection of life, property, and individual liberty." The Platt Amendment also provided for a North American naval base at Guantanamo, a site still occupied by the United States against the objections of the Cuban government. Cuban products now went to North American markets, and the island became, in essence, a political protectorate of the United States. Twice, in 1905 and in 1917, the United States intervened militarily under the Platt provision.

A British–American agreement set up the International Sugar Committee to control the sale of Cuban sugar, dividing the export market exclusively between the two countries and giving them the power to establish the price. U.S. investment in Cuba, in addition to sugar refineries and lands, included mining, communications, and the railways. The U.S. Federal Reserve Bank established its only foreign branch in Havana. By 1926 U.S. direct investment on the island totaled nearly $1.4 billion.

Two political parties developed, the Liberals and the Conservatives. In 1925 Liberal candidate Gerardo Machado was elected president for a 4-year term. In 1927, Machado changed the constitution, extending the presidential term to 6 years and had himself reelected, which in essence destroyed the party system in Cuba. During the Machado presidency, student and university activism grew. Julio A. Mella, a law student and secretary-general of the Student Federation, organized a national student congress. He later founded the Popular University José Martí, patterned on the Popular University González Prada, established by Victor Raúl Haya de la Torre and José Carlos Mariátegui in Peru, to expand education to the working class. Strongly antiimperialist and highly critical of the role of the United States, Mella worked with the Mexican Enrique Flores Magón to organize the Cuban Communist Party in 1925. Through Mella's efforts students began to attack the increasingly dictatorial government of Machado, who responded by jailing Mella. After his release, Mella left for exile in Mexico. Opposition to the Machado dictatorship continued at the University of Havana, where students organized the University Student Directorate, which focused anti-Machado sentiment in Havana. The directorate leadership was ousted from the university, ending the first phase of struggle against Machado.

However, the economic collapse of 1929 caused a precipitous drop in the world price of sugar, followed by political unrest and severe repression. The assassination of Mella in Mexico and the increased repression by Machado led to a second directorate in 1930, which began organizing open demonstrations against the government. The new leadership included future president Carlos Prío Socarrás, Raúl Roa (later foreign minister under Fidel Castro), and Eduardo Chibas, future founder of the Cuban People's Party (Orthodox). A clash with police killed one of the student leaders and brought the closing of the university by Machado. Now known as the "Generation of 1930," the students turned to urban violence. Directorate leaders were arrested, as were most of the faculty, including physiology professor Ramón Grau San Martín. Other groups developed in opposition to the increasingly unpopular Machado. U.S. Ambassador Summer Welles tried to mediate the conflict between Machado and his opposition but failed, and a general strike, uprisings among the unionized sugar workers, and an army revolt forced Machado into exile in August 1933. He was replaced by Carlos Manuel de Céspedes, son of the hero of 1868, who restored the 1901 constitution. The new government immediately received U.S. backing, aimed at isolating the most radical forces.

Directorate leaders continued to agitate against the government, accusing Céspedes of being too close to Machado and the United States. Students demanded a new constitution plus social and economic reforms. Government plans to freeze army promotions and reduce pay led to a takeover of the army by noncommissioned officers headed by Sergeant Fulgencio Batista. Batista, who had worked as a stenographer at the military trials of the students under the Machado regime, invited directorate leaders to a meeting. Together they agreed to a coup and on the composition of a new government, ousting Céspedes in September 1933. Although Batista did not accept a post in the new government, the action placed him in a position where he dominated politics through the control of the army for the next 26 years.

The new government was headed by Professor San Martín, whose short-lived government initiated important social and nationalist legislation. For example, Antonio Guiteras, minister of government, nationalized the Cuban electrical system. Simultaneously, a series of workers' protests, land confiscations by peasants, and a takeover of sugar mills by sugar workers resulted in strong opposition to the new government from Cuba's wealthy elites and U.S. Ambassador Welles. Behind the scenes, Batista and Welles conspired to bring down the new government as the army withdrew its support of San Martín.

Prior to Batista's election in 1940, a new progressive and democratic constitution was enacted. Like Mexico's 1917 constitution, it was oriented toward social and economic rights. In the second elections held under the new constitution, San Martín was elected president in 1944. He ran on the ticket of the Cuban Revolutionary Party (Auténtico), which was an outgrowth of the student movements of the 1930s. He had been living in exile in Miami and returned only after his election. A second Auténtico president, Carlos Prío Socarrás, a student leader of the 1930s, was elected in 1948.

The Auténtico program stressed progressive policies but quickly became identified with extremes of corruption. A new political party, the Cuban People's Party

(Orthodox), formed around the leadership of Eduardo Chibas, also a member of the Generation of 1930. University students, critical of Auténtico corruption, became a source of support and leadership for the Orthodox. The party's youth wing was led by Fidel Castro, a law student at the University of Havana. The popularity of the new party indicated that it would win the presidency in the 1952 election, even though Chibas had committed suicide a year earlier. Castro was an Orthodox candidate for congress.

In a surprise move, Batista launched a military coup in March 1952, removing Prío Socarras. He canceled the upcoming election and appointed himself president. The new Batista government catered to U.S. policy interests by adopting an anticommunist position and by breaking formal diplomatic relations with the Soviet Union. Washington responded with military assistance grants of $1.5 million annually from 1954 to 1956 and doubled this figure during the 1957–1958 period. A military mission assisted in training Batista's army. Cuba was opened up to increased American investment, and Havana became an ever more popular gambling and nightclub center just a few miles off the Florida coast. American fascination with Cuba had begun in the 1920s during prohibition, when U.S. citizens went to Cuba to drink and gamble in facilities operated by North American mobsters. In the 1950s, organized crime and the Batista government cooperated in personal enrichment.

Revolution

The opposition to the new Batista government was centered in the urban areas. Following the example of the Generation of 1930, students organized urban guerrilla warfare, using the universities as sanctuaries from the national authorities. In Havana, students formed the Revolutionary Directorate under the leadership of José Antonio Echeverría. On the other end of the island, in the city of Santiago de Cuba, Frank País, son of a Protestant minister, organized students at the University of Santiago.

Castro gathered a number of students and workers around him and sought to begin a national uprising by capturing the army barracks at Moncada, Santiago, and the Céspedes barracks in Bayamo. They attacked on July 26, 1953. In the ensuing battles, most of the attackers were killed, and Castro was captured. At his trial, Castro defended himself, saying "History will absolve me." He was sentenced to prison on the Isle of Pines (now renamed the Isle of Youth) but released after 22 months as part of a general amnesty by Batista under popular pressure. An agreement between Castro and País created the 26th of July Movement (M-26-7), named for the date of the Moncada barracks attack. After Castro had made a number of appearances in continued opposition to Batista, he was advised to leave the country and began to enlist and train a guerrilla army in Mexico. There, he met and began work with an Argentine doctor, Ernesto "Ché" Guevara, who had been in Guatemala with the government of Jacobo Arbenz until the Central Intelligence Agency (CIA)–backed overthrow of that government in 1954. After successful fundraising among anti-Batista Cubans, Castro bought a yacht, the *Granma,* from a retired American couple. In November 1956, he loaded the *Granma* with eighty-two men and sailed for Cuba, landing in Oriente Province. In a coordinated effort, País tried to divert the attention of Batista's forces to the city of Santiago; but the invaders were met by army units and almost completely defeated. The survivors, including Castro, his brother Raúl, and Ché Guevara, took refuge in the Sierra Maestra mountains.

For the next 2 years, the war against Batista proceeded on two fronts, the 26th of July movement guerrilla campaign in the Sierra Maestra of eastern Cuba and an urban resistance campaign consisting of several different political groupings. During 1957 the guerrillas worked to consolidate their position in the mountains by recruiting local peasants to join them and to provide logistical support. During this period, the 26th of July movement articulated its political program and publicized it with the aid of a small radio transmitter and the favorable coverage given their movement by a *New York Times* reporter, Herbert Matthews.

Meanwhile, many Cubans were already bombing government installations, executing police, and undermining confidence in the Batista government. In March 1957, the Revolutionary Directorate under the leadership of Echeverría tried to kill Batista in an armed attack on the presidential palace. The attempt failed and resulted in the death of Echeverría and most of the directorate leadership. Other nonstudent armed revolutionary groups included Civic Resistance (affiliated with the 26th of July movement); the Montecristi movement of progressive army officers led by Colonel Ramón Barquín, which attempted a failed coup against Batista; and the Puros, who briefly held the Cienfuegos naval station in September 1957. Batista responded to the rebellion with widespread repression. Close to 20,000 Cubans would die in the struggle between 1953 and 1959, mostly civilians.

The ultimate military success of the 26th of July Movement was surprising in both its quickness and its small numbers at the beginning. Of the eighty-two men who boarded the *Granma* in Mexico, only twelve made it to the mountains. After a year of accumulating a few hundred cadre, the guerrillas launched their first attacks in early 1958, just a year before their ultimate triumph. Batista's defeat began in May 1958 when his army carried out an ill-fated all-out offensive against the rebels in the Sierra Maestra. The turning point was a 10-day battle in Jigue when the rebels surrounded a government unit of greater firepower and defeated them. Following that defeat, the morale of Batista's primarily conscript army was very low. Seizing the moment, the 26th of July movement went on the offensive. In the decisive battle at Santa Clara in December 1958, the rebel forces under the leadership of Ché Guevara and Camilo Cienfuegos totally routed Batista's forces and the army collapsed. Batista had no reliable defenses around him in Havana, and on December 31, 1958, he fled the country. Victory came to the 26th of July movement even sooner than it had expected.

Beyond the broad outlines of the military campaign just detailed, the triumph of the 26th of July Movement was a complex phenomenon. It was not a mass-based revolutionary war by a peasant army like those that occurred in China or Vietnam. Peasants were recruited to the 26th of July movement and gave it important support, but the guerrilla army, 800 as late as September 1958, was primarily a force of students, professionals, and workers from Cuba's middle sectors. The Cuban insurrection was not an urban proletarian revolution. Organized labor, whose ranks were heavily influenced by the communist People's Socialist Party (PSP), opposed the 26th of July movement until almost the very end, when the communists gave their belated support.

The Museum of the Revolution, located on the edges of Old Havana, is the former presidential palace. It was constructed between 1913 and 1920. Tiffany's of New York decorated the interior. The palace was the site of an unsuccessful assassination attempt on Fulgencio Batista in March 1957. *(Photo by Catherine A. Kocy)*

The 26th of July Movement also carried out a broad alliance strategy that culminated at a July 1958 meeting in Caracas, Venezuela, where the Revolutionary Democratic Civic Front was organized, encompassing almost all of the anti-Batista forces. The front, combined with the military weakening of Batista, eroded U.S. government support for the regime. In March 1958, under pressure from the Senate, the U.S. State Department placed an arms embargo on Cuba. In December, the Eisenhower administration repeatedly placed pressure on Batista to step down. However, the U.S. opposition to Batista was predicated on the assumption that the moderate anti-Batista forces would dominate the new government. That assumption proved to be erroneous.

Revolution in Power

On January 8, 1959, Castro and the 26th of July Movement entered Havana. He noted that the U.S. military had prohibited the Liberator Army under General Calixto García from entering Santiago de Cuba in 1898 and that history would not be repeated. Castro took no position in the new government but set about consolidating Cuba's military forces under his command. He sent one of his trusted lieutenants, Cienfuegos, to relieve Barquín, who had taken command of Batista's remaining troops. Forces of the directorate initially refused to disarm and had to be persuaded to accept Castro's authority.

Castro and his allies from the Sierra Maestra were committed to a program of radical social and economic reform, and they soon set out on a course to consolidate control over state power. The victory over Batista came so quickly that most of the old political structures were intact. Only a few thousand of Batista's closest allies left the country. Most of the landowning elite, businesspeople, professionals, and clergy stayed, hoping that they could influence the course of the new government and protect their considerable privileges. Well aware that their radical plans would encounter stiff resistance among those committed to only minor change, Castro and his allies moved to isolate his opponents one by one. In mid-February 1959, Castro accepted the position of prime minister and began to push through measures that would distribute wealth and increase support in the rural areas. In May, an agricultural reform act limited the size of most farm holdings to under 1000 acres. This measure destroyed the largest holdings, including U.S.-owned sugar properties, several of which exceeded 400,000 acres. Land was distributed to thousands of rural workers, and the government moved to improve conditions on the large farms it now controlled. As a result, support for the revolution increased throughout the countryside. The passage of the Rent Reduction Act resulted in the transfer of about 15 percent of the national income from property owners to wage workers and peasants.

A literacy campaign sent thousands of young volunteers to rural areas. Literacy was increased, and the young supporters of the revolution learned firsthand about the conditions of the rural areas. The government also began building hundreds of new schools and training thousands of additional teachers. Health care was extended to the entire population for the first time with the construction of rural clinics and hospitals. Many private and racially segregated facilities such as clubs and beaches were opened to the public. These radical social and economic measures carried out in the first year of the revolution often involved mass mobilizations, which served to unite the poor majority of Cuban citizens behind the government. These measures also served to identify the movement's political enemies, who exposed themselves through their vociferous opposition to the changes. Moderates in the government, such as acting President Manuel Urrutia Lleó, resigned in protest in June 1959, taking much of the leadership of the old democratic parties and landed elite into exile with them. Simultaneously, the use of revolutionary tribunals to judge and then execute approximately 500 members of Batista's police and security agencies was popular with the Cuban masses but forced many of those who had been associated with the old regime to seek refuge abroad. One by one those political forces that opposed the radical direction of the revolution dropped away until only the revolutionary core remained, primarily the cadre of the 26th of July movement from the Sierra Maestra and a few allies from the Revolutionary Directorate, who increasingly assumed key cabinet posts and took control of the government bureaucracy. The final element in the revolutionary coalition was the PSP. Castro made a formal alliance with them in late 1959, not completely trusting them but desirous of using their organizational skills in the reconstructed government bureaucracies. Their inclusion in the government also served to drive out the remaining anticommunist elements.

The increasingly radical direction of the revolution in 1959–1960 led to a direct confrontation with Washington. The U.S. government had begun to realize that it

Mobilized literacy workers in Cuban Literacy Campaign.

had a potential major problem with Cuba when Castro left Washington following a visit in 1959 without requesting significant U.S. aid. Up until that point, U.S. officials had expected to control Cuba through the normal give-and-take of foreign aid. By April 1959, the Cuban leadership had already decided on a series of radical changes and were not seeking approval in Washington. At the time Castro left Washington, Cuba still maintained the Batista policy of nonrecognition of the Soviet Union. However, this policy began to change; and in December 1959, an official Soviet journalist was admitted to Havana. In February 1960, Soviet First Deputy Premier Anastas Mikoyan paid a visit and a Soviet–Cuban trade agreement was signed. Ché Guevara went to Eastern Europe soon after and lined up $100 million in credits for industrialization in Cuba. Relations with the Soviet Union offered a balance and an alternative to dominance of American power in Cuban affairs. Formal diplomatic relations were reestablished between the two countries in May 1960.

The Cuban economy depended on sugar. A U.S. quota system had allocated Cuba a 2.8 million ton market at a predetermined and subsidized price considerably above the world market. This amounted to significant U.S. governmental aid to Cuba. One of the first actions of friendship by the Soviet Union was the February 1960 purchase of Cuban sugar. As U.S.–Cuban relations worsened, the Soviet Union agreed to purchase 2.7 million tons of Cuban sugar if the American government reduced its quota. The Soviet Union also began to supply Cuba with oil. Cuba has a small domestic supply of petroleum but only enough to meet about 15 percent of national needs. With a shortage of foreign exchange, Cuba found it increasingly difficult to keep refineries supplied with imported oil, mostly from Venezuela. In

April 1960, the first shipment of Soviet oil arrived in exchange for Cuban products. American oil companies, which owned Cuba's refineries, advised by the U.S. secretary of the treasury, refused to refine the oil. The refineries were taken over by the Cuban government, and Washington responded by eliminating Cuba's sugar quota, the backbone of the Cuban economy.

The confrontation between Havana and Washington had been building throughout 1959 and 1960. The Cuban government began regulating the U.S.-owned Cuban Telephone Company in March 1959. The confrontation over the oil refineries resulted in the first nationalizations in July 1960, and they were followed quickly by the seizing of U.S.-owned sugar plantations in August, foreign banks in September, and more businesses in October. Late in 1960 the United States broke diplomatic relations with Cuba, and in January 1961 the Eisenhower administration instituted an embargo on most exports to Cuba. The Agrarian Reform Law of May 1959 laid the groundwork for eventual seizure of many large American properties with an offer of 20-year bonds for payment; the United States, rejecting the bonds, demanded "prompt, adequate, and effective compensation." By December 1959 the CIA began to recruit Cuban exiles, and in March 1960 Eisenhower decided to arm and train an exile force for the purpose of invading the island and precipitating the overthrow of the Castro government.

John Kennedy assumed the presidency of the United States in January 1961 and with it the responsibility for the group of Cuban exiles, now training in Central America under CIA direction. In Cuba, Castro had inaugurated the Committees for the Defense of the Revolution (CDR), organized block by block in the cities, to guard against opposition and to enlist support for the government. In the mountains of Escambray, a group of anti-Castro guerrillas maintained harassment of government troops; but at U.S. request, they stopped action until the exile forces were ready. In April, the exiles invaded Cuba at the Bay of Pigs but were stalled by local militias, while in the cities the CDR quickly pointed out persons in opposition, who were immediately arrested before any of them could support the invasion. The major result of the American intervention was the consolidation of Castro's position by creating a solid identification between the antiimperialism of Cuban tradition and the victory of the forces under Castro. Soon after the defeat of the exile force at the Bay of Pigs, Castro declared the "socialist" character of the Cuban Revolution. Socialist countries supported Cuba, with the Soviet Union honoring its promise to buy 2.7 million tons of sugar. The People's Republic of China bought a million tons; other socialist nations, 300,000 tons.

From the declared commitment to socialism in April 1961 to the campaign to produce 10 million tons of sugarcane in 1970, the Cuban Revolution moved through its most idealistic period. Domestically, the revolution sought to create a thoroughly homegrown socialist economy marked primarily by lack of market incentives. Shared sacrifice and a drive for self-sufficiency were the primary driving forces in economic development. The leadership sought to diversify the Cuban economy while instituting a policy of industrialization. New products such as cotton were introduced to the island with the hope of reducing the island's dependence on foreign inputs. At the time of the revolution, the United States had $1 billion invested in Cuba. U.S. companies controlled 40 percent of the sugar crop

and 55 percent of the sugar mill capacity; more importantly, the U·
the major buyer of Cuban sugar. In return for preferential entry
U.S. markets, Cuba was required to open its market to U.S. manufac..
this undercut the development of domestic industries. There were numerou..
tortions—Cuba exported raw sugar but imported candy; it produced vast quantities of tobacco but imported cigarettes. Cuban economic policy of the 1960s was
designed to reverse this reality. The determination to end dependence on sugar
production took the extreme form of plowing over vast acreage of sugar lands and
planting new crops, but these efforts largely failed due to the lack of expertise and
appropriate climatic conditions.

During the 1960s, the Cuban government also borrowed a strategy of heavy
industrialization from the Soviet Union, but these efforts yielded only limited success because of Cuba's particular conditions and the lack of trained personnel. Following the failure of the "balanced growth" model, Cuba turned to an approach
labeled the "turnpike model." Instead of seeking to diversify the economy immediately, Cuba would give priority to sugar production by increasing the cultivated
acreage and increasing mechanization. Earnings from sugar export would be used to
import machinery to diversify agricultural and industrial production on a sounder
basis. Other sectors were also developed, especially the production of cattle, fishing,
and citrus fruit. Cement, nickel, and electricity were also expanded with assistance
of machinery from the Soviet Union. During this period (1964–1970), the nationalization of the Cuban economy was completed. All industry, commerce, and finance
and 70 percent of agricultural land were controlled by the state. This period was
marked by a great ideological debate over socialist economic strategy. The basic
question was whether a largely underdeveloped country like Cuba could primarily
use moral incentives to motivate greater productivity in the workforce or whether
it was necessary to use some sort of material incentives. Cuban Communist leader
Carlos Rafael Rodríguez argued that, given Cuba's low level of development, the
workers could not be expected to have sufficient consciousness for appeals to the
good of the society; increased productivity needed to be rewarded with higher
wages and bonuses. This "market socialism" position was also advocated by Soviet
advisers.

The more radical position, argued by Guevara, was that economic organization could be totally centralized, with resources allocated to enterprises according
to plan rather than market forces. Central to this argument was that workers could
be motivated without material incentives to work for the collective, the common
good. After some experimentation with both models, Castro endorsed Guevara's
approach in 1966; and that period culminated in the revolutionary offensive of 1968–
1970, which focused on large-scale investment in sugar with the aim of harvesting
and processing 10 million tons of sugar in 1970. The concentration of resources on
production entailed further sacrifices from the populace, but the primary goal was
to finance industrialization without further debt. It was also hoped that the success
of the campaign would be paid off by higher levels of production throughout the
society from increased industrialization.

The 1970 sugar harvest was a massive undertaking that involved workers from
all sectors and volunteers from around the world; although close to 10 million tons

ere cut, major processing problems cut the final harvest to 8.5 million tons, far short of the goal. It was a significant blow to the prestige of the revolution, and production dropped in several key sectors outside of sugar. The failure of the revolutionary offensive led to a reassessment of the goals and strategies of the revolution in economic development as well as in other areas. It was recognized that more attention had to be paid to productivity, perhaps at the sacrifice of some egalitarian goals. It was also realized that economic independence from the Soviet Union could not be achieved in the short run.

Concurrent with the changing economic realities, the end of the 1960s brought some changes on the international front. During the 1960s, the Cuban leadership advocated an uncompromising stance toward Latin American elites and the United States. Castro's Second Declaration of Havana saw revolution as inevitable in Latin America due to class oppression, economic exploitation, and oligarchical domination by pro-United States repressive regimes. Havana sympathized with such prospects and saw it as "the duty of every revolutionary to make the revolution." As a strategy, Castro called for armed revolution on a continental scale. The Cubans gave direct material support to revolutionary movements in Nicaragua, Guatemala, Venezuela, and Colombia. Guevara, a leader of Cuba's own revolution, went to fight in Bolivia, where he was killed in 1967. Two conferences during this era epitomized the commitment of the Cuban leadership to the strategy of revolutionary guerrilla warfare. In 1966, Castro convened the Conference of Solidarity of the Peoples of Asia, Africa, and Latin America, where, in his keynote speech, the Cuban leader attacked U.S. imperialism, Latin American elite governments, and all political movements that opposed the necessity of armed struggle, including communist parties. The strategy of guerrilla warfare was confirmed at the Latin America Solidarity Conference the following year in Havana. While this strategy struck a responsive chord among revolutionaries throughout the Americas, the policy did isolate Cuba within the hemisphere. Its support for armed guerrilla movements made normal relations with most governments in Latin America impossible and even served to bring Castro in conflict with significant leftist forces in the region. Castro directly attacked the reform-oriented approach of the region's communist parties as a betrayal of revolutionary principles. Most communist parties in the hemisphere had renounced armed struggle as a viable strategy for power and were pursuing reforms within existing Latin American political structures.

Decade of the 1970s—Economic Changes

The decade of the 1970s in Cuba saw a more sober approach in economic policy making, internal governance, and foreign affairs. In hindsight, this was the decade where the Cuban Revolution was successfully institutionalized. The longevity of the Cuban revolutionary project was secured in a series of crucial policy shifts following the failure of the sugar harvest. As a starting point, the party and Castro himself took full responsibility for the shortfall. There was no significant scapegoating, nor did the events result in a purge of party leadership. The response to the failure was policy initiatives in economics and politics that were probably long overdue. The changes were not instituted hastily but rather introduced gradually over the course of the next decade.

The changes in the economic arena were considerable. The failure of the economic projects of the 1960s led the Cuban leadership to reluctantly conclude that the only viable economic strategy was to move toward economic integration with the East European Council for Mutual Economic Assistance (CMEA). This was a difficult decision for the revolutionary leaders because it meant that the diversification of the Cuban economy that they had so desperately sought in the 1960s would have to be placed largely on hold. Integration into the CMEA meant that Cuba would primarily concentrate on the production of sugar, nickel, and citrus products in return for oil, manufactured goods, and canned foods. This arrangement worked in large measure because Cuba received a guaranteed return for its exported primary products, something it could not likely have obtained in the open world capitalist market. Cuba received an especially favorable exchange rate on Soviet oil for its sugar. This arrangement essentially shielded Cuba from the dramatic rise in world energy prices that occurred between 1973 and 1982, devastating many Third-World economies. The Soviet demand for Cuban sugar was high, and by the early 1980s Cuba was importing more Soviet oil than it needed, allowing for the resale of millions of barrels into the world market for hard currency. This export of oil became a valuable project for Cuba and allowed for the further raising of the Cuban standard of living. By the mid-1980s, 85 percent of Cuba export– import was with the CMEA countries. The only major trade that remained with the capitalist world was the prized Cuban tobacco. During this period, Cuba did not abandon its goal of increasing food self-sufficiency and developed more domestic industries, but inevitably these efforts did take a back seat to meeting the production goals for the CMEA.

The growing certainty of the economic deals made with the CMEA on a multi-year basis allowed for a new emphasis on planning that included reactivation of the state Central Planning Board (JUCEPLAN). Prices and investments were centrally controlled, although in the 1970s there was some decentralization of economic planning to local and regional authorities. Without great fanfare there was also a shift away from the 1960s emphasis on solely moral incentives toward the use of material incentives to raise levels of production. The shift clearly had ideological overtones that were welcomed by the Soviet advisers, but the change also occurred because, unlike in the 1960s, the improved state of the economy gave the government a much greater ability to carry out a program of worker bonuses. Even with all of these changes, the period of 1970–1989 was not one of unbroken progress for the Cuban economy. After a brief period of accelerated growth in the early 1970s, the first 5-year plan (1975–1980) fell far short of its goals. The economy did grow again in the first half of the 1980s, buoyed in part by the profitable reexport of Soviet oil during a period of high world oil prices. Throughout this period, there continued to be problems of lower than expected worker productivity.

During this time, the Cuban consumer did not always directly benefit from the overall growth of the economy because of its primary export orientation, but the wealth redistribution policies of the revolution did result in a significant sharing of the benefits of CMEA membership. In 1970, virtually all consumer goods were rationed; but by the mid-1980s, only 30 percent of income was being spent on rationed goods and, by 1989, the ration had all but been eliminated. By the end of the 1980s, Cuba had constructed one of the most egalitarian societies in the world, free of the malnutrition and hunger that marked most of its Central American and

Caribbean neighbors. However, even at Cuba's height, the Cuban consumer still suffered from a lack of variety and quality of goods available to buy. When the economic shocks of 1989 intervened, Cuba had not yet achieved a fully developed socialist economy.

Political Process

The 1970s saw an overhaul of the Cuban political process with the institutional-izing of the formal organs of government power, known as People's Power. These institutions, created islandwide in 1976, represented a shift in governance structures from the first phase of the revolution. The 1960s had seen the consolidation of the Cuban Communist Party (PCC) and the utilization of the neighborhood-based CDR as dual governing organs. The CDR were designed in 1960 for security purposes, reporting on the activities of counterrevolutionaries and supporting governmental policy. At their peak, they numbered 3 million members; but as the 1960s wore on, active membership declined somewhat and they became primarily responsible for neighborhood ideological education and social organization and communicating government decisions to the masses. The leadership recognized that the CDR could not rule the country and that task was given to the PCC created in 1965. The PCC's origins can be traced to 1961 when the alliance with the old Communist Party (PSP) was formalized with the creation of the Integrated Revolutionary Organization (ORI). It was viewed as temporary, and with 16,000 members it was reorganized in 1963 into the United Party of the Cuban Socialist Revolution (PURSC). The PURSC was then acknowledged by the Soviet Union as a legitimate communist party. The final stage of party development began in October 1965 with the launching of the PCC, an organization modeled after the Soviet one. It had a small politburo at the top composed primarily of Sierra Maestra veterans and a handful from the old PSP, a central committee of a few hundred members, and a National Party Congress that was to meet every 5 years to establish broad policy guidelines. Actually, there was little change in governance style for several years. The first party congress was not convened until 1975; in the interim, decision making revolved almost exclusively around the small core of 26th of July movement veterans who had led the revolu-tion from its beginning. However, after 1975 the party and its formal structures grew in importance. By 1980 party members occupied nearly all of the important positions with the state ministries, the armed forces, and the education system. Like other communist parties, it was a limited-membership organization, never encom-passing more than 15 percent of the population. Party members are selected care-fully to ensure that they are fully dedicated to the tasks of the revolution. They are expected to be model citizens and modest in their personal lives. Most of them start early, beginning as Young Pioneers when teenagers, then becoming Young Com-munists when they enter adulthood, and finally party members a few years later. Their material rewards are generally limited, yet they have always been favored by somewhat easier access to housing and consumer goods and are able to travel more abroad.

The Cuban government never functioned as smoothly or as efficiently as the creators intended. During the early years, costly planning and administrative mistakes were made, some the result of inexperience and others the result of adopting inappropriate Soviet models. The limitation of the CDR as a feedback mechanism was also acknowledged after the failure of the 10-million-ton campaign in 1970. In response, popular participation in policy implementation was proposed through newly created government organs called People's Power. Following a trial run in Matanzas province in 1974, the institutions were established nationwide in 1976. Still in operation today, People's Power is composed of municipal, provincial, and national assemblies that are assigned the task of supervising government agencies within their jurisdictions and at the national level, formulating laws and regulations for the society as a whole. The first People's Power elections were held in 1976 following the ratification in a national referendum of a new constitution. The country is divided into 169 municipalities and then into electoral districts where roughly every 1,000 to 1,500 voters (fewer in some rural areas, more in other areas) elect one representative to a Municipal Assembly of People's Power for a term of two and a half years. In each of these constituent districts, an electoral committee is appointed to oversee the nomination of candidates. The district is broken down into subdistricts, each of whom can propose a candidate. This process usually produces several candidates from each district, and by law there must be at least two nominees; an uncontested election is not permitted. The electoral commission investigates all candidates and publishes its results. Candidates are not permitted to campaign and can be disqualified if they are judged to be doing so. Runoff elections are often necessary to obtain a majority vote. In the 2007 municipal elections 15,236 delegates were chosen from over 35,000 candidates. In 3,028 constituencies a second round of voting was necessary because no candidate received a majority in the first round. Participation in the first round of voting was 96.5 percent even though voting in Cuba is not mandatory. Of the elected delegates, 26.8 percent are women and 16.8 percent are young people. There is traditionally considerable turnover among municipal delegates. In 2007 only 5,775 were holdovers from the previous assemblies.

Municipal deputies must spend part of each week available to their constituents to receive their complaints or opinions. Every 6 months there is a formal accountability session at which complaints, suggestions, and other community interests are raised with the delegate. The delegate must then attempt to resolve the matter or provide an explanation at the next accountability session. If the constituents are not satisfied with a delegate, he or she can be recalled or voted out in the next election. Usually only about half of the delegates are reelected. Deputies are not professional politicians and are generally given time off from their full-time jobs to carry out these functions. Some have compared their position to that of county supervisors in the U.S. system, providing a link to the local population with only limited powers of their own. The municipal assembly has committees responsible for such areas as education, health, and economic affairs. In 1989 people's councils—groups of delegates from within a municipality—were created in Havana to make government more accessible. By 1993 the people's councils were adopted throughout the country. In the original system, the municipal deputies were also responsible for electing provincial and national deputies in indirect elections. They elected delegates from lists provided by a nominating committee headed by a representative of the Communist Party and made up of members of a wide range of civic organizations. This indirect system was replaced by significant electoral reform carried out for the 1993 elections.

The Provincial People's Power Assemblies can propose projects and assign priorities to housing, hospitals, and other projects. The provincial legislatures and their executives act as an intermediary between national policy and its execution at the local level. The provincial government allocates its budget, received from the national level, among the various municipal units. This is done by collecting requests and advice from the lower levels. The assemblies are responsible for selecting the directors for industries, for moving personnel from one job to another, and for replacing persons who are removed or retire. However, not all enterprises report to the provincial level; some report directly to the national level.

The highest organ of government is the 614-member National Assembly of People's Power. As the legislative body of Cuba, the assembly passes the budget, confirms heads of ministries, makes laws, selects Supreme Court justices, and sets basic economic policies. It meets only infrequently to ratify decisions and draw public attention to national issues. The primary work of the assembly, as in many other legislative bodies worldwide, is done in standing committees. These committees investigate and prepare reports and proposed laws to be debated during National Assembly sessions. Their role is mainly consultative and investigative and they conduct public hearings. The assembly, whose deputies are elected for 5-year terms, also appoints a thirty-one-member Council of State to run the government on a day-to-day basis between assembly sessions. The president of the council is chosen by the assembly and is both head of state and head of government. This gives him the power to nominate the first vice president, five other vice presidents, and members of the Council of Ministers, all of whom are subject to confirmation by the assembly. In January 2008 Fidel Castro was reelected to the National Assembly but one month later, citing reasons of health, declined to be nominated for another term as president. Raul Castro accepted nomination and was elected to replace his brother. In addition to its executive functions, the Council of State can legislate by issuing decree laws when the assembly is not in session. The Council of State also is responsible for the court system. The composition of the National Assembly is interesting. The largest single group, of 173, are leaders of local levels of government; but the second largest group, of 145, are workers, peasants, cooperative workers, educators, health-service employees, and others directly linked to production and services. Thirty-five are members of the armed forces, and thirty are writers or other cultural workers. Not surprisingly, the Communist Party apparatus is well represented, with sixty-four functionaries. Overall, in the 2002 elections, 72.9 percent of the elected municipal delegates were party members. About 15 percent of the Cuban population belongs to the party.

The PCC is not legally an institution of the government, but by constitutional mandate and in political practice it rules the country. Over half of those originally elected at the municipal level were party members, and of the 481 delegates first elected to the National Assembly, 441 were party members. The Council of State was always dominated by the veterans of the Sierra Maestra and now is dominated by the younger generation of Communist Party leaders. In a very important development of the last 10 years, the day-to-day management of the Cuban state has passed to a generation of leaders who came of age after 1959. The key players Ricardo Alarcon, president of the National Assembly, Carlos Lage, vice president o. the Council of State, and Felipe Perez Roque, foreign minister. The direction of the Communist Party officially lies in its National Congress, which adopts new national plans and elects the Central Committee, the ongoing policy-making body of the party. The committee meets in plenary session at least once every year and officially is the highest body of the party between sessions of the party congresses. Selection to the committee is prized, a mark of honor and prestige in Cuban society. The 150-member Central Committee works as a planning body and shadows the implementation of party policies by the government. Virtually every person of importance in Cuba is a member or alternate member of the Central Committee, from generals and provincial heads to top medical people and administrators. Little is known about the internal workings of this body, but it is said to operate on the basis of consensus since the formal existence of factions is prohibited. It has surely been the scene of important political policy discussions, especially in the time period since 1989.

The Secretariat, selected from the membership of the Central Committee, is officially its executive body and is responsible for carrying out the committee's policies between yearly meetings. To oversee the work of the Secretariat, the Political Bureau (or Politburo) is elected from the Central Committee to run the party. In the Political Bureau lies the political power of decision. The Political Bureau's twenty-four members control both the party and important posts in the government. Until his illness Castro was not only the first secretary of the party but also commander-in-chief and president of the Council of State and the Council of Ministers. His brother Raúl was second secretary, first vice president, and minister of the armed forces. Members of the Political Bureau also head the Ministry of Culture, the Confederation of Cuban Workers, the sugar industry, the Ministry of Agriculture, and the Ministry of Interior.

The unions, with a special place in Cuban politics, differ from other organizations and interest groups. The unions' general secretary is a member of the Political Bureau, and the national committee of the Confederation of Cuban Workers (CTC) and its national directorate have the right to initiate laws, a power otherwise restricted to government organs. Normally, the minister of labor is a member of the CTC and the trade unions are guaranteed positions on the Central Committee and in the leadership of the provincial and municipal party organizations. Within the National Assembly and other government bodies, the CTC acts as an interest group, not independent of the PCC but sometimes representing an alternate perspective.

The special role of unions flows in part from Cuba's self-declaration as a workers' state and because the unions predate the revolution (the CTC was founded in 1939) and have played a historical role in Cuban politics. Further, support of organized labor is vital to the Cuban economy. Workers are especially encouraged to become party members, where they make up the majority. In theory, the unions have the right to strike; but in practice, it has never been exercised. However, there is a natural tension between the unions and the state-run management over wages and work rules. Management wants to increase production quotas and keep work rules flexible, while the unions express contrary interests. It is often the

ɲn that mediates such conflicts, but disagreements can be taken to
for resolution.

political opposition in Cuba does not exist. The PCC is the only
.. party, and throughout the years of the revolution those persons who
...ve sought to pursue a political position against it have faced significant state
repression, usually in the form of jail terms. Even today, Amnesty International
acknowledges 80 political prisoner cases. The great majority of the political dissidents have gone into exile; and as a result, political opposition inside Cuba today
is weak. With active support of the U.S. government representatives on the island,
political opposition has shown some signs of life in recent years. The Verela Project
succeeded in collecting thousands of signatures calling for constitutional reform;
however, the government rejected the petition, and in 2003 seventy-five political
dissidents were arrested and many jailed with long prison terms. Beyond formal
political opposition, is it possible to speak of a civil society in Cuba independent of
the PCC and the government? In the mid-1980s, the government permitted society
to form new associations "from below." It was a recognition that neither the huge
mass organizations (CDR, CTC, etc.) nor the specialized professional associations
provided for the diversity of Cuban society. The civil associations grew slowly at
first and then, during the economic crisis of the 1990s, rapidly. Today, there are some
2150 associations registered in Cuba. The greatest number are fraternal–philosophical, including 420 Masonic lodges. The others range from sports clubs to scientific
and technical groups. Two hundred of them are nationwide. To receive legal recognition from the state, an association must also be approved by the state organization
in the sphere related to it. The number of successful new associations approved
demonstrates that barriers are not insurmountable, but the approval of new civil
associations has been limited since February 1996 because of the intensification of
U.S. economic pressure on Cuba and the subsequent hardening of Cuba's domestic
policies. This slowing of the pace of growth in civil society demonstrates the wari-
ness with which such independence is viewed in party circles.

International Relations

The 1970s and 1980s also saw a reorientation of Cuba's foreign relations. The 1960s
had been marked by an uncompromising revolutionary internationalism that clearly
aligned Cuba with revolutionary causes throughout the world, especially in Latin
America. As a consequence, Cuba was largely in a position of diplomatic isolation
except for its growing political and economic ties with the Soviet Union and its
allies. All of Latin America, with the exception of Mexico, had broken relations with
Cuba in the 1960s. Exceptions to Cuba's isolation included normal relations with
Mexico, Canada, and Spain, despite U.S. pressure on those countries. However, two
events in the late 1960s helped foster a shift in Cuba's international relations. First,
in 1967, Castro's confidant Ché Guevara was killed in Bolivia attempting to lead
revolutionary forces. Guevara's death came at the end of a series of defeats suffered
by revolutionary groups that the Cubans had backed in Latin America. Guevara's
defeat led to a reevaluation of the perspective that had argued that the Cuban model
of insurrection could be easily copied elsewhere in Latin America. Second, Soviet

pressure on Cuba began to take effect. The Soviets had always been uneasy about support for guerrilla warfare and Cuba's outspoken criticism of reform-oriented Latin American communist parties, but the pressure did not become severe until Castro was brought into line following the Soviet invasion of Czechoslovakia. Castro's first instinct was to criticize Soviet behavior in that invasion, but it quickly became clear that deviations from Moscow's perspective would have severe economic consequences for Cuba.

Soon after, the election of Richard Nixon brought the prospect of U.S–Soviet détente and with it a strong desire by the Soviet Union to downplay revolutionary rhetoric in the Third World. Cuba largely complied with Soviet pressure and began to stress diplomatic initiatives in Latin America, resulting in the reestablishment of relations with Argentina, Peru, and Chile. These three countries had undergone shifts to the left and saw the reestablishment of relations with Cuba as part of a foreign policy shift away from total domination by the United States. Later political changes, particularly the military coups in Chile and Argentina, damaged these relations, although ties with Argentina were never suspended. By the mid-1970s Cuba had shifted its own policy toward more normalized relations with other countries of the Americas, but the general political circumstances, particularly the domination of Latin America by military regimes, made a significant breakdown of isolation difficult. It was within that context that Cuba began to project itself more aggressively within the Nonaligned Movement (NAM) and within Africa.

Cuba's role in Africa in the 1970s signaled the beginning of a new era of foreign policy that was to be marked by an expansion of Cuban power and influence—an end to Cuba's isolation. Cuba had aided Algeria and Zanzibar in the 1960s, but the actions of the 1970s were qualitatively different. By the end of the decade, Cuba had 35,000 troops on the continent aiding the revolutionary governments of Ethiopia and Angola against foreign invasions while also providing wide-ranging civilian support from medicine to education. Crucial to the respect Cuba gained throughout the Third World was the role that 10,000 Cuban troops played in repelling a South African incursion into Angola in 1975. Similarly, more than 13,000 Cuban troops were instrumental in 1978 in repelling a Somalian invasion of Ethiopia that had been inspired by the United States. These actions would not have been possible without the political and financial support of the Soviet Union, but they allowed the Cuban government a visible opportunity to project its commitment to revolutionary internationalism on a world scale.

Cuba's successes in Africa led directly to a prominent role for Castro in NAM, an organization of Third-World countries that grew in prestige during the 1970s. In 1979, at the ministerial conference of NAM, Cuba received strong endorsement of its Africa policies; and in September 1979, at the sixth NAM summit in Havana, Castro was elected to the presidency of the organization. The presidency of NAM represented a new high of prestige for Castro and revolutionary Cuba, yet Castro's term as president was not without its setbacks. Cuba lost prestige within the organization when it backed the unpopular Soviet invasion of Afghanistan. However, Cuba's setbacks over Afghanistan were reversed during the crisis over the Falklands/Malvinas in 1982. Overt U.S. support for the British during that brief war gave Cuba the opportunity to rally Latin American nations on a nationalistic basis against the United States, thus helping to break down Cuba's isolation from Latin America. A major trade deal with Argentina ensued soon after the crisis, and the systematic reestablishment of relations with the rest of Latin America proceeded throughout the 1980s. By the end of the decade, Cuba was extending its trade with most of Latin America and Cuban leaders, including Castro, were welcome and prominent participants at Latin American and Caribbean political meetings.

Parallel to successes in Africa and with NAM, Cuba also played an important role in the Central American/Caribbean region in the early 1980s as a supporter of the revolutionary governments that emerged in Grenada and Nicaragua in 1979. Cuba's relationship with the Nicaraguan revolutionaries was long-standing, going back to the founding of the Sandinista National Liberation Front (FSLN) in 1961. During the dark days of the FSLN, its leaders often lived in exile in Cuba before returning in the late 1970s to lead a successful revolution against the Somoza dictatorship. The Sandinista uprising received more direct support from countries such as Costa Rica and Venezuela, but once the FSLN attained power, Cuba and Nicaragua established a close relationship. Cuba provided important material support and considerable revolutionary advice.

By 1983 Cuba's fortunes in the international arena were on a strong upward path, but there was a cost for these gains. As it had in earlier times, Cuba became a target of the United States because of its successes. There had been a brief thaw in United States–Cuba relations after 1977 when diplomatic missions were reopened in each country and the ban on U.S. citizens traveling to Cuba was lifted. However, the long-standing trade embargo was not lifted, and by 1979 Cuba was being harshly attacked for its policies in Africa. When Ronald Reagan assumed the presidency in 1981, Cuba's relations with Grenada and Nicaragua were attacked and the ban on U.S. citizen travel to Cuba was reinstated. Cuba's deep involvement continued in Nicaragua through the decade, but the Sandinistas lost power in the 1990 elections after a long and debilitating war with the United States.

Cuban Response to the Collapse of the Soviet Union

Dramatic changes began in Cuba with the fall of the Berlin Wall in November 1989 and were accelerated by the collapse of the Soviet Union at the end of 1991. These events impacted Cuba so strongly because at the beginning of 1989 virtually all of Cuba's foreign trade (87 percent) was with the Soviet Union and other socialist countries of CMEA. Cuba was dependent on CMEA for most of its energy supplies, fertilizer, machine tools, and canned foods. The CMEA arrangement to purchase Cuban sugar, nickel, and other primary products had led to significant economic and social progress after 1970, but the sudden and unexpected loss of these markets wrecked the Cuban economy. In 1989, Cuba imported 13 million tons of oil from the Soviet Union, but by 1992 it was able to import only 6 million tons, all of it at world market prices. The importing of canned food from Eastern Europe was ended altogether. By 1993 Cuba had lost 75 percent of its import capacity, and the country's economic activity contracted by 50 percent. Outside of the context of war, no modern economy had been so devastated in the twentieth century. The destruction of the economy resulted in the return of rationing for basic necessities. Rationing was not new to revolutionary Cuba; but in the 1980s it had been largely eliminated, and a system of "parallel markets" had allowed consumers to add to the food available in the subsidized state markets. Since these parallel markets depended to a large measure on food imported from Eastern Europe, they disappeared virtually overnight in 1991 as rationing was reintroduced.

The return to rationing was clearly a setback for Cuba, but it also meant that the country was not abandoning its socialist principles. The hardships were to be shared, and no one was to be left on his or her own. The equitable rationing of goods was in stark contrast to most of the rest of Latin America, where "structural adjustment programs" often resulted in food prices beyond the means of the majority, who are poor and in consequent malnutrition. In addition to rations, other dramatic measures were introduced to rescue the economy and maintain the productivity of the people. To maintain food production in the context of fuel shortages, more than 80,000 oxen were imported to take the place of tractors. In an attempt to deal with the dramatic reduction in public transportation, 600,000 bicycles were imported from China into a country where there was no tradition of cycling. To earn immediate hard currency, a program to dramatically increase the tourism industry was implemented despite the social problems, such as drugs and prostitution, that came along with it. From just a $165 million industry in 1989, tourism revenues grew to $850 million in 5 years as successful foreign investments in new facilities were attracted from Europe and Latin America. Today, tourism is the primary engine of the Cuban economy; with 2 million visitors annually and revenues of close to $2.5 billion, it has permitted the Cuban economy to be reinserted into the world's capitalist system. The tourism sector thrives even though U.S. visitors make up less than 5 percent of the total, the majority coming from Canada, Latin America, and Western Europe. However, tourism brings with it inevitable challenges to a socialist system, including prostitution and inequality. In addition, after many years of sharp growth, tourism revenues leveled off in 2006 and 2007. To meet tourist and national needs, Cuba's purchases abroad and subsequent debt has risen.

To spur foreign investment, changes were made in Cuban law to allow full recovery of investments in 3 years and relatively easy repatriation of profits. Taxation in the first years of investment was also sharply reduced. Latin American businesspeople, particularly Mexicans, were seriously courted by the Cuban government. An early fruit of this initiative was the decision by Domos, a Mexican telecommunication company, to invest heavily in updating the Cuban phone system. By 1994 over 150 foreign–Cuban joint ventures were under way, comprising over $1.5 billion invested from many other countries, including Spain, Canada, Germany, and Israel. The bulk of the activity was in tourism, where investors have insisted on a quick turnaround of profits in hard currency, thus limiting the positive impact on the economy. These efforts have been limited by the aggressive efforts of the U.S. government to prevent foreign business investment in Cuba. First, the Torricelli bill in 1992 and then the Helms-Burton legislation of 1996 tightened the long-term U.S. embargo on Cuba by punishing firms that make investments on the island. Although the legislation, especially Helms-Burton, has caused friction between the

United States and its allies, its presence does represent an obstacle to Cuba's further reintegration into the current world economy.

By the middle of 1994, the economic freefall continued and the Cuban economy and society seemed to be headed for disaster. In practice, the ration was not providing enough for people to eat, and the amount of time spent in lines obtaining the basic necessities was further undermining the remaining economic production. Discontent with the economic situation boiled over during the summer of 1994 as several incidents surrounding the hijacking of boats in Havana Harbor brought out people in demonstrations against the government for the first time since 1959. However, ultimately the Cuban leadership was successful in defusing the situation and beginning a slow turnaround of the economy that continues to the present day. The Cuban government opened up its ports in August 1994 and allowed thousands of discontented Cubans to go to the United States, where their arrival created a political crisis for President Bill Clinton. The crisis ended with a new immigration agreement between the United States and Cuba in September 1994, and the United States ended its long-standing policy of granting political asylum to all Cubans leaving the island. Under the new policy, refugees reaching U.S. soil are still granted the right to apply for asylum, but those intercepted at sea are returned to Cuba. A new agreement, signed in May 1995, allows for the legal immigration of up to 20,000 Cubans per year to the United States. In practice, the U.S. government has rarely permitted 20,000 Cubans per year to migrate, thus in effect continuing to encourage illegal emigration from the island. For many years, the two countries regularly discussed immigration issues, but in 2004 the George W. Bush administration suspended the talks indefinitely.

On the economic front, the Cuban government initiated a series of reforms that were designed to encourage private investment. The most important and successful project has been the reopening of private agricultural markets, where the producers sell directly to the public. Begun in late 1994, these markets resulted in a better food situation for the average Cuban and served to restore the value of the Cuban peso. Another important reform allowed the licensing of a wide range of individual service businesses, from tailors to barbers to small restaurants in private homes. A major economic decision in 1993 allowed for the legalization of the dollar for use by the Cuban population as a whole. The circulation of the dollar had become too widespread for the government to ignore, so the decision was made to legalize it for the purposes of better control. It is now estimated that $700 million to $950 million a year flows into the Cuban economy from Cubans living in the United States. Dollar legalization had a sound economic foundation, but the political and social ramifications have been negative. Pursuit of the dollar increases prostitution, overvalues jobs in the tourist sector, and privileges those in the society who have the good fortune to have relatives in the United States. At the end of 2004 the Cuban government ceased the use of the U.S. dollar as the currency of the tourism industry, instead adopting the convertible peso as the exclusive currency and pegging it at 82 U.S. cents per peso. One of Cuba's most dramatic economic reforms began in the sugar industry in 2002. Since that time, in an effort to dramatically reduce the historic role that sugar has played in the Cuban economy, seventy of the island's 150 sugar mills have been closed, 3.4 million acres of land have been

Mechanized Cuban-made sugarcane harvesters and their proud operators in Cuban cane field. *(Photo by Patrice Olsen and Harry E. Vanden)*

taken out of sugarcane (some 62 percent of the total land use previously devoted to the crop) and allotted to other agricultural uses, and the number of workers employed in sugar production has been reduced by one-quarter, with the 100,000 laid-off workers guaranteed their former wage as they retrain for new occupations. As a result sugar production is now just over 2 million tons per year.

The other aspect of Cuban economic recovery was the attraction of modest amounts of foreign capital into Cuba's main production areas of sugar and nickel mining. Although the investments were small, they helped Cuba reverse its economic freefall; with a gain of 2.5 percent in 1995 and more substantial gains of 7.8 percent and 2.5 percent in 1996 and 1997, respectively, Cuba's growth rate slowed in 1998 to 1.2 percent but rebounded to 6.2 percent in 1999. Between 2000 and 2006, the Cuban economy grew at an average annual rate of 3.0 percent. This growth has left the overall Cuban economy almost on par with its 1989 level. Despite the modest economic growth, the daily lives of average Cubans revolve around obtaining the basic necessities of life. Waiting in long lines to obtain rationed food and commuting by bicycle or waiting for inconsistent public transportation cuts sharply into worker productivity, which must improve if the Cuban economy is to prosper. These difficulties of life are not unique to Cuba, but what makes it an interesting place to study is that Cuba has gone through this dramatic crisis while trying to maintain its socialist principles. In Cuba, unlike the former communist countries in Europe, there is no full-scale embracing of a market economy. In speech after speech, Castro reiterated that Cuba would not return to a capitalist past. This means that the sacrifice has been shared. The free medical and educational systems have been maintained. In part because there has been shared sacrifice, there has been no social explosion, which many predicted. However, maintenance of the system remains a challenge in the face of growing inequalities caused by an economy dependent primarily on tourism and remittances and the pent-up material demands of the younger generation. The rule of Raul Castro since July 2006 has hinted at possible new economic strategies with more market orientation but few concrete changes have emerged.

Cuba underwent significant changes in the 1990s, but those changes generally did not extend to its relations with the United States. As Cuba plunged into economic crisis at the beginning of the decade, U.S. policy focused on attempting to prevent Cuba from reintegrating into the world economy. In 1992, Congress passed and President George H. W. Bush signed the Cuba Democracy Act, which sought to tighten the 30-year-old embargo by cutting off third-country trading to Cuba by U.S. companies. The legislation also specified that the only acceptable political change in Cuba was the total removal of the PCC from power. U.S. policy makers fully expected the revolutionary government to fall quickly in the absence of its socialist allies in Europe. When the collapse did not occur, new legislation drafted in Congress by Jesse Helms and Dan Burton sought an even tighter embargo on Cuba by punishing virtually every enterprise from any country that sought to make new investments on the island. Initially opposed by the Clinton administration because of vigorous opposition from U.S. allies, the Helms-Burton legislation was passed into law in 1996 following an incident in the Straits of Florida when the Cuban Air Force shot down airplanes of a Miami-based exile group that had entered Cuban airspace. Tensions between the two governments also grew over continued U.S. government support for groups seeking the overthrow of the Cuban government. However, opposition to the embargo within the United States continued to build. In early 1998, the U.S. Chamber of Commerce began a public campaign against the embargo, citing worldwide opposition to it and its inconsistency in light of U.S. trade with China and Vietnam, other countries where the Communist Party remains in power. As a result of the campaign, many Republican lawmakers, especially in Midwest farm states, began calling for a lessening of the embargo to allow for the sale of food and medicines. In 2000, legislation permitting the sale of food and medicine was passed by the U.S. Congress and signed by President Clinton. By 2007 Cuba was purchasing over $400 million per year in U.S. agricultural products, placing it in the top twenty-five receivers of such products among U.S. trading partners. However, Cuba received no reciprocity of access to U.S. markets other than a limited number of U.S. citizens travelling to Cuba and U.S. citizens sending remittances to relatives in Cuba. It remained the basic policy of the U.S. government to work for the overthrow of the Cuban socialist system, and the Bush administration stepped up those efforts on a number of fronts. In 2002, the U.S. interests section in Havana became more bold in its cooperation with Cuban opponents of the government and then in 2004 stepped up its effort to tighten the embargo. Travel of U.S. citizens to the island, including that of Cuban Americans, was sharply curtailed; and efforts were made to significantly reduce the amout of U.S. remittances sent to the island.

Cuba entered the new millennium as controversial as ever. Fidel Castro, now the aging revolutionary hospitalized with a serious illness, commands attention and respect around the world. The United States, the world's only remaining superpower, still works for his destruction. Cuba has changed dramatically in many ways since 1989 as it constructs a new economy out of the ruins of its ties with the socialist East. Steadfastly refusing to renounce its past, Cuba seeks to define socialism for the new century by retaining the significant social achievements of the revolution in the framework of an economy fueled by foreign investment and private initiative. It is not yet clear that Cuba can successfully find that path, especially in the context of a U.S.-dominated world; but the Cuban Revolution has successfully defied the odds so many times before that betting against its success may be a risky proposition.

Chronology

1898 Cuba achieves independence from Spain during Spanish-American War; Cuba occupied by U.S. troops until 1902

1901 Platt Amendment to new Cuban constitution gives the United States the right to intervene in Cuba to "maintain government adequate for the protection of life, property, and individual liberty"

1906 American governor appointed to replace Cuban president

1925 Gerardo Machado becomes president and rules in dictatorial manner

1933 Machado overthrown by popular revolt

1934 U.S. President Franklin Roosevelt abrogates Platt Amendment, provisional government overthrown by "sergeants' revolt" led by Fulgencio Batista

1940 Batista elected president under a new constitution

1944 Opposition candidate Grau San Martín elected president

1952 Batista takes over government in a coup

1953 Young rebels, led by Fidel Castro, attack Moncada military barracks in Santiago and are captured and jailed

1955 Batista declares amnesty, Castro flees to Mexico

1956 In July, rebels led by Castro travel by boat to east end of Cuba; only a dozen escape battles with armed forces and take refuge in Sierra Maestra Mountains

1958 Guerrilla war starting in mountains spreads and defeats Batista's force at end of year

1959 Castro creates coalition government in January; in June, moderates in cabinet resign, leaving effective control to Castro and the 26th of July movement

1961 In January, United States breaks relations with Cuba and imposes trade embargo; invasion at Bay of Pigs by CIA supported by Cuban exiles defeated by Cuban army

1962 United States confronts Soviet Union over its placement of missiles in Cuba; "Missile Crisis" ends with Soviets pulling missiles out in exchange for U.S. promise never to invade Cuba

1965 Cuban Communist Party (PCC) formed

1970 Failed 10-million-ton sugar harvest leads to economic and political reform

1976 New system of local, provincial, and national assemblies creates People's Power

1986 PCC begins "rectification" plan in response to economic slowdown and bureaucratic inefficiencies

1989 Collapse of communist regimes in Eastern Europe begins process of economic reform

1994 Confrontation with the United States over refugee exodus; private agricultural markets reinstated
1998 Visit of Pope John Paul II
2004 George W. Bush administration institutes new measures to tighten the U.S. embargo
2006 Fidel Castro enters hospital with undisclosed illness, presidential duties temporarily transferred to Raul Castro
2008 Citing reasons of health Fidel Castro steps down as Cuban president while remaining head of the Communist Party. Raul Castro is elected to a five year presidential term.

Bibliography

Anderson, Jon. *Che Guevara: A Revolutionary Life*. New York: Grove Press, 1997.

Azicri, Max, and Elsie Deal, eds. *Cuban Socialism in The New Century: Adversity, Survival, and Renewal*. Gainesville: University of Florida Press, 2004.

Blight, James and Philip Brenner. *Sad and Luminous Days: Cuba's Struggle with the Super Powers after the Missile Crisis*. Lanham, MD: Rowman and Littlefield, 2007.

Brenner, Philip, et.al. *A Contemporary Cuba Reader: Reinventing the Revolution*. Lanham, MD: Rowman and Littlefield, 2007.

Castro, Fidel, and Frei Betto. *Fidel and Religion: Castro Talks on Revolution and Religion with Frei Betto*. New York: Simon and Schuester, 1987.

Chaffee, Wilber, and Gary Prevost, eds. *Cuba—A Different America*. Savage, MD: Rowman & Littlefield, 1992.

Deutschmann, David, and Deborah Shnookal. *Fidel Castro Reader*. Melbourne: Ocean Books, 2007.

Erisman, Michael. *Cuba's Foreign Relations in a Post-Soviet World*. Gainesville: University of Florida Press, 2002.

Guevara, Ernesto Ché. *Episodes of the Cuban Revolutionary War*. New York: Pathfinder Press, 1996.

Hart, Armando. *Aldabonazo: Inside the Cuban Revolutionary Underground*. New York: Pathfinder Press, 2004.

Kirk, John. *Between God and Party: Religion and Politics in Revolutionary Cuba*. Tampa: University of South Florida Press, 1989.

Luis, Julio Garcia. *Cuban Revolution Reader*. Melbourne: Ocean Press, 2007.

Matthews, Herbert. *Revolution in Cuba*. New York: Charles Scribner's, 1975.

Morales Dominguez, Esteban, and Gary Prevost. *U.S.–Cuban Relations: A Critical History*. Lanham, MD: Lexington Books, 2008.

Murphy, Catherine. *Cultivating Havana: Urban Agriculture and Food Security in Years of Crisis*. San Francisco: Food First Books, 1999.

Pérez, Louis A. *Cuba: Between Reform and Revolution*. New York: Oxford University Press, 1988.

Roman, Peter. *Cuba's Experience with Representative Government*. Boulder, CO: Westview Press, 1999.

Sanchez, German. *Cuba and Venezuela: An Insight into Two Revolutions*. Melbourne: Ocean Press, 2007.

Saney, Isaac. *Cuba—A Revolution in Motion*. London: Zed Books, 2004.

Sarduy, Pedro Pérez, and Jean Stubbs. *AfroCuba: An Anthology of Cuban Writing on Race, Politics, and Culture*. Melbourne: Ocean Press, 1993.

Smith, Wayne S. *The Closest of Enemies: A Personal and Diplomatic Account of U.S.–Cuban Relations since 1957*. New York: Norton, 1987.

Stricker, Pamela. *Toward a Culture of Nature: Sustainable Development and Environmental Policy in Cuba*. Lanham, MD: Lexington Books, 2007.

Whiteford, Linda, and Laurence Branch. *Primary Health Care in Cuba: The Other Revolution*. Lanham, MD: Rowman and Littlefield, 2007.

FILMS AND VIDEOS

Fidel. Cuba, 2000.
If You Only Understood. Cuba, 1998.

The King Does Not Lie: The Initiation of a Shango Priest. United States, 1992.
Nothing. Cuba, 2001.
Memories of Underdevelopment. Cuba, 1968.
The Uncompromising Revolution. United States, 1992.

WEBSITES

www.granma.cu *Granma International* (newspaper of the Communist Party).
www.radiohc.org/index.html Radio Havana.
www.cubagov.cu Cuban government (official).

VENEZUELA

GUYANA

SURINAME

FRENCH
GUIANA

COLOMBIA

Amazon River

AMAZON RAINFOREST

Recife

PERU

*BRAZILIAN
HIGHLANDS*

San Francisco River

Salvador

BOLIVIA

Brasília

CHILE

Belo Horizonte

Rio de Janeiro

PARAGUAY

São Paulo

Map of
BRAZIL

N

W ✶ E

S

150 0 150 300 Miles

Scale 1:24,000,000

URUGUAY

ARGENTINA

FOURTEEN

Brazil

Wilber Albert Chaffee

Introduction

A continental nation, Brazil dominates South America, occupying half of the territory and bordering on all the other South American nations except Ecuador and Chile. One of the giants among nations, Brazil is fourth largest in area, the fourth largest democracy, and the largest Catholic country. If Brazil were turned 180 degrees on the globe, its southernmost point would reach as far north as the border between North and South Carolina. The Amazon River, draining much of the land east of the Andes, carries twelve times the volume of water of the Mississippi and is navigable by ocean freighter across the width of Brazil, making the Peruvian city of Iquitos a seaport. The Amazon, itself, is the world's largest rain forest.

With 190 million people, half of South America's population, Brazil's population is the fifth largest in the world. Starting originally as a group of Portuguese colonies, today's population is a mix of the indigenous Amer-Indians, descendents of slaves brought from Africa, members of originally European immigrant families, especially Portuguese, Germans, Lebanese, and Italians, and over a million of Japanese ancestry. As a result, Brazil is second only to Nigeria in terms of persons of African ancestry and has the largest Japanese population outside of Japan. Sixteen of Brazil's cities have a population of a million or greater. The metropolitan areas of Rio de Janeiro and São Paulo have 11 million and 18 million people, respectively.

Brazil is one of the BRIC countries (Brazil, Russia, India, China) that are expected to be among the world's six largest economies by 2050. It publishes 60 percent of the literature of South America and has an important national literature generally

Thanks to Diva for careful editorial work.

unknown in much of the rest of the world. Authors include Euclides da Cunha, Machado de Assis, Rachel de Queiroz, Carlos Drummond de Andrade, Guimarães Rosa, Jorge Amado, and Clarice Lispector. Brazil's Globo television system is one of the largest commercial networks in the world, with its programming going into Portugal and Africa.

Proud of their country, Brazilians will tell you "God is a Brazilian."

A Brief Political History

European contact with what is today Brazil came with the landing in 1500 of Pedro Alvares Cabral at Coroa Vermelha in today's state of Bahia while sailing from Portugal to Asia via the Cape of Good Hope, and the first permanent Portuguese settlement was founded in 1532 at São Vicente in São Paulo. Subsequently, Portugal established colonies, called *capitanias* (captaincies), to harvest brazilwood for textile dyes, beginning in the northeast, the territory that bulges east toward Africa. Brazilian land proved to have good soil to expand the cultivation of sugarcane, brought from the Azores, which was followed by a massive slave trade from Portuguese colonies in Africa to tend the sugarcane and its processing in giant *engenhos* (sugar mills).

Political power was centered in *municipios* (municipalities) dominated by agricultural elites, who also controlled the politics of the captaincies. Although the Portuguese crown eventually established a viceroyalty, first in Bahia and later in Rio de Janeiro, the captaincies essentially reported directly to Lisbon. Border conflicts developed with Argentina, beginning a tradition of competition over leadership in South America.

In 1808, as a result of Napoleon's invasion and conquest of Iberia, the Portuguese royal family fled from Lisbon and established the new capital of their empire in Rio de Janeiro. For the first time, national politics in Brazil was centralized, technical schools were established, and printing presses brought in. A sense of nationhood began to develop as the captaincies became provinces. With the defeat of Napoleon, the royal family returned to Lisbon in 1821, leaving the crown prince, Dom Pedro de Bragança, as regent. At the urging of the Brazilians, Dom Pedro proclaimed the independence of Brazil in 1822, becoming its first emperor, Dom Pedro I. Under the constitution of 1824, the emperor had "moderating power," allowing him to "watch over the maintenance of the independence, equilibrium, and harmony of the other political powers," a power that allowed him to dissolve the congress and form a new government. The independence under the emperor maintained Brazil as a single country, avoiding the disintegration that happened with Spanish colonies, and the provinces now became states.

In 1831 Dom Pedro I abdicated in favor of his 5-year-old son, Dom Pedro II, and the country was ruled by a regency until 1840, when the young emperor, at the age of 15, assumed full royal powers. Dom Pedro II reigned rather than ruled. Although the country was centralized in name, control from Rio de Janeiro was light-handed, seldom interfering with the politics of the states. Two political parties developed, the Liberal Party and the Conservative Party, representing the patriarchal oligarchies that controlled the states. The parties alternated in forming the federal government and served at the emperor's pleasure.

During the later part of Portuguese colonial rule and much of the Brazilian monarchy, the British dominated Brazilian trade and its economy under special treaty rights. They supplied English manufactured goods and bought most of Brazil's exports, which were primary products, especially cotton, sugar, and minerals.

One of the few national actions was the war with Paraguay (1865–1870), which gave what may be the first real sense of nationalism, a national military hero, the Duque de Caxias, Luiz Alves de Lima e Silva, and the first counterweight to the extreme federalism of Brazil in the form of an active national military. The Paraguayan War also highlighted the essential military weakness of Brazil, its lack of infrastructure, especially in its interior, and the difficulties in executing a war even against a nation as small and weak as Paraguay. The need for national economic development, as a result, came from the military, which saw itself as the only force really interested in the good of the nation as a whole.

Slavery became a continuingly contentious political issue, with the British pressuring Brazil to end the slave trade; and in 1871, the Law of the Free Womb made anyone born after that date a freeman. Professional groups from the cities and military positivists, followers of French Positivist leader Auguste Comte who believed that scientific methods could be applied to society and to politics, led the fight for emancipation of the slaves, establishment of the republic, and development. In 1888, while the emperor was visiting Europe, his daughter, Princess Isabel, as regent and under pressure from the army that had declared that hunting escaped slaves was beneath its honor, abolished slavery. The following year the military, headed by Marshal Manuel Deodoro da Fonseca, overthrew the monarchy and declared Brazil a republic, and the positivist slogan "Order and Progress" became part of the new flag.

The republic adopted a constitution, modeled on the American constitution, with a nationally elected president permitted one 4-year term. Federal funds began to be used to create a national infrastructure of roads and railways, initiating a long period of economic growth. By 1894, politics became the politics of the governors, with no national political parties, each state having a Republican Party. By tacit agreement between the two major states, São Paulo and Minas Gerais, the presidency was traded between them every 4 years in *"café com leite"* (coffee with milk) politics; São Paulo's economy dominated with the growing of coffee, while Minas Gerais produced dairy goods. In this strongly federal system, the congress served as a meeting place where legislation covered only those points agreed to by the states in negotiation with the federal president. Although there was a federal military, the states all had their own militias under the command of the governors, in some cases rivaling the national army in power. Opposition to the power of the two states included attempts by Brazil's best-known statesman, Rui Barbosa, who had been a part of the Second Hague Conference in 1907, to win the presidency. Other opposition came from a group of military officers, dominated by young lieutenants (*tenentes*), who revolted against the government in the 1920s but failed to overturn the system. The 1929 Depression brought about the loss of income from coffee exports and increasing discontent with the traditional politics of the Old Republic. Defeated in 1930 as presidential candidate, Getúlio Vargas of the state of Rio Grande do Sul, along with dissident military including many of the *tenentes*, successfully ousted the old government and inaugurated the Second Republic. Vargas was made provisional president by the congress.

Vargas dominated Brazilian politics from 1930 until 1954, navigating among conflicting interests of the states, differing military factions, and ideological political parties such as the *Integralistas*, modeled on Europe's fascism, and the Communists, led by Plinio Salgado and by former *tenente* leader Luis Carlos Prestes, respectively. Centralization of Brazilian politics became a reality for the first time since the early 1800s as Vargas replaced elected governors who did not support him with appointed *interventors* but faced a rebellion in 1932 that lasted several months when the state of São Paulo reacted against the imposition of *tenente* João Alberto as *interventor*. Vargas, who believed in the virtues of a rural culture and economy, faced a strong internal migration of agricultural workers who were streaming to the cities. As increasing urban population without jobs threatened political order,he sought ways of increasing industrial employment to absorb the growing urban workforce, a process that developed into a strategy of import substitution, reflecting his xenophobia. This fit the nationalist and developmentalist sentiments of the military, which increasingly became the major support of Vargas. In 1934, a new constitution was written and the congress elected Vargas to the presidency. The constitution, which did not allow for reelection, called for elections in 1938. As the election approached, political parties began to support candidates; but in 1937, backed by the army, Vargas declared the *Estado Novo* (New State), making official his dictatorship. He presented a new constitution, eliminated political parties, and further increased his authority by centralizing fiscal power. A corporative system of state-sponsored unions kept labor both under control and supportive of the government and a system of labor courts, modeled on the Italian system, was created to eliminate industrial conflict. Both strikes and lockouts were declared against the public interest, while other legislation established a minimum wage and protection for labor. Vargas cultivated his image as the *pai dos pobres* (father of the poor).

As World War II approached, Vargas sensed the eventual victory of the Allies and negotiated Brazilian involvement in the war with the United States. With American financial and technical support, he gained the construction of the first integrated steel plant of Latin America at Volta Redonda, in the state of Rio de Janeiro, and the training of the Brazilian Expeditionary Force, which then sailed to Europe and fought alongside American troops in the Italian campaign.

The involvement of the Brazilian military with U.S. troops created a long-term relationship between officers of the two militaries. The technological and industrial resources available to the American troops impressed upon the Brazilians the need for accelerated economic development. Additionally, strong friendships were developed that extended into the mid-1980s and resulted in close cooperation between the armed forces along with acceptance of North American views on global ideological conflict.

A strong argument erupted, dominating economic policy debate in the late 1940s. Industrialists, with Roberto Simonsen as their spokesperson, wanted protection from foreign competition, including high tariff barriers and restriction of the entry of foreign capital. Opposing him, economist Eugenio Gudin believed that Brazil's future lay in the export of primary products and called for low tariffs and foreign investments. The debate took place in the newspapers, but Simonsen's position mirrored the sentiments of Vargas and the arguments coming from the Economic Commission for Latin America (ECLA) in Santiago, Chile, augmenting the import substitution strategy of economic development.

Democratic Interlude

At a time when Brazilian troops were fighting in Europe against dictatorship, the *Estado Novo* of Vargas seemed out of place to many Brazilians and pressure for elections built. Vargas began the process of developing two political parties, encouraging the organization of the Social Democratic Party (PSD) by a group of *interventors* representing the interests of their states but also including industrialists and large landowners, and the Brazilian Labor Party (PTB) built around urban labor and a system of control over workers. Opposition to Vargas, including many of the *tenentes*, created the National Democratic Union (UDN). General Eurico Dutra was launched as a candidate of a PSD–PTB coalition, while the UDN nominated *Brigadeiro* Eduardo Gomes, a *tenente* hero and head of the air force during World War II. Vargas was forced to resign in October 1945, and Dutra was elected president by popular vote. A new constitution, written in 1946, completed the move to democratic rule.

Vargas returned to the presidency in 1950, winning election as the PSD–PTB candidate, easily defeating Gomes' second attempt as a candidate. His term in office was marked by a tilt toward economic nationalism, especially the creation of Petrobras, the national oil company. The Vargas presidency was full of allegations of corruption, much of them coming from the pen and voice of Carlos Lacerda, newspaper publisher and governor of Rio de Janeiro. Told by the military leadership that he was no longer acceptable as president, Vargas committed suicide in the presidential palace in 1954, leaving behind a statement blaming his death on a "sea of mud" and a "campaign of international groups joined with national groups" seeking control of Brazilian resources. Vargas became a political martyr, which turned the tables on his tormentors.

Scheduled presidential elections went forward, the PSD–PTB candidate, Minas Gerais governor Juscelino Kubitschek, winning. Kubitschek, a physician of Czech ancestry, campaigned promising "fifty years progress in five." With his inauguration in 1956, he quickly set out a "program of targets," including the construction of a new capital, christened Brasília, to be located in the country's interior. Much of the economic program was authored by Celso Furtado, an economist who had been working at ECLA. An automobile industry came into being, encouraged by special treatment of foreign manufacturers, who were given a protected market, bringing a major surge of import substitution, while a program of roads and other infrastructure charted new routes throughout Brazil. The fast-paced growth brought employment, increasing inflation, and charges of corruption. Kubitschek finished his term with a display of confidence and accomplishment, moving the capital from Rio de Janeiro to the newly constructed Brasília. However, rural unrest was beginning, and labor felt left out.

In early 1961, UDN candidate and São Paulo governor Janio Quadros became Brazil's new president. He had campaigned with a broom as the symbol of his pledge to sweep the country clean of corruption. A major attempt to stabilize the economy failed, mostly due to the refusal of the Congress to approve harsh austerity measures. In August, after only 7 months in office, Quadros tendered his resignation, apparently in an attempt to gain stronger presidential powers, but was surprised when the Congress accepted it. João "Jango" Goulart, who had been minister of labor under Vargas and Kubitschek's vice president, had been elected vice president again under Quadros. At the time of the president's resignation, Goulart was visiting the People's Republic of China, lending credence to belief that he was sympathetic to communist ideas. Goulart was sworn in as president, but dissatisfaction with Goulart, the result of recession, increasing inflation, fears of his leftist rhetoric, and his failure to punish a military mutiny, resulted in a joint military–civilian coup at the end of March 1964, a coup hailed by the United States as saving Brazil from communism.

The Military in Politics

The involvement of the military in Brazilian politics certainly did not begin with the 1964 coup. The history of Brazil includes intimate inclusion of the military beginning with the Paraguayan war in the middle of the nineteenth century. Later, military officers eliminated the monarchy, taking over the presidency for the first two postimperial administrations, those of Generals Deodoro da Fonseca and Floriano Peixoto. At that time, the officers assumed the *poder moderador* (moderating power) earlier exercised by the emperor, beginning a long history of insertion into politics. This was followed by the *tenente* uprisings, first in 1922 with the "18 of the Fort" at Copacabana in Rio de Janeiro and 2 years later with the 1924 revolt centered in São Paulo. The revolt was followed by the march of the young military officers, led by Captain Luis Carlos Prestes, through the interior of the country, trying to overthrow the landed oligarchy in an attempt to correct perceived maladies in the political system. It was the same beliefs that led to a split in military ranks in 1930 and support for the overthrow of the lame-duck presidency of Washington Luís, placing Getúlio Vargas in Rio de Janeiro's Catete Palace (then Brazil's White House).

Later, the military became the opposition to Vargas, and every presidential election from 1945 until 1980 had a military officer as one of the two major candidates. When Vargas was pressured out of the presidency in 1945, his elected replacement was army Chief of Staff General Eurico Dutra, opposed by *Brigadeiro* Eduardo Gomes, survivor of the Copacabana Fort uprising of 1922. Four years later, Vargas won the presidency, with Gomes again being defeated. In 1955, Kubitschek was elected president, opposed by former *tenente* leader Marshal Juarez Távora and 4 years later, Jânio Quadros won the presidency against opposition candidate Marshal Henrique Lott.

Generals as Presidents

Following the overthrow of President Goulart in 1964, the Congress, pressured by the military, voted to make army Chief of Staff General Humberto Castelo Branco president. He abolished old political parties and replaced them with an official party, the National Renovating Alliance (ARENA), and a single opposition party, the Brazilian Democratic Movement (MDB). Political power was centralized in the executive, who could make laws without the consent of Congress, and Congress was temporarily closed. The election of presidents was transferred from popular vote to indirect election by an electoral college made up of members of Congress, and the election of governors and mayors of major cities was also made indirect. A major shift in power occurred when the federal government reduced the distribution of tax revenues, retaining more in Brasília and controlling expenditures. Before 1964, close to 55 percent of federally collected revenues were passed on to the states and municipalities; in the next 20 years, that figure dropped to 30 percent. During the military regime (1964–1985), elections continued and generals who became president took off their uniforms and served only 5-year terms. The military manipulated election laws, created and joined states, and used the economy in order to maintain control, especially where their dominance of voting in the smaller northeastern states meant a majority in the Senate.

Castelo Branco began the process of taming inflation, then running at more than 50 percent a year, by fiscal reform and monetary restriction. A veteran of the Brazilian Expeditionary Force in Italy, he aligned Brazil with the policies of the United States in a doctrine of national security that included repression of suspected communists. A series of institutional acts, decrees that bypassed legislative approval, centralized control of the government and suspended political rights for many prominent citizens.

A hard-line military faction, critical of the administration of Castelo Branco and its economic reforms, controlled the next election and made General Arthur Costa e Silva president in 1967. He brought a new economic team into the government, headed by a young professor of economics from the University of São Paulo, Antonio Delfim Netto. Delfim Netto increased available credit, especially in agriculture, and began a process of fast economic growth that lasted from 1968 to 1974, averaging almost 11 percent a year, the "Brazilian Miracle." Production costs were reduced by control of wages, and exports were promoted. A massive cerebral hemorrhage incapacitated the president in mid-1969, but the military leadership refused to allow the civilian vice president to take office and instead selected General Emílio Médici as the new president.

Médici continued the economics of Delfim Netto and met opposition to the government, including urban guerrilla warfare and the kidnapping of foreign diplomats, with increased repression, including the disappearance of suspects. At the same time, the rapid growth of the economy brought increased social mobility and national pride. The continued growth of the economy served to legitimize military rule despite a rising vote for the opposition MDB.

General Ernesto Geisel, part of the same military group as former president Castelo Branco, became president in 1974, announcing a policy of moving the country back toward democracy. He brought in a new economic team that faced problems of increasing inflation and petroleum price increases. International borrowing and increased investment by the state sought to rekindle the growth pattern, as the opposition politicians grew stronger. State-owned companies dominated the economy, running much of industry, mining, and banking. Geisel restored the political rights of many who had been exiled, only to find them winning contested elections for governorships and other offices. General João Figueiredo, selected by Geisel to succeed him in 1979, faced continuing deterioration of the economy, with slowed growth and increasing inflation. A serious recession began in 1982 as foreign investment stopped and the servicing of Brazil's debt, now the largest among developing countries, overwhelmed the budget. A new independent labor union formed under the leadership of autoworker Luiz Inácio da Silva, popularly known as "Lula," breaking the control that the government had maintained over workers since the administration of Vargas. Professional groups and the Catholic Church openly expressed the realities of military repression of civilians.

A new election law attempted to split the opposition by allowing new political parties to form and required all parties to have the word *Party* in their name. ARENA became the Social Democratic Party (PDS) and the MDB became the Brazilian Democratic Movement Party (PMDB). At the same time, new parties were organized. Lula organized the Workers' Party (PT) and Leonel Brizola, governor of Rio de Janeiro, founded the Party of Democratic Workers (PDT). Massive popular demonstrations, *diretas ja!* (Direct Elections Now!), filled the streets with demands for election of the next president by popular vote. Figueiredo refused, and the PDS split over the issue, with some members leaving the party to form the Party of the Liberal Front (PFL). In the next presidential election, both candidates were civilians and the opposition won the indirect election with a coalition of the PMDB and the PFL, called the Democratic Alliance.

The "New Republic"

The day before the inauguration in March 1985, president-elect Tancredo Neves of the PMDB underwent emergency surgery and vice president-elect, José Sarney, temporarily took over the office, shortly thereafter assuming the presidency when Neves died. Brazil now had a civilian president who had earlier been head of the military-aligned PDS and a congress controlled by the leadership that had opposed the military.

Sarney faced a serious economic crisis of high inflation and slow growth. A group of young economists came forward with new theories on how to halt the inflation without the orthodox recessionary measures normally prescribed. At the end of February 1986, the theories were put into effect with the Cruzado Plan, which froze wages and prices while increasing the income of the lowest-paid workers. The resulting new demands brought employment as industry used existing capacity for production. Despite recommendations of economists that the plan be modified because demand exceeded productive capacity, Sarney refused. The Plan's immediate success catapulted Sarney's popularity, while preparations went ahead for an election of congressional deputies, many senators, and governors. The great importance of the election was that the combined deputies and senators would also become a constituent assembly, writing a new constitution to replace the military's. Sarney's allies overwhelmingly won the election, but the Cruzado Plan collapsed immediately after as inflation soared and growth came to a halt by the end of the year.

The new 1988 constitution provided liberal benefits for many formerly left out of social services and distributed a larger portion of the federal tax receipts to the states and municipalities. A split in the PMDB resulted in the creation of the Brazilian Social Democratic Party (PSDB), led by senators displeased with the rightward swing of the PMDB resulting from former ARENA members who had switched parties. Sarney, who had successfully campaigned for a 5-year presidency (later changed to 4 years), completed his term in March 1990, while inflation soared to over 80 percent a month.

The new president, Fernando Collor de Mello, had beaten labor leader and organizer of the PT Lula da Silva in the first direct election for a president since 1960, winning 52.6 percent of the runoff election. Governor of the small northeastern state of Alagoas, Collor was the youngest president in Brazil's history, campaigning against corruption in politics and established politicians and running as a candidate of a new party he created solely for the election. He promised that no one who had served previous governments would be in his cabinet. His most audacious appointment was a 36-year-old woman, Zélia Cardoso de Mello, as minister of economics, a combination of the former ministries of finance and planning.

To control inflation, Collor immediately froze all savings accounts in the country, temporarily lowering inflation. Additionally, he believed that Brazil's import substitution strategy needed to be replaced with an economy open to the global market and began a process of privatization of the state-owned industries, including the National Steel Company at Volta Redonda. A scheduled lowering of tariffs on imports reduced the barriers that protected Brazilian industry from international competition. Thus, Brazil embarked on a new economic course, sloughing off decades of state-led growth and protectionism.

Collor, secure in his popular election and coming into office as the Cold War's abrupt ending invalidated the national security doctrine, began to reduce the influence of the military, including cutting its budget and eliminating nuclear weapons research. He also continued reducing the long-standing antagonisms with Argentina. In the spring of 1991, Collor signed the Treaty of Asunción, creating a common market among the countries of Argentina, Uruguay, Paraguay, and Brazil. Known by its abbreviated name, Mercosur (Market of the Southern Cone) effectively increased the internal market for the products of the two largest economies in South America.

As the economic stabilization policies of the new government proved ineffective, inflation returned. In spring 1992, Collor's younger brother, Pedro, publicly stated that the president was receiving funds in exchange for political favors. A congressional investigation produced evidence that resulted in Collor's impeachment, followed in December by his resignation and a vote by the Congress to remove his political rights for 10 years. The impeachment proceedings of Collor were the first in Latin American history in which a president had been legally removed from office through constitutional processes. Brazil's fledgling democratic institutions had passed a major test.

Vice President Itamar Franco, succeeding to the presidency, continued Collor's privatization initiative and other stabilization programs. The most important action he took was the appointment of Senator Fernando Henrique Cardoso, first as foreign minister, then as finance minister. The president gave Cardoso full support in a program to end the long-standing inflation that had plagued Brazil for decades and was then running at more than 20 percent a month. The new finance minister brought together a team of economists, many of whom had developed the Cruzado Plan, and with them instituted a new stabilization program, the Real Plan, named after the new currency put into circulation. By July 1994, the Real Plan had brought inflation down dramatically and Cardoso became a candidate for the presidency in the fall elections.

In the election, the only two significant candidates were Cardoso, leader of the left-of-center PSDB in coalition with the right-of-center PFL, and PT candidate Lula da Silva, who had narrowly lost to Collor in the previous election. Cardoso had an international reputation as a scholar, having coauthored a book in the 1960s that examined the problems of economic development in Latin America in relation to its dependence on the capitalist economy of the industrialized nations of Europe and North America. Cardoso won the election and enjoyed marked popularity as the continued success of the Real Plan meant a better standard of living for much of the population, especially the poor.

Cardoso came to office as the man who defeated inflation, and his continuing legitimacy largely depended on continuing success at holding inflation down. Successive governments in Brazil had used inflation to pay for budget deficits, and the deficits in turn fed inflation. A major issue has been the necessity of reforming the budget in order to hold down inflation. Even though the government's coalition in Congress enjoyed sufficient votes to pass reforming legislation, party discipline was not adequate for fiscal reform as deputies often voted contrary to their parties' position. The policy of privatization continued during the Cardoso administration, effectively ending public sector industry. Congress did agree to amend the constitution to permit the president, governors, and mayors to run for a second consecutive term, a break with Brazil's past and allowing Cardoso to run for reelection in 1998, claiming the need for a second term to finish the job of restructuring the economy. Cardoso's presidency ended with major problems of unemployment and lack of growth unresolved, as well as a high level of federal debt.

Lula da Silva handily won the 2002 presidential election despite fears of some that he would abandon the reforms of the previous government. The new administration exhibited strong continuity in terms of inflation control and fiscal austerity while launching the program *Fome Zero* (No Hunger) to guarantee sufficient food to the nation's poorest sectors. He constructed a congressional coalition sufficient to amend the constitution, bringing social security and tax reforms that had not been previously possible. At the same time, he began a drive to expand Brazil's exports, especially to South Africa, India, and China.

Political Economy

In many ways, Brazil's politics have been defined by its economy. Initial European interest in Brazil, especially by the Portuguese, focused on the export of primary products including brazilwood as a dye, sugar, gold, diamonds, coffee, and rubber. By the first part of the twentieth century, coffee had become synonymous with images of Brazil. Today, primary products remain a major part of the export economy, with iron ore, soybeans, orange juice, and frozen chickens surpassing coffee.

However, industrial manufactures now exceed the value of primary products, with exports of steel, airplanes, automobiles and automotive parts, consumer durables, and electronic equipment.

By the 1930s Brazilian economists and planners began to realize that the future development of the country required diversification and industrialization. The ability to compete in the international market of industrial goods was questioned, and Brazil began implementing a strategy of import substitution with its allied policy of trade barriers, including high tariffs, to protect the new domestic industries. Brazilian governments, starting with construction of the National Steel Company at Volta Redonda in the 1940s, began the development of state-owned industry, soon followed by the creation of a state-owned oil company, Petrobras. Electric power and telephones also were taken over by the government, along with major investment in transportation and many other areas. The government became the major owner of industry and employer in the country as the import substitution strategy was pushed with low-interest loans.

The import substitution strategy of Vargas continued with the Kubitschek government, now augmented by theoretical studies from ECLA, promoted by Brazilian economist Celso Furtado, which claimed lack of development resulted from structural dependence on Europe and the United States. In the private sector, the development of the automobile industry brought with it many associated companies as parts suppliers and service industries grew. Brazil went from being a supplier of coffee to being a highly diverse industrialized country, producing aircraft, weaponry, subway cars, electronics, pharmaceuticals, petrochemicals, textiles, and footwear.

The military, despite its opposition to Vargas and dislike of Furtado, continued and expanded the strategy of import substitution, giving the federal government control over a major portion of the economy. Diversification of agricultural exports accompanied diversification in import substitution industry. The military gave negative interest loans to agribusiness for expansion and new products, knowing that it was the fastest way of increasing exports. Part of the increase came with the development of the alcohol-from-sugar program for automobile fuel in response to the dramatic rise in imported petroleum prices in the 1970s.

During the late 1960s and early 1970s, the rapidity of economic growth earned Brazil considerable international attention. The growth was financed by reducing the labor value of production through limiting wage increases, funds from the national pension program, and foreign loans. Beset with persistent payment problems, Brazil turned to foreign borrowing in the 1970s. Banks pushed loans as a result of the glut of petrodollars they were accumulating from oil producers who had raised prices dramatically. The ability to borrow ended when the oil price collapse of the late 1970s dried up the ready availability of foreign loan capital.

Inflation became a characteristic of the Brazilian economy, fed in part by federal and state expenditures exceeding tax revenues. Much of industry was oligopolistic, faced little competition domestically, and was protected by high tariffs from less expensive foreign products. As a result, prices could be set to guarantee profits without regard to quality or costs. Wages were indexed to inflation, their value set by government standards rather than by collective bargaining.

During the 1980s, the economy stagnated as inflation increased, the worst conditions since the 1929 Depression, creating the "lost decade." The combination of depression and inflation was a major factor in the loss of power of the military and its decision to allow a return to democratic rule. The civilian governments of Sarney and Collor tried unsuccessfully to stabilize the economy with various antiinflation plans.

The Collor government began a major change in Brazil's economic policies, privatizing state-owned companies, inviting greater foreign investment, and lowering tariff barriers to imports. The opening to the international market reversed a 60-year policy of autarky, publicly owned industry, and import substitution. These actions continued under the brief administration of Franco and were followed by the first successful stabilization effort headed by Cardoso—an action that propelled him into the presidency. Among Cardoso's initiatives was the expansion of Mercosur, bringing in Chile and Bolivia as associate members, with the objective of eventually including all of South America in a common market.

To the surprise of many, President da Silva continued many of the economic policies of the Cardoso administration. Brazil continued the effort to expand Mercosur to all of South America and became the cochair with the United States on negotiations for the Free Trade Area of the Americas but led opposition to it on the basis of American protectionism. Along with India, Brazil organized opposition to a new round of World Trade Organization talks due to the failure of Europe, the United States, and Japan to reduce agricultural subsidizes and open their markets to goods from developing countries. The alcohol from sugar programs expanded, giving Brazil an important initiative in reducing greenhouse gases, and cars were designed to use it for fuel. Greatly increased exports moved Brazil into a positive current account, especially supplying China with soybeans and iron ore.

Geography of Inequality

Brazil is divided into states, varying geographically in size from the huge state of Amazonas to small states like Alagoas. Populations of the states also represent great differences, with a population of more than 30 million in the state of São Paulo and only 300,000 in Amapá. Elected governors and state legislatures govern states, which in turn are divided into some 5000 municipalities, in some way equivalent to U.S. counties, each with its mayor and municipal council. Brasília is the site of the federal government, located in the Federal District near the center of the southern part of the country. Today, the Federal District has over 2 million people and has become a hub that connects the interior of the country with the industrialized southeast.

The Brazilian Institute of Geography and Statistics (IBGE) divides the country into five regions: North, Northeast, Southeast, Center-West, and South. The North, comprised of the states of Pará, Amazonas, Acre, Rondônia, Roraima, Amapa, and Tocantins, is the area of the Amazon basin with Manaus and Belém being the only two major cities. This is the area of Brazil's vast rain forest, the home of most of Brazil's remaining Indians. This region borders the Guianas, Venezuela, Colombia, Peru, and Bolivia, yet has few roads or other land transport. The Northeast, a region of drought, desert, and poverty, has long existed with a sugar economy and subsistence farming. The Office for the Development of the Northeast (SUDENE), charged with improving the living conditions among the northeastern states, has not made a significant difference in its 40 years of existence. All the states have an Atlantic coast, with the cities of Fortaleza, Recife, and Salvador being major ports and state capitals. Northeastern states are Maranhão, Piauí, Ceará, Rio Grande do Norte, Paraíba, Pernambuco, Alagoas, Sergipe, and Bahia. The Northeast's population includes many descendents from the African slave trade and Salvador, Bahia, is known as the capital of African Brazil. The Southeast consists of the states of Rio de Janeiro, Espírito Santo, Minas Gerais, and São Paulo and is the economic powerhouse of Brazil and the region with the greatest population. The Center-West, a new frontier for Brazil, contains the states of Mato Grosso, Mato Grosso do Sul, and Goiás, along with the Federal District of Brasília. The South is comprised of the states of Rio Grande do Sul, Santa Catarina, and Paraná, the most European part of Brazil, with much of the population tracing ancestry back to Germany and Italy.

Brazil's geography of inequality underpins its system of economic and political power. The northeast is poor, literacy is low, and infant mortality high. Political power still resides in the hands of traditional families, while much of the population lives by subsistence farming and the area is devastated every few years by drought. The southeast and south are industrialized, with the state of São Paulo's economy exceeding that of Argentina and that of the state of Minas Gerais being greater than that of Chile or Peru. Additionally, São Paulo is the center of the country's banking, agribusiness, and service industries.

A shift in the population has taken place, changing the major locus of poverty. In the last 60 years, Brazil has gone from an agrarian to an overwhelmingly urban society—now 80 percent of the population—with peasants pushed off the land, especially in the northeast, by drought and capital-intensive agriculture, moving to the major cities seeking work in the increasingly industrialized economy. The result is seen in the thousands of *favelas*, the squatter housing built on swamps, vacant lots, and hillsides, which are a prominent and permanent part of the urban landscape. Often lacking adequate running water or sewage, their populations run into the millions.

The geography of inequality is not only regional, it appears in the deep class divisions, in great differentials of educational opportunity, and in income maldistribution. The income of the upper 10 percent of society is twenty-six times that of the lowest 40 percent. Brazil has the greatest wealth inequalities of any major nation in the world.

A Culture of Discrimination

AFRO-BRAZILIANS

To the first-time visitor to Brazil, the apparent lack of racial discrimination in a population which exhibits every human color seemingly demonstrates a color-blind society. In the 1940s, Brazilian anthropologist Gilberto Freyre gave legitimacy to the concept of racial democracy with his studies of social history encapsulated in his book *The Masters and the Slaves* (*Casa-Grande & Senzala*). Census takers have found over 100 words used to express the multitude of ethnotypes present in the society. Possibly the most popular and best-known Brazilian is soccer star Edson Arantes do Nascimento, better known as Pelé, an Afro-Brazilian; and Machado de Assis, a mulatto and founder of the prestigious Brazilian Academy of Letters, has been called Latin America's greatest literary figure.

However, behind this surface lies a pervasive racism. Despite the fact that a majority of Brazilians have some African ancestry, persons of color are poorly represented in politics and less so in the professions. A cursory examination of poverty shows income levels decreasing as complexion darkens. A visit to the universities finds few of color among either the faculty or the students. The officer corps of the military, and especially the navy, remains almost exclusively white.

Organized reaction against discrimination exists in muted form, not emerging as a significant interest group. Racial discrimination is constitutionally illegal. Furthermore, since the end of slavery in 1888, there have been no "Jim Crow" laws in Brazil. A result is that Afro-Brazilians have not had a focus in their battle for equality. In 2003, some universities instituted affirmative action programs to increase the number of Afro-Brazilians.

Advances have been made in recent years. An Afro-Brazilian was elected governor of one of the smaller states, and another was elected mayor of Brazil's largest city, São Paulo, in 1996. In 1999, the second Afro-Brazilian was promoted to the rank of general. One of the most important politicians in Rio de Janeiro is Benedita da Silva, an Afro-Brazilian woman from the *favelas* who has been federal deputy, senator, governor of the state, and cabinet minister. In 2003, an Afro-Brazilian was appointed to the Supreme Court.

WOMEN

Traditionally, Brazilian culture calls for the man to be the breadwinner and the woman to be housewife and mother. Men control Brazilian society, but with women entering the workforce in rapidly increasing numbers, this culture has been changing. Two forces have brought this change. First, the decreasing value of labor in production, partly the result of the "wage squeeze" during the military regime and partly due to restructuring of the economy. Both have exacerbated income inequality and led to many families requiring more than one income. Second, an increasing number of educated women are claiming the right to personal careers and professions. On an average, the income of a black woman is one-quarter that of a white man.

The changing role of women also appears in Brazil's political life. Only in the decade of the 1990s did women emerge onto the political scene as elected officials and decision makers. The PT has been a vehicle for a number of them. In addition to Benedita da Silva, women have been elected mayors of important cities, including Luiza Erundina and Marta Suplicy in São Paulo and Maria Luiza Fontenelle in Fortaleza. In 1994, the state of Maranhão elected Roseana Sarney, the daughter of former president José Sarney (1985–1990), as the first female governor. She was subsequently reelected in 1998 and briefly in 2002 was a presidential candidate, instead elected a federal senator. A few women have been appointed to cabinet positions, the most notable being Zélia Cardoso de Mello, appointed by President Collor as minister of the economy. Erundina and da Silva also have had cabinet positions. Rosinha Matheus, wife of former governor Anthony Garotinho, was elected governor of Rio de Janeiro in 2002, defeating the incumbent da Silva. Two women sit on the Supreme Court, and another is governor of a major state.

The Political System

Unlike most Latin American countries, which became republics on gaining their independence from monarchical European countries, Brazil adopted a constitutional monarchy system including a bicameral legislature with a population-based lower house of deputies and a senate representing states. The legal system, carried over from the Portuguese colonial period, was based on the Napoleonic code rather than on English common law as in the United States. As mentioned, Brazil, too, became a republic but only at the end of the nineteenth century, in 1889.

A major problem in Brazilian elections is the manner in which federal deputies and state legislators are elected; Brazil has an open-list, proportional election. Deputies and members of the state legislatures are not elected from individual districts but at large from the state, each state acting as a single election district. The candidates with the most votes win the seats of the state. As a result, candidates compete against other members of their own party. While it is necessary to be affiliated with a party in order to be a candidate, winners have little loyalty to their parties and often change party to gain an improved position. Additionally, this method of proportional representation strengthens various interest groups that would not be able to elect a representative in a local district but can win sufficient votes in the states to elect a favored candidate. This puts a premium on coalition building while weakening party structure and party discipline.

Election to executive positions—the president, governors, and mayors—requires a majority of valid votes cast. If no candidate obtains a majority on the first ballot, the two candidates with the most votes compete in a runoff election.

Voting is required in Brazil, and the 1988 constitution extended the franchise both to illiterates and to 16-year-olds, greatly increasing democratization and essentially giving the franchise to all adults. This total opening was gradually obtained in different intervening constitutions until the one of 1988, which marked a final and major shift away from the restricted franchise adopted in 1891, when only literate males could vote.

Brazil's constitution, written in 1988 in an atmosphere of reaction against the centralization and excesses of the military regime, has a strong liberal content, including bringing rural workers into the social security system for the first time and expanding labor rights. The most important decentralizing provision of the constitution required that substantial federal revenues be passed on to the states and municipalities. The constitution has been amended, especially during the Cardoso administration, in order to change the distribution of funds so as to balance the federal budget, refederalizing federal control, a balance essential to the control of inflation. Yet, governors have often successfully prevented amendments that would reallocate monies.

The President

The president and vice president are elected directly every 4 years, with the right of a single reelection. The presidential residence is the Palácio da Alvorada (Palace of the Dawn) and presidential offices are in the Palácio do Planalto (Palace of High Plain) in the capital of Brasília.

Historically, the president of Brazil has functioned largely independently of the Congress. The 1988 constitution reduced the power of the presidency in relation to the Congress, giving the Congress virtual veto of any presidential action. In reality, however, the faction-ridden Congress has not used its power effectively, and the president has been able to use provisionary measures to legislate, which the Congress has accepted despite its power to overturn them. This power was reduced in a constitutional amendment that limited the use of the measures and required the Congress to act on them. A leader of the government in the Congress introduces legislation for the executive and tries to shepherd it into law. The president can veto legislation but can be overridden by a second congressional vote.

The president constructs a cabinet to give representation to various interest groups. The ministry of finance (*fazenda*) along with the president of the Central Bank administer the economic policies. Often, there are serious rivalries between ministries, the personalities of the president and the ministers determining which of them dominates policy. Usually, the business community is consulted before the president chooses economic ministers. The ministry of labor will go to someone who has links to unions. Cabinet positions are used to bring different parties into the government, with deputies and senators given positions. In this manner, presidents can form a legislative coalition to support policies, with the expectation that the cabinet members will be able to obtain their parties' votes for executive-sponsored legislation. Accepting a cabinet or other executive position does not mean losing a legislative seat but only temporarily surrendering it to an elected alternate legislator and reclaiming the seat when he or she returns to the legislature. The foreign ministry, known as Itamaraty, operates largely independently of the foreign minister, who acts more as a spokesperson for foreign policy.

A major change has been the creation of a single ministry of defense, replacing the traditional ministries of the army, navy, and air force as well as the chief of staff of the armed forces. The new ministry is headed by a civilian, and the military report to the minister. This change has greatly reduced the role of the military in Brazilian politics, possibly to its lowest point since the mid-nineteenth century, with the de facto end of the moderating power they assumed at the empire's end in 1889.

The president also nominates federal judges. If the president leaves the country, the vice president, followed by the presidents of the Senate and the House, becomes acting president until his or her return.

The 1988 constitution expanded the role of the office of the General Prosecutor of the Republic, giving him or her the ability to investigate and prosecute crime independent of political pressures. The office is in many ways equivalent to the attorney general in the United States, but in other ways the general prosecutor's office is a fourth branch of government as it has constitutionally guaranteed functional and administrative autonomy.

The Legislature

Brazil has a bicameral legislature. In the lower Chamber of Deputies (Câmara dos Deputados), representation is based on the population of each state, with deputies elected every 4 years. The Federal District and territories also have congressional representation. The constitution stipulates that each state has a minimum of eight and a maximum of seventy deputies. This distribution strongly favors the smaller and poorer states of the north and center-west over the more populous and richer state of São Paulo.

The upper house of senators (Senado), has three from each state. Senators are elected for 8 years, half of them every 4 years. Each senator is elected with first and second alternates, who replace the senator if he or she leaves office, through either death, removal, or acceptance of another position. Senators frequently leave their seats, often to run for mayor or governor or to become a member of the cabinet. If a senator wishes to return to his or her seat, the alternate reverts to his or her previous position.

In addition to legislation, the houses of Congress can initiate parliamentary commissions of inquiry to investigate possible legal irregularities. Like the United States, the Chamber of Deputies has the right of impeachment and the Senate, the trial of the impeachment.

The Courts

The Supreme Court has eleven judges, nominated by the president and confirmed by the senate. Justices serve until a mandatory retirement age of 70 and the president of the court serves a 2-year term based on seniority. The court deals with federal issues and the constitutionality of legislation and is the final court of appeal. Additionally, there is the Supreme Court of Justice, which rules as a final court of appeal on criminal cases. The judiciary also includes a number of separate court systems to deal with specific areas of jurisdiction.

A national labor court system arbitrates between labor and management. All the courts have regional and local lower courts. Labor courts were set up in the 1930s under the administration of Getúlio Vargas to reduce the cost of strikes and to use labor unions as an arm of presidential power. Today, the courts still mediate industrial conflict, being a holdover of the corporatist institutions set up at that time. An electoral court system controls elections, making sure that candidates have the necessary credentials, that voting is honest, and that the elections take place in accordance with the law. A military court system, as its name implies, handles cases involving members of the armed forces, under military law.

The judicial system of Brazil is the weakest of the branches of government. This is partly the result of a lack of a tradition of judicial independence and partly of the fact that law is based on the Napoleonic code rather than on judicial interpretation, as in the common law system. A recent constitutional amendment requires lower courts to honor Supreme Court decisions, and decisions often are not final as there are a number of ways to appeal rulings. Yet, the courts have been strong enough to declare some legislation unconstitutional and to play a significant political role.

Political Parties

Several parties have significant representation in Brazil. Lula da Silva, the current president of Brazil, is the leader and principal organizer of the Workers' Party (PT), the furthest left of the major parties. Originally the greatest support for the PT lay in the industrial cities of São Paulo, in the south, and major urban areas but the anti-poverty measures of the da Silva administration have given him strong support in the northeast. It is the only political party with party discipline and has grown in importance consistently since its organization. In 2002, the PT formed a coalition with the Liberal Party, taking on businessman José Alencar as the vice presidential candidate. After winning the presidency, the administration of da Silva moved to the center left and maintained many of the policies of the previous administration.

The Party of the Brazilian Democratic Movement (PMDB) is a centrist party that originated as the opposition party that the military allowed during its regime. In addition to membership traced back to its antimilitary origin, many former members of the military's ARENA, following its unpopularity, changed party loyalty and joined the PMDB.

The Democrat Party (DEM) is the renamed Party of the Liberal Front (PFL), which resulted from a 1984 split in the PDS over the demand for direct election of the president. Today, the right-of-center DEM generally represents the political elite of the northeastern states and landowner interests but is enjoying increased representation in the south and southeast.

The Brazilian Social Democratic Party (PSDB), which includes former president Fernando Henrique Cardoso, split off from the PMDB in 1988. Although its candidates lost the presidency in the 2002 and 2006 elections, it won a number of important governorships, including those of three of the five most important states, São Paulo, Rio Grande do Sul, and Minas Gerais.

In addition to these larger parties, there are many smaller parties with a few deputies in the Congress. Among them is the former Brazilian Communist Party, which changed its name to the Popular Socialist Party. In the 1998 and 2002 presidential elections, Ciro Gomes was its candidate, going on to become the minister of national integration in the da Silva administration. Gomes earlier had been a member of the PSDB, governor of Ceará, and minister of finance. The Communist Party of Brazil, which earlier had split from the Brazilian Communist Party, remains. The Liberal Party has a strong base in the Evangelical churches of Brazil. ARENA underwent a number of changes, first becoming the Party of Social Democracy (PDS), finally becoming the Progressive Party (PP), the most conservative of Brazil's major parties. The Democratic Worker's Party (PDT) takes a nationalist and left-of-center political position and is strongest in the states of Rio de Janeiro and the southern states.

Throughout these permutations, it bears repeating that the Brazilian genius for short-term coalition building at the expense of party building is the dominant style of political action, while federalism continues as the institutional matrix of its politics.

Interest Groups

Major interest groups have organized delegations within the legislature, largely made possible by the system of proportional representation that allows candidates identified with the group to receive sufficient votes in a state to win a seat. Many of these groups cross party lines and are formally organized in the legislature, among them are the agricultural interests, banking, soccer clubs, construction industry, private schools, Evangelical churches, and retired persons.

BUSINESS

Business in Brazil is organized within each state by federations of industry, a hold-over from the corporatist 1930s. The São Paulo State Federation of Industries (FIESP) is the most powerful of these federations as the state has close to half the country's industry. FIESP maintains a major research office and financially supports particular political candidates. More than any other group, it represents the interests of Brazilian business, and presidents usually ask the advice of the federation in selecting finance ministers in matters of the economy. The Brazilian-American Chamber of Commerce wields considerable influence as a result of investment by multinational corporations.

UNIONS

Parallel to business are the labor unions, which function under the Consolidation of Labor Laws, originally created by Getúlio Vargas in 1943. The General Confederation of Workers (CGT) is the official confederation of unions, based on the corporate structure put in place by Vargas and funded by union dues, equivalent to a single day's pay each year, collected and dispersed by the Ministry of Labor. The system of official unions gave the government virtual control of labor for almost 50 years. A second major confederation is the CUT, an independent union originally organized under the leadership of Lula da Silva by the metal workers of São Paulo's automobile industry in the early 1980s. The CUT has grown at the expense of the CGT as unions feel that their interests are better represented by the independent nature of the new federation. The CUT has been affiliated with the PT but over time developed an independent policy position. A union economic research institute, the Interunion Department of Statistics and Socioeconomic Studies (DIEESE), sponsored by CUT in São Paulo, has been able to challenge government statistics on wages, employment, and buying power of wage earners. A third confederation is the Union Power (Força Sindical), which takes a less militant position than the CUT and has developed, in part, from efforts of the American Federation of Labor–Congress of Industrial Organizations (AFL-CIO) to create a labor leadership modeled on the North American experience. Rural workers, generally left out of traditional industrial unions, are represented by the National Confederation of Workers in Agriculture (CONTAG), growing first under military sponsorship and later independently, using the right to administer government social programs for its membership as a means of enlisting members. The CONTAG affiliated with the CUT in 1996.

BANKING

Banking is big business in Brazil. Until the Real Plan stabilization, banking profits were extremely high; and with their financial power, came political power. With inflation under control, many private banks have gone bankrupt and the political power of the banking industry has diminished; but the banks still maintain a substantial voice. A serious problem was the state banks, controlled by governors, who often used their financial power for political purposes. The restructuring of private banking and privatization of state banks required a major federal program in the mid-1990s to save the financial system, costing over $50 billion. Foreign banks bought a number of the banks, especially from Spain.

Public Employees

Public employment is well organized in Brazil at all levels. Federal employees are particularly well positioned and effective at protecting their jobs and salaries through the trade union lobby the Interunion Department of Legislative Staff (DIAP) and the National Confederation of Federal Public Servants (CNESF). On a number of occasions, presidents of Brazil have tried to reduce federal expenditures by cutting the oversized bureaucracy, but they have often had their attempts defeated as members of Congress have responded to the lobbying of the legislative staff. In 2003, the CNESF, which represents some 900,000 civil servants, split off from the CUT, mostly over pension benefits.

Agrarian Reform

Much-needed land reform has long been lacking in Brazil. A number of governments have placed laws on the books or made statements about the need for reform, including the newly instituted military regime in 1964; but nothing adequate has yet been done to make land and agricultural credits available to the many who seek them. In the 1950s, the peasant leagues gained headlines in their occupation of land in the northeast. Much of Brazil's agricultural land is held for investment and lies fallow, and ownership is highly concentrated. Other land is part of large agribusiness companies. The Movement of Landless Rural Workers (MST) has become a potent political force in Brazil. It has taken over land, called for a land-reform program, and created dramatic demonstrations of its demands, including a massive march on Brasília and occupation of government buildings. Battles with landowners have resulted in a number of deaths. The PT and the CUT have recognized the legitimacy of the MST claims and allied with it, and the Catholic Church has called for recognition of its needs. Although the largest land reform program in Brazil's history was carried out during the Cardoso administration, it did not come close to filling the demands for land. The da Silva administration has promised extensive land reform but has insisted that the MST not act outside the law.

Landowners

Strong opposition to land reform comes from the *fazendeiros* (landowners) and the *coroneis* (colonels), traditional political bosses in the northeastern states. Well organized in the Rural Democratic Union (UDR), owners' interests are well represented in the Congress as the Parliamentary Front of Agriculture. It can count on more than a third of the votes in the two houses and has successfully prevented any effective land reform. During the writing of the 1988 constitution, it was part of a coalition called the Big Center (Centrão), which wrote effective protection of its interests. Its continuing power comes from its ability to control voting in rural areas, particularly in the smaller states of the northeast, which dominate the senate because of their number. As a result, the UDR can block any legislation contrary to its interests, yet its support is necessary for any action that the executive wishes to get through Congress.

Students

Politics in Brazil, as in most of Latin America, begins in the universities. Students seeking political careers first enter university politics, usually associating themselves with a national political party. One of the first organizations to be repressed by the military was the National Union of Students, operating since the 1930s, which reappeared as civilian rule returned. Students were in the forefront of the protests calling for the impeachment of President Collor and can get a hearing in the highest levels of the government on issues pertaining to education. Yet, they have not regained their influence under the postmilitary governments, but a political party will offer outgoing presidents of the union backing for election to Congress and a subsequent political career.

ORGANIZED RELIGION

Brazil is the most populous Catholic country, and the Church remains an important force. The Church historically has been identified with the social and political elite, and demonstrations by the faithful against the Goulart government were an important factor in legitimizing the 1964 coup. During the 1960s, much of the Church became strongly committed to liberation theology, with its championing of the poor. Under the leadership of the Brazilian National Confederation of Bishops (CNBB), base communities were developed for worship and to provide needed services. The base communities fostered the organization of new groups that made demands on the government. Among the new groups that found inspiration in the base communities was the new trade union movement. During the military regime, priests often were spokespersons for opposition to authoritarian rule. The Archdiocese of São Paulo gathered reports on human rights violations, which were published in 1985 under the title *Brasil: Nunca Mais (Brazil: Never Again)*, which went to fourteen editions. The military governments came to view many priests and bishops as supporters of left-wing policies and antithetical to their intentions of cleansing the country of communism. Like the military governments, the Vatican has seen danger in liberation theology. Liberal priests have been silenced, and the archdiocese of a powerful cardinal who supported the new theology was reduced in size and influence. Over the last decade, as the older generation of Brazilian bishops retired, new bishops who are opposed to liberation theology have replaced them. Yet, the Church is by no means monolithic, as the CNBB, like Brazilian federalism itself, has proved a flexible institution capable of accommodating its different factions. The Church speaks out on questions of morality and doctrine. It has opposed artificial birth control but has not been able to prevent its advocacy by the government, especially in the highly successful program to reduce human immunodeficiency virus (HIV) infection. The lack of an adequate number of priests along with a well-financed effort by Evangelical groups has resulted in the fast growth of non-Catholic churches, especially Evangelicals. The most prominent of them is the domestically createdUniversal Church of the Reign of God, with over 2500 congregations, which has successfully used television to promote membership and has expanded abroad, including to the United States. With the open-list proportional elections, the Evangelical churches have elected a significant number of representatives who represent an important interest bloc in the Câmara dos Deputados.

Another religious interest in Brazil comes through Umbanda and Candomblé, based on West African Yoruba religion brought by slaves. Not well organized politically, its influence cannot be measured due to the blending of many of its rituals and gods with Catholic worship. Yet, politicians carefully honor its expression and accept its voice when raised.

The Amazon

The Amazon region makes up almost 60 percent of Brazil's territory, thinly populated except for a few cities like Manaus yet important in terms of its biodiversity and effects on the global climate. Brazil's borders with seven other countries run through the Amazon, and vast areas are set aside as homelands for Amer-Indians. The indigenous peoples have suffered dramatically as disease and occupation by persons seeking gold have decimated their populations.

Part of the concern has been the destruction of vast areas of the rain forest, amounting to 14 percent of the area in 10 years, for lumber, minerals, and farm land. During the military governments, an ill-conceived road-building project, the Trans-Amazon Highway, tried to open the area for agriculture. In response, environmental groups have tried to save the Amazon, most significantly by promoting sustainable development. Conflict between ranchers and environmentalists climaxed in the 1988 assassination of Chico Mendes, a leader of the rubber tappers (*seringueiros*) by a local landowner and his son. Mendes had lobbied hard nationally and internationally, winning the "Global 500" award given by the United Nations for his work in organizing extraction reserves which restricted the destruction of the rain forest. He had also organized the tappers into a union and helped found the National Council of Rubber Tappers. His lobbying led to the suspension of a loan from the Inter-American Development Bank for road building in the area. In 2005, Sister Dorothy Stang, a 74-year-old American nun who had worked for sustainable development and had come into conflict with ranchers and loggers, was assassinated.

Brazil Today

Brazil must be counted as one of the world's great emerging markets, with a maturing democracy and a stabilized and growing economy after 40 years of inflation. The country has embraced the global economy and the political consequences of that choice. The transition to democratic rule was managed successfully, with increased power to the legislature and the judiciary and measures that reduce the role of the military in domestic politics. Politically, pervasive corruption remains a serious characteristic among Brazilian politicians, undermining trust in the government and in democracy itself. Presidents of both houses of Congress, members of Congress, governors, and cabinet members have been forced out of office but so far none has been incarcerated. Election to Congress is used as a protection against prosecution for public thievery. Corruption is less acceptable; in the 2002 election, a significant number of important politicians who had been accused of corruption were eliminated in the first round of voting, including former governors of Minas Gerais and São Paulo, former president Collor, and the former mayor of São Paulo. Economically, the tradition of inflation, debt financing, and oligopolistic industry has been broken. New social programs in education, social security, and public health have been put into place. Internationally, Brazil has emerged as the leading power in both the politics and economy of South America, with almost no historic differences with neighbors and leadership in a regional economic bloc that has significant political ramifications. A major foreign policy objective is a permanent seat on the Security

Council of the United Nations. In 2004, Brazil sent troops to Haiti as head of a U.N. peacekeeping operation. Brazil has taken international leadership in a South–South effort, along with India and South Africa, to improve international trade and open the industrialized world to products from lesser developed countries.

Despite advances, Brazil retains a legacy of social problems that threaten its future. Poverty, inequality, and ignorance require resources not presently available to the government. Urban infrastructure continues to fall behind need as droughts and mechanization of agriculture drive rural populations into cities. Land reform and agricultural credits for small landholders are part of an unfulfilled agenda. Northeast Brazil still lacks adequate opportunities for employment, and infant mortality rates are among the world's worst. Unfortunately, what Brazilians call "the social debt" and inequities in wealth, have no immediate solution, but important advances have been made since 1994: Poverty levels dropped significantly with the end of inflation under the Cardoso administration, along with improvements in primary education, actions continued under the Da Silva government, which also created the *Bolsa Familia* (family stipend), a combination of the *Fome Zero* program, the *Bolsa Escola*, which gives money to poor families that keep their children in school, and the Basic Benefit provided to persons in extreme poverty. Two other major problems are those of environmental protection and of urban violence. Brazil must address growing environmental issues, among them serious urban pollution and the destruction of the Amazon rain forest. In the major metropolitan areas, drug lords control the *favelas* and threaten general public order. Policing is hampered by low salaries for police, the firepower of the criminals, and organizational limitations on cooperation among police agencies.

Growth is returning as investment pours into Brazil and its exports increase. The only question is whether the growth will be sufficient to both absorb the increasing numbers of persons entering the workforce each year and at the same time give jobs to the many already out of work or underemployed. Industrial restructuring as a result of privatization and international market competition reduced blue-collar jobs and brought a wave of unemployment. At the same time, protectionist barriers in industrialized countries have limited purchase of Brazil's exports, especially of agricultural products. Yet the sale of its commodities has greatly improved economic conditions and the country, for the first time in its history, is a creditor rather than a debtor nation. At the same time, a leveling of income has meant a major movement of the population out of the lower income classes and into middle income socio-economic status (Class C).

Brazil is a nation of superlatives, but one that threatens it is that of the greatest wealth and income inequality among major nations of the world. The great question is whether Brazil's democracy and economic reforms can be maintained and advanced at the same time great problems remain. That is, can successive governments pay the "social debt"?

Chronology

1500 Sighting of and landing on Brazilian territory by Pedro Alvares Cabral
1808 Portuguese royal family arrives in Brazil and makes Rio de Janeiro capital of the Portuguese Empire

1822   Portuguese crown prince Dom Pedro I declares Brazil an independent nation and himself emperor
1888   Elimination of slavery
1889   Overthrow of emperor and establishment of the first republic by the military
1922   Week of modern art; revolt of Copacabana Fort
1924   Revolt of the *tenentes* in São Paulo and beginning of the Prestes Column's march through the interior
1930   Overthrow of the first republic and assumption of the presidency by Getúlio Vargas
1937   Vargas established the *Estado Novo* (New State)
1945   Vargas forced out of office, Marshal Dutra elected president
1954   Vargas, elected president in 1950, commits suicide
1956   Election of Juscelino Kubitschek and beginning of the construction of Brasília
1961   President Jânio Quadros resigns, succeeded by Vice President João Goulart
1964   Military coup ousts Goulart and generals assume presidency, beginning 21 years of military rule
1985   Tancredo Neves, a civilian, elected president
1988   New constitution written
1990   Direct election of Fernando Collor de Mello, defeating Luiz Inácio Lula da Silva
1992   President Collor de Mello impeached, resigns; succeeded by Vice President Itamar Franco
1994   Real Plan stabilizes economy; Fernando Henrique Cardoso elected president, defeating Lula da Silva
1998   Cardoso elected for a second term, again defeating da Silva
1999   Military ministries replaced by a single civilian minister of defense
2002   da Silva elected president
2006   da Silva re-elected for second term; Brazil announced the liquidation of its debts with the International Monetary Fund and the Paris Club

Bibliography

The following books in English will give a broad picture of various aspects of Brazil. Additionally, there is a vast Portuguese-language literature for those able to read it. Fortunately, Spanish speakers can read Portuguese materials relatively easily.

Ames, Barry. *The Deadlock of Democracy in Brazil*. Ann Arbor: University of Michigan Press, 2000.
Bresser Pereira, Luis Carlos. *Economic Crisis and State Reform in Brazil: Toward a New Interpretation of Latin America*. Boulder, CO: Lynne Rienner, 1996.
Cardoso, Fernando Henrique. *The Accidental President of Brazil: A Memoir*. New York: Public Affairs, 2006.
Chaffee, Wilber Albert. *Desenvolvimento: Politics and Economy in Brazil*. Boulder, CO: Lynne Rienner, 1998.
Eakin, Marshall C. *Brazil: the Once and Future Country*. New York: St. Martin's Press, 1997.
Evans, Peter. *Dependent Development: The Alliance of Multinational, State, and Local Capital in Brazil*. Princeton, NJ: Princeton University Press, 1979.
Font, Mauricio A., and Anthony Peter Spanakos, eds. *Reforming Brazil*. Lanham, MD: Lexington Books, 2004.
Furtado, Celso. *The Economic Growth of Brazil: A Survey from Colonial to Modern Times*. Berkeley: University of California Press, 1968.
Geddes, Barbara. *Politician's Dilemma: Building State Capacity in Latin America*. Berkeley: University of California Press, 1994.
Hagopian, Frances. *Traditional Politics and Regime Change in Brazil*. New York: Cambridge University Press, 1996.
Keck, Margaret. *The Workers' Party and Democratization in Brazil*. New Haven: Yale University Press, 1992.

Kingston, Peter R. *Crafting Coalitions for Reform: Business Preferences, Political Institutions, and Neoliberal Reform in Brazil*. University Park, PA: Pennsylvania State University Press, 1999.

Kinzo, Maria D'Alva, and James Dunkerley, eds. *Brazil since 1985: Economy, Polity and Society*. London: Institute of Latin American Studies, University of London, 2003.

Levine, Robert M., and John J. Crocitti, eds. *The Brazil Reader: History, Culture, Politics*. Durham, NC: Duke University Press, 1999.

Lewin, Linda. *Politics and Parentela in Paraiba: A Case Study of Family-Based Oligarchy in Brazil*. Princeton, NJ: Princeton University Press, 1987.

Mainwaring, Scott. *The Catholic Church and Politics in Brazil, 1916–1985*. Stanford: Stanford University Press, 1986.

Page, Joseph A. *History and Cultures: The Brazilians*. Reading, MA: Addison-Wesley, 1995.

Scheper-Hughes, Nancy. *Death Without Weeping: The Violence of Everyday Life in Brazil*. Berkeley: University of California Press, 1992.

Silverstein, Ken, and Emir Sader. *Without Fear of Being Happy: Lula, the Workers Party in Brazil*. New York: Verso Press, 1991.

Skidmore, Thomas E. *Politics in Brazil: 1930–1964, An Experiment in Democracy*. Oxford: Oxford University Press, 1967.

——. *The Politics of Military Rule in Brazil, 1964–85*. Oxford: Oxford University Press, 1988.

Stepan, Alfred, ed. *Democratizing Brazil: Problems of Transition and Consolidation*. New York: Oxford University Press, 1989.

FILMS AND DVDS

Black Orpheus. Brazil, 1959.
Dona Flor and Her Two Husbands. Brazil, 1976.
Central Station. Brazil, 1998.
Pixote. Brazil, 1981.
Bye Bye Brazil. Brazil, 1979.
City of God. Brazil, 2002.
Eu, Tu, Eles (Me, You, and Them). Brazil, 2000.
Carandiru. Brazil, 2003.
The House of Sand, 2006.
The Year My Parents Went on Vacation, 2006.
Three Blood Brothers (Três Irmãos de Sangue, 2007.
City of Men (Cidade dos Homens), 2007.

WEBSITES

www.brasilemb.org Brazilian embassy.
www.planalto.gov.br President's office.
www.senado.gov.br Brazilian Senate.
www.fazenda.gov.br Brazilian Finance Ministry.
lanic.utexas.edu Latin American Network Information Center (LANIC).
www.brasa.org Brazilian Studies Association.
www.pt.org.br Worker's Party.

BOLIVIA

PARAGUAY

BRAZIL

*Pacific
Ocean*

Rio de la Plata

●Córdoba

Rosario ●

URUGUAY

Buenos Aires

CHILE

Map of
ARGENTINA

N
W E
S

100 0 100 200 300 Miles

Scale 1:45,000,000

**Falkland Islands
(Islas Malvinas)**

FIFTEEN

ARGENTINA

Aldo C. Vacs

Argentina is located in the Southern Cone of South America. The country is shaped like an inverted triangle, with the northern base bordering on Bolivia, Paraguay, and Brazil; the eastern side on Brazil and Uruguay; the western side on Chile; and the apex pointing toward Antarctica. Its territory comprises about 2.8 million square kilometers, making it the eighth largest country in the world and the second largest in Latin America (after Brazil). The Andes Mountains run from the Bolivian border to Tierra del Fuego and separate Argentina from Chile. Argentina exhibits a great diversity of physical features, productive capacity, and demographic patterns. The northern region has subtropical weather, the central has a temperate climate, and the southern displays cold temperatures. The northwest is quite arid and poor but has small subtropical areas and a string of fertile valleys where most of the population, including a substantial *mestizo* component, resides. Cuyo, in the Western central region, is also arid but contains a number of oasis settlements that facilitate fruit and wine production and in which most of the population, largely of Spanish and Italian descent, is concentrated. The Gran Chaco, which includes savannas and subtropical forests, is located in the north central and eastern region, where most of the small remnants of the indigenous population live together with groups of European descent devoted to the production of cotton, tobacco, tea, and yerba mate. Patagonia, in the south, contains arid plateaus where sheep are raised and fertile valleys where fruit is produced; but it remains scarcely populated. The Pampas, in the central eastern portion of Argentina, are among the most fertile grasslands in the world; and their temperate climate and adequate rainfall facilitate the large-scale production of grains and the raising of livestock. Most of the country's population live in large urban concentrations located in the Pampas region, including the capital city, Buenos Aires, as well as Rosario, La Plata, Mar del Plata, and Bahía Blanca as well as their respective suburban areas and satellite cities.

Argentina has a population of about 40 million people, most of European ancestry. In the late nineteenth and early twentieth centuries, massive waves of immigrants from Italy, Spain, central Europe, Russia, and the Middle East substantially altered the size and composition of the Argentine population. Between 1870 and 1914, the population grew from about 2 million to 8 million people, of whom close to one-third were foreign-born. After 1930, European immigration declined, but the country attracted large numbers of immigrants from neighboring countries. Most of these immigrants together with large contingents of the existing rural population settled largely in the cities, making Argentina one of the most urbanized countries in Latin America. By 1914 more than 50 percent of the population was living in urban concentrations; by 2000 it was estimated that close to 90 percent of the total population lived in urban areas.

From an economic perspective, Argentina has been a relatively rich country, particularly in the Latin American context. Between the 1870s and 1930, the country experienced rapid economic growth, which led to the emergence of large middle and urban working classes and expansion of political participation. The Great Depression brought about the end of economic prosperity, political stability, and social progress and inaugurated a period of growing confrontation during which Argentina's situation steadily declined. Between the 1940s and the early 1980s, the fluctuations between populist but fragile liberal democratic regimes and increasingly repressive military dictatorships contributed to economic stagnation, a growing concentration of income and wealth in the hands of the elites, and worsening poverty and marginality among the working and middle classes. Since the early 1980s, the establishment and consolidation of liberal democracy ended the darkest period of Argentina's political history, restoring the respect for human rights and providing for popular participation and political stability. However, the implementation of stringent free market policies reinforced inequitable patterns of income distribution, generated unemployment, increased poverty, fostered the multiplication of social problems, and led to political instability, resulting in an electoral turn toward more redistributionist and state-led policies in recent years.

Political Evolution

From Colony to Oligarchic Republic

Most of the territory currently occupied by Argentina was settled throughout the sixteenth and seventeenth centuries by two groups of Spanish colonizers: one arrived by land from Peru, occupying the northwestern area of current Argentina and spreading toward the south and southeast; another came by sea from Spain and colonized the areas comprising the Río de la Plata basin. The inhabitants of the northwestern region remained linked to the viceroyalty of Peru, supplying food, beasts of burden, and textiles demanded by the Peruvian and Upper Peruvian (Bolivian) silver-mining economy. The colonists who settled in the margins of the Río de la Plata and in the areas along the Paraná and Uruguay Rivers produced hides for export to Spain and engaged in legal as well as illegal commercial activities, including the smuggling of goods to and from Great Britain.

From the Spanish crown's perspective, the economic importance of both regions was limited: there were neither precious metals nor other valuable raw materials, there was only a scarce number of sedentary Indians whose labor could be exploited in agricultural activities, and the lack of conditions for a plantation economy prevented the introduction of large numbers of slaves. However, the strategic and commercial importance of the Río de la Plata area and specifically of Buenos Aires, its main city, increased in the late colonial period as it became a barrier against Portuguese territorial expansion and an entry point for commercial transactions with the hinterland. The continuous territorial disputes with Portugal transformed Buenos Aires into a crucial defensive outpost and led to the creation of local militias. The commercial role of the city and the Pampas region was bolstered during the eighteenth century by the increasing demand for hides in Europe and, in the late eighteenth and early nineteenth centuries, by the export of salted meat, particularly to the slave plantations of Brazil and the Caribbean.

The creation in 1776 of the viceroyalty of the Río de la Plata (comprising current Argentina, Uruguay, and portions of Bolivia, Paraguay, and Chile) with Buenos Aires as the government seat reinforced this trend and permanently shifted the balance of power in favor of the *porteño* (port city) elites. At the same time, this shift in the balance of power sharpened the conflict between the oligarchies of the interior, which zealously defended their political autonomy and tried to protect the regional economies from foreign competition, and the Buenos Aires elites, who tried to attain political supremacy and championed free trade.

Argentina's independence from Spain, secured between 1810 and 1816, was the culmination of a process involving growing tensions between the creole landed and commercial oligarchies, who had gradually concentrated most economic resources in their hands, and the Spanish rulers and administrators of a declining empire, who excluded these elites from political participation and wanted to preserve an outmoded mercantilist system. The first two decades after independence were marked by a succession of civil wars between the *Unitarians*—supporters of the prerogative of Buenos Aires to establish a centralized national government and promote free trade—and the *Federalists*—regional groups who steadfastly defended provincial autonomy and espoused economic protectionism. The confrontation between these two groups resulted in a period of civil wars accompanied by rapid economic decline.

This violent stalemate was temporarily broken after the inauguration in 1829 of Juan Manuel de Rosas as governor of Buenos Aires, a position he occupied with only a brief interruption until 1852. Rosas, a rich landowner from Buenos Aires province who defined himself as a Federalist, was able to establish his ascendancy on the federal *caudillos* (political–military strongmen) of the interior and to quell successive Unitarian challenges. Rosas' peculiar brand of federalism embodied the interests of the traditional cattle ranchers and exporters of hides and salted meat from Buenos Aires, who wanted a peaceful climate in which they could export their products, import manufactures, profit from the customs revenues generated by the port of Buenos Aires, and control the conduct of foreign relations. In exchange for this, they were inclined to leave provincial authority in the hands of local *caudillos*, maintaining harmonious relations with the provincial elites who shared their aversion to any change in the economic status quo, traditional class structure, and forms of political domination.

However, after two decades of dictatorial rule, the inability of the Rosas regime to promote the kind of political and economic changes that many among the elites believed were necessary to overcome the country's isolation and relative stagnation led to an alliance between interior and coastal groups interested in fostering a process of capitalist agrarian development. The fall of Rosas in 1852 was followed by a short period of internal conflict as the Buenos Aires and provincial elites clashed over the definition of the political and economic design of the emerging state. Finally, through a suitable combination of military force, political concessions, and economic might, the agrarian and commercial exporting elites of Buenos Aires were able to assert their hegemony and establish new conditions for political stability and economic growth, completing the occupation of the national territory, implementing free market and free trade policies, and creating a stable oligarchic political regime. This group consolidated its supremacy and prevented internal discord by forging an alliance between the Pampean and regional elites and appealing to the use of force and fraud when necessary to win elections.

Political stability facilitated Argentina's economic modernization and reinsertion into the world political economy as a producer and exporter of grains and beef. Between 1862 and 1916, successive administrations confronted the problems of the scarcity of labor, capital, skills, infrastructure, and technology by promoting massive immigration, attracting foreign investment, fostering education, implementing an ambitious program of public works, and encouraging the introduction of new techniques for cattle raising, grain cultivation, and food processing, storage, and transportation. Thus, by World War I, Argentina had become a major world exporter of beef, grains, and wool. The population had increased fivefold and was becoming mainly urban. There was a growing number of middle- and working-class people concentrated in the largest cities, especially in Buenos Aires, and the per capita income was higher than in several European countries.

However, the emergence of politically disenfranchised middle-class and urban working-class sectors and the existence of some provincial elites who felt excluded from the economic bonanza resulted in growing opposition to the oligarchic regime. Middle-class and marginal elite groups converged in the creation in 1892 of the Unión Cívica Radical (UCR, Radical Civic Union), the first and oldest mass party in Argentina, which fought for the expansion of political participation. In turn, the increase in the number of immigrants and urban workers led both to the rise of the anarchist movement and to the creation in 1894 of the Socialist Party, which sought significant political and socioeconomic changes.

The Ascent and Fall of Mass Democracy

Between 1892 and 1912, the Radicals, under the leadership of Hipólito Yrigoyen, engaged in armed revolts and practiced electoral abstention to force the Conservative elite to make political concessions. The emergence of militant labor and leftist political organizations, the growing pressure coming from the middle-class opposition, and the realization on the part of the oligarchy that the Radicals, despite their name, did not intend to alter the existing economic and social structures prompted the decision to liberalize the political system. In 1912, the reformist wing of the ruling Conservative Party passed a law instituting obligatory universal male suffrage and enacted guarantees to make voting secret and unconstrained. Afterward, the UCR began to participate successfully in a series of contests that culminated in 1916 with the election of Yrigoyen as president.

The period of 1916–1930 was one of democratic political stability characterized by the predominance of the UCR at the national and provincial levels. The Radical administrations focused their initiatives on the political arena, promoting the enlargement of the electorate and the displacement of conservative groups from power positions; but they introduced only minor changes in the socioeconomic domain. Federal interventions reduced the influence of conservative political groups that, unlike other Latin American traditional elites, could not rely on the electoral manipulation of a pliable peasantry, whose presence was practically negligible in the Argentine agrarian capitalist system. However, the oligarchic groups did not attempt to eliminate the democratic regime as long as the Radicals protected the existing socioeconomic structures. Thus, the Radical administrations' progressive policies were limited to favoring the urban and rural middle sectors through state patronage and social and educational policies and to satisfying some of the demands of the urban workers through the creation of an embryonic social security system, price controls of wage goods, and mediation in labor conflicts.

This period of political stability and social peace ended when the crash of 1929 and the ensuing Great Depression led to an abrupt decline in export revenues. The collapse of the economy led to an acute fight for economic shares between different socioeconomic groups. At the same time, the crisis reduced the margin of maneuver of the Radical administration, which was unable to sustain its state patronage or to overcome the structural causes of the economic crisis. Moreover, in his old age, President Yrigoyen seemed to have lost the ability to deal effectively with the growing political and economic problems challenging his administration. In these circumstances, the landed and commercial elites were able to mobilize part of the discontented middle class and to incite some army officers to overthrow the elected government. The coup d'état of September 1930—orchestrated by the traditional oligarchy, supported by middle-class groups, and implemented by the armed forces—signaled the end of the era of Argentina's political stability and the beginning of more than five decades of continuous disarray.

The leader of the 1930 coup, General José F. Uriburu, attempted between 1930 and 1932 to establish an authoritarian regime whose corporatist features resembled Italian fascism. However, the oligarchy and a substantial portion of the military and middle sectors opposed Uriburu's project and forced him to allow the emergence of a façade democracy. The banning of the UCR and the use of electoral fraud and coercion facilitated the coming into power of Conservative administrations that attempted to restore the old oligarchic regime by limiting political participation and favoring export-oriented economic growth based on a close commercial association with Great Britain.

Throughout the so-called infamous decade (1930–1943), the ruling Conservative groups attempted to re-create the "paradise lost" of the oligarchic regime, when their political domination was uncontested and the export–import model of growth reigned supreme. However, it soon became clear that in the international and domestic circumstances engendered by the Great Depression, this goal was unattainable. The Conservative governments of the 1930s and early 1940s realized that even the substantial economic concessions made to Great Britain were not able to revive the prosperity based on the traditional export–import model. The rise of a new model of economic growth, import substitution industrialization (ISI), became inevitable as the decline in export revenues and the consequent scarcity of hard currency reduced the capacity to import and created opportunities and incentives for the rise of local manufacturing. This economic transformation would have significant social and political consequences that ultimately would lead to the end of Conservative rule.

The emergence of an industrial elite producing consumer goods for the domestic market, the decline in agricultural exports and the consequent rural stagnation, the escalating pace of rural–urban migration associated with the new employment opportunities in the emerging industrial sector, the influential political role played by the military after 1930, the growing discontent of the middle sectors with Conservative electoral fraud and economic policies, the demands of labor organizations, and the rise of nationalism created a volatile situation that could not be adequately controlled by the conservative regime. The beginning of World War II reinforced some of these trends—such as the need to produce domestic manufactures, the growing importance of the military, and the rise of democratic and nationalistic demands by different groups—and created the opportunity for the military to oust the Conservative administration without significant opposition.

The Rise and Decline of Peronism

The 1943 coup was plotted by a secret military lodge made up of nationalistic and authoritarian officers who sympathized with the fascist ideology and wanted to maintain Argentina's neutrality during World War II. Among those who participated in the coup, Colonel Juan D. Perón rapidly emerged as the most skillful political figure. Palace coups engineered by Perón removed the two initial military presidents from office. Finally, a close Perón associate, General Edelmiro Farrell, became president (1944–1946); and with his backing, Perón concentrated in his hands the vice presidency, the ministry of war, and the newly created secretariat of labor and social welfare. Afterward, using the power and resources of these offices, Perón organized a coalition that included his military supporters and an emerging state-controlled labor movement. Faced with Perón's growing power, his military and civilian adversaries tried to oust him; but this attempt failed when, after a few days of incarceration, Perón was rescued by a massive mobilization of workers who demanded his release on October 17, 1945. Eva Duarte, a young actress who had become Perón's companion in 1944, offered him continuous support during the crisis, and they married shortly afterward. Eva Perón—Evita, as she became popularly known—rapidly emerged as a prominent political figure in her own right, helping gather support for Perón among the poorer sectors of the population.

After Perón's release, a divided military heeded the growing demands for democratization and called for elections to be held in early 1946. Both Perón and his adversaries tried to mobilize and organize their supporters into broad political coalitions. On the Peronist side, the state-supported labor organizations created the Partido Laborista (Labor Party), while some former radical and conservative politicians established the so-called Renovating Junta of Radicalism, which counted on the support of several nationalistic middle-class groups and provincial political organizations. Both parties endorsed Perón as their presidential candidate but maintained separate lists for other offices. The opposition front included Radicals, Socialists, Communists, and Conservatives that formed an electoral alliance called Unión Democrática (Democratic Union). Alliance members agreed to support the presidential candidate nominated by the Radicals but presented their own candidates for other offices. In the February 1946 elections, Perón won the presidency with 54 percent of the vote and his supporters carried most provinces, securing substantial majorities in Congress.

A new political era, the era of populism, had started. The 1946 elections signaled the end of the Radical electoral predominance, the Conservative ability to manipulate the political process, and the capacity of minor parties, such as the socialists, to gain congressional seats. Perón's victory rested on the support of the new urban working-class electorate fostered by the internal migrations and industrialization, the rural population and the inhabitants of the poorer provinces, and sectors of the lower middle class grateful for his economic and social initiatives. After his inauguration, Perón cemented a state-dominated populist alliance whose fundamental pillars were organized labor, the industrialists producing for the domestic market, and the nationalistic military groups favorable to rapid industrialization. This populist regime favored strong state intervention in the economy to promote industrialization, income redistribution policies favorable to organized labor and civilian and military bureaucracies, and nationalization of crucial sectors of the economy (public utilities, transportation, and foreign trade).

The Peronist government maintained the democratic forms (periodic elections, division of powers, and political party competition) but engaged in a number of semiauthoritarian practices, such as restricting the freedoms of expression, assembly, and strike; controlling the judiciary; manipulating the mass media and the educational system; imposing political constraints on public employees, union leaders, and education workers; and harassing and persecuting adversaries. As a result, the chances of the opposition parties to compete successfully for power were considerably reduced, and they began to favor a military coup as the only alternative to what they defined as an increasingly "totalitarian" regime.

The Peronist economic policies and political practices were relatively successful in the early postwar years as Argentina benefited from the use of war-accumulated reserves and the recovery of the international economy while workers, industrialists, and the military remained united behind a government that satisfied their demands. Meanwhile, Peronism expanded its basis of electoral support by extending the franchise to women in 1947 and establishing the women's branch of the party. Evita played a central role in encouraging these decisions and became the leader of the women's branch of the Peronist Party. She also performed a crucial role in strengthening the regime by offering social welfare services through the Eva Perón Foundation, overseeing organized labor, and promoting the public veneration of Perón's leadership in her speeches and publications.

Evita, in a characteristic gesture, addressing her followers from the balcony of the Casa Rosada during Peronist rallies in Buenos Aires' central square, the Plaza de Mayo. (*Photo provided by the Department of Documentary Photographs, Argentine National Archive*)

In 1949, Perón called for a constitutional convention that, amid strong objections from the opposition, instituted the possibility of presidential reelection, an option that had been forbidden by the 1853 constitution. Peronist union leaders, female activists, and some elected officials tried to nominate Evita as vice presidential candidate; but faced with strong military opposition and affected by failing health, she was forced to decline the nomination. In 1951, Perón was reelected president, gathering 65 percent of all votes cast.

At the time of his second inauguration in 1952, Perón confronted growing difficulties as changes in the international economic situation, declines in domestic agricultural production, balance-of-payments deficits, inflation, and economic stagnation led to a renewed fight for economic shares among the members of the Peronist coalition. Perón's inability to restore economic prosperity and satisfy the conflicting demands of his followers reinforced the trend toward authoritarianism.

The increasingly repressive characteristics of his political initiatives—declaration of a state of siege and internal war, takeover of newspapers and growing censorship, forced membership in the Peronist Party and other organizations, and open confrontation with the Catholic Church—weakened his regime and strengthened the resolve of the opposition to remove him by any means. Evita's death in 1952, the multiplication of the allegations of corruption, and a number of scandals involving Perón and his associates contributed to undermine the regime's popularity and made it increasingly difficult to mobilize supporters in its defense. Perón's misguided policies, which fluctuated between using more repression and making concessions, fostered the unity of the anti-Peronist forces. Finally, in September 1955, after a series of failed revolts, a faction of the military supported by the opposition parties and the Catholic Church succeeded in overthrowing the regime. Perón fled the country and was replaced by a military administration, which very rapidly became involved in internal feuds concerning how to deal with the defeated Peronists and what kind of program to implement to replace Perón's populist policies.

AUTHORITARIANISM AND LIMITED DEMOCRACY

After the fall of the Peronist regime, a succession of antipopulist civilian and military governments attempted with scarce success to overcome Argentina's political, economic, and social crises by introducing a new political economic model to foster growth and political stability. The forces that overthrew Perón agreed that the decline of the classic ISI model required the rejection of Perón's income redistribution and nationalistic policies and a new economic strategy that would include adjustment programs to reduce the growing balance-of-payments deficits, incentives for foreign investment in order to attract new capital and technology, and stabilization plans to eliminate inflation. Notwithstanding their different origins, composition, and ruling styles, the governments established during this period practiced exclusionary or repressive policies toward important sectors of the population, particularly against Peronists, who until 1973 were totally or partially banned from participating in elections. Meanwhile, to different degrees, these governments maintained state intervention in the economy while trying to shift the country's industrialization strategy in a new direction, one that combined relative protection and support for local producers with incentives for foreign investment and the welcoming of financial capital in an attempt to promote exports (especially of manufactures), foster international competitiveness, and modernize the most dynamic sectors of the economy.

These attempts failed due to a number of economic situations, including the relative scarcity of foreign investment, inflationary pressures, hard currency shortages, and state mismanagement. More important yet, the groups favored by the populist regime, such as organized labor and state-dependent industrialists, were able to outlast its fall and struggled to preserve or augment their respective shares of a dwindling economic pie while looking at the state as the means to attain their sectoral goals. Ultimately, this confrontation led to growing inflation, social conflict, and a progressive government paralysis that intensified the economic crisis and heightened political instability.

Between 1955 and 1976, Argentina had a succession of authoritarian military and partially democratic civilian governments that were unable to overcome this stalemate. This failure affected the military administrations established in 1955–1958, 1962–1964, and 1966–1973, all of which were forced to step down and allow for a transition to civilian rule to escape political and economic disaster. The civilian governments of Arturo Frondizi (1958–1962) and Arturo Illia (1964–1966), elected thanks to the military ban on Peronism, were overthrown by the same military after they proved unable to solve the country's problems.

Finally, in the 1970s, faced with urban insurrections and the rise of guerrilla movements, the military and its allies allowed the electoral participation of Peronism—but not of Perón himself—in an attempt to restore some degree of stability. This led to the election in March 1973 of Perón's personal delegate, Héctor J. Cámpora, who resigned 3 months after his inauguration so a new election, in which Perón could participate, could be held. Faced with the internal divisions affecting the Peronist movement, Perón attempted to maintain a neutral position by nominating his wife, María Estela Isabel Martínez de Perón (Isabel Perón), as the vice presidential candidate. The formula of Perón–Perón won the October 1973 presidential elections with 62 percent of the votes, but Juan Perón died in July 1974. He was succeeded by his widow, who exacerbated, through a combination of governmental mismanagement, corruption, and authoritarian practices, the domestic strife. In early 1976, Argentina was in complete turmoil with Peronist and Marxist guerrilla groups, including the Montoneros and the Ejército Revolucionario del Pueblo (ERP, the Revolutionary Army of the People), fighting against the military and paramilitary organizations while strikes, lockouts, and demonstrations proliferated in a context of economic stagnation, spiraling inflation, and political crisis.

Military Regime and State Terror

In March 1976, the armed forces overthrew Isabel Perón and started the so-called process of national reorganization. This Argentine version of bureaucratic authoritarianism lasted until 1983. The military junta closed Congress and provincial legislatures, removed all elected officials and Supreme Court justices, banned the activities of political parties, placed labor and some business organizations under military control, and enacted other measures aimed at controlling political life. The new regime also unleashed a wave of repression that surpassed all previous authoritarian experiences. A brutal system of state terror was institutionalized, with multiple military, paramilitary, and police groups trying to annihilate the opposition. This campaign of extermination, which the military itself called a "dirty war," was aimed at eliminating not only the armed guerrilla groups and their sympathizers but also any kind of dissent. To achieve this end, the regime used multiple terrorist methods, including murder, "disappearance," incarceration in clandestine concentration camps, jailing, torture, exile, and looting opponents' property. More than 10,000—according to some estimates, as many as 30,000—disappeared after being abducted, tortured, and assassinated by the security forces. Hundreds were killed in armed confrontations, while thousands more were forced into exile. The military rulers were also determined to eliminate the socioeconomic and political factors that led to Argentina's economic decline, social strife, and political instability. They agreed with a number of influential members of the elite and technocratic experts that the roots of the crisis were found in the existence of an interventionist state and a semiclosed economy typical of the ISI strategy. These advisers believed that the loosening of free market forces would not only create the conditions for renewed economic growth but also discipline the social actors' behavior, destroying the socioeconomic and political bases for the emergence of populist regimes. After a free market and trade liberalization program had been fully implemented, the different socioeconomic and political groups would perceive the futility of trying to influence public policies in their favor because the market, not the state, would assume the role of allocating resources and distributing income. As a result, the main cause of Argentina's high level of social conflict and political mobilization would be eliminated and governability would be restored. Once this happened, the military and its civilian allies envisioned the establishment of a more stable and less participatory political regime in which some form of restricted electoral competition would finally be authorized. However, the military regime was unable to attain its goals. The restrictions imposed by the armed forces on the monetarist economic team, which included a ban on reducing military budgets and privatizing military-controlled state enterprises, the formulation of misguided economic policies (especially those that led to overvaluation of the local currency), the persistent refusal of the economic agents to modify their state-oriented expectations and behaviors, and the worsening external financial conditions, led to economic disaster. At the same time, growing domestic and foreign condemnation of the dictatorship's atrocious human rights violations helped to isolate and weaken the military regime. Domestically, this opposition was spearheaded by several human rights organizations, led by the Mothers of the Plaza de Mayo, a group of mothers of the disappeared that since 1977 congregated every Thursday at Buenos Aires' main public square in front of the presidential palace demanding information about their relatives and an end to illegal repression. Internationally, the courageous activities of the human rights groups and the shock generated by a number of state terrorist activities—such as the kidnapping of Jacobo Timmerman, director of the newspaper *La Opinión*, and the disappearance and assassination of several priests and well-known personalities—resulted in condemnation of the Argentine regime by nongovernmental human rights organizations (such as Amnesty International and Americas Watch), the United Nations and Organization of American States human rights commissions, and several developed nations' governments, including the United States under the Carter administration and Western European governments.

In 1982, faced with a foreign debt crisis, economic stagnation, and growing domestic discontent, the government attempted to solve its problems by embarking upon an anticolonial military venture. The recovery of the Falkland Islands (Islas Malvinas), controlled by the British and claimed by Argentina, appeared to offer the perfect chance to unify the nation behind the government, regain some prestige for the military, and legitimize the regime. However, the confrontation with Great Britain ended in a complete Argentine defeat, and the domestic backlash forced the military to call for elections and transfer power to the civilians.

The authoritarian regime had failed to attain its ultimate goals but succeeded, through brutal repression and application of regressive economic policies, in changing Argentina's socioeconomic structure; reducing the power of organized labor; weakening the middle class; creating conditions for the growth of large, diversified

Members of the military junta that ruled after the 1976 military coup and waged a "dirty war" against their opponents, which resulted in thousands of assassinations and "disappearances." From left to right: Admiral Emilio Massera, General Jorge Videla, and Brigadier Orlando Agosti. (*Photo provided by the Department of Documentary Photographs, Argentine National Archive*)

domestic economic groups and foreign corporations devoted to export activities; and reducing the state economic role and its commitment to policies aimed at protecting low- and middle-income groups. The Argentine society that emerged from the military process was much more heterogeneous and fragmented than the one that had facilitated the rise of populism. These new economic and social conditions facilitated the acceptance of liberal political and economic prescriptions to promote stability and growth.

THE RETURN TO DEMOCRACY

The collapse of the military government convinced a majority of the Argentine population not only that authoritarian regimes were unable to solve the country's problems but also that they inflicted a staggering cost in human lives, civil rights, and social welfare. This majority was inclined to support parties and candidates that offered the highest likelihood of consolidating a stable democracy and rejecting authoritarian deviations. Even those groups that had supported the military regime and benefited from its policies recognized that without a solid political foundation the free market model they favored was not going to last. At the same time, the acknowledgment that earlier state-led experiences had been unable to overcome the country's structural deficiencies and the simultaneous perception that socialist and populist regimes were crumbling the world over convinced many Argentines that liberal economic policies were the only option to solve the crisis.

The democratically elected administrations of Raúl Alfonsín (1983–1989) and Carlos S. Menem (1989–1995, reelected 1995–1999) enjoyed the advantage of political legitimacy but confronted numerous economic obstacles inherited from the military. The basic elements of a liberal democracy, such as periodic elections, party competition, and majority rule with constitutional limitations, were preserved. However, there was also a growing concentration of power in the executive branch, which limited legislative participation and judicial control over important decisions as the country turned toward a free-market economy.

The UCR led by Alfonsín won the 1983 elections by a wide margin of votes. It was favored in that occasion by the popular feeling that the Radicals would maintain their traditional respect for democratic liberties, the presidential candidacy of a relatively charismatic leader, and the fear that the Peronists would persist in embracing some of the authoritarian practices used in the past. Moreover, the military government's policies had promoted a process of deindustrialization that eroded Peronism's traditional basis of electoral support by substantially reducing the number of industrial workers and weakening the strength of organized labor. In these conditions, it was possible for the Radicals to consolidate their basis of electoral support among the middle class and to make inroads among the growing number of self-employed and nonunionized workers.

The Alfonsín administration implemented economic plans that combined orthodox liberal stabilization measures with some unorthodox ones aimed at protecting middle- and low-income sectors. At the same time, it attempted to fulfill its promises to bring the military personnel responsible for human rights violations to trial and to depoliticize the armed forces. However, the economic policies failed to overcome the domestic resistance of the Peronist Party and organized labor to free market policies and the business groups' refusal to accept government controls on wage, fiscal, and exchange policies. As the civilian opposition grew, the military also defied the human rights policies of the administration and engaged in a series of revolts that compelled Alfonsín to make concessions, greatly reducing the number of officers that could be punished for their deeds during the "dirty war." Moreover, foreign banks, the International Monetary Fund (IMF), and the governments of developed countries gradually withdrew their economic support for the administration, worsening the situation.

The growing disenchantment of large sectors of the population with the economic, social, and human rights policies of the Radical administration led to a decline in its popularity. Meanwhile, the Peronists were able to complete their process of internal reorganization on a more democratic basis, eliminating some unpopular figures from the party's leadership and projecting an image of moderation that attracted the support of not only the working class but also some middle-class sectors. On the right, other groups were also able to increase their appeal among middle- and upper-class groups by denouncing the Radicals' vacillating economic policies and by calling for a more coherent strategy of economic liberalization. In 1987, the Radicals were soundly defeated by the Peronists in the midterm congressional elections and lost a number of important governorships.

In 1988, Menem won the Peronist primaries and became the party's presidential candidate, emphasizing populist themes that appealed to the majority of the party members. Meanwhile, as the 1989 presidential elections approached, government attempts to regain control over the situation failed. In this context, Menem secured his victory with 51.7 percent of the votes, and the Peronists won a majority of the gubernatorial and congressional positions in dispute.

After the elections, the paralysis of the Alfonsín administration combined with the misgivings concerning Menem's populist economic and social promises worsened the crisis. The already high rate of inflation was replaced by hyperinflation, with prices rising more than 120 percent per month. Real wages collapsed, igniting a social explosion and forcing the presidential declaration of a state of siege. Finally, Alfonsín resigned in late June to facilitate Menem's early presidential inauguration a few days later.

LIBERAL DEMOCRACY AND FREE MARKETS

To the surprise of his followers and adversaries alike, the new president embraced economic and political ideas opposed to the traditional Peronist policies. The populist promises of a "productive revolution" and huge wage raises were replaced by a free market economic program executed by some of the most representative figures of Argentina's economic and technocratic elites. Menem's project, the construction of a "popular market capitalism," required dismantling of the interventionist state conceived in the 1940s by Perón, which had survived the assault of successive military and civilian administrations. However, the Peronist tradition of personalistic leadership and the subordination of the Peronist Party and unions to the government continued, facilitating the concentration of power in the hands of the president.

The Menem administration formulated a series of ever more radical neoliberal economic and social policies that resulted in sweeping market reforms. All state enterprises and services were privatized and transferred to domestic or foreign owners, including the phone, airline, railroad, shipping, coal mining, highway, steel, armaments, and petrochemical companies; postal and insurance services; public television and radio stations; and an array of other public utilities and firms controlled by the state. Most economic activities were deregulated, a number of regulatory agencies were eliminated, and there were massive dismissals of public employees. Government monetary control was minimized, and a new currency was created (the peso replacing the austral) that was freely convertible in dollars at a parity rate of 1 for 1. In the external sector, the opening of the economy included implementation of free trade policies, such as the removal of tariff and nontariff barriers and the elimination of most subsidies, liberalization of rules concerning financial and investment flows, and acceptance of a foreign debt-for-equity approach.

These economic policies accomplished some impressive results: inflation was contained, the economy grew at a significant rate (6.1 percent in 1990–1994), the rate of exchange remained unchanged, and capital inflows increased. At the same time, the program reinforced the trends toward regressive income distribution, higher unemployment, concentration of wealth, oligopolization of the economy, growing trade deficits, and decline of the provincial economies most affected by federal budget cuts. Nevertheless, electoral support for the administration among the population increased significantly as these measures generated economic stability and made the return of inflation unlikely.

In other areas, Menem followed a course that bolstered his political preeminence. In the labor movement, the administration reacted forcefully against its opponents, dismissing state workers, imposing obligatory arbitration in private sector conflicts, and giving legal recognition only to pro-government unions. The right to strike was limited by presidential decree, wage and salary raises were linked to increases in productivity, and union control of workers' health and other social services were reduced.

Inside the Peronist Party, Menem supporters were appointed to the leading positions, reinforcing the subordination of the party and the congressional delegation to the president. The nomination and appointment of judges sympathetic to the administration eliminated many of the potential obstacles to the use of executive decrees to implement controversial policy initiatives and a law increasing from five to nine the number of justices packed the Supreme Court with Menem loyalists. At the same time, Menem cemented good relations with influential military officers by pardoning the former members of the ruling juntas and other military personnel still incarcerated for their responsibility in human rights violations. Although internal military divisions and frictions were not completely eliminated, these concessions and the promotion of more professionally oriented officers made it possible to defeat new revolts of small discontented groups and considerably reduced military pressures on the administration.

In 1994, Menem successfully promoted a constitutional reform that would permit his reelection. Negotiations with the president of the UCR, Alfonsín, resulted in an agreement in which, in exchange for supporting the reform, the opposition obtained the president's promise to replace three pro-Menem Supreme Court justices with less partisan personalities and a commitment to support constitutional provisions aimed at limiting executive power, shortening presidential and senatorial tenures, creating the post of chief of cabinet, reforming the judiciary, and reinforcing controls on the administration. A combined Peronist–Radical majority in the constitutional assembly secured passage of these reforms.

The 1995 general elections resulted in a major victory for Menem, a tremendous defeat for the Radicals, and the rise of a center-left coalition, the Frente País Solidario (FrePaSo), made up of leftist groups, Peronist dissidents, and some provincial organizations that opposed Menem's economic and human rights policies. Menem was reelected for the 1995–1999 term with close to 50 percent of the votes, while the Peronists won most congressional and gubernatorial races. The Radicals gathered less than 17 percent of the votes and FrePaSo obtained close to 30 percent of the votes, doubling its congressional representation.

The 1995 vote confirmed the preference of the population for the continuity of an administration that had secured economic and political stability. It also showed the radical's inability to overcome the negative consequences of the hyperinflation, social turmoil, and political debacle characteristic of the final months of the Alfonsín administration. The electoral rise of FrePaSo made it clear, however, that a significant portion of the population opposed the administration policies and preferred a less orthodox economic strategy aimed at generating employment and income redistribution; less stringent social, educational, and health programs; different military and human rights policies; and more control over the executive's actions.

The Decline of Economic Neoliberalism and Political Upheaval

Throughout his second administration, Menem was faced with a decline in economic growth, a dramatic rise in unemployment, and severe socioeconomic crises in some of the provinces.

As the congressional elections of 1997 approached, the main opposition forces, the UCR and FrePaSo, realized that an electoral alliance would have excellent prospects of defeating the Peronists. The rise in unemployment, numerous allegations of corruption and police brutality, and the growing insecurity and distrust of the judiciary affected the government's popularity, particularly in the larger cities and most populated provinces. Thus, the leaders of the two main opposition groups agreed on establishing an electoral front—the Alliance for Work, Justice, and Education— and advocated a program calling for the creation of jobs, elimination of corruption, and increased educational, health, and other social expenditures. This political approach succeeded, and the alliance obtained more than 45 percent of the votes versus 36 percent for the Peronists, who lost their absolute majority in the Chamber of Deputies.

These results opened a period of intense political competition in anticipation of the presidential elections of 1999. The Peronists became involved in an internal struggle for the presidential nomination that pitted the governor of Buenos Aires province, Eduardo Duhalde, against Menem, who indicated his interest in running for a third term but ultimately failed to remove the constitutional ban on a third consecutive term. The alliance nominated the Radical mayor of the city of Buenos Aires, Fernando de la Rúa, for the presidency and Carlos Alvarez, a leader of FrePaSo as the vice presidential candidate.

Throughout the presidential campaign, the alliance benefited from the dissensions inside the Peronist Party; the Menem administration's inability to overcome the economic recession, reduce unemployment, and eliminate corruption; and Duhalde's incapacity to prevent a number of police scandals in Buenos Aires province. On October 24, 1999, the alliance won the presidential elections with 48.5 percent of the votes versus 38.1 percent for the Peronists while increasing its congressional representation and gaining some governorships. On December 10, 1999, de la Rúa and Alvarez were inaugurated president and vice president. However, soon the alliance began to be affected by internal dissension as it became clear that the president and the Radical leaders were going to neither alter substantially the economic, social, and foreign policies followed by Menem nor engage in a strong anticorruption campaign. In October 2000, Vice President Alvarez resigned after his calls for a stronger stance against corruption were ignored by the president. The alliance remained in place but was considerably weakened by this resignation as well as by a ministerial reshuffle that indicated de la Rua's intention to maintain and deepen the neoliberal course followed by his predecessors.

In the second half of 2001, amid growing recession and unemployment, the de la Rúa administration faced a rising tide of withdrawal of dollar-denominated deposits from the banks and was forced to suspend these withdrawals to prevent a generalized collapse of the financial system. This measure infuriated middle-class depositors, whose life savings were frozen, and led to multiple manifestations of discontent that very rapidly converged with the protests of the unemployed and impoverished groups, resulting in massive street demonstrations, lootings, and violent confrontations with the security forces. Groups of unemployed demonstrators known as *piqueteros* (picketers) blocked main highways and bridges demanding jobs, food, and subsidies while, at the same time, organizing soup kitchens and community health and educational services. Middle-class and low-income demonstrators took to the streets of the main cities calling for the resignation of the authorities and the renewal of the political establishment, demanding "Que se vayan todos!" (They all must go!). Simultaneously, neighbors in different cities began to organize *asambleas de barrio* (neighborhood assemblies) in which, independent from the political parties, people organized demonstrations against the government and discussed proposals to solve local problems. As the intensity of the opposition and the level of the violence increased, the president attempted to solve the crisis by declaring a state of siege, and trying to negotiate the creation of a national unity government with the Peronists. On December 20, after these attempts to control the situation failed, de la Rúa resigned his office.

The resignation marked the beginning of a chaotic political period in which the absence of a vice president led to successive congressional attempts to nominate a new president. In a matter of days, three different Peronist politicians were inaugurated and resigned as they could not control the situation. The convertibility of the peso into dollars ended, a default on the external debt was announced, and the peso declined to a third of its value. Finally, the fear that the crisis could end in a catastrophic collapse of the system led politicians and representatives to come to an agreement on supporting the appointment to the presidency of Eduardo Duhalde, the former governor of Buenos Aires, vice president and defeated Peronist presidential candidate in 1999.

Duhalde was inaugurated on January 1, 2002, and remained in power until May 25, 2003. During this short period, the Duhalde administration was able to restore some degree of stability in the economic, social, and political realms. In the enomic sphere, the "convertibility" experience came to a formal end, and the value of the peso stabilized at 3 pesos for a dollar. Depositors were forced to exchange their dollar-denominated funds at a third of their value in pesos or to accept promises of long-term repayment in dollars at low interest rates. Negotiations were initiated with the IMF, World Bank, and foreign lenders to restructure the debt and reschedule payments. Some progress was made in improving the socioeconomic situation by introducing payments to the unemployed, engaging in some public investment, and increasing some of the expenditures on health, education, and housing. At the same time, Duhalde skillfully managed the political situation by announcing that he would not run for election in 2003, allowing different Peronist candidates to emerge, and selecting the relatively unknown Nestor Kirchner, the governor of the southern province of Santa Cruz, as his favorite. In the 1970s, Kirchner, together with his wife, Cristina Fernández, had been members of the leftist Peronist Youth while they were studying at La Plata, the capital of Buenos Aires province. After the 1976 coup, the Kirchners moved to Santa Cruz, keeping a low profile until redemocratization. In the 1980s and 1990s, they became again politically active in the Peronist movement. He had been elected governor of Santa Cruz and his wife became a federal senator. Duhalde supported Kirchner as a presidential candidate in the expectation that as governor of a small province with a good image but lacking a national political machine of his own, Kirchner would be able to defeat Menem but remain unable to challenge Duhalde's control of the Peronist party.

The main contestants in the April 2003 presidential elections included three Peronist candidates (Kirchner, Menem, and Adolfo Rodríguez Saá, the brief December 2001 provisional president who had declared the debt in default), one Radical (Leopoldo Moreau), a former Radical who had been briefly economic minister under de la Rúa (Ricardo López Murphy), and another former Radical representative with left populist leanings (Elisa Carrió). The results showed an ample dispersion in the electoral preferences of the population: Menem received 24.5 percent of the votes, Kirchner 22.2 percent, López Murphy 16.4 percent, Rodríguez Saá 14.1 percent, and Carrió 14 percent. These results required a second voting round to be held in May 2003 between the two candidates with the most votes. However, it soon became clear through polls that Kirchner could count on sufficient support to easily beat Menem. After considerable hesitation and under strong political pressure, Menem finally decided to withdraw his candidacy, making it possible for Kirchner to be declared the winner and assume the presidency on May 25.

Once inaugurated, Kirchner was able to increase and cement his popularity by implementing a number of redistributive economic policies, progressive social measures, human rights initiatives, and nationalistic foreign policies in the context of a rapidly recovering economic situation. While the economy grew and unemployment declined, favored particularly by the increase in the prices of export commodities, the Kirchner administration formulated policies aimed at promoting job creation, increasing unemployment benefits, improving health and educational services, and maintaining an adequate level of governmental expenditures, even when faced with presure from the IMF and bankers to increase the fiscal surplus to repay the foreign debt. A tough stance was taken in the negotiations with private foreign creditors that resulted in the exchange of most of the debt at more favorable conditions and a considerable decrease in debt payments. With support from Venezuela, the debt with the IMF was canceled, eliminating the IMF's oversight of the country's economic policies and facilitating the abandonment of orthodox free market programs. The economy recovered steadily and by the end of Kirchner's tenure it was growing at an annual rate of more than 8 percent. Hard currency reserves had risen to $35 billion and the balance of the trade remained highly positive. In this context of economic growth and increasing domestic consumption, the main problems faced by the administration were energy shortages, relative price misalignments, and the possibility of increasing inflation.

The Kirchner administration supported and implemented a number of legal, judicial, and symbolic initiatives destined to punish human rights violations that had been forgiven by previous administrations. Thus, the rescission of the amnesty laws led to the detention, trial, and incarceration of a number of human rights violators who had escaped prosecution or been freed in previous years. Museums and memorial sites were created to remember the victims of the state terrorist activities and the role of human rights organizations was officially recognized and supported. In the foreign policy sphere, the government distanced itself from the United States, particularly by refusing to support the Bush administration policies toward Iraq, the creation of a hemispheric free trade area, and militarization of the anti-drug traffic efforts; established closer relations with Cuba and Venezuela; adopted a tougher position in negotiations with foreign lenders and multilateral credit institutions; and promoted closer integration with Brazil and the other members of MERCOSUR as well as the incorporation of new members such as Venezuela.

Politically, Kirchner took advantage of his growing popularity and the weakness of the opposition to build his own political base. His approach led to a series of internal Peronist confrontations that divided the party into different factions but succeeded in the creation of a substantial base of support that comprised Peronist groups as well as sectors of other organizations, including portions of Radical, provincial, and center-left parties. In the 1995 congressional and gubernatorial elections, "Kirchnerist" candidates running under different labels succeeded in winning a plurality of the disputed seats and governorships. Most important, President Kirchner's wife, Cristina Fernández, who had been until then a senator representing the province of Santa Cruz, ran for the senate in the largest province—Buenos Aires—and defeated the wife of Eduardo Duhalde and his powerful political machine. With these electoral results, Kirchner secured control over the Peronist party, Congress, and most provincial administrations and was able to consolidate his administration's turn away from conservative market policies and toward center-left populist ones.

As the presidential elections of 2007 came closer, Kirchner's popularity remained high and the expectations were that he would be re-elected. However, in a surprising decision, he decided not to run and to support the presidential candidacy of his wife, Cristina Fernández. In the general elections of October 2007, Cristina Fernández de Kirchner won in the first round with 45.3 percent of the votes over Elisa Carrió who obtained 23 percent, Roberto Lavagna (a Peronist and former economics minister under Duhalde and Kirchner) with 17 percent, and the also Peronist Alberto Rodríguez Saá, who received 7.6 percent of the votes. For the first time in Argentine history, not only had a woman been elected president, but the two candidates receiving the most votes were women The vice presidential candidate who accompanied Cristina Fernández was Julio Cobo, the Radical governor of the Province of Mendoza, who had joined together with other Radical politicians for the "Kirchnerist" electoral coalition, Frente para la Victoria (Victory Front). Cristina Fernández was inaugurated on December 10, 2007, announcing in her inaugural speech that she would continue to implement domestic and international policies similar to those formulated by her husband, focusing on the elimination of poverty, promotion of social welfare, the pursuit of an independent foreign policy and regional integration, women's issues, and the defense of human rights.

Politics and Power

CONSTITUTIONAL FRAMEWORK AND POLITICAL INSTITUTIONS

The Argentine constitution, promulgated in 1853 and amended on different occasions, is currently in effect after having been rescinded or suspended during different periods of authoritarian rule. The 1853 constitution instituted a republican and representative political system with moderate federal features. It provided for a division of powers between the executive, legislative—divided into a Chamber of Deputies and a Senate—and judicial branches while upholding a presidentialist regime. The constitution guarantees a number of individual rights, among them freedom of association, speech, and press; protection of domicile, correspondence, and private activities against unwarranted government searches and interference; equality before the law; right to a public trial; and prohibition of retroactive application of any laws. Freedom of religion and freedom of public worship are also sanctioned, but the Catholic Church maintains a privileged position, enjoying economic support from the federal government. In economic terms, the 1853 constitution was extremely liberal, establishing the inviolability of private property, espousing free trade and market principles, promoting foreign immigration and investment, and opening internal rivers to free navigation.

The 1853 constitution was amended but remained largely unchanged until 1949, when a convention convened by President Perón—in circumstances defined as illegal by the opposition—introduced substantial reforms, including the possibility of presidential reelection and endorsing state economic intervention, limitations on private property rights, nationalization of natural resources, public utilities, credit, and foreign trade. After Perón's overthrow, the military government declared the 1949 constitutional reform null and void and summoned a new constitutional convention, which adjourned after having approved a single new article guaranteeing workers' rights, minimum wages, and social security benefits. In 1994, under Menem, a constitutional convention shortened the duration of the presidential and vice presidential mandate to 4 years and established direct popular presidential elections with a system of run-off voting (that replaced the electoral college). It also introduced new constitutional rights and guarantees, including consumer, children's, and the indigenous population's rights, and endorsed legislation establishing women's right to occupy at least one-third of all elected positions.

The executive branch consists of the president, the vice president, and the cabinet. Executive power is vested in the president, who can appoint and remove the ministers at will, except the chief of cabinet, who is answerable to the president but politically responsible to Congress and can be removed through a nonconfidence vote. The president and vice president are elected directly by popular vote through a runoff system for a 4-year term with the possibility of immediate reelection for one additional period. The president is the "supreme chief of the nation," whose powers include the general administration of the country, the appointment of administration officials, the implementation of laws, the right to introduce laws before Congress and to veto or approve legislation in part or as a whole, and the conduct of foreign relations. The president is the commander-in-chief of the armed forces and nominates Supreme Court justices and members of the diplomatic corps for confirmation by the Senate. The president can also declare, with the approval of the Senate, a state of siege, temporarily suspending some civil liberties in case of external attack or internal rebellion. Argentina follows a presidentialist tradition, concentrating in the presidents a large amount of power that makes it possible for them to often dominate the legislative and judicial branches.

The legislative branch consists of two houses: the Chamber of Deputies and the Senate. According to the constitution, the deputies represent the nation as a whole, while the senators represent the provinces and the Federal District. Congress has the power to make all laws and regulations, levy taxes and establish the budget of the central government, ratify or reject treaties and integration accords, authorize the executive to declare war, declare a state of siege and intervene in a province, and accept or reject the resignation of the president and vice president. Both chambers possess similar powers, and their approval is required to pass most legislation. To override a presidential veto, two-thirds of the votes in both chambers are required.

Judicial power at the national level is exercised by the Supreme Court of Justice and the lower courts created by Congress. The judicial branch is formally independent but, in practice, has been affected by external interferences and internal problems. The judiciary has often been subordinated to political authorities; judges and judicial personnel have been removed and replaced for political reasons, and the executive has disregarded judicial decisions. Compounding these problems, the judiciary has been plagued by slow procedures, frequent reversals of precedents, lack of citizen access, occasional corruption, and political disagreements between its members.

Until the early 1990s, Argentina had a significantly large and diversified public sector composed of the central administration, decentralized agencies, and state enterprises. Since the rise of Peronism in the 1940s, the public sector has grown very rapidly as the regulatory, distributive, and productive functions of the state expanded. The central administration has been highly bureaucratic in its procedures and clientelistic in its recruitment and composition. Attempts made by successive civilian and military governments to increase efficiency, reduce size, and attract better-qualified candidates were contradicted and frustrated by the inability of these same administrations to forego clientelistic practices and risk political and social confrontations. Menem was more successful at reducing the size of the state, but clientelistic practices, bureaucratic procedures, and corruption still plague some areas of the public administration.

According to the constitution, the twenty-three provinces and the Federal District retain all power not delegated to the federal government. Each province elects its own legislature and governor, but the constitution makes governors the "natural agents" of the federal government, in charge of enforcing the national constitution and laws. Contributing to reinforce the subordination of the provinces to the central authority is the federal government's power to take over and replace local officials with federal appointees when the "republican form of government" is endangered by internal conflicts. Because the courts have declined to define the notion of "republicanism," arguing that it is a political matter, federal authorities can define these circumstances very broadly and assume control of a province without judicial interference.

Main Political Parties

Unión Cívica Radical. The Radical party emerged as the first Argentine modern mass party demanding the end of the oligarchic regime and renewal and moralization in the political, electoral, and administrative spheres. It was supported by diverse groups, including university students, marginal members of the elite, and middle- and low-income creole sectors. In 1896, Hipólito Yrigoyen became the leader of the party and began to expand its basis of support by recruiting new members among the immigrant-descent urban middle class and workers. The promulgation, in 1912, of an electoral law that guaranteed free, universal male, obligatory suffrage facilitated Yrigoyen's presidential victory in 1916. Under Yrigoyen, the Radicals also favored some nationalistic and statist policies and implemented moderate redistributive and social policies, although without affecting the essential characteristics of the agriculturally based export–import model.

In the 1930s, after the overthrow of Yrigoyen, the Radicals were prevented from coming back to power by the use of repression, proscription, and fraud. After being defeated by the Peronists in 1946, Radicalism remained the main opposition and adopted a program calling for nationalization of natural resources, strategic industries and services, state intervention in the economy, income redistribution, and an independent foreign policy while denouncing the Peronist violations of civil liberties and political freedoms.

After supporting the military coup that ousted Perón, the Radicals split into two different parties: the Intransigent faction, led by Arturo Frondizi, and the People's faction, led by Ricardo Balbín. In the elections of 1958, after having reached an agreement with Perón, Frondizi was elected president with Peronist support but rapidly lost it and was overthrown in 1962. In 1964, taking advantage of the proscription of Peronism, the People's Radicals won the presidential elections. The new president, Arturo Illia, implemented some modest nationalistic and redistributive policies while respecting most constitutional freedoms and guarantees until he was overthrown by the military in 1966.

In the 1970s, the People's faction was able to obtain the exclusive use of the UCR name. Two major internal groups emerged during this period: one, led by Balbín, embraced moderate positions, favored alliances with other political parties, and maintained a friendly approach toward Perón; another, led by Raúl Alfonsín, favored more nationalistic and redistributive economic policies and opposed collaboration with Perón. Although losing two successive presidential elections to the Peronists in 1973 and being unable to prevent the military coup of 1976, Balbín remained leader of the party until his death in 1981. In 1982, when the military announced the call for elections, Alfonsín gained control over the party and became its successful presidential candidate. The Radical defeat in the 1989 presidential elections, hyperinflation, the electoral decline in successive congressional elections, and secret negotiations with Menem on constitutional reform eroded Alfonsín's popularity but were not enough to completely upset his control over the party machine. In the late 1990s, the Radicals were able to regain some of their popularity among the middle sectors by denouncing the socioeconomic difficulties and corruption associated with the Menem administration. The conformation of the alliance with the center-left FrePaSo helped to facilitate this recovery, and by 1998 the Radicals were once again in a competitive political position. In November 1998, Fernando de la Rúa, president of the Radical party and mayor of the city of Buenos Aires, won the open primaries organized by the alliance and became its presidential candidate for the 1999 elections. De la Rúa's victory in the presidential elections temporarily strengthened the Radical party, but very soon the decline of his administration led to factional splits and reduced the party's popularity to its lowest historical level. During the 1990s and early 2000s, different groups, such as those led by Elisa Carrió, split from the party and established their own political organizations while a number of Radical provincial factions became integrated into the Kirchnerist support front (known as Radicals K), including the one led by Julio Cobos from the province of Mendoza, who became vice presidential candidate in the ticket led by Cristina Fernández. In the 2007 general elections, the Radical party supported the candidacy of Roberto Lavagna, whose coalition came third with 17 percent of the votes. Nevertheless, the Radical party still maintains its organization and enjoys an important presence in Congress and at the provincial and local levels, making it feasible for it to regain its electoral chances.

Peronist Party. The Peronist Party was created in 1946 after Perón's victory in the presidential elections. Throughout Perón's first presidency (1946–1952), the party, which after the introduction of women's suffrage in 1947 was divided into male and female sections, played a secondary role in the Peronist movement. The party was reduced to mobilize Peronist voters at election times and to disseminate the *doctrina justicialista,* an ideology advocated by Perón that represented a third option between capitalism and communism and called for social class cooperation, state intervention, nationalistic policies, and nonalignment in order to build an Argentina that would be economically independent, socially just, and politically sovereign. During Perón's unfinished second presidency (1952–1955), the party's importance increased as Perón's authoritarian turn led to attempts to establish partisan control on the civil service and socioeconomic organizations.

After Perón's fall, the party became an underground political organization subordinated to the exiled leader, conveying Perón's orders to his followers. However, Perón was unable to prevent the emergence of the so-called neo-Peronist Parties that, with the support of some union leaders, were determined to develop a "Peronism without Perón." Most of these parties had a brief existence, but a few of them established provincial roots and remain active today.

In the 1970s, Peronism was formally reorganized as the Justice Party (Partido Justicialista, PJ). Perón remained the party chief, with the right to appoint or remove the party authorities and select its electoral candidates. However, internal factions—including union leadership, guerrilla groups, professional politicians, and youth organizations—were vying for power. Perón tried to reestablish his authority and prevent further divisions by becoming president and nominating his wife for vice president, but his death in 1974 cleared the way for violent internal confrontations.

After the 1976 military coup, Peronism was banned and many of its leaders were jailed, persecuted, or killed by the military. The party resurfaced in 1982 but split into a so-called *verticalista* faction—interested in maintaining the power of the traditional political and union bosses and continuing the tradition of hierarchical control from the top as practiced by Perón—and a number of *antiverticalista* groups—which tried to introduce more democratic procedures and elect a new leadership. The *verticalistas* succeeded, appointing Isabel Perón president of the party and nominating traditional politicians and union bosses as candidates for most elective offices. The nondemocratic features of this process, the unsavory personalities and activities of some of the Peronist candidates, and the growing popularity of Alfonsín combined to produce the defeat of the PJ in the 1983 elections. The confrontation between *verticalistas* and *antiverticalistas* resumed, with the former considerably weakened and the latter strengthened by these results. By the late 1980s, Carlos Menem, a provincial governor and vice president of the party, appealed to populist and nationalistic rhetoric to prevail in the first open party primaries and went on to win the presidential election of 1989. After his inauguration, Menem reasserted his control over the party by becoming its president. Attempts made by groups opposed to Menem to maintain some influence failed, and the party remained under the control of the president's supporters, although new internal divisions emerged as Menem's second presidential term came to an end. In 1998 and 1999, Menem tried unsuccessfully to nullify the constitutional article that made it impossible for him to run for a third presidential term but confronted growing opposition from important party figures such as Eduardo Duhalde, the governor of Buenos Aires province, who finally became the Peronist presidential candidate in the 1999 elections. Duhalde's defeat left the party in disarray, and a number of Peronist leaders, including the elected governor of Buenos Aires, Carlos Ruckauf, other governors, and Menem himself, began to compete to gain control over the party machine in anticipation of the 2003 presidential elections. The collapse of the de la Rúa administration led to a period of dramatic internal confrontation within the party from which Duhalde emerged as the winner, consolidating his control over the party machine. After Duhalde supported the presidential candidacy of Kirchner, a new internal party struggle developed between the two politicians that ended with the victory of Kirchner although the party remained divided into competing factions. As a result, in the 2007 general elections, various Peronist groups supported different candidates in the presidential, gubernatorial and congressional elections.

Other Parties and Coalitions. Besides the Radicals and Peronist Party there has been a continuous presence in the Argentine political scene of a number of minor parties and coalitions. On the left, there have been multiple organizations—including socialists, communists, and other groups—that, at different times, played a role in the electoral contests, especially in the urban areas, but that have been affected by their inability to overcome ideological divergences, avoid factionalism, and compete successfully for the working- and middle-class voters who support the Peronist and Radical parties. On the right, there have been a series of provincial parties that have remained influential at the local level but have been unable to organize a successful conservative alliance at the national level. In the last few years, there were several center-left and center-right parties and coalitions that attained relative success for brief periods but that disintegrated rapidly or became relatively uninfluential after a short time. At the time of the 2007 elections, the most relevant of these coalitions on the center-left was the Civic Coalition Confederation led by Elisa Carrió, which ended second in the presidential election and substantially increased its congressional representation; on the center-right the most important of these coalitions were the Advanced Nation coalition led by Roberto Lavagna, who ended third in the presidential elections, and the Republican Proposal led by the businessman Mauricio Macri, who was elected mayor of the city of Buenos Aires.

INTEREST GROUPS

The Military. The modern Argentine armed forces were organized as a professional institution during the late nineteenth century and remained subordinated to the civilian authorities until 1930. Since then, the military has not only organized coups and established authoritarian regimes but also played a crucial political role under most civilian administrations, exercising indirect control and vetoing government initiatives. Most officers have embraced conservative positions and supported the creation of a political system characterized by limited participation, hierarchical order, and an emphasis on domestic national security. However, agreement of these basic points has not prevented the emergence of factions that disagreed on the best methods to attain these goals or that were motivated by personalistic and group ambitions.

After overthrowing Perón in 1955, the coup leaders purged Perón's supporters from the officer corps but split into moderate and radical anti-Peronist factions, a division that would linger until the 1970s. The continuous capacity of Peronism to obtain electoral majorities and the civilian administrations' inability to suppress it resulted in the military coups of 1962 and 1966. In 1966, General Juan Carlos Onganía banned all political parties and established a bureaucratic authoritarian regime. However, growing economic and social problems accompanied by urban revolts and the rise of guerrilla movements led to Onganía's removal by his fellow officers and to a call for elections in which Peronism was finally allowed to participate.

In 1976, the armed forces overthrew Isabel Perón and inaugurated an authoritarian regime that, unlike previous ones, divided power equally among the three branches and attempted to create a system in which the military as an institution exercised power. However, as the difficulties accumulated, the military split once again into opposing factions: one group tried to implement less orthodox economic policies while establishing closer ties with conservative and provincial parties in order to co-opt their support; another group favored market policies and opposed any kind of political opening. The latter tried to overcome the crisis by increasing repression and arousing nationalistic feelings through the recovery of the Falkland/Malvinas Islands. The defeat on the islands forced the military to call for elections that resulted in a Radical victory.

Under Alfonsín, the military budget was greatly reduced and the power of the civilian authorities was strengthened. Members of the three military juntas were tried and sentenced to prison for human rights violations. However, as the number of officers brought to trial increased, the military multiplied its demonstrations of discontent and refused to testify before civilian judges. Faced with growing disobedience, Alfonsín tried to limit the number of military officers under judicial investigation by supporting a law that extinguished any penal action against officers if they were not indicted within 60 days after the promulgation of the law. When this was not enough to satisfy the military and a revolt erupted, Alfonsín supported a "due obedience law" that exempted most officers from trial, with the exception of those who had been top commanders during the "dirty war."

The concessions made by Menem, especially the pardons for the members of the juntas, satisfied most of the military and diminished support for the rebellious groups, making it possible to defeat and expel them from the ranks. After this, the military remained subordinated to the civilian government, performing its professional activities and exhibiting no signs of being interested in meddling in the political arena. This stance was not modified even when, in early 2001, a judge declared the unconstitutionality of the laws passed under Alfonsín, renewing the possibility of bringing to trial those officers accused of human rights violations. Although vehemently opposed to this decision, the military did not revolt as it had done in the past, preferring in this case to appeal the decision to higher courts. The military and human rights policies implemented by Kirchner, which included the replacement of the high military command and the resumption of trials for human rights violations committed during the period of military rule, have also displeased the armed forces, but once again, the military has preferred to use constitutional channels and means to convey its disatisfaction.

The Catholic Church. The Catholic Church has played an influential role in Argentine politics, as either a supporter or an opponent of specific policies implemented by different governments, particularly in the educational and social areas. The 1853 constitution instituted freedom of belief but granted Catholicism a privileged position by requiring the federal government to finance the Church and the president and vice president to be Catholic.

The Catholic Church has supported those governments which promised to implement policies that corresponded to a conservative interpretation of Catholic teachings, disregarding the authoritarian or democratic origins of these administrations. When some governments formulated policies that clashed with these notions, the Church conducted political campaigns aimed at reversing these measures and sometimes to remove the governments responsible for them. For example, the Church supported Perón because he promised to maintain religious education in public schools and to follow Catholic social teachings, but when Perón decided to eliminate religious education, promulgate a divorce law, and legalize prostitution, the Church became a crucial participant in the coalition that overthrew him.

The majority of bishops and cardinals have been consistently conservative, even during the 1960s and 1970s when less traditional attitudes proliferated in the rest of Latin America. The emergence in Argentina of a group of progressive priests who embraced liberation theology was a phenomenon restricted mainly to the rank and file. Most Church authorities welcomed the military coups of 1966 and 1976, especially because right-wing nationalistic figures associated with the Church were appointed to important positions.

Throughout the 1976–1983 period, most Church dignitaries supported the military regime or adopted neutral positions and only a few bishops and archbishops openly opposed the authoritarian government, although some members of the Church (including bishops, priests, and lay associates) were killed, jailed, and persecuted. After the restoration of democracy in 1983, the most conflictive aspects of Church–state relations were focused on family, cultural, and educational issues. Under Alfonsín, the Church hierarchy unsuccessfully opposed the passing of a divorce law and a more liberal family code. This defeat strengthened the influence of a more moderate group of bishops who emphasized the moral role of the Church but distanced themselves from open political actions. Under Menem, the Church hierarchy initially adopted a more supportive attitude than during the Alfonsín administration in the expectation that the new president, who had opposed the divorce law and advocated the Church's social teachings, would follow a less secular course. However, some members of the hierarchy criticized the application of economic policies that affected the poor and generated unemployment, while others denounced the pardons given by Menem to the military. Under Kirchner the Church confronted the administration on issues such as reproductive rights and AIDS policies and was threatened by the resumption of human rights trials that resulted in the condemnation of some priests involved in the repressive activities and the dismissal of chaplains associated with the military and security forces.

Organized Labor. Argentina's long tradition of well-organized and relatively powerful labor organizations started in the late nineteenth century. The first unions were formed by European immigrants, particularly skilled workers, who embraced anarchist and socialist ideologies. In the 1940s, Perón was able to skillfully manipulate the labor movement through a combination of rewards for his supporters (collective bargaining, official recognition, social benefits) and elimination of his opponents (denial of legal recognition and benefits and removal from office). By 1945, the General Confederation of Labor (CGT) was under the control of Peronist union leaders, many of them newly elected, and the numbers of unionized workers increased rapidly. In October 1945, a workers' mobilization forced the release of Perón from confinement and cleared the way for his presidential campaign. After Perón's inauguration, union membership became obligatory for most workers, the number of unionized workers greatly increased, and their wages and benefits improved. The CGT remained firmly under the control of Perón, who eliminated political dissidents and appointed loyal members of small unions to lead the organization.

After Perón's fall, the CGT and most unions were taken over by the military; however, in elections held in 1956, a majority of the unions elected Peronist leaders, and in the early 1960s, the Peronists regained control of the CGT. Although persecuted and banned by different military and civilian governments, organized labor became an important political actor able to use its mobilization capacity to support Peronism and strengthen or weaken the administrations established between 1958 and 1976.

Under the 1976–1983 authoritarian regime, the CGT was taken over by the military and some influential labor leaders who tried to oppose the military rulers were kidnapped and killed or forced into exile. As the economic crisis erupted, union leaders led some demonstrations and strikes but remained weak and disorganized. Only after the Falklands/Malvinas crisis were the multiple labor factions able to overcome part of their differences and to reestablish a unified CGT under Peronist control.

After the defeat of the PJ in the 1983 elections, confrontations within the CGT became more acute and created the opportunity for the rise of new labor leaders. In 1986, the CGT regained legal status and pursued a number of goals, among which the most important were the recomposition of real wages, the control of social services, and the promulgation of a new law on trade unions; but its ability to exact concessions from the government was limited by its lack of internal unity.

Some labor leaders negotiated with the Radical government and secured the appointment of one of their own as minister of labor. The Alfonsín administration sent to Congress a package of labor legislation reestablishing collective bargaining, maintaining union-provided social services, and strengthening the rights of organized labor. However, after the Radical electoral defeats, this alliance collapsed and most union leaders went back to the Peronist fold and organized several general strikes.

After his inauguration, Menem saw an independent CGT as an obstacle to the smooth implementation of a neoliberal program. Collaborationist union leaders were appointed to government positions and tried to gain control over the CGT, which split into two rival organizations: one of them stated its complete loyalty to the administration and supported the neoliberal economic plan; the other declared its support for Peronism but opposed the economic policies and warned that it would continue to fight for higher wages and against dismissals. In late 1992, public employees' and teachers' unions joined by other smaller organizations formed a new labor organization that strongly opposed the neoliberal economic policies, denounced the official CGT as collaborationist, and established political links with the opposition. In 1994, a group of Peronist unions, led by the transportation workers' union, broke away from the CGT and formed another organization, the Movement of Argentine Workers (MTA), demanding tougher opposition to the government's labor and welfare policies. Meanwhile, as a result of Menem's neoliberal policies, the number of workers affiliated with unions had decreased from 50 to 35 percent while the number of self-employed and nonunionized workers had increased substantially. In 2000, sectors of organized labor confronted the de la Rúa administration and called for strikes to oppose a new labor law that would weaken job stability and curtail the application of collective bargaining agreements. However, the divisions inside the labor movement prevented the creation of a unified front, and the labor reform promoted by the government was passed with the support of the CGT's moderate union leaders against MTA resistance. After de la Rúa's fall, the labor movement was reunified into a single CGT that by 2005 was led by Hugo Moyano from the truck drivers' union. Under Moyano, the CGT maintained a relatively friendly approach toward the Kirchner administration but there were internal labor disputes for the leadership positions, with the opponents to Moyano beginning to demand his replacement. In late 2007, Moyano demanded wage raises to compensate for inflation and clashed with the newly elected president, Cristina González, who announced her intention to promote a "social pact" that would try to prevent wage and price increases and to avoid involvement in labor's internal disputes.

In the late 1990s, in the context of the socioeconomic crisis, two important social movements emerged in Argentina: the *piqueteros* (pickets) and the recovered factories movement. The *piquetero* organizations are made up of unemployed workers who demand jobs and economic support by demonstrating in the streets and blocking important roads and bridges. They have evolved into a number of unemployed workers' groups that have been able to obtain subsidies from the government and exercise some degree of political influence, especially during the Kirchner administration, although they remain divided between softliners (open to cooperation with the government) and hardliners (embracing more radical positions). The recovered factory movement is made up of workers who have taken over closed factories and other enterprises (such as hotels and service companies), transforming them into self-managed units. There are about 150 of these recovered companies with more than 15,000 workers. They have counted on some moderate support on the part of the Kirchner administration but many of them face important economic and legal challenges and the movement itself remains divided into different currents, weakening the ability to advance its demands.

Business Associations. Argentine business associations are organized along sectors of economic activity, including agricultural, industrial, commercial, and financial interests. Among the agricultural associations, the most powerful are the Argentine Rural Society, which represents the interests of the largest and wealthiest landowners—cattle raisers and grain producers—and the Argentine Rural Confederation, which represents the interests of the medium to large agricultural producers, including cattle breeders and grain producers. Both organizations strongly defend private property rights—opposing any land reform—and advocate free market and trade policies. In the 1990s, they became the strongest supporters of Menem's economic policies, particularly welcoming the elimination of exchange controls, the elimination of regulations and agricultural state boards, and the measures directed to reduce labor costs. After the collapse of the neoliberal policies, they maintained a strong opposition to any tax increases and introduction of new regulations but due to the high profits associated with the rise in the price of export commodities these measures did not affect these sectors as strongly as they expected.

The Argentine Agrarian Federation initially represented tenant farmers and afterward small and medium-sized farmers engaged in mixed agricultural and cattle-raising activities that produce mostly for the domestic market. Politically, it has usually opposed authoritarian regimes and supported democracy, favoring some degree of state intervention to enlarge the domestic market and protect small producers. It has been less supportive of neoliberal policies, expressing concern about the decline of the domestic market and the increase in agricultural imports and maintaining a closer cooperation with the Kirchner administration.

The most important industrial association is the Argentine Industrial Union, whose membership and influence expanded as the ISI process developed. The organization was controlled by the large industrialists from Buenos Aires who opposed Perón's labor policies. After becoming president, Perón dissolved the organization and replaced it with another that represented the interests of the smaller industrialists of the interior and those that emerged as a result of the Peronist industrializing policies. After Perón's fall, the Industrial Union was restored and continued to represent the larger domestic and foreign industrial companies that supported a moderately liberal economic approach, although it also favored some state intervention and protection to promote its interests.

The 1976–1983 military regime recognized the Argentine Industrial Union as representative of all industrial groups, but two factions emerged: one that represented the large industrial groups with liberal economic positions and another that represented the smaller industrial groups of the interior and favored some degree of state intervention. Under Menem, the former backed most of the neoliberal policies, while the latter expressed reservations concerning the rapid opening of the economy and the decline of the domestic market. Under Kirchner, economic growth led to an industrial recovery that benefitted particularly those sectors producing for the domestic market.

The Argentine Chamber of Commerce represents the interests of the commercial sector but also includes among its members representatives of the insurance, transportation, and financial companies. It has always defended the free market system, advocated free trade, and called for the lifting of price controls and state regulations. In political terms, it has traditionally supported conservative civilian and military governments while opposing those that followed populist and state-led strategies. In the 1990s, it became one of the strongest supporters of Menem's neoliberal policies and stated its opposition to some of the redistributionist and state interventionist policies implemented by Duhalde and Kirchner.

Bank organizations include the Association of Banks of the Argentine Republic, the Association of Argentine Banks, and the Association of Banks of the Interior of the Argentine Republic. The first represents the interests of the largest banks, more than half of which are foreign-owned. The other two associations represent the interests of smaller banks mostly of local capital. All of them support liberal economic principles, including free financial and exchange markets, but differ on the roles to be played by foreign capital and the state. While the first one supports unrestricted free movement of capital and complete lifting of most financial regulations, the other two favor some regulations to prevent the concentration of capital in the largest foreign and national banks.

WOMEN'S ROLE

Women's participation in Argentina's labor force has been increasing steadily since the 1940s, with 61 percent of women participating in the labor force as of 2007. However, around two-thirds of female workers are concentrated in the service sector. Wages for women were estimated to be on average one-third lower than those for men. In educational terms, women have fared better, having attained a higher level of literacy and high school attendance than men and representing a substantial proportion of university students, including those in traditionally male-dominated careers such as law, medicine, and engineering.

In the political realm, women have played an increasingly important role, particularly since their enfranchisement in the late 1940s. Since the turn of the century, Argentine women have fought for the right to vote and participated in political party activities, particularly in left and center-left parties. The emergence of Peronism in the 1940s was associated with the rise to prominence of Evita Perón, who became one of the twentieth century's leading political figures and has remained a revered icon for a substantial sector of the population. She was instrumental in securing the extension of the right to vote to women in 1947 and became the leader of the women's sector of the Peronist Party until her death in 1952. After 1947, women became active participants in many of the political parties, were elected to the national and provincial legislatures, and were appointed members of different cabinets, although in a lesser proportion than men. In 1973, Isabel Perón—Juan Perón's third wife—was elected vice president of the country in a formula headed by her husband. After Perón's death in 1974, she became the president of the country until she was overthrown by the military coup of March 1976.

Women played a crucial role during the last military dictatorship (1976–1983) in the struggle for human rights and democracy. The Mothers (and Grandmothers) of the Plaza de Mayo became the main opponents of the military junta, openly denouncing the terrorist tactics of the regime and demanding the return of the disappeared. Through their brave actions, which cost them heavily in terms of repression and persecution, the Mothers were able to call world attention to the brutality of the military government and to mobilize sectors of the Argentine population in the demand for respect for human rights and the establishment of democracy. After the transition to democracy, the Mothers and other human rights organizations in which women play a fundamental role have continuously demanded the investigation and condemnation of those responsible for terrorist practices and the return of the children of the disappeared.

In the 1990s, in order to increase women's formal political representation, a constitutionally endorsed law required that political parties reserve every third place on their lists of candidates for women. The implementation of this quota law, the first in the world of its kind, led to a rapid increase in the number of women elected to office; currently around 40 percent of the seats in Congress are occupied by women representing different parties. Also, there has been an increase in the number of women in ministerial and secretarial positions and running for executive office at the provincial level since the reestablishment of democracy, but the proportion of women appointed and elected to these offices remains relatively low. The 2007 general elections resulted in the presidential victory of Cristina Fernández de Kirchner with 45 percent of the votes, and the runner up was another woman, Elisa Carrió, who gathered 23 percent. In her inaugural address, the new president mentioned that it could be harder for a woman to lead her country but emphasized that she will be guided by the example of Eva Perón and the Mothers and Grandmothers of the Plaza de Mayo in her attempts to eliminate poverty, defend human rights, and punish their violations.

Looking Forward: Argentina's Political Prospects

In the 1980s and 1990s, the Argentine political–economic situation was characterized by the gradual consolidation of a liberal democratic regime and the implementation of neoliberal economic policies. This development surprised many analysts familiar with the country's evolution in the twentieth century. In the past, these elements were clearly antagonistic: liberal democratic governments felt threatened by the local versions of populism and were unable to stand the negative reactions generated by the attempts to implement free market policies; populist regimes were perceived as incompatible with liberal democracy and neo-liberal economic programs because they often engaged in authoritarian practices and favored state intervention in the economy; and economic liberal programs were implemented through authoritarian means by the elites and the military due to their inability to gain electoral support and popular backing for free market policies. The inability to reconcile these elements became an important factor in fostering the periodic outbursts of political, economic, and social instability that resulted in Argentina's traditional merry-go-round of military and civilian governments since 1930.

The current situation, characterized by the stability of a constitutional liberal democratic regime with successive elected administrations able to implement neo-liberal and populist policies without generating the collapse of democracy represents a scenario that would have been considered implausible in the past. Nevertheless, the stability of the emergent Argentine liberal democracy is still an issue when considering the strength and durability of the commitment to this regime by different domestic groups. In Argentina, support for liberal democracy depended on a number of political variables, such as the degree of devastation brought about by authoritarian regimes and the intensity of the population's revulsion against these regimes, the depth of the popular belief in the legitimacy of democracy, the ability of democratic governments to establish effective institutional arrangements, and the existence of representative political parties. However, when confronted with the rise of tensions between market and democracy, the elected administrations of Alfonsín, Menem, de la Rúa, and Kirchner turned in different degrees to solutions that, without eliminating the liberal democratic features of the regime, represented a consistent effort to concentrate political power in the executive branch, limit the participation or influence of organized political and socioeconomic groups in the decisions, and establish direct relations between personalistic leaders and an atomized civil society.

The fact that the concentration of power in the executive and the implementation of neoliberal policies had facilitated a rise in corruption and generated unprecedented levels of unemployment and poverty among the population led to changes in the political situation. Election results in the late 1990s indicated that these problems facilitated the growth of a center-left coalition interested in implementing policies aimed at reducing arbitrariness and corruption while lessening unemployment and poverty. This trend was temporarily interrupted by the unfortunate experience of the de la Rúa administration, but immediately after its fall, there was a renewed tendency to abandon the neoliberal economic policies and move in the direction of reintroducing some redistributive and welfare policies. In these conditions, the prospects for the consolidation of liberal democracy in Argentina are still brighter than they have been since the 1920s, but the stability of the regime is still threatened by the existence of socioeconomic inequities and political weaknesses that could foster popular discontent and result in domestic upheaval.

Chronology

1516 First Spanish expedition arrives at Río de la Plata

1536 First foundation of Buenos Aires; the city is abandoned in 1540

1580 Second foundation of Buenos Aires

1776 Creation of the viceroyalty of Río de la Plata

1806–1807 British invasions repelled by *criollo* militias

1810 *Criollo* government junta replaces Spanish authorities

1816 Declaration of independence

1816–1829 Civil wars between federal and centralist factions

1829–1852 Dictatorship of Juan Manuel de Rosas

1853 National constitution molded on U.S. presidentialist system adopted

1853–1861 Sporadic civil war between Buenos Aires elites and provincial leaders

1862–1880 Consolidation of oligarchic regime led by agro-exporting Buenos Aires elites

1880–1916 Economic prosperity generated by export–import growth model and political stability under oligarchic regime

1916–1930 Mass democracy under elected middle-class radical administrations: Hipólito Yrigoyen (1916–1922, 1928–1930) and Marcelo T. de Alvear (1922–1928)

1930–1943 Great Depression and economic crisis in Argentina; military coup overthrows Yrigoyen; return of oligarchy to power and beginning of import substitution industrialization

1943–1955 Rise and fall of Juan D. Perón's populist regime

1955–1966 Political instability characterized by succession of military governments and limited democratic regimes

1966–1973 Military regime in power; socioeconomic crisis, urban explosions, and guerrilla warfare

1973–1976 Return to democracy under Peronist elected government; President Perón dies in office (1974) and is replaced by his widow and vice president Isabel Perón; growing socioeconomic and political tensions; violent confrontations between guerrilla groups and military

1976–1983 Military regime, "dirty war," and economic crisis; invasion of Falkland Islands and defeat (1982); military call for elections (1983)

1983–1989 Radical party wins elections; Raúl Alfonsín elected president; growing economic and social problems; hyperinflation and political crisis

1989–1995 Peronist candidate Carlos S. Menem elected president for 1989–1995; Menem implements free market economic policies and attains political preeminence; constitution amended allowing for presidential reelection (1994)

1995–1999 Menem reelected president; consolidation of market economy; growing socioeconomic problems and accusations of corruption

1999 Electoral alliance between Radical party and FrePaSo wins presidential election; Fernando de la Rúa and Carlos Alvarez elected president and vice president, respectively, for 1999–2003

2000 Vice President Alvarez resigns in October, denouncing lack of effective governmental action against corruption; alliance between radicalism and FrePaSo remains but is considerably weakened

2001 President de la Rúa is forced to resign in December amid socioeconomic crisis and popular demonstrations; brief period of political turbulence with three different presidents

2002 On January 1, Eduardo Duhalde is inaugurated president

2003   Nestor Kirchner is elected president in April and inaugurated in May
2007   Cristina Fernández de Kirchner is elected president in October and inaugurated in
December

Bibliography

Brysk, Alison. *The Politics of Human Rights in Argentina: Protest, Change, and Democratization*. Stanford, CA:
Stanford University Press, 1994.

Corradi, Juan. *The Fitful Republic: Economy, Society and Politics in Argentina*. Boulder, CO: Westview Press,
1985.

Di Mauro, José Angel. *¿Que se vayan todos? Crónica del derrumbe político*. Buenos Aires: Corregidor, 2003.

Epstein, Edward, ed. *The New Argentine Democracy: The Search for a Successful Formula*. Westport, CT:
Praeger, 1992.

Hodges, Donald C. *Argentina's "Dirty War": An Intellectual Biography*. Austin: University of Texas Press,
1991.

James, Daniel. *Resistance and Integration: Peronism and the Argentine Working Class, 1946–1976*. Cambridge:
Cambridge University Press, 1988.

Lewis, Paul. *The Crisis of Argentine Capitalism*. Chapel Hill: University of North Carolina Press, 1990.

O'Donnell, Guillermo. *Bureaucratic Authoritarianism: Argentina, 1966–1973, in Comparative Perspective*.
Berkeley: University of California Press, 1988.

Page, Joseph. *Perón: A Biography*. New York: Random House, 1983.

Peralta Ramos, Mónica, and Carlos Waissman. *From Military Rule to Democracy in Argentina*. Boulder, CO:
Westview Press, 1987.

Potash, Robert. *The Army and Politics in Argentina, 1928–1945: Yrigoyen to Perón*. Stanford, CA: Stanford
University Press, 1969.

———. *The Army and Politics in Argentina, 1945–1962: Perón to Frondizi*. Stanford, CA: Stanford University
Press, 1980.

Rock, David. *Argentina, 1516–1987: From Spanish Colonization to Alfonsín*. 2nd ed. Berkeley: University of
California Press, 1987.

———. *Politics in Argentina, 1890–1930: The Rise and Fall of Radicalism*. London: Cambridge University
Press, 1975.

Simpson, John, and Jana Bennet. *The Disappeared and the Mothers of the Plaza*. New York: St. Martin's Press,
1985.

Smith, William C. *Authoritarianism and the Crisis of the Argentine Political Economy*. Stanford, CA: Stanford
University Press, 1989.

Snow, Peter, and Luigi Manzetti. *Political Forces in Argentina*. 3rd ed. Westport, CT: Praeger, 1993.

Timmerman, Jacob. *Prisoner without a Name, Cell without a Number*. New York: Vintage Books, 1982.

Films

The empty ATM (Wide Angle 4). United States, 2003. Documentary examines the 2000–2001 economic, social, and political crisis and explores how Argentines dealt with the collapse of their
economy.

The Garden of Forking Paths. (Americas Program 1): United States, 1993. Documentary examining Argentina's political, economic, and social development in the twentieth century.

Las Madres: The Mothers of Plaza de Mayo. United States, 1985. Documentary about the courageous role
played by the mothers of the "disappeared."

The Official Story. Argentina, 1985. On the "dirty war," the disappeared, and their repercussions on
Argentine society.

La República Perdida I/La República Perdida II. Argentina, 1983/1985. Documentaries focused on the
twentieth-century political history of Argentina that explore the causes of instability.

Tango Bar. Argentina, 1988. The story of the tango is narrated against the background of Argentina's
1976–1983 dictatorship.

Websites and Other Sources

Information on current Argentine events is available in English through the Foreign Broadcast Information Service–Latin America as well as the foreign news sections of the *Miami Herald, New York Times, Wall Street Journal,* and *Washington Post.* Access to the main Argentine newspapers and magazines is easily secured through the internet on a daily and weekly basis. Among the main newspapers are the following: *Clarín* (www.clarin.com.ar), *La Nación* (www.lanacion.com.ar), and *Página/12* (www.pagina12.com.ar).

Political information can be obtained at different sites, including the Latin American Network Information Center (LANIC) maintained by the University of Texas, which offers a wealth of data and numerous links to different sites in Argentina and abroad dealing with governmental institutions, political parties, human rights, media and academic research centers (http://info.lanic.utexas.edu/la/argentina/).

SIXTEEN

CHILE

Eduardo Silva

Introduction

Long and narrow, Chile clings to the western edge of South America's Southern Cone. Hugging approximately 3000 miles of Pacific coastline from Peru to Tierra del Fuego and separated from Argentina by the majestic Cordillera de los Andes, the country averages only about 100 miles in width. Chile's territory also includes possessions in Oceania and Antarctica. The country's length ensures a great variety of climate. The mineral-rich, sparsely populated northern third (Arica to Atacama) is one of the driest deserts in the world. The central third (Coquimbo to Llanquihue), where the bulk of the population lives, ranges from semiarid to mild Mediterranean to wet temperate and constitutes the agricultural heartland, dairy center, and timber capital of the nation. Temperate climate continues to the extreme south, dominated by a spectacular geography of islands and fjords, where sheep ranching, fishing, oil, and timber extraction predominate.

Blessed with a strong democratic tradition, Chile overcame near civil war in the early 1970s, economic chaos, and a harsh military dictatorship to emerge as a model of economic and political stability in the 1990s. Since 1990, democratically elected governments have managed the neoliberal economic model inherited from the military government in a manner that, with the exception of the Asian crisis–induced economic slowdown of 1998–2002, ensured sustained growth. Moreover, while political turmoil engulfed Venezuela, the central Andes, and Argentina in the late 1990s and early 2000s, Chile consolidated democracy..

The darker legacies of Chile's military government temper this rosy assessment. Chile may be a model for neoliberal economics and democratic stability, but it suffers from the socioeconomic and environmental imbalances that radical neoliberal models generate. In 2007, after 16 years of democratic rule, Chile was still a more unequal country than before the dictatorship, garnering it the dubious distinction of having one of the worst income distributions in Latin America. Moreover, for all its growth Chile's economy had not developed much beyond the agromineral export profile of traditional underdeveloped nations and paid a heavy cost in terms of environmental degradation and natural resource depletion. Meanwhile, its political stability rested, in part, on anti-democratic institutions. Those institutions protected the privileges of upper-class social groups. Although successive center-left governments abrogated most of those "authoritarian enclaves" by 2008, the political practices they created still affect electoral politics and the policy process. Meaningful reform of the dictatorship's labor code, regressive tax code, and the electoral system still await.

Chile is a heavily urbanized country; 85 percent of its approximately 16.3 million people live in cities and towns, mostly in the central part of the nation (about 5 million live in metropolitan Santiago, the capital city). At 2 percent, the annual population growth rate is on the lower end for Latin America. Most Chileans are *mestizos*, the descendants of sixteenth- and seventeenth-century Iberian European conquistadors and the local native population. Waves of non-Iberian European immigrants did not contribute greatly to the Chilean population; but of those who reached Chile most became part of the upper middle class professional and commercial strata inserted between *mestizo* employees and white persons of Spanish heritage who comprise the upper classes. Lacking a plantation economy, persons of African descent are a negligible component of the population. Nevertheless, racism manifests itself in a strong correlation of skin color and Native American features to socioeconomic status. In general, the more European-looking, the higher the status. Since the 1980s, Asians have also arrived in Chile in greater numbers, following Chile's opening to international trade.

Political Economy

Since 1975, Chile has applied a neoliberal economic model, which has delivered sustained, high economic growth rates for most of the time between the mid-1980s and 2004. Following the neoliberal prescriptions of the Washington Consensus, its economy is very open to international trade and finances. Openness to trade significantly diversified the economy. Although copper still contributes heavily to export earnings, the emphasis on comparative advantage has intensified agro-exports in fruits, timber, fish, wine, and other minerals, such as molybdenum. The financial services, construction, and commercial sectors also expanded notably. Manufacturing, after a period of decline due to the dismantling of protection and subsidies of the earlier import substitution industrialization (ISI) period, restructured, stabilized, and even exports. In addition to these modifications, rapid economic growth stimulated a tight labor market up to 1998, which together with low inflation contributed to rising wages. Privatized pension funds and health insurance, in addition to capital inflows from abroad, provided ample investment funds for the Chilean economy. The Asian crisis–induced recession of 1998–2002 had a negative impact on these trends, but employment and investment have picked up again with the resumption of economic growth in 2000, albeit not to previous levels.

The governing center-left coalition (now in its fourth term) maintained the neoliberal model inherited from the military government. Macroeconomic stability, with a special emphasis on inflation control, receives priority. Due to extensive privatization, with the exception of copper mining the state renounced public enterprise as a development tool. It mainly relies on fiscal and monetary policy to direct the economy. Economic growth and increased welfare spending dramatically reduced poverty from 40 percent of Chileans in 1990 to 17.5 percent in 2006 and lowered indigency to under 5 percent of the population. Content with their accomplishments, official Chile (the government and those close to it) and Conservatives alike see little need for change.

Because of their growing complacency Chile's center-left governments neglected serious problems generated by the neoliberal model. The commitment to inflation control overvalues the currency, hurting exporters and suppressing policies that reactivate economies during downturns. Lack of state direction inhibited a transition from an agromineral extractive economy to one capable of adding value to those products and developing technology. Also, although absolute poverty has declined, the highly unequal distribution of the nation's wealth has not changed since the military government, when it became even more concentrated than before. By the same token, Chile's education policy and other barriers—such as the pro-business labor code—limit opportunity for social mobility for the majority, who are not members of the relatively small middle class or the tightly knit circles of the rich, the well-born, and the powerful. Accumulating tensions contributed to unexpected mass demostrations by students and copper and forestry workers in 2006 and 2007 who felt the government was too remote and insensitive to their grievances despite the fact that president Michelle Bachelet had campaigned on a platform of citizen participation.

Political History

Geography, natural resource endowments, and fierce armed resistance by the Araucanian people left their stamp on the social, political, and economic development of Chile. In colonial times, the Captaincy General of Chile was a far-flung outpost of the Spanish Empire that began at the valley of the Aconcagua River, considerably south of its contemporary northern border. In contrast to Peru, Bolivia, and Mexico, the relative absence of gold and silver gave the social and economic structures of colonial Chile a decidedly agrarian foundation. Most creole wealth, power, and privilege flowed from control over large estates: the *encomienda* and the *hacienda*. This system engendered a rigid class structure with harsh labor exploitation. *Encomenderos* (conquistadors and their descendants who received land grants and rights to the labor of the natives on it) lorded over an Indian and *mestizo* workforce, who, in return for a plot of land, owed unrestricted fealty and labor to the landlord. In addition to the *encomenderos*, public officials, the high clergy, and merchants rounded out the colonial elite. This stratified, repressive, rigid social system had an enduring legacy. From colonial days until the present, relatively small, closely knit networks of elites have defended the exploitative underpinnings of their wealth and privilege vigorously.

Chile secured its independence from Spain in 1818. Between then and 1830, family, personal, and ideological conflicts contributed to a period of political instability. This era ended when the Conservative oligarchy defeated the Liberals, who had challenged the privileges of the traditional landowning and merchant oligarchy, in the civil war of 1829–1830, thus paving the way for the autocratic republic (1831–1871). The constitution of 1833 established a centralized and authoritarian government featuring strong presidentialism. A series of constitutional reforms eroded the autocratic republic between 1870 and 1875 and granted greater powers to the legislature, which protected the interests of traditional agrarian and merchant elites.

President José Manuel Balmaceda challenged the considerable power of the legislature (which overrepresented the oligarchy) when legislators blocked his reform-minded economic and social policies. This confrontation erupted in the civil war of 1891, ending 50 years of political stability and ushering in the parliamentary republic (1891–1924) after Balmaceda's defeat. During the parliamentary republic Congress dominated the presidency. Political and fiscal disorder during this period sparked constitutional reform that culminated in the constitution of 1925, a document that reestablished presidential rule and introduced direct popular elections for both chambers of Congress.

Chile underwent substantial socioeconomic change between 1860 and the early twentieth century, principally with the emergence of the mining industry, especially after the War of the Pacific (1879–1883) against Peru and Bolivia. Victorious, Chile annexed the Bolivian province of Atacama and the Peruvian provinces of Tarapacá and Arica. This act deprived Bolivia of its access to the Pacific Ocean and gave Chile vast mineral wealth—first nitrate and then copper. Mining brought three changes. First, it created a new, very wealthy social group, mine owners, who became part of the socioeconomic elite of Chile. Second, mining ushered in an enduring characteristic of Chile's economic system: control of its principal export product by foreign economic interests, initially the British in the case of nitrate and later the United States with copper. Third, mining necessitated miners, most of whom came from rural Chile. Ruthlessly exploited and repressed, they provided the foundation for working-class organization.

Between 1891 and 1920, the parliamentary republic served Chile's agromineral, financial, and merchant oligarchy and British economic interests well. In keeping with the worldwide spread of free market capitalism under British hegemony free trade, a minimalist state almost entirely devoted to the maintenance of internal order, and brutal labor repression reigned. However, socioeconomic change pressured the stability of this political regime. Urbanization and the expansion of mining, industrial, and service wage labor under harsh working conditions generated spontaneous labor organizing. Urbanization and Chile's nitrate-fueled economic boom also swelled the ranks of the middle classes who built reformist political parties with links to labor. They supported anti-clericalism, labor reform, public education, tariff barriers to stimulate industrialization, more taxes on land and business, and direct election of the president.

Mounting political instability engulfed Chile between 1920 and 1932 as conservative and reformist governments fought to protect or modify the privileges of the traditional socioeconomic groups of the oligarchy. The struggle brought down the parliamentary republic in 1924 and ushered in the constitution of 1925, which remained in force until 1973. Democracy, however, remained elusive as a succession of dictatorships gripped Chile, first under the quasi-fascist rule of Carlos Ibáñez del Campo (1927–1931) and then military juntas, some of which were quite progressive. Chile returned to full political democracy with the second election of Arturo Alessandri as president in 1932 (his first had been 1920–1924 and March–Oct. 1925). His administration marked the beginning of 40 years of uninterrupted democratic rule, a period that ended with the violent overthrow of Salvador Allende in 1973.

Conservatives, Reformers, and Revolutionaries

The political system that emerged from the ruins of the parliamentary republic was highly presidentialist and centralized; the presidency initiated most legislation; and all important decisions were made in the capital, Santiago. The Congress mainly negotiated bills with the presidency, fine-tuning them to the interests of the political parties and their constituencies. However, the Congress had the power to kill bills. When no candidate won a clear majority in presidential elections, the Congress nominated the president from the top two vote-getters. This occurred with some frequency, and a tradition formed in which the Congress ratified the candidate with the most votes.

During this period Chile had a tripolar party system. On the right were the Conservative and Liberal Parties, the Radical Party and later the Christian Democrats occupied the center, and the Socialist and Communist Parties dominated the left. The right mostly represented the interests of socioeconomic elites (the upper and upper middle classes), although social conservatives of the middle and even working classes, usually staunch Catholics, also voted for it. Most middle classes supported centrist parties, although anticlerical forces from the upper class also swelled the ranks of the Radical Party, and some sectors of organized labor later backed the Christian Democrats. Usually, however, urban labor and much of the lower middle class sustained the Socialist and Communist Parties. Because of *inquilinaje* (a servile form of sharecropping), rural labor remained a captive voting bloc for conservatives.

Each pole of this party system advocated different policies to promote economic development and social peace. The right supported a good business climate, one that favored investment opportunities over redistribution of the national wealth to less advantaged social groups. By and large, conservatives also opposed labor rights. The center was more reformist. Centrists proposed greater state involvement in the economy to promote industrialization through public ownership, planning, and regulation; and they sought land reform to modernize agriculture. Centrists also championed social reforms in education, health, and housing and pledged support for organized labor. The left embraced the same causes; the difference lay in their ideological and programmatic emphasis. Influenced by Marxism, leftists unabashedly pronounced that the concentration of private property in the hands of a few was the root of social and economic inequality in Chile. Therefore, state involvement in the economy should be greater than that advocated by more middle class–oriented centrist parties, and more radical land reform was required. Revolutionaries called for the abolition of most or all private businesses. Leftists believed in strong support for organized labor (higher wages, benefits, and rights) and generous fiscal expenditures for social reforms.

The flexibility of centrist parties was key to the political stability of Chile's tripolar multiparty system in which each pole mustered roughly a third of the votes. Because they frequently won the highest plurality, they had to be willing to enter into governing coalitions with either the moderate right or left, depending on circumstances. This ensured policy moderation and majorities in the Congress with which to pass legislation. Knowing that they might become part of governing coalitions also kept the right and left poles of the system from radicalizing and, thus, from destabilizing the system. However, because presidents could only win by pluralities, when parties of the right and left won, they too had to be flexible and enter into governing coalitions with centrist parties.

Alessandri's second administration (1932–1938) followed the logic of this political system. He took office determined to restore political order, to generate economic recovery from the Great Depression, and to implement mild labor reforms based on the Labor Code passed during his first administration. However, Alessandri's rightward drift induced the Radical Party to join the Popular Front, an electoral and governing coalition dominated by the centrist Radical Party that included the Socialist and Communist Parties. This electoral strategy ushered in three Radical Party administrations between 1938 and 1952.

Pedro Aguirre Cerda's Popular Front government (1938–1941) established the foundations of Chile's political economy for the next 25 years. It cemented an enduring, albeit implicit, multiclass coalition of industrialists, the middle class, and urban labor that supported ISI with redistribution and promotion of labor rights. Reformist centrist and left political parties mediated that coalition and established policies that appeased landowners. However, redistributive measures were a constant source of tension. Making good on the promise of greater social justice in a country with high levels of social inequality proved to be extraordinarily difficult.

After Aguirre Cerda's death in office in 1941, successive Radical Party administrations drifted to the right. Under pressure from the United States and the right wing of the Radical Party, the government of Gabriel González Videla (1946–1952) outlawed the Communist Party, despite the fact that it had accepted the party's electoral support to win the presidency. Feeling betrayed socialists and communists allied and ran their own presidential candidates.

A disenchanted electorate, augmented by the female vote, put an end to 14 years of Radical Party–led Popular Front coalition tactics with the election of independent Carlos Ibáñez del Campo to a second presidency. His center-right presidency marked the tone of political conflicts for the next 20 years. First, the center-right feared the electoral resurgence of an independent left. Second, in three-way presidential elections minority governments in which presidents won by a plurality were the rule (Ibáñez del Campo claimed 47 percent of the vote). Third, inflation and a sluggish economy were the principal economic issues, generating fierce political maneuvering over fiscal, monetary, foreign exchange, and trade policies. Balance of payment deficits in the national accounts fueled inflation. Fighting inflation required stabilization policies—tight fiscal and monetary policies (reducing government expenditures and increasing interest rates).

The next president, Jorge Alessandri (son of Arturo Alessandri), ran as an independent backed by the Conservative and Liberal Parties. However, Alessandri won with less than one-third of the ballots cast (31.6 percent), an alliance of the Socialist and Communist Parties headed by Salvador Allende came in a close second (28.9 percent), and a new centrist political force, the Christian Democratic Party under Eduardo Frei Montalva, garnered 20.7 percent. Alessandri's administration (1958–1964) ushered in a period in which minority governments of the right, center, and left attempted to impose their own solutions to Chile's socioeconomic problems. These conditions fueled a leftward drift, radicalization, and polarization of Chilean politics.

Alessandri's promarket, antilabor policies did little to solve Chile's socioeconomic problems; but they did alienate the center-left and the left, which perceived those policies to be an onslaught against hard-earned gains. Certain they could not win the presidency in 1964 and fearful of the left's chances in a serious three-way race, the Conservative and Liberal Parties decided not to present a candidate. This electoral strategy boosted the center-left, now dominated by the Christian Democratic Party under Eduardo Frei, which won handily with 56 percent of the vote. Salvador Allende, again the standard-bearer of the Communist–Socialist alliance, garnered 39 percent. The candidate of the Radical Party finished a poor third.

The Christian Democrats came into office with a reformist socioeconomic program. The "Revolution in Liberty" addressed the social problems of the urban poor by stressing housing, education, and neighborhood self-help organizations. Land reform would aid the rural poor and, it was hoped, boost agricultural productivity. A controlled opening of the economy to imports, partial nationalization with compensation of U.S.-dominated copper mines, and promotion of export diversification into fishing and timber were intended to invigorate the Chilean economy. Political opposition and renewed inflation hampered implementation of the "Revolution in Liberty" for the last half of the Frei administration. Polarization deepened as the Conservative and Liberal Parties united in the National Party in 1966. This was a response to the leftward drift in the center of gravity of the Chilean party system. The more radical wing of the Christian Democratic Party gained ascendancy, and revolutionary splinter groups of the Communist and Socialist Parties gathered visibility.

The 1970 presidential election was a three-way race between Jorge Alessandri on the right, Christian Democrat Radomiro Tomic for the center-left, and Salvador Allende for the traditional left at the head of Unidad Popular (Popular Unity). Unidad Popular included the Socialist Party, the Communinst Party, the Radical Party, the firebrand Revolutionary Movement of the Left (Movimiento de Izquierda Revolucionario), and a breakaway faction of the Christian Democrats. Their platform promised a democratic, peaceful road to socialism. It stressed nationalization, income redistribution, a reform of labor relations in favor of workers, creation of a unicameral congress, and reform of the education and judiciary systems. To

the shock of the overconfident right Unidad Popular won the presidential election, albeit with a plurality of the slimmest margin: 36.3 percent to Alessandri's
34.9 percent. The event was one of the defining moments of Chile's contemporary
political history.

Maneuvers to block Allende's ascension to office began immediately, including a bungled U.S.-backed plan to induce a coup d'état by kidnapping the commander-in-chief of the armed forces, René Schneider. All failed and Unidad Popular
took office in early 1971 amid great expectations by both supporters and detractors. Initial policies for the Chilean path to socialism followed three tracks. The
first track stressed demand-stimulus measures to increase the purchasing power
of wage labor, thereby boosting the sales of manufactured goods and services to
the benefit of industrialists and merchants. The idea was to allay the fears of the
upper and middle classes by fueling economic growth that all could benefit from
while simultaneously wooing labor votes away from centrist parties, especially
the Christian Democrats. The strategy worked in 1971 as Chile experienced strong
wage and gross domestic product (GDP) growth. The second component involved
nationalization of industry. Unidad Popular sought to build up the state sector,
encourage joint ventures between the public and private sectors, and maintain a
substantial private sector. Initial efforts concentrated on foreign concerns in mining,
manufacturing, and services. These led to strong confrontations with U.S.-owned
Anaconda and Kennecott mining and the International Telegraph and Telephone
company. However, Chilean property owners, with the exception of the small and
underdeveloped financial sector, were not affected and, for the most part, raised
no alarm. Accelerating agrarian reform and the organization of the peasantry was
the third major policy area. This immediately created friction between the landed
oligarchy and Unidad Popular, although for most of 1971 these tensions remained
isolated.

Conflict sharpened progressively from mid-1971 on as Unidad Popular
directed nationalization policy more and more at large-scale domestic companies. In part, Unidad Popular wanted to break the economic power of the Chilean
business sectors that opposed the government, believing that would break their
political power as well. Instead, it galvanized upper-class opposition to Allende's
government.

Meanwhile, an economic crisis fueled by deficit spending and falling investment began to engulf Chile. This turned the middle class and medium and small
business against Unidad Popular. Mounting labor strife and the creation of an alternative commercial distribution system for basic consumer goods to counter mounting scarcity, the Juntas de Abastecimiento Popular, further stiffened opposition by
those groups.

In December 1971, confrontation over all of these pressing issues culminated
in the formation of a broad coalition of the middle class, medium- and small-scale
businesspeople, and large-scale business groups against Unidad Popular: the Private Sector National Front. To break the back of the bourgeoisie, Allende's government responded with a nationalization policy targeted against the nation's most
important consumer durables, food processing, pulp and paper, beverages, construction, and fishing companies. Meanwhile, the Christian Democratic Party's

efforts to negotiate nationalization policy with Unidad Popular finally collapsed in mid-1972.

Class conflict mounted quickly afterward. Business staged a massive lockout, the "Bosses' Strike" that began in August 1972. Labor countered by breaking into factories and running down inventory to keep production going. A month-long trucker's strike—clandestinely financed by the U.S. Central Intelligence Agency (CIA)—broke out in October in tandem with more massive lockouts. Labor answered by organizing alternative transportation systems. After this, conservative political parties and the Christian Democratic Party united in an electoral alliance, the Democratic Confederation, to sweep the March 1973 congressional elections. The plan, to gain a two-thirds majority in Congress to impeach Allende, failed as Unidad Popular increased its popular vote from 36 percent to 44 percent. Electoral support for opposition parties dropped from 64 percent during the 1970 presidential election to 54 percent. These electoral results and the violent social conflict that engulfed Chile afterward set the stage for the military's intervention.

It should be noted that from the very beginning the U.S. government did everything in its power to help set that stage. The United States contributed to economic destabilization—making the economy scream—by denying loans to Chile from the U.S. Agency for International Development, the Export–Import Bank, the Inter-American Development Bank, and the World Bank. Its intelligence services helped organize Chilean rightists and financed the survival of crucial conservative news media (*El Mercurio*) as well as key events, such as the trucker's strike. Yet, despite high levels of confrontation, the ferocity of the military's coup against Allende on September 11, 1973, took everyone by surprise. It was a well-orchestrated combat operation against a revolution that was mostly rhetoric with respect to its capacity for armed resistance. In the terror that followed, thousands lost their lives, thousands more were arrested and tortured, and tens of thousands went into forced or voluntary exile.

Military Government

The Chilean armed forces had intervened in politics to resolve a deep societal crisis, which they attributed to the failings of a developmental model that fed class conflict. Therefore, during its first year of rule, the military junta searched for a development model altogether different from Chile's past. The junta found it in neoliberalism. Neoliberal ideology offered a vision of the economy, society, and the state capable of eradicating state-led development and Marxism. The military had largely achieved its goal when it handed the reins of power over to civilians in 1990.

The military inherited a chaotic economy. Extravagant fiscal deficits fed hyperinflation, expropriation paralyzed industry and commerce, and investment was nonexistent. The U.S.-trained neoliberal economists that advised the junta argued that sound, sustained economic growth depended on monetary stability, reestablishing a free market economy in which the private sector was the engine of growth, and building an economy open to international competition and foreign investment. These advisors were known as the "Chicago boys" because most of them had received graduate degrees from the economics department of the University of Chicago, where they studied with Milton Friedman, a Nobel Prize–winning monetarist. To wring inflation and other price distortions out of the economy, they implemented an orthodox economic stabilization program. Between 1975 and 1978, price controls were lifted, interest rates were increased, and fiscal spending was slashed. Constructing a free market economy, however, required additional measures. The junta's economic team privatized a considerable portion of Chile's mixed economy (especially the industrial and financial sectors but not the nationalized mining sector) and deregulated the financial system. Thoroughgoing trade reform, especially tariff barrier reduction, restructured Chile's economy from industries producing for domestic markets toward sectors with a comparative advantage: mining, fishing, fruits, and timber. The commercial (import–export business) and construction sectors also boomed. Generous conditions for foreign investors lured external capital back into the country. Beginning in 1979, the Chicago boys privatized the pension system now largely administered by Pension Fund Administraters (AFPs), health-care insurance by creating Private Health Insurance Plans (ISAPRES), and the educational system via vouchers and crafted a labor code that institutionalized the emasculation of organized labor. In addition to these measures, the Chicago boys decentralized political administration by giving regions and municipalities more authority over local issues.

The military government also restructured Chilean politics. It established a highly centralized, closed, authoritarian political system. It closed Congress indefinitely, banned all political parties, and purged state institutions and universities. The Junta persecuted socialists, communists, and other far-left groups mercilessly; many died or suffered torture, imprisonment, and exile at the hands of the consolidated intelligence services of the armed forces and the national police force. Pinochet, the commander-in-chief of the army, centralized power in his person and pronounced himself president of the nation.

Although Pinochet maintained order with iron-fisted rule, he and his supporters among the upper classes wanted to legitimate authoritarianism. They wrote a new constitution, submitted it to a plebiscite in 1980, and had it approved by a wide margin under questionable electoral conditions. The constitution of 1980 was designed to guide Chile through a transition from military rule to a protected democracy. It awarded the military guardianship over the political system and safeguarded the privileges of property by making it virtually impossible to reform the free market economic system. The transition itself was to begin in 1988 with a plebiscite to decide whether Pinochet would continue as president. If the plebiscite ratified him for another 8-year period (to 1997), elections for Congress would be held in 1989. If the plebiscite rejected Pinochet, then open elections for the presidency and for a Congress would be held in 1989. Naturally, Pinochet and his supporters fully expected to win riding the crest of economic good times and the disarray of disheartened opposition political forces.

The economic cataclysm that beset Chile with the onset of the Latin American debt crisis changed that rosy script. Between 1982 and 1983, GDP plunged by 15 percent. The financial system collapsed as firms and banks became insolvent and went bankrupt because they could no longer roll over their debt at cheap interest rates. Unemployment soared to 33 percent. The middle classes lost their savings.

This economic crisis shook Pinochet's regime to the core. His unconditional support for the Chicago boys and orthodox deflationary policies in a depressed economy aroused a powerful opposition movement. As discontent mounted, the union movement organized protests. The first mass mobilization, held in May 1983, succeeded beyond the leadership's wildest dreams. Opposition political parties quickly took over the protest movement, and mass demonstrations against Pinochet's rule were held on an almost monthly basis until 1986. Two blocs quickly vied for control of this movement: the Christian Democratic–led Democratic Alliance and the Communist-led Popular Democratic Movement. Yet, the military government managed to defuse the political opposition. It played for time by engaging the Democratic Alliance in negotiations for a transition from authoritarian rule. The Democratic Alliance wanted to substantially amend the 1980 constitution to remove the tutelary powers of the military and overrepresentation of conservatives. Pinochet temporized to blunt the political impact of mass mobilization. The restoration of vigorous economic growth as of 1984 further dulled the power of the opposition. After a failed attempt on Pinochet's life in 1986, mass mobilization ended and the political transition followed the timetable and institutional structure set by the junta.

Despite these setbacks, the opposition to Pinochet did not come away completely empty-handed. It struggled successfully for free and fair elections for the 1988 plebiscite, a significant accomplishment as it turned out. Moreover, the Democratic Alliance emerged as the more important of the two opposition movements, and its member parties learned how to work together more efficiently. This political force, now calling itself the Coalition of Parties for the No (the "no" vote was a ballot against Pinochet), soundly defeated him in the plebiscite (54.7 to 43 percent). The military, agreeing to abide by the terms of the 1980 constitution, and mollified by the opposition's promise not to alter the free-market economic model, accepted defeat and set presidential and congressional elections for December 1989. The resurrection of political parties in the mid-1980s also extended to the center-right, which, being in full agreement with the military government, had disbanded their political organizations. The more traditional conservatives of the old National Party formed National Renovation, while libertarians (free marketeers connected to the military government) established the Independent Democratic Union.

These were the political forces that contested the founding election of Chile's new democracy and that have dominated Chilean politics since then. In 1989, the center-left opposition bloc, now calling itself the Coalition of Parties for Democracy (CPD), backed the candidacy of Patricio Aylwin, a conservative Christian Democrat who, as president of the senate in 1973, had staunchly opposed Allende. On the center-right, National Renovation and the Independent Democratic Union supported the candidacy of Hernán Büchi, the architect of Chile's strong economic recovery based on more flexible management of free market economics. A populist banker-businessman, Francisco Javier Errázuriz, also ran on the right. The presidential election results mirrored the plebiscite. Aylwin won with 55.2 percent of the vote. Conservatives garnered 44.8 percent, but those votes were split between Büchi (29.4 percent) and Errázuriz (15.4 percent). The far left, by contrast, fared poorly. Aylwin and the CPD took office in March 1990.

Power and Politics

Since 1990, four successive administrations of the center-left CPD have governed Chile, Patricio Aylwin (1990–1994), Eduardo Frei Ruiz-Tagle (1994–2000), Ricardo Lagos (2000–2006), and Michelle Bachelet (2006–2010), Chile's first female president. Alywin and Frei, both from the Christian Democratic Party, symbolized centrist control of the coalition, and Lagos' presidency closed a cycle in Chilean political history. He was a lifelong Socialist, who had been a cabinet member under Allende. However, Chile's governability was no more threatened by him than by the other two because the top leadership of the CPD's political parties, including socialists, developed a remarkable consensus over the correctness of the neoliberal model and of working within the boundaries of the 1980 constitution. Bachelet, also of the Socialist party, and whose father had been killed by the Junta for not supporting the coup, was ideologically more to the left insofar as she wanted to push social welfare and human rights issues. In practice, however, she has followed the established pattern by settling on a course of modest reform.

True to their promise to the military government and true to the ideological conversion of its leadership, CPD governments maintained the free-market political economy inherited from the dictatorship. Rapid, sustained economic growth and its benefits consolidated support for neoliberal economics in the CPD. Between 1984 and 1997, the neoliberal economic model produced rapid, sustained economic growth of approximately 7 percent per year with low inflation, virtually balanced budgets, and a high investment rate. Growth slowed to an average of 2.3 percent between 1998 and 2003 (largely due to the Asian financial crisis), which was still much better overall than the performance of its neighbors. Since then the economy has been expanding between 4 and 5 percent per year with a large budget surplus and tightening labor markets. In 2007 inflation, at around 7 percent, surged, but is expected to subside to the more ususal 3 percent once high world energy and copper prices stabilize and decline. Because all four administrations of the CPD supported the free-market economy inherited from the dictatorship and exercised policy moderation, serious challenges to conservatives on the issues that had torn Chile apart in the past—property, profits, and the social order—were no longer on the political agenda.

Nevertheless, the CPD's mild reformism differentiates its governments from the military dictatorship or, presumably, a future government of the center-right. They addressed many issues that required urgent attention given the previous regime's repressive character and neglect. Human rights, expanding state revenue, alleviating poverty, and providing more health care and education topped the list. The CPD also supported new social issues, such as the rights of women and ethnic minorities and the environment, and strove to rid the 1980 constitution of its authoritarian enclaves. On balance, the CPD accomplished a great deal between 1990 and 2008.

It consolidated democracy, maintained economic stability and growth, addressed social equity issues, and recognized new social movements.

The undemocratic institutions to constrain the sovereign will of the people in the 1980 constitution structured much of power and politics after 1990. These institutions established a "protected democracy" that conferred extraordinary powers on conservative political forces to defend the neoliberal socioeconomic model imposed by the military government from anything but modest reform. Those institutions shaped a policy-making process that generally produced a compromise bill in which the core interests of the center-right were strongly protected, or else the bill died.

Key "authoritarian enclaves" included reserve domains of autonomy for the armed forces and the Supreme Court (for more details, see the section on government institutions). However, over time, especially in relation to human rights issues, those capabilities have been curtailed and invoked less and less. The powers of the Senate and the electoral system constituted the main tethers with which the 1980 constitution tied the democratic regime to the military government's neoliberal socioeconomic order. All legislation must have the approval of both chambers of the Congress. However, until the end of Lagos' administration the constitution reserved a number of senate seats for appointment from conservative institutions (initially appointed by Pinochet himself). Because of these "designated senators" right-wing forces generally enjoyed a majority and could kill a bill if they were unwilling to compromise with the center-left-dominated Chamber of Deputies on core issues. As a result, occasionally center-left governments compromised strongly with conservatives, to the point of gutting bills. Even then, when conservatives did not wish to compromise, they simply vetoed bills. Thus, an intransigent center-right (and a frequently complacent CPD) ensured that reforms, if passed, never challenged the neoliberal model imposed by the military government.

The electoral system, still in force, favors conservative political forces by overrepresenting them. First, the boundaries of electoral districts for both the Chamber of Deputies and the Senate give more weight to areas that had voted heavily for Pinochet in the 1988 plebiscite. Second, the binomial electoral system also benefits conservatives in lower house elections. Each district elects two deputies. A party coalition must obtain double or more votes than the competing coalition to win both seats. If it does not, the minority coalition automatically wins a seat. This system ensures that the second largest bloc, frequently supporters of Pinochet and conservative parties, can win one out of every two contested seats with only one-third of the vote, which is the historic percentage of the vote for the right. The binomial electoral system also encourages coalition building in a multiparty system, which reduces the danger of ideological polarization and party system fragmentation that contributed to the collapse of democracy in 1973.

All four CPD presidencies patiently chipped away at these authoritarian enclaves, which they had been trying to abrogate since the coalition first formed in 1983. Significant constitutional reform to restore Chile to full political democracy proved beyond the powers of the first two CPD administrations. Constitutional amendments require two-thirds support of all deputies and senators. Given the conservatives' interest in the maintenance of military guardianship and veto power over socioeconomic policy, up to 2005 they had approved relatively minor changes. The first set of reforms was negotiated in 1989 after Pinochet's defeat in the October 1988 plebiscite and before the first general election in December 1989. Fifty-four mostly minor reforms were approved in a plebiscite on July 30, 1989, largely with the help of the center-right National Renovation Party. Among the more significant ones was the restoration of full electoral competition by lifting the ban on the Communist Party and other erstwhile left-wing revolutionary parties. Furthermore, the leadership of labor unions and interest group associations was once again open to militants of political parties. The number of elected senators was increased from 26 to 38, which reduced the proportion of designated senators in that chamber. The president would no longer have the power to dissolve the Chamber of Deputies, and civilian representation was increased on the National Security Council to reach parity with military members. During Aylwin's administration, in November 1991, the Congress approved amendments to local government. They replaced presidentially appointed local officials with directly elected mayors. In February 1994, the length of the presidential term was reduced from 8 to 6 years, and in May 2000 the Lagos administration passed a bill that stripped outgoing presidents of the right to become senators for life.

In 2005, in a breakthrough for Chilean democracy the CPD and the opposition agreed on significant constitutional reforms. These included the abolition of the designated senators, presidential authority to dismiss military commanders, reducing the National Security Council to an advisory role, and cutting the presidential terms from 6 to 4 years. Significantly, however, the binomial electoral system remains. Conservatives remained staunchly opposed to the CPDs preference for proportional representation. Analysts believe the opposition negotiated these reforms for several reasons. The CPD by then had appointed five non-military senators loyal to the government; Pinochet and close identification with the dictatorship had become an electoral liability, and those at odds with the CPD had, by then, mostly resigned.

Despite these constitutional amendments, over time the authoritarian enclaves generated enduring informal political norms and practices. Hence by the end of 2007, 2 years into Bachelet's government, the Chilean policy process had not changed much. The CPD leadership remained committed to the neoliberal economic model, largely because it had delivered sustained economic growth and macroeconomic stability. A tradition of close political negotiation with the private sector and conservative political parties ensured only mild reform of labor, social welfare (health, pensions, aid to families), and education that only minimally distorted markets. However, ideologicial conversion, the strength of right-wing forces, and a predilection for consensus were not the only obstacles to more signficant social reforms. Important conservative elements in the CPD (especially in the Christian Democratic Party) also opposed them. The rest of this section examines the evolution of social policy and human rights reform under 17 years of CPD rule.

Reducing high rates of poverty and indigence inherited from the dictatorship was a high priority for the CPD. In the late 1960s, the percentages of Chileans living in poverty and indigence stood at 22 and 6 percent, respectively. Toward the end of the military government, those rates soared to 38 and 17 percent, respectively. Social policy under the CPD reduced those numbers to 17 percent below the poverty line in 2006. These improvements relied mainly on the use of market mechanisms, such as expansion of the labor market (higher employment) via sustained economic growth, improvements in real wages, and low inflation. However, increases in minimum wages, job training programs, and expansion of social programs targeting benefits to the poorest citizens also contributed. Despite the CPD's proactive stance it could not reduce the sharp increase in income inequality that was one of the darker legacies of the dictatorship's neoliberal economic and social reforms.

The CPD also pledged to build up public health care and education. Government expenditures for public health doubled between 1990 and 2004 and expanded even more during Bachelet's government. As a result, public health care, on which 75 percent of Chileans rely, has improved. The private health insurance system under the ISAPRES, which only about 25 percent of Chileans can afford, remained unaffected by these changes. Still, analysts concluded both the public and private systems are underfunded. Thus, the Lagos administration passed a law (Plan AUGE) that reformed the financing of the health-care system to make quality service more acessible to all for a predetermined list of illnesses regardless of whether individuals are enrolled in the public or private system.

Chile has a literacy rate of about 96 percent and a high level of average schooling (about 8 years). The military government thoroughly reformed the education system by privatizing and decentralizing it. The system included public municipal schools, private schools with state subsidies (student voucher system), and elite, exclusive totally private schools. Due to a high level of social-class-based inequities in the system, high school students organized surprising mass mobilization in 2006, the first year of Bachelet's government. After some fierce and much criticized repression, Bachelet sponsored a reform of the education system to address the worst inequities. Unfortunately, conservative forces supportive of the privatized decentralized system hijacked the reform proceess and only midly reformed the existing one. The compromise bill is expected to pass in 2008. The main innovations were the creation of a superintendency within the Ministry of Education to ensure and enforce the quality of schooling across the system; oversight by the Ministry of Education of expenditure of state subsidies by the schools; and reorganization of school grades into 6 years of elementary and 6 years of "middle-level" education (as it used to be before the military government). Signficantly municipalities still controlled schools and subsidized private schools remained for-profit businesses.

By 2000 it became clear that the private pension system contained a number of design flaws that excluded large numbers of people from receiving a pension or guaranteeing an unacceptably low one. Bachelet's government proposed a mild pension system reform targeted to these vulnerable groups. First, poor people who because of their employment history never opened AFP accounts would receive a small guaranteed minimum pension ($75,000 or about US$150 per month). Second, persons with small monthly incomes over their working life (and hence with limited savings capacity) would have their AFP pensions subsidized on a sliding scale by the state, but in no case could AFP and state subsidy surpass 200,000 pesos (about US$400) per month. Third, people could open the equivalent of individual retirement accounts. Fourth, to increase competition and (hopefully) lower high administrative fees of the AFPs, banks may offer pension services. By December 2007 serious negotiation over the reform bill among major political parties had ended and it is expected to pass in 2008.

Tax hikes initially financed increased social spending. The Aylwin administration negotiated tax increases with the center-right, which used its majority in the Senate to set new rates at levels that were comfortable for business. Although the manufacturer's association (Sociedad de Fomento Fabril) opposed any new taxes, most business groups and National Renovation were more pragmatic. In fact, they insisted that the corporate tax portion of those increases be earmarked for social expenditures. Congress renewed the tax reform law, which had a short sunset clause, toward the end of the Aylwin administration. Although the rates were lowered, they remained higher than under the military government. In 2001, the Lagos government reformed the tax code by lowering personal income tax and raising taxes on corporations.

Bachelet took a different tack to finance increased social spending for health, pension, and education reform. Given the difficulty in hiking taxes, her government drew on the budget surplus. President Lagos had mandated that the Chilean state should maintain an average budget surplus of 1 percent of GDP. However, unusually high copper prices, Chile's largest export item, raised the actual surplus to about 7 percent of GDP. Futhermore, Bachelet lowered the surplus mandate to 0.5 percent of GDP, an amount which still insured long term fiscal solvency.

Despite the decline in overall poverty rates, improved real wage indexes, public health care, education, and expanded social safety nets, the Concertación's social policies have not challenged the neoliberal model. As a result, Chile has made little progress toward becoming a more egalitarian society. Successive Concertación governments failed to alter Chile's highly skewed distribution of national income, which became one of the most unequal in Latin America during the military government. By some indicators, the concentration of income has worsened since the return to democracy.

Severe repression of workers and their organizations during the dictatorship placed labor relations high on the CPD's policy agenda. However, successive administrations made little headway in reforming the mostly probusiness clauses of the military government's labor code. The key issues for the labor movement, a major constituency of the CPD, were strengthening union organization, increasing finances, improving job security, increasing membership, and expanding the right to strike. The Chilean private sector, represented by the Confederation of Production and Commerce (CPC) along with conservative political parties, used the institutions of Chile's protected democracy (especially the Senate) to gut successive labor reform bills under Aylwin and Lagos. All that the labor code reforms of 1994 and 2001 managed were some minor changes on issues such as collective negotiation, job security, and permitting labor confederations. The upshot has been that unionized labor initially increased after democratization, only to suffer a clear decline. As a percentage of the employed labor force, unionized workers increased from 10 percent in 1986 to 15 percent in 1992 and steadily declined to just over 10 percent in 2004. The CPD's lack of unqualified and vigorous support of labor's core demands has cooled relations between organized labor and the governing coalition. Changes in the composition of the economy also contribute to the decline of organized labor. These include the expansion of seasonal labor (in agriculture and the fishing and tourist industries, for example); deindustrialization as a result of Chile's neoliberal economic model; the stagnation of economic sectors with a tradition of strong unions, such as the mining sector; and the growth of economic sectors with a tradition of weak unionization, such as services and commerce.

The labor code's subcontracting rules were especially generous to the private sector and the issue exploded during the first year of Bachelet's government. Large firms subcontracted workers from employment companies and saved money by not having to pay benefits, wages at scale, and by sweating labor. Subcontracting rules also impeded unionization at the workplace. In 2006 subcontracted copper workers protested subcontracting rule abuse, organized wildcat strikes, and violently clashed with riot police. In the aftermath of these confrontations, Bachelet passed a law that reformed subcontracting rules in 2007. The major accomplishment was that the contracting firm would henceforth be obligated to pay the social security contributions of subcontracted workers. In the past that had been the subcontracting firm's reposnsiblity, but they frequently dodged it.

In addition to these traditional issues, the CPD embraced new social movements whose issues had received scant, if any, recognition by the military government. During the military government, the feminist, environmental, and indigenous people's movements mostly aligned with opposition political forces. They survived by establishing nongovernmental organizations that carried out research and organized people. The military government suffered their presence, kept them under close surveillance, and usually ignored their policy recommendations. However, because of their connections to the political parties of the CPD, once Chile redemocratized, many of these researchers and activists were called upon to formulate policy in their respective areas of expertise. They headed and staffed the technical commissions that drafted the electoral platform and governing program of the CPD on gender, environment, and indigenous peoples. Later, they entered public service in government agencies created by the Aylwin administration to address these issues. However, all of these new state agencies were firmly subordinated to traditional socioeconomic and political concerns such as economic growth and the consolidation of political democracy. None gained cabinet status, and some had only administrative budgets, meaning they could not execute policy. They could only propose policy to the relevant ministries, which may or may not act upon those proposals. (For more details, see the section on interest groups.)

Deepening economic development presented further challenges to the CPD's reign. Although Chile's neoliberal economy was stable and growing and although the nation had succeeded in diversifying the commodities it exports, its economy was still essentially an agromineral extractive one. In 2005, as in the 1950s and 1960s, the challenge was still one of adding value to those commodities and generating whole new industries in Chile, increasing wages, building service industries, and accelerating economic growth. As promised during the transition to democracy in the 1990s, the CPD has relied on the market rather than planning and industrial policy to achieve those goals. Hence those challenges go largely unmet. Instead, the CPD concentrated on foreign economic policy. All CPD administrations have embraced a policy of open regionalism. Chile has been very active in the Asian Pacific Economic Cooperation (APEC). It has also pursued associate status in Mercosur (the Southern Cone Common Market) and finally signed a free trade agreement with the United States and the European Union in 2003.

Surprisingly, the most positive developments in redemocratized Chile occurred in the area of human rights. The military government unleashed a ferocious campaign of terror, especially between 1973 and 1977, in which 3000 persons died and about 30,000 were subjected to torture. Since 1990, the issue has divided the Chilean polity, arousing strong passions on both sides: conservatives, who felt the violence was justified, and leftists and reformists, who suffered it or believed human rights violations to be crimes against humanity. The CPD built its approach on three principles: truth, justice, and reparation. Truth involved the investigation and full public disclosure of the extent of human rights violations with respect to victims and methods. Justice referred to the military: making the perpetrators accountable. Reparation entailed compensating victims and their families. Yet, both the Aylwin and Frei administrations recognized that they lacked the political power to address the question of justice, that is, to bring human rights violators to trial. Given the nature of Chile's transition to democracy, the armed forces remained politically strong and used their prerogatives to protect themselves from prosecution. With backing from conservative political forces, which look to the military—and Pinochet personally—as the saviors of Chile and the guardians of neoliberal order, there was no question of overturning the amnesty the military government had decreed for itself in 1978. In 1998, Pinochet's and the military's position seemed unassailable.

For these reasons, the Aylwin administration concentrated on truth by establishing the Truth and Reconciliation Commission, also known as the Rettig Commission. The commission investigated human rights violations that involved deaths and disappearances. It gave a full accounting of victims, the methods used by the security branches of the armed forces and the police, and the judiciary's condoning of state terror. It was hoped that this public accounting and an amnesty for most of the remaining political prisoners in Chile would begin the process of reconciliation. The Aylwin government also addressed reparations by compensating the families of victims who had died or disappeared. With respect to justice, the CPD pushed through pardons for most of the remaining political prisoners. It also managed a slight reorientation of military justice: some cases would be tried by civilian, rather than military, courts.

In 2000, President Lagos and the Socialist Party came into office with a strong commitment to see justice done. To everyone's surprise, by 2005 Pinochet's political fortunes had reversed dramatically due to unrelenting efforts to prosecute him and other military human rights violators for their crimes. It all began in October

1998, when Senator Pinochet traveled to Great Britain for medical reasons. While Pinochet was in London, Tony Blair's Labour government arrested him pending extradition to Spain for human rights violations. Pinochet languished under house arrest for 16 months in Britain until he was pronounced medically unfit for extradition and trial in Spain and flown back to Chile where President Frei had promised to initiate legal proceedings against him. Although Pinochet's supporters gave him a hero's welcome, the Lagos administration upheld the government's commitment to let the courts decide whether Pinochet should stand trial. Between 2001 and his death in 2006 Pinochet's case wound its way through the legal process. Although he was never brought to trial these events demonstrated the Chilean political elites' confidence that the nation had overcome the conflicts of yesteryear.

The Pinochet affair was very salutary for Chile. His absence precipitated renewed calls for truth (full disclosure of where bodies were buried, who killed them, and how) and justice (trials for at least some of the perpetrators). Once Pinochet was back in Chile, the Lagos administration established a negotiating committee (*mesa de diálogo*) that included representatives from the military. Initial agreements, which later became law, centered on the issue of disclosure. Persons with knowledge of where bodies were buried were not required to reveal who had committed the killings. As a result, the military issued startling, painful, and highly embarrassing accounts of what happened to many of the disappeared. Eventually, a government report released in November 2004 compiled these admissions of guilt, calculating that 3000 people had been killed and 30,000 had been tortured. The government then announced that those who had suffered torture would receive reparations. Meanwhile, in a startling turn, the commander-in-chief of the army issued a statement admitting institutional responsibility for this sad chapter of Chilean history. The air force issued a similar declaration. Meanwhile, the *Carabineros* (national police) and the navy admitted that individuals may have committed excesses. In addition to these developments, the Supreme Court and lower courts were finding ways around the amnesty law, and it is very likely that some military personnel will be brought to trail.

On balance, then, in 2008 Chile had less to fear from the conflicts of the past than many Chileans thought when the transition to democracy began in 1989. Tensions over potentially destabilizing issues such as human rights, constitutional reform, economic development, and social policy were institutionally channeled. For example, human rights and constitutional questions wound their way through the legal and legislative systems or were settled in executive branch–sponsored negotiations between the parties involved. The debate over economic development and social equity did not, by and large, exceed the normal political differences over levels of taxation and regulation common in developed democratic countries. The venue for such debates was the proper one: the legislature, rather than rule by presidential decree. Major anti-democratic features of the 1980 constitution were abrogated.

However, these positive steps fall short of meaningful advances in helping Chile to become a more egalitarian society and of ameliorating its environmental degradation. Chile's income distribution remains one of the most unequal in Latin America;

its labor code is one of the most regressive; and, despite reforms under Lagos and Bachelet, access to decent health, education, and housing are still mainly restricted to the 25 percent of the population that can afford it. On many of these measures, Chile has barely recovered to standards that existed before military rule, although the figures are an improvement over those prevalent during the dictatorship. Chile achieved economic stability but at the cost of making a fetish of economic growth. Social mobilization by students and workers in 2006 and 2007 suggests that many Chileans are frustrated with the remote, technocratic nature of Chilean politics that leaves little room for effective citizen participation and that concentrates on small adjustments to the neoliberal model that do not really address their fundamental concerns.

Chilean Government Structures

POLITICAL INSTITUTIONS

The military government's administrative decentralization program divided Chile's territory into fifteen regions, including the Santiago metropolitan area. Each region is headed by an intendant (*intendente*) appointed by the president. Regions were divided into the traditional fifty-one provinces, each headed by a governor also appointed by the president. In November 1991, the Congress approved constitutional changes to local government whereby appointed mayors would be directly elected.

Executive power is vested in the president, who serves a 4-year term, and successive reelection is not allowed. Presidents are directly elected by absolute majority; in the absence of a clear-cut majority, the two top vote-getters compete in a run-off election (or second-round vote). The presidency is the strongest branch of the political system. It initiates most bills, and the presidency's full weight behind a bill can overcome opposition through compromise. Moreover, the presidency has a strong role in the maintenance of internal order. The presidency is assisted by the National Security Council that includes the president of the republic, the presidents of the Supreme Court and the Senate, and the heads of the armed forces (army, navy, air force) and of the national militarized police (*Carabineros*).

The legislative branch consists of a bicameral Congress located in the port city of Valparaíso (about an hour and a half by road from Santiago, the capital city). It is not as powerful an institution as it had been before 1973 since it meets fewer days than it did before 1973 and its oversight capacity and the competence of its committees are diminished. The Senate consists of thirty-eight members and the Chamber of Deputies has 120 seats.

The judicial branch of government consists of a twenty-one-member Supreme Court, sixteen appellate courts, major claims courts, and local courts. Supreme Court justices are appointed by the president of the republic from a slate of five names proposed by the court itself. Each appellate court has jurisdiction over one or more provinces. The Supreme Court exercises its duties in separate chambers consisting of at least five judges each. These chambers are presided over by the most senior member or the president of the court. The judicial system also includes special courts, such as juvenile courts, labor courts, and military courts in time of peace. Moreover, the background of the Supreme Court justices generally favors the interests of upper-class socioeconomic groups that support neoliberalism. Pinochet stacked the court with relatively young judges who were friends of the outgoing regime. Thus, on constitutional issues, the Supreme Court generally supports the conservative position, especially in relation to private property rights and expropriation.

The 1980 constitution granted the armed forces significant tutelary power over civilian political forces, especially center-left ones. However, in practice, by 2008 they had practically ceased to exercise many of their prerogatives, especially in relation to the National Security Council where the military lost the right to convoke it. As of 2006 the presidency gained the power to fire commanders in chief. Still, military doctrine and promotion of general officers are free of civilian oversight. The president of the republic may nominate the commander-in-chief of the armed forces only from a list of five names submitted by the military and can only remove him before the 4-year term is up under the most extraordinary of circumstances. Moreover, internal security laws give military courts expanded jurisdiction over judicial issues that are usually the purview of civilian courts. This hampers expeditious investigation of human rights abuses committed during the military government.

MAIN POLITICAL PARTIES

Chile has a strong, well-institutionalized political party system. It remains a tripolar multiparty system with many of the traditional parties still active, although, of course, important new parties exist. The core of the old National Party formed National Renovation (RN), a center-right party based on traditional conservative values that includes some moderates and occasionally is willing to negotiate key policy issues with center-left administrations that have dominated Chilean politics since the transition. A "new right" also developed. Close collaborators of the military government, especially among the economic technocrats, formed the Independent Democratic Union (UDI). The UDI, a libertarian party, is less inclined to compromise with centrist or center-left political parties. The RN and UDI have managed to form electoral coalitions for presidential races, now called the Alliance for Chile, but relations between the two parties are frequently strained.

The center is dominated by the Christian Democratic Party (PDC). The PDC retains its traditional factions: conservatives (*guatones*), leftists (*chascones*), and centrists (*renovadores*). Ideologically, the PDC continues to rely on social-Christian doctrine. Yet, the party has evolved in that it is no longer a confessional one. The Radical Party is another traditional centrist party that remains on the political scene. It has moved to the center-left ideologically and has joined the Socialist International.

The left changed substantially, especially the Socialist Party (PS). After significant internal turmoil, dissension, and splits, the PS experienced an ideological transformation by renouncing Marxism and the class struggle and becoming a European-style social democratic party. It is, essentially, a moderate center-left party styled after England's Labour Party led by Tony Blair and the socialist parties of Spain under Felipe González, France under François Mitterand and Lionel Jospin, and Germany under Gerhardt Schroeder. These parties are searching for a "third way," a middle ground between free market capitalism and orthodox Socialism. The Party for Democracy (Partido por la Democracia, PPD) is another moderate center-left party that formed following one of the initial splits of the PS. Both the PS and the PPD renounced social revolution and socialist state building. They no longer supported nationalization, extensive industrial policy, the strong mixed economy, full employment, or the comprehensive welfare state. They softened their commitment to labor rights and more equal distribution of the national wealth. Party leadership accepted free market economics and settled for putting a human face on capitalism, meaning a commitment to maintaining social safety nets, education, health care, and civil society participation in political decision making. Meanwhile, the Communist Party of Chile (PCCh) retains its Marxist roots, although it no longer actively advocates violent revolution. In that sense, it seems to have embraced an ideological posture similar to that of European communists in the 1980s. Further to the left but also, for the moment, eschewing revolution are the Revolutionary Movement of the Left (MIR) and the Movimiento Patriótico Manuel Rodríguez, whose origins lay in the armed resistance to the military government.

In a significant departure from the past, the electoral system encourages coalition building among political parties. Ironically, the center-left has forged the most enduring one: the CPD, which has won four successive presidential races (1989, 1993, 1999, and 2005). As of the mid-1990s, it included four major political parties: the Christian Democrats, the Socialist Party, the Party for Democracy, and the Radical Party. The more notable element of this coalition was the taming of the left, including the strongly reformist wings of both the Christian Democrats and the Radical Party. Speculation over the future of the CPD abounds given growing tensions within it and electoral gains by conservatives.

Right-wing political parties have had more difficulties forging enduring electoral pacts. Generally, National Renovation and the Independent Democratic Union join forces for presidential races and go their separate ways afterward. Not winning the presidency may be part of the problem; there are fewer incentives for long-term concerted action. However, substantial differences in conservative ideology and willingness to negotiate with the center-left also divide them. Nevertheless, Alliance for Chile candidates have done well in the last two presidential elections.

Interest Groups

WOMEN

Chilean women have a history of second-class citizenship and discrimination in relation to men. However, as the twentieth century progressed, they made advances. They won the right to vote in 1949 and obtained wide access to education, including university education. Women have also become more visible in the business world at the mid-managerial level, although the board room remains a predominantly male preserve. Female participation in the nonprofessional labor force has also increased since the 1970s, especially in nondomestic services (food services, sales, secretarial) and nontraditional industry (fruit packing, canneries, poultry dressing and packaging). Thus, traditional gender roles are increasingly under challenge among both the middle and working classes.

Women have become an important political force in Chile. The women's movement was a vital force in the opposition to the military regime, especially in organizing the vote that defeated Pinochet in the decisive plebiscite of October 5, 1988. In newly redemocratized Chile, female politicians in municipalities and in the national legislature are more numerous than ever before, representing the full political spectrum. They also occupy numerous government posts, including cabinet posts. In December 2005 former Defense Minister Michelle Bachelet became the first female president of Chile. She has appointed many more women to cabinet posts, reaching parity with men. Former Foreign Minister Sonia Alvear headed the Christian Democratic Party in 2007. Also in 2004, the passage of a divorce law—over strenuous objection of the Catholic Church—heralded a victory for gender relations in Chile. Despite these advances, women still suffer from gender discrimination, not only in the workplace but also socially. Women, and married women in particular, are subjugated to men where property and legal guardianship of children are concerned.

In the governments of the CPD, gender issues have received far more attention than in the past. In January 1991, the Aylwin administration created the National Women's Service, SERNAM, to incorporate a gender perspective into public policy. SERNAM's immediate focus was to reduce discrimination against women in access to employment, housing, education, and credit. Longer-term objectives were aimed at improving the position of women with respect to men. They included dismantling institutionally rooted gender inequalities that hindered equal rights for women, easing the responsibility of females for home and child care, and stopping the sexual division of labor by integrating women into the labor market.

Overall, SERNAM did not succeed in promoting its longer-term goals or, sadly, many of its shorter-term ones either. This was largely due to the agency's firmly subordinated place on the Concertación's policy agenda. The agency did not enjoy cabinet rank and had only an administrative budget. As a result, SERNAM concentrated on forming working teams with the relevant departments of other ministries. These teams generated research that its members hoped would be useful in policy debates. Under these conditions and in the interest of compromise with conservative political forces, SERNAM played a more limited role than its staff envisioned. Existing programs operated mainly as government services rather than as foci to encourage the empowerment, organization, and participation of women in the community, unions, and social organizations. Thus, SERNAM lacked a strongly organized social base to help push its agenda forward.

INDIGENOUS PEOPLES

Although the vast majority of Chileans are *mestizos* or of European heritage, some 3 percent of the population are native peoples, mostly Araucanian or Mapuche, who still inhabit the forested region of south central Chile (Bío-Bío and Araucanía). In the twentieth century, the vanquished Mapuches (whose armed resistance continued into the 1880s) suffered from widespread discrimination and second-class citizenship. Until 1973, close-knit Mapuche communities based on family groupings retained common lands called *reducciones,* which they worked communally or as individual family parcels. Communal property and a separate identity for indigenous peoples clashed with the dictatorship's neoliberal ideals. In 1978, the military government broke up the *reducciones* and replaced them with family farms, which could be bought, mortgaged, and sold to cultivate individualistic, competitive, and economic maximizing behavior among the Mapuche. Thus, the dictatorship hoped to obliterate Mapuche identity and culture, a strategy begun after the coup when the military broke Mapuche organizations by subjecting their leaders to death, torture, imprisonment, and exile.

The governments of the CPD have attempted to redress some of the worst discriminatory policies of the military government and earlier. A vibrant indigenous peoples' movement has also emerged. All told, approximately 900,000 people claiming Mapuche heritage currently live in Chile, most of them exploited and poor. In 1989, while Patricio Aylwin was still a candidate for the presidency, the CPD signed an agreement with the indigenous peoples of Chile. In it, the CPD committed itself to the promulgation of a new law that would recognize ancestral culture and rights. Aylwin's government partially delivered on this promise by passing a new Indian law in 1993. The law recognized ancestral lands. It protected them by making them inalienable and established a fund to buy back lands that had been usurped by Chileans since the beginning of the century, when the reservations originally had been established. The law also promoted multiethnicity, legally recognized Indian communities, encouraged participation in policy making, and acknowledged the need for socioeconomic development. The National Corporation of Indigenous Development (CONADI) now administers indigenous affairs.

The Indian law was an important progressive step, but, of course, much remains to be done. For one, CONADI would benefit from more independence from the presidency. The removal of directors who sided too openly with indigenous communities against the development projects of important private firms hurt the legitimacy of the institution among indigenous peoples and their allies. It transformed the Indian representatives on CONADI's council into state functionaries. The commitment to socioeconomic development for indigenous peoples was lukewarm at best. Simmering, at times violent, land conflicts continue; and the all-important issue of autonomy for indigenous peoples has barely been touched.

Environmental Movement

The CPD also welcomed previously marginalized environmentalists into their fold and vowed to address Chile's environmental problems. The Aylwin administration created the National Commission for the Environment (CONAMA) and in 1994 passed the Comprehensive Environmental Act. CONAMA, a small agency without cabinet rank, was structured as an interministerial commission chaired by the top troubleshooter and right hand to the president of the republic, the minister of the general secretariat of the republic. Its heart is the technical secretariat, whose principal function is to oversee the implementation of environmental impact reports for new public and private economic development projects. Pollution abatement, rather than natural resource extraction, is CONAMA's principal focus. Meanwhile, all of the ten line ministries with environmental functions retained their jurisdictions and implement resolutions taken in the interministerial meetings of CONAMA. CONAMA's consultative council incorporates civil society and business in the policy process.

The Comprehensive Environmental Act turned mandatory environmental impact reporting into the main instrument of environmental policy. The "polluter pays" principle is the second major instrument to force compliance with environmental regulations. However, the requirement is weak because the burden of proof rests with the prosecution. The act emphasizes gradualism. This means prioritizing problems and applying only small, incremental changes to deal with the most urgent ones. Still, the environmental movement has used environmental impact reporting provisions to mount legal challenges to new ventures in resource extraction, which are sometimes successful.

Overall, CONAMA and the Comprehensive Environmental Act are weak institutional and legislative instruments to tackle Chile's formidable environmental problems, which include high levels of pollution in urban and rural areas and rapid rates of extraction of natural resources, such as fisheries. CONAMA does not have the mandate, political backing, or staff to effectively tackle environmental problems. The Comprehensive Environmental Act reinforces this condition. Why? Political leaders are fearful that more vigorous environmental action may hamper economic growth. Thus, Concertación administrations bow to pressure from conservative political forces. Still, CONAMA represents official recognition of the issue and is an advance over previous conditions. Things may change, however. Bachelet's government introduced a bill to Congress for the creation of a Ministry of the Environment to give environmental policy more muscle. Environmentalists welcome the initiative, especially since the eruption of a bruising conflict over the proposed damming of more than ten rivers in pristine southern wilderness areas to generate hydroelectric power for central Chile. Such a ministry might help resolve frequently violent conflicts over forested lands between big timber companies and indigenous peoples.

Organized Business

The most influential economic interest groups are business, finance, and agriculture. Each of the major economic sectors has a sectoral peak association. The most powerful ones are the Industrial Development Society (SFF), the National Agriculture Society, and the National Chamber of Commerce, which organize industrialists, landowners, and merchants, respectively. The SFF takes a very hard line with respect to the maintenance of Chile's protected democracy. The National Mine owners' Society, the Chilean Builders' Chamber, and the Banking and Financial Institutions Association round out the most important business interest groups. In practice, these associations mostly represent the interests of large-scale businesspeople. The six major sectoral associations have formed an encompassing peak association, the Confederation for Production and Commerce (CPC). The CPC defends the general interests of business in the policy process. Its views represent a consensus of those of its six member organizations.

Organized Labor

Labor organizations emerged significantly weakened after 18 years of military rule and repression. The old, Marxist-dominated Sole Workers' Center (CUT) was broken up by the military government, which allowed labor organizations only at the plant level. An unofficial, Christian Democrat-led, anti-Marxist confederation, the Workers' Democratic Center, was tolerated. The Copper Workers' Confederation remained the most militant union. It spearheaded the protest movement of 1983 and formed the core of the National Workers' Commando and the National Labor Union Coordinator (CNS). In 1988, the CNS became the Unitary Workers' Confederation (CUT), which remains Chile's principal labor confederation. It is a grouping of industrial, professional, and mining unions led by leftist Christian Democrats and elements of the left, including the Communist Party. Overall, the union movement is not as strong as it was before the military government. Restricted collective bargaining, weak strike laws, open shops, low membership (slightly over 10 percent of all employed workers in 2004), and other measures have limited organized labor's ability to represent its interests. As of 2006, however, the labor movement has become more militant in frustration over its electoral support being taken for granted by the CPD.

Catholic Church and University Students

The Catholic Church, students, and intellectuals also play a role in Chilean politics. During the Pinochet period, the Church promoted human rights and gave aid to the poor and dispossessed. Its political role has declined with redemocratization, dedicating itself mainly to defending traditional family mores. In practice, that has translated into blocking abortion and divorce laws in Congress and maintaining bans on contraceptives such as the "morning after pill." Despite their efforts, Chile passed a divorce law in 2004, after which the Church retrenched in defense of right to life. Until recently, the student movement was not as active as it had been historically in Chile, but its organizations continued to produce future leaders of the major political parties. However, in 2006 high school students, principally, with support from university students and some professors mobilized massively for a month, frequently clashing with police who were strenuously repressing them. This action precipitated the aforementioned education reform act, which should become law in 2008. Meanwhile, intellectuals, especially those with advanced degrees from foreign universities (with a heavy concentration in economics), have become very influential. They swell the ranks of the technocracy that advises all elected political leaders in and out of government. Lastly, the environmental, women's, and indigenous people's movements have also gained more recognition.

Conclusion

After 17 years of center-left CPD rule, Chile has consolidated democracy and the free-market economy. Since 1990 Chile has enjoyed regular, fair, and free elections among well-established, institutionalized, programmatic political parties with freedom of expression and association. The significant authoritarian institutions that initially "protected democracy" have either been eliminated or so weakened that they no longer pose a threat, as is the case with military autonomy. Moreover, as has historicaly been the case, Chile's basic state institutions—the executive, the legislative, the judiciary—function reasonably well and, in comparison to other Latin American countries, have been relatively free of corruption, occasional scandals notwithstanding. By the same token, all four CPD governments have maintained the free-market economy inherited from the military dictatorship. However, they have steadfastly implemented mild social reforms to put a more "human face" on neoliberalism, especially in poverty reduction, health care, and most likely in pensions and education. Equally important, huge strides were made on the human rights issue, to the point where some of the perpetrators have gone to trial and prison and reparations have been paid to survivors of the disappeared and to persons who were tortured.

Naturally, problems remain. Chile is a country in which market efficiency guides economic and social policy, and where establishment sociopolitical elites and significant portions of the population accept the inequalities of the market. Income inequality stands at historically high levels and ranks among the highest in Latin America. Despite reforms, many people have limited or no access to decent health care services, education, and housing. The price system (the market) ensures the allocation of these services to entrenched, rigid social status groups. The student and labor mobilizations of 2006 and 2007 suggest a growing disenchantment and frustration with CPD complacency and its remote, technocratic governing style. Although the country is doing well economically they believe the fruits of sustained economic growth disproportionately benefit politically powerful socioeconomic elites at their expense. The CPD's inability, and frequently unwillingness, to pass meaningful labor code reform and redistributive tax reform symbolizes the problem. In 2006–2007 the boondoggle of the "Trans-Santiago," a poorly designed and implemented reorganization of bus transport in the capital city, crystallized resentment and disenchantment with a technocratic style of government that citizens believed did not really care about people and their problems.

These issues—and long tenure in office—create mounting tensions in the CPD between factions that prefer more redistribution of the national wealth and factions that support the status quo. Complicating matters, these factions cut across party lines. Open conflict has led to the expulsion of prominent party leaders in the CPD and the PPD. Meanwhile, Bachelet, unfortunately, appears unable to impose discipline within the CPD. This fuels speculation that the Alianza might win the next presidential election if it can produce a good candidate and the CPD cannot. Should that come to pass, a government of the center-right would probably play down human rights, reduce government social spending, privatize remaining public assets more aggressively, resume business deregulation, put economic regionalism on the back burner, and cut back state support for feminism, the environment, and indigenous peoples. However, such policies would not endanger Chilean democracy, they would be part and parcel of the give and take of democratic politics.

Chronology

1536 Diego de Almagro extends Spanish conquest to Chile; colonial period shapes social and economic systems; perennial Indian wars in central Chile against Mapuches

1810 Chile begins independence movement from Spain

1818 With help from Argentine General José de San Martín, General Bernardo O'Higgins finally liberates Chile from Spain; Chile becomes a republic

1833 Autocratic republic begins when Diego Portales' new authoritarian constitution ends political instability and sets the groundwork for the Portilian state, which lasts until 1898

1839 Chilean military defeats Peru–Bolivia confederation in a war that began in 1836

1879 War of the Pacific against Peru and Bolivia over mining concessions breaks out

1883 Chile wins War of the Pacific and permanently gains provinces of Arica, Tarapacá, and Antofagasta; Bolivia loses access to Pacific Ocean

1891 Civil war against president José Manuel Balmaceda ends autocratic republic, beginning of parliamentary republic

1925 Chile's Portilian constitution replaced by the constitution of 1925; political instability engulfs Chile and returns in 1932 with election of Arturo Alessandri to presidency

1949 Women receive the right to vote

1970 Salvador Allende elected president at the head of Popular Unity, a coalition of leftist political parties; Chile begins the peaceful, democratic road to socialism; political and social polarization over nationalization of industry, land reform, and other sociopolitical issues tears the country apart

1973 On September 11, the armed forces, headed by General Augusto Pinochet, overthrow Popular Unity and a U.S.-backed military junta takes political power; several years of state terror follow

1975 Radical neoconservative experiments in economic and social reform begin

1978 Military government approves an amnesty law for all security personnel involved in human rights violations

1980 A new constitution with many authoritarian enclaves is approved in a questionable plebiscite

1988 End of military rule; the Christian Democrat–led opposition coalition, with help from the U.S. government, defeats General Pinochet in a plebiscite on his continued rule in October

1990 Christian Democrat Patricio Aylwin becomes president of redemocratized Chile at the head of a broad center-left coalition of political parties known as the CPD; his government introduces progressive legislation to redress the worst excesses of the military government and extends presidential terms to 6 years; record economic expansion continues

1994 Christian Democrat Eduardo Frei, Jr., begins a second CPD administration

1998 Asian economic crisis triggers recession in Chile; Pinochet taken into custody in Britain pending extradition charges to Spain for human rights violations

2000 Lagos wins runoff election and begins third government of the CPD; Pinochet released from custody in Britain, returns to Chile to face legal proceedings for human rights violations; economic growth resumes

2004 Army and air force admit institutional responsibility for systematic human rights violations in Chile; Pinochet again declared fit to stand trial

2005 CPD candidate Michelle Bachelet becomes the first female president of Chile in second-round voting

2006 General Pinochet dies

Bibliography

Angell, Alan, and Benny Pollock, eds. *The Legacy of Dictatorship: Political, Economic, and Social Change in Pinochet's Chile*. Liverpool, G.B.: University of Liverpool Press, 1993.

Argüelles, Pilar, and Ricardo Fredes, eds. *Chile: The Other September 11*. Melbourne: Ocean Press, 2003.

Austen, Robert. *The State, Literacy, and Popular Education in Chile, 1964–1990*. Lanham, MD: Lexington Books, 2003.

Baldez, Lisa. *Why Women Protest: Women's Movements in Chile*. Cambridge: Cambridge University Press, 2002.

Bauer, Arnold J. *Chilean Rural Society from the Spanish Conquest to 1930*. New York: Cambridge University Press, 1975.

Borzutzky, Sylvia. *Vital Connections: Politics, Social Security, and Inequality in Chile*. Notre Dame: University of Notre Dame Press, 2002.

Borzutzky, Sylvia, and Lois Hecht Oppenheim, eds. *After Pinochet: The Chilean Road to Democracy and the Market*. Gainesville: University Press of Florida, 2006.

Collier, Simon. *Chile: The Making of a Republic, 1830–1865*. Cambridge: Cambridge University Press, 2003.

Collins, Joseph. *Chile's Free Market Miracle: A Second Look*. Monroe, OR: Food First, 1995.

Drake, Paul. *Socialism and Populism in Chile, 1932–1952*. Urbana: University of Illinois Press, 1978.

Drake, Paul W., and Iván Jaksic, eds. *The Struggle for Democracy in Chile, 1982–1990*. Rev. ed. Lincoln: University of Nebraska Press, 1995.

Edwards, Sebastián, and Alejandra Cox-Edwards. *Monetarism and Liberalization: The Chilean Experiment*. Cambridge: Ballinger, 1987.

Ellsworth, P. T. *Chile: An Economy in Transition*. New York: Macmillan, 1945.

Ffrench-Davis, Ricardo. *Economic Reforms in Chile: From Dictatorship to Democracy*. Ann Arbor: University of Michigan Press, 2002.

Fleet, Michael. The *Rise and Fall of Chilean Christian Democracy*. Princeton, NJ: Princeton University Press, 1985.

Foxley, Alejandro. *Latin American Experiments in Neoconservative Economics*. Berkeley: University of California Press, 1983.

Garretón, Manuel Antonio. *Incomplete Democracy: Political Democratization in Chile and Latin America*. Chapel Hill: University of North Carolina Press, 2003.

Gil, Frederico. *The Political System of Chile*. Boston: Houghton Mifflin, 1966.

Gil, Frederico, Ricardo Lagos, and Henry Landsberger, eds. *Chile at the Turning Point: Lessons of the Socialist Years, 1970–1973*. Philadelphia: Institute for the Study of Human Issues, 1979.

Hojman, David. *Chile: The Political Economy of Development and Democracy in the 1990s*. Pittsburgh: Pittsburgh University Press, 1993.

——, ed. *Neoliberalism with a Human Face? The Politics and Economics of the Chilean Model*. Liverpool, UK: University of Liverpool Press, 1995.

Kaufman, Edy. *Crisis in Allende's Chile: New Perspectives*. New York: Praeger, 1988.

Kaufman, Robert. *The Politics of Land Reform in Chile, 1950–1970*. Cambridge, MA: Harvard University Press, 1972.

Kay, Cristóbal, and Patricio Silva, eds. *Development and Social Change in the Chilean Countryside: From the Pre-Land Reform Period to the Democratic Transition*. Amsterdam: Centrum voor Studie en Documentatie van Latijns Amerika, 1992.

Kirsch, Henry W. *Industrial Development in a Traditional Society: Entrepreneurship and Modernization in Chile*. Gainesville: University of Florida Press, 1977.

Loveman, Brian. *Chile: The Legacy of Hispanic Capitalism*. 2nd ed. Oxford: Oxford University Press, 1988.

Mamalakis, Markos. *Growth and Structure of the Chilean Economy: From Independence to Allende*. New Haven, CT: Yale University Press, 1976.

Martínez, Javier, and Alvaro Díaz. *Chile: The Great Transformation*. Washington, DC: Brookings Institution, 1996.

Montecinos, Verónica. *Economists, Politics, and the State: Chile 1958–1994*. Amsterdam: Centrum voor Studie en Documentatie van Latijns Amerika, 1998.

Monteón, Michael. *Chile and the Great Depression: The Politics of Underdevelopment, 1927–1948*. Tucson: Arizona State University Press, 1998.

Moran, Theodore H. *Multinational Corporations and the Politics of Dependence: Copper in Chile*. Princeton, NJ: Princeton University Press, 1974.

O'Brian, Philip. *Allende's Chile*. New York: Praeger, 1976.

——. *The Pinochet Decade*. London: Latin American Bureau, 1983.

Oppenheim, Lois Hecht. *Politics in Chile: Democracy, Authoritarianism, and the Search for Development*. Boulder, CO: Westview Press, 1993.

Oxhorn, Philip D. *Organizing Civil Society: The Popular Sectors and the Struggle for Democracy in Chile*. Philadelphia: Pennsylvania State University Press, 1995.

Paley, Julia. *Marketing Democracy: Power and Social Movements in Post-Dictatorship Chile*. Berkeley: University of California Press, 2001.

Petras, James. *Politics and Social Forces in Chilean Development*. Berkeley: University of California Press, 1970.

Petras, James, and Fernando Leiva, with Henry Veltmeyer. *Democracy and Poverty in Chile: The Limits of Electoral Politics*. Boulder, CO: Westview Press, 1994.

Pollack, Marcelo. *The New Right in Chile, 1973–97*. New York: St. Martin's Press, 1999.

Roxborough, Ian, Philip O'Brien, and Jackie Roddick, eds. *Chile: The State and Revolution*. London: Macmillan, 1977.

Scully, Timothy. *Rethinking the Center: Party Politics in Nineteenth and Twentieth Century Chile*. Stanford, CA: Stanford University Press, 1992.

Sigmund, Paul. *The Overthrow of Allende and the Politics of Chile, 1964–1976*. Pittsburgh: Pittsburgh University Press, 1977.

Silva, Eduardo. *The State and Capital in Chile: Business Elites, Technocrats, and Market Economics*. Boulder, CO: Westview Press, 1996.

Solimano, Andrés, Eduardo Aninat, and Nancy Birdsall, eds. *Distributive Justice and Economic Development: The Case of Chile and Developing Countries*. Ann Arbor: University of Michigan Press, 2000.

Spooner, Mary Helen. *Soldiers in a Narrow Land: The Pinochet Regime in Chile*. Berkeley: University of California Press, 1994.

Stallings, Barbara. *Class Conflict and Development in Chile*. Stanford, CA: Stanford University Press, 1978.

Stevenson, John Reese. *The Chilean Popular Front*. Westport, CT: Greenwood Press, 1945.

Tulchin, Joseph, and Augusto Varas. *From Dictatorship to Democracy: Rebuilding Political Consensus in Chile*. Boulder, CO: Lynn Rienner, 1991.

Valenzuela, Arturo. *Chile: Politics and Society*. New Brunswick, NJ: Transaction, 1976.

——. *The Breakdown of Democratic Regimes: Chile*. Baltimore: Johns Hopkins University Press, 1978.

Valenzuela, Arturo, and Samuel Valenzuela, eds. *Military Rule in Chile: Dictatorship and Opposition*. Baltimore: Johns Hopkins University Press, 1986.

Verdugo, Patricia. *Chile, Pinochet, and the Caravan of Death*. Coral Gables, FL: North-South Center Press, 2001.

Vylder de, Stephen. *Allende's Chile*. Cambridge: Cambridge University Press, 1976.

Weeks, Gregory. *The Military and Politics in Postauthoritarian Chile*. Tuscaloosa: University of Alabama Press, 2003.

White, Judy, ed. *Chile's Days of Terror: Eyewitness Accounts of the Military Coup*. New York: Pathfinder Press, 1974.

Winn, Peter. *Victims of the Chilean Miracle: Workers and Neoliberalism in the Pinochet Era, 1973–2002*. Durham, NC: Duke University Press, 2004.

——. *Weavers of Revolution*. New York: Oxford University Press, 1986.

Wright, Thomas C. *Landowners and Reform in Chile: The SNA 1919–1940*. Urbana: University of Illinois Press, 1982.

FILMS AND VIDEOS

The Battle of Chile. United States, 1976.

Chile, Obstinate Memory. United States, 1997.

Details of a Duel: A Question of Honor. Chile/Cuba, 1988.

In Women's Hands. United States, 1993.

Microchip al Chip. Chile, 1991.
The Pinochet Case. Chile, 2001.
La Frontera. Chile. 1991.
Under Construction. Chile, 2000.
Estadio Nacional. Chile, 2001.
I Love Pinochet. Chile, 2001.
Wichan: The Trial. Chile, 1995.

WEBSITES

www.lanic.utexas.edu Latin American Information Network, best source for data, mostly in Spanish.
www.iadb.org Inter-American Development Bank.
www.larcdma.sdsu.edu/humanrights San Diego State University, Human Rights.
www.ILO International Labor Organization.
www.labl.com/countries/chile Chilean–American Chamber of Commerce.
www.economist.com
www.washingtonpost.com

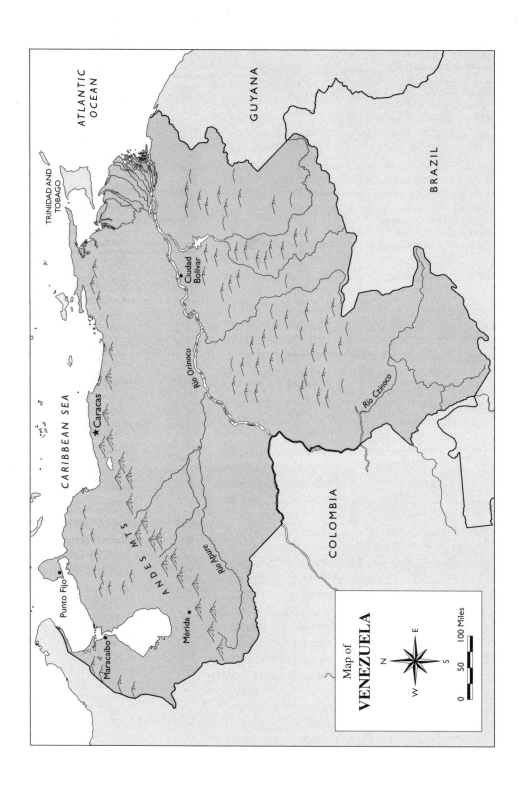

ATLANTIC
OCEAN

TRINIDAD AND
TOBAGO

GUYANA

BRAZIL

CARIBBEAN SEA

Caracas ★

Punto Fijo •

Maracaibo •

Mérida •

A N D E S   M T S

Río Apure

Río Orinoco

Ciudad
Bolívar •

Río Czinoco

COLOMBIA

Map of
VENEZUELA

N
W   E
S

0   50   100 Miles

SEVENTEEN

VENEZUELA

Daniel Hellinger

Venezuela's recent history is a tale of two coups—failed ones. The first was led by Lieutenant Colonel Hugo Chávez against the elected government of President Carlos Andrés Pérez in February 1992. The politicians running the country called people to the streets to defend democracy but were shocked to discover that public sympathy was overwhelmingly on the side of Chávez, who became an overnight hero.

Ten years later, it was Chávez, elected president in December 1998 (and again in July 2000), who had to face down a military conspiracy. The rebellious generals acted in alliance with politicians from two political parties that had dominated Venezuelan politics for 40 years and with a broader coalition of groups threatened by the popular president's move to a more radical program in 2001. Chief among these latter groups were executives of the state-owned oil company (Petróleos de Venezuela, PDVSA), union bosses allied with the old political elite, and owners of the major broadcast media and most important newspapers. On April 11, 2002, this cabal placed President Chávez under arrest, alleging that he had ordered troops to fire on unarmed opposition demonstrators. They swore in the president of the Venezuela Chamber of Commerce (FEDCAMARAS) as the new president, and proceeded to close the elected National Assembly and suspend constitutional rights.

Then a remarkable thing happened. Venezuela's poor, whom Chávez calls "*el soborano*," began to descend from the poor *barrios* that cling to the mountainsides above the Caracas valley and surrounded the presidential palace. In other cities throughout the country people massed at government buildings and military bases, demanding restoration of their elected president. After 48 hours, loyal military units restored Chávez to power. In December 2003, the opposition tried a second time to force the president's resignation. PDVSA executives, cooperating with the old union bosses, shut down for 3 months the vital oil industry, which generates a quarter of the country's economy, 80 percent of its exports, and half of the government's revenues. With help from retirees, lower level employees, and experts from other oil exporting countries, the government once again emerged victorious.

Two years later, in August 2004, a more peaceful confrontation took place in the form of a recall election, won convincingly by Chávez. In December 2005, the opposition, facing defeat again, decided to boycott the elections for the National Assembly (Venezuela has no Senate), which resulted in a complete sweep of seats by the coalition of parties backing Chávez. An opposition candidate did contest the December 2006 presidential election, but Chávez was re-elected resoundingly.

Although the opposition still dominated the private media, and most of the domestic economy remained in private hands, *anti-chavistas* had been dislodged from the military and PDVSA, the two most powerful institutions within the country. Although still subject to periodic elections and the possibility of a recall at some time, few checks on the president's power remained. Conversely, one might say that the president was in a unique position to deliver on the promises he made during the campaign, particularly his intention to accelerate the transition of Venezuela to "socialism of the twenty-first century," a goal that he first announced in 2005.

Signs in 2007 indicated another turn toward a more radical, even revolutionary agenda. Constitutional reforms scheduled for a popular vote in December would have extended the president's term from 6 to 7 years and permitted indefinite re-election of the chief executive. The package also included defining new socialist property sectors (in addition to continuing rights of private property), creating a new branch of government built upon networks of locally based communal councils, and permitting the national government to redraw the system of state and local government. But much to the surprise of most of the international media, and indeed a surprise to both Chávez and his opposition, the Venezuelan voters rejected the reforms by one percentage point on December 2, 2007.

Elsewhere in the world, *chavismo* was being watched because the Venezuelan leader had become the most outspoken critic of U.S. hegemony and capitalist globalization, seen by many in the world as a hero but by some in Washington as the newest member of the Axis of Evil. An even more compelling reason is that Venezuela has the fortune (or "misfortune," some would say) of possessing the world's seventh largest reserves of conventional oil, largest in Latin America (see Table 23). If heavy oil, not yet technologically or economically feasible to exploit fully, is counted, more hydrocarbons lie under Venezuelan soil than in the entire Middle East. Venezuela's polarized politics are too important for the world to ignore.

Geography and People

The Spaniards who visited the coast of Venezuela in 1499 observed natives in the Lake Maracaibo region (today the northwest state of Zulia) using a black, sticky substance to repair and caulk their canoes. They called it "devil's excrement." Four hundred fifty years later, some Venezuelan nationalists, including Juan Pablo Pérez

TABLE 23.   Greatest Oil Reserves by Country, 2006

Rank	Country	Proved Reserves (Billion Barrels)
1	Saudi Arabia	266.8
2	Canada	178.8
3	Iran	132.5
4	Iraq	115.0
5	Kuwait	104.0
6	United Arab Emirates	97.8
7	Venezuela	79.7*
8	Russia	60.0
11	United States	21.4

*Venezuela announced in 2007 that proven reserves had risen to over 100 billion barrels. If heavy nonconventional oil is included, Venezuela has the largest reserves in the world.

Source: Federal Reserve Bank of Dallas, based on data for *Oil and Gas Journal.*

Alfonzo, a former oil minister and cofounder of the Organization of Petroleum Exporting Countries (OPEC), would say that his country was "drowning in the devil's excrement" because a flood of imported consumer goods was threatening to obliterate traditional values and customs.

Venezuela is approximately the size of Texas and Oklahoma combined. In addition to the Lake Maracaibo region, oil and gas are found in the eastern states of Monagas and Anzoátegui, which is also rich in bauxite and iron and in hydroelectric power provided by the mighty Orinoco River. Along the border with Colombia, the high Andes run through three western states; a lesser spur (although some peaks reach nearly 9000 feet) runs along the northern, Caribbean coast. Most of Venezuela's 25 million people, 87 percent of them urban, live in these northern highlands; one of every five Venezuelans lives in metropolitan Caracas. The western and central states are ideal for growing coffee, the major export before the oil boom commenced in the 1920s. Before coffee, there was cacao, produced mostly in coastal plantations in a region called Barlovento, which remains today deeply marked by African culture. Today, the northern coast's fine beaches brim with tourist potential.

The eastern slopes of the Andes give way to plains, *los llanos,* where cattle ranches predominate. Farther south is the Sabana Grande, famous for diverse and exotic flora and fauna, home to most of Venezuela's small indigenous population. (Some indigenous people inhabit the peninsula west of Lake Maracaibo.) In the Sabana lies legendary El Dorado, which tempted Spanish conquistadors to undertake fruitless, tragic expeditions in search of gold and later inspired H. G. Wells to write *The Lost World.* Spectacular mountain outcroppings, called *tupuys,* interrupt the Sabana; from one of them descends Angel Falls, the highest waterfall in the world.

The majority of Venezuelan people are *pardos,* their term for racially mixed people whose ancestors were Europeans, Africans, and (to a lesser extent) indigenous inhabitants of the region. In the Andean west, the population is more generally *mestizo.* In Barlovento and much of the coast, descendants of African slaves remain the majority. Upper- and middle-class Venezuelans are more likely to have lighter skin, but little remains of the original oligarchy that owned the cacao plantations, *los amos del valle*, or "lords of the valley." Many perished or were ruined during Venezuela's war for independence and nineteenth-century civil wars. Lighter-skinned Venezuelans are more likely descendants of immigrants who came in the late 1800s or post-World War II. In the 1970s, Venezuela experienced an influx of Latin Americans fleeing violence and dictatorship, attracted by the oil boom of that era. These immigrants included hundreds of thousands of Colombians working today in the informal sector.

Race and Gender

Race has become an explicit and important part of Venezuela's politics. Chávez grew up the son of a schoolteacher in the small city of Sabaneta, in the state of Barinas, located where the *llanos* meet the Andes. His appearance is typical of *pardos*, who on their African side are often descended from slaves who fled the coastal plantations for the sparsely populated interior. The great oil-induced migration of the twentieth century saw the *pardo* population shift from rural areas to the city *barrios*.

Although patriarchical and *machista*, Venezuelan society in the *barrios* (poor neighborhoods) is held together by women. Alejandro Moreno, a sociologist and priest who has lived many decades in the *barrios*, argues that they are populated not by "men and women" but by "mothers and their boys." Although the first generation of migrants has given way to a generation more rooted in urban living and more thoroughly socialized by mass media, the traditions and attitudes of *barrio* dwellers still create a somewhat different world from the "modern" sectors, especially in Caracas. In these poor neighborhoods many Venezuelans live by the close personal ties that marked the country in its rural, agricultural past. Chávez, who left Barinas to take up a military career and get an education, is regarded by many of Venezuela's poor majority today as *their* president, in contrast to the government officials and businesspeople who live in the glittering skyscrapers and cafes in the valley below. Moreno (1998, 5) summarized Chávez' charismatic appeal to these Venezuelans: "What is important is not what he speaks but what speaks inside him. In him speaks the convivial relations of popular Venezuela, of convivial man. . . . An elderly woman expressed it very well: 'For me, it's like my own son is president.'"

In past democratic transitions, Venezuela's women often played a crucial role in organizing resistance to authoritarianism. Their solidarity toward oil workers, often taking in their families and collecting support funds, made possible the partial victory in the oil strike of December 1936. Women's organizations were among the sectors of civil society organized and pressuring for Venezuela's first, abortive experiment with democracy in 1945–1948. Without their risky underground work, Venezuela's most recent dictatorship might not have been toppled in 1958. After these transitions, women generally returned to the domestic sphere with relatively few concessions to their needs. Some progress on gender equality and family rights was accomplished in the post-1958 period, but the poorest women, especially those working in domestic labor, were generally left out of the gains. Probably no country in the world makes a fetish of Western standards of female beauty more than Venezuela. Venezuelans have won more beauty contests than any other nationality, and beauty queens often move on to careers not only in show business but in journalism and politics as well. Irene Sáez, a former Miss Universe, was a prominent mayor and for several months in 1998 the leading presidential candidate in the polls. The endless pageants held throughout the country have also encouraged schools to teach women how to conform to what critics call a "Venus culture," as well as a vast cosmetic surgery industry dedicated to altering (including "whitening") women's appearance to conform more to European standards.

Women are a key sector because they often are community leaders, essential to the prospects for the government's long-run goals of creating an economy based on social solidarity and unleashing the creative power of people in grassroots projects. This reality is reflected in several respects. New laws extend labor rights and benefits to women working in the domestic sector. The Bolivarian Constitution of 1999 uses gender-neutral language (for example, referring to *venezolanas y venezolanos*). The constitution broadens reproductive rights, much to the dismay of the Catholic hierarchy, but not to the satisfaction feminists who wanted a clearer affirmation of abortion rights. A Women's Bank funded by the state provides women with credits and education for micro-enterprises and cooperatives, although these programs are often compromised by clientelism and favoritism toward government supporters. The government acknowledges that violence and discrimination against women remain major obstacles to development, but it has failed on several occasions to move decisively in this field.

Venezuela's History and Its Uses Today

In 1982, then-Lieutenant Hugo Chávez met with other young officers to form what would become the Bolivarian Revolutionary Movement (MBR-200, later just MBR). They swore an oath of allegiance under the same tree that, according to Venezuelan mythology, shaded Simón Bolívar and his collaborators when they swore to liberate the country from Spain. Disillusioned by the squandering of the oil boom of the 1970s, the young officers pledged to fight corruption, reform the armed forces, and "rescue the values of the nation." These values were defined in their minds by three historical leaders: Bolívar, *El Libertador;* Simón Rodríguez, his teacher; and Ezequiel Zamora, a nineteenth-century *caudillo* famed for his egalitarian social program.

After defeating Spanish forces near Maracaibo in 1821, Bolívar and his allies proclaimed the Republic of Gran Colombia, embracing present-day Ecuador, Colombia, Panama, and Venezuela. The civil war for independence, which came to a close later that year, had seen over 400 battles on Venezuelan soil, reducing the population by one-third. Although Venezuela's cacao was highly prized for its quality in Europe, the region had been an underpopulated backwater of Spain's American empire. African slaves constituted less than 10 percent of the approximately 900,000 people who lived in the vast territory in the late colonial system, but their labor and culture were fundamental to the colonial economy. Those who had not freed themselves by fleeing to the vast interior plains and mountains were set free by manumission in 1854. However, most *negros* and *pardos* remained victims of forced labor through perpetual debt peonage, a mass of discontented males available to fill the ranks of *caudillo* armies.

Bolívar had sought to transform the social structures of slavery and peonage to lay the basis for republican government. This meant creating a new national culture by synthesizing European ideas with the traditional knowledge of the indigenous people. The idea of blending indigenous with European knowledge was a main theme in the work of Rodríguez, who warned against wholesale imitation of European ways in the South American environment. "We must innovate or fail," he warned. In 2002, Chávez adopted the name *Missión Robinson*, appropriating one of Rodríguez's pseudonyms, for a mass campaign to eradicate illiteracy.

The *criollos* allied with Bolívar joined the independence cause to escape Spanish economic controls, not to pursue republican ideals. Their notion of a republic was one where their narrow class and regional interests were represented, not one embracing those of all races and social classes. Confronted with their resistance to social change, Bolívar sought near dictatorial power, contradicting some of the very ideals he espoused. The Liberator had championed the pan-American ideal of a united continent, capable of dealing equitably with the United States, which, he feared, would impose on Latin America "misery in the name of democracy." As his dream of a united and progressive republic slipped away, Bolívar bitterly ruminated that he had attempted to "plow the sea." In the year of Bolívar's death, 1830, General José Antonio Páez, whose fierce *llanos*-based army had been crucial to winning the independence war, declared Venezuela's independence from Gran Colombia. Bolívar's admirers formed a liberal opposition to the conservative Páez, but for a generation Bolívar remained a largely discredited figure in the minds of Venezuela's ruling class.

Bolívar's image would be rehabilitated and exalted after a devastating civil war, the Federal War of 1858–1863. Liberals, united behind a call for a less centralized federal system, fought conservatives. In fact, the lofty principles articulated by both sides masked a vicious factional struggle within the landed oligarchy. However, one liberal general, Ezequiel Zamora, earned a reputation for brilliance in battle and for his commitment to land and liberty for the masses. Zamora rallied the peasants, who could become legally indebted for life at 10 years old and who had to carry passbooks to show they owed no labor to landowners, with his cry of *"Temblar a la oligarchía"* ("Make the oligarchy tremble"). Even the liberal *criollos* were alarmed. Legend has it that the bullet that felled him in battle was fired by one of his fellow officers. Chávez today invokes the egalitarian mythology of Zamora and brands his political enemies with the *caudillo*'s battle cry against oligarchy.

The liberals prevailed in a bloodbath that took between 60,000 and 100,000 lives, approximately 5 percent of the population. The promises made to the peasants were quickly forgotten. The Liberal General Antonio Guzmán Blanco, who dominated Venezuelan politics between 1870 and 1888, imposed social peace among regional *caudillos* and began a heavy-handed modernization program. An admirer of all things French, the "illustrious American" set about building railroads, highways, and new public buildings with funds borrowed from abroad, corruptly administered. Guzmán created a cult around the figure of Bolívar, creating Bolivarian societies, establishing national holidays, renaming the national currency after the Liberator, and building monuments in even the tiniest Venezuelan villages. These measures fostered a Venezuelan national identity, but the underlying export-oriented, agrarian economy and social indolence remained. At the end of Guzmán's rule, only 19 percent of the population was literate, and regional *caudillos* ran their local fiefdoms.

The relative peace of the Guzmán decades ended when a new sector of land-owners, mostly coffee growers and dairy farmers from the Andean states, rose in rebellion against bankers, merchants, and government officials in Caracas. In 1899, after another round of civil war, the Andeans, led by General Cipriano Castro, triumphed. An Andean general would govern Venezuela for all but three of the next 59 years.

Castro was simultaneously nationalist, authoritarian, and populist. He ran afoul of European powers when he refused to honor foreign investments and debts contracted by the old regime and by rival *caudillos*. In 1902, Britain, France, Germany, and Italy blockaded the Venezuelan coast. An alarmed United States, invoking the Monroe Doctrine, brokered a compromise; but in 1908, Washington leapt at the opportunity to oust Castro by supporting a coup. Another Andean general, Juan Vicente Gómez, established a dictatorship that would last until his death in December 1935. A ruthless tyrant who ran the country like it was his personal *hacienda*, Gómez was nonetheless also a state builder. He put Venezuela's fiscal house in order by improving the customs bureaucracy, and he continued Castro's work of building and training Venezuela's first professional army. With improved communications and highways, Gómez was able to deploy his well-trained and well-armed troops to defeat regional *caudillos* and their peasant armies. Guzmán had run Venezuela as first among equal *caudillos*. Gómez established himself as the nation's single, dominant *caudillo*.

Oil Changes Everything

In 1922, 14 years after Gómez came to power, oil drillers struck the first enormous gusher, and Venezuela was forever changed. In 1921, coffee exports had generated nine times the earnings of oil exports, which totaled 5.3 million bolívars (Bs.). Five years later, oil exports shot up to Bs. 259 million, more than double the earnings of coffee and cacao combined. In 1935, oil generated Bs. 676.8 million, sixteen times what coffee and cacao exports generated in the same year. The greatest flow of wealth was to Gómez and his circle of family and cronies, to whom he had awarded concessions subsequently sold to the foreign oil companies, who benefited from liberal terms offered by a state and oligarchy with little knowledge of the industry or value of its product. Still, the flow of dollars from oil exports washed over Venezuela's traditional, poor social structure with the force of an economic tidal wave. Peasants fled brutal conditions and rural indolence for new opportunities in oil camps and cities. A new working class in the oil camps appeared. Venezuelans became employed as drivers, port and railroad workers, construction workers, etc. Imports soared, creating opportunities for merchants. A small but growing middle class began to promote its interests and think about wresting power away from the Gómez tyranny.

In 1928, when a group of university students was arrested after a protest, spontaneous work actions and protests broke out, eventually leading to their release and exile. From abroad, one member of this "Generation of 1928," Rómulo Betancourt, whose name would become synonymous with the struggle for electoral democracy and who would become one of the leading statesmen of twentieth-century Latin America, developed a plan to replace Gómez with a government broadly representative of Venezuelan society. His strategy, the founding doctrine of the party legally registered as Acción Demócratica (AD) in 1941, consisted of (1) antiimperialism, which meant challenging the oil companies (*imperialismo petrolero*) and capturing a "just share" of profits for the nation; (2) using the profits ("sowing the oil," according to one Venezuelan intellectual) to modernize and diversify the economy and to improve living conditions (health, education, housing, etc.); and (3) democracy based on universal suffrage and a direct vote for the president, to create a political base for this project.

Some say that the twentieth century finally arrived in Venezuela on the day that Gómez, the last caudillo, died in his bed in December 1935. Widespread rioting and looting of the property of *gomecistas* greeted the news. Alarmed, the civilian leaders returning from exile and the generals who succeeded Gómez in the period between 1936 and 1945 sought middle ground. In late 1936, an oil workers' strike forced concessions from the government but also led to the exile of Betancourt and others. Both the moderate left and Communists continued to operate in clandestine fashion during an era of "soft" repression.

The two factions became bitter enemies, especially in their competition for control of the small but strategic unionized workers. Ultimately, Acción Democrática, legalized under that name in 1941, prevailed, in part because Betancourt worked tirelessly to organize not only workers but peasants and the middle class. AD became a truly national party, with branches in every neighborhood and town. It extended its dominance when it came to power after a coup in 1945.

The president overthrown that year was General Isaías Medina Angarita, a hero to *chavistas* today. Medina is remembered as a progressive president who took advantage of the strategic importance of oil during World War II to negotiate a new relationship with the oil companies. Essentially, in exchange for legalizing questionable concessions gained during the Gómez era, the companies conceded that the Venezuelan government's powers of taxation were sovereign, not limited by contract. The state's share of oil profits rose from 8 percent to more than half.

Medina did not complete his term. He had negotiated a transitional agreement with AD, but a compromise candidate was incapacitated by illness, and the agreement fell apart. Some ambitious middle-class officers, disgruntled that Medina had failed to cleanse the military of *gomecista* cronies, conspired with Betancourt and AD to overthrow Medina in October 1945. AD subsequently won three national elections by overwhelming majorities. Today, whenever the opposition raises the issue of the failed coup of 1992, Chávez recalls that AD first came to power via a coup.

For 3 years (the *trienio*) the AD government implemented a program of housing construction, education reform, land reform, peasant and labor organizing, and public investment. It enjoyed massive popular support but had many powerful enemies. The Communists were furious as *adeco* organizers used the Labor Ministry to help push rivals out of unions. On the other hand, Venezuelan business sectors did not distinguish between union organizing and Marxism. Rafael Caldera, who had begun his career in 1936 by organizing a Catholic student movement in opposition to the secular *adeco* youth movement, organized an opposition Christian Democratic party, the Independent Political Electoral Organizing Committee (COPEI). COPEI was small relative to the status it would achieve in the post-1958 era, but it was reinforced by the influence of the Church hierarchy, which was hostile to AD's secular education reforms.

AD cadres were often zealous about revolution, but party leaders had grown cautious, if not conservative, about the pace of change. Betancourt and the *trienio* government were pragmatic. The oil companies negotiated hard, but they were happy with a deal struck with Betancourt to share profits "fifty-fifty." More farsighted sectors in the U.S. foreign policy establishment understood that Betancourt was a reformist, not a communist; but Washington's swing to the right in the Cold War environment meant that all leftists, especially those with a Marxist past, were regarded with suspicion. AD's enemies at home exploited the hostile atmosphere. Amid rumors of a coup, the novelist Rómulo Gallegos, the *adeco* president, and Betancourt refused the request of leftist union leaders to arm militias to defend the government. On November 24, 1948, some of the same officers who had acted against Medina overthrew Gallegos. In 1952, another Andean general, Marcos Pérez Jiménez, seized full dictatorial power.

The Punto Fijo Regime and the Rise and Fall of "Partyarchy"

Pérez Jiménez tried to combine populism, in the form of lavish spending on construction and massive housing projects, with heavy-handed authoritarianism. By 1958, corruption, inefficiency, and cold-blooded murder of political opponents alarmed many military officers who sensed that the institution was alienating itself from Venezuelan society. The business community was alarmed when the regime began to renege on debts and contracts. With Betancourt, Caldera, and other veteran leaders in exile, young Communist and *adeco* cadres led an increasingly effective resistance in the swelling slums of Caracas and other large cities. In January 1958, after an abortive coup demonstrated opposition within the armed forces, Pérez Jiménez fled the country. A provisional government took power and planned for elections in December 1958.

The winner was Rómulo Betancourt and AD. Ten years of exile and dictatorship had noticeably changed the political climate. Washington and the Venezuelan business community now saw Betancourt as a moderate, much preferred to leaders like Fidel Castro, who after 1959 began to take Cuba down a revolutionary and eventually communist path. Caldera, Betancourt, and other party leaders agreed to power sharing, both to isolate the right and to exclude the Communists from a role in the new system. Church leaders now could rely upon COPEI, though not a confessional party, to represent their interests. The military accepted civilian control (notably, congressional approval of promotions) in exchange for autonomy over operational affairs (e.g., command left in military hands). Business leaders accepted unions and a regulated economy; in exchange, the government would make good on debts as well as subsidize and protect new industries, continuing the import substitution programs of the *trienio* and Pérez Jiménez.

The power-sharing agreement was signed in October 1958, just before the December elections, at Caldera's Caracas villa, Punto Fijo. Although not required, Betancourt included members of the other parties in his cabinet. This practice was abandoned by Caldera after he won the December 1968 election, but the two major parties, AD and COPEI, continued to cooperate to ensure their dominance—at the same time as they bitterly contested each other for power within the political condominium. The contest was over distribution of oil revenues, which in 1958 seemed uncertain because new Middle Eastern producers were threatening Venezuela's market share. When the U.S. administration refused to negotiate an agreement to guarantee Venezuela access to the U.S. market, the Betancourt government dispatched its oil minister, Pérez Alfonzo, to the Middle East to propose cooperation, eventually leading to OPEC. Alfonzo became known as the "father of OPEC," but he worried that oil earnings were stifling, not encouraging the economic development that Betancourt had hoped would flourish under democracy. Alfonzo urged the country to conserve its oil resources for the future, not exhaust them in a short term quest for profits.

The exclusion of the Communist Party of Venezuela (PCV) and Betancourt's limited reform agenda alienated the left. The PCV and young *adecos* had borne the human cost of organizing resistance to the dictatorship. The leftist wing of AD, which included most of its youth, formed the Movement of the Revolutionary Left (MIR) and began to criticize Betancourt. Betancourt fully backed the Kennedy administration's hard line against the Castro regime in Cuba, while younger Communists and the MIR dreamed of their own revolution *à la Cubana*. Although most of the older PCV leaders resisted, their youth and the MIR took to armed struggle, finding some support in the poor housing blocks inhabited by recent migrants from the countryside. The main guerrilla army, the Armed Forces of National Liberation (FALN), received some support from Cuba but faced a Venezuelan military armed and trained by the United States.

For most of the 1960s Venezuela suffered from a violent insurgency and government crackdowns on dissent. Betancourt's government enjoyed electoral legitimacy and the advantages of both oil income and support from Washington. As defeat loomed, some guerrillas turned to urban terrorism, further dissipating their support. Defeat should have been evident when in the face of calls for boycotts Venezuelans turned out in large numbers for the 1963 elections, won by AD's labor leader, Raúl Leoni. In 1968, another election took place, and this time Rafael Caldera, the COPEI founder, triumphed over a divided AD, resulting in the first peaceful transfer of power via election in the country's history. Caldera, although regarded as a staunch anti-communist, took the initiative to offer amnesty to the guerrillas. Beginning in 1969, most of them put down their arms; many returned to politics, sometimes becoming legislators and even cabinet members in governments led by politicians they had vowed to overthrow. Teodoro Petkoff, a legendary guerrilla leader known for his daring escapes from prison, founded the Movement toward Socialism (MAS), made up mostly of young Communists who made a self-critique of the failure of the guerrilla war and were disillusioned by the Soviet invasion of Czechslovakia in 1968. Petkoff moved full circle from revolutionary leftist to Minister for Planning in the second government of Caldera (1994–1998), where he helped implement market-oriented reform policies. He left MAS rather than follow the party into an alliance with the *chavistas*. He later became editor of a prominent opposition newspaper.

Former guerrillas Alfredo Maneiro (deceased in 1982) and Pablo Medina were cofounders of Causa R (Radical Cause), an influential worker-oriented political party that emerged in the late 1980s. Another former guerrilla leader, Douglas Bravo, never accepted amnesty or renounced armed struggle and remained head of Bandera Roja (Red Flag). Bravo, Medina, and other leftists made contact in the 1980s with Lieutenant Hugo Chávez and other young officers discontented with the Punto Fijo system. They became allies of Chávez in a failed coup attempt of February 1992, but some turned against Chávez. Others stayed loyal, including Alí Rodríguez, who served at different times as president of the state oil company, oil minister, and foreign minister.

By 1973, the insurgency had been defeated and the political party system created by the Pact of Punto Fijo had reached maturity. An opposition candidate, COPEI's Caldera, had won an election (1968) and assumed power, then returned it after AD's victory in December 1973. Unlike most Latin American countries, no truly conservative party existed; both major parties saw the role of the state as essential to "sowing the oil" in economic development. Small right-wing conspiracies in the military had been crushed. Both AD and COPEI dominated the political landscape but conceded a quota of influence to smaller leftist parties, products of splits from the AD and the PCV. The most important of these parties was MAS. MAS's attempt to reconcile socialist ideals with democratic politics attracted many intellectuals, but for some leftists the party was too reformist. A handful of original MAS members, including Maneiro, defected from the party to undertake a more long-term, grass-roots strategy of organizing poor *barrios* in Caracas and the growing working class in the new steel and aluminum enterprises in eastern Guayana, which became the bases for Causa R.

How did a conspiracy between a handful of unsuccessful guerrillas and discontented young army officers become a mass force to dislodge the politicians associated with the Punto Fijo regime? Several factors converged.

Rising and Frustrated Expectations. For most of the century, living standards and social mobility were rising in Venezuela. During the OPEC oil boom of the 1970s, all things seemed possible. The Venezuelan government took in $2.6 billion in oil earnings in 1973, about two-thirds of all revenues received. In late 1973, oil prices quadrupled. As a result, in 1974, revenues shot up to $8.9 billion. The *adeco* president, Carlos Andrés Pérez, winner of the 1973 elections and a protégé of Betancourt, called his national plan for using the oil earnings *"manos a la obra"* ("Let's get to work"), but much of his program was sheer populism. He used the windfall to raise the minimum wage, eliminate unemployment entirely, create vast new steel and aluminum industries, subsidize industries and agriculture, and expand social benefits. Inflation was controlled by keeping the bolívar at 4.3 to the dollar, which made it cheap for nearly everyone to get dollars for travel abroad or to buy imported goods. Prices were capped. Life was so good that Venezuelans sometimes refer to this period as the era of *"Tan barato, dame dos!"* ("So cheap, I'll take two!").

In 1976, Venezuela nationalized (peacefully, legally, with compensation) the oil industry, creating in its place a state holding company, Petroleos de Venezuela S.A. (PDVSA). Now, the state controlled the entire bonanza. In his eagerness to transform Venezuela overnight into an industrial powerhouse, Pérez borrowed heavily against future earnings. International banks, struggling under a global recession, were eager to lend. By 1978, it looked like the bubble might burst; but then came a second round of oil price hikes of 1980, following the Iranian Revolution and the outbreak of war between Iraq and Iran. In 1981, the government took in $21.6 billion from oil revenues, accounting for over 90 percent of government revenues. The COPEI president, Luis Herrera Campins, elected in December 1978, had promised to be more frugal; but instead, he rode the new wave of petrodollars.

Unfortunately for Herrera Campins and Venezuela, the OPEC oil boom was coming to a close. In 1982, oil earnings fell about 25 percent, and the price per barrel was in free-fall. The massive new industries started by Pérez were uncompetitive internationally and riddled with corruption, in need of continual subsidies to set off losses. There was the foreign debt to pay as well. With elections pending in December 1983, Herrera Campins tried to avoid devaluation, which would lead to higher prices and falling wages. He bled PDVSA dry of its accumulated savings, but it was not enough. On a day that Venezuelans call "Black Friday," February 28, 1983, he devalued the bolívar. The days of "4.3" and zero unemployment were over. The poverty rate soared, and Venezuelans began to ask who was to blame.

Corruption. As living conditions fell, the problem of corruption in government seemed to get worse. Pérez and Herrera Campins were second-generation party leaders. Around them were politicians, speculators, and wealthy businessmen who did not share the zeal for democracy and honesty that characterized most of the generation of Betancourt and Caldera. Pérez himself was touched by scandal, though he escaped censure. Herrera Campins was never accused of corruption, but several high *copeyanos* were. Venezuelans could now see that the Christian Democrats were little different from the *adecos*. Between 1983 and 1988, the administration of President Jaime Lusinchi (AD) touched new depths of corruption. Wealthy Venezuelans showed a special fondness for Florida real estate and imported whisky.

Generals, senators, ministers, and business elites siphoned millions of dollars into their pockets and then safely abroad; at the grassroots, petty corruption became a way of life. Tollbooth operators would turn in only a fraction of their collection, cutting in their bosses and keeping their jobs as long as they belonged to the right party. Bureaucrats demanded "service payments" (bribes) to attend to public business. Since the corruption enveloped generals and admirals, most of the military seemed well integrated into the system of graft and patronage. No one knew that within its ranks were officers like Chávez, disillusioned with Punto Fijo democracy and inspired by the ideals of Bolívar.

Ideological Crisis. Recall that Betancourt's plan for Venezuela 50 years earlier had linked democracy to antiimperialism (wresting control of oil profits) and development ("sowing the oil" in economic development). Between 1983 and 1987, Venezuela actually suffered a net loss of $17.3 billion in capital due to debt payments and capital flight. After nationalization, no longer could failures be blamed on *imperialismo petrolero*. Elites tended to blame the people for the economic disasters of the post-1980 period; in their view, the oil rents had made them lazy, deceived into believing that the country was wealthy. The people had a different perspective: if the country once was wealthy but the people were poor, then those at the top had to be held accountable.

From Decay to Collapse of the Punto Fijo System

When Pérez won a second term in 1988, he campaigned as a populist who would restore the good times. Pérez surely knew that it was not within his power to return to the *"tan barato"* days, but he probably also did not know the full dimensions of the crisis until he took office after a lavish inauguration that was more like a coronation, which only reinforced popular beliefs that the country remained wealthy. The population was shocked when Pérez announced what he thought was obvious and inevitable: an austerity program and structural adjustment agreement with the International Monetary Fund (IMF). Public employment was to be frozen, price controls eased, wages held in check, and so on.

Neoliberal, market-oriented ideas have found less traction in Venezuela than elsewhere: the state owns nearly all heavy industries, such as petrochemicals and metallurgy. Almost all industries and agriculture are heavily subsidized; when oil prices are high, local industries cannot compete with imports; when oil prices are low, demand slackens. Banks rely extensively on government deposits and borrowing, opening significant opportunities for corruption and patronage. Venezuela's private capitalists often built their fortunes on land and money speculation or by collecting commissions as go-betweens in government contracts and concessions. Hence, while there was some sentiment for selling off state-owned heavy industries and infrastructure (e.g., telecommunications), the constituency for sweeping, market-oriented change was small.

On the morning of Monday, February 27, 1989, gasoline prices were due to rise. Microbus owners were angry because they were not allowed to pass along the increase to their riders. They attempted to collect anyway, and an angry mob burned a microbus, lighting a fuse. By the end of the day, widespread looting and rioting, which became known as the *Caracazo*, had spread to 22 cities. Police, poorly paid and sharing the same conditions as their neighbors, organized the systematic looting of many stores, especially where merchants, believing that price controls would soon be lifted, had hoarded goods. Shocked, Pérez hesitated; but by Tuesday evening things seemed to be calming down. Then, Pérez sent the army to occupy neighborhoods and to recover some of the looted goods. In the resulting violence, human rights groups estimate that over 1000 died.

This use of the army angered the young Bolivarian officers, increasing their numbers and determination to act. On February 14, 1992, Venezuelans and foreign observers were shocked to learn that a coup was under way. When it failed, Pérez supporters asked the captured leader to go on television to appeal to his supporters to lay down their arms.

Lieutenant Colonel Hugo Chávez complied. Uninformed, wearing his red para-trooper's beret, Chávez took responsibility (in contrast to the politicians), made the appeal, but told his comrades that their objectives had failed "for now." He spoke less than a minute, but the effect was electrifying. The politicians expected people to rally to democracy; suddenly, thousands of youth were sporting red berets on the street. Amid a clamor in Congress, with politicians condemning the coup and one *adeco* calling for the execution of its leaders, the *eminence gris* of the system, Rafael Caldera, rose to speak. (Betancourt had died in 1981.) He condemned the coup but, to the astonishment of the politicians, recognized the plotters' widespread support and reflected on why the people had lost faith in the system.

Pérez and his economic program were finished. Street demonstrations became daily occurrences. A second failed coup attempt in November 1992 showed that normalcy had not returned. In 1993, Congress ousted Pérez on a trumped-up charge of illegally diverting funds. A caretaker government gave way to Caldera, who won the December 1993 election after splitting from COPEI, the party he had founded nearly 50 years earlier. For the first time, the integrity of the elections was seriously called into question. Andrés Velásquez, a metal worker and leader of a movement to democratize the Confederation of Venezuelan Workers (CTV), nominated by Causa R, ran third in official results but claimed he had won; in the end, though, victory was awarded to Caldera. The new president, who had extended amnesty to the guerrillas after 1968, sought national reconciliation by freeing Chávez and other imprisoned officers. The old Christian Democrat promised to find an alternative to neoliberalism, but by the end of his term, much to the anger of the voters, he ended up with a package of economic policies resembling those of his disgraced predecessor.

As the December 1998 elections approached, it seemed likely that Venezuela's next president would come from outside the traditional party system, due in part to political reforms enacted after the *Caracazo*. Direct election of governors, previously appointed by the president, permitted regional politicians to establish independent bases of support. Early leaders in the polls were Irene Sáez, the mayor of a middle-class Caracas suburb, and Henrique Salas Römer, governor of the populous state of Carabobo. Then Chávez abandoned his advocacy of abstention and entered the race. Sáez proved more image than substance. Her candidacy collapsed after she accepted the endorsement of COPEI, a sign of the popular contempt for the tra-ditional parties. AD's candidate, its secretary general, never gained any traction. Meanwhile, Chávez surged. COPEI and AD at the last moment threw their sup-port to Römer, which may have cost the candidate more than he gained. Prohibited by law from using Bolívar's name for partisan purposes, Chávez called his "elec-toral movement" the Movimiento Quinta República (Fifth Republic Movement) or MVR (*V* here is a Roman numeral, referring to the founding of a "fifth" Venezuelan republic). Chávez won 56 percent of the vote as the candidate of the MVR and some smaller parties united in a coalition called the Polo Patriótico (PP).

In the Punto Fijo era, Venezuela's political parties had insinuated themselves into almost every area of organized social life—unions, neighborhood associations, women's groups, student organizations, peasant associations. The parties ran slates of candidates against one another for control of these organizations. Victory meant a larger share of the state's oil income (often called "rent"), which subsidized all of these organizations in one form or another. For example, unions were mostly funded by state revenues, not dues. Union leaders controlled major banks and services (e.g., tourist facilities), which compromised their relationship with workers and worsened the problem of corruption. Contracts often included lucrative commissions for the negotiators. Conversely, control over oil rents gave the party leaders immense patronage and power over the rank and file.

Iron discipline prevailed in internal party matters and legislative matters. A vote against the directive of the party leadership on even the smallest matter was political suicide. Many elected officials or officers of civic groups were "parachutists," that is, individuals from other regions, unknown to the voters or members, imposed by central party authorities after the process of internal struggles among different factions. This politics was in part the legacy of the disciplined internal party structures created in the 1930s and 1940s, when the parties operated illegally and adopted internal rules similar to those used by the Communists. One analyst called this state of affairs "partyarchy," and it did not disappear with the election of President Chávez. One major issue confronting the new president would be how to cleanse the political system of these practices.

In the 1990s, citizen movements demanded change beyond the limited reforms enacted after the *Caracazo*. Middle-class groups, like Queremos Elegir ("We Want to Choose"), called for single-member district representation and mandatory primaries. Venezuela's system of proportional representation seemed highly democratic, but it was deeply flawed. The lists of candidates were determined from the top down by national party leaders. Voters cast ballots by marking an X over a party symbol. From the national Congress and largest union organizations down to the smallest neighborhood councils and high school student groups, AD and COPEI fought one another, often making tactical alliances with smaller parties but combining their power against newcomers unwilling to be co-opted. By the 1990s, most Venezuelans were ready for major change. Chávez made the centerpiece of his 1998 campaign the outright call for a constituent assembly to rewrite the constitution, while Römer hesitated to call for such a sweeping change.

Another major issue of the 1998 campaign was oil policy. In the 1990s, PDVSA executives had successfully pushed through an *apertura petrolera* (oil opening), permitting foreign capital into the oil fields through service contracts, joint ventures, and shared risks. PDVSA, usurping the role of the Ministry of Mines and Energy, offered highly attractive terms designed to radically boost production with relatively little investment of its own. Company executives urged that Venezuela leave OPEC unless the organization abandoned its quota system; some floated the idea of selling private shares in the company. PDVSA acquired a network of refineries and stations (e.g., the U.S. company CITGO). PDVSA management claimed it was merely attempting to secure markets, but critics saw the maneuver as a way to hide

President Chávez speaks. (*Ministry of Information, Venezuela*)

profits by transferring them abroad, manipulating accounts, and selling crude to its own affiliates at deep discounts.

The collapse of oil prices after the Asian economic crisis of 1998 ruined PDVSA's plans. Chávez accused company executives of selling out the national patrimony in order to maintain their own high salaries and privileged lifestyle. The managers and professionals associated with PDVSA would become the nucleus of forces that tried to topple the president via a coup, an industry shutdown, and finally a recall referendum. The executives sought to save the company from Chávez; Chávez sought to save the country from the company.

Venezuela's "Bolivarian" Constitution and Institutional Framework

Upon assuming office, Chávez moved boldly to sweep away the old institutions that underpinned the traditional parties. He called and won a referendum to convene the Constituent Assembly, with most delegates to be chosen one to a district, to write a new constitution. The single-member district formula magnified the victory of Chávez and his coalition, the PP. They had an overwhelming majority in the assembly, which convened on August 9, 1999. Now it was the old party leaders' turn to complain about lack of democracy.

The Constituent Assembly renamed the country the Bolivarian Republic of Venezuela, an affirmation that Chávez' revolution intended to invoke the Liberator's philosophy for its underlying principles. Like many constitutions in Latin America, the new charter guaranteed people an extensive list of social and economic rights that are beyond the capacity of the government to fulfill, but these commitments reaffirmed Chávez' agenda of social inclusion. That is, they affirmed the principle that economic policy making should prioritize the needs of those threatened with exclusion from the social benefits of oil income and vulnerable to the impersonal forces of capitalist globalization.

International human rights treaties to which Venezuela is a signatory are given preeminence over national laws. Indigenous rights (three delegates to the Constituent Assembly were allocated directly to indigenous organizations) were given unprecedented recognition. All rights typically associated with liberal democracy were recognized, although there were potential areas of conflict. For example, although freedom of speech and press were guaranteed, a right of the people to "truthful information" was also guaranteed. Critics argued that this provision as well as a new media law (passed in 2004) violate international and hemispheric obligations in the area of press freedoms. In response, *chavistas* accused the Venezuelan media of saturating the country with commercials, minimizing educational programs for children, and transmitting perhaps the most violent programming in the Americas. The constitution and a new media law gave the government significant regulatory power, which defenders saw as necessary to ensure media responsibility, while critics feared censorship.

The Bolivarian constitution established a unicameral National Assembly, elected mostly by a first-past-the-post system of representation, which tends to exaggerate majority power and underrepresent minority interests. Where the new constitution is most innovative is in regard to citizen participation and the configuration of branches of government. In addition to the usual three branches (executive, legislative, judicial), the constitution creates a "citizen's power" branch, an attempt to incorporate Chávez' idea of "protagonistic" democracy. Venezuela's new system would, on the one hand, be representative and pluralist but, on the other hand, also promote direct participation by the people. The attorney general, a national ombudsman, and a comptroller were to be chosen by the new National Assembly after consultation with a council composed of groups in civil society, such as human rights organizations. Provisions permitting recall of elected officials and referendums were also designed to give citizens a protagonistic role in Venezuela's new democracy.

The new National Assembly elected in 2000 was supposed to legislate enabling laws, but instead the parties cut deals with one another in making the appointments. Also, instead of subjecting new, major legislation to widespread popular debate, the assembly granted President Chávez emergency powers for 1 year to decree legislation in a broad range of policy areas, including land reform, oil policy, education, etc. Chávez waited almost the entire year to act. When he did, he acted strongly in favor of popular interests, but the process was hardly evocative of a "protagonistic" role for the people.

Reform of the judiciary has been very controversial as well. In the late Punto Fijo era, the courts were heavily politicized. When rich and powerful figures were unhappy with the decision of one court, they could usually find a judge tied to their party willing to lend a sympathetic ear and issue a conflicting opinion or, at the appeals level, to reverse a finding. However, contrary to the image often portrayed by the international media, the politicized nature of the courts does not always work in Chávez's favor. For example, the Supreme Court decided on highly technical and convoluted grounds that military officers involved in the short-lived 2002 coup could not be put on trial for their actions.

On the whole, international jurists have praised efforts to reform Venezuela's court system but questioned the move by the National Assembly, controlled by the *chavistas*, to make it easier for a simple majority to confirm nominees for the Supreme Court, expand the size of the court, and facilitate the removal of judges considered corrupt or derelict in their responsibilities. These were seen as an attempt by Chávez to pack the court with his supporters, while the president argued these changes were needed to fight corruption and overcome obstructionist tactics by the opposition.

After his re-election in December 2006, President Chávez announced he would follow through with a promised reform of the 1999 Bolivarian Constitution, and he appointed a committee of his supporters to make proposals to go before the National Assembly and then the people in a referendum in December 2007. The most controversial change would have extended the presidential term from 6 to 7 years and substitute indefinite re-election for a two-term limit established in 1999. Why did the proposals fail? The opposition portrayed the proposals as a naked grab for power by the president, and to some extent even supporters of the president seemed to agree. Even if they did not vote "no," many abstained. Chávez mustered 3 million votes less than he received in the December 2006 reelections.

Among other changes included in the package of changes was one to change the "geometry of the state" and another to create new property forms. The former proposal would create a new branch of government, popular power, defining communes as the building blocks of the "socialist state." Although continuing to guarantee private property rights, the reformed constitution would have created several forms of collective property intended to consolidate the growth of a sector of "solidarity," made up of micro-enterprises, cooperatives, and farms using sustainable and appropriate technologies ("endogenous development").

Although the reforms went down to defeat, Chávez was likely to attempt to implement some of them through legislation and, perhaps to hold another referendum before his term expires in early 2013. For that reason, it is worth examining the proposals a little further. Already by law, the communes remain part of municipalities and states but are empowered to allocate funds provided directly by the central government to local organizations. This task is supposed to be carried out by councils formed by *voceros* (spokespersons), a term deliberately chosen to stress that these leaders were not to be considered "representatives" but conduits for the preferences of local organizations united in grassroots *consejos comunales* (community councils), constituted by about 200 families in urban areas. State and local municipal authorities continue to have resources of their own. Just whether and in what form elected officials will collaborate with the councils was far from clear. Critics, both inside and outside *chavismo*, fear they will become little more than clientelist networks. Chávez sees the *consejos* as instruments to fight clientelism and corruption.

After the reform commission submitted its proposals, the National Assembly approved a number of additional provisions, including one to the original reforms.

One would give the president power during "states of exception" to suspend constitutional rights of free speech and the Venezuelan equivalent of habeas corpus, which drew criticism from human rights organizations at home and abroad. This provision drew criticism from the government's own human rights ombudsman and from the former vice president, but its supporters said that the coup of April 2002 and the problems arising from several natural disasters showed the need for such a measure.

The president tried to make the referendum a popularity contest, which meant of course that the opposition was able to take even higher expectations away from what was a narrow defeat. However, the proposals also provoked for the first time deep debate among intellectuals and leaders identified with *chavismo*. Wouldn't the existence of parallel state and local governance structures create inefficiency and confusion? Wouldn't the new communal councils be susceptible to cooptation by a state with enormous resources (oil profits) at its disposal? Might not a future government use suspension of rights against the *chavistas* themselves? The commission that developed the reform proposals was closely supervised by Chávez himself. Once again, said the critics, Chávez was reinforcing a strong cultural tendency toward personalism and presidentialism, a criticism that was amplified in the weeks after the election. For its part, the government argued that the reforms were necessary to speed redistribution of resources to benefit the poor and lay the legal foundation for a more participatory form of democracy and society. Where critics saw a centralization of power, the government's defenders said that formally granting local councils constitutional status and allocating budgetary resources directly to them was a step toward decentralization. The domestic opposition and the international media repeatedly characterize Chávez as "authoritarian" or a "dictator." His democratic credentials were tested by the extremely narrow defeat of his constitutional reform proposals in the December 2007 referendum. Chávez confounded his critics by accepting the results. The result also gave a boost to the credibility of the country's beleaguered National Electoral Commission. So in defeat, the Venezuelan president could take some solace in the improvement of his international reputation.

Political Actors in Bolivarian Venezuela

The collapse of *puntofijismo* in 1998 left Venezuelan politics in an extremely fluid and polarized state, bitterly divided around the figure of Chávez himself. The contending forces were aligned against one another in coalitions of loosely organized parties, movements, and interest groups.

CHAVISMO OR "OFICIALISMO"

Chávez and his coconspirators viewed the Bolivaran Revolutionary Movement (MBR) as a military–civilian movement. To a degree, that conception of the armed forces and the people joined together to transform society remains his conception of how his movement will function. When Chávez abandoned advocating abstention and launched his presidential candidacy in 1998, it was necessary to create the MVR. The MVR joined some smaller parties, including MAS (prompting the defection of

Petkoff and some other historic leaders of this party) and Patria Para Todos (PPT, or Fatherland for All) to form the PP. The PPT was the product of divisions in Causa R and included some of the former guerrillas who had worked clandestinely with the MBR and supported the 1992 coup attempt by Chávez. The party's electoral base was small, but it brought to the coalition organizing experience and a circle of intellectuals with expertise in oil. One of them, Alí Rodríguez, became the main architect of the government's new oil policies, which included reinvigorating OPEC, imposing higher royalties on new foreign investment in oil, reducing PDVSA's international holdings, and reasserting control of the Ministry of Mines and Energy over the company. Besides his government positions, Rodríguez served as secretary general of a reinvigorated OPEC in 2001–2002.

A veteran leftist politician, Luis Miquilena, was the MVR's first leader, controlling internal affairs with Chávez' blessing. Miquilena adroitly steered the Constituent Assembly, but his tactics in the subsequent National Assembly reminded many *chavistas* too much of the Punto Fijo era. In the 1998 campaign, Miquilena had lined up support for Chávez from sectors in banking, commerce, and mass media; but these interests naturally expected influence in return. Miquilena's willingness to cut deals with the traditional parties signaled a degree of moderation and pragmatism, but many *chavistas* saw cronyism and corruption growing in the ranks of their revolution.

Chávez has repeatedly tried to engineer a transition from this style of politics. He discarded Miquilena in 2001 and initially announced he planned to reconstitute the MBR, but the MVR continued to be more suitable for passing legislation in the Assembly and preparing for elections. After the coup of April 2002, Chávez tried to consolidate the popular insurgency on his behalf by encouraging Bolivarian Circles, but these too began to wither and to lack the staying power of the MVR. However, the MVR proved inept in preparing for the 2004 recall elections, so Chávez stepped in to create "electoral battle units," which proved invaluable to his victory. However, once again the politicians of the MVR and other parties seemed unable to put aside their hierarchical tendencies. The parties brokered deals to present slates of nominees for local elections in October 2004. An attempt to organize primaries for local elections in May 2005 ended in confusion. Slates of candidates for the December 2006 National Assembly were again developed through bargaining between the MVR and smaller, allied parties, leaving many *chavistas* at the based disillusioned.

Chávez once more sought to institutionalize participatory politics by calling for formation of the Unified Socialist Party of Venezuela (PSUV) after his re-election in December 2006. The MVR leadership immediately dissolved itself and proclaimed its loyalty to the PSUV, but some smaller parties balked. Initially to be founded in March, it was not until late October that internal elections for a founding convention got underway. Some leaders claimed that over 5 million Venezuelans, approximately a quarter of the adult population, had joined the party by late 2007, but the fact that only 4.3 million voters said "yes" to the constitutional reform makes that number highly questionable.

Venezuelan culture is greatly shaped by the influence of the state's control of petrodollars, exacerbating a tendency throughout Latin America toward strong executive authority and hierarchy. Even before it had a program and a charter, the

PSUV had instituted a disciplinary committee. To the obstacles facing participatory democracy in Venezuela one must add the charismatic leadership of Chávez himself. The president desperately seeks to prevent career politicians and bureaucrats from coopting the Bolivarian revolution and re-creating the ills of the old Punto Fijo system. The president may be sincere in his objectives, but he has not yet proven capable of empowering and trusting his own ministers, and he at times shows an intolerant streak toward dissent, even within the ranks of his own supporters. A major question in the aftermath of the December 2007 vote was whether the president was capable of learning from his own mistakes.

THE OPPOSITION

The opposition has proved even more inept at organizing itself. In 2001, *antichavistas* formed an alliance, the Coordinadora Democrática (CD). It was neither very coordinated nor democratic. First it alienated most of the population by participating in the short-lived coup of 2002 and the shutdown of the oil industry for 3 months beginning in December 2002. Then, the CD tried to discredit the outcome of the 2004 recall election, flying in the face of the verdict of international observer teams. Facing defeat in the 2005 elections for the National Assembly, opposition forces at the last moment called for abstention, much to the consternation of several parties and leaders who had wished to participate. Turnout was low, but not enough to discredit the *chavista* victory, leaving the opposition with no representation in the national legislature. By 2006, the opposition had lost influence in virtually all important arenas in Venezuelan politics except one—the private media—and even there some broadcast outlets and newspapers apparently decided to moderate their tone rather than face extinction.

For the December 2006 election, most of the opposition united around the candidacy of Manuel Rosales, governor of Zulia, the most populous state and home to Lake Maracaibo's oil production. Rosales was a former *adeco* and one of a handful of politicians to have survived the rising *chavista* tide. Chávez defeated him with a resounding 63 percent of the vote, but for the first time the opposition candidate accepted defeat. The *antichavista* opposition had taken the first step toward broadening its appeal. Its fortunes may be enhanced if significant numbers of *chavistas* become disenchanted with the PSUV. However, success, in the form of victory at the polls in December 2007 raised new questions. Could the opposition stay united for future battles, or will the temptation of gaining spoils of office cause internal squabbling? Could the opposition develop an appealing program, not just represent *antichavista* sentiment? The president, despite defeat, still maintained high approval ratings entering 2008.

Business organizations in Venezuela are extremely weak in comparison to the behemoth that is PDVSA. After President Herrera Campins virtually expropriated (and wasted) $5 billion in accumulated profits in 1983, company executives began to look for independence from the state. PDVSA was held in high repute, both nationally and internationally, as a well-run meritocracy; PDVSA executives and professionals saw themselves as an island of competence in a sea of corruption and profligacy. Accustomed to First-World incomes and standards of living, working closely with international oil executives, PDVSA executives aggressively

pursued an agenda of attracting foreign investment through joint ventures and service agreements, which meant loosening restrictions in the 1975 nationalization law.
Company presidents publicly advocated for Venezuela to leave OPEC. Some Venezuelan oil experts proposed privatization of the company by distributing shares to
citizens. Luis Giusti, president of PDVSA during the second Caldera administration
(1994–1998), was considered a possible presidential candidate. The collapse of oil
prices in 1998 undermined Giusti and strengthened Chávez and critics of the company, such as Rodríguez. Although the foreign oil companies do business with the
government, the former executives of PDVSA and Chávez became mortal enemies
of each other.

A dozen or so family groups (Mendoza, Cisneros, Boulton, etc.) own the bulk
of service and manufacturing industries, and family and friendship connections
have always counted for much. *"Este señor tiene sus cosas en orden"* ("This gentleman has his arrangements in place") was, and remains (to the dismay of many
chavistas), an important recommendation for doing business with private or public entities.

The most important private business association is the Federación de Cámaras y
Asociaciones de Comercio y Producción de Venezuela (FEDECAMARAS), whose
president, Pedro Carmona, briefly assumed the presidency in the short-lived coup
of April 2002. However, in the aftermath of Chávez' victory in the recall referendum
of August 2004, FEDECAMARAS seemed ready to abandon intransigent opposition. FEDECAMARAS's labor counterpart, the CTV, was historically dominated
by AD, much the way labor and the Institutional Revolutionary Party in Mexico
were mutually related. CTV leaders formed a powerful sector within the party and
often pressed labor demands, but in the end party interests held sway over those
of workers. The CTV seemed helpless after 1983 to stem rising unemployment and
deteriorating living conditions. Corruption was rife within the labor bureaucracy.
In the late 1980s, a labor democracy movement emerged, much of it organized by
Causa R.

In December 2000, President Chávez called a referendum on a proposal to
democratize the CTV and labor in general. He won but with a small majority
and high rates of abstention. In subsequent elections marked by fraud and confusion, Carlos Ortega, an *adeco* labor bureaucrat from the oil sector, was elected CTV
president. *Chavistas* then launched a rival confederation (UNT, National Workers'
Union), which has gained ground but left organized labor deeply divided. Workers
in general seem to reject the corrupt and unresponsive leadership of the past, but
they also resist being subordinated to the interests of any political party, including
the MVR. Many middle-class Venezuelans, fed up with AD and COPEI, supported
Chávez in the December 1998 election and then participated in the process of popular input that shaped the 1999 Bolivarian Constitution. The radical turn of *chavismo*
in November 2001 was the catalyst for a shift in their attitude. In the capital, many
united behind an organization called SUMATE ("Join UP"), which claims to be nonpartisan and independent but has received significant infusions of money from the
U.S. taxpayer-financed National Endowment for Democracy (NED).

The catalyst for the coup of April 2002 was a series of decree laws that Chávez
proclaimed just as a 1-year grant of authority from the National Assembly was

about to run out. The most controversial of the decrees were three in the areas, respectively, of land reform, fishing, and oil. The first two, although not directly threatening the middle class, were portrayed by opposition forces in the national media as attacks on private property. The third, by unilaterally increasing the government's share of oil revenues and moving oil policy out of the hands of PDVSA executives, was depicted as a policy that would drive away foreign investment and politicize control over the motor force behind the national economy. To fears about the direction of government economic policy must be added middle-class resistance to government plans to assert more influence over Church-controlled schools, which are heavily subsidized by the state.

In December 2001, the CD called a modestly successful one-day civil strike to protest the policies. Emboldened by the response, the group escalated actions and began to plot with military officers disgruntled with the president's determination to reorient the armed forces toward development projects at home. The opposition called a mass demonstration in front of PDVSA headquarters for April 11 after another two-day civic strike. By this time the private broadcast networks and major newspapers were cooperating in efforts to force the president from office, running advertisements calling people out to the rally.

In what seemed spontaneous but later was revealed to have been part of a plan to provoke a coup, the leader of the labor federation associated with AD called on several hundred thousand people assembled in front of PDVSA to march on the presidential palace, where the president's supporters were waiting. Violence broke out. The media blamed it entirely on the *chavistas* and said that Chávez had ordered the military to repress the people in the streets. Dissident generals arrested the president and said he had resigned, which Chávez denies to this day. The stage was set for the remarkable events described at the beginning of this chapter.

Then came the 3-month oil shutdown, which opposition figures call a "strike" and government supporters call the "oil sabotage." Once again, the government triumphed, conceding nothing more than a commitment to abide by the results of a recall election, the opposition gathered sufficient signatures to force one constitutionally. Now SUMATE came to the front, taking the lead in the subsequent petition campaign. After a series of legal battles and mediation by former U.S. President Jimmy Carter and his Carter Center, the recall election took place on August 15, 2004.

SUMATE's stubborn rejection of the outcome cost it considerable national and international prestige. Its prestige suffered further when, against the wishes of several prominent opposition figures interested in running for president in 2006, the organization joined AD and COPEI in urging abstention in the 2005 National Assembly elections. This decision turned a near-certain government landslide into a clean sweep. When SUMATE attempted to coordinate an opposition primary in summer 2006 to choose a presidential candidate, the leading figures settled the competition among themselves rather than allow the organization to stampede them into another round of abstention.

The eventual unity candidate, Manuel Rosales, the governor of Zulia state, created a new party, *Nuevo Tiempo* (New Times), as a vehicle for his ambitions. Another small party, but one with a significant influence among the middle class in Caracas, is *Primero Justicia* (Justice First). It offers a neoliberal ideological platform, which currently has limited appeal in Venezuela outside of affluent areas of the capital. A few other small parties, some splinter groups from AD, COPEI, and the *Movimiento al Socialismo* (MAS; once the country's largest leftist party) make up the rest of the highly fragmented opposition.

The most influential opposition stronghold remains the media. In early 2007, President Chávez instructed the Ministry of Communications not to renew the broadcast license of RCTV, one of the four large private TV and radio networks. The station's license was up for renewal, and its role in actively promoting the coup of April 2002 and PDVSA work stoppage were cited, among other reasons, for denial. Critics seized on the decision as a violation of press freedoms, but the other three stations continued to broadcast. Meanwhile, the state broadcast media continued, in violation of law, to propagandize in favor of the government.

As the December 2007 referendum on the Constitution approached, the opposition at first showed its divisions. AD, COPEI, and some other small opposition parties urged abstention and even threatened street actions to disrupt the election. SUMATE took an ambiguous position, clearly against the reforms but careful not to take a position on abstention. Others, such as *Nuevo Tiempo*, sought to postpone the vote, sensing that a prolonged debate would weaken the government's chances. But the turning point came when retired general Raul Baduel, the former defense minister and a *chavista* hero for having stood with the president during the 2002 coup, broke with Chávez and severely criticized the government. It seemed likely that Baduel would enter politics himself; furthermore, the defection of such a prominent and popular soldier likely has caused some dissent within military ranks, something that is difficult to measure with any certainty.

Neutral actors are hard to find in the Venezuelan drama. The Church is relatively weak. Most of the hierarchy joined the CD, but many clergy working in the poor *barrios* are inclined toward Chávez. The situation is more complicated and opaque for that other pillar of internal rule in Latin America, the military. The failure of the April 2002 coup gave the president an opportunity to purge the officer ranks of disloyal elements. Many Venezuelan officers have embraced their participation in missions (many funded directly by PDVSA) in the *barrios* and poor rural areas. Still, there are reports that some officers are disgruntled with the new missions, feeling that they do not befit their vocation and training. Still others are loyal to the original goals of the MBR and have embraced the new constitution, but these "constitutionalists" do not necessarily transfer this loyalty to the person of Chávez.

Venezuelan society witnessed an explosion of popular organizations among women (especially in cooperatives), *barrio* residents, indigenous peoples, environmentalists, human rights activists, etc. Some organizations are linked to the Bolivarian movement or SUMATE, but many jealously guard their independence. The Venezuelan Program for Human Rights Education and Action (PROVEA) criticizes both the government and opposition for excesses and violations of rights. In a highly polarized political context, where the media seem hopelessly politicized and partisan, PROVEA is one of the few reliable non-partisan sources of information on what is happening within the country.

From Survival Politics to Revolution

In his first 2 years, Chávez focused on sweeping away the old political class, but his economic policies were not radical. He maintained payments on the international debt, did not reverse any privatizations of the 1990s, sought to create incentives for foreign investment, and even retained for a time the conservative finance minister inherited from the Caldera administration. In 2000, Chávez did not so much reverse field as begin to implement programs aimed at improving social conditions. Especially controversial was Plan Bolívar 2000, which charged the army with projects aimed at repairing and building housing, schools, clinics, and subsidized markets in the *barrios*. Critics say Chávez has eroded military professionalism and created a quasi-military state. Others say that Chávez has given the army a popular mission and used its training to benefit, not repress, the people, as has so often been the case in Latin America.

President Chávez' victory in 1998 raised popular expectations, but Chávez inherited an economy in free-fall, low oil prices, and a smaller share of profits (a legacy of contracts signed during the *apertura*). Then, in December 1999, heavy rains devastated much of the coastline, leaving over 10,000 people dead in the worst natural catastrophe in a half-century. Between 2001 and 2003, the government had to contend with the impact of the short-lived coup and 3-month oil stoppage. The stoppage cost the country $9 billion, 9 percent of its annual gross domestic product. The economy contracted by 8.9 percent in 2002 and 9.4 percent in 2003. Poverty stood at 55 percent of the population in that year. In 2004, the economy began to grow at a very high annual rate, between 7 and 12 percent, and by 2006 the official poverty rate fell to just over 30 percent. This figure does not fully reflect improved conditions, as health programs and subsidized markets (MERCAL) provide benefits to poor people that are not directly reflected in income statistics. The ability of the government to reduce poverty can be attributed to three factors: global oil prices, the government's ability to collect a high proportion of the resulting profits, and the political will to channel revenues into social spending. Many analysts simply treat the first factor as exogenous, a stroke of luck attributable to the seemingly unquenchable thirst of India and China for energy. This overlooks the role that Chávez played in reversing the decline of OPEC's ability to control production. Emphasis on prices also tends to obscure the important impact that the new oil law of 2001 had on the government's share of revenues. The new law slightly reduced taxes but increased royalties, which are easier to collect and are levied directly on exports. New policies also ensured that profits from overseas operations, such as Citgo in the United States, would be returned home.

The third factor involves political will. President Chávez carries a deep personal commitment to a redistributive policy, but also is politically motivated. A significant boost in social spending through various popular missions helped ensure the president's smashing victory in the recall election of 2004. Chávez has allowed much social spending to be carried out directly by the oil company, instead of moving profits from the PDVSA into state coffers. This is a deliberate attempt to cultivate popular support for state ownership and to make it difficult to contemplate privatization in the future. In 2006, PDVSA spent over $13 billion on social missions and grassroots economic projects, almost as much as what is spent by the central government itself. However, there was little fiscal oversight, and even pro-*chavista* media reported many incidences of corruption. Furthermore, these funds were never channeled into the state treasury, which limited democratic control over them by the National Assembly.

The opposition has seized on these shortcomings. It also raises the question of whether economic growth and poverty reduction could survive a decline in oil prices. Were prices to collapse due to a sudden downturn in the high-growth Asian economies, the consequences would be enormous for the entire global economy, not just Venezuela. If Asian economies continue to expand, the outlook is probably for continued high oil prices. However, a modest fall in prices might cause problems as well. Governments and citizens grow accustomed to levels of spending, and any cuts can reverberate in declining public approval. The government's 2008 budget anticipated oil prices of approximately $50, about half of what they were in early 2008.

Entering 2008, the government, despite high oil prices, was facing some challenging economic and political problems. Inflation was reaching 20 percent and the bolivar was overvalued, continuing to discourage export diversification and encouraging cheap imports. Far and away, Venezuelans see personal security (crime) as a serious problem that needs to be addressed. And there were signs of popular discontent with the performance of *chavista* governors and mayors. Advancing loftier revolutionary goals may be difficult if some of these down-to-earth issues are not effectively addressed.

Land reform is another controversial policy in *chavista* Venezuela. Over 130,000 families received state-owned land, alleviating inequality in a country where 70 percent of agricultural land was owned by 3 percent of the population. In 2005, the reform was extended to unused private lands, and land occupations, especially in the western state of Zulia, have increased tensions. The government also carried out an urban land reform, offering deeds to homeowners in poor urban neighborhoods but only after residents agreed to form community organizations to settle property disputes and establish boundaries. The government accepted Cuba's offer of 12,000 doctors willing to live and work in the poorest areas, a program called "*Barrio adentro*"(Inside the neighborhood). The opposition criticized this program as an attempt to "Cubanize" the nation, a serious mistake as access to medical treatment proved extremely popular.

The Chávez government hopes to achieve sustainability by training doctors, teachers, and other needed personnel. For example, the plan is to gradually replace the Cubans with Venezuelan doctors trained at Cuba's international medical school and at the new Bolivarian University. The plan's success depends not only on training sufficient numbers to relieve the Cubans but also on the more difficult task of creating a mindset of service and sacrifice among the newly trained professionals.

Just as important, however, are plans to construct a sector of the economy that is characterized by solidaristic social relations, appropriate technology, and community responsibility. Among the measures taken in this area are:

- The creation of an estimated 130,000 cooperatives. Of this number, 30,000 apparently had ceased functioning either because they were ill conceived, lacked sufficiently trained members, or were merely fronts to defraud the government. Learning from failures and building on successes will be crucial to making this sector successful.

- Creation of "endogenous poles of development" in rural areas. These are intended to be model agricultural cooperatives that will produce for subsidized markets in the cities. Government planners hope that these centers will induce some reverse migration from the cities to the countryside, a laudable goal that will be very difficult to achieve. This is in addition to rural land reform, which had benefited over 130,000 families by 2005.
- Comanaged (shared management by workers and executives) state-owned enterprise, leading in some cases to fully worker-managed enterprises in the future. However, some labor union leaders are unhappy with the pace of nationalization of factories that were taken over by workers during the 3-month work stoppage of 2003–2004. Others object that decisions continue to be made with little worker input in many of the supposed comanaged firms.
- Micro-enterprises with community responsibilities. Many of these enterprises are headed by women.

Even with all of these experiments and with the renationalization of several companies that were fully or partly privatized (communications, airlines, aluminum, oil, etc.) before 1998, the private sector's weight in the economy had actually grown relative to the public sector by 2007. This result can be attributed to the sharp increase in petrodollars circulating through the economy, which has greatly boosted commerce. For example, car sales in 2006 were up 55 percent over the previous year. High oil prices and a strong currency (i.e., Venezuelans need fewer *bolivares* to buy dollars and other foreign currencies) make it easy to import consumer goods, which in turn disadvantages local producers.

So while the opposition fears that Chávez seeks to import the Cuban model into Venezuela, some leftist *chavistas* question just how the solidaristic economy is to either overtake or relate to the mainstream macro-economy, something that the president has not addressed. Some resent the growth of a *"boli-bourgeoisie,"* referring to bankers and commercial interests that have made a truce, if not an alliance, with the government, to benefit from the oil boom.

The viability of the *chavista* project not only depends on the vagaries of global oil markets, it depends on the degree to which other international economic and political forces permit experimentation. Chávez's foreign initiatives have included arms purchases from Russia, new trade deals with Iran, and attracting investments from oil-thirsty China and India.

President Chávez often employs hyperbole for political expediency or effect. In Washington, U.S. officials often do the same, painting his regime as totalitarian and connecting it to terrorism for their own political ends. To cite one example, something that barely makes a ripple in the U.S. media but is fully disseminated in Venezuela, the United States Air Force Chief of Staff and the Undersecretary of Defense submitted a paper, *Strategic Initiatives* (October 24, 2007), to the Congress and asserted that the Air Force needs a new long-range bomber to deal with potential enemies, among them Venezuela. They argued without embarrassment, "Venezuela's leaders have embarked that country on a path that might deny us access to that country or its neighbors in the near future. Clearly we need a new penetrating bomber with the range, payload and survivability and lethality to project our nation's power."

The government has launched several initiatives toward strengthening hemispheric economic integration. These include Telesur, a television satellite network for broadcasting Latin American produced programs; PetroSur and PetroCaribe, which offer joint energy projects, and the Bolivarian Alternative for the Americas (ALBA), an alternative to the U.S.-promoted Free Trade Area of the Americas (FTAA). In contrast to the FTAA, modeled on NAFTA, ALBA would include a social charter on labor and human rights and a fund to invest in least developed areas. A major step toward this objective was overcome when Brazil and six other countries agreed in 2007 to the founding of Banco del Sur (Bank of the South), which is intended to offer financing alternatives to loans from the International Monetary Fund and World Bank, which often come with strings attached.

The projects are often proposed with rhetoric that exceeds reality, but the very fact that progress, however modest, has been made on all fronts indicates that Chávez has made significant progress toward his overall strategic goal—to use oil diplomacy (1) to reduce Venezuela's dependence on the U.S. market; (2) to encourage Pan Americanism along lines originally conceived by Bolívar, as Latin American unity capable of dealing with the United States on equal terms; and (3) to cooperate with other nations seeking to shift the world from a unipolar system under U.S. hegemony to a multipolar one.

Just what twenty-first-century Socialism would look like was not so clear, as President Chávez prepared to lead the country through new experiments in governance and popular economics. Perhaps an opposition blogger, Katy, on *Caracas Chronicles* (caracaschronicles.blogspot.com), ruminating on the weak state of the opposition, put her finger on one of the few conclusions about which most observers agree.

Chávez and *chavismo* have changed Venezuelan politics, yet Chávez seems to be the only politician who has understood this. The poor in Venezuela have long been neglected, a fact few people dispute these days. And Chávez has brought about a sense of empowerment in people previously disenfranchised. Whether this empowerment is real or not is beside the point—what matters is that they feel empowered.

Chronology

Pre-1499   Sparsely inhabited—estimated 350,000 inhabitants

1499–1810   Colony of Spain; hides and cacao are chief exports

1728   Crown creates the Compania Guipuzcoana with trade monopoly until 1777; source of *criollo* frustration

1810   Era of independence wars begins, first under leadership of Francisco Miranda, then after 1816 under Simón Bolívar; independence declared in 1811; last Spanish garrison falls in 1823

1830   Conservative General José Antonio Páez leads break-up of Gran Colombia and establishment of Venezuela as an independent republic; brief period of relative peace soon disturbed; by 1888 the country has experienced 730 battles and 26 major insurrections

1850s   Rise of coffee economy in the Andes

1858–1863 Federal War: population falls from 1.9 million to 1.6 million, heads of cattle fall from 12 million to 1.8 million

1870–1888 Antonio Guzmán Blanco rules as head of alliance of *caudillos*

1899 Andean coffee oligarchy in ascent; General Cipriano Castro takes power

1901 Europeans blockade Venezuelan coast in support of unsuccessful revolt by opponents of Castro; United States intercedes to settle European demands of Castro government

1908–1935 Juan Vicente Gómez, last *caudillo,* subordinates country to his rule; modernizes army and finances

1922 Oil boom commences; Gómez benefits

1935–1945 Gómez dies; succeeding period of liberalization; parties emerge

1943 President (General) Isaías Medina achieves reform of oil laws and forces companies to accept power of state to subject them to taxation

1945–1948 Rómulo Betancourt and his Democratic Action (AD) party govern; radical, modernizing, democratically elected (after initial coup of 1945); government agrees to 50–50 sharing of profits with oil companies

1948 Coup leads to populist and repressive dictatorship of General Marcos Pérez Jiménez

1958 Dictatorship overthrown; pact of Punto Fijo among parties; Betancourt, leader of the AD political party wins presidency in December elections

1960–1968 Guerrilla warfare ends with defeat of leftists inspired by Cuban Revolution

1973 Election of Carlos Andrés Pérez; Organization of Oil Exporting Countries (OPEC) oil boom; attempt to modernize overnight; heavy debt contracted; corruption emerges as serious issue; new industries in east; second boom in 1978 following Iranian Revolution, price of oil falls after 1981

1977 Oil companies nationalized; Petroleos de Venezuela S.A. (PDVSA) formed

1983 Devaluation of bolívar (previously 4.3:1) marks end of boom; oil prices and economy in free-fall

1989 After winning December 1988 election with a populist campaign, Pérez announces International Monetary Fund restructuring plan, followed by the *Caracazo;* riots in 23 cities leave over 1000 dead

1992 Colonel Hugo Chávez, head of "Bolivarian" movement formed in the military, leads unsuccessful coup on February 12 against Pérez; second coup in November also fails, but Pérez eventually forced from office by Congress

1994 Rafael Caldera, participant in pact of 1958, becomes president following break from his party, the People's Independent Electoral Organizing Committee (COPEI), and victory in December 1993 election; oil company managers move toward privatization under "oil opening," urge break from OPEC

1998 President Hugo Chávez elected in December as AD and COPEI support collapses; he reverses oil policy and his followers, elected to special assembly, write the new constitution; country renamed the "Bolivarian Republic of Venezuela"; Chávez elected again in 2000, inaugurated for 6-year term in 2000

2000 Second OPEC oil summit convened by Chávez in Caracas

2002 In April, attempted coup by opposition reversed by mass pressure unleashed from *barrios,* loyalty of key military leaders, and international condemnation, despite support from Washington; in December, oil company executives lead call for general strike with mixed success; informal economy continues, but 2-month shutdown of oil industry devastates the economy; loyal oil workers reopen industry with international help from OPEC countries; production largely restored by April 2003

2003 Government launches "missions" to improve literacy and health care in *barrios;* involvement of military generates controversy

2004 After long political and legal battle, with international mediation, government agrees to recall referendum under terms of the 1999 constitution; Chávez wins nearly 59 percent of vote, marked by high turnout; opposition divided and demoralized as Chávez announces "deepening" of Bolivarian Revolution

2005 In January, Chávez declares himself for a "socialism of the twenty-first century" in a speech at the World Social Forum in Porto Alegre, Brazil; in December, the progovernment coalition sweeps all seats in elections for the National Assembly as a result of a divided opposition's decision to abstain

2006 Manuel Rosales, opposition candidate, concedes victory to Chávez in December elections; Chávez wins with 63 percent of vote in election marked by high turnout, but he fails to achieve announced goal of 10 million votes

2007 Threatening to expel noncompliant members of his government, Chávez calls on all supporters to join the new Unified Socialist Party of Venezuela (PSUV); he leads call to amend constitution to lengthen his term, permit indefinite re-election, and give constitutional status to community councils, among other provisions; National Assembly adds change allowing suspension of some freedoms during states of emergency; on December 2, the reform packages narrowly lose in a referendum

Bibliography

Alexander, Robert Jackson. *Rómulo Betancourt and the Transformation of Venezuela*. New Brunswick, NJ: Transaction Books, 1995.

Betancourt, Rómulo. *Venezuela: Oil and Politics*. Boston: Houghton Mifflin, 1998.

Buxton, Julia. *The Failure of Political Reform in Venezuela*. Aldershot, UK: Ashgate, 2001.

Coppedge, Micahel. *Strong Parties and Lame Ducks: Presidential Partyarchy and Factionalism in Venezuela*. Stanford, CA: Stanford University Press, 1998.

Coronil, Fernando. *The Magical State: Nature, Money and Modernity in Venezuela*. Chicago: University of Chicago Press, 1997.

Crisp, Brian. *Democratic Institutional Design: The Powers and Incentives of Venezuelan Politicians and Interest Groups*. Stanford: Stanford University Press, 2000.

Ellner, Steve. *Organized Labor in Venezuela, 1958–1991: Behavior and Concerns in a Democratic Setting*. Wilmington, DE: Scholarly Resources, 1993.

Ellner, Steve, and Daniel Hellinger, eds. *Venezuelan Politics in the Chávez Era: Class, Polarization, and Conflict*. Boulder, CO: Lynne Rienner, 2003.

Ewell, Judith. *Venezuela and the United States: From Monroe's Hemisphere to Petroleum's Empire*. Athens: University of Georgia Press, 1996.

Friedman, Elisabeth J. *Unfinished Transitions: Women and the Gendered Development of Democracy in Venezuela*. University Park: Pennsylvania State University Press, 2000.

Gott, Richard. *In the Shadow of the Liberator: Hugo Chávez and the Transformation of Venezuela*. London: Verso Press, 2000.

Hellinger, Daniel. *Venezuela: Tarnished Democracy*. Boulder, CO: Westview Press, 1991.

Hillman, Richard. *Democracy for the Privileged: Crisis and Transition in Venezuela*. Boulder, CO: Lynne Rienner, 1994.

Jones, Bart. *Hugo! The Hugo Chavez Story from Mud Hut to Perpetual Revolution*. Hanover, NH: Steerforth Press, 2007.

Karl, Terry Lynn. *The Paradox of Plenty: Oil Booms and Petro-States*. Berkeley: University of California Press, 1997.

Kozlof, Nicolas. *Hugo Chávez: Oil, Politics and the Challenge to the U.S.* London: Palgrave Macmillan, 2007.

Lynch, John. *Simón Bolívar: A Life*. New Haven, CT: Yale University Press, 2006.

Marcano, Cristina, and Alberto Barrera Tyszka. *Hugo Chávez: The Definitive Biography*. New York: Random House, 2007.

Martz, John. *Acción Democrática: Evolution of a Modern Political Party in Venezuela*. Princeton, NJ: Princeton University Press, 1966.

McCoy, Jennifer, and David Myers, eds. *The Unraveling of Representative Democracy in Venezuela*. Baltimore: Johns Hopkins University Press, 2004.

Mommer, Bernard. *Global Oil and the Nation State*. Oxford: Oxford University Press, 2002.

Moreno, Alejandro. "Editorial," *Heterotopia*. 4:10 (September–December 1998).

Naím, Moisés. *Paper Tigers and Minotaurs: The Politics of Venezuela's Economic Reforms*. Washington, DC: Carnegie Endowment for International Peace, 1993.

Rabe, Stephen G. *The Road to OPEC: United States Relations with Venezuela, 1919–1976*. Austin: University of Texas Press, 1982.

Wilpert, Gregory. *Changing Venezuela by Taking Power: The History and Politics of the Chávez Government*. London: Verso, 2007.

FILMS AND DOCUMENTARIES

Oriana. Venezuela, 1991. A young woman returns to her family home in the jungle.

¿Puedo Hablar? 2007. Documentary about 2006 presidential election attributes Chávez's popularity to genuine concern for poor but raises issues about his personal accumulation of power.*The Revolution will not Be Televised*. Ireland, 2003. Irish film crew in Caracas to make pro-Chávez documentary finds itself in the presidential palace during the April 2002 coup.

Shoot to Kill. Venezuela, 1990. Carlos Azpurua's feature film on violence and law in a Caracas *barrio*.

Turmoil. United States, 2002. Documentary on political conflict in Venezuela.

Venezuela, A 21st Century Revolution. Great Britain, 2004. Organizing popular movements in Venezuela.

WEBSITES

www.derechos.org.ve The best independent reports on Venezuela are from the respected human rights agency PROVEA (website is in Spanish).

www.venezuelanalisis.com A well-organized and readable English-language website with a decidedly pro-Chávez slant.

www.vheadline.com Another site generally favorable to *chavismo*.

www.vcrisis.com Comparable *antichavista* English-language source, somewhat shrill but informative.

www.analitica.com More staid but clearly *antichavista*.

www.petroleumworld.com Oil-related developments affecting Venezuela.

www.eluniversal.com/eng_index.shtml Some articles from *El Universal*, once among Caracas' most respected newspapers but turned harshly *antichavista* (in English).

www.entornointeligente.com An anti-Chávez media portal linking articles from major newspapers in Venezuela.

www.rethinkvenezuela.com/index.html Progovernment views are distributed in the United States by the Venezuela Information Office.

www.aporrea.org Venezuela's burgeoning grassroots media sector.

EIGHTEEN

COLOMBIA

John C. Dugas

At the beginning of the twenty-first century, Colombia is a country beset with a host of complex problems. Although a formal constitutional democracy with an extensive history of civilian rule, Colombia's political regime has often been restrictive in character and has frequently failed to provide effective guarantees of basic civil rights and liberties to its citizens. It currently faces two well-established leftist guerrilla movements, vicious right-wing paramilitary groups, some 3 million internally displaced refugees fleeing from violence in the countryside, a deeply entrenched drug trade based upon the cultivation and processing of coca and opium poppies, and intense pressure from the United States to stop the drug trade at the source. Alongside these seemingly intractable problems, however, Colombia is notable for the dynamism of its cities and the entrepreneurial spirit of its people. In the cultural realm, its artists demonstrate impressive creativity, ranging from the Nobel Prize– winning novelist Gabriel García Márquez and the world-renowned painter/ sculptor Fernando Botero to the popular music sensations of Shakira, Juanes, and Carlos Vives. The political arena itself is striking for the sheer valor of many nonviolent political activists, the historical capacity for compromise of political elites, and the notable ability of ordinary citizens to "muddle through" repeated crises.

Despite this intriguing mix of characteristics, until recently Colombia has been among the least studied of the major Latin American nations. Nonetheless, this neglect has eased significantly over the past two decades as Colombia's role in drug trafficking and the sharpening of its internal armed conflict has prompted sustained attention from both journalists and scholars.

Colombia is located in the northwest corner of South America, adjoining the Panamanian isthmus and sharing borders with Venezuela, Brazil, Peru, and Ecuador. At 440,000 square miles in area, it is the fourth largest Latin American country in size, slightly larger than the states of California and Texas combined. Colombia is dominated by the Andes Mountains, which enter the country at its southern border with Ecuador and split into three principal ranges running northward. The country's two most important rivers, the Magdalena and the Cauca (which eventually joins the Magdalena), flow in a northward direction between these ranges, ultimately emptying into the Caribbean. The majority of Colombians live in cities and towns located in the intermountain basins and plateaus of the Andes. The country's extensive low-lying areas are known as "hot country" (*tierra caliente*) since the temperature is significantly warmer than the more temperate clime of the mountains. In the north, a vast expanse of largely flat hot country begins toward the lower course of the Magdalena River and lies adjacent to the Caribbean Sea. The other major area of hot country lies to the east of the Andes; here are located Colombia's great plains, known as the *llanos*, as well as the Amazon rain forest farther south and east. Most of *tierra caliente* is relatively sparsely populated, particularly the *llanos* and the Amazon region. Colombia's population of 44 million is the third largest in Latin America, exceeded only by Brazil and Mexico. Most Colombians are *mestizo*, that is, of mixed indigenous and European origin, with smaller numbers of Caucasians, Afro-Colombians, indigenous peoples, mulattos (of mixed African and European origin), and *zambos* (of mixed African and indigenous origin). Spanish is the principal language, although indigenous languages are still spoken in some regions and are recognized as official by the 1991 constitution. The vast majority of Colombians identify themselves as Roman Catholic; nevertheless, evangelical Protestantism is growing rapidly, and there is a small Jewish community. Some indigenous communities also practice their traditional religions.

Economic and Social Context

As a Spanish colonial possession, Colombia's economic significance was primarily as a producer of gold for the mother country. Indeed, Colombia was the principal source of gold in the Spanish Empire, even though the amount produced paled in comparison with the silver mined in Mexico and Peru. Secondarily, the port of Cartagena served as a major base for the Spanish navy in the Caribbean, as well as a major entry point for both African slaves and European imports destined for the interior of the colony. Nevertheless, Colombia's economic development was largely stagnant throughout the colonial period. It never developed significant exports outside of gold, hampered by the high costs of transportation from the more populated areas of the Andes to the coastal ports of Cartagena and Santa Marta.

In the aftermath of independence, Colombia's economic development was constrained by the destruction wrought by the war as well as by the continued high costs of transportation. Even though it had now gained complete freedom of trading partners, it had few exports other than gold that could justify the costs of transporting goods across the Andes from the populated interior of the country. Thus, throughout the 1820s and 1830s, Colombia's exports were relatively small and dominated by gold. As late as the mid-1840s, gold still accounted for nearly three-fourths of Colombian exports. Nonetheless, economic elites made concerted efforts to introduce tropical commodities that could be profitably exported. The most important of these was tobacco, which by the mid-1860s began to exceed gold in export earnings. Other tropical exports during this period included animal hides, indigo, brazilwood, cinchona bark (for the production of quinine), and cotton.

Ultimately, the most important export commodity introduced to Colombia during the nineteenth century was coffee, first cultivated in the Santander region of the easternmost range of the Andes, where it had spread from its origin in western Venezuela. Subsequently, coffee began to be grown throughout the Colombian Andes but particularly in the central Andean range in the region of Antioquia and to its south. Coffee accounted for less than 2 percent of export earnings during the early 1840s but grew to nearly 50 percent of export earnings by 1898. By 1950, coffee accounted for over 70 percent of Colombia's export earnings and had provided much of the foreign exchange required for the country's incipient industrialization. While some coffee was produced on large estates, the predominant mode of cultivation was that of small to medium-sized family farms. Thus, unlike cases such as El Salvador that were dominated by expansive coffee estates, Colombia's coffee industry was largely rooted in independent family farmers. Some scholars have suggested that this characteristic had a conservatizing effect on Colombian society, especially since the country's leading industry was overwhelmingly Colombian-owned and -operated.

In the second half of the twentieth century, the Colombian economy underwent significant changes, becoming both more industrialized and more diversified in its economic output. The economic dominance of coffee gradually declined, and by 2006 coffee accounted for less than 7 percent of the country's legal export earnings. Simultaneously, the country experienced a significant growth in nontraditional exports, such as cut flowers, bananas, textiles, shoes, clothing, and processed food. Even more significant was the expansion of mining and the production for export of coal, nickel, and especially oil. Although Colombia remained a major producer and exporter of unprocessed commodities into the twenty-first century, it also experienced a notable process of industrialization, particularly after 1950. Like most Latin American countries, Colombia adopted a policy of import substitution industrialization (ISI) after mid-century, designed to promote domestic industry by encouraging the production of goods that had previously been imported from abroad. Such a policy was an amalgam of protectionist tariffs, preferential credit, tax incentives, and subsidized electricity rates for industry, as well as the creation of state-owned industries where private capital was unwilling to invest. In the 1950s and 1960s, most industrial production occurred in relatively light industries; however, by the 1970s industrialization had expanded into more technologically sophisticated areas, such as plastics, petrochemicals, and automobile assembly.

Despite their embrace of ISI, Colombian policy makers avoided the high degree of state intervention pursued by other Latin American countries. Indeed, from the mid-twentieth century to the present, economic policy has been broadly conservative in nature: import substitution was complemented by a growing emphasis on export promotion, monetary and fiscal policy remained fairly cautious, agrarian

reform was limited at best, and labor policy was generally conservative. Such policies have clearly responded to the interests and pressures exerted by economic
elites, as opposed to the demands of labor unions or peasant movements. Nonetheless, Colombia's macroeconomic policies have also helped it avoid many of
the harsh extremes experienced by its neighbors. For example, during the "lost
decade" of the 1980s, Colombia was the only South American country that did
not experience a single year of negative economic growth; it avoided the extreme
hyperinflation that plagued many of its neighbors and was the only major debtor
country in Latin America that did not have to restructure its debt. Colombia was
also among the last of the countries in the region to embrace economic liberalization (doing so in the early 1990s), and its immediate effects were less harsh than
those experienced by many other Latin American countries.

Caution and moderation have thus been the prevalent watchwords of economic
policy makers in Colombia for decades; however, this has certainly not implied a
broad societal satisfaction with the socioeconomic status quo. In the countryside,
capitalist agricultural development caused tremendous social upheaval for Colombian peasants. It promoted a model of development that relied increasingly upon
the concentration of land ownership, the availability of cheap wage labor, the
introduction of advanced agricultural techniques, and large-scale farm production. This conflicted with an alternative "peasant model" of agrarian development
that entailed fairly widespread distribution of land among numerous small holders engaging in more traditional agricultural production based upon family labor.
As a result of this basic clash, contemporary Colombia has experienced numerous
agrarian conflicts, which continue to occur and are largely rooted in disputes over
land ownership. Land distribution has long been skewed in favor of large landholders. A World Bank study published in 2004 found that small and medium-size
farmers constituted 97 percent of all landowners but controlled only 34 percent of
agricultural property, whereas the largest landowners were only 0.3 percent of all
rural landowners but held 45 percent of rural property. Such a condition reflects
both the historical limitations of agrarian reform in Colombia as well as the absence
of an effective national peasant movement. The most important peasant movement in Colombian history, the National Association of Peasant Users, or ANUC
(Asociación Nacional de Usuarios Campesinos), was founded in 1967 but fell apart
in the late 1970s and early 1980s as a result of internal divisions and state repression.
Unfortunately, the inequality of land distribution has worsened since the 1980s as
the drug trade has produced a "counter-agrarian reform" in the countryside: large
traffickers have invested their profits in the countryside, frequently using coercion
to force peasants off their land. In turn, both leftist guerrillas and right-wing paramilitaries have recruited the bulk of their forces from among peasants, who encounter few viable alternatives in the countryside (other than direct participation in the
drug trade as cultivators of coca or opium poppy). All of this constitutes part of the
internal armed conflict in Colombia (discussed below), which has produced some
3 million internal refugees, most of them peasants fleeing from the crossfire among
guerrillas, paramilitaries, and state security forces.

In contrast to the peasantry, urban workers in Colombia have had a fairly long
tradition of national organization and a somewhat greater influence on state pol-

icy. In 1936, the first important national labor confederation, the Confederation of Colombian Workers, or CTC (Confederación de Trabajadores de Colombia), was established and became an ardent supporter of the liberal administrations of the 1930s and early 1940s. A new labor confederation, the Union of Colombian Workers or UTC (Unión de Trabajadores de Colombia), was founded in 1946 under the auspices of the Catholic Church. The UTC shared certain ideological affinities with the Conservative Party, and Conservative politicians in turn saw value in promoting an alternative to the Liberal-dominated CTC. The 1960s and 1970s witnessed the growing autonomy of the CTC and the UTC from the traditional political parties, but the labor movement was plagued by a divisiveness that sharply restricted its power. For example, in the early 1960s, long-standing disagreements between Liberals and Communists within the CTC resulted in the expulsion of the latter and the establishment of a new Communist-dominated labor confederation in 1964, the Trade Union Confederation of Colombian Workers or CSTC (Confederación Sindical de Trabajadores de Colombia). A fourth national labor confederation, the General Confederation of Labor or CGT (Confederación General de Trabajo), was founded in 1971, rooted in Christian Democratic principles. The lack of a single national labor confederation, the weakening of the two traditional labor confederations, and the growing importance of unaffiliated independent trade unions clearly diluted the potential power of the labor movement.

Beginning in the 1980s, however, attempts were made to consolidate the Colombian labor movement. In 1986, the United Central Organization of Workers or CUT (Central Unitaria de Trabajadores) was founded, bringing together the former CSTC, the majority of independent trade unions, and a significant number of trade unions and federations previously affiliated with the CTC and the UTC. Two years later, in 1988, the Confederation of Democratic Workers of Colombia or CTDC (Confederación de Trabajadores Democratica de Colombia) was established, uniting the majority of the former UTC, some trade unions previously affiliated with the CTC, and other independent trade unions. In 1992, the CTDC merged with the CGT. Despite this febrile activity, the Colombian labor movement remains characterized by a debilitating divisiveness. In 2005, the labor movement was divided into the majority CUT, representing 66.6 percent of unionized workers, the CGT (13.5 percent of unionized workers), the CTC (5.5 percent of unionized workers), with the remaining 14.4 percent of unionized workers unaffiliated with any of the labor confederations. The strength of the Colombian labor movement is also undermined by its limited extension among the working class. Of the approximately 18 million Colombian workers in 2005, only 831,000 were unionized, representing just 4.6 percent of the working population. The organized labor movement has also been among the foremost victims of Colombia's ongoing political violence. For example, between the August 2002 inauguration of President Alvaro Uribe and July 2007, there were 391 murders of trade unionists in Colombia, more than in the rest of the world combined.

Pressure from organized labor has been instrumental in achieving legislation that favors the Colombian working class; however, such legislation has also tended to place constraints on labor protests and labor organization. This double-edged nature of labor legislation was evident from early on. Thus, while Law 83 of 1931 recognized for the first time the right of workers to organize, it also contained an open shop clause that served the purpose of hindering union formation. Likewise, Law 6 of 1945 contained a number of benefits for Colombian workers, but effectively prevented the organization of industrywide unions, thus curtailing the potential power of the labor movement. During the National Front period (1958–1974), at the same time that labor legislation expanded some guarantees for trade unions and their members, it also endeavored to place limits on the number of strikes and to thwart the unionization of state employees. More recently, Law 50 of 1990 and Law 789 of 2002 contained limited benefits for workers, but their primary thrust was to aid employers by giving them greater flexibility to dismiss workers. Such results demonstrate that the organized labor movement shares with the peasantry a relatively weak position in the balance of power among social classes in Colombia.

The dominant classes in Colombia, comprised largely of national economic elites who own or control the principal private productive assets of land and capital, exercise significant power in the economic realms of agriculture, industry, finance, and commerce. The interests of these sectors are articulated and defended by a variety of producer associations (*gremios*), ranging from relatively small regional groups to large national organizations. Although particular sectoral interests of the dominant classes occasionally come into conflict, there exists substantial consensus on such fundamental issues as the defense of private property, limited state intervention, conservative social policies, and opposition to the leftist guerrilla movements. The first Colombian producer association, the Agricultural Society of Colombia, or SAC (Sociedad de Agricultores de Colombia), was founded in 1871 to promote the interests of large farmers. The SAC was followed by the creation in 1927 of the National Federation of Coffee Growers, or FEDECAFE (Federación Nacional de Cafeteros). Although membership was open to all coffee growers, in practice the FEDECAFE represented the interests of the largest coffee producers and exporters. Perhaps the most prominent of all the producer associations is the National Association of Industrialists, or ANDI (Asociación Nacional de Industriales), which was established in 1944. This organization primarily represents Colombian industrial enterprises but has extended membership to businesses in the areas of agriculture, commerce, finance, and insurance.

A number of other producer associations wield significant influence, although their efforts have been dedicated largely to the promotion and defense of their particular sectoral interests. In the agricultural sector, a prominent defender of the interests of large-scale ranchers has been the National Livestock Federation, or FEDEGAN (Federación Colombiana de Ganaderos), founded in 1959. Several producer associations have been formed to represent the specific interests of commercial farmers of rice, cotton, sugarcane, milk, poultry, and flowers. This pattern was repeated in the industrial realm, where producer associations emerged to foster the development of specific industries such as plastics, textiles, paper, cement, and pharmaceuticals. Retail establishments also have their own association, the National Merchants Federation, or FENALCO (Federación Nacional de Comerciantes), founded in 1945. Likewise, the banking sector has been represented since 1936 by the Colombian Bankers Association, or ASOBANCARIA (Asociación Bancaria de Colombia), and more recently by the National Association of Financial Institutions, ANIF (Asociación Nacional de Instituciones Financieras).

Colombian producer associations, in contrast to the peasantry and the labor confederations, have traditionally exerted considerable influence on the formation of state policy. Although it would be misleading to portray them as controlling the reins of the state, the producer associations have enjoyed relatively easy access to state policy makers, and their concerns have received significantly more attention than those raised by the peasantry or by organized labor. This is not to say that their proposals or critiques have always been accepted. Indeed, the relative autonomy of the state has allowed it to occasionally enact policies seemingly in opposition to the interests of producer associations. A recent example of this was the neoliberal "economic opening" carried out during the administrations of Virgilio Barco and César Gaviria in the early 1990s, which subjected many Colombian industries to greater international competition. Nonetheless, there is little to suggest that national economic elites have lost significant power relative to the peasantry or organized labor at the beginning of the twenty-first century.

Despite these significant societal divisions, all Colombians experienced major demographic transformations since the mid-twentieth century. Between 1950 and 2007, the population more than tripled in size, growing from 12.6 million to 44.3 million. Moreover, this growth in population was accompanied by significant urbanization. Colombia moved from being a predominantly rural society in 1950 to a largely urban society by 2005, when 75.9 percent of the population resided in urban areas. However, the latter half of the twentieth century also witnessed a rapid decline in population growth, from 3 percent per year in the early 1960s to 1.6 percent per year by 2005. Population growth slowed largely as the result of a sharp decrease in the country's total fertility rate, which dropped from an average of nearly seven children per woman in the 1950s to an average of 2.6 children per woman by 2005. The marked decline in population growth also accompanied a significant improvement in the living conditions of the average Colombian. Between 1950 and 2005, life expectancy at birth increased by over 20 years, giving the average Colombian born in 2005 a life expectancy of 72.6 years. At the same time, the infant mortality rate dropped from 123 deaths per 1000 live births in the early 1950s to 24.4 deaths per 1000 live births in 2005.

In spite of these improvements in socioeconomic conditions, Colombia in 2007 continued to be classified by the World Bank as a lower middle-income country, with a gross national income per capita of $2020. It is characterized by significant income inequalities and high levels of poverty, with about 17.8 percent of the population living on less than US$2 per day, and 7 percent doing so on less than US$1 per day. By 2007, Colombia had largely recovered from a severe economic recession that had shaken the country in the mid-to-late 1990s. Nonetheless, it continued to experience relatively high levels of unemployment, reaching 12.8 percent in the first trimester of 2007. The administration of President Alvaro Uribe sought to jumpstart the economy by signing a sweeping free trade agreement with the United States. Nonetheless, the accord faced stiff opposition from U.S. and Colombian labor unions, the left-wing Alternative Democratic Pole party, and Democrats in the U.S. Congress. In addition to their deep-seated economic concerns, opponents cited the history of violence against trade unionists and argued that the trade accord should not move forward until Colombia makes progress in convicting those who have murdered labor organizers. By the end of 2007, the future of the U.S.–Colombia Free Trade Agreement was still uncertain.

Political History

The first inhabitants of present-day Colombia most likely arrived from the north, crossing into the territory from the Panamanian isthmus and gradually populating both the Andean highlands and the lower *tierra caliente*. At the time of the Spanish conquest, the indigenous population comprised various groupings of Caribs, Arawaks, and Chibchas. The Chibchas were predominant, consisting most notably of the Tairona people of the Sierra Nevada of Santa Marta close to the Caribbean and the more populous Muisca people inhabiting the plateaus of the easternmost range of the Andes. The Muiscas were, in fact, the largest group of indigenous people to be found between the Maya of Central America and the Incan Empire. Spanish explorers first encountered Colombia in 1499, when Alonso de Ojeda led a voyage that passed along the Guajira peninsula. In 1510, the first attempt at colonization was made, with the founding of the town of San Sebastián along the Gulf of Urabá near the Panamanian isthmus. Nonetheless, that settlement did not endure, and it was not until 1525 that Spaniards established their first permanent city, Santa Marta, on the Caribbean coast. Beginning a decade later, the Muiscas were subdued by a Spanish expedition into the interior of the country led by Gonzalo Jiménez de Quesada, who founded the capital city of Bogotá in 1538 near the site of a Muisca town of similar name. For most of the colonial period, present-day Colombia was governed from Lima, forming part of the Viceroyalty of Peru. However, in 1739, the territory was elevated to the status of viceroyalty in its own right, the Viceroyalty of New Granada, which also comprised modern Venezuela, Ecuador, and Panama.

Colombia achieved its political independence in the violent revolutionary struggles that shook the continent after Napoleon deposed King Ferdinand VII of Spain in 1808. Although the struggle for independence began in 1810, royalist forces were not defeated in Colombia until August 7, 1819, when Simón Bolívar routed the Spanish at the Battle of Boyacá. Even then, fighting continued in various parts of Colombian territory until 1823. The nineteenth century was tumultuous for the new country. Just a decade after its independence, the Republic of Colombia experienced a severe dismemberment as both Venezuela and Ecuador broke away to form independent countries in 1830. The remainder of the century was marked by a series of civil wars between the Liberal and Conservative Parties, which today are among the oldest continuously functioning political parties in all of Latin America.

The parties originated in disputes between the followers of Bolívar (who died in December 1830) and those of Francisco de Paula Santander, Bolívar's vice president during the war for independence and later president of Colombia (1832–1837). Bolívar's followers emphasized the need for social order and favored a leading role for the Catholic Church in society; in the 1840s, they formally organized themselves into the Conservative Party. Santander and his followers, meanwhile, stressed the importance of liberty and sought a greater separation between church and state. By the 1840s they too had congealed into a political organization, the Liberal Party. Conservatives also tended to favor centralized political administration and economic protectionism, while Liberals supported federalism and free trade; nonetheless, these distinctions were not always clear and, in any case, were subordinate to the church–state controversy. Ideological differences between the two parties helped to foment seven major civil wars in Colombia during the second half of the nineteenth century: 1851, 1854, 1860–1862, 1876, 1885, 1895, and 1899–1902. In only one of these conflicts, the civil war of 1860–1862, was the challenging party (in this case, the Liberal Party) able to conclusively defeat the political party in power. Nevertheless, the wars helped to reinforce party identity among both elites and the lower-class Colombians, who did much of the fighting and dying. The bloodiest of these conflicts, the War of a Thousand Days (1899–1902), produced an estimated 100,000 deaths. This war also weakened Colombia significantly, facilitating the separation of Panama in November 1903.

U.S. complicity in the separation of Panama is one of the more dismal episodes in U.S.–Latin American relations. The U.S. and Colombian governments had negotiated the Hay-Herrán Treaty of 1903, which authorized the United States to construct and operate a canal across the isthmus of Panama, which was then the northernmost department of Colombia. Nevertheless, the Colombian Senate, concerned about the amount of payment as well as the abrogation of Colombian sovereignty in the proposed Canal Zone, rejected the treaty unanimously in August 1903. President Theodore Roosevelt was outraged by the decision, calling the Colombians "contemptible little creatures," "jack rabbits," and "foolish and homicidal corruptionists" and famously remarking that "You could no more make an agreement with the Colombian rulers than you could nail currant jelly to a wall." The United States thereupon encouraged secessionist leaders in Panama, intervened to ensure that Colombian military forces could not put down the insurrection, and then quickly recognized the independence of the rebel government. Within 2 weeks, the Roosevelt administration negotiated a new canal treaty with representatives of the fledgling Panamanian government. Colombians bitterly held the United States responsible for the Panamanian secession. In 1921, the U.S. government belatedly agreed to pay Colombia an indemnity of $25 million for the loss of Panama.

Despite the recurring political violence between Liberals and Conservatives, Colombia lacked sustained periods of military rule, a factor that helped the two political parties to establish themselves as the primary actors in Colombian politics. Indeed, much of Colombia's political history can be understood as a struggle between the Liberal and Conservative Parties for control of the state. Between 1863 and 1885, the Liberal Party dominated, governing under a constitution that was federalist, secular, and politically liberal. From 1886 to 1930, the Conservative Party ruled under a constitution that centralized political authority and reestablished Church privileges. Unfortunately, the frequent exclusion of the opposite party from positions of power during these periods of party dominance fomented both ill will and the not infrequent civil wars. In 1930, the Conservative Party split in the presidential election, allowing the Liberal candidate to win and ushering in a new era of

Liberal Party dominance. The Liberals attempted to expand the electorate, limit the influence of the Church, and respond to the demands of peasant and urban labor movements. Growing urbanization appeared to consolidate the Liberal Party as the majority party during this time period. Nonetheless, in the 1946 presidential elections, the Liberal Party split, fielding two presidential candidates, which permitted Conservative candidate Mariano Ospina Pérez to win.

La Violencia

The period from 1946 to the early-1960s has come to be known as *La Violencia*, a bloody sectarian conflict between the Liberal and Conservative Parties in which approximately 200,000 people died. *La Violencia* began in the aftermath of the 1946 elections as Conservatives and Liberals fought over the spoils of political office at the local level. This violence greatly intensified after the assassination of the popular Liberal Party leader Jorge Eliécer Gaitán on April 9, 1948. Gaitán was a populist politician of lower middle-class background who had become a self-made man, a brilliant criminal lawyer, and in 1947 the leader of the Liberal Party. Gaitán was a charismatic speaker who appealed directly to the lower and lower middle classes, often through mass rallies and parades. He employed an antielite discourse, arguing that oligarchs from both political parties exploited the state for their own benefit while ignoring the needs of the masses. In contrast, Gaitán explicitly identified himself with the lower classes, proclaiming famously "I am not a man, I am a people!" Gaitán was the most likely presidential candidate of the Liberal Party for the 1950 elections. His unfortunate assassination marked both the end of his populist movement and the escalation of *La Violencia*.

Gaitán's murder immediately resulted in a massive urban insurrection in Bogotá (the *Bogotazo*), which destroyed large parts of the city and resulted in a bloody military operation to regain control. Shocked by the violence of the *Bogotazo* and afraid of losing its political control over the masses, a faction of the Liberal Party immediately joined the Conservative administration of Ospina in an effort at bipartisan government. Nonetheless, the partisan friction continued, paralleled by the continuation of violence in the towns and countryside. The antagonism between the national leaders of the political parties was also renewed, and in May 1949 the Liberal Party withdrew from the Ospina administration. When Liberals in Congress subsequently threatened to impeach President Ospina in 1949, the Conservative government declared a state of siege, closed Congress, and suspended civil liberties. The Liberals, alleging a lack of electoral guarantees, withdrew from the presidential election of November 1949, resulting in the unopposed election of Conservative Laureano Gómez.

The election of Gómez represented a victory for the most extreme wing of the Conservative Party. Militantly partisan, the Gómez administration precipitated a heightening of *La Violencia*. Indeed, of the approximately 200,000 deaths during the period of *La Violencia*, over 50,000 of them occurred in the first year of the Gómez administration. By this time, Liberal guerrilla movements had organized in several areas, while the Conservatives utilized the military apparatus of the state to defend their partisan cause. Violence was prevalent throughout the country, with the exception of the Caribbean coast and the southwestern department of Nariño. In much of the countryside, traditional rivalries between villages that were predominantly Liberal or Conservative erupted into conflict. In the cities, the violence was less intense; but even there, acts of political violence occurred, most notably the ransacking of the offices of the major Liberal newspapers by Conservative mobs and the destruction of the homes and headquarters of Liberal Party leaders. Perhaps the most disturbing development from the point of view of political elites was the utilization of violence as a means of addressing nonpartisan social conflicts. Indeed, while largely partisan in nature, *La Violencia* often spiraled out of control in the form of rural banditry, local political vendettas, and violent efforts to confront large landowners or, alternatively, to plunder small landholders. The continuation of *La Violencia*, along with the attempt by the Gómez administration to impose a new corporatist-style constitution, deepened preexisting divisions within the Conservative Party. More moderate Conservatives, led by former President Ospina, began to conspire with the military against Gómez. This eventually led to Gómez' ouster in a military coup by General Gustavo Rojas Pinilla in June 1953.

Rojas Pinilla came to power with the support of both Liberals and the Ospinista wing of the Conservative Party. This support was grounded in the belief that the general could stem the tide of violence and pave the way for a return to civilian rule. Although the military government of Rojas Pinilla did have notable initial success in quelling *La Violencia*, it was unable stop the conflict completely. Indeed, in 1956, the toll from violent conflict had risen again to over 11,000 deaths, a level comparable to the latter years of the Gómez administration. Moreover, although Rojas Pinilla had assumed power with no evident desire to consolidate his position, it soon became clear that he sought to perpetuate his stay in power by creating a political base of support through populist social reforms and appeals to labor. Disillusioned with this course of events, leaders from both political parties began to oppose Rojas Pinilla. In July 1956, the Liberal politician (and former president) Alberto Lleras Camargo met with former Conservative president Laureano Gómez in Spain, where he was living in exile. The two leaders signed the Pact of Benidorm, which articulated the decision by their respective political parties to oppose Rojas Pinilla, and which led to a series of subsequent agreements aimed at restoring bipartisan civilian government. Resistance to the military regime culminated in May 1957 when Rojas Pinilla was removed from power by a five-man military junta that was to serve as an interim government until bipartisan civilian rule was restored in 1958.

THE NATIONAL FRONT REGIME (1958–1974)

The new bipartisan civilian regime was known as the National Front. It epitomized the notion of a "pacted democracy," wherein political elites negotiate compromises that protect their fundamental interests, thereby facilitating the process of democratization. In the case of the National Front, the pacted democracy was secured by a rigid agreement that provided for power sharing by the two traditional parties and extensive mutual guarantees to protect the parties' interests. Specifically, the National Front was founded upon the twin pillars of alternation in power and parity of power. With regard to alternation, the agreement provided that the presidency was to alternate every 4 years between the Liberal Party and the Conservative Party for a period of 16 years. Parity, in turn, referred to the strictly equal division of political power between the two parties. First, all popularly elected bodies were to be equally divided between the Liberal and Conservative Parties regardless of the electoral results in a given district. This provision applied to the Senate and the Chamber of Representatives, the departmental assemblies, and the municipal councils. Within each party's (equal) allotment, seats were to be awarded by proportional representation according to the number of votes won by different party factions. Second, all cabinet appointments as well as all positions in the judicial branch were to be divided equally between the two parties. Third, government officials as well as administrative appointments at all levels of government were to be named on the basis of parity between Liberals and Conservatives. An exception was made for career civil service bureaucrats and military appointees. Finally, the National Front agreement required a two-thirds majority vote for the approval of nonprocedural measures in all popularly elected bodies. This measure gave added assurance to the parties that their fundamental interests would be protected.

In effect, the National Front agreement institutionalized bipartisan rule in Colombia. It created a political regime that was civilian in character but not particularly democratic in nature. This restricted democracy generally respected civil liberties but limited political participation to the Liberal and Conservative Parties. Third parties were formally excluded from direct participation in politics. The political regime also allowed for direct elections, but these had no bearing on the partisan composition of elected bodies since parity was predetermined. Such restrictions on democratic rule were justified as necessary for bringing stability to a deeply divided society. To the surprise of many observers, the National Front system survived the 16-year period intact, with two Liberal presidents (Alberto Lleras Camargo, 1958–1962, and Carlos Lleras Restrepo, 1966–1970) alternating with two Conservative presidents (Guillermo León Valencia, 1962–1966, and Misael Pastrana Borrero, 1970–1974). The National Front was successful in restoring and consolidating civilian rule in Colombia, which has lasted to the present time. Moreover, the National Front put an end to the fierce party-based violence that had been ubiquitous since the mid-1940s. Partisan violence declined steadily during the early years of the National Front until it was virtually extinguished by 1966. Although the National Front witnessed the upsurge of other modes of societal violence, particularly with the emergence of leftist guerrilla movements, the partisan conflicts of *La Violencia* were largely left behind.

Unfortunately, the National Front regime also had the unintended consequences of fragmenting and depoliticizing the traditional Liberal and Conservative Parties, of entrenching clientelism as their primary means of mediating between the state and society, and of drastically reducing their responsiveness to the demands of a modernizing and restive country. All of these changes, in combination with the absolute exclusion of other political parties and movements from power, provided fertile ground for incipient left-wing guerrilla movements. The Colombian guerrillas were themselves rooted in *La Violencia* since many of their leaders were former combatants from that period. Nonetheless, unlike the Liberal guerrillas of the previous era, the leftist guerrillas of the 1960s and 1970s sought to overthrow the established political and socioeconomic order. By the 1970s, four principal guerrilla movements were active in Colombia: the Colombian Armed Revolutionary Forces, or FARC (Fuerzas Armadas Revolucionarias de Colombia); the Army of National Liberation, or ELN (Ejército de Liberación Nacional); the Popular Liberation Army, or EPL (Ejército Popular de Liberación); and the April 19th Movement, or M-19 (Movimiento del 19 de Abril).

The FARC originated in response to a 1964 military campaign against a number of communist-oriented peasant self-defense groups in regions of southern Tolima and southwestern Cundinamarca. From its beginnings, the FARC attempted to establish ties to the peasantry in its zones of influence, particularly in areas of recent colonization. It also maintained close links to the Colombian Communist Party and adhered to the party's strategy of "the combination of all forms of struggle." The ELN was a Cuban-inspired guerrilla movement begun by Colombian students who sought to establish a socialist regime. It initiated military operations in January 1965 with an attack on the town of Simacota in Santander. The ELN became the most orthodox of the Colombian guerrilla movements, never wavering from its original goal of socialist revolution or its view of the government as "bourgeois" and, thus, an absolute enemy with which negotiations were impossible. The EPL originated in the Sino-Soviet split of the mid-1960s, which caused a division in the Colombian Communist Party and the creation of the Maoist-oriented Marxist- Leninist Communist Party of Colombia, or PCC-ML (Partido Comunista de Colombia–Marxista-Leninista). The EPL was established in 1967 as the armed wing of the PCC-ML. It was originally heavily influenced by Maoist thought, with its focus on the peasantry and its corresponding strategy of a prolonged popular war. However, the EPL broke with Maoism in 1980 and expanded its radius of action to include urban areas. M-19 was born in 1973 out of the merging of two sectors that were dissatisfied with the existing revolutionary movements: one sector consisted of individuals who had been expelled from the Communist Party and the FARC, while the other was comprised of members of the socialist wing of the National Popular Alliance (Alianza Nacional Popular, or ANAPO), a political movement led by the former dictator Rojas Pinilla. Indeed, the name of the guerrilla movement came from the date of April 19, 1970, when the presidential election was allegedly stolen from Rojas Pinilla. M-19 was the least orthodox of the Colombian guerrilla movements, highly nationalistic and originally urban in nature.

THE POST-NATIONAL FRONT PERIOD (1974–1990)

The National Front regime formally ended in 1974 with the termination of bipartisan presidential alternation and congressional parity. Nonetheless, other aspects of parity remained in place until the early 1990s. Specifically, a 1968 constitutional reform extended for 10 years bipartisan parity in the appointment of cabinet officers, governors, mayors, and non-civil service administrative positions. Even after 1978, the constitution required the president to "give adequate and equitable participation" to the principal opposing party in appointments to these positions. Despite these restrictions, 1974 marked the return of unrestrained party competition for the presidency, Congress, departmental assemblies, and municipal councils. Elections between 1974 and 1990 showed that the Liberal Party clearly had become predominant in Colombia, winning the majority of seats in the Chamber of Representatives and the Senate in every election. Its congressional domination peaked in 1990 when it won 61.8 percent of the seats in the Chamber and 63.1 percent of the seats in the Senate. The Conservative Party retained its position as a solid minority, generally capturing between 30 and 40 percent of the seats in Congress. Third parties, meanwhile, typically garnered less than 5 percent of congressional seats.

The Liberal Party also dominated the presidency between 1974 and 1990: of the five presidents elected in this period, four were Liberals. The sole Conservative elected to the presidency in this period (Belisario Betancur, 1982–1986) was able to achieve office only after a split in the Liberal Party caused it to field two presidential candidates. Nonetheless, in an important sense, competition between the two dominant political parties no longer mattered. In the aftermath of the National Front, ideology had largely ceased to differentiate the Liberal Party and the Conservative Party. Although factions of the Conservative Party might speak with greater insistence about the need to return to traditional morality and to maintain close relations with the Catholic Church, few programmatic differences remained between Colombia's two historic parties. Both could be described fairly as mainstream catchall parties dependent upon multiclass support.

Despite their electoral dominance, by the 1980s both the Liberal Party and the Conservative Party appeared to be in crisis. Although both parties defended the interests of the upper strata of Colombian society, neither had shown itself willing to address effectively the concerns of the lower and middle sectors of society. In addition, the rigidity of the political regime, deep-seated clientelism, and widespread political violence hindered the emergence of new political parties that might serve as real alternatives to the bipartisan monopoly of power. The result was a deepening crisis of political legitimacy, reflected in declining party identification, widespread political apathy, high rates of electoral abstention, a growing number of civic strikes and protests, and the intensification of organized violence against the established political regime.

In particular, the repressive policies of the Liberal administration of Julio César Turbay (1978–1982) generated growing sympathy for the guerrilla movements, especially for the M-19, which came to symbolize opposition to the increasingly unpopular Turbay government. Ironically, although Turbay sought to crush the guerrillas militarily, the FARC, the EPL, and the ELN all grew in numbers and expanded their activities during his administration. This period also witnessed the emergence of several new, although relatively small, guerrilla movements: the indigenous Quintín Lame Armed Movement (Movimiento Armado Quintín Lame); the Workers' Revolutionary Party, or PRT (Partido Revolucionario de los Trabajadores); and the Movement of the Revolutionary Left, or MIR (Movimiento de Izquierda Revolucionaria).

The Conservative administration of Belisario Betancur (1982–1986) sought to radically change the repressive approach of its predecessor by carrying out a policy of democratic reform and peace negotiations with the guerrilla movements. The policy achieved limited success, most notably in the passage of an amnesty law in 1982 and the signing of peace accords with the FARC, EPL, and

M-19 in 1984. Nonetheless, the Betancur peace process soon confronted a number of obstacles, including congressional resistance, military opposition, economic crisis, and the failure of all sides to comply with the peace accords. By the end of the Betancur administration, the ELN, the EPL, and the M-19 were all once again engaged in armed conflict with the state. Nonetheless, the FARC maintained a tenuous cease-fire with the state and had launched a legal political movement, the Patriotic Union, or UP (Unión Patriótica). Lamentably, soon after its founding, literally thousands of UP members began to be assassinated, largely by right-wing paramilitary forces but with the apparent participation or acquiescence of state security forces. This systematic campaign against UP militants, which would continue for years, is one of the greatest human rights tragedies of recent Latin American history.

The Liberal administration of Virgilio Barco (1986–1990) was marked by increased violence on the part of all of the armed actors, with a concomitant worsening of the human rights situation. The first 2 years of Barco's government were marked by heightened guerrilla violence, including the return of the FARC to direct combat with the state and the failure to initiate any substantive peace talks. Nonetheless, by 1988 the M-19 had become convinced of the need to demobilize and reenter civilian life. After a period of lengthy negotiations, the M-19 signed a peace accord and turned in its arms in March 1990. Meanwhile, right-wing paramilitary groups, which had taken root in the early 1980s, began to flourish as they benefited from an influx of drug money and the collaboration of certain sectors of the state security forces. Despite a variety of distinct origins, in the 1980s the various types of paramilitary groups began to merge in practice, becoming offensive (as opposed to defensive) military groups whose sole raison d'être was to fight against leftist guerrillas and their presumed supporters. Indeed, the principal strategy of the paramilitaries was to target and kill individuals who constituted the support network of the guerrillas as well as anyone who was believed to sympathize with the guerrillas.

The Barco administration also had to confront the growing power and violence of drug cartels. In 1989, the violent activities of drug traffickers, particularly the Medellín cartel, reached a critical threshold, highlighted by the assassination of several prominent political figures. The most notable of these was Luis Carlos Galán, a popular Liberal senator and the clear favorite to become president in the 1990 elections. After Galán's murder in August 1989, Barco announced a series of far-reaching state-of-siege decrees intended to break the back of the drug cartels, which were labeled by the president as "the common enemy." During the 4 weeks following Galán's assassination, some 10,000 persons were arrested and the state took possession of hundreds of buildings, airplanes, vehicles, and weapons, along with 4.7 tons of cocaine.

In the face of this intense state crackdown, the Medellín cartel issued its own declaration of war against the Colombian state. The cartel began a campaign of terror that shook Colombian society with its blatant violations of international humanitarian law and whose principal weapons were intimidation, dynamite attacks, car bombs, kidnappings, and assassinations, primarily of civilians. By the end of September 1989, the drug traffickers had carried out more than 140 dynamite attacks against government offices, banks, businesses, hotels, and schools. It was during this period that the United States began a policy of massive security assistance for the War on Drugs. The George H. W. Bush administration supported President Barco's declaration of war against the Medellín cartel by announcing the 5-year, $2.2 billion Andean Initiative. Beginning with the Andean Initiative and continuing through the present, the bulk of the counternarcotics aid that the United States has sent to Colombia has been military in nature.

THE 1991 CONSTITUTION AND BEYOND

Paradoxically, the Medellín cartel's vicious war against the state during 1989–1990 was key to the subsequent democratization of the Colombian political regime. The drug traffickers' violence, in combination with the apparent incapacity of the state to respond adequately to it, highlighted public discontent with the existing political regime. An enterprising movement of student activists took advantage of this crisis of legitimacy and successfully pushed politicians from the traditional parties to support the election of the National Constituent Assembly to draft a new constitution. In 1991, the assembly met for 5 months to draw up the constitution, with the explicit purpose of broadening and deepening Colombian democracy. The possibility of participating in the assembly also served as a concrete incentive for the reincorporation into civilian life of the EPL and two smaller guerrilla movements, the PRT and the Quintín Lame. All signed peace accords with the government, demobilized, and engaged actively alongside former guerrillas of the M-19 in helping to write the new constitution.

The 1991 constitution itself represented a significant step toward the democratization of the Colombian political regime. Among other measures, it eliminated all vestiges of the exclusionary National Front regime, introduced an extensive bill of citizen rights, provided for a variety of new participatory mechanisms (including the popular election of governors), and curtailed the president's state-of-siege emergency powers. The new constitution, however, did not undertake significant reforms with regard to the political party system or the state security forces. Of equal importance, the 1991 constitution did not function as a viable political pact to end the ongoing conflict, primarily because neither the FARC nor the ELN guerrillas participated in its drafting and, thus, did not feel compelled to respect the new constitutional order.

In the aftermath of the 1991 constitution, the Liberal and Conservative parties initially continued to dominate Colombian politics. However, the traditional two-party system was undermined by a package of constitutional amendments approved in 2003 that sought to establish more cohesive and responsible parties. Thus, in the 2006 congressional elections, the Liberal and Conservative parties together garnered only 35.3 percent of the seats in the Senate (down from 83.3 percent as recently as 1998) and 38.6 percent of the seats in the Chamber of Representatives (down from 81.4 percent in 1998). A democratic leftist party, the Alternative Democratic Pole (*Polo Democrático Alternativo*), won 9.8 percent of the seats in the Senate and 4.8 percent in the Chamber, and its presidential candidate came in second with 22.0 percent of the vote, nearly twice the votes of the official Liberal Party candidate.

THE DRUG TRADE IN COLOMBIA

To the outside world—and to chagrin of most of its citizens—Colombia is synonymous with drug trafficking. The powerful drug cartels of the 1980s and 1990s developed from modest and disperse drug-trafficking activities in Colombia in the 1960s and early 1970s. Originally focused on the production and transportation of limited amounts of marijuana, by the late 1980s the drug trade had shifted largely to cocaine and had come under the control of the Medellín and Cali cartels. Between them, the cartels were estimated to control between 75 and 80 percent of the Andean cocaine traffic, employ nearly 100,000 Colombians, and derive annual incomes of between $2 and $4 billion. In the 1990s, both the Medellín and Cali cartels were dismantled but without any significant drop in the amount of cocaine exported. Instead, the drug industry became more fragmented, with dozens of small to medium-sized trafficking organizations taking over the terrain of the big cartels. Colombia also became a major producer of opium poppy, from which heroin was refined and exported to the United States.

The effects of the drug trade on the Colombian economy have been decidedly mixed. On the positive side, drug trafficking has contributed to the nation's trade surplus, provided employment for significant numbers of Colombians, and opened channels of upward mobility for some members of the lower social classes. On balance, however, the economic effects of drug trafficking have been negative. The influx of narcodollars has tended to revalue the Colombian peso, which has placed pressure on the country's traditional industries. Moreover, the climate of violence associated with drug trafficking has encouraged domestic capital flight and generally discouraged investment. Much of the investment that does take place is directed into unproductive enterprises valued more for their ability to launder drug money than to produce a profit. Of particular concern, the violence accompanying the drug trade has increased the costs of doing business by forcing companies to spend significant amounts on security measures. The enormous profits of the drug trade have grossly inflated the price of land, goods, and services in the trafficking areas and in major cities. The drug trade has also contributed to turning Colombia into a net importer of food as a result of the conversion of cropland into marijuana and cocaine fields and the employment of peasants to grow and process the drug crops. Finally, the drug trade has enormously increased the level of corruption throughout the economic system.

Whatever the ultimate economic balance, the more lasting consequences for Colombia have occurred in the political realm. In the 1980s and 1990s, drug cartels relied extensively on both bribery and violence against state officials to protect their trafficking activities. All too often, Colombian police officers, soldiers, judges, and elected officials were faced with the excruciating choice of *plata* or *plomo*; that is, they could accept "silver" (*plata*) in the form of a bribe to look the other way, or "lead" (*plomo*) in the form of a bullet if they chose to confront the traffickers. More recently, drug trafficking organizations have sought to enter the political realm directly, primarily through the paramilitary organizations that they have long financed or controlled. In a scandal that unfolded in 2006–2007, some twenty-seven Colombian politicians, including fourteen sitting members of Congress, were arrested for their close ties to the paramilitaries. Most analysts agree that the principal factor that prompted the paramilitaries to enter the political realm was to ensure protection from extradition and long prison sentences in the United States for drug trafficking offenses. Despite the tremendous amount of resources dedicated by U.S. and Colombian officials to fighting the drug trade over the past three decades, the U.S. State Department acknowledged in 2007 that Colombia remains the source of almost 90 percent of the cocaine entering the United States and is the primary source of heroin used east of the Mississippi River.

SOCIAL MOVEMENTS IN COLOMBIA

Colombian guerrillas, paramilitaries, and drug traffickers tend to dominate the headlines, particularly in the U.S. media. Nonetheless, Colombia also has a vibrant civil society characterized by diverse social movements seeking to transform the country peacefully. Colombian social movement organizations range from religious bodies to environmental groups to an incipient women's movement. By way of example, it is instructive to examine briefly the role played by a student movement, the indigenous movement, and the human rights movement in their efforts to enact democratic change in Colombia.

The Colombian student movement of 1989–1990 is an important example of how social movements have played a key role in transforming Colombian politics. Although student movements tend to be ephemeral and focused largely on reforming higher education, a student movement emerged in Colombia in 1989 that played a key role in bringing about the constituent assembly that drafted the 1991 constitution. The origins of this student movement lay in the assassination of presidential candidate Luis Carlos Galán on August 18, 1989. One week after Galán's assassination, an estimated 15,000 to 20,000 students from Bogotá universities conducted a silent march to his grave. At the cemetery, the students proclaimed their rejection of all types of violence, demanded respect for human rights, and issued a call to reform those institutions that contributed to the national political crisis. In addition, they announced the creation of a united student movement that would work to provide answers to the country's crisis. The student movement soon decided to promote a National Constituent Assembly to reform the country's rigid constitution, with the goal of broadening and deepening Colombian democracy. Ultimately, the students persuaded the country's political leadership to support a plebiscite on the possibility of convoking a National Constituent Assembly, which garnered 86.6 percent of all votes cast. Although the student movement itself eventually dissolved, the resultant 1991 constitution stands as a testimony to the creative power of a social movement.

The Colombian indigenous movement demonstrates the difficulties and achievements of a more lasting social movement. The indigenous population in Colombia is relatively small, consisting of slightly less than 1 million persons, and is fragmented into eighty-one distinct ethnic groups that speak sixty-four different languages. Nonetheless, a contemporary indigenous movement began to organize in the early 1970s in the department of Cauca, seeking to defend indigenous lands and customs. The success of this original movement was soon replicated elsewhere. Between 1971 and the mid-1980s sixteen indigenous organizations were created in other departments of Colombia, eventually coming together to form the National Indigenous Organization of Colombia (ONIC, *Organización Nacional Indígena de Colombia*) in 1982. The Colombian indigenous movement was not free from internal tensions, which at times erupted into conflict between the stronger regional organizations and the ONIC. Nonetheless, the movement's organizations shared an interest in recovering indigenous territory, achieving greater autonomy for indigenous communities, and protecting indigenous culture. The most notable achievements of the indigenous movement came about in the 1991 National Constituent Assembly, in which they elected two representatives to the seventy-member body. These delegates worked with other sympathetic delegates to introduce several articles to the 1991 constitution that explicitly protected indigenous culture, language, territory, and traditional forms of governance. The Colombian indigenous movement today continues to rely extensively on these constitutional guarantees as it struggles to defend its interests, especially against paramilitary units, drug traffickers, and guerrilla movements that encroach on indigenous territory to promote their own agendas.

Finally, the human rights movement is among the most overlooked yet crucial of the social movements working to transform Colombia today. The Colombian human rights movement began during the repressive years of the administration of Julio César Turbay (1978–1982) with the creation of the Permanent Committee for Human Rights (*Comité Permanente para los Derechos Humanos*). It was soon joined by a variety of national and regional human rights organizations, many of which focus on specific aspects of human rights abuses in Colombia, such as the Association of Families of Detained and Disappeared Persons in Colombia (ASFFADES, *Asociación de Familiares de Detenidos-Desaparecidos en Colombia*); the Office for Human Rights and Displacement (CODHES, *Consultoría para los Derechos Humanos y el Desplazamiento*); the Colombian Commission of Jurists (CCJ, *Comisión Colombiana de Juristas*), which produces sophisticated studies of human rights and international humanitarian law in the context of Colombia's civil conflict; the Center for Research and Popular Education (CINEP, *Centro de Investigación y Educación Popular*), which maintains the country's most widely consulted database on human rights violations, and the Free Country Foundation (*Fundación País Libre*), which focuses on kidnappings. Given the country's internal armed conflict, the promotion and defense of human rights places human rights defenders at considerable risk. Indeed, Colombian rights workers have been subjected to assassinations, disappearances, torture, death threats, and smear campaigns seeking to undermine their work. These attacks have been carried out primarily by paramilitary units and sectors of the state security forces, and secondarily by guerrilla movements, and have been aimed at creating a climate of fear that will deter human rights workers from continuing their activities. The Colombian human rights movement today plays a crucial role in keeping the issue of human rights at the forefront of national and international debates, particularly at a time when the national climate of opinion favors a military solution to Colombia's civil conflict.

The other two major parties in Congress, Radical Change (Cambio Radical) and the Social Party of National Unity (*Partido Social de Unidad Nacional*, better known as the *Partido de la U*), were new parties comprised largely of former Liberals and Conservatives who broke away from the traditional parties to support the reelection of President Alvaro Uribe in 2006. It is unclear whether these parties will continue to exist after Uribe's presidency and, if not, whether their adherents will return to the folds of the Liberal and Conservative parties. The Colombian party system is thus unstable at the beginning of the twenty-first century, but the days of the exclusive two-party system appear to be over.

Much of the violence perpetrated by drug traffickers eased during the Liberal administration of César Gaviria (1990–1994). The Gaviria government prioritized ending the violence of the drug cartels and, to that end, guaranteed traffickers a reduced sentence and non-extradition if they surrendered to authorities and confessed to at least one crime. However, most of the key traffickers, including the notorious leader of the Medellín cartel, Pablo Escobar, chose to wait until the 1991 National Constituent Assembly passed a constitutional article explicitly banning extradition before taking advantage of Gaviria's generosity. In June 1991, Escobar and his top lieutenants surrendered to Colombian authorities. However, when the Gaviria administration decided to transfer them to a more secure prison in July

1992, Escobar and nine of the top leaders of the Medellín cartel escaped. Drug-related violence again surged until state security forces killed Escobar in December 1993 and the Medellín cartel was dismantled. The victory, however, was ephemeral since the rival Cali cartel quickly took over the Medellín cartel's business and no significant reduction in drug trafficking took place. Meanwhile, the Gaviria administration engaged in peace negotiations with both the FARC and the ELN guerrilla movements, in Caracas, Venezuela (1991), and in Tlaxcala, Mexico (1992); however, neither of these efforts came to fruition.

Colombia's internal conflict deepened during the Liberal administration of Ernesto Samper (1994–1998). Unfortunately, Samper's term quickly became mired in a serious drug scandal, in which the president was accused of receiving several million dollars from the Cali drug cartel for his election campaign. Although Samper steadfastly denied the charges, the accumulation of evidence led to two unsuccessful attempts in Congress to impeach the president. The U.S. government never believed Samper's claims of innocence and exerted tremendous pressure to force his resignation. In both 1996 and 1997, the Clinton administration decided to "decertify" Colombia in its annual review of international cooperation with the United States in its War on Drugs. A more personal rebuke was the decision by the State Department in 1996 to cancel Samper's visa to the United States. U.S. pressure had contradictory effects. On the one hand, it provoked angry charges of U.S. intervention in Colombian internal affairs and rallied many Colombians to the defense of Samper. On the other hand, it pushed the Samper administration to dismantle the top leadership of the Cali cartel in 1995, as well as to strengthen penalties for drug trafficking and to reform the 1991 constitution to once again allow for the extradition of Colombian citizens to stand trial abroad.

Unfortunately, Samper's preoccupation with the drug scandal and his accompanying loss of credibility undermined his administration's efforts to deal with the armed conflict. Both left-wing guerrilla movements and right-wing paramilitary groups expanded significantly during the Samper administration and both had become increasingly reliant upon the drug trade, directly or indirectly, to finance their armed activities.

The Conservative administration of Andrés Pastrana (1998–2002) engaged in a fitful dialogue with the FARC leadership for over 3 years, during which the guerrillas were ceded a 16,000-square-mile demilitarized zone intended to facilitate peace talks. Nonetheless, the talks ultimately failed to produce much more than a detailed agenda for negotiations. Over time, the Pastrana administration grew increasingly concerned about abuses committed by the FARC in the demilitarized zone, whereas the FARC repeatedly charged the government with failing to act decisively to curtail the cruel actions of the paramilitary forces. The peace talks broke down definitively in February 2002 when the government ordered the military to retake the demilitarized zone. In the meantime, parallel peace talks with the smaller ELN guerrilla movement likewise proceeded in a halting fashion, with few results to show by the end of Pastrana's term in office.

Even as Pastrana talked peace with the Colombian guerrilla movements, he was determined to repair relations with the United States. He was thus willing to intensify the war on both drug traffickers and the growing number of peasant cultivators of coca. Pastrana found that the destruction of the Cali cartel—like the destruction of the Medellín cartel before it—had produced little effect on the overall quantity of drugs being shipped from Colombia. Rather, the drug trade had simply fragmented as several dozen small to intermediate-sized trafficking organizations took the place of the powerful cartels. Moreover, the drug trade had expanded into the production of heroin from opium poppies. The war on drugs in Colombia became notably more militarized under Pastrana, particularly under the auspices of "Plan Colombia," a comprehensive strategy supposedly developed by the Pastrana administration but in fact largely devised by the United States. In principle, Plan Colombia was a multifaceted program designed to eradicate illicit crops, support a negotiated settlement with the guerrilla movements, revive the moribund Colombian economy, and provide aid for judicial institutions, human rights, and alternative development. In practice, however, Plan Colombia largely became a conduit for U.S. military and police assistance. Most of the U.S. funds went to train and equip new counternarcotics battalions within the Colombian army. Underlying this effort was a strategy known as the "push into southern Colombia," in which the newly formed counternarcotics battalions would move into areas of coca production such as Putumayo and Caquetá that were dominated by the FARC guerrillas. Critics rightly feared that the United States was being drawn ever more deeply into Colombia's long-standing internal armed conflict.

The election of Alvaro Uribe, a hardliner and dissident Liberal, as the president of Colombia in 2002 reflected the growing frustration and disillusionment of much of the Colombian populace with regard to the ongoing conflict. Uribe had been critical of the peace process during the Pastrana administration and promised to reestablish firm state authority throughout the country. Once in office, Uribe worked assiduously to strengthen the state security forces and to ensure that they were deployed effectively throughout the country. He courted the George W. Bush administration, successfully garnering continued U.S. military assistance. By 2007, Uribe's security policies had produced significant results, with a considerable decline in most indicators of violence, including kidnappings, extrajudicial killings, and massacres. Much of this decline is explained by the extensive demobilization of right-wing paramilitary units across the country, a process begun under the Uribe administration in 2003. Over the next 3 years, some 31,000 members of paramilitary groups formally demobilized. Nonetheless, this process was undermined by lax penalties for even the most egregious crimes committed by paramilitary forces, as well as by the reemergence of newly armed groups. Indeed, despite the demobilization, some twenty-two paramilitary groups with upwards of 3000 members were reported to be operating in Colombia in 2006.

Uribe's "iron fist" approach to the guerrilla movements made him initially reluctant to consider peace negotiations, particularly in the aftermath of the Pastrana administration's failed efforts. Nonetheless, exploratory talks began in late 2005 between the Uribe administration and the ELN guerrillas in Havana, Cuba. Despite promising signs, as of the end of 2007 these talks had yet to produce a substantial agreement. Uribe was even less inclined to negotiate with Colombia's

largest guerrilla organization, the FARC. Nonetheless, pressured by the international community as well as by Colombian civil society, the Uribe administration in
2007 began to consider seriously the possibility of a prisoner-for-hostage exchange
with the FARC, in which some forty-five political hostages held by the FARC would
be exchanged for FARC prisoners held by the Colombian government. Nonetheless,
hopes for such a humanitarian exchange were temporarily dashed in November
2007, when Uribe publicly terminated the facilitating role that had been played by
President Hugo Chávez of Venezuela.

President Uribe's relative success in improving the security situation in
Colombia, along with the steady recovery of the economy from the recession of
the mid-to-late 1990s, helped to bolster his public approval ratings, making him
one of the most popular Colombian presidents in decades. Uribe rode this popularity to re-election as president in May 2006 with 62.4 percent of the vote. Despite
this popularity, Uribe remained the object of significant criticism from both labor
organizations, which disapproved of his neoliberal economic policies, and human
rights groups, which expressed concern over the growing number of extrajudicial
killings perpetrated by state security forces and the impunity in which these cases
remained.

Meanwhile, in the aftermath of September 11, the Bush administration dropped
all pretenses of supporting Colombian state security forces solely for counternarcotics purposes. Rather, key U.S. officials began to reformulate U.S. policy using
the rhetoric of "counterterrorism" and referring to the nonstate armed actors in
Colombia, particularly the FARC, as terrorist organizations posing a threat to
regional security. Legislation passed in July 2002 allowed U.S. security assistance
to be used "against activities by organizations designated as terrorist organizations," thus officially breaking with the long-standing policy that U.S. military
aid to Colombia be utilized solely for counternarcotics purposes. Between 2000
and 2007, the United States provided over $4 billion in military aid to Colombia,
making it the largest recipient of U.S. aid outside the Middle East and Afghanistan. This money went toward purchasing dozens of helicopters, the creation of
new army and navy brigades, and the training of thousands of Colombian military and police. Literally hundreds of U.S. troops and private contract personnel were on the ground in Colombia, working as military trainers, intelligence
gatherers, spray pilots, and mechanics, among other duties. Meanwhile, congressional opponents of U.S. security assistance to Colombia successfully introduced
human rights conditions that needed to be met for the full amount of military
aid to be released. However, despite unequivocal evidence of continuing human
rights violations by Colombian state security forces, the U.S. State Department
consistently certified Colombia's human rights record, thus allowing the aid to
be disbursed.

The Colombian Political Regime: Constitutional Structure and Actual Practice

State authority is formally exercised in Colombia today in accordance with the 1991
constitution, which defines Colombia as a "decentralized, unitary Republic, with

autonomous territorial entities, democratic, participatory, and pluralist" (Article 1). Administratively, the country is divided into thirty-two departments, each of which has an elected governor and a departmental assembly that can pass administrative decrees governing areas such as public works, tourism, and socioeconomic development. Departments, in turn, are subdivided into municipalities (roughly the equivalent of U.S. counties), each of which has an elected mayor and municipal council. Despite appearances to the contrary, Colombia is a unitary state—not a federal state—since departments and municipalities are strictly limited in their competencies by the constitution and national legislation.

At the national level, the executive branch is led by the president, who is both head of state and head of government. The president and vice president are elected by national popular vote for 4-year terms. If no candidate receives a majority of votes in the presidential election, a runoff election is held between the top two candidates. Although the 1991 constitution originally limited the president to one term in office, a 2005 constitutional amendment allows the president to be re-elected for a second consecutive term. The president governs with the aid of a cabinet of appointed ministers and traditionally has exercised tremendous political power. The 1991 constitution did place some limits on that power by removing the ability to appoint departmental governors, weakening the president's veto power, limiting the president's ability to issue legal norms, and restricting the president's ability to govern under "state-of-siege" decrees. Nevertheless, the presidency remains the key political office in Colombia. This is especially true since the executive branch enjoys extraordinary fiscal powers: all budgetary bills must originate in the executive branch and Congress can only increase spending in a given area with the written authority of the respective cabinet minister.

The legislative branch consists of a bicameral Congress elected through a system of proportional representation for 4-year terms. There are no term limits that restrict reelection. The 102-member Senate has 100 members elected in a single national electoral district and two indigenous members elected by indigenous communities. The Chamber of Representatives is elected in departmentally based districts, with each department granted a minimum of two representatives and an additional representative for every 250,000 inhabitants. In addition, the Chamber has four seats set aside for Afro-Colombians (2), political minorities (1), and Colombians living abroad (1). In the 2006–2010 legislature, this translated into 166 representatives. Congress has traditionally suffered from a lack of public confidence due to such practices as absenteeism, nepotism, corruption, foreign junkets made at taxpayers' expense, and extensive pork barrel legislation. The 1991 constitution attempted to address some of these concerns by establishing strict eligibility requirements for candidates to Congress, explicit conditions under which a member of Congress could be removed from office, and strict conditions for travel abroad. The 1991 constitution also strengthened the legislative branch by giving Congress the power to override presidential vetoes more easily, to censure executive cabinet members, to modify legislative decrees issued by the president, and to limit the president's authority under the declaration of a state of siege.

The judicial branch is organized into several functional jurisdictions. The "ordinary" jurisdiction covers civil, criminal, commercial, labor, and family law matters and works through a hierarchical system of municipal courts, circuit courts, superior courts, and the Supreme Court. The Supreme Court is a 23-member body that hears appeals from lower-level courts and has the authority to investigate the president, members of Congress, and other high government officials. Members of the Supreme Court serve 8-year terms and are ineligible for reappointment. They are chosen through a system known as "cooptation," in which the court itself selects its own new members from a list of eligible candidates proposed by the Superior Council of Judicial Affairs, a body created by the 1991 constitution to ensure the independence of the judiciary. The "administrative" jurisdiction deals with disputes arising from official public acts as well as the acts of private entities performing public duties. It adjudicates these matters through departmental courts and the Council of State, a 27-member body that serves as the highest administrative court in the country. Like the justices of the Supreme Court, the magistrates of the Council of State serve 8-year, nonrenewable terms and are chosen by cooptation from among candidates postulated by the Superior Council of Judicial Affairs. Finally, the "constitutional" jurisdiction is the realm of the Constitutional Court, a nine-member body created by the 1991 constitution and dedicated to determining the constitutionality of a wide range of laws, bills, referenda, and treaties. The justices of the Constitutional Court also serve for 8-year, nonrenewable periods. However, unlike the magistrates of the other two superior courts, each justice of the Constitutional Court is elected by the Senate, from a slate of three candidates nominated by the president, the Supreme Court, and the Council of State, respectively.

The 1991 constitution transformed the previous judicial system, in which judges were responsible for the entire sequence of investigating a crime, issuing a verdict, and sentencing the criminal. Under the new system of justice, a separate, independent body investigates a crime and prosecutes the accused before the judge, whose responsibility is now limited to that of judging and sentencing. The leading role is played by the newly created Office of the General Prosecutor (the Fiscalía General), which is charged with "investigating crimes and accusing the suspected infractor before the corresponding courts of law" (Article 250). The general prosecutor, who serves for a period of 4 years, is selected by the Supreme Court from among three nominees chosen by the president. Another 1991 reform related to the judicial branch is the establishment of the Human Rights Ombudsman (*Defensor del Pueblo*), whose task is to promote and protect human rights in Colombia. As such, the Ombudsman has a number of responsibilities, including education, preparation of legislation, petitioning of habeas corpus, and preparation of special legal actions to defend the basic rights of citizens. The Human Rights Ombudsman is chosen by the Chamber of Representatives from a slate of three candidates nominated by the president. Finally, the 1991 constitution establishes special indigenous legal jurisdictions. Within these jurisdictions, indigenous authorities are allowed to exercise judicial functions in accordance with their own norms and procedures, as long as these are not contrary to the law and constitution.

The formal, constitutional exercise of power as delineated in the 1991 constitution is constrained in actual practice by several significant factors. First, the historic weakness of the Colombian state means that its territorial reach is often limited, particularly in more rural, inaccessible parts of the country. Although the Uribe administration successfully established a police presence in all 1105 Colombian municipalities, this presence is frequently limited to a single small station incapable of fully controlling the municipality, particularly in its rural zones. The lack of an effective state presence, and the absence of education, health, and other public services has allowed the de facto control of certain areas by guerrilla movements, drug trafficking organizations, or paramilitary units. Second, despite the good intentions of the 1991 constitution, the Colombian political system continues to function largely through a system of broker clientelism, especially outside of the major urban areas. That is, politicians use their access to office to distribute specific state benefits such as government jobs, government-financed scholarships, and access to government-provided social services in return for votes on election day. Such a system subverts the notion that all citizens should have equal access to state benefits. Third, beyond the distorting influence of broker clientelism, Colombian elections continue to be marred by outright vote-buying and by the armed intimidation of both voters and candidates in some areas, particularly by the guerrilla movements and the remaining paramilitary units. Such practices clearly undermine the ability of Colombian authorities to conduct "free and fair" elections. Fourth, Colombian presidents since the mid-twentieth century have tended to govern under the auspices of a "state of siege." Declaring a state of siege in order to confront issues of public order allows presidents to exercise legislative as well as judicial power. Although the 1991 constitution instituted safeguards to restrict and regulate the state of siege, the mechanism continues to be used by Colombian presidents. Reliance on a state of siege for governance undermines democracy through undue accumulation of power in the hands of the executive. Finally, Colombian democracy continues to be weakened by the direct and indirect participation of the state security forces in human rights abuses in their conduct of the war against the leftist guerrillas. An eventual resolution of Colombia's long-standing civil conflict is likely to happen only when state security forces fully respect the civil and political rights of all Colombian citizens, particularly noncombatants caught in the midst of war.

Chronology

1526 Santa Marta, the oldest permanent Spanish city in Colombia, is established

1538 Gonzalo Jiménez de Quesada founds the city of Bogotá after subduing the Muiscas

1739 The Viceroyalty of New Granada is permanently established with its capital at Bogotá; it encompasses present-day Colombia, Venezuela, Ecuador, and Panama

1810 The struggle for independence from Spain begins as Caracas, Cartagena, Bogotá, and other cities in the Viceroyalty of New Granada form their own self-governing juntas

1816 Spanish troops under General Pablo Morillo reestablish Spanish rule throughout most of the former Viceroyalty of New Granada

1819 Patriot troops under the leadership of Simón Bolívar defeat the Spanish at the Battle of Boyacá

1830   Venezuela and Ecuador separate from Colombia; Bolívar, in increasingly ill health, relinquishes power and dies shortly thereafter

1863   A new constitution introduces a radically federalist system of governance; the Liberal Party dominates under this constitution for the next two decades

1886   Under the leadership of Rafael Núñez, a rigidly centralist constitution is adopted; the next four and a half decades are a period of Conservative dominance in government

1899–1902   The War of a Thousand Days, a major civil war between Liberals and Conservatives, produces some 100,000 deaths and contributes indirectly to the loss of Panama

1903   A Panamanian uprising occurs with the complicity and armed intervention of the United States; U.S. diplomatic recognition of the fledgling government is immediate and solidifies the independence of Panama from Colombia

1930   The Liberal Party wins the presidency for the first time in over four decades, after the Conservatives split their votes between two candidates

1936   The first agrarian reform law is adopted in Colombia; also, Colombia's first nationwide labor confederation is established, the Confederación de Trabajadores Colombia (CTC)

1946   A Conservative, Mariano Ospina Pérez, assumes presidency for the first time in 16 years, after the Liberal vote is split between the moderate Gabriel Turbay and the populist Jorge Eliécer Gaitán; in the aftermath of the election, violent outbreaks occur between Conservatives and Liberals

1948   Liberal leader Gaitán is assassinated, producing mass rioting in Bogotá and throughout the country; Violent incidents continue until large portions of the country are caught up in an undeclared civil war between the Liberal and Conservative Parties— *La Violencia*

1949   Laureano Gómez, an extreme Conservative leader, wins an unopposed election to the presidency after the Liberal Party withdraws from the race; political violence between Liberals and Conservatives intensifies

1953   General Gustavo Rojas Pinilla overthrows Gómez in a military coup and assumes the presidency

1957   Rojas Pinilla resigns and goes into exile; a national plebiscite endorses the creation of the National Front regime, which establishes a government in which the presidency alternates between Liberals and Conservatives for a period of 16 years and all positions in government are distributed evenly between the two parties

1964   The last vestiges of the partisan violence between Liberals and Conservatives—*La Violencia*—are eliminated

1964–1967   Three major guerrilla organizations take up arms against the Colombian state— the Cuban-inspired Ejército de Liberación Nacional (ELN), the Marxist-Leninist Fuerzas Armadas Revolucionarias de Colombia (FARC), and the Maoist Ejército Popular de Liberación (EPL)

1973   The nationalist leftist Movimiento 19 de Abril (M-19) guerrilla movement takes up arms

1974   The National Front regime formally comes to an end with the election of Alfonso López Michelsen, a Liberal, to the presidency

1982   Belisario Betancur, a Conservative, assumes the presidency and begins peace negotiations with the Colombian guerrilla movements, eventually achieving cease-fire agreements with the M-19, the FARC, and the EPL

1985   The Unión Patriótica (UP) is created as part of the peace negotiations with the FARC; in November, an M-19 detachment seizes the Supreme Court building in Bogotá and is exterminated along with half of the Supreme Court justices when the army takes it back

1989   President Virgilio Barco declares war against the Medellín drug cartel, which responds with a full-fledged campaign of car bombings, terrorist attacks, and kidnappings

1990   The M-19 turns in its arms and agrees to participate in electoral politics as a legal political movement

1991   A new constitution is drafted to deepen Colombian democracy; the constitutional assembly includes several delegates from guerrilla movements that have disarmed, including the M-19, the EPL, the Quintín Lame, and the Partido Revolucionario de Trabajadores (PRT). Pablo Escobar, leader of the Medellín cartel, turns himself in to Colombian authorities

1993   State security agents kill Escobar, who had escaped from prison the previous year, and the Medellín cartel is dismantled

1994   Ernesto Samper, a Liberal, assumes the office of the president amidst charges that he accepted money from the Cali drug cartel to finance his presidential election

1995   Colombian state security forces dismantle the Cali cartel; president Samper survives an impeachment process in the Chamber of Representatives

1996   Samper survives a second impeachment process in the Chamber of Representatives; the United States decertifies Colombia in its annual assessment of international cooperation in the War on Drugs

1997   The United States again decertifies Colombia in its annual review of international cooperation in the War on Drugs

1998   Andrés Pastrana, a Conservative, assumes the office of the presidency and begins peace negotiations with the FARC, ceding them a 16,000 square mile demilitarized zone to facilitate peace negotiations

1999–2000   President Pastrana, in conjunction with the Clinton administration, promotes Plan Colombia; the bulk of U.S. funding for Plan Colombia goes toward military and police assistance in an intensification of the War on Drugs

2002   Peace negotiations with the FARC break down and the Colombian armed forces retake the demilitarized zone; Alvaro Uribe, a dissident Liberal, is elected president, promising to take a hard line against the leftist guerrilla movements; the United States explicitly allows its military assistance to be used against Colombian guerrilla forces

2003   President Uribe enters into peace negotiations with several right-wing paramilitary movements, resulting in the demobilization of some 31,000 armed fighters by 2006

2006   Alvaro Uribe is reelected president with 62.4 percent of the vote

Bibliography

Alesnia, Albert. *Institutional Reforms: The Case of Colombia.* Cambridge, MA: MIT Press, 2005.

Bergquist, Charles, Ricardo Peñaranda, and Gonzalo Sánchez, eds. *Violence in Colombia 1990–2000. Waging War and Negotiating Peace.* Wilmington, DE: Scholarly Resources, 2001.

Bowden, Mark. *Killing Pablo: The Hunt for the World's Greatest Outlaw.* New York: Penguin Books, 2001.

Braun, Herbert. *Our Guerrillas, Our Sidewalks: A Journey into the Violence of Colombia.* 2nd ed. Lanham, MD: Rowman & Littlefield, 2003.

Bushnell, David. *The Making of Modern Colombia: A Nation in Spite of Itself.* Berkeley: University of California Press, 1993.

Chepesiuk, Ron. *Drug Lords: The Rise and Fall of the Cali Cartel.* Wrea Green, UK: Milo Books, 2003.

Crandall, Russell. *Driven by Drugs: U.S. Policy toward Colombia.* Boulder, CO: Lynne Rienner, 2002.

Dix, Robert H. *The Politics of Colombia.* New York: Praeger, 1987.

Drexler, Robert W. *Colombia and the United States: Narcotics Traffic and a Failed Foreign Policy.* Jefferson, NC: McFarland, 1997.

Dudley, Steven. *Walking Ghosts: Murder and Guerrilla Politics in Colombia*. New York: Routledge, 2004.

Giraldo, Javier. *Colombia: The Genocidal Democracy*. Monroe, ME: Common Courage Press, 1996.

Hartlyn, Jonathan. *The Politics of Coalition Rule in Colombia*. Cambridge: Cambridge University Press, 1988.

Hartlyn, Jonathan, and John Dugas. "Colombia: The Politics of Violence and Democratic Transformation." In *Democracy in Developing Countries: Latin America*. 2nd ed. Edited by Larry Diamond, Jonathan Hartlyn, Juan J. Linz, and Seymour Martin Lipset. Boulder, CO: Lynne Rienner, 1999.

Kirk, Robin. *More Terrible than Death: Massacres, Drugs, and America's War in Colombia*. New York: Public Affairs, 2003.

Kline, Harvey. *State Building and Conflict Resolution in Colombia, 1986–1994*. Tuscaloosa: University of Alabama Press, 1999.

Martz, John D. *The Politics of Clientelism: Democracy and the State in Colombia*. New Brunswick, NJ : Transaction Publishers, 1997.

Molano, Alfredo. *The Dispossessed: Chronicles of the Desterrados of Colombia*. Chicago: Haymarket Books, 2005.

———. *Loyal Soldiers in the Cocaine Kingdom: Tales of Drugs, Mules, and Gunmen*. New York: Columbia University Press, 2004.

Oquist, Paul H. *Violence, Conflict, and Politics in Colombia*. New York: Academic Press, 1980.

Palacios, Marco. *Between Legitimacy and Violence: A History of Colombia, 1875–2002*. Durham, NC: Duke University Press, 2006.

Posada-Carbó, Eduardo, ed. *Colombia: The Politics of Reforming the State*. New York: St. Martin's Press, 1998.

Randall, Stephen J. *Colombia and the United States: Hegemony and Interdependence*. Athens: University of Georgia Press, 1992.

Richani, Nazih. *Systems of Violence: The Political Economy of War and Peace in Colombia*. Albany: State University of New York Press, 2002.

Roldán, Mary. *Blood and Fire: La Violencia in Antioquia, Colombia, 1946–1953*. Durham, NC: Duke University Press, 2002.

Safford, Frank, and Marco Palacios. *Colombia: Fragmented Land, Divided Society*. Oxford: Oxford University Press, 2002.

Tate, Winifred. *Counting the Dead: The Culture and Politics of Human Rights Activism in Colombia*. Berkeley: University of California Press, 2007.

Taussig, Michael. *Law in a Lawless Land: Diary of a Limpieza in Colombia*. New York: The New Press, 2003.

Thoumi, Francisco E. *Political Economy and Illegal Drugs in Colombia*. Boulder, CO: Lynne Rienner, 1995.

Vásquez Perdomo, María Eugenia. *My Life as a Colombian Revolutionary: Reflections of a Former Guerrillera*. Philadelphia: Temple University Press, 2005.

Welna, Christopher, and Gustavo Gallón, eds. *Peace, Democracy, and Human Rights in Colombia*. South Bend, IN: University of Notre Dame Press, 2007.

World Bank. *Colombia Poverty Report*. 2002. www.worldbank.org.

Zamosc, Leon. *The Agrarian Question and the Peasant Movement in Colombia: Struggles of the National Peasant Association 1967–1981*. Cambridge: Cambridge University Press, 1986.

FILMS AND VIDEOS

Maria Full of Grace. United States/Colombia, 2004.
Welcome to Colombia. Colombia/France, 2003.
Plan Colombia: Cashing in on the Drug War Failure. United States, 2003.

WEBSITES

Center for International Policy—Colombia Project, http://www.ciponline.org/colombia A comprehensive source of information in English on current developments in Colombia and U.S. policy initiatives.

http://www.colombiaemb.org/opencms/opencms Colombian Embassy in Washington, D.C.

http://bogota.usembassy.gov United States Embassy in Bogotá, Colombia http://www.gobiernoenlinea.gov.co. Colombian government gateway to major government offices, ministries, etc.

http://www.hchr.org.co. U.N. High Commissioner for Human Rights Office in Colombia, the U.N. Office dedicated to the promotion and defense of human rights in Colombia.

http://www.usofficeoncolombia.com U.S. Office on Colombia, an independent organization helping Colombian civil society groups to educate U.S. decision makers about the impact of U.S. policy on the region.

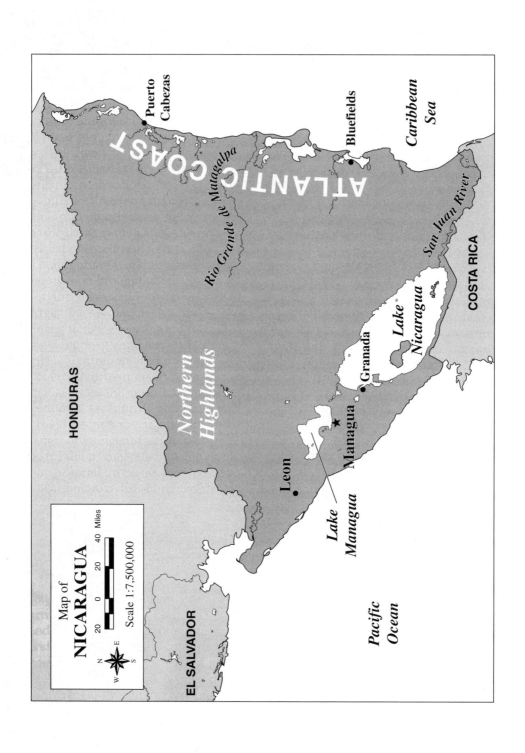

NINETEEN

NICARAGUA

Gary Prevost and Harry E. Vanden

Introduction

Nicaragua, located at the geographic center of Central America, is the largest and most sparsely settled of the Central American republics. Its 57,143 square miles make it about the size of the state of Iowa. Its population of 5.3 million, which has grown rapidly in the last two decades, is concentrated on the Pacific coast side of the country. It has three distinct geographic regions: mountains in the north, a narrow Pacific coastal plain containing two large lakes, and a wider Atlantic coastal plain. The Pacific plain is part of a trough that connects the Atlantic and Pacific Oceans through the San Juan River Valley. For more than a century this region has been viewed as having great potential for a new interoceanic canal. There is considerable volcanic activity in the northwestern part of the country, with three volcanos reaching 5000 feet emerging from Lake Nicaragua.

Most of Nicaragua has considerable potential for agricultural production. Occupying nearly half of the country, the Caribbean lowlands are composed primarily of hot, humid tropical rain forest and swamps. They are not conducive to long-term productive agriculture, and less than 10 percent of the population lives there. The central highlands and western lowlands have been much more hospitable to human habitation and agricultural production. The central region is especially good for coffee production, while the western lowlands support a wide range of agricultural products, such as cotton, rice, and sugar.

Nicaragua is favored not only with above-average natural resources and climatic conditions but also with several other advantages. Unlike some Latin American countries, it is not overpopulated. Arable land is adequate for the size of the population. Much of the country has a relatively homogeneous population, with no significant racial, linguistic, or religious differences. Most Nicaraguans are Roman

Catholic, speak Spanish, and are *mestizo* (mixed Spanish and Indian ancestry). The exception to this homogeneity is the Atlantic coast region, which is quite different. This region has an English-speaking black population with a Caribbean heritage and a small native indigenous population of Sumo and Miskito Indians. Despite its abundant natural resources, Nicaragua has remained one of the poorest countries in the hemisphere, with low per capita income and short life expectancy. It is also a country that has had more than its share of political violence and oppression. However, Nicaragua also falls within a select group of countries worldwide that has experienced a highly unusual phenomenon—social revolution. The events of the 1970s and 1980s in Nicaragua, the era of the Sandinista revolution, warrant Nicaragua's inclusion as a case study in this volume. It shares many characteristics with its Central and Latin American neighbors, but it was the brief period of revolutionary fervor that makes Nicaragua stand out. Yet, in order to understand the historical context of the events of 1978–1990, it is necessary to review Nicaraguan history.

As Thomas Walker has observed in his treatment of Nicaraguan history, the patterns of conflict that have marked modern Nicaragua did not begin with the Spanish conquerors of the sixteenth century. The region was inhabited by indigenous groups of South American origin that occupied the less hospitable eastern regions, while the western side was colonized by Meso-American groups from the north. There was little contact between the two groups, but within the western region there were clear patterns of warfare, slavery, and involuntary servitude. Spanish conquerors reached Nicaragua from Panama in 1522, making their first contact with indigenous people on the western plains. The expedition, under the leadership of Gil González, was seeking to obtain gold and converts to Christianity and was apparently successful on both counts. It also discovered the possible water link between the Atlantic and Pacific using the San Juan River and Lake Nicaragua. The initial contact was not without violence, however, as a legendary chief, Diriangen, offered armed resistance to the Spanish. In 1524, under the leadership of Francisco Hernández de Córdoba, the Spanish imposed their control over the region and founded the settlements of Grenada and León.

The Spanish conquest of Nicaragua had a profound and devastating impact. The existing indigenous population of around 1 million was reduced within a few decades to just tens of thousands. Some deaths occurred in battles with the Spanish, but most came from diseases that the Spanish introduced, such as measles and influenza, for which the local population had no immune defenses. Slavery was also a factor in reducing the population. As many as 400,000–500,000 natives were put in bondage during the early period; many were shipped out of the country. Demand for slaves was especially high from Peru. By the 1540s the Indian population of western Nicaragua had dropped below 50,000 and continued to decline afterward. The legacy of this devastation is that the more populated western part of Nicaragua is predominantly a *mestizo* culture with little trace of its indigenous past except for a significant number of cities and towns with native names. Today, few contemporary residents understand the significance of the long-forgotten histories behind these names.

Another legacy of the colonial period is the rivalry between the cities of León and Grenada. Grenada was originally designated by the Spanish to be the administrative center. As a result, it was populated by the aristocratic class, while colonizers of lower social status settled León, which was projected to be primarily a fortress city on the northern reaches of the colony. However, León emerged as the administrative capital, and aristocratic Grenadans had to endure centuries of rule by a city they viewed to be inferior. This resentment boiled into open warfare on occasion as the two cities also developed an economic rivalry. Wealth in aristocratic Grenada was based primarily on cattle, while the León economy was more commercially oriented and included international trade. For much of the colonial period, Nicaragua was an underpopulated, impoverished corner of the Spanish Empire. The economy, with its severe labor shortages, supported the wealthy lifestyles of the upper class in León and Grenada but was insufficient for more widespread prosperity.

The end of the colonial era did not bring any great relief to Nicaragua's difficult position. It won its independence in stages, first as a part of the Mexican Empire in 1821. It then became a member of the Central American Federation in 1823 and finally emerged as a sovereign state in 1838, when it withdrew from the federation. Internally, most of the nineteenth century after independence was marked by constant battles between León and Grenada for control of the country. By then, the Leonese had come to call themselves "liberals" and the Grenadinos had identified themselves as "conservatives." In a pattern that was to repeat itself, the chaos created by the internal conflict combined with the departure of the Spanish allowed outside forces to exert significant influence over Nicaragua.

British interests established a protectorate over the Atlantic region, known as the Autonomous Kingdom of Mosquitia, which lasted for most of the nineteenth century. U.S.-based Commodore Cornelius Vanderbilt's transit company became involved in moving California-bound gold prospectors across Nicaragua in 1849. Simultaneously, the British claimed control over the mouth of the San Juan River on the Atlantic coast, threatening the Vanderbilt operations. In 1850, the United States and Great Britain attempted to diffuse the conflict by signing the Clayton-Bulwar Treaty, in which they agreed to cooperate on the development of any transoceanic transit route. The treaty was negotiated and signed without involving the government of Nicaragua, establishing a pattern of disregard for Nicaragua's sovereignty that has continued to the present.

The Clayton-Bulwar Treaty did not end conflict in Nicaragua. In 1855, the Liberals of León hired an American soldier of fortune, William Walker, to lead their army against Grenada. Under Walker's leadership, the Liberal army triumphed and Walker became the de facto president of Nicaragua. He instituted Liberal reforms, including the encouragement of foreign investment and development of Nicaragua's natural resources. Initially, Walker's activities were supported by the U.S. government. However, the British and other Central American governments were taken aback by what seemed to be a bold imperialist act by the United States. Nicaraguans of both political parties also began to turn against Walker when he legalized slavery and established English as the country's official language. Now seen as a hated foreigner, Walker came under attack from forces armed by the British, other Central American governments, and even private U.S. interests who feared he had become a liability to stable commerce in the region. In 1857, the U.S. government brokered a deal that sent Walker into exile. He returned in 1860 but was unsuccessful in regaining control and was defeated and executed. The final defeat of Walker in 1860 by a combined Central American force ushered in a 30-year period of rule by the Conservatives, who quelled numerous uprisings and established a semblance of a stable, yet traditional, government.

The Modern Era

The beginning of a modern national consciousness in Nicaragua that included the Indian and *mestizo* masses emerged toward the end of the nineteenth century. Only then did a few intellectuals begin to look toward their distant indigenous past to rediscover the nation's historic identity and transcend the narrow Hispanicism that had often constrained national politics, thought, and literature. Although the Liberal reform movement did not develop in Nicaragua until the late nineteenth century, it carried a vision of society similar to movements in Mexico (under Benito Juárez) and elsewhere in Latin America. José Santos Zelaya's Liberal revolution of 1893 marked the beginning of the modern Liberal movement in Nicaragua. Although constrained by traditional European-style liberalism, Zelaya endeavored to centralize state power. He introduced some progressive ideas and began to challenge the traditional oligarchy and the power of the Catholic Church. His successful drive to recover the Atlantic coast from British colonialism also stimulated the growth of a national consciousness. Supported by elements of the national bourgeoisie, Zelaya introduced reforms that soon alarmed the Conservative forces and threatened the interests of the United States, which was antagonistic to the growth of a vigorous, independent national capitalist class in Nicaragua.

As Zelaya faced increasing internal and external pressure, his regime degenerated into a dictatorship. In 1909, Washington forced him to resign before he could implement his plans to modernize Nicaragua. Using various pretexts, the United States sent in Marines to reinstate Conservative rule and ensure the dominant position of U.S. capital. As U.S. intervention increased over the next years (the Marines again landed in 1912, to prop up the regime of Adolfo Díaz, and did not leave until 1924), antiinterventionist sentiment grew among the Nicaraguan people. With the outbreak of a new Liberal uprising against a Conservative coup in 1925 and the U.S.-inspired reinstallation of Adolfo Díaz as president, the struggle began to take on clear nationalist and antiimperialist overtones. The Marines once again intervened. It was at this point that Augusto César Sandino returned from Mexico and joined the now strongly nationalist Liberal struggle. Although Sandino encountered open hostility from the upper-class head of the Liberal army, José M. Moncada, he was able to arm and organize his own Liberal band and participate in the increasingly successful offensive.

Sandino was born into poverty in southern Nicaragua in 1895. As a young man, his nationalist instincts were fueled when he witnessed the humiliation of Liberal General Benjamín Zeledón by U.S. Marines in 1912. Between 1923 and 1926 Sandino worked in Mexico as a mechanic in the oil industry of Tampico; it was there that his eclectic political philosophy was formed through contacts with anarchists, Free Masons, and supporters of the Mexican Revolution. The Liberal struggle was met with enthusiastic support from the masses, who participated in growing numbers. However, as these forces were in sight of a clear military victory, the United States arranged a compromise solution that was accepted by Moncada and eventually supported by all the Liberal generals, save one—Sandino. Thereafter, large numbers of peasants, miners, artisans, workers, and Indians who had fought with Sandino followed him to the Segovias, a remote mountain region in the north. From here, he began a guerrilla war.

The first Sandinista struggle continued from 1927 to 1933, and Sandino's growing army made life very difficult for the Marines. Their political work and the increasing sophistication and tenacity of their popular guerrilla war had gained the support of many Nicaraguans, growing numbers of Latin Americans, and a few informed North Americans. The intensity of the conflict with the Marines forced Sandino and his followers to upgrade their military tactics and strengthen their ties with the rural masses who supported their struggle.

This was one of the first modern examples of the power of a guerrilla army with popular support against a technologically superior invader, even when the latter was bolstered by a significant national mercenary military force. Mobile guerrilla bands as the components of an egalitarian people's army, political as well as military organization, integrated political and military actions, close ties to the peasants, and, most importantly, popular support and involvement—such were the legacy from Sandino's war. More than three decades later, these lessons were put to use by the leadership of the next generation, the Sandinista National Liberation Front (FSLN).

Yet, although Sandino's political support had enabled him to gain a military victory, he disbanded his army before he could achieve far-reaching political and economic change. After his death at the hands of Anastasio Somoza's National Guard (1934), most of Sandino's followers were soon killed by the U.S.-trained National Guard. Some Sandinista columns fought on for a few more years in remote areas, but they too were eventually forced to abandon systematic armed resistance. All that remained was the legacy of Sandino and the example of his army, which lived on in the popular mind for some time, nourished by eyewitness accounts and first-hand stories from Sandinist survivors.

Nicaragua returned to more traditional authoritarian rule as Somoza took direct control of the government in 1936. He instituted an increasingly repressive family dictatorship that—mostly because of its close ties to the United States—would endure until militarily defeated by the FSLN in 1979. However, despite bloody repression and the intense vilification of Sandino and his followers, sporadic popular struggle continued through the 1930s, 1940s, and 1950s, although at a relatively low level. This period of struggle included military actions by both old Sandinists and younger patriots such as the "Generation of '44." Somoza proved to be one of the best friends of the United States and was warmly received by Franklin Roosevelt in Washington. By the 1950s Nicaragua was a fully dependent producer of primary goods (mostly coffee and cotton) and an integral part of the U.S. system of political and economic control in the Western Hemisphere. There were occasional armed actions by old Sandinists and other Nicaraguans who could no longer countenance the heavy-handed political and economic manipulation that characterized the Somozas and their friends. Students and workers occasionally demonstrated against the regime, but they lacked any clear ideological perspective in which to place their efforts. Opposition to the dictatorship came to be symbolized by the sincere but elitist Conservative Party. Even the Nicaraguan Socialist Party (founded as a pro-Moscow communist party in 1944) often collaborated with the traditional politicians and Somoza-controlled unions, at the workers' expense. Somoza had taken over the Liberal Party and even went so far as to make pacts (in 1948 and 1950) with the Conservative Party in an attempt to co-opt the only major focal point of opposition to his regime.

Carlos Fonseca and the Roots of the FSLN

It has been said that Nicaragua is a land of poets and that poets often reflect the popular will. Rigoberto Lopez Pérez was one of the Nicaraguan intellectuals who directly felt the far-reaching cultural implications of a dependent dictatorship that was subservient to the United States. He, like Cuban poet José Martí, felt compelled to exchange pen for pistol to liberate his country. In 1956, the young poet assassinated Somoza. In so doing he not only avenged Sandino but also spurred a reexamination of national conscience that increasingly challenged the status quo. The dictator's eldest son, Luis, took over the reigns of power and became the next Somoza to rule. A new wave of guerrilla activities broke out in the countryside; one of the more famous of these was led by Ramon Raudales, a veteran of Sandino's army. The university students also began to show a new militancy, and for the first time, a small group began to study Marxist theory. The Nicaraguan Socialist Party (PSN) had been founded in 1944 and maintained the closest of ties to the Soviet Union. Like most Latin American communist parties prior to the 1960s, its ideology was modeled after that of Soviet Stalinism. It was thus ill equipped to creatively fuse Marxism with the national reality of Nicaragua. Nonetheless, the party was virtually the only institution in the country where Marxist ideas were taken seriously. As such, it attracted the attention of emerging young student radicals like Carlos Fonseca and Tomás Borge.

Fonseca was born in Matagalpa in northern Nicaragua. His mother was a cook and his father, a worker in a U.S.-owned mine. Borge was a secondary school classmate and close friend. Fonseca became a political activist at an early age. At 16, he participated in a strike at his school, demanding the removal of a medallion depicting Somoza from the school's crest. At 17, he and Borge discovered the writings of Marx and Engels in the bookstore of poet Samuel Meza and read and studied these philosophers. He soon drifted toward the PSN, and in 1955, at the age of 19, he joined the party. Fonseca enrolled in law school in León the following year and, with Silvio Mayorga and Borge, formed a cell of the PSN's youth group.

Fonseca began studying Nicaraguan history that year and later traced the roots of the rebellion to the numerous attempts of the Indians to resist Spanish conquest. He also identified with the rebellion in 1821 led by Cleto Ordoñez against the annexation of Nicaragua by Agustín de Iturbide, the Emperor of Mexico. Other nineteenth-century Nicaraguans that Fonseca identified with included those who sought a united Central America, particularly Francisco Morazán; those who fought the American adventurer William Walker in the 1850s; and those who participated in the War of the Indians in 1881. Fonseca saw the latter, an uprising of Indian and *mestizo* people against the ruling elite of Matagalpa, as a forerunner to Sandino's war. He also carefully studied Sandino's thought and politicomilitary activities and found great inspiration in his struggle against the Marines, strong class consciousness, and internationalism. Later, he began to be disillusioned by the reformist approaches of the PSN and sought a new vehicle for change based on the methodology of armed struggle. The key turning point was the shooting of four students during anti-Somoza demonstrations in 1959 and the tepid response of PSN leaders to the National Guard's actions.

Fonseca's disenchantment with the PSN did not involve a rejection of Marxism but rather a belief that the PSN was abandoning the use of Marxism as a dynamic philosophy. The guerrilla war in Cuba and the example of the Cuban Revolution had already inspired guerrilla activity in the late 1950s. Like many young Latin American revolutionaries, Fonseca and his collaborators were much taken by Fidel Castro's 26th of July movement and believed that guerrilla warfare was the best method of achieving political change. Deported to Guatemala in April 1959 following student demonstrations in León, Fonseca went briefly to Cuba. Then, with advice from Ché Guevara and practical assistance from the Cuban government, he joined up with the Rigoberto López Pérez column in the Honduran border region. The column was composed of a group of fifty-five Nicaraguans, Cubans, and other Latin Americans. The column was surprised and massacred; Fonseca was wounded but made his way to Cuba for convalescence. He became convinced of the need for a new political formation, and in July 1961 the FSLN was formally launched in Tegucigalpa, Honduras, by Fonseca, Borge, and Mayorga. The FSLN consisted of just twelve militants, including Colonel Santos López, a veteran of the Sandino-led struggle against the U.S. Marines in the late 1920s, and Victor Tirado López, later, like Borge, one of the nine members of the FSLN's National Directorate. According to Borge's prison writings, the name of the organization and its clear link to Sandino was suggested and fought for by Fonseca. The figure of Sandino was and continued to be a significant factor in shaping the political philosophy of the FSLN.

Drawing heavily on the Cuban revolutionary experience and the writings of Guevara and Castro, the Sandinistas reinterpreted Sandino. They drew on the revolutionary thought of other Latin Americans, such as Peruvian José Carlos Mariátegui. By studying Nicaraguan circumstances in light of similar wars in Cuba, Vietnam, and elsewhere, the Sandinistas were able to build on Sandino's tactics and infuse their movement with a coherent ideology. The Sandinistas believed that the only road to power was through armed struggle. Like other young Fidelistas throughout Latin America, they felt that launching rural guerrilla warfare was all that was necessary to convince the people, beginning with the peasantry, to take up arms and join the guerrillas. In Nicaragua, as elsewhere in the region, this was a fundamental and very costly error; and the FSLN's first attempts at guerrilla warfare met with defeat. The new Sandinistas had failed to do what their namesake had done well—mobilize the local populace on the side of the guerrillas through well-planned political and organizational activity coordinated with and part of the armed struggle. Some of the FSLN's best cadres became isolated and surrounded at Pancasán in mid-1967. Most were killed as the National Guard closed its trap on the guerrillas. Like the Fidelista guerrilla currents all over Latin America, they suffered a disastrous military setback. However, unlike many other guerrilla movements in Latin America, the Sandinistas were able to learn from their early mistakes. They demonstrated a great capacity for self-criticism and were thus able to transcend their initial error of isolating themselves from the masses. They were able to fashion a strategy that eventually would bear fruit.

In the period after Pancasán, the FSLN's increased prestige brought many new recruits, especially from among students and youth in the cities. The FSLN began to establish what it called "intermediate organizations"—student, worker, neighborhood, and Christian movements. The success the Sandinistas were having in winning *campesinos* to their cause in the mountains alarmed Somoza and his U.S. advisers. Large-scale counterinsurgency operations were launched. Peasants suspected of collaborating with the FSLN "disappeared," were tortured, and were murdered. The counterrevolutionary terror became so intense that the guerrillas were forced farther and farther back into the mountains and progressively separated from the inhabited areas where they had been gaining support.

Simultaneously, other powerful sectors of Nicaraguan society were beginning to undergo change. Progressive sectors within the Catholic Church became more concerned with the conditions of the lower classes. Motivated by this concern and the ideas of liberation theology, they intervened actively in the process of social change. As discussed in Chapter 6, after the Latin American bishops' meeting at Medellín in 1968, a section of the Latin American Church became involved in the struggle for social change. In Nicaragua, the key institution was the Institute for Human Advancement (INPRHU), which began to organize using the methodology that Brazilian educational philosopher Paulo Freire had developed. Numerous Christian popular organizations emerged in the 1970s as the struggle against Somoza deepened. Eventually, an important unity was struck between the FSLN and these forces when prominent church figures such as Ernesto and Fernando Cardenal and Miguel D'Escoto became part of the FSLN. What is most significant about the Nicaraguan case and the FSLN is that this historic gulf between Marxist and Christian forces was bridged not simply through a brief tactical alliance but through the integration of progressive Christians into the revolutionary movement. The result of this unity was that the political philosophy of the FSLN, and in particular its attitude toward Christianity, became unique among revolutionary parties with Marxist origins.

The growing strength of the political opposition coincided in the late 1960s and early 1970s with a growing crisis within the ruling Somoza dynasty. In June 1967, the third Somoza, Anastasio Jr., came to power in a blatantly rigged election. This election came on the heels of the death of Luis Somoza, who had ruled since the death of his father. Luis ruled in a manner that allowed for economic modernization under the aegis of the Kennedy administration's Alliance for Progress and for modest political reform that gave the presidency to two Liberals outside of the Somoza family, René Schick Gutiérrez and Lorenzo Guerrero. Unlike his brother Luis, Anastasio Jr. was a military man and his arrival at power signaled the end of an era of cosmetic liberalization and a return to more blatant authoritarian dictatorship. This approach was underscored by the bloody suppression of a protest rally shortly before the 1967 election. Once in power, Anastasio Jr. turned away from the civilian power base of the Liberal Party that his brother had rejuvenated and much more toward the use of military power to maintain family rule. Positions throughout government that were filled with technocrats by his older brother came increasingly to be filled by officers of the National Guard loyal to the Somoza family but without governing expertise. By 1970, corruption and incompetence became more widespread as the family more openly used public office for private enrichment. Anastasio Jr. also more blatantly ignored the Nicaraguan constitution. According to that document, he was to step down when his term expired in 1971; but through a pact with Conservative leader Fernando Aguero, he circumvented the rules and was elected to a new presidential term that was to last until 1981.

Turning Point for Revolution

Most observers argue that a key turning point for the regime was the Christmas earthquake of 1972, which cost the lives of 10,000 people and destroyed central Managua. Passing on the opportunity to be magnanimous with the family fortune in the face of the disaster, Somoza chose to turn the catastrophe to short-term personal advantage. He and his associates used their control of the government to channel international relief funds into their own pockets, primarily through the self-awarding of government contracts and the purchase of earthquake-damaged land and industries. Popular resentment against the government began to build among all classes when it became clear that Somoza used the tragedy to his own advantage. Donated international relief supplies were often sold by the government or given to friends of the Somoza family. Emergency housing funds from the U.S. government went disproportionately into the construction of luxury homes for Guard officers, while the homeless poor had to settle for wooden shacks they constructed themselves. Reconstruction of the city's roads and drainage system was also badly mismanaged. Somoza lost not only whatever support he may have had among the poorer classes but also the loyalty of the country's economic elite. Somoza's competitors in the business world were outraged by the manner in which he largely shut them out of the earthquake reconstruction. He also levied new taxes and then proceeded to exempt his own businesses. After 1973, large segments of the business community went elsewhere with their political support, eventually to the revolutionaries.

The political crisis of the Somoza regime and the earthquake came at a time when the FSLN was not well poised to take advantage. After Pancasán, the movement survived but did not prosper. By 1972, the revolutionaries had fewer than 500 cadres within Nicaragua, and much of the leadership, including Fonseca, was living in exile in Cuba. Realizing that popular sentiment against the dictatorship was building, the FSLN made a spectacular reentry into Nicaraguan politics on December 27, 1974, with the seizure of the home of a wealthy Somoza supporter who was hosting a party for the U.S. ambassador. An FSLN commando unit held more than a dozen foreign diplomats and Nicaraguan political leaders hostage for several days and forced Somoza to release Sandinista political prisoners, pay a large sum of money, and broadcast and publish FSLN communiqués. This action surprised many Nicaraguans since Somoza had declared the guerrilla challenge to be dead.

Somoza's response to the FSLN action served to deepen the crisis of his regime. He imposed martial law and sent his National Guard into the countryside to destroy the FSLN. In pursuit of that objective, the Guard carried out arbitrary imprisonment, torture, and murder of hundreds of peasants. These brutal acts were not the first committed by the Guard, but the political landscape had changed. Catholic priests in rural areas documented these actions, and the Nicaraguan Church hierarchy, which had previously supported the Somoza dynasty, denounced its human rights violations. The Church's changed stance gave international notoriety to Somoza.

However, even as the regime weakened, the path to political change was not entirely clear. For its part, the FSLN was severely divided over the proper strategy to employ against Somoza. Three tendencies emerged, formalized at a meeting of the National Directorate in Cuba in 1975, the first convening of that body since 1970.

The three tendencies were called Prolonged People's War, Proletarian, and Insurrectionist or Tercerista.

The three tendencies finally converged around the tactical and strategic questions brought to the fore by the upsurge of mass struggle that opened in late 1977 and as the urban masses moved into action after the murder of Conservative opposition leader and well-respected newspaper publisher Pedro Joaquín Chamorro in early 1978. After the first serious confrontation between the urban masses and the National Guard—the uprising in the Indian community of Monimbó in February 1978—the Insurrectionist tendency shifted its strategy almost exclusively to prepare for insurrection in the cities. The Insurrectionists also participated in the Broad Opposition Front (FAO) through their supporters in the "Group of Twelve." The twelve were prominent middle- and upper-class opponents of Somoza, including Sergio Ramírez, later elected vice president on the FSLN ticket in 1984. All opposition forces soon united under the banner of the National Patriotic Front (FPN). The FPN took on the character of a united front, drawing in the trade unions, two of the three factions of the old PSN, student groups, and organizations such as the Popular Social Christian and Independent Liberal Parties—all under FSLN hegemony. Finally, the experience of the September 1978 attempt at insurrection—which the Insurrectionist tendency spearheaded most enthusiastically—taught the need for better organization and preparation. The cumulative effect of these lessons, and the massive organized mobilization that resulted, paid off in June 1979 as the FSLN coordinated a massive popular insurrection.

As the summer of 1979 approached, the Somoza dictatorship became increasingly isolated. Despite his increasingly dismal prospects, Somoza was unwilling to compromise and launched what proved to be a fatal strategy. He ordered the bombing of civilian areas in order to deny his adversaries food and shelter. It failed because the FSLN suffered few casualties and bombing served to further rally popular support behind the rebels. Faced with imminent defeat, Somoza fled the country on July 17, 1979. He went first to the United States and then into exile in Paraguay, where he was assassinated 14 months later by Argentine revolutionaries. His demise ended one of the most durable dictatorships—46 years—in Latin American history.

On July 19, 1979, the Sandinistas marched into Managua and established a revolutionary government that was dominated by the FSLN but also contained political actors from the non-Sandinista opposition to Somoza, including Chamorro's widow, Violeta. The new government reflected the relationship of forces that existed at the time that the guerrilla war triumphed. The FSLN, confident that it had a mandate for significant social, political, and economic change, set about the process of creating a revolution in Nicaraguan society. The Sandinistas remained in power for 11 years, until 1990, when, following an electoral defeat at the hands of a coalition headed by Violeta Chamorro, the FSLN handed over power and retreated to the position it held through the first years of the twenty-first century—that of leading opposition party.

The FSLN in Power

As the Sandinistas consolidated their political control after July 1979, more moderate elements of the victorious coalition left the government. After the initial euphoria of the revolutionary victory died down, the revolutionary leadership engaged in actions that suggested the participation and grassroots democracy that had been initially envisioned as part of the Sandinista program might be sidetracked. Power became concentrated in the upper echelons of government and in the FSLN's National Directorate. Later, as the United States and its allies pressured the Nicaraguan leadership to bring the regime more in line with Western-style political systems, steps were taken toward a system of representative democracy that the dominant group in the Sandinista leadership hoped would satisfy many of its detractors and thus increase the legitimacy of the Nicaraguan government in the eyes of the West, a legitimacy that was never received.

The political challenge that faced the Sandinistas as they assumed political power in July 1979 was significant. The revolutionaries had come to power at the head of a broad anti-Somoza front that had many different conceptions about the future of Nicaragua. The middle- and upper-class opponents of Somoza grounded in the nation's traditional opposition parties—Conservatives, Independent Liberals, and Social Christians—were interested primarily in gaining political power for themselves within traditional Nicaraguan political structures. Their commitment to social change was limited at best. They were largely interested in perpetuating the traditional authoritarian system but without the dictator Somoza and his Liberal Party.

The Sandinistas and their supporters in the peasantry as well as the urban poor wanted a far more radical transformation. They were more interested in the end product of social change than in the particular forms of political structures. However, much of the Sandinista leadership was skeptical of a narrow definition of democracy that reinstated the traditional party system, minimized direct popular participation, and did not include a social and economic dimension. Sandinista leaders believed that democracy did not begin or end with elections. Because the Sandinistas were primarily interested in social change, they initiated a political process that would favor newly formed mass organizations of workers, peasants, women, and youth. Their direct involvement was embodied in the Council of State, which exercised legislative authority from 1979 to 1984. The council, which would eventually expand to fifty members, included representatives from the traditional political elites (e.g., Conservative Party), Superior Council of Private Enterprise or COSEP (business organizations), and the Catholic Church. However, while the Sandinistas sought input from these groups, the majority of the council were representatives of organizations loyal to the Sandinistas and committed to comprehensive social change. Key groups included the Association of Nicaraguan Women Louisa Amanda Espinosa (AMNLAE, the national women's organization), Sandinista Youth (JS 19-J), the Association of Rural Workers or ACT (the peasants' organization), and the Sandinista Workers Confederation or CST (a union organization). In granting a majority of seats to these grassroots organizations, the Sandinistas were virtually guaranteeing the projection of significant social change through the legislative process while at the same time breaking the hold of the traditional elites on the Nicaraguan political process. Fully aware of the political direction in which the Sandinistas were taking the revolution and the consequences for their political and economic interests, key elite members of the broad anti-Somoza front, including Violeta Chamorro, withdrew from the provisional government in protest over the composition of the Council of State. Faced with that challenge, the FSLN leadership restructured the executive branch with a smaller representation of non-Sandinistas and began to move the revolutionary process in a more radical direction. In the first 4 years of Sandinista power, the revolutionary government recognized trade unions, organized significant land reform, passed measures guaranteeing women's rights, expanded health care and education, and broadened its diplomatic contacts to include the East European socialist countries and the Nonaligned Movement (NAM). These actions served to galvanize opposition to the Sandinistas both within Nicaragua from the former elites and from the U.S. government.

Consolidating Political Institutions

Despite its obvious advantages to the furtherance of a revolutionary program, especially the involvement of grassroots organizations, the Sandinistas did not consider the Council of State to be a permanent body but rather a transitional one until elections could be held. Elections were promised in 1979, but the Sandinistas argued that significant preparation was needed for them to accurately reflect the will of the Nicaraguan people. International pressures grew on the FSLN to hold the elections sooner rather than later. The context for the elections also changed with the full-scale launching of the Contra War against Nicaragua by the United States in 1981–1982. Hoping to utilize the elections to legitimize Sandinista political power, the FSLN modeled its government and electoral process after Western examples. The president would be directly elected for a 6-year term and, as in the French system, would hold more power than the legislative branch. The National Assembly was created as a unicameral body, with selection primarily by proportional representation (the number of seats being directly proportional to the percent of the vote for each party). Very little consideration was given to retaining a direct legislative role for the mass organizations. Some Sandinistas privately raised concerns about the loss of grassroots initiative, but by 1983–1984 defeating the counterrevolution (*contras*) had become the dominant task. Priority was ultimately given to gaining support in the Contra War from Western governments, something that was never achieved to any significant degree. Ironically, the primary support for the FSLN in the Contra War came from Cuba and the Soviet Union, neither of which saw Western-style elections in Nicaragua as a positive. Within Nicaragua, the FSLN sought to legitimize its policies by defeating the traditional parties in the electoral arena. Ultimately, key elite actors, who were by now supporting the war against the Sandinistas either overtly or covertly, boycotted the elections and thereby undermined the legitimacy of the process in the eyes of much of the Western world. In any case, the November 4, 1984, elections in Nicaragua were significant in that a revolutionary party competed for political power with elite-oriented parties. The negotiated electoral law defined parties as entities that could vie for political power, a far cry from the special status reserved for the vanguard party in Marxist–Leninist states. The result was also a rare event in Nicaraguan history—an honest election. There was real electoral competition among seven different parties, three to the right of FSLN and three to the left. After a history of rigged elections and limited suffrage, the 1984 elections, open to all Nicaraguan citizens 16 years of age and above, helped embed in the Nicaraguan nation a notion of representative democracy that had been severely lacking. Despite the boycott of rightist parties, armed threats by the contras, and a U.S. government campaign against the legitimacy of the elections, participation was extremely high: 93 percent of those eligible registered and, of these, 75 percent voted on election day. The big winners were the Sandinistas, who garnered 62.9 percent of the votes for president and vice president and 62.3 percent of the National Assembly votes. Although political conditions prior to the election were not perfect, the voting itself did not see the type of corruption and vote fraud that had been so common in countries like Guatemala and El Salvador. The government and its policies were openly criticized during the campaign, and the opposition was able to win one-third of the seats in the National Assembly.

The 1984 elections also laid the groundwork for successful national elections in 1990, 1996, and 2001 that saw the defeat of the Sandinistas and the successful transfer of political power. However, the 1984 elections were not an unqualified success for democracy. As was pointed out earlier, grassroots organizations lost their direct representation and now were dependent almost exclusively on representation through the FSLN party. Throughout its years in power, pressed by its continuing war with the U.S.-backed contras, the FSLN operated as a top–down vanguard revolutionary movement. Party leaders rejected the idea of creating a mass party in 1979, and through the 1980s and most of the 1990s decision making was tightly controlled through the nine-member National Directorate; party ranks remained small, only a few thousand.

The 11 years that the Sandinistas were in power were tumultuous ones both in Nicaragua and throughout Central America. Within Nicaragua, the FSLN attempted revolutionary transformation on a scale rarely seen in Latin America. At the same time in the 1980s, civil wars raged in nearby El Salvador and Guatemala as rebel movements similar to the FSLN made serious bids for power. The region also became a prime battleground for the implementation of a U.S. conservative vision of a continuation of the Cold War between the United States and the Soviet Union. U.S. president Ronald Reagan made the defeat of the Sandinistas and their removal from power a high priority of the U.S. government. To this end, the United States armed and financed a counterrevolutionary war against Nicaragua throughout the 1980s, utilizing primarily the forces of the defeated dictator Somoza operating out of bases in Honduras. By the end of the decade, the FSLN, with significant Soviet assistance, defeated militarily the counterrevolutionaries (contras) but at great costs. More than 30,000 lives were lost, and the country's economy was devastated. Weary of the war and facing the continued hostility of the United States, the Nicaraguan people voted the FSLN out of power in the February 1990 elections. To the surprise of many observers, the Sandinistas handed over the reigns of power to the incoming Chamorro administration in April 1990. In doing so the FSLN became the first revolutionary group in Latin American history to cede power to an opposition force through an election.

The 1990 Election and After

Since 1990, three conservative governments have sought to reverse the policies and programs of the Sandinistas. Violeta Chamorro's National Opposition Union

(UNO) and Arnoldo Alemán's Constitutional Liberal Party (PLC), elected in 1996, succeeded in significantly undermining FSLN programs. This has also been the case under the administration of Enrique Bolaños from 2002 on. However, they have not succeeded in their goal of marginalizing the FSLN. The Sandinistas emerged from the 1990, 1996, and 2001 elections as the leading opposition force with political control in several municipalities, including Managua.

Although the FSLN had been able to maintain unity while it was in power, most of the other parties have not been able to overcome the traditional Nicaraguan proclivity for factionalism and internecine struggle. If traditional factionalism had held sway in 1990, there would have been some twenty opposition parties on the ballot. This would have splintered the opposition vote and allowed the FSLN an easy victory. Realizing this, the George H. W. Bush administration pushed for a unified opposition coalition and strongly encouraged the selection of a fresh opposition candidate who could serve as a symbol around which the opposition could rally. Although lacking political experience, Violeta Chamorro filled this role very well. With U.S. support, she was able to edge out Enrique Bolaños, a traditional political leader and head of COSEP (who successfully ran for president in 2001), and become the UNO candidate. By the time of the election, the U.S.-supported unity of UNO had held. Included in the new coalition were parties that traced their origins to the old Conservative and Liberal Parties as well as social democratic parties, social Christian parties, a party tied to contra leaders, and even two communist parties—the PSN and the Communist Party of Nicaragua (PCdeN).

The Sandinista leadership knew that conditions were bad, but they thought their political base could endure a little longer while they employed the human and material resources at their disposal to win the election. They also realized that they were playing a high-stakes game and that the United States had designated huge sums of money for the UNO campaign. This was epitomized by the 1989 U.S. congressional authorization of $9 million in overt funding for the opposition. It was to be dispensed through the National Endowment for Democracy.

Up to the time of the February election, it seemed that the Nicaraguan revolution might be able to build on the experiment with socialist democracy that developed in Chile in the early 1970s. Down to the eve of the election, most opinion polls suggested that the Nicaraguan people would ratify the socialist, mixed-economy experiment and continue with Sandinista democracy. However, the Sandinistas' stunning defeat at the hands of the U.S.-sponsored UNO suggested that the *demos* (the people) were not entirely satisfied with Sandinista rule or the type of socialist democracy that was developing in Nicaragua. Careful analysis of the facts suggests that the low-intensity conflict that the Bush administration waged against Nicaragua had disastrous effects on the economy. Also, the Nicaraguan government was not well prepared to manage the deteriorating economic conditions or respond to the growing hostility to conscription for the Contra War.

By 1988 inflation had reached some 36,000 percent, real wages had fallen to 29 percent of their 1980 value, milk consumption had fallen by 50 percent, and production reached levels that were abysmally low. In that same year, the deteriorating economy began to heavily impact daily life and increasingly became a subject of intense public concern. The government clearly assigned blame to the United

States. However, like the neoliberal policies the Chamorro administration later followed, the government response was an austerity program that was modeled on the programs that Brazil and Argentina employed in 1985 and 1986 and, as such, fell disproportionately on the poor.

When the results of the election were counted, the UNO had won a landslide victory, with 54.7 percent of the votes compared to 40.8 percent for the FSLN. The FSLN was defeated throughout the country, even in previously strong FSLN working-class districts in Managua. The UNO gained fifty-one of the ninety-two National Assembly seats and control of 101 of 132 municipal councils.

The newly refined electoral framework was imperfect, but it still provided a mechanism by which a growing desperation with conditions could be registered. The 1990 election proved to be a very effective means of registering a massive protest vote and sanctioning the Sandinista government. Many political observers celebrated the 1990 election as a return of democracy and the end of one-party dominance. Yet, one could equally argue that it was the beginning of an imposed regime that resulted from economic and military pressure from the United States and its allies and from pro-U.S. conservative groups inside Nicaragua. During the election, these forces employed a variety of tactics to induce a majority of the population to vote against the Sandinista government. In all, the United States had invested heavily in supporting opposition forces in Nicaragua—some $26 million in overt and covert aid since the 1984 election. *Newsweek* suggested that $5 million in covert funds had been used for the 1990 election alone. Overt funding for the election was estimated at $12.5 million. The authoritarian decision-making style by the government and the arrogance of many government and FSLN party leaders also convinced many other voters to sanction the party in office the only way they could: by voting for the only viable opposition—UNO.

In an action that further reduced the possibility of a return to a one-party-dominant regime under Sandinista control, the Sandinista government engaged in what came to be a very controversial action. Soon after the 1990 election, they rushed legislation through the National Assembly that granted title to confiscated property to those who had occupied it during the Sandinista years. While this did give title to some peasants and cooperatives and other small property owners, it also gave quite a few Sandinista leaders title to expensive properties they had used or been awarded as compensation for their years of service and sacrifice. Known as the *Piñata*, it came to be regarded as a way for the Sandinista leadership to enrich themselves before leaving office. As time progressed and poverty among the masses increased, the *Piñata* bred increasing resentment, helped erode support for the Sandinistas, and seemed to confirm the growing popular perception that government, while paid for by the many, was by and for the few.

The Chamorro Years, Alemán and Bolaños

In retrospect, it would seem that the 1990 election marked the beginning of a return to political decision making by political and economic elites that was conducted far from institutions in which the masses could exercise any real power. Indeed, the next 6 years saw the development of a political system that was increasingly characterized by intense competition among political elites. Nor were important concerns addressed; as unemployment and poverty became more generalized and income and wealth more concentrated, it became increasingly clear those aspects of economic democracy that had grown during the earlier years of Sandinista rule were severely eroded by successive waves of neoliberal policies and elite politics. These policies were continued under successive administrations. In 1990, it seemed that the real electors were not the majority who voted for the UNO but the external and internal economic elites who had engineered the Sandinista electoral demise. It was their demands—and not those of the common people—that would get the greatest attention. What the majority that voted for the UNO did not realize was that Violeta Chamorro had been chosen as an electoral tool to unseat the Sandinistas. Thus, there would be strong pressure to dismantle the type of state apparatus and policies that had developed under Sandinista rule, implement a conservative neoliberal economic program, strengthen traditional parties, and further reduce the power and size of the mass organizations and the Sandinista party. Nor would these changes give the masses any appreciable power in the new system.

The mass mobilizations at the time of the revolution and during the first years of Sandinista rule also set the stage for an often tenacious popular resistance against many of the unpopular economic policies that the Chamorro government tried to implement. As resistance was worn down, elements of the new policies were, however, gradually put in place.

President Daniel Ortega (left, wearing hat and bandana and shaking hands) campaigning in the 1990 Nicaraguan elections. Recast in jeans, cowboy boots, and bandana, Ortega was portrayed by FSLN as a rock star–like friend of the people. He lost to UNO candidate Violeta Chamorro. Defeated again in 1996 and 2001, Ortega returned in triumph to the presidency through the 2006 elections. *(Photo by H. Vanden)*

By 1991 it was becoming increasingly apparent that the Chamorro government was unable to solve basic economic problems for the common people. The fact that conditions actually deteriorated after the 1990 election did little to convince the masses of the ultimate utility of Western-style representative democracy. Nor were conflicts and centripetal forces limited to the Sandinista party.

The National Assembly became a focal point for political competition and deal making. While the economy continued to deteriorate, political conflict increased. A dispute between the president and many assembly members of her own UNO coalition in 1992 worsened the situation. This angered the other UNO delegates, who questioned the legitimacy of the institution and began to boycott assembly sessions. They believed that the understanding on which their coalition was based had been betrayed and further accused Chamorro and Antonio Lacayo of collaborating with the Sandinistas in a cogovernment. On the left, worker and peasant organizations and the increasingly militant ex-Sandinista fighters (*recompas*), who had still not received land, accused the Sandinista leadership of collaborating with the government at their expense. Former contras (*recontras*) who had not received their promised land also became increasingly militant.

Further, many factors converged in 1994 to precipitate a crisis that shook the Nicaraguan state to its very foundations. There was a movement to reform the 1987 constitution. Pushed by a coalition made up of parties and individuals who currently did not have easy access to power, the reforms envisioned increasing the power of the National Assembly at the expense of the executive. The constitutional reforms would take away the president's power to tax and spend by decree without legislative approval, prohibit nepotism, expand constitutional liberties, abolish the draft, clarify the right to private and other forms of property, reduce the presidential term from 6 to 5 years, and stipulate that a second round of voting would need to be held in those elections where the leading candidate did not get at least 45 percent of the vote. The net effect would have been to considerably strengthen the legislature at the expense of the presidency and (through the prohibition against nepotism) to eliminate Antonio Lacayo from future governmental positions, including that of the presidency. Begun in 1993, this process gained momentum during 1994. It led to much heated discussion between the two branches of government, but no consensus or compromise was reached. When the package of constitutional reforms was finally sent to the executive in January 1995, President Chamorro did not promulgate them. The situation worsened when the legislature would not accept Chamorro's recommendations for Supreme Court justices and instead sent their own list back to the executive, who in turn refused to appoint them. This left the nation's highest court without a quorum. The severity of the crisis was such that it took the combined effort of the major donor nations to convince the governmental institutions that cooperation was necessary to move beyond the breach.

The 1996 Elections and the Evolving Party System

As the 1996 elections approached, the FSLN began to ally itself with Minister of the Presidency Antonio Lacayo's newly formed National Project. The Sandinista Renovation Movement (MRS) was making common cause with the Christian Democratic

Union, Virgilio Godoy's Independent Liberal Party, Miriam Arguello's Popular Conservative Alliance, the Nicaraguan Democratic Movement (MDN), and the National Conservative Party (PNC). The strongest contender for the 1996 presidential election was Managua's conservative mayor, Arnoldo Alemán. Alemán was using his PLC to gain control of the now factionalized old Liberal Party (including Liberal groups who were allied with Somoza). In the end, this strategy and his successful public works campaign in Managua combined to give him victory in the first round of the election. His Liberal Alliance was also a big winner elsewhere, winning many municipalities, including Managua, and forty-two of ninety-three seats in the National Assembly. The FSLN won thirty-six seats in the assembly and the smaller parties, fifteen.

In 1996, it was the vestiges of the old Liberal Party reorganized as the Liberal Alliance that had once again united to claim victory. The FSLN's 11 years of party dominance had been refuted in the 1990 and again in the 1996 elections. Although still a power contender, it was far from being the dominant party in Nicaragua. The MRS, led by Sergio Ramírez, ran as a separate party; but it won only a small percentage of the vote. Other political groupings were fractionalized as well. There were twenty-four parties on the ballot, but Alemán's Liberal Alliance and the FSLN secured 89.8 percent of the votes. (Sandinista presidential candidate Danial Ortega came in a distant second with 38 percent of the vote compared to Alemán's 51 percent.) In the first months of Alemán's rule, there was a strong upsurge in returning *Somocistas*, and shortly after the election Somoza's nephews returned to Nicaragua to reclaim much of Somoza's property. Indeed, Alemán's administration soon became known or its favoritism, if not outright corruption. By entering into a pact with Alemán, the FSLN further eroded its legitimacy in the eyes of many. This helped to explain Ortega's significant loss to Enrique Bolaños and the PLC-led Liberal Alliance in 2001.

The election in November of that year saw a similar outcome to the 1996 election as old-line politician and former head of the major business grouping (COSEP) Bolaños led the Liberal Alliance to victory over Sandinista candidate Ortega with a resounding 56 percent of the vote compared to Ortega's 42 percent. After less than 2 years in office, the Liberal Alliance had splintered. In the municipal elections in November 2004, the Sandinistas swept at least 90 of the country's 152 municipalities, including Managua and 15 of the 17 department capitals. Ortega and the FSLN forged an alliance with the Alemán wing of the Liberal Alliance, who had turned against Bolaños after he spearheaded an anticorruption drive that implicated Alemán. After Alemán was removed from the National Assembly and forced to submit to a criminal trial, he was convicted of taking more than $7 million and sentenced to a prison term of 20 years. Further, by making this controversial alliance with former enemy Alemán and his PLC, the Ortega-led FSLN became a potent force in the legislature with the ability to move the National Assembly to pass legislation increasing the legislative body's power at the expense of the president. Though they have maintained political space for the left in Nicaraguan politics, it remains to be seen if indeed the Sandinistas have protected the achievements of their revolution, especially in agrarian reform, workers' rights, and women's rights. Some Sandinistas and former Sandinistas see the FSLN as just one more party that is more interested in competing for power than improving the conditions of the masses. Its election, through continued questionable agreements with the Liberals, in 2006 only served to reinforce that negative view of the FSLN among many.

Neoliberalism and the Economy

The Chamorro, Alemán, and Bolaños regimes proved especially accommodating to the compilation of external forces advocating the globalization process. As Nicaragua became subject to neoliberal policies and ever more integrated in the globalized economy, its national economy continued to deteriorate, as did its balance of payment deficits, which reached close to $12 billion in 1994. Internal economic conditions continued to deteriorate for the masses, with decreases in real income, official unemployment figures in excess of 50 percent, and reduced medical and educational services for the masses. Though economic growth increased after 1995, the persistence of poverty and unemployment and a growing movement to reduce social services suggested that the effects of neoliberal policies on the masses were far less positive than promised and often imposed increased hardships. Indeed, the data underline the general trend that the U.N. Human Development Program noted in its *Human Development Report 1999*, that—in contradiction to neoliberal premises—without an active role by government to ensure equity and human services, the forces of globalization do not necessarily support human advancement at all.

Based on the advice of its new conservative economic consultants and the U.S. State Department's Agency for International Development, the World Bank, and the International Monetary Fund (IMF), the new regimes began the process of globalization by implementing neoliberal policies. This process proceeded from 1990 to 1996 under Chamorro and was continued under the even more conservative regime of Alemán from 1996 to 2002 and by Bolaños thereafter. In 1998, Nicaragua suffered a severe setback when it was hit by Hurricane Mitch, causing some 9000 deaths and $10 billion in damage.

However, even though neoliberalism was implemented with a great deal of enthusiasm, the results of these policies were not always what was desired. In the early 1990s, the greatest inflow of capital did not come from investments but rather from aid and assistance programs from donor nations and international institutions. This trend continued. Further, the value of exports actually fell by $87 million from 1990 to 1992, while the value of imports increased by $237 million during the same period. This led to a balance of payment deficits of $610 million in 1992 and of $428 million in 1994. By the mid-1990s the external debt had reached almost $12 billion, making it the highest per capita debt in the world. Nicaragua became a member of the most indebted nations club and began to ask for debt forgiveness as a way of surviving. Even after much of its indebtedness was forgiven, by the end of the decade, its external debt was still at $8 billion. Further, the neoliberal repayments were devastating. Under the terms of the 1994 structural adjustment agreement, Nicaragua had to pay an average of $280.7 million a year in principal and interest payments. Just the debt service payments represented 60 percent of export value. Indeed, in the post-Sandinista period, better than half of government revenues (and sometimes as much as 70%) were designated for debt service payments. In 1997, the government spent more than twice as much on foreign debt payments as it did on health care and education combined. The net effects for the Nicaraguan people have been harsh indeed. As the external debt again mounted, Nicaragua was classified as one of the IMF's Heavily Indebted Poor Countries. In 2004, it qualified for debt reduction, when the IMF and World Bank forgave $4.5 billion in debt.

There were, however, some economic successes. The end of the Sandinista period was marked by extremely high inflation—it was more than 30,000 percent in 1988. Under neoliberal policies, it was drastically reduced. Inflation fell to 13.4 percent in 1990, 3.5 percent in 1992, and 12.4 percent in 1994. It has remained in check. After negative growth in the early 1990s, the economy finally started to grow in the mid-1990s: 3.2 percent in 1994, 4.3 percent in 1995, and 4.2 percent in 1998. This represented a major turnaround.

Social Conditions

The greatest question is, however, what the effects of the neoliberal policies have been. Unemployment in the mid-1990s was some 54 percent. By 1999 unemployment was officially put at 22 percent but considered much higher by most. The greatest growth in jobs had been in the informal sector, which offered no pension or other benefits. Wealth became more concentrated, and the distribution of income worsened. Half of the population lived in poverty, and 19.4 percent lived in absolute poverty. The richest fifth of the population received 65 percent of the income, while the poorest fifth received only 3 percent. These same percentages continued into the next century. Services had also fallen. For instance, medical consultations per capita fell 21 percent from 1990 to 1994 as the availability of health care was reduced. Living conditions for the masses fell to levels close to those in Haiti, and the per capita gross domestic product did as well (a little more than $400 per year in the mid-1990s and less than $400 per year by 2000). Conditions improved slightly with economic growth at between 1.5 and 2.5 percent by 2003 and 2004, but with some 22 percent unemployment and 35 percent underemployment, the per capita income remained one of the worst in the hemisphere at less than $800 annually, and what income there was remained very poorly distributed. Misery was widespread.

Nicaraguan Government Structures

Similar to other Latin American governments, Nicaragua has four independent branches of government: executive, legislative, judicial, and electoral. As is often the case in Latin America, the executive branch is the most powerful. The president heads the state's executive branch, where he is both head of state and head of government. The administrative apparatus under presidential control is rather large, with sixteen ministries and thirty-five independent agencies having cabinet rank. The appointive powers of the president are extensive, including all ministers in the Council of Ministers and vice ministers and numerous other high-level functionaries. The president chooses the chief and associate justices of the Supreme Court but from a list provided by the National Assembly.

The National Assembly is composed of ninety members elected by proportional representation from nine administrative regions, plus the defeated presidential candidates. The assembly's most important powers are budgetary oversight, the ability to summon the president and ministers, and a role in naming Supreme Court justices, members of the electoral council, and the controller general. The National Assembly also has an extensive system of standing and special committees, although the work of the body has been weakened by limited resources. When the National Assembly acted primarily to back up the president during the Sandinista years, it never developed an independent stance. However, divisions within UNO between 1990 and 1996 allowed the assembly to become more of a player in its own right. In 1995, reforms also strengthened the hand of the assembly vis-à-vis the executive branch. After the 2001, elections, the Liberal Alliance held fifty-three seats, the FSLN thirty-eight and the Conservative Party one.

Courts in Nicaraguan and Latin American history have not played a role similar to that of their North American neighbors. As a unitary state, Nicaragua does not have a formal checks and balances system. The lack of judicial review of laws leaves the Nicaraguan courts with the role of applying and interpreting laws rather than making them. The Supreme Court has sixteen judges elected for 5-year terms by the National Assembly. It is organized into four divisions, each responsible for a specific realm of law: civil, criminal, constitutional, and administrative.

The fourth branch of government, the Supreme Electoral Council, is intended to ensure that electoral administration is nonpartisan. Established in 1983, it performed well in the 1984 elections and was in significant measure responsible for the legitimacy of the hotly contested 1990 elections. Under the leadership of Sandinista Mariano Fiallos, it set a high standard for honesty and competence. Unfortunately, this organ's reputation was damaged by widespread irregularities in the 1996 election and a restructuring in 2000 that guaranteed partisan appointees from the Liberal Party and FSLN.

As a unitary state, Nicaragua is divided into fifteen departments and two autonomous regions (the Atlantico Norte and the Atlantico Sur).

Interest Groups

The Sandinistas were out of political power at the level of the national government from 1991 to2007, but any discussion of interest groups in contemporary Nicaragua must bear a strong input from the Sandinista era. Many of the key sectors and organizations that influence politics in Nicaragua today emerged during the 1980s. Many were originally a part of FSLN structures, but after 1990 they moved to a more independent position. As is true elsewhere in Latin America, the most powerful traditional groups, such as large landowners and large-scale entrepreneurs, did not work through organizations but maintained direct links with the governments of Chamorro, Alemán, and Bolaños.

WOMEN

In the area of women's rights, the gains of the 1980s were numerous, including paid maternity leave; equal access to education; legal equality in relation to divorce, adoption, and parental responsibility; a measure of economic independence; and the inclusion of sex education in the school curriculum. Of course, these gains occurred in the context of a very traditional male-oriented society and with a Sandinista government that often resisted women's demands out of a lack of commitment to women's rights and a deference to the Roman Catholic hierarchy. However, even with those limitations, women had emerged by 1990 as much greater players in Nicaraguan politics and society than ever before.

The gains women achieved during the Sandinista period were undermined in 1990 and after. On the positive side, the legal framework was largely maintained. Successive post-Sandinista regimes and the Catholic Church have sought to restrict the right to unilateral divorce by either party, but so far the Sandinista-era law has been sustained. However, the legal framework put in place by the Sandinistas had many serious limitations for women's rights. Examples of loopholes in the legal code of the revolutionary period included abortion, violence against women, democratization of the family, lack of an equal-pay provision, and protection for gays and lesbians. Despite pressure from some women, abortion was never decriminalized. The Sandinista leadership made it clear that it was unwilling to go against the Catholic Church on this issue. However, during the 1980s, abortion became widely tolerated and few prosecutions occurred. Since 1990, the Managua women's hospital stopped performing therapeutic abortions, and the procedure has been driven entirely underground. The pro-government media presented powerful antiabortion measures, and these dovetailed with the traditional Catholic Church's wider campaign of promoting a more traditional role for women. Nicaragua also took a backward step with the passage of antisodomy laws in 1999. Prior to this measure, Nicaraguan law had been silent on such questions. The conservative framework of laws concerning women and the family allowed the Nicaraguan delegation at the U.N. Population Conference in Cairo in 1994 to line up with the Vatican against the mildly progressive majority document.

Nonetheless, the greater involvement of women in the public life of Nicaragua was an important advance of the 1980s. AMNLAE was one of the strongest mass organizations during the Sandinista years. Women's organizations have lost power since 1990. Indeed, on many fronts, the position of women was under strong attack in Nicaragua. The country's economic crisis bore heavily on women because so many were heads of households and because they bore a disproportionate burden of household production and reproduction. Desperate economic circumstances resulted in a greater occurrence of prostitution. There were a variety of new groups organized around concrete issues such as violence against women and women's health, including abortion.

WORKERS

A significant expansion of workers' rights, especially the right to form unions and engage in collective bargaining, was a definitive achievement of Sandinista power. Prior to 1979, only about 30,000 Nicaraguans (less than 10 percent of the workers) were trade union members, and strikes or even collective bargaining were made virtually impossible by the Somoza regime. By the end of the 1980s, there were more than 2000 workplace unions, with some 55 percent of the working population unionized. New laws enacted by the National Assembly guaranteed the right to strike and collective bargaining. Some trade union rights, including the right to strike, were suspended during the Contra War; but strikes occurred throughout the 1980s. Most labor confrontations were settled through dialogue with the FSLN.

The arrival in power of the Chamorro government in 1990 brought new challenges for the labor movement. The privatization process was not limited to the agricultural sector; state-owned manufacturing, utility, and service industries were also targeted. As in the rural areas, the initial instinct of the union movement was total opposition to privatization, and large demonstrations, including factory occupations, occurred during the summer of 1990. However, divisions within the working class and the absolute commitment of the government led to the privatization process going forward.

The Sandinista-affiliated FNT mobilized often during the Chamorro presidency, mounting big strikes in 1990, 1991, 1992, and 1995. These mobilizations delayed, but did not stop, the government's austerity programs. However, by the end of the Chamorro period, organized labor was worn out. Its decline in influence continued under the Alemán and Bolaños administrations. Today, it maintains a presence in Nicaraguan politics but with a significantly smaller role than during the Sandinista period. The main groups are the FNT, a Sandinista grouping comprised of eight labor unions; the Permanent Congress of Workers (CPT), a grouping of four non-Sandinista labor unions; and the independent Nicaraguan Workers' Council.

BUSINESS

The last 25 years have seen considerable swings in the strength of this traditional interest group. After holding considerable influence during the long years of Somoza family rule, the business community was largely marginalized during the Sandinista years. The influence of COSEP and the business community improved with the election of Chamorro but not as quickly as might have been expected. The election of Alemán in 1996 with Bolaños as vice president completed the business community's return to its former status. The disposition of the property question in 1997 demonstrated that strength. The Alemán-dominated National Assembly passed a new property law that strengthened the position of former owners. With the election of former COSEP head Bolaños to the presidency in 2001, the business organization became even more powerful. However, there is evidence that their power has been weakened under the new Ortega presidency.

RURAL GROUPS

Agrarian reform was at the top of the list of Sandinista achievements because it is often cited as the single most important development of the 1980s in Nicaragua. Nicaragua was primarily an agrarian country. By 1990, the agrarian reform had affected more than half of the country's arable land, benefiting some 60 percent of all rural families. Also by 1990, the majority of farms were in the hands of small- and medium-sized producers, in contrast to the historic maldistribution of land going back to colonial times. Initially, the Sandinista land reform had concentrated on creating a significant state sector for agro-export; but beginning in 1985, much greater emphasis was placed on land distribution to individual *campesinos*. By 1989, the small private producers and the cooperatives were responsible for 47 percent of all agricultural production. The *campesino* sector benefited from the government's policy of easy credit terms and technical assistance along with state-run processing and storage facilities, but heavy-handed government control in the countryside eroded Sandinista support. In one of its final acts in 1990, the outgoing Sandinistaled National Assembly passed laws designed to protect the agrarian reform from its possible dismantling by future governments. While the laws could not make up for 10 years of failure to grant the necessary titles, they provided a legal basis to struggle for the maintenance of this gain.

The large-scale return of former owners, mainly self-exiles who had developed business interests in Miami, led to many confrontations and mobilizations. These mobilizations led to the July 1990 general strike, which demanded the repeal of Decrees 10–90 and 11–90. The FNT received assurances that no further land would be returned, but in reality the government continued its privatization and land-return policies behind the scenes. The ability of the rural union movement to carry out a resolute struggle against the return of lands was undermined by cross-cutting interests. In some instances, farm workers welcomed former landlords, hoping that their return would bring new capital into their farms. In other instances, the government's firmness in moving forward with privatization persuaded some farmers to accept what they thought was the best deal they could get. At the end of the Sandinista period, nearly 12 percent of the country's farmland was state-owned under the rubric of the Area of People's Property (APP). This area declined slowly after 1985 as Sandinista agrarian policy shifted toward the distribution of individual plots, but it remained largely intact and became a key target of the Chamorro counterreform. Many of the 70,000 workers on state farms were affiliated with the Sandinista-led Rural Workers' Association (ACT) and were seen as a significant Sandinista power base to be attacked. The National Union of Farmers and Ranchers (UNAG) emerged from the Sandinista years as one of the strongest and most independent mass organizations but gradually lost power and is now subsumed under the FNT labor umbrella.

Initially, the ACT sought to prevent the privatization process entirely, but it retreated from this position as a result of division within its ranks. Eventually, the union accepted the government's policy with several stipulations. The speed with which this privatization was carried out is demonstrated by the fact that by the end of 1993 the ACT reported that the agricultural APP had been 100 percent privatized. In the face of these policies and pressures, it is not clear how long Nicaragua's relatively democratic distribution of land can be maintained.

ARMED FORCES

Sometimes overlooked in recitations of revolutionary achievements, especially by outside observers, was the elimination of the repressive apparatus of the Somoza regime and its replacement by an army and police force under civilian political control. When the Sandinistas handed over state power in 1990, they left behind army and police institutions imbued with a revolutionary consciousness and insulated from penetration by North American institutions. At the time of the 1990 elections, there were about 96,000 soldiers, and by mid-1994 the number stood at 17,000. The retirement of Humberto Ortega in early 1995 and his replacement by a less controversial Sandinista officer, General Joaquín Cuadra, was hailed by many as a further depoliticizing of the armed forces. Cuadra is from a Nicaraguan oligarchic family and is a cousin of Antonio Lacayo, influential adviser to President Chamorro. By the end of 1995, the Sandinista label had been removed from the organization.

The nature of the strongly Sandinista military changed over time. The army was not absorbed into the framework of U.S. domination, as was true for virtually every other Latin American army except that of Cuba. Nor had it engaged in the systematic human rights abuses so common in Nicaragua's northern neighbors in Central America. Nicaraguan citizens did not have to fear arbitrary death or detention as they did during the Somoza era. The army also remained strictly neutral during the protracted political stalemate between the executive and legislative branches in 1994 and 1995. The professionalism of the army helped defuse the potentially volatile confrontation. In numerous incidents, the army was deployed in labor disputes, especially in the countryside, where it has acted in support of former landowners attempting to recover their land from occupying workers.

The deterioration of the police as a progressive force occurred with even greater speed. The ministry of the interior was renamed the ministry of government, and the Sandinista police became the national police. Chamorro appointee Carlos Hurtado became the new high official, replacing Tomás Borge. New uniforms were issued, and police units in riot gear were commonly deployed in the capital, a departure from the Sandinista era. In 1992, Managua mayor Arnoldo Alemán created a new municipal police force (highly visible in the capital with their red berets). After initial hesitation, the police were used as strikebreakers. In the most dramatic confrontation to date, three people were killed when a force of over 600 antiriot policemen opened fire on protesters in the Managua neighborhood of Villa Progreso during a transportation strike in May 1995. During the 1980s the Sandinista police gained a reputation for honesty and discipline. Much of that reputation is now gone. Bribery and corruption have developed on a widespread basis in the context of the desperate economic situation and low police salaries. Both the military and the police have, however, remained under civilian contron and are not prone to intervention in the political process, as is the case in Guatemala and Honduras.

INDIGENOUS PEOPLE

After initial serious mistakes, the Sandinista government enacted an autonomy statute for Nicaragua's Atlantic coast that is a significant achievement for the rights of the indigenous peoples of the Americas. Nicaragua's Atlantic coast, rich in minerals and other natural resources, had long been exploited with no care for the environment or the non-Hispanic population that lived there. The region encompasses 56 percent of Nicaragua's territory, but with a population of some 350,000, it has less than 10 percent of the population. Roughly two-thirds of the region's people are *mestizo* immigrants who came to the region from the west in search of land. However, the rest of the population is indigenous, with the largest group (75,000) being Miskitos who live in small communities throughout the Atlantic coast region. There are also small communities of Creoles, the name used by descendants of Africans. Initially, the Pacific coast–based Sandinistas continued the same pattern of dominant relations with the Atlantic coast. After serious confrontation with Central Intelligence Agency (CIA)–sponsored Indian rebel groups in the early 1980s, however, the government entered into dialogue with the Atlantic coast residents. This dialogue resulted in a 1987 autonomy statute that guaranteed the rights of the indigenous groups to their own language, culture, and communal forms of land ownership. In addition, the statute recognized the rights of the different groups in regard to the development of natural resources. Also established were regional government assemblies with direct representation from each ethnic group. The statute allowed for the transference of considerable authority to these governments, especially in the areas of taxation and resource development.

Post-Sandinista governments have challenged the autonomy process. Basically, Managua used flanking tactics to undermine the rights of the residents of Nicaragua's Atlantic coast. Rather than seeking any formal reversal of the autonomy statute, the central government simply ignored the law and created its own approach to the region. In April 1990, Chamorro created the Institute for the Development of the Atlantic Coast (INDERA). For 4 years, the meager resources allotted for the coast were channeled through INDERA rather than the regional autonomous councils. The Managua government used INDERA to divide the different coast groups by pitting them against each other. With shifting political alliances, both Atlantic coast regional governments passed motions rejecting INDERA in 1994, and the central government eliminated the agency and proceeded to carry out all programs for the coast through national-level ministries.

The greatest challenges to the coast today are growing environmental destruction and the lack of control over its natural resources—fishing, forestry, and mining. According to the spirit of the autonomy law, control over the coast's resources was to be vested with the regional government bodies. The central government ignored this aspect of the law or used local leaders sympathetic to the central government to conclude deals on the exploitation of resources that are detrimental to the region's interests.

POLITICAL PARTIES

Historically, Nicaraguan politics were largely dominated by two parties, Liberals and Conservatives. The Liberals had their base in the university town of León, with a tenuous link to the ideas of democracy and progress. The Conservatives were based in Grenada and its traditional Catholic values. Their rivalry was fierce, often escalating to civil war. Few, if any, honest elections were conducted prior to 1979. The Somozas captured the Liberal Party. The Conservatives were their main opposition, tolerated only as long as they were no real threat to the family's entrenched power.

As David Close has written, the creation of a competitive political party system came in 1982 when the FSLN-dominated Council of State passed a political parties law. The passage of this law was significant because it moved FSLN away from Leninist principles and opened the legal possibility of a Sandinista electoral defeat. Under the law, the number of parties in Nicaragua grew rapidly, with seven contesting the 1984 election. By 1990 more than thirty parties had been registered, although the election turned into a two-way contest when the parties opposed to the Sandinistas came together under the banner of UNO. After 2000, changes in the electoral laws and pact politics between the PLC and the FSLN reduced the number of parties competing at the national level. By the time of national elections in 2001, the Conservative Party had become so weak that it was able to win only one seat in the National Assembly, clearing the way for Liberal and Sandinista dominance.

FSLN. The FSLN remains the largest and best-organized political party in Nicaragua, and the fruits of that residual organization were demonstred in their 2006 electoral victory. However, the party has changed considerably since its time in power in the 1980s. Since 1990, divisions have reemerged among the Sandinistas, although not along the same lines as in the 1970s. After a bitterly divisive party congress in May 1994, the FSLN broke into two separate political organizations in January 1995 with the departure from the party of several key figures, including former Nicaraguan Vice President Sergio Ramírez. Many prominent intellectuals, including Ernesto and Fernando Cardenal, also left the party. Many of those who left formed the MRS, which was formally launched as a political party at a congress in May 1995. The gulf between those who stayed in the FSLN and the newly formed MRS was quite wide.

During 1992 and 1993, divisions had developed within the party over the political course that the party's National Directorate was pursuing as an opposition party. FSLN leadership pursued a tactical alliance with the Chamorro government. Later, a similar strategy was pursued with the Alemán faction in the National Assembly after he became president. These alliances gave the FSLN no real control but meant that it was seen as bearing some of the responsibility for the dire economic circumstances of the country. In practice, FSLN support for social and economic stability meant that the economic interests of the popular sectors took a back seat in the political priorities of the FSLN. Important elements in the resurgent popular movements, especially the trade unions, showed marked displeasure with the FSLN leadership. This opposition first came into the open in July 1993 with the publication of an open letter signed by twenty-nine prominent Sandinistas that called for the party leadership to distance itself definitively from the Chamorro government and resume close affiliation with the social base of the FSLN, the workers and peasants.

The May 1994 congress represented a solid victory for the Democratic left tendency, which dominated the elections to the new Sandinista Assembly and National Directorate. The congress, however, also laid the groundwork for the split that occurred several months later. The spirit of the congress was deeply divisive and marked by harsh personal attacks. In a seemingly vindictive act, Ramírez was excluded from an expanded National Directorate despite his prominent position in the party and leadership of an obviously important minority grouping. The party was also suffering from the widespread belief, both inside and outside the party, that individual members unfairly benefited from the distribution of goods that occurred during the transition to the Chamorro government (the *Piñata*). Daniel Ortega came to dominate an ossifying party apparatus, consistently engaged in partisan politics within the party, and established himself as the Sandinista *caudillo*. This occurred despite a 1998 scandal involving strong accusations of Ortega's persistent sexual abuse of his stepdaughter, Zoilamérica Narváez. The party's involvement in the *Piñata*, its questionable pacts with the PLC and Alemán, ongoing internal dissension, defections, and the MRS breakaway combined with its loss of moral authority and failure to articulate a credible alternative to the neoliberal economic policies of the government to ensure defeat at the hands of Alemán in the 1996 elections and of Bolaños in 2001. The victory of FSLN candidate Herty Lewites in the 2001 mayoral election in Managua and the FSLN rout of the PLC in the municipal elections in 2004 lifted the party's prospects, and it paved the way for its return to power in the 2006 elections. Benefitting from the failure of the previous administrations of Chamorro, Alemán, and Bolaños to solve the country's social and economic problems, the

Sandinistas returned to power when Daniel Ortega won the presidency with 38 percent of the vote and thirty-eight of eighty-six seats in the National Assembly. The victory was aided by constitutional and political deals with the PLC; the death in early 2006 of Herty Lewites, a potentially strong independent candidate; and the general leftward trend of Latin American voting in the new century. The constitutional deal struck between Ortega and Alemán allowed a candidate to avoid a run-off by getting 35 percent of the vote and a lead of at least 5 percent. Ortega narrowly achieved that threshold in 2006. Demonstrating that the FSLN was just a faint echo of the revolutionary party of the 1970s, the party ran a low-key, uncontroversial, and nonconfrontational campaign. In a particularly opportunistic move just before the election the FSLN courted support from the Catholic Church when it supported a bill banning theraputic abortions, a long-standing practice in Nicaragua.

Liberal Parties. With the disintegration of the anti-Sandinista UNO coalition in the mid-1990s, the liberal PLC emerged as the key anti-Sandinista force. The PLC broke with the official liberal party of the Somozas, the PLN, in the late 1960s over Anastasio Somoza, Jr.'s, decision to assume the presidency in the 1967 elections. It participated as part of the FSLN's opposition in the Council of State but before the mid-1990s was not a significant force. However, solid party-building activities after 1990, previously unused by any party other than the Sandinistas, quickly catapulted the party into a strong position. Its first national presence came with its 1994 victories in the Atlantic coast regional elections.

Although Alemán became the party's central leader and won the presidency in 1996 under the PLC banner, he was not a longtime member. The PLC recruited Alemán, the mayor of Managua under the UNO government, calculating that his reputation as a strong leader who got things done would make him an excellent candidate.

The other strong partner in the Liberal Alliance that contested the 1996 election was the Independent Liberal Party. Founded in 1944 to oppose the continuation of the Somozas in power, this party had strong anti-Somoza credentials and participated in the revolutionary struggle and the first revolutionary government. Its senior leader, Virgilio Godoy, was elected vice president under Violeta Chamorro in 1990, although sharp divisions with the UNO coalition reduced the power of the vice president.

In the 2001 elections, Bolaños became the standard bearer of the PLC, easily defeating Ortega. The combined Liberal Alliance also won a clear majority of fifty-three seats in the National Assembly. As a movement developed for the prosecution of Alemán for his legendary corruption, fissures began to appear amongst the Liberals. By vigorously supporting the eventual trial and imprisonment of Alemán, Bolaños alienated the bulk of the PLC, which sought leniency for their leader. By 2004 the Alemán faction of the PLC had entered a temporary coalition with the Ortega-led Sandinistas to try to force President Bolaños from office. This effort failed but in the process weakened the Liberal Alliance and paved the way for the FSLN victory in 2006.

Conclusion

Nicaragua's future course is yet to be definitively determined, but it should be noted that the conservative forces, strongly aided by the United States, have clearly gained the upper hand in the context of a world situation favorable to their neoliberal program and the continuing failure of the FSLN leadership to provide a coherent alternative. As the new millennium got under way, Nicaragua continued to slide back to many of its traditional ways.

- The great majority of Nicaraguans were living in grinding poverty with little immediate hope of redemption. Nicaragua remained the poorest country in the hemisphere after Haiti.
- Reminiscent of its traditional dependence, Nicaragua was ever more closely tied to the advanced industrial countries of the West as a producer of primary products and recipient of their aid. It had followed State Department, IMF, and World Bank advice to implement neoliberal reforms, only to gain one of the highest per capita debts in the world.
- Starting with the presidential term of Arnoldo Alemán, the country returned to traditional personalistic politics marked by increasing authoritarian tendencies, frequent accusations of blatant favoritism and corruption, and ever more partisan party politics conducted by the political elite.
- Power and personalism were overshadowing government and party institutions. Pacts and political arrangements often defined the rules of political competition and law making more than the courts or constitution.
- Strikes and demonstrations against unpopular policies characterized political life in the 1990s, and the populace displayed high levels of political alienation and disillusionment with political institutions.
- Mass organization and popular mobilizations seemed to be two of the few remaining ways for the masses to meaningfully participate in the political process.
- Liberation theology and the popular (Catholic) Church continued to come under attack from the conservative Catholic Church hierarchy and lost a great deal of their previous influence.

This list was compiled prior to the FSLN's 2006 victory but remains fundamentally accurate. One year into its new term in office, the government has undertaken a few initiatives reflecting its modest electoral promises to the country's majority poor. Its most important program, Zero Hunger, has been slow off the mark. The program has some promise, as it gives real resources like animals and seeds to poor people, but its implementation and ultimate success remain a large question mark. To a remarkable extent Ortega's economic policy is just as neoliberal and pro-IMF as that of Bolaños. This should not be surprising given the Sandinista business sector and Ortega's desire to retain a reasonable climate for foreign investment. To the degree that Ortega's return to power has represented a real shift it is in the foreign policy arena. To date, Ortega has been able to maintain good relations with Washington while joining Chavez's Bolivarian Alternative (ALBA) and welcoming Iranian President Ahmadinejad to Managua. These gestures are more than just revolutionary nostalgia as both Venezuela and Iran have announced significant projects of material aid to Nicaragua. The strong and committed base of local FSLN activists are clearly energized by the return to national power by their party. The party is seeking to harness their power through the newly created CPCs (Councils of Citizen Power). These organs seek to co-opt the power of the independent grass-roots organizations that developed during the 16 years that the FSLN was out of power behind the programs of the new Ortega administration. The new CPCs can give the grassroots organizations direct access to the presidency but in the process their cherished independence is weakened, the classic dilemma for civil society organizations. If this access leads the Sandinista government to real solutions to the country's long-standing problems, Ortega's return to power will be a turning point in Nicaraguan political history, but it is equally possible given the lack of any real checks on presidential power and Ortega's neoliberal tendencies, the FSLN's return to power will be short-lived and unsuccessful in transforming Nicaragua.

Chronology

1522 Spanish reach Nicaragua

1821 Nicaragua becomes independent

1823–1838 Nicaragua becomes part of Central American Federation

1855 William Walker takes over Nicaragua

1908 Marines occupy Bluefields

1912–1924 Marines occupy Nicaragua

1926–1933 Marines again occupy Nicaragua; Sandino leads guerrilla war

1934 Sandino assassinated

1936–1957 Anastasio Somoza dictatorship

1957 Anastasio Somoza assassinated; son Luis becomes president

1961 Sandinista National Liberation Front (FSLN) founded in meeting in Tegucigalpa, Honduras

1967 Anastasio Somoza, Jr., becomes president

1960s FSLN guerrilla fronts repeatedly destroyed, forcing shift to coordinated political and military action

1974 Reemergence of FSLN guerrilla activity with seizure of Somoza associates at a holiday party

1975–1977 Carlos Fonseca Amador killed; FSLN splits into three factions; Insurrectionists (Tercerista faction) shift strategy from rural guerrilla warfare to urban insurrection and broad alliances

1978 FSLN commandos seize National Palace; September insurrection in major cities defeated by National Guard

1979 Reunification of FSLN; final offensive defeats *Somocista* forces and Junta of National Reconstruction (JGRN) takes power on July 19

1980 National literacy crusade; Violeta Chamorro and Alfonso Robelo leave Governing Council of National Reconstruction (JGRN); Council of State, dominated by Sandinista mass organizations, assumes legislative power

1981 U.S. government begins covert financing of ex-National Guardsmen

1982 Nicaraguan government imposes state of emergency after contra attacks

1983 Visit of Pope John Paul II highlights conflict between official Church and revolution; Nicaragua joins Contadora peace process

1984 Elections held; Daniel Ortega elected president, and Sandinistas win 63 percent of the seats in the National Assembly

1985 United States declares economic embargo against Nicaragua

1986 World Court rules that United States is in violation of international law for its support of the contras; National Assembly elaborates new constitution

1987 Constitution approved; National Assembly passes autonomy statute for the regions of the Atlantic coast

1988 Nicaraguan government institutes harsh austerity measures in the face of declining productivity and 36,000 percent inflation; Sapoa agreement is signed between the contras and the Nicaraguan government; Hurricane Joan devastates the country, particularly the Atlantic coast region

1990 Elections are held in Nicaragua, and the final results give 55 percent to the UNO and 41 percent to the FSLN; Violeta Chamorro assumes the presidency; the Nicaraguan Workers' Front (FNT) is formed with 200,000 members

1996 Arnoldo Alemán elected president, defeating Daniel Ortega and the FSLN

1998 Hurricane Mitch hits Nicaragua, causing many deaths and widespread destruction

2001 Enrique Bolaños elected president at head of Liberal Constitutional Party (PLC) for 2002–2007 term, defeating Sandinista candidate Daniel Ortega, 56 percent to 42 percent

2004 Arnoldo Alemán found guilty of corruption and sentenced to 20 years; Sandinistas win vast majority of municipalities in countrywide municipal elections

2006 Daniel Ortega and the FSLN return to power in narrow electoral victory

Bibliography

Black, George. *The Triumph of the People*. London: Zed Books, 1981.

Close, David. *Nicaragua: The Chamorro Years*. Boulder, CO: Lynne Rienner, 1999.

Dye, David R. *Democracy Adrift, Caudillo Politics in Nicaragua*. Cambridge, MA: Hemispheric Initiatives, 2004.

Gilbert, Dennis. *Sandinistas*. Oxford: Blackwell, 1988.

Millett, Richard. *Guardians of the Dynasty*. Mary Knoll, NY: Orbis Books, 1977.

Norsworthy, Kent. *Nicaragua—A Country Guide*. Albuquerque, NM: Inter-Hemispheric Education Resource Center, 1990.

Prevost, Gary, and Harry E. Vanden, eds. *The Undermining of the Sandinista Revolution*. London: Macmillan, 1997.

Robinson, William. *A Faustian Bargain*. Boulder, CO: Westview Press, 1993.

Schoultz, Lars. *Beneath the United States, A History of U.S. Policy Toward Latin America*. Cambridge, MA: Harvard University Press, 1998.

Spalding, Rose. *Capitalists and the Revolution in Nicaragua*. Chapel Hill: University of North Carolina Press, 1995.

Vanden, Harry E., and Gary Prevost. *Democracy and Socialism in Sandinista Nicaragua*. Boulder, CO: Lynne Rienner, 1993.

Vilas, Carlos. *State, Class, and Ethnicity in Nicaragua*. Boulder, CO: Lynne Rienner, 1989.

Walker, Thomas, ed. *Nicaragua without Illusions*. Wilmington, DE: Scholarly Resources, 1997.

——. *Nicaragua: Living in the Shadow of the Eagle*. 4th ed. Boulder, CO: Westview Press, 2001.

FILMS AND VIDEOS

Deadly Embrace: Nicaragua, the World Bank and the International Monetary Fund. United States, 1999. Available through Ashley Eames, Wentworth, NH, 03282.

Fire from the Mountains. United States, 1987.

Nicaragua: From the Ashes. United States, 1982.

Thank God and the Revolution. United States, 1981.

Map of
BOLIVIA

N
W E
S

| 0 | 100 | 200 km |
| 0 | 100 | 200 miles |

Rio Mamore

Riberalta

Cobija

PERU

Lake
Titicaca

Nevado
Sajama

Amazon Basin

Rio Beni

Trinidad

Rio Mamore

★ **LA PAZ**

Cochabamba

Oruro

Santa
Cruz

Sucre

Rio Lauca

Potosi

ATACAMA DESERT

SOUTH
PACIFIC
OCEAN

Tarija

A N D E S

Altiplano

CHILE

66 ARGENTINA

BRAZIL

Puerto
Aguirre

Rio Paraguay

PARAGUAY

60

TWENTY

BOLIVIA

Waltraud Q. Morales

Introduction

Landlocked within the heart of South America and often neglected by policymakers and scholars alike, Bolivia is a microcosm of the formidable challenges and revolutionary changes sweeping across Latin America today. A land of ancient indigenous civilizations and great geographical and social contrasts, Bolivia is one of the most ethnically diverse countries in the hemisphere, and also one of the poorest and least developed. The country has a long tradition of political instability and experienced a major social revolution in 1952 to redress historic oppression and inequities—especially among its majority Indian population. Indeed, the spirit and everyday reality of revolutionary struggle and militancy of its people not only persists today but seems unrivaled in contemporary Latin America. Since 2000, that militancy has erupted numerous times to sweep aside unpopular, and even democratically elected governments, provoking a series of ominous pronouncements by Bolivia watchers: "a crisis of representation," "a failed state," "a second Bolivian Revolution," or "another uncompleted revolution."

In December 2005, the unprecedented election of President Evo Morales Ayma sharply focused the world's attention on Bolivia and the evolving social and political drama. Bolivians and foreign observers alike hoped that the election of Morales, a populist, indigenous leader of the country's Coca Growers' Union, would stabilize the country's shaky government and contain the social turmoil. However, when Bolivia's first democratically elected indigenous president embarked on a revolutionary path of constitutional reform and economic and social redistribution, these hopes faded as confrontations in the Constituent Assembly between Morales's supporters and conservative forces moved to the streets.

Relations with the United States and the new government also deteriorated. Washington policymakers, who had been opposed to Morales's ascendancy from the outset, were dismayed but divided over how to respond. The Bolivian president's rhetoric was stridently anti-American, and Evo—as he was popularly called—embraced leaders on America's blacklist from Venezuela's Hugo Chávez and Cuba's Fidel Castro to Iran's Mamoud Ahmadinejad. However, Morales's election created a dilemma for the United States and its avowed policy of "democratic enlargement" in Latin America and beyond.

With his strong indigenous and activist credentials, Evo Morales represented the historically oppressed ethnic and economic outgroups, which helped elect him by the strongest popular majority in any election to date—unequivocal proof of Bolivian democracy at work. Moreover, his cabinet was more diverse and inclusive in gender, class, and ethnicity than any before. Morales once explained that Bolivia was a multiethnic democracy in theory and that his goal was to make it a reality. If in the face of this democratic mandate, the Bush administration publicly demonstrated antipathy to Morales (as the U.S. Ambassador did in 2002) it would strengthen anti-democratic forces in Bolivia and elsewhere and expose the blatant hypocrisy of U.S. policy.

In many ways the 2005 presidential election was historic. It marked not only an important milestone for indigenous rights in Bolivia and Latin America, but also a political—even revolutionary—turning point for the struggling Andean nation. The election represented a break with entrenched elites and traditional political parties. It reflected the expansion of democracy, and the unprecedented triumph of nontraditional groups and leaders, representing women, citizens of color, and the poor underclass. It also initiated a search for new political and economic models.

Several developments had favored the outcome. Bolivians were fed up with the devastating consequences of economic neoliberalism and Washington-style privatization and globalization. A grassroots anti-globalization movement, which had achieved great momentum after 2000, spearheaded a return to the state-centric economic principles that had inspired the 1952 National Revolution. Moreover, Bolivians were tired of constant U.S. interference in the country's domestic affairs, especially energy and anti-drug policies. In a groundswell, voters reacted by electing a leader whose popularity grew by challenging and defying Washington's agenda. Also, earlier constitutional reforms, which had decentralized political power, had permitted radical, grassroots social movements to participate directly in elections and bring a number of nontraditional candidates—like Morales—to office.

Ultimately, history will record the fate of President Morales and his revolutionary experiment, and whether his election broke the cycle of protest that paralyzed Bolivia since 2003, or brought it to a head. One thing was assured: there was no turning back the clock. Bolivian politics and society would never be the same.

Geopolitical Overview

Bolivians argue that the country is a "prisoner of geography" and victim of adversity—landlocked and reduced by half because of territorial losses since independence. Many Bolivians also believe that this constricted geopolitical status has hindered economic development. Nevertheless, Bolivia is the sixth largest country in Latin America—larger than Texas and California combined or twice the size of France. The country is also extremely diverse in topography and climate zones, ranging from the frigid high Andes and Andean plateau (*Altiplano*) and the temperate intermountain valleys, to the lush, tropical savannahs and forests of the Amazon Basin. Bolivia shares with Peru Lake Titicaca, South America's highest and largest lake. On the *Altiplano* ancient Indian peoples developed hundreds of varieties of potatoes and tended various camelid animals like the llama, alpaca, and vicuña, as do Bolivians today. Lower elevations were rich in fruits and vegetables and served then as now as the country's grainery.

For most of its post-conquest history the Bolivian economy was dependent on rich silver and tin mines of the high *Altiplano* (intermountain plateau) along the western spine of the Andean range. Mining was both a blessing and a curse, creating a persistent monoculture and boom economy that skewed economic development and virtually every other aspect of the country's social and political life. The popular description of Bolivia as "a beggar on a throne of gold" captures the perversity of the extractive monoculture. Mining also ensured the enslavement of Bolivia's majority highland Indian population—Aymara and Quechua peoples—who to this day, despite the near-virtual depletion of the mines and great tin collapse in 1985, continue to eke out a meager livelihood deep in the bowels of the earth. The infamous Cerro Rico of the colonial city of Potosí, which supplied Spain and the industrializing powers of Europe with mountains of silver to mint their coins and feed mercantilist expansion, has been tunneled into Swiss cheese as hazardous excavation and scavenging by poor Indians continues there and in other mines.

During the heyday of the tin era in the first half of the twentieth century, Bolivian tin mines provided 30 percent of the world's annual production. Even today, although production is below 10 percent of exports, mining remains an important, if greatly diminished, economic activity in Bolivia. Indeed the collapse of the tin economy in 1985 and the massive layoffs and mine closures directly led to Bolivia's other boom resource—coca leaf cultivation—and its integration into illegal Andean cocaine production and the global drug trade. Thousands of desperate indigenous and *mestizo* miners migrated to the central and eastern lowlands of the country to cultivate coca leaf. Because of the lack of transportation and other basic infrastructure, coca was the only crop that withstood the long trips to market and commanded a decent price. Soon Bolivian coca was shipped raw or semiprocessed as cocaine paste to the refiners, middle men, and exporters of the Colombian drug cartels. Millions in illicit drug money poured into the country, sustaining the ex-miners and other desperate *campesinos* but also distorting Bolivia's economic development as black markets in foreign currency exchange and consumer goods crowded out the legitimate economy and weakened the control of the state.

As in most of Latin America, wealth and power in Bolivia meant land, which belonged to a handful of landowners, probably less than 2 percent of the post-independence and pre-revolutionary population. The predominantly Indian peoples of the *Altiplano*, inter-Andean valleys, and semitropical and tropical lowlands were largely landless, having been stripped of their communal holdings (or *ayllus*) by the twentieth century. On the eve of the 1952 Revolution, Indian peasants (called *Indios* before the revolution and *campesinos* after) were engaged primarily in agriculture but were basically landless, as some 6 percent of landowners held 92 percent of cultivable land. Despite significant land reform in the decade after 1952, reconcentration of ownership since has generated a powerful Landless Movement (*Movimiento Sin Tierra*, or MST), especially in the *Oriente* or eastern lowlands.

Because the majority of the population originally settled on the *Altiplano*, Bolivia is viewed by much of the world as an Andean and Indian country. However, two-thirds of the country's land mass lies in the semitropical and tropical lowlands or *Oriente*. Migration and economic expansion, especially in the department and city of Santa Cruz, shifted the economic and much of the political power away from the indigenous and *mestizo* populations of the highlands and into the hands of the European-looking lowlanders. Evo Morales's election and reforms directly challenged those interests, and inflamed regional and racist tensions. At the heart of the conflict, however, is economics. Land is very concentrated in the hands of cattle barons and soybean producers, and the expanding hydrocarbon sector, especially natural gas, is located in the lowlands. This region, historically rife with secessionist movements, in many ways represents the other, "white" Bolivia. Nevertheless, the *Oriente* is also home to marginalized indigenous groups that have become politically mobilized in the last two decades through the land reform movement. Despite their regional ties, many lowland Indians see opportunity in Morales's election.

Historically, regionalism was a dominant force because political power inevitably followed economic power. Before the silver boom of the sixteenth century, Sucre—still the constitutional capital of Bolivia today—was the political capital. Later Potosí—the city of silver—became a thriving metropolis and the colony's political and economic center. With the demise of the silver economy and rise of the great tin empires in the nineteenth century, both economic and political power shifted to La Paz—today's de facto capital—but only after a brief civil war in 1898. Similarly, the relocation of Bolivia's economic center to Santa Cruz and its wealth to the *Camba* (lowlander) elites of the *Oriente* has shifted political power away from La Paz. However, the shift is incomplete and is contested by the Kollas or highlanders of the *Altiplano*, especially by President Morales, and the Aymara and Quechua indigenous social movements that he represents.

Early History

From 7500 B.C.E. until 1532 A.D., the pre-Columbian empires of the Tiwanaku, Aymara, and Incan peoples dominated the territory from the Pacific coast to the Andean highlands. Despite the absence of written records, these early indigenous cultures were rich in oral traditions and artifacts. They domesticated the Andean llamas and alpacas and developed a complex agricultural system of farming and grain supply. Of these cultures, the Tiwanakan peoples were the ancestors of the Aymara, the pre-Incan Indians of Bolivia, who had established a vast empire and capital at Tiwanaku. Their cosmology and religion influenced the Incan and other pre-Incan peoples, and their complex social and economic organization was copied by the Incas. The civilization's demise is a mystery—perhaps the result of ecological disaster or conquest. In its place on the *Altiplano* around Lake Titicaca emerged the regional kingdoms of the Aymara.

Around 1460, soldiers of the Quechua empire of the Incas defeated the decentralized Aymaras and, despite numerous rebellions, incorporated them into their Pan-Andean empire of 8 to 10 million inhabitants. The Incan social structure evolved into a rigid pyramid of agriculturally based classes wherein land was held in common through *ayllus* (agricultural cooperatives), and royal monopolies controlled the mines and animal and forest resources. An ancient involuntary labor system, the *mita*, provided the armies of workers and soldiers for the empire. By the sixteenth century, despite its high level of development and relative prosperity, the empire began to decline and assisted by treachery and firepower the Spanish invaders conquered it in 1532.

Colonial Rule (1532–1809)

During the sixteenth century the Spanish established colonial Bolivia's governing center on the mineral-rich *Altiplano,* under the Audiencia of Charcas (Upper Peru) with its administrative seat in Sucre. Mining dominated the colonial economy and established a two-class society of wealthy Spaniards and impoverished Indians. By 1650, Potosí, the Villa Real of Carlos V, was the richest and most populated city of the New World reportedly with 160,000 inhabitants. Mineral exploitation, however, dislocated the indigenous population, distorted the rural economy, and increased class and race inequities. Although there was a caste system under Incan rule, the *encomienda* system of the Spanish overlords destroyed the indigenous way of life and abuses of the *encomienda* and *mita* worsened the exploitation of the indigenous underclass. In the mines hundreds of thousands of Indian slaves perished because of subhuman conditions and disease—perhaps 15 percent in the first 50 years of the colony. On the land, Indians served as the feudal aristocracy's serf labor, their lives determined by their overlord. In 1776, administrative centralization reduced the relative autonomy of the Audiencia of Charcas, and colonial Bolivia reported to the newly established Viceroyalty of Buenos Aires. This reorganization, the French Enlightenment, and the fact that only Spanish-born officials could hold important governing positions and own lucrative properties invited native rebellion. Spanish colonial misgovernment, which had provoked bloody Indian insurgencies in Bolivia in the late eighteenth century, such as the uprising by Túpac Katari in 1780 and 1783, now inspired the *mestizo* and *creole* independence movement.

Independence and Caudillo Rule (1809–1879)

In July 1809, an independence uprising in La Paz, led by Pedro Domingo Murillo, established a popular citizens' council and a governing junta, but was quickly quashed by troops from Lima and a counter-coup in La Paz. However, the next year when the Viceroyalty of La Plata in Buenos Aires rebelled, uprisings erupted throughout Bolivia. Although Bolivian forces fought the Fifteen Years' War, liberation only came after major victories in the rest of Latin America by Generals José de San Martín, Antonio José de Sucre, and Simón Bolívar. Finally in April 1825, at the

Battle of Tumusla, Alto Peruvian independence from Spain was assured. Bolívar never intended an autonomous Alto Perú, however, as competition among post-independence power centers began to interfere with his plans for a united South America, the idea of an independent Bolivia as a buffer state gained favor.

In July 1825 highland patriots assembled to decide their future: independence, incorporation with Lower Peru, or annexation by Argentina. As both Peru and Argentina now supported an independent Alto Perú, the highland delegates had only Bolívar's opposition to overcome. To that end, they named the new country after Bolívar, and made him its first president. The official date of independence of the Republic of Bolívar was August 6, celebrating Bolívar's victory at the Battle of Junín in 1825. However, despite being elected for life, Bolívar served as president for mere months, and soon returned to Gran Colombia to pursue his failing dream of a greater South America.

Bolivia's first constitutionally elected president was Antonio José de Sucre (1826–1828), who struggled to rebuild the war-torn and bankrupt country, but was soon removed when Peru invaded in 1828. Finally in 1829, the election of Andrés de Santa Cruz realized a decade of relative stability and a series of legal, educational, and fiscal reforms. Because Santa Cruz had a Quechua mother who claimed to be the direct descendant of the last Inca ruler, he is considered Bolivia's first *mestizo caudillo*. Santa Cruz dreamed of a greater Peruvian-Bolivian Confederation that would mirror the ancient Incan political system, and briefly unified the two countries in 1836. In so doing he upset the fragile South American status quo; both Argentina and Chile declared war, exiled Santa Cruz, and abolished the confederation in 1839.

Great political turmoil followed as military strongmen or *caudillos* fought over who would rule Bolivia. Finally, in 1848, General Manuel Isidoro Belzú seized the presidency. A *mestizo* with pronounced Indian features, he was affectionately called "Tata Belzu" by the indigenous masses. He was the typical bigger-than-life *caudillo*, terrified of assassination and revolt, but whose populist policies favored the Indians and oppressed classes. Finally, José María Linares became Bolivia's first civilian president in 1854 and pursued sweeping fiscal, administrative, and judicial reforms. He was forced to impose authoritarian rule to thwart the incessant coup plotting; nevertheless, in 1861, General José María de Achá, his Minister of War, overthrew him and became president.

In 1864, Mariano Melgarejo, the most reviled of Bolivia's *mestizo* tyrants whose brutality and corruption earned him the epithet *el caudillo barbaro*, was responsible for the loss of Bolivia's rich Matto Grosso region to Brazil and Atacama province to Chile. His secret deals with Chilean nitrate companies and the 1866 Mejillones Treaty hastened the War of the Pacific. That same year an unpopular land decree seized and sold off communal Indian lands and instigated peasant riots. He was overthrown in 1871 by General Agustín Morales, who annulled the agrarian reform and renegotiated the disastrous agreements.

Finally in 1873, the civilian governments of Adolfo Ballivián and Tomás Frías broke through the military rivalries and attempted to resolve the looming territorial crisis with Chile but were powerless against the hawks in the army and General Hilarión Daza, who seized power. Foolishly underestimating the Chilean threat, in 1878 Bolivia's Congress levied a ten-cent tax on nitrate exports by the British-Chilean Nitrates and Railroad Company of Antofagasta, and provided Chile and allied foreign capitalists the perfect pretext for war.

The War of the Pacific (1879–1884)

More than a territorial dispute, the War of the Pacific of 1879 was the first of several resource wars that dismembered or impoverished Bolivia. Geopolitical rivalry and economic imperialism were two important external causes, but Bolivia's internal instability and regionalism were also to blame. The *Altiplano* remained the country's center of gravity, and the fledgling republic, weakened by revolts and corrupt and inept leaders, failed to exert control over its distant provinces. Until the discovery of fertilizer riches, the Pacific Coast was sparsely settled and ignored by highland governments. The poverty and backward economy also meant there was scant Bolivian capital available to develop the guano and nitrate resources. On the other hand, Chilean entrepreneurs and British commercial interests had formed a partnership and were already engaged in profitable mining and shipping to Europe the natural agricultural fertilizers of Bolivia's Atacama region. Moreover, geopolitically, Chile was a fierce rival of Peru and Argentina and was intent on dominating the Pacific Coast.

The territorial dispute became serious after the discovery of guano and nitrates in 1840. Clashes over competing Chilean and Bolivian claims led to conflict in 1857 and 1863. Bolivia was simply too weak to defend its sovereignty militarily, and so it turned to diplomacy. In 1866 the First Treaty of Limitation between Bolivia and Chile (the Mejillones Treaty) established the boundary at the 24th parallel, and a shared exploitation zone between the 23rd and 25th parallels. A Second Treaty of Limitation in 1874 ended the zones of shared economic exploitation, and, most important, exempted Chilean companies operating in Bolivian territory from any new taxes for the next 25 years.

Unfortunately, in 1878 President Daza implemented a ten-cent tax on each hundred pounds of nitrates exported from Bolivian territory, violating the 1874 Treaty. In response, the British-Chilean Nitrates and Railroad Company of Antofagasta refused to pay the tax, and the Chileans sent a battleship, which seized the Bolivian port of Antofagasta in February 1879. Chile gave Bolivia a 24-hour ultimatum to accept arbitration. When Bolivia refused, Chile occupied the entire Pacific Coast south of the 23rd parallel, and in April 1879 declared war against Bolivia and Peru.

Bolivia's forces were demolished early on; they were unprepared and their leaders were inept and irresponsible. By 1880 Bolivia was spent and Peru was forced to bear the brunt of the war. Finally, in October 1883 Peru signed a separate peace treaty with Chile, ceding a large swath of its coastal territory. Bolivia signed a truce in 1884, which left Chile in de facto possession of all Bolivia's coastal territory. A final peace treaty was not signed until 1904 and even this treaty, as far as Bolivia is concerned, remains in dispute.

In large part, the Pacific War was a natural consequence of growing Chilean hegemony and the aggressive expansion of global capitalism. Nevertheless, Bolivia's misgovernment contributed to the country's defeat. In reaction, civilians took over.

Republican Government (1880–1932)

Civilian rule centered on competing elites and their political parties representing special ethnic and class interests. These civilian politicians were members of a new white and *mestizo* ruling class of silver and tin mining barons and their business associates and remnants of the old landed aristocracy. For 50 years until the Great Depression and Bolivia's tragic involvement in the Chaco War, they relied on a system of limited franchise and control of government by personalist leaders beholden to the mining plutocracy, in effect making Bolivia "a state that tin owned." Despite its serious drawbacks, this ruling system provided the necessary political stability for state formation and economic growth.

Two major political parties developed during the War of the Pacific. The Liberal Party wanted to continue the war and the Conservative Party pressed for a negotiated peace. The Conservatives represented the interests of the silver magnates who dominated Bolivian politics until the Civil War of 1899, which ended the era of the Conservative Party oligarchy and the regional influence of Potosí and Sucre—Bolivia's official capital. The Liberals, victors in the regional clash, were allied with the up-and-coming tin-mining elite and the increasing economic power of the highland industrial and commercial interests in Oruro and La Paz, which became Bolivia's effective capital after the revolt. In addition, Liberals favored secular and federalist rule and Conservatives supported Roman Catholicism and unitary government. However, these differences did not run deep; leaders of both parties represented civilian rule and the predominantly white privileged class. In principle, both parties believed that constitutional government would bring the stability and national unity needed for economic prosperity.

With the franchise limited to less than 5 percent of the population, instability and violence were contained as partisan and electoral disputes replaced military coups. However, representative government remained precarious as Bolivian politicians generally lacked a civic culture of compromise and honest stewardship. Nevertheless, despite the elite infighting and outright electoral manipulation by the ruling party, the opposition could obtain a sizable legislative representation in the early decades of republican rule. After a relatively free election in 1884, the election of 1888 turned violent, and the Conservative Party winner controlled the presidency until the Liberal revolt of 1899. In turn, from 1900 to 1920 the Liberal Party oligarchy monopolized power until a coup by disaffected Liberals, who had founded the new Republican Party and ended the Liberal monopoly.

By 1920 the regional and economic power base that dominated the country until 1952 was firmly in place. Between 1900 and 1927 the world demand for industrial metals—especially tin—reached its zenith. The incredible profits bankrolled Bolivia's big three tin magnates—Carlos Aramayo, Mauricio Hochschild, and Simon Patiño— and their control of the country's economy and government. The Patiño holdings alone provided 50 percent of Bolivia's total tin production. A *mestizo*, "white collar" mine worker, Patiño struck it rich with a small mine in Potosí and consolidated his mining empire buying out British and Chilean mining interests in 1910 and 1924.

The state treasury was so dependent on the low taxes on tin exports that the big three tin barons in effect exerted a virtual veto power over the government. Tin production, which was controlled by the companies and the volatile global market, increased Bolivia's economic dependency. The state promoted free market and free trade policies that benefited and enriched the mining capitalists but contributed to the government's chronic budget deficits. However, the government was in a bind: tin provided essential employment, foreign exchange, and government revenue. Reforms were not only impossible but unthinkable as long as the private tin companies "owned" most politicians and public officials and were protected by the conservative military. This entrenched political-economic control of the tin oligarchy and associated establishment interests was known as *la Rosca*.

The Republican Party's seizure of power in 1920 marked the shift from two-party oligarchic rule to a volatile populist multiparty system. The Republicans soon split into the rival factions of the aristocratic Daniel Salamanca and populist Bautista Saavedra. As president Saavedra (1921–1925) put down labor and Indian unrest; he also indebted Bolivia to Wall Street bankers and encouraged Standard Oil of New Jersey to prospect for oil in the Chaco region. The opposition, including the new Nationalist Party of Hernán Siles, which won the 1925 elections, denounced his policies.

By 1930, the country was in deep economic and political crisis. The U.S. stock market crash a year earlier had precipitated a crash in global tin prices. With the treasury virtually bankrupt and the economy in shambles, the country's dependence on tin became a double-edged sword. In July 1930 President Siles attempted to change the constitution and remain in office, but a bloody citizens' revolt, the "constitutionalist" revolution, removed him. Daniel Salamanca was elected president. In all respects his presidency was a failure. Not only were his domestic policies ineffective and repressive, but his foreign policy was catastrophic. He aggressively expanded Bolivian control over the Chaco region, and escalated a minor border clash with Paraguay into war.

Already by the eve of war, major changes were underway. The 1930 revolt marked a shift in Bolivian politics from palace coups to populist mass action and direct street democracy. The economic depression and the war undermined the political power of the tin oligarchy and made it vulnerable to a populist and nationalist backlash. Most important, the war turned the military against the *Rosca* and its political hegemony.

The Chaco War and the Coming of Revolution (1932–1951)

Bolivia's defeat in the Chaco War created the social and political preconditions for revolution in 1952. The defeat was an unexpected and devastating blow to Bolivian national pride. Bolivians had expected a quick, easy victory over Paraguay, which they considered to be a weaker, third-rate power. As with the War of the Pacific a century earlier, the war was not simply for territory but for resources. The Gran Chaco was largely a sparsely populated wasteland of a quarter of a million square miles in the heart of the continent and the boundary dispute between Bolivia and Paraguay preceded independence. In 1920 rumors of rich oil deposits revived the competition between the two countries, and to this day, many Bolivians believe that foreign oil companies (i.e., Standard Oil and Royal Dutch Shell) had a surreptitious role in the war.

A hawk, President Salamanca surrounded himself with like-minded ultrana-tionalists. He had pilloried his predecessor for cowardice and was obsessed with restoring Bolivia's honor. Despite the economic recession, he sank millions of pesos that Bolivia did not have into armaments, preparing for the right moment to strike against Paraguay. As diplomatic efforts stalled and tensions escalated, on July 18, 1932, Salamanca ordered the army to preemptively seize a strategic water source in the desert-like region. The war had begun. Despite the speeches and parades, the war was not popular; the general staff had warned that the country was not ready and many Bolivians and Paraguayans favored a diplomatic solution. The military's warnings proved prescient as the war bogged down into a litany of defeats. In early 1935 Paraguayan forces had advanced within miles of Bolivia's oil centers and the war's command center. The Bolivians drove them back and recaptured the oil region. With both sides spent, a protocol of peace and cease-fire was signed in June 1935.

Why had Bolivia lost the war when observers (including the Paraguayans) had anticipated its victory? Who was to blame for defeat? Bolivia in 1932 had three times Paraguay's population and seven times its soldiers and outgunned Paraguay by as much as ten to one. From the outset, military and civilian dissension, corruption, and incompetence were to blame. On the eve of war the general staff had resigned in protest because Bolivia was not prepared for war. There had been four commanders in 3 years, and three armies were destroyed in the field; in the middle of the war, the army mutinied and arrested the president. Defeat was costly. Over 100,000 men had died on both sides and both countries were crippled with massive national debts. However, for Bolivia the social and political consequences of the Chaco defeat were revolutionary. The war and defeat were catalysts for fundamental social change that swept away the tin oligarchy and the traditional political class and began the grad-ual integration of Bolivia's indigenous peoples into national life. War and defeat created both the psychological and structural conditions for radical change.

In the post-war period, an anti-establishment political coalition emerged com-posed of veterans, labor unions, peasant syndicates, and student activists, led by two populist military reformers, Colonels David Toro and Germán Busch. Fore-most, the military reformers were nationalists who also stood for social justice, economic development, and popular participation. Anti-imperialism united them; they rejected the stranglehold of foreign capital and the tin *Rosca* on Bolivia. They were harbingers of the 1952 Revolution. In 1936 Toro and Busch, who believed that Bolivia's problems could *not* be solved within the traditional political system but instead were the direct consequences of that system, preempted the May elections with a military coup. As president of a civilian-military junta, Toro promised to defend the interests of workers and veterans, reduce poverty, and restore Bolivia's economic sovereignty. His government operated under a vague rubric of socialism and had formed an alliance with old-style Republican Socialists and a new Social-ist Party of syndicalist and Marxist persuasions. The mix was highly volatile and it disturbed Busch.

Fearing a coup against him, Toro made a bold move: he nationalized the U.S.-owned Standard Oil of Bolivia. The 1937 expropriation was the first seizure of a U.S. company in Latin America, predating by a year the Mexican nationalization. It was immensely popular: Standard Oil had come to represent all the evils of imperialism.

Toro and Busch favored nationalist and corporatist economic policies and rejected the special privileges of the tin interests and foreign investors. They were soon under attack by conservatives and radicals alike. As partisan dissension increased, Busch overthrew Toro in July 1937, but upheld the nationalization. He institutionalized the reforms of the 1936 Revolution through a constitutional convention, which elected him president in May 1938, and began to draft a new constitution. For the first time, the political left took part. The 1938 Constitution was radical and progressive. It established the social function of private property and state control over the economy. An educational reform promised free, universal education, and indigenous schools and the 1939 Bush Labor Code granted the right to unionize and strike, and improved working conditions. However, unable to control the political turmoil that the reforms unleashed, in April 1939 Busch assumed dictatorial powers. Before his suicide in 1939, he nationalized the Mining Bank and secured the state's right over the nation's mineral wealth. In the end the Toro and Busch constitutional reforms were beaten back by political chaos and polarization between the forces of financial privilege and radical extremism—a valuable lesson for later reformers and revolutionaries alike. The military alone was unable to impose social change without the support of civil society, which was deeply divided. Most turmoil was the consequence of the post-war mobilization of radical social movements and political parties, and the resistance of the oligarchy and its *políticos* to their loss of influence to this new class of political actors. The war had discredited the traditional parties, allowing anti-establishment nationalist and Marxist parties to emerge.

As the party of the 1952 Revolution, the Nationalist Revolutionary Movement (*Movimiento Revolucionario Nacionalista*, or MNR) was the most important nationalist party. Although the MNR had ties to supporters of Toro and Busch, the party was not formed until 1941. Its middle-class founders were student activists, war veterans, and journalists who denounced imperialism and the *Rosca* as the foreign and class enemies of the people. Led by Víctor Paz Estenssoro—Bolivia's first revolutionary president—the MNR program emphasized its patriotic, socialist, revolutionary, and nationalist character. A central goal was economic independence. Another nationalist party, the Bolivian Socialist Falange (*Falange Socialista Boliviana*, or FSB) was founded in 1937 and survived several decades after 1952 as the only organized opposition to the MNR. Influenced by Spanish fascism, the party was fundamentally anti-communist and elitist.

Several Marxist parties were also founded in the 1930s and 1940s but lost importance after the revolution. The Party of the Revolutionary Left (*Partido de la Izquierda Revolucionaria*, or PIR) had antecedents in the leftist student and workers' movements but its leaders were suspicious of the MNR, and mistakenly allied with the oligarchy in the 1940s. Of parties on the left, the PIR was more moderate and mirrored the MNR, proposing a multiclass, nationalist bourgeois revolution. Its program called for a statist economy, agrarian reform, and nationalization of mining and petroleum resources. Despite its base in the radical labor movement, notably the influential Confederation of Bolivian Workers (COB), the PRI was a bankrupt party by 1950.

The Revolutionary Workers' Party (*Partido Obrero Revolucionario*, or POR), also developed from the socialist left of the 1920s (and became affiliated with Leon Trotsky's

Fourth International), but was more radical than the PIR. Its leader, Tristán Marof, provided the historic phrase—mines to the state, land to the Indian—that became the fighting words of the 1952 Revolution. Despite its name, the Revolutionary Workers' Party appealed primarily to university students and middle-class Marxist intellectuals. Unfortunately, the POR was split into two factions. One group espoused a populist synthesis of Marxism and indigenism akin to the Peruvian Marxist, José Carlos Mariátegui. The second group agitated for a Leninist revolution by a vanguard party of the proletariat, and creation of a socialist state of workers and peasants. The POR became the party of the Bolivian Mine Workers' Federation (*Federación Sindical de Trabajadores Mineros de Bolivia,* or FSTMB) that was founded in 1944.

Threatened by the post-war radicalism, the oligarchy formed a coalition of the traditional parties, propertied classes, and conservative military and began to systematically dismantle the Busch reforms. In 1940 the oligarchy's candidate and popular war hero, General Enrique Peñaranda, won the presidency handily, although indicative of the changing times the leftist PIR candidate received an unprecedented 17 percent of the vote. Peñaranda's government established close relations with the United States and received substantial economic and military assistance. With war in the Pacific interrupting U.S. access to tin, Bolivia became the major supplier; as a result U.S. influence over Bolivia's internal affairs increased. The conservative government renewed debt payments (suspended since 1931) to American banks, signed a tin agreement on terms favorable to the United States, and indemnified Standard Oil for the expropriation of its properties.

These policies inflamed the opposition. As dissension in Congress and labor unrest increased, the government declared martial law and cracked down on the MNR and strikers. In December 1942 a massacre at the Catavi Mine left hundreds of striking miners dead. Such repression forged an alliance among the miners, labor, the MNR, and the reformist military. In December 1943 Lieutenant Colonel Gualberto Villarroel overthrew Peñaranda and was elected president in August 1944. The new government included the MNR and younger officers of the nationalistic military lodge. The United States and the oligarchy denounced Villarroel's government as "Nazi," and indeed the reformers were ideologically divided and confused by rightist socialist and leftist tendencies. The common denominator, however, was nationalism and anti-imperialism. The government stood on the side of the dispossessed—miners, labor, and the indigenous peoples. Villarroel held the first Indian Congress in 1945 that abolished involuntary servitude. Although the reform was not enforced, it provided hope and momentum to the indigenous movement.

The oligarchy instigated an uprising in July 1946. A mob attacked the presidential palace, murdered Villarroel, and hung his body from a lamppost in the main plaza. For the next 6 years the oligarchy and conservative military repressed all political and social opposition. In 1949 a Catavi mine massacre left several hundred striking miners dead, and a brief MNR-led civil war ended violently. However, in May 1951 the MNR presidential candidate, Víctor Paz Estenssoro, ran from exile and won a plurality. Before the National Congress could decide the outcome, the oligarchy handed the government to the military, which annulled the elections, and appointed a general as interim president. These unconstitutional actions, culminating two decades of frustrated reforms, prompted a revolutionary uprising.

From Revolution to Military Dictatorship (1952–1982)

The Bolivian Revolution began with the Battle of La Paz on April 9, 1952. The revolt by the MNR and workers and miners was aided by the city's police force that provided the rebels with arms. After 3 days of heavy fighting the urban rebellion triumphed and Víctor Paz Estenssoro returned from exile and was sworn in as president on April 16. As Latin America's second social revolution since the Mexican Revolution, the Bolivian Revolution initiated radical political and socioeconomic change. Among the revolution's major reforms were universal suffrage and education, land reform, nationalization of the mines, and incorporation of the Indian into national life. By abolishing literacy tests, the 1952 voting law established real democracy for the first time as the number of eligible voters quintupled to a million voters. Most of these were illiterate indigenous peoples, who were 60 percent of the population and had never been accorded full citizenship rights. In 1951 a mere 5 percent of Bolivians voted; in 1960 this figure had risen to 26 percent. To win elections, political parties would now have to appeal to an increased and more diverse electorate.

The 1953 Agrarian Reform Decree abolished feudal debt servitude and restored the collective properties of indigenous communities. However, because the MNR had delayed enactment, the reform legalized earlier seizures by indigenous peasants and confiscated only large estates. Nevertheless, land reform broke the hold of the landed aristocracy and helped empower the Indian. In 1952 land ownership was highly inequitable: some 5 percent of landowners held over 90 percent of the land. Of over 70 percent of Bolivians in agriculture, most were indigenous peasants who were largely landless.

The 1952 Act of Bolivia's Economic Independence nationalized major mining enterprises and created the state Bolivian Mining Corporation (*Corporación Minera de Bolivia*, or COMIBOL). The state now controlled most of the country's tin production and foreign exchange earnings, and although the economic impact was huge, the benefits to the government and people of Bolivia were less than anticipated. First, to gain diplomatic recognition and economic assistance from the United States, the MNR government (against the opposition of the radical labor sector of the party) compensated the tin barons at a significant loss to the treasury. Second, by 1952 the private mines were aging and had limited production and capitalization so that in effect, the state assumed additional expenses and liabilities. Finally, Bolivia was in an economic crisis because of the drastic cuts in the U.S. tin quota. On the other hand, U.S. aid to Bolivia, among the most generous in the region, was conditional and served to control and moderate the revolution. For example, the government's new Petroleum Code privileged U.S. corporate investment over the Bolivian State Petroleum Enterprise. U.S. aid was also linked to the draconian stabilization program imposed by the International Monetary Fund (IMF) in 1956 to control the crippling inflation. Thus, despite revolutionary rhetoric, MNR policies could not achieve the country's economic independence.

Despite opponents' charges of communism, the revolution was primarily nationalist and led by a middle-class party. MNR leaders had forged a multiclass coalition of intellectuals, students, miners, workers, and peasants; indeed Víctor Paz

Estenssoro had argued that a Bolivian revolution would succeed only by a broad alliance of classes. However, the party's ideological and class diversity—an asset in making the revolution—became a liability once in power. The MNR's original program of national autonomy and economic development was moderate and purposely vague, but the alliance with workers and miners and the struggle for power radicalized the party. Nevertheless, as the government's revolutionary legislation transformed the landscape of traditional Bolivia, the MNR became more divided between moderate and radical wings.

Influenced by the Mexican model, the MNR attempted to institutionalize the revolution by a corporatist system of party control over civil society and the military. The MNR government created a new military loyal to the party and co-opted national peasant and labor unions. To control the powerful labor movement, the MNR formed the Bolivian Labor Central (*Central Obrero Boliviano*, or COB) and affiliated labor with the MNR, including the largest union of mine workers, the FSTMB. Although the leftist MNR labor leader Juan Lechín headed both unions, the party's hold over labor remained partial. Not only was the proletarian left at odds with the MNR's mainstream, middle-class orientation, but also labor zealously guarded its autonomy.

In the rural sector the MNR government founded the National Peasant Confederation (*Confederación Nacional de Trabajadores Campesinos de Bolivia*, or CNTCB). Nevertheless, indigenous peasant leaders were suspicious of political parties and despite MNR affiliation, peasant organizations could not always be controlled. Instead, as with labor, the MNR tended to exert its influence indirectly and contain the potentially powerful indigenous movement by manipulating internal leadership and factional struggles. This divisive governing strategy, rather than providing a loyal base for the MNR government, split the party. During the presidency of Hernán Siles Zuazo (1956–1960) the party's ruling coalition was fragmented further as the government turned against labor interests and used the military to quell peasant unrest.

Already before 1960, the MNR, composed of three factions—the pragmatic reformers of Víctor Paz Estenssoro, the conservative nationalists of Hernán Siles, and the proletarian left of Juan Lechín—was unraveling as sectors split off and formed independent parties. A governing pact had promised each leader a presidential term but the pact was broken when Paz Estenssoro was re-elected in 1960 and 1964, ironically to reduce party dissension and maintain U.S. support. By 1964 with only the Paz Estenssoro wing of the original MNR remaining, the party's failure to unite Bolivian society and to institutionalize the revolution invited a military counterrevolution.

A junta of officers of the reorganized army and Air Force General René Barrientos Ortuño removed Paz Estenssoro. A key motivation behind the coup was the need for social order; days earlier the army had clashed with striking miners, students, and teachers. Barrientos, in a populist, charismatic style not unlike that of Evo Morales, cultivated the Quechua indigenous leaders of his native Cochabamba, and justified the military takeover as a restoration of the revolution. In 1966 Barrientos was elected president with the help of his new Military-Campesino Pact. This alliance gave him (and subsequent military presidents) the ability to control civil society, especially the miners and proletarian left, and impede the return of civilian democratic rule. Although Barrientos preserved major reforms, he pursued conservative and repressive policies. Military takeovers and bloody confrontations in the mines and military administration of the unions "disciplined" labor. A new investment code and pro-business climate favored U.S. corporations and the new homegrown moneyed elite. The military institution, imbued with U.S. counterinsurgency training, viewed any political opposition as communist subversion. This was the political and social climate when Ernesto "Ché" Guevara launched his guerrilla *foco* experiment in Bolivia in 1967.

Ché Guevara misunderstood the Bolivian reality and miscalculated the opposition to Barrientos. As a result his attempt to spark a popular insurgency in Bolivia that would provoke an aggressive, Vietnam-style U.S. military intervention and incite a continental-wide revolution failed. The clandestine guerrilla front established in Bolivia's inaccessible and isolated southeastern jungles never generated more than a handful of recruits or the curiosity of local inhabitants. An effective counterinsurgency effort among the Bolivian military and the U.S. military and CIA ended in Guevara's capture and death in October 1967. This was Barrientos' finest hour; subsequently his hold on the government slipped and he died unexpectedly in a helicopter crash in 1969.

After his death a brief civilian interregnum was cut short by General Alfredo Ovando Candia, a nationalist reformer intrigued by the Peruvian military model of "revolution from above." Ovando organized a civilian-military cabinet of the "national left" and reversed the policies of Barrientos. Labor unions were permitted to reorganize, miners' wages were increased, and civil liberties were restored. However, because the leftist ruling coalition of progressive military and young civilian reformers was unstable and lacked broad support, social unrest increased. In a popular move in October 1969 Ovando nationalized the installations of U.S. Gulf Oil, which had paid close to $2 million to the Barrientos government for special concession in oil and gas production. Gulf (and the major oil producers) retaliated with a boycott of Bolivian crude, causing the Ovando government to lose $14 million in revenues. In turn, the United States severely reduced economic aid. In September 1970, a besieged Ovando promised Gulf Oil $78 million in compensation.

A month later General Juan José Torres seized power and forged ahead with his military-led revolutionary populism. Torres welcomed a Popular Assembly of progressive and Marxist parties and social movements, which debated and enacted revolutionary policies. As the country became more ideologically polarized, direct action by students and property seizures by workers and peasants contributed to rising instability and violence. Finally in August 1971, the conservative military and Hugo Banzer Suárez, supported by the regional business interests in Santa Cruz, cut short Torres' radical experiment.

President Banzer patterned his elitist and authoritarian rule—a Bolivian-style bureaucratic authoritarianism—on that of the Brazilian military and its brand of repressive order and progress. Banzer's policies protected the newly prosperous middle class and economic elite of the Media Luna (southeastern lowlands, especially Santa Cruz) whose interests in mining, import–export, petroleum, and agribusiness fueled economic growth, but he repressed labor, peasants, students, and most political parties. By 1974 he dispensed with democratic pretense altogether and in an *auto-golpe* established a personalist dictatorship. Banzer's neoliberal economic policies welcomed foreign investors with generous investment laws; a new Petroleum Code brought new exploration by a number of U.S. oil companies. Foreign banks provided hefty loans and the U.S. government tripled the level of military and economic assistance.

However, by 1977 the political pressure for a return to civilian government was intense. There were major demonstrations around the country and a hunger strike in the main cathedral of La Paz. Relations with Washington soured as the Carter administration championed democracy and human rights. When an economic crisis compounded the unrest, Banzer was forced to promise elections and move up the electoral timetable. Despite high expectations, the three elections held between 1978 and 1980 were sullied by fraud and military intervention. In August 1979 international dignitaries invited to the swearing in of the first civilian president elected in over a decade were disappointed when the Bolivian Congress could not decide. After an interim president was sworn in, the military removed him within months. In another interim appointment in November 1979 Lidia Gueiler Tejada, president of the Chamber of Deputies, briefly served as Bolivia's first woman president. She narrowly escaped an assassination attempt intended to derail upcoming elections. Nevertheless, the 1980 elections went forward and Hernán Siles received 39 percent of the vote. However, because he lacked an absolute majority, a run-off vote was to be held in the Congress.

Instead General Luis García Meza, the infamous cocaine general, seized power. Bolivia became known as the country that cocaine bought. An admirer of Chilean dictator Augusto Pinochet, García Meza justified the violation of civil liberties and brutal repression as a battle against Bolivia's "Marxist cancer." Every sector of civil society was victimized as hundreds were killed during the military's yearlong rampage. Moreover, García Meza and his Minister of Interior were close to major drug cartels. Bolivia became an international pariah as the United States and Latin American governments refused to recognize the rogue regime. In a cosmetic move in August 1981 the military high command forced out García Meza and normalized relations with the United States. However, the musical chairs of generals continued over the next 14 months. As demonstrations, road blockages, and general strikes immobilized the country, the military turned to Congress, which revalidated the 1980 elections. Four chaotic years and nine presidents later, in October 1982 Hernán Siles took office.

Transition to Democratic Rule

After 18 years of militarism the expectations for democracy were unrealistic. The populist program of Siles was unable to resolve the severe economic crisis or contain the political and social instability. The civilian government had inherited a $5 billion foreign debt and insufficient resources to make even the interest payments. In 1984 an IMF stabilization program and neoliberal policies to control rampant inflation imposed such hardship that close to 2 million Bolivians faced starvation. Under these extreme economic conditions, Siles was unable to contain Bolivia's militant labor movement and maintain democratic rule. Political parties and their infighting were also to blame for the mixture of instability and stalemate. Conservative parties controlled Congress and opposed the government's progressive legislation, forcing Siles to rule by executive decree. Parties on the left, including the government's ruling coalition, were also dissatisfied and agitated for more radical measures and a greater share of political spoils. Vice President Jaime Paz Zamora often clashed with Siles; there were rumors that he and factions in the military were conspiring to unseat the president. Two army colonels linked to drug activity attempted a "cocaine coup" to forestall the government's investigation into the military–drug connection. In June 1984 Siles was kidnapped and held by the elite anti-narcotics force until the American ambassador intervened.

Thus the return to democracy proved chaotic and precarious. During the 3 years of the Siles presidency (1982–1985) political crises, coup plots, and general strikes paralyzed the country. Indicative of the chronic governing instability, there were some six cabinets and seventy-five ministers in that brief time. By late 1984, fearing imminent military intervention and anxious to preserve civilian rule, Siles agreed to early elections. Thus in an ironic twist of fate in August 1985 Víctor Paz Estenssoro, who had presided over the 1952 Revolution, was in office to roll back its key policies. His solution to the national crisis was "democracy with authority," or a strong dose of repression and counterrevolution. Paz Estenssoro and his Historic-MNR party narrowly defeated former dictator Hugo Banzer and his right-wing party (National Democratic Action, ADN). Although Banzer received the most popular votes, there was no majority. In the horse-trading in Congress, the votes of leftist deputies proved decisive and Paz Estenssoro was elected because their animosity toward Banzer was greater than their dislike of Paz Estenssoro.

Learning from the mistakes Siles had made, Paz Estenssoro engineered a governing pact, appointed ministers based on political expediency, and ruled by executive decree. His second Planning Minister, Gonzalo Sánchez de Lozada, was a prominent mining entrepreneur and the key economic adviser behind the draconian New Economic Policy (*Nueva Política Económica*, NPE). This neoliberal austerity program drastically reduced the workforce in the mines and bureaucracy, devalued the peso, and held the line on wages. The economy was in severe recession because of astronomical levels of inflation and the crash in the world tin market in 1985. The government shut eleven state mines and fired more than 13,000 miners. When Bolivia's workers resisted with a national strike Paz Estenssoro imposed martial law and arrested and exiled hundreds of union leaders.

Paz Estenssoro's "Pact for Democracy" between the major parties, the MNR and ADN, guaranteed him the political leverage and legislative majority to exert control. However, as the 1989 election neared, the MNR terminated the pact, forcing Paz Estenssoro to govern by states of siege. Despite improvements in inflation and international credit, the NPE was a partial solution that increased social inequities and exposed the contradiction inherent in democracy with authority.

Political pundits caricatured the major contenders in the May 1989 elections as the "three look alikes." There was Hugo Banzer of the ADN, who had narrowly lost the last election. The MNR put up Sánchez de Lozada, nicknamed "Goni" and mocked for his gringo Spanish. He had been raised in the United States and graduated from the University of Chicago, where he had acquired his free market fervor. The third presidential hopeful was Jaime Paz Zamora, former vice president and leader of the Leftist Revolutionary Movement or MIR party. The economy rather than human rights and drug trafficking dominated the campaign, and voters, nostalgic for the economic growth during Banzer's dictatorship, rationalized away its abuses. Thus, Banzer was predicted to win. Although both Sánchez de Lozada and Banzer each garnered 23 percent of the vote and Paz Zamora only 20 percent, a deal in Congress between former enemies gave the presidency to Paz Zamora. The MIR–ADN pact created a National Unity government that divvied up the ministries between the two parties.

Paz Zamora's policies were more of the same: neoliberal austerity and martial law to contain strikes and demonstrations. Despite his rhetoric, the political style of Paz Zamora was not very different from that of his uncle, Víctor Paz Estenssoro; both had replaced revolutionary populism with hard-line pragmatism. Minimally, these conservative policies consolidated civilian government at the expense of popular democracy but at the same time provided a degree of stability necessary for renewed economic growth.

Was the era of the old-style revolutionary populism, which had dominated Bolivian politics since the Chaco War, irrevocably over? Had Bolivian politics shed its ideological passion and gravitated to the center? Or would a new populism arise to challenge the political accommodation and revive the revolutionary tradition? In large part, a new populism was in the making. After economic "rationalization" by two pseudo-democratic administrations, the militant Bolivian labor and miners movements had largely been subdued and replaced by grassroots indigenous and coca leaf growers' organizations. These movements posed a formidable challenge to the conservative political establishment.

Prodded by the United States, the administrations of Víctor Paz Estenssoro and Paz Zamora (as well as three subsequent governments) enacted aggressive anti-narcotics policies. Domestic legislation and the 1990 Andean Initiative sought to limit the cultivation of the coca leaf and control its distribution, threatening the livelihood of traditional coca growers and recent highland entrants who became integrated into the illegal coca paste and cocaine production networks of the Andean drug cartels. Despite increased external pressure and anti-narcotics assistance that militarized the Andean drug war in the late 1980s, the majority of Bolivians viewed drugs primarily as a U.S. problem and as one of demand rather than supply. The Paz Zamora government took this position publicly and attempted to diffuse international opprobrium with the mantra that "coca is not cocaine," and to emphasize a development over policing strategy with the "Coca for Development" campaign.

However, until the progressive power consolidation of the Cochabamba Coca Growers' Confederation in the 1990s, which culminated in the election of Evo Morales, the confederation's leader, as president, the pro-coca campaign had limited political impact. The hard-line anti-drug and neoliberal economic policies of the administrations of Sánchez de Lozada and Hugo Banzer were partly to blame. Between 1993 and 1997 President Sánchez de Lozada and the MNR technocrats enacted constitutional and economic reforms that rolled back the few remaining vestiges of the revolution. Major state enterprises, including mining and petroleum, were privatized. Although Víctor Hugo Cárdenas, an Aymara Indian, served as vice president, Bolivia's indigenous citizens had less rather than more political influence.

The government of Hugo Banzer (1997–2001) tightened these policies with an extensive forcible coca eradication program and economic austerity that further incited the coca growers and worker–peasant unions in the highland and tropical regions of the country. Both governments applied repressive policing to control the mounting strikes and demonstrations, especially in 1999, a year that had the lowest economic growth in a decade. By 2000 the political temperature had reached a boiling point. Nevertheless, the United States and international aid agencies hailed Bolivia as a "miracle" of economic stabilization and coca eradication. The IMF and World Bank granted Bolivia over $1 billion in debt forgiveness and Banzer's "Zero Coca" campaign reduced the traditional crop to the lowest level in decades. Then in 2000 a corruption and drug trafficking scandal and violent protests in Cochabamba against water privatization, the first "Water War," shook the Banzer government. The old dictator, dying of cancer, turned over the government to his vice president, Jorge Quiroga Ramírez.

The young U.S.-educated technocrat, however, was unable to calm the political and social unrest. Cochabamba erupted again in violent demonstrations and clashes with the military in the second Water War against the government's water privatization contract with the multinational corporation, Bechtel. Most Bolivians viewed water as a natural birthright and resisted the staggering increase in rates. At the same time the daily protests and roadblocks by peasant coca growers in the Chapare and Yungas regions escalated. Violent clashes between the military and growers finally forced Quiroga to suspend coca-leaf eradication and the controls on its marketing.

These social movements, although important in themselves, were also symbolic of the mounting frustration and resistance to the counterrevolutionary policies under civilian and semidemocratic governments since 1982. In particular, Bolivia's indigenous majority rejected the privatization (Law of Capitalization) and globalization agenda of the country's technocratic and westernized political class, which seemed to benefit them and the foreign corporations more than the popular classes. The 1994 and 1995 constitutional reforms (Law of Popular Participation and Law of Administrative Decentralization, respectively), which had emphasized the nation's multiethnic and pluricultural character, decentralized its administrative structure and provided more economic and political resources to more than 300 newly created municipalities, local communities, and regional governments. By giving indigenous civil society more opportunities for participation, these measures further mobilized and empowered the indigenous movement, which was then in a unique position to challenge the political establishment in the 2002 and 2005 presidential elections.

Indigenous Resurgence and Populist Democracy

In the decades after the revolution, Bolivia's peasant unions served as the vehicle for indigenous organization. Founded in the late 1970s, the Confederation of Peasant Unions (*Confederación Sindical Única de Trabajadores Campesinos de Bolivia*, or CSUTCB), was headed until 1988 by Genaro Flores, the Aymara leader of the indigenist party, the Túpac Katari Revolutionary Liberation Movement. Resistance to the drug war and neoliberalism radicalized and unified peasants and indigenous groups, which used direct action tactics—strategic roadblocks, property seizures, hunger strikes, mass rallies, marches and "chew-ins" of the sacred coca leaf—to undermine and topple civilian governments.

CIVIC ASSOCIATIONS AND INDIGENOUS PEOPLES

Since 1994 and especially since 2000, grassroots associations and social movements have proliferated in Bolivia and achieved unprecedented political clout. The 1994 Law of Popular Participation and the 1994 Law of Civic Associations and Indigenous Peoples permitted associations of native and indigenous peoples, traditional communities (*ayllus* and *markas*), civic associations, and local neighborhood committees to participate in the electoral process directly without the mediation of political parties. Candidates of these associations could run for election to the presidency, congress, mayoral offices, and constituent assemblies. The law also provided that 50 percent of seats for popular associations be reserved for women.

The result has been the grassroots empowerment of a host of specialized interests and social movements, and the decline of traditional political parties and rise of new ones formed out of previous civic associations and indigenous groups. For example the second most important party in government in 2005 is PODEMOS, which arose in 2004 from the political alliance Alianza Siglo XXI, and successfully ran in recent elections. For the first time in 2004 more than 600 citizens associations were organized to compete in municipal elections; of these 344 were legally recognized by the Electoral Court and actually participated in the electoral process. Similarly, the native organizations (*organizaciones originarias*) of indigenous peoples have been recognized by the Electoral Court which has made special allowances for traditional customs if written language is not used. In the 2004 municipal elections, sixty-five candidates represented indigenous peoples organizations. In 2005 hundreds of civic and indigenous organizations played an increasingly influential role in the first direct elections for departmental prefects (state governors).

MAJOR INTEREST GROUPS AND SOCIAL MOVEMENTS

Since the 1952 Revolution and especially after the return to democratic government in 1982, interest group representation and radical, grassroots social movements have extended into the areas of human rights, indigenous concerns and cultural rights, student organizations, and women's committees, as well as the traditional organizations representing peasants, unions, business, agricultural, industrial, and commercial interests. Especially dominant since 2000 have been anti-globalization social movements, the coca growers' federations, the indigenous peoples' organizations of both the highlands and tropics, and the various autonomy movements of native peoples and departmental civic associations. Some of the more prominent include the following.

- Aid for Peasants-Indigenous of the Oriente, Apoyo para el Campesino-Indígena del Oriente Boliviano (APCOB)
- Assembly of Guaraní People, Asamblea del Pueblo Guaraní (APG): Promotes land and citizenship rights for lowland Indians
- Assembly for Peoples' Sovereignty, Asamblea por la Soberanía de los Pueblos (ASP): Peasant and indigenous organization opposed to privatization and transnationalism
- Bolivian Confederation of Indigenous Peoples of the Oriente, Confederación Indígena del Oriente, Chaco y Amazonía de Bolivia: Also before 1989, Central Indígena de Pueblos y Comunidades Indígenas del Oriente Boliviano (CIDOB)

- Bolivian Confederation of Private Entrepreneurs, Confederación de Empresarios Privados de Bolivia (CEPB): Conservative business association with national and regional branches
- Bolivian Permanent Assembly of Human Rights, Asamblea Permanente de Derechos Humanos de Bolivia (APDHB)
- Bolivian Workers Central, Central Obrero Boliviano (COB): One of the oldest unions
- Bolivian Mine Workers' Federation, Federación Sindical de Trabajadores Mineros de Bolivia (FSTMB): One of the most militant workers' unions but largely inactive today
- Center of Indigenous Peoples of Beni, Central de Pueblos Indígenas del Beni (CIDOB)
- Confederation of Colonists of Bolivia, Confederación Sindical de Colonizadores de Bolivia (CSCB): Pro-indigenist and land movement
- Confederation of Peasant Unions of Bolivia, Confederación Sindical Única de Trajajadores Campesinos de Bolivia (CSUTCB)
- Coordinator of Water and Life, Coordinadora de Agua y Vida (same as next)
- Coordinating Committee in Defense of Water, Coordinadora en Defensa del Agua: Led by Oscar Olivera of the Cochabamba "Water War"
- Departmental Association of Coca Producers, Asociación Departamental de Productores de Coca (ADEPCOCA)
- Federation of Neighborhood Councils of El Alto, Federación de Juntas Vecinales El Alto (FEJUVE): Led by Abel Mamani, and active in the 2005 El Alto Water War opposing privatization by Aguas de Illimani and French company, and the 2003 Gas War; Mamani was appointed Minister of Water in the Morales government
- Federation of Peasant Women of the Tropics of Cochabamba, Federación de Mujeres Campesinas del Trópico de Cochabamba: Women's coca growers union once led by Leonilda Zurita
- Federation of Private Entrepreneurs of Santa Cruz, Federación de Empresarios Privados de Santa Cruz
- Housewives Committee of Siglo XX, Comité de Amas de Casa de Siglo XX: Association of miners' wives once headed by peasant indigenous woman Domitila Barrios de Chungara
- Landless Movement, Movimiento Sin Tierra (MST): Indigenous land reform movement
- Pro-Santa Cruz Civic Committee, Comité Cívico Pro-Santa Cruz: Santa Cruz organization for autonomy that opposes the new constitution and policies of Morales
- Regional Workers Center, Central Obrero Regional (COR): Active in El Alto Water and Gas Wars
- Six Federations of Coca Growers of the Tropics of Cochabamba, Seis Federaciones del Trópico de Cochabamba: Represents six regional federations of local coca growers unions and some 40,000 peasant coca growers; the federation supported the founding of MAS
- Union of Cruceño Youth, Unión Juvenil Cruceñista: Santa Cruz pro-autonomy student group active in anti-Morales demonstrations

By 1988, the national Peasant Coca Growers' Union and Juan Evo Morales Ayma became the voice of the *cocalero* movement, and the Indians' right to grow the sacred leaf soon evolved into demands for greater indigenous rights and autonomy. The steady militarization of the drug war provoked daily confrontations between the military and the special narcotics control forces and the peasantry, irrevocably rupturing the Military-Peasant Pact, which had served to neutralize the indigenous and *campesino* majority for decades. In the struggle and as a consequence of the 1994–1995 participation and decentralization reforms, the peasants', workers', and indigenous unions and social movements developed intimate ties with the parties of the left and elected an unprecedented number of *campesino* and Indian delegates to the legislature.

BOLIVIA'S RADICAL WOMEN ACTIVISTS

The role of Bolivian women in social movements and political activism has increased exponentially in the last decade. Hunger strikes by wives and mothers during the dark days of the Banzer dictatorship and other military governments ultimately served to rally civil society and provide impetus for democratization and human rights. Two women represent different generations and experiences but share in common the struggle against repression, inequality, and injustice.

Domitila Barrios de Chungara is a valiant woman of Bolivia's gritty mines, who was the head of the Housewives Committee of Siglo XX (*Comité de Amas de Casa del Siglo XX*) during the era of military and repressive governments of the late 1960s and 1970s. She was arrested and beaten defending her livelihood, family, and home. A pioneer of the Bolivian women's movement, Domitila struggled against the macho society in the mines and oppression of the working class. Although of indigenous (Aymara and Quechua) descent, she rejected her Indian roots in an era when to be Indian was to be ashamed.

Leonilda Zurita Vargas is another valiant woman activist, younger and more empowered. She is a congresswoman (deputy) in Bolivia's Chamber of Deputies for the Movement toward Socialism (MAS). As a *cocalera* and leader of the Federation of Peasant Women of the Tropics of Cochabamba, she has also been on the frontlines of the U.S. drug war in Bolivia and the struggle against forcible coca eradication in the Chapare. She was jailed and harassed by police for union organizing and in 1995 led a women's march and 12-day hunger strike to protest the violence in the Chapare. In 2004 she became an international celebrity when the U.S. government suspended her visa because she was on the terrorist blacklist. American officials claimed that she was responsible for the deaths of police and anti-narcotics officers during protests near Cochabamba. However, she was never tried or found guilty and the charges had been dropped.

For Leonilda as for Domitila, activism was a necessity, not a choice. Like Domitila she grew up poor with a large number of siblings; her father died when she only two, and in Domitila's case it was her mother. Both were responsible for raising the younger children in the family. Leonilda was of Quechua roots and grew up in the lowland jungles of the Chapare without running water or electricity. Since her childhood, her family grew coca and survived on a meager plot of land. She explained why she organized marches and demonstrations and became the first female president of the coca growers with words that echoed Domitila's earlier experience in the mines: "We are organized, because we are traumatized."

In large part, this also explains the great rise in Bolivian women's activism in the last decades, and the exceptional growth in their numbers in the Congress, in municipal and regional government, civic and neighborhood associations, political parties, and in the cabinet and administration of Evo Morales—the most gender inclusive and diverse ever. As for Domitila and Leonilda, women's organizing and empowerment have been the direct outcome of the struggles to survive that have shaped their lives.

The Aymara leader, Felipe Quispe Huanca, known as *el Mallku* or the Eagle, headed the CSUTCB and an Indian political party, the Pachakuti Indigenous Movement (MIP) that competed with the MAS party of Morales in recent elections. In 2002 Morales came close to an electoral victory when the U.S. Ambassador Manuel Rocha spoke out against his candidacy. In 2005, after 3 years of social and political turmoil, the Indian majority, the country's largest voting bloc, came out in force to make one of their own Bolivia's first democratically elected indigenous president. These elections, therefore, marked a historic turning point in Bolivia's political development: the spectacular power transition from traditional establishment parties to newcomer, socialist and pro-indigenist parties. It is instructive to consider in greater detail how this major shift came about.

The re-election of Sánchez de Lozada in 2002 created the conditions that furthered the transition to a new era of anti-establishment, populist government. First, the electoral outcome revealed a country split among opposing interests: the more traditional MNR of Sánchez de Lozada (23 percent), the MAS and Evo Morales (21 percent), and the conservative lowlander and regional interests of the New Republican Force (NFR) of Manfred Reyes Villa (21percent). The remainder of the vote went to Jaime Paz Zamora's MIR (16 percent) and Felipe Quispe's MIP (6 percent). The radical and pro-Indian vote was on the rise (MAS and MIP with 27 percent). The MAS promised to end the U.S.-led coca eradication program and renationalize the sectors of the economy that had been privatized. The electoral campaign was especially tawdry, racked by corruption scandals and mud-slinging and exceptionally expensive, at over $5 million in a country where the majority of the population lived below the poverty line and the national debt remained in the billions. The competition assailed Morales as a drug trafficker and Marxist. When none of the candidates received the necessary majority, an interparty governing pact in the run-off election in Congress handed the presidency to Sánchez de Lozada— the least popular candidate according to polls.

However, the MNR-dominated government endured a mere 15 months. In 2003 social protests erupted over Sánchez de Lozada's tax increase in February and plans to market Bolivian natural gas via Chilean ports in the September–October Gas War. After the deaths of more than 100 protestors in the bloody confrontations between the military and the popular social movements that year, Sánchez de Lozada was forced to turn over the government to Vice President Carlos Mesa Gisbert. An independent, honest broker without the support of either establishment or anti-establishment political parties, Mesa was unable to resolve the smoldering political crisis. Despite the successful July 2004 referendum on Bolivia's gas resources and the revised Hydrocarbon Law of May 2005, which increased the tax on new gas fields, Mesa reluctantly conceded to early presidential elections in 2005. The endemic violence and instability confirmed that the traditional political parties and ruling establishment had lost legitimacy and that fundamental reforms were necessary to restore peace and normalcy.

The presidential election of December 2005 sealed the unprecedented power transition between Bolivia's nonindigenous ruling elite and its indigenous majority. Moreover, the turmoil and conflict since 2000 had effectively mobilized major social sectors against the establishment. To some extent as in 1952, a diverse, multiclass combination of urban and rural groups, indigenous highlanders and lowlanders, *mestizos*, the poor, the middle-class, intellectuals, and certain regional interests had voted for Morales and his party's radical agenda to "Refound the Nation." The MAS program included a new constitution, renationalization of the hydrocarbon sector and the mines, suspension of coca eradication, restoration of statist-socialist economics, and indigenous and regional autonomy. In effect, the election, which Evo Morales won by a landslide majority of 54 percent of the popular vote, provided him the national mandate to effect a second Bolivian revolution on the foundations of the first.

Crisis of Reform and Autonomy

The contemporary Bolivian crisis is both of democratic representation and state effectiveness. Since the return to democracy in 1982, the pursuit of neoliberal economic policies has disadvantaged poor and indigenous citizens unequally and unfairly, and weakened the governing capacity of the Bolivian state and its ability to redress socioeconomic inequities. Moreover, the pro-market and pro-export orientation of the majority of Bolivian governments (civilian and military alike) after 1964 has benefited the more prosperous southeastern departments of the country disproportionately, especially the economic and business elites of Santa Cruz. Since 1964, the traditional political parties and military authoritarians have shared in and protected these regional economic interests and their preeminent influence over the national government. However, with the expansion of democratic participation by Bolivia's indigenous majority these interests can no longer be guaranteed within the existing political system by either authoritarian or democratic means. Thus this power shift toward socialist and indigenist groups has revived old secessionist tendencies and encouraged the recent demands for the regional autonomy of Bolivia's four southeastern departments (Santa Cruz, Tarija, Beni, and Pando) or the Oriente or Media Luna region.

A critical power struggle is underway. It has economic, racist, class, ideological, regional, and nationalist dimensions. The democratic consolidation and decentralization of the 1990s facilitated the entry and participation of indigenous voters and candidates in national politics to an unprecedented degree. Nevertheless, despite electoral successes and an impressive increase in indigenous legislators to Congress, the conservative political establishment continued to effectively block popular reforms and progressive change. Democratic gains were unable to achieve and to sustain alternative economic development and governance strate-

---

BOLIVIAN NATIONAL CONGRESS
2005 POLITICAL PARTY REPRESENTATION IN BOLIVIAN CONGRESS

Party	Seats in Senate	Seats in Chamber of Deputies	Total Seats in Congress
Movement Toward Socialism (MAS)	12	72	84
Democratic Social Power (PODEMOS)	13	43	56
National Unity Front (UN)	1	8	9
Nationalist Revolutionary Movement (MNR)	1	7	8
Total	27	130	157

Bolivian Government

There are three branches of government: the executive, the legislative, and the judicial. Except for the judiciary, which has its seat in the legal or constitutional capital of Sucre, the other branches are based in the working capital of La Paz. The executive branch includes the president, the vice president, and fourteen cabinet ministers. Bolivia's president serves as both the head of state and the head of government and has a 5-year term of office. A presidential candidate must receive an absolute majority of the popular vote (51 percent). Until the 2005 elections no candidate received such a strong mandate. Therefore, Bolivia's presidents were determined by a run-off election in Congress.

The legislature is the *Congreso Nacional* (National Congress) with the *Cámara de Diputados* (Chamber of Deputies or House of Representatives) of 130 deputies, and the *Cámara de Senadores* or *Senado Nacional* (Chamber of Senators or National Senate) with twenty-seven senators (see Bolivian National Congress).

The judiciary includes the *Corte Suprema de Justicia de la Nación* (Supreme Court of Justice of the Nation), and the *Tribunal Constitucional* (Constitutional Tribunal). The Supreme Court consists of twelve judges who are elected by a two-thirds vote of the Congress.

---

gies, especially ones that favored socialist and pro-poor and pro-indigenist policies. Bolivia's weak system of "pacted democracy" repeatedly delivered partisan and pro-establishment compromises that ignored the wishes of a majority of the electorate. Although democracy increased mass mobilization and incorporation of traditionally excluded groups, it failed to translate into the empowerment of and the delivery of state services to the poor and indigenous sectors of society. Therefore, as political opportunities and economic expectations increased, legitimacy and satisfaction with government and the political system declined, creating the perfect scenario for an escalating crisis of relative deprivation and popular insurrection.

The election of Evo Morales has not resolved this crisis. It has deferred and redefined it into a national struggle between radical reform and regional autonomy. As Bolivian civil society matures in comprehensiveness and complexity (encompassing hundreds of civic and neighborhood committees, women's movements and household associations, and indigenous territorial base communities), the task of democratic governance has become more difficult for presidents, especially ones

BOLIVIAN PRESIDENTS SINCE 1930: ELECTED, UNELECTED, AND INTERIM

Carlos Blanco Galindo, 1930–1931
Daniel Salamanca Urey, 1931–1934
José Luis Tejada Sorzano, 1934–1936
David Toro Ruilova, 1936–1937
Germán Busch Becerra, 1937–1939
Carlos Quintanilla Quiroga, 1939–1940
Enrique Peñaranda del Castillo, 1940–1943
Gualberto Villarroel López, 1943–1946
Néstor Guillén Olmos, 1946
Tomás Monje Gutiérrez, 1946–1947
Enrique Hertzog Garaizabal, 1947–1949
Mamerto Urriolagoitia Harriague, 1949–1951
Hugo Ballivián Rojas, 1951–1952
Víctor Paz Estenssoro, 1952–1956
Hernán Siles Zuazo, 1956–1960
Víctor Paz Estenssoro, 1960–1964
Víctor Paz Estenssoro, 1964
René Barrientos Ortuño. 1964–1969
Alfredo Ovando Candia, 1969–1970
Luis Adolfo Siles Salinas, 1969

Juan José Torres Gonzáles, 1970–1971
Hugo Banzer Suárez, 1971–1978
Juan Pereda Asbún, 1978
David Padilla Arancibia, 1978–1979
Wálter Guevara Arze, 1979
Alberto Natusch Busch, 1979
Lidia Gueiler Tejada, 1979–1980
Luis García Meza Tejada, 1980–1981
Celso Torrelio Villa, 1981–1982
Guido Vildoso Calderón, 1982
Hernán Siles Zuazo, 1982–1985
Víctor Paz Estenssoro, 1985–1989
Jaime Paz Zamora, 1989–1993
Gonzalo Sánchez de Lozada, 1993–1997
Hugo Banzer Suárez, 1997–2001
Jorge Quiroga Ramírez, 2001–2002
Gonzalo Sánchez de Lozada, 2002–2003
Carlos Mesa Gisbert, 2003–2005
Eduardo Rodríguez Veltze, 2005
Juan Evo Morales Ayma, 2005–

like Morales with an unprecedented but polarizing mandate. The Morales administration has attempted to diffuse discontent and meet rising expectations by pursuing two related objectives: greater representational openness and transparency in government; and an increase in the authority, resource base, and effectiveness of the state. The deliberations of the Constituent Assembly (composed of 255 delegates elected and convened in 2006) and the passage of the New Political Constitution (*Nueva Constitución Política*) in December 2007 addressed the first objective. The "nationalization" of the petroleum and gas resources on May Day 2006, and the renegotiation of international contracts with transnational corporations on terms more beneficial to the state furthered the second objective.

The problem, however, is that these reforms have generated a backlash from domestic and international interests, especially the autonomy movement of the Pro-Santa Cruz Civic Committee and the departmental prefects of the Media Luna. Fiercely opposed to the draft constitutional charter, which they consider illegal and anti-democratic because it was passed without the opposition delegates present, the leaders of the four southeastern provinces have increased their efforts toward greater self-rule. If the Morales administration is unable to address and defuse these regional demands, autonomy could escalate into outright secession, which in turn could provoke a reaction by Bolivia's armed forces and tear the country apart. Moreover, there is no consensus on what autonomy and self-rule entails and for whom.

Autonomy basically refers to the direct election of regional political authorities. Among MAS supporters, autonomy also means decentralization and greater self-rule and citizenship rights for indigenous communities, including Guaraní and lowland Indian groups. Media Luna leaders, however, have trivialized self-rule and land rights for native communities as chopping Bolivia into thousands of pieces. Nevertheless their demands for autonomy are more radical and extensive. These entail regional control over natural resources and police, and the retention of two-thirds of the tax revenues generated in the departments (instead of it going to the central government). These measures will provide regional elites (wealthy businessmen and landowners) the economic, political, and legal means to reject or undermine proposed constitutional reforms and protect regional prerogatives from indigenous and socialist encroachments.

With the country polarized between competing autonomies, identities, and agendas, a "war of referendums" is in the offing for 2008 and beyond. The timing, wording, and legal requirements of these popular plebiscites will be critical. So far, President Morales has called for an emergency referendum wherein voters can recall him and the country's departmental prefects. Further, a national referendum must be held to approve the new constitution, and special referendums are to be held if any of its 408 articles is not approved. Meanwhile regional-level referendums are being speedily organized to pass autonomy statutes in Santa Cruz and other Media Luna departments. Moreover, if these referenda are held first, the results could influence and complicate (and potentially defeat) the national constitutional referendum.

The challenges facing Bolivia in the years ahead are indeed staggering and unpredictable. Too many questions remain unanswered and problems unresolved. If democracy is able to weather the social crisis over revolutionary reforms and reactionary autonomy struggles, perhaps national integrity and unity can be preserved. And if Evo Morales succeeds in his government's ambitious goal to "Refound Bolivia," the country may become a more equitable and representative land for all of its citizens.

BOLIVIA: MAJOR POLITICAL PARTIES SINCE 1952

- Civic Solidarity Union, Unión Cívica de la Solidaridad (UCS)
- Conscience of the Fatherland, Conciencia de Patria (CONDEPA)
- Democratic Popular Unity, Unidad Democrática y Popular (UDP)
- Democratic Social Power, Poder Democrático Social (PODEMOS)
- Leftist Revolutionary Movement or Movement of the Revolutionary Left, Movimiento de Izquierda Revolucionaria (MIR)
- Movement Toward Socialism, Movimiento al Socialismo (MAS)
- Nationalist Democratic Action, Acción Democrática Nacionalista (ADN)
- National Unity Front, Frente de Unidad Nacional (UN)
- Nationalist Revolutionary Movement, Movimiento Nacionalista Revolucionario (MNR)
- New Republican Force, Nueva Fuerza Republicana (NFR)
- Pachakuti Indigenist Movement, Movimiento Indígena Pachakuti (MIP)
- Socialist Party, Partido Socialista (PS); formerly known as Bolivian Socialist Vanguard, Vanguardia Socialista de Bolivia (VS)
- Túpac Katari Revolutionary Liberation Movement, Movimiento Revolucionario Túpac Katari de Liberación (MRTKL)

Evo Morales and Hugo Chávez. *(STR/AFP/Getty Images)*

Chronology

900–1000   Classical Period of Tiwanaku

1100–1400   Rise and development of Aymara kingdoms

1400–1500   Incan conquest of Aymara and establishment of the Kollasuyo

1532   Spanish conquest of Inca Empire by Francisco Pizarro

1538   Spanish colonize Upper Peru and establish the Viceroyalty of Lima

1545   Discovery of *Cerro Rico* (Silver Mountain) of Potosí

1548   Establishment of the Audiencia of Charcas with its seat in Sucre

1730   Indigenous rebellion in Cochabamba against Spanish authorities

1780–1782   Indian rebellion of Túpac Amaru (José Gabriel Condorcanqui)

1825   Liberation of Upper Peru and declaration of Bolivian independence

1825–1828   Marshall Antonio José de Sucre elected president and establishes Bolivia's first republican government

1829–1839   Rule by General Andrés de Santa Cruz

1835–1839   Creation of the Peru-Bolivian Confederation by General Santa Cruz; Chile invades and defeats Santa Cruz

1841   Peru invades but is defeated ending attempts to annex Bolivia

1860s–1870s   Guano, nitrates, and silver discovered in Atacama region

1879–1884   War of the Pacific; Bolivia is defeated and becomes landlocked

1880–1899   Civilian and Conservative Party rule of the Silver Oligarchy

1899   Federal Revolution of the Liberal Party; power shifts to La Paz and the Tin Oligarchy

1904   Peace Treaty of War of the Pacific signed

1920   Rebellion by Bolivia's indigenous peoples is repressed

1923   Miners' revolt is suppressed with violence and bloodshed

1932–1935   Bolivian defeated in Chaco War with Paraguay

1936–1939   Military reform governments of Colonel David Toro and Colonel Germán Busch

1937   President Toro nationalizes Standard Oil Company

1939–1943   Conservative government of General Enrique Peñaranda

1943–1946   Military reform government of Major Gualberto Villarroel and MNR

1944   Founding of the Bolivian Mine Workers' Federation (FSTMB)

1945   First National Indigenous Congress

1946   Overthrow and hanging of President Villarroel

1946–1952   Return of rule by mining oligarchy

1951   Nationwide elections are overturned and military takes over

1952   Bolivian National Revolution (April)

1952–1964   MNR governments of Víctor Paz Estenssoro and Hernán Siles Zuazo

1952   Universal Suffrage Decree

1953   Land reform and nationalization of the mines

1955   Educational Reform Decree

1964–1969   "Restorative Revolution" of General René Barrientos

1965–1967   Ernesto Ché Guevara active in Bolivia; death of Ché (October 1967)

1969–1970   Military populist government of General Ovando and nationalization of the Bolivian Gulf Oil Company (October 1969)

1970–1971   Military leftist government of General Juan José Torres

1971–1978   Military coup and dictatorship of General Hugo Banzer Suárez

1978   Miners' wives launch hunger strike in La Paz cathedral to protest government repression and demand national amnesty

1979   Massacre of All Saints by military results in more than 200 dead; Lidia Gueiler Tejada heads an interim government as Bolivia's first woman president

1980   Cocaine coup by General Luis García Meza preempts electoral process; U.S. and European governments suspend aid

1982   Return to democracy; Congress revalidates 1980 election of Hernán Siles Zuazo

1982–1985   Left of center civilian government of Hernán Siles Zuazo; hyperinflation and instability forces early elections

1985–1989   MNR Government of Víctor Paz Estenssoro; his "democracy with authority" imposes neoliberal New Economic Policy (NPE)

1985   Crash of world tin market sends Bolivian economy into recession

1986   Mine closings and 23,000 miners lose jobs; escalation of U.S.–Bolivian anti-narcotics operations

1988   Law on the Regulation of Coca and Controlled Substances (Law 1008) criminalizes coca leaf cultivation in most of the country

1989–1993   Presidency of Jaime Paz Zamora

1989   Chapáre coca-growing federations sponsor first national *Día de Acullico* or Day of Coca-leaf Chewing

1990   Andean Drug Summit in Colombia officially militarizes the Bolivian drug war; lowland indigenous peoples March for Territory and Dignity secures land rights

1993–1997   Presidency of Gonzalo Sánchez de Lozada and Víctor Hugo Cárdenas as Bolivia's first indigenous vice president

1997–2001   Presidency of Hugo Banzer; forcible coca eradication and militarization of the 1998 "Zero Coca" or "Plan Dignity" policy and economic austerity provokes strikes and roadblocks by coca growers and worker-peasant unions

2000   "Water War" protests in Cochabamba over water privatization by the Bechtel Corporation forces government to impose martial law (February–April); month-long peasant roadblocks seal off La Paz (September–October); rise of Bolivian Landless Movement (MST)

2001   An ill Banzer resigns a year early and Vice President Jorge Quiroga Ramírez takes over

2001–2002 President Jorge Quiroga continues political and neoliberal policies; cancellation of the Bechtel water privatization project; unrest as coca growers protest coca eradication; Evo Morales, leader of the coca growers' federation, is ousted from Congress but runs for president in 2002 elections in which his MAS party has strong showing

2002 Gonzalo Sánchez de Lozada wins June elections

2003 Bloody January–February protests over proposed tax hike; more bloodshed during September–October "Gas War" protests derails Sánchez de Lozada presidency on October 17; Vice President Carlos Mesa Gisbert becomes interim president

2004 President Mesa holds July referendum and 80 percent of voters approve proposed new Hydrocarbon Law

2005 Congress approves new Hydrocarbon Law increasing taxes on gas and oil for new fields but Mesa does not sign it and is forced by rising protests to call elections; Evo Morales wins the presidency in a landslide victory as Bolivia's first elected president of indigenous heritage and promises to "Refound the Nation"

2006 May Day "renationalization" of Bolivia's hydrocarbons and energy sector; Constituent Assembly elections (July) to rewrite the constitution; Santa Cruz approves autonomy agenda

2007 Bloody clashes in Sucre between pro- and anti-Morales supporters and Constituent Assembly delegates pass draft of new constitution in military garrison; Constituent Assembly moves to Oruro and approves proposed constitutional charter despite boycott by opposition delegates from eastern lowlands; four lowland departments promise to hold referendum on autonomy

2008 National and departmental referendums on the new constitution and autonomy provisions

Bibliography

Arnade, Charles W. *The Emergence of the Republic of Bolivia.* New York: Russell & Russell, 1970.

Barr, Robert R. "Bolivia: Another Uncompleted Revolution." *Latin American Politics and Society.* Vol. 47, No. 3 (Fall 2005): 69–90.

Barrios de Chungara, Domitila. *Let Me Speak! Testimony of Domitila, a Woman of the Bolivian Mines.* New York: Monthly Review Press, 1978.

Benner, Susan E., and Kathy S. Leonard, eds. and trans. *Fire from the Andes: Short Fiction by Women from Bolivia, Ecuador, and Peru.* Albuquerque: University of New Mexico Press, 1998.

Crabtree, John, Gavan Duffy, and Jenny Pearce. *The Great Tin Crash: Bolivia and the World Tin Market.* London: Latin America Bureau, 1987.

Crabtree, John, and Laurence Whitehead, eds. *Toward Democratic Viability: The Bolivian Experience.* Oxford: Palgrave, 2001.

Dangl, Benjamin. *The Price of Fire: Resource Wars and Social Movements in Bolivia.* Oakland, CA: AK Press, 2007.

Dunkerley, James. *Rebellion in the Veins: Political Struggle in Bolivia, 1952–1982.* London: Verso, 1984.

Eaton, Kent. "Backlash in Bolivia: Regional Autonomy as a Reaction against Indigenous Mobilization." *Politics & Society,* Vol. 35, No. 1 (March 2007): 71–102.

Gill, Lesley. *Teetering on the Rim: Global Restructuring, Daily Life, and the Armed Retreat of the Bolivian State.* New York: Columbia University Press, 2000.

Grindle, Merilee, and Pilar Domingo, eds. *Proclaiming Revolution: Bolivia in Comparative Perspective.* London: Institute of Latin American Studies, University of London, 2003.

Guevara, Ernesto Ché. *The Bolivian Diary of Ernesto Ché Guevara.* Ed. by Mary-Alice Walters. New York: Pathfinder, 2000.

Klein, Herbert S. *A Concise History of Bolivia.* Cambridge: Cambridge University Press, 2003.

——. *Bolivia: The Evolution of a Multi-Ethnic Society.* 2nd ed. New York: Oxford University Press, 1992.

Kohl, Ben, and Linda Farthing. *Impasse in Bolivia: Neoliberal Hegemony and Popular Resistance.* New York: Zed Books, 2006.

——. "The Price of Success: Bolivia's War against Drugs and the Poor." *NACLA Report on the Americas* 35 (July/August 2001): 35–41.

Kornbluh, Peter. "The Death of Ché Guevara: Declassified." National Security Archive, George Washington University. Available online at http://www.gwu.edu/~nsarchiv/NSAEBB/NSAEBB5/

Ledebur, Kathryn. "Bolivia: Clear Consequences." In Coletta A. Youngers and Eileen Rosin, eds. *Drugs and Democracy in Latin America: The Impact of U.S. Policy,* pp. 143–184. Boulder, CO: Lynne Rienner, 2005.

Lehman, Kenneth. D. *Bolivia and the United States: A Limited Partnership.* Athens: University of Georgia Press, 1999.

Malloy, James M. *Bolivia: The Uncompleted Revolution.* Pittsburgh, PA: University of Pittsburgh Press, 1970.

Malloy, James M., and Eduardo A. Gamarra. *Revolution and Reaction: Bolivia, 1964–1985.* New Brunswick, NJ: Transaction, 1988.

Menzel, Sewall H. *Fire in the Andes: U.S. Foreign Policy and Cocaine Politics in Bolivia and Peru.* Lanham, MD: University Press of America, 1996.

Mitchell, Christopher. *The Legacy of Populism in Bolivia: From the MNR to Military Rule.* New York: Praeger, 1977.

Morales, Waltraud Queiser. *Bolivia: Land of Struggle.* Boulder, CO: Westview Press, 1992.

——. *A Brief History of Bolivia.* New York: Facts on File, 2003.

——. "Militarising the Drug War in Bolivia." *Third World Quarterly.* Vol. 13, No. 2 (1992): 353–370.

——. "Responding to Bolivian Democracy: Avoiding the Mistakes of Early U.S. Cuban Policy." *Military Review* (July-August 2006): 27-34.

NACLA Report on the Americas. "Bolivia Fights Back." Vol. 38, No. 3 (November/December 2004).

Nash, June. *We Eat the Mines and the Mines Eat Us: Dependency and Exploitation in Bolivian Tin Mines.* New York: Columbia University Press, 1979.

Olivera, Oscar. *Cochabamba: Water War in Bolivia.* Trans. by Tom Lewis. Cambridge, MA: South End Press, 2004.

Painter, James. *Bolivia and Coca: A Study in Dependency.* Boulder, CO: Lynne Rienner, 1994.

Postero, Nancy Grey. *Now We Are Citizens: Indigenous Politics in Postmulticultural Bolivia.* Stanford, CA: Stanford University Press, 2007.

Powers, William. *Whispering in the Giant's Ear: A Frontline Chronicle from Bolivia's War on Globalization.* New York: Bloomsbury, 2006.

Sánchez, José H. *The Art and Politics of Bolivian Cinema.* Lanham, MD: Scarecrow Press, 1999.

Santos, Rosario, ed. *The Fat Man from La Paz: Contemporary Fiction from Bolivia.* New York: Seven Stories Press, 2000.

Van Cott, Donna Lee. *From Movements to Parties in Latin America: The Evolution of Ethnic Politics.* New York: Cambridge University Press, 2005.

Yashar, Deborah J. *Contesting Citizenship in Latin America: The Rise of Indigenous Movements and the Postliberal Challenge.* Cambridge: Cambridge University Press, 2005.

FILMS AND DOCUMENTARIES

Films by Director Jorge Sanjinés

Banderas del Amanecer. 1982. Political events of 1979–1982, including the failed elections, military repression, coup of García Meza, and the return to democracy.

La Nación Clandestina. 1989. Indian Sebastían Mamani denies his class and indigenous roots and culture and plays a repressive role during dictatorships.

El Enemigo Principal. 1973. *Campesino* seeks revenge against *hacendado* who took his land away.

El Coraje del Pueblo. 1971. The Courage of the People; The Night of San Juan; Repression during the government of General Barrientos, especially of labor and peasant groups under pretext of fighting Ché's guerrilla threat.

Yawar Malku or *Blood of the Condor.* 1969. Classic film on Bolivia.

Ukamau. 1966. Indian peasant and abuse by *hacendado* as peasant tries to get revenge for the rape of his wife.

Other Bolivian Films and Documentaries about Bolivia

American Visa. 2005. A Bolivian professor who, after being denied a U.S. visa, gets involved in assorted criminal activities.

The Devil's Miner. 2006. Independent Lens Documentary of two Bolivian brothers that live in poverty with their mother in mountains of Bolivia and work in Cerro Rico mine.

The Bolivian Diary. 1996. Ché Guevara is executed by the Bolivian Army (aided by the CIA). Guevara's diary, a personal account of his attempt to foment revolution in Bolivia.

El Violín/The Violin. 2007. A Mexican-Bolivian production about an aging traveling musician who gets caught up in a peasant revolt.

Evo Pueblo. 2007. The history of a young farmer of the Bolivian plateau that becomes the first indigenous president of Bolivia.

Fire on the Amazon. 1993. In Bolivia's Amazon basin, corporate cattle ranches are replacing the rain forest, Rubber Trapper Union leader Santos forges an alliance with Indians to protest deforestation and is assassinated.

Hijos de la Montaña de Plata. 2006. Hard life of Bolivia's miners.

Our Brand Is Crisis. 2005. About the selling of Bolivian presidential election of Gonzalo Sánchez de Lozada in 2005.

Quién Mató a la Llamita Blanca/Who Killed the White Llama? 2006. About a young Bolivian couple who transport cocaine to Brazil and are chased by wily U.S. anti-narcotics agents.

WEBSITES

Bolivian Information, Gateways, and News

http://www.comunica.gov.bo/ Agencia Boliviana de Informacíon; official government news information.
http://www.tni.org/drogas/andina/andina.htm Acción Andina.
http://www.bolivia.com Bolivia News Portal.
http://www.boliviaweb.com Boliviaweb.
http://www.bolpress.com Bolivia Press.
http://www.bolivianet.com Bolivianet.
http://boliviasolidarity.org Bolivia Solidarity Network.
http://www.americas.org/country/country.asp?country=Bolivia Americas Bolivia Resource Center.
http://ain-bolivia.org Andean Information Network.
http://lanic.utexas.edu/la/sa/bolivia LANIC links to Bolivia media resources.
http://www.bolivianstudies.org Bolivian Studies Association.
http://www.cedib.org Bolivia Press by CEDIB (Centro de documentación e investigación boliviano).
http://www.democracyctr.org Democracy Center.
http://Econoticiasbolivia.com Econoticias; a media resource that provides news coverage and regular reports critical of neoliberalism and state repression in Bolivia.
http://www.globalexchange.org/countries/americas/bolivia/ Global Exchange.
http://bolivia.indymedia.org Indymedia Bolivia.
http://www.erbol.com.bo/ Live Radio from La Paz.
http://www.noticiasbolivianas.com Noticias Bolivianas; News aggregator for all Bolivian newspapers.
http://upsidedownworld.org Upside Down World: Alternative news outlet critical of neoliberalism and its struggles in Bolivia.
http://www.zmag.org/lam/boliviawatch.cfm ZNET's Bolivia Watch.

Human Rights/Drug Policy

http://drcnet.org Drug Reform Coordination Network.
http://wola.org/bolivia Washington Office on Latin America.
http://www.witness.org Lawyers' Committee for Human Rights.

APPENDIX 1
Presidential Elections

Argentina

2007 Presidential Election

Candidate	Party	Percentage
Cristina Fernandez de Kirchner	Front for the Victory Alliance	44.9
Elisa Carrió	Civic Confederation Coalition (CCC)	23.0
Roberto Lavagna	Agreement Alliance UNA (AC–UNA)	16.9

2003 Presidential Election: Round One

Candidate	Party	Percentage
Carlos Saul Menem	Front for Loyalty Alliance/ Union of the Democratic Center Party	24.3
Nestor Kirchner	Front for Victory Alliance	22.0

Note: Presidential candidate Carlos Saul Menem announced that he would withdraw from the second-round presidential race. According to Argentina's electoral law, Menem's withdrawal cleared the way for his opponent, Nestor Kirchner, to be named president by default.

Bolivia

2005 Presidential Election

Candidate	Party	Percentage
Juan Evo Morales Ayma	Movement Toward Socialism (MAS)	53.7
Jorge Quiroga	Democratic and Social Power (PDS)	28.6
Samuel Doria Medina	National Unity Front (FUN)	7.8

2002 Presidential Election

Candidate	Party	Congressional Votes
Gonzalo Sanchez de Lozada	Nationalist Revolutionary Movement (MNR)	84
Juan Evo Morales Ayma	Movement Toward Socialism (MAS)	43

According to the Bolivian Constitution, the Congress decides who will be the president between the two candidates with the highest number of votes if neither candidate has received more than 50% of the votes.

Brazil

2006 Presidential Election: Round 1

Candidate	Party	Percentage
Luís Inácio Lula da Silva	Worker's Party (PT) / Liberal Party (PL)	48.6
Geraldo Alckim	Brazilian Social Democratic Party (PSDB)	41.6
Heloisa Helena	Socialism and Freedom Party (PSOL)	6.9

2006 Presidential Election: Round 2

Candidate	Party	Percentage
Luís Inácio Lula da Silva	Worker's Party (PT) / Liberal Party	60.8
Geraldo Alckim	Brazilian Social Democratic Party (PSDB)	39.2

2002 Presidential Election: Round 1

Candidate	Party	Percentage
Luís Inácio Lula da Silva	Worker's Party (PT) / Liberal Party (PL)	46.4
José Serra	Brazilian Social Democratic Party (PSDB) / Brazilian Democratic Movement Party (PMDB)	23.2
Anthony Garotinho	Brazilian Socialist Party (PSB)	17.9

2002 Presidential Election: Round 2

Candidate	Party	Percentage
Luís Inácio Lula da Silva	Worker's Party (PT) / Liberal Party (PL)	61.4
José Serra	Brazilian Social Democratic Party (PSDB) / Brazilian Democratic Movement Party (PMDB)	38.6

Chile

2005 Presidential Election: Round 1

Candidate	Party	Percentage
Michele Bachelet Jeria	Democratic Agreement (CD)	46.0
Sebastian Piñera Echeñique	National Renewal (RN)	25.4
Joaquín Lavín Infante	Independent Democratic Union (UDI)	23.2

2005 Presidential Election: Round 2

Candidate	Party	Percentage
Michele Bachelet Jeria	Democratic Agreement (CD)	53.5
Sebastian Piñera Echeñique	National Renewal (RN)	46.5

1999 Presidential Election: Round 1

Candidate	Party	Percentage
Ricardo Lagos Escobar	Party for Democracy (PPD)	48.0
Joaquín Lavín Infante	Independent Democratic Union (UDI)	47.5

1999 Presidential Election: Round 2

Candidate	Party	Percentage
Ricardo Lagos Escobar	Party for Democracy (PPD)	51.3
Joaquín Lavín Infante	Independent Democratic Union (UDI)	48.7

Colombia

2006 Presidential Election

Candidate	Party	Percentage
Alvaro Uribe Velez	Colombia First	62.2
Horacio Serpa Uribe	Liberal Party (PL)	31.8
Carlos Gaviria Diaz	Alternative Democratic Pole (PDA)	22.0

2002 Presidential Election

Candidate	Party	Percentage
Alvaro Uribe Velez	Colombia First	53.1
Horacio Serpa Uribe	Liberal Party (PL)	31.8

Costa Rica

2006 Presidential Election

Candidate	Party	Percentage
Oscar Arias Sanchez	National Liberation Party (PLN)	40.9
Ottón Solís Fallas	Citizen Action Party (PAC)	39.8
Otto Guevara Guth	Liberation Movement (ML)	8.5

2002 Presidential Election: Round 1

Candidate	Party	Percentage
Abel Pacheco de la Espriella	Christian Social Unity Party (PUSC)	38.6
Rolando Araya Monge	National Liberation Party (PLN)	31.1
Ottón Solís Fallas	Citizen Action Party (PAC)	26.9

2002 Presidential Election: Round 2

Candidate	Party	Percentage
Abel Pacheco de la Espriella	Christian Social Unity Party (PUSC)	58.0
Rolando Araya Monge	National Liberation Party (PLN)	42.0

Note: According to the Costa Rican Constitution, a candidate needs a minimum of 40 percent of the popular vote to be elected without a second round of voting.

Dominican Republic

2004 Presidential Election

Candidate	Party	Percentage
Leonel Fernández	Dominican Liberation Party (PLD)	56.7
Hipólito Mejia	Dominican Revolutionary Party (PRD)	34.0

2000 Presidential Election

Candidate	Party	Percentage
Hipólito Mejia	Dominican Revolutionary Party (PRD)	49.9
Danilo Medina	Dominican Liberation Party (PLD)	24.8
Joaquín Balaguer	Social Christian Reformist Party (PRSC)	24.7

Ecuador

2006 Presidential Election: Round 1

Candidate	Party	Percentage
Alvaro Noboa Vicente Taiano	Institutional Renewal Party of National Action (PRIAN)	26.8
Rafael Correa Delgado Lenin Moreno Garcés	Movement Alliance (PAIS/PS–FA)	22.8
Gilmar Gutiérrez Borbúa	Patriotic Socialist Party (PSP)	17.4

2006 Presidential Election: Round 2

Candidate	Party	Percentage
Rafael Correa Delgado Lenin Moreno Garcés	Movement Alliance (PAIS/PS–FA)	54.8
Alvaro Noboa Vicente Taiano	Institutional Renewal Party of National Action (PRIAN)	43.3

2002 Presidential Election: Round 1

Candidate	Party	Percentage
Lucio Edwin Gutiérrez Borbua	Patriotic Socialist Party (PSP) Pluri-National Pachakutik Movement–New Country (MUPP–NP)	20.4
Alvaro Fernando Noboa Pontón	Institutional Renewal Party of National Action (PRIAN)	17.4
Leon Roldós Aguilera	Republican Party (PR)	15.4

2002 Presidential Election: Round 2

Candidate	Party	Percentage
Lucio Edwin Gutiérrez Borbua	Patriotic Socialist Party (PSP) Pluri-National Pachakutik Movement–New Country (MUPP–NP)	54.8
Alvaro Fernando Noboa Pontón	Institutional Renewal Party of National Action (PRIAN)	45.2

El Salvador

2004 Presidential Election

Candidate	Party	Percentage
Antonio Saca	National Republican Alliance (ARENA)	57.7
Schafik Handal	National Liberation Front Farabundo Martí (FMLN)	35.6
Hector Silva	United Democratic Center (CDU)	3.9

1999 Presidential Election

Candidate	Party	Percentage
Francisco Flores	National Republican Alliance (ARENA)	52.0
Facundo Guardado	National Liberation Front Farabundo Martí (FMLN)–Christian Social Union (USC)	28.9
Rubén Zamora Rivas	United Democratic Center (CDU)	7.6

Guatemala

2007 Presidential Election: Round 1

Candidate	Party	Percentage
Alvaro Colom Caballeros	National Unity of Hope (UNE)	28.2
Otto Pérez Molina	Patriotic Party (PP)	23.5
Alejandro Giamattei	Grand National Alliance (GANA)	17.2

2007 Presidential Election: Round 2

Candidate	Party	Percentage
Alvaro Colom Caballeros	National Unity of Hope (UNE)	52.8
Otto Pérez Molina	Patriotic Party (PP)	47.2

2003 Presidential Election: Round 1

Candidate	Party	Percentage
Oscar Jose Rafael Berger Perdomo	Progressive Party/Reform Movement (PP-MR-PSN)	34.3
Alvaro Colom Caballeros	National Unity of Hope (UNE)	26.4
José Efraín Ríos Montt	Republican Guatemalan Front (FRG)	19.3

2003 Presidential Election: Round 2

Candidate	Party	Percentage
Oscar Jose Rafael Berger Perdomo	Progressive Party/Reform Movement (PP-MR-PSN)	54.13
Alvaro Colom Caballeros	National Unity of Hope (UNE)	45.87

Haiti

2006 Presidential Election

Candidate	Party	Percentage
René García Préval	Front for Hope (LESPWA)	51.2
Lesly Francois Sa Manegat	Rally of Progressive National Democrats (RDNP)	12.4
Charles Hanry Jean Marie Baker	Respect (Respé)	8.2

2000 Presidential Election

Candidate	Party	Percentage
Jean-Bertrand Aristide	Fanmi Lavalas	91.8
Arnold Dumas	Independent	2.0

Note: There were widespread allegations against Fanmi Lavalas of electoral fraud during the 2000 election.

Honduras

2005 Presidential Election

Candidate	Party	Percentage
Manuel Zelaya	Liberal Party (PLH)	49.9
Porifirio Lobo	National Party (PNH)	46.2

2001 Presidential Election

Candidate	Party	Percentage
Ricardo Maduro Joest	National Party (PNH)	52.2
Rafael Piñeda Ponce	Liberal Party (PLH)	44.3

Mexico

2006 Presidential Election

Candidate	Party	Percentage
Felipe Calderón	National Action Party (PAN)	36.4
Andrés Manuel López Obrador	Coalition for the Good of All (CBT)–Democratic Revolutionary Party (PRD)	35.3
Roberto Madrazo	Institutional Revolutionary Party (PRI)	21.5

2000 Presidential Election

Candidate	Party	Percentage
Vicente Fox Quesada	National Action Party (PAN)	42.5
Francisco Labastida Ochoa	Institutional Revolutionary Party (PRI)	36.1
Cuauhtémoc Cárdenas Solórzano	Democratic Revolutionary Party (PRD)	16.6

Nicaragua

2006 Presidential Election

Candidate	Party	Percentage
Daniel Ortega Saavedra	Sandinista National Liberation Front (FSLN)	38.0
Eduardo Montealegre Rivas	Liberal Nicaraguan Alliance (ALN)	28.3
José Rizo Castellon	Constitutional Liberal Party (PLC)	27.1

2001 Presidential Election

Candidate	Party	Percentage
Enrique Bolaños Geyer	Constitutional Liberal Party (PLC)	56.3
Daniel Ortega Saavedra	Sandinista National Liberation Front (FSLN)	42.3

Panama

2004 Presidential Election

Candidate	Party	Percentage
Martín Torrijos	Revolutionary Democratic Party (PRD)	47.7
Guillermo Endara	Solidarity Party (PS)	30.9
Miguel Alemán	Arnulfista Party (PA)	16.4

1999 Presidential Election

Candidate	Party	Percentage
Mireya Moscoso	Arnulfista Party (PA)	44.9
Martín Torrijos	Revolutionary Democratic Party (PRD)	37.6
Alberto Vallarino	Christian Democratic Party (PDC)	17.5

Paraguay

2003 Presidential Election

Candidate	Party	Percentage
Nicanor Duarte	National Republican Association (ANR)	37.1
Julio Cesar Franco	Authentic Radical Liberal Party (PLRA)	23.9
Pedro Fadul	Mother Country Movement (MPQ)	21.3
Guillermo Sanchez	National Union Party of Ethical Citizens (PUNCE)	13.5

Peru

2006 Presidential Election: Round 1

Candidate	Party	Percentage
Ollanta Humala	Union for Peru (UP)	30.6
Alan García	Peruvian Aprista Party (PAP)	24.3
Lourdes Flores	National Unity (UN)	23.8

2006 Presidential Election: Round 2

Candidate	Party	Percentage
Alan García	Peruvian Aprista Party (PAP)	52.6
Ollanta Humala	Union for Peru (UP)	47.4

2001 Presidential Election: Round 1

Candidate	Party	Percentage
Alejandro Toledo	Possible Peru (PP)	36.5
Alan García	Peruvian Aprista Party (PAP)	25.8
Lourdes Flores	National Unity (UN)	24.3

2001 Presidential Election: Round 2

Candidate	Party	Percentage
Alejandro Toledo	Possible Peru (PP)	53.1
Alan García	Peruvian Aprista Party (PAP)	46.9

Uruguay

2004 Presidential Election

Candidate	Party	Percentage
Tabaré Ramón Vásquez Rosas	Progressive Encounter-Broad Front-New Majority (EP-FA-NM)	51.9
Jorge Larrañaga	National Party—Whites (PN-B)	34.9
Guillermo Stirling	Colorado Party (PC)	10.6

1999 Presidential Election: Round 1

Candidate	Party	Percentage
Tabaré Ramón Vásquez Rosas	Progressive Encounter (EP)	38.5
Jorge Luis Battle Ibañez	Colorado Party (PC)	31.3
Luis Alberto Lacalle de Herrera	National Party–Whites (PN-B)	21.3

1999 Presidential Election: Round 2

Candidate	Party	Percentage
Jorge Luis Battle Ibañez	Colorado Party (PC)	54.1
Tabaré Ramón Vásquez Rosas	Progressive Encounter (EP)	45.9

Venezuela

2006 Presidential Election

Candidate	Party	Percentage
Hugo Rafael Chávez Frías	Movement for the Fifth Republic (MVR)	62.8
Manuel Rosales	Independent	36.9

2000 Presidential Election

Candidate	Party	Percentage
Hugo Rafael Chávez Frías	Movement for the Fifth Republic (MVR)	59.5
Francisco Arias	Independent	37.5

Sources: Georgetown University and Organization of American States Political Database of the Americas, http://www.georgetown.edu/pdba. Derksen, Wilfried. Elections Around the World, http://www.agora.stm. it/elections/election.htm. electionguide.org, http:// 209.50.195.230/ eguide/resultsum/uruguay_pres04.htm.

APPENDIX 2
Recent Legislative Elections

Argentina

2005 Chamber of Deputies and Senate Elections

Party	Percentage (Deputies/Senators)	Number of Seats (Deputies/Senators)
Front for Victory (FV)	29.9/45.1	50/14
Radical Civic Union (UCR)	8.9/7.5	10/2
Alternative for a Republic of Equals (ARI)	7.2/6.9	8/0
Justicialist Party (PJ)	6.7/0.7	9/1

2001 Chamber of Deputies and Senate Elections

Party	Percentage	Number of Seats (Deputies/Senators)
Alliance (Radical Civic Union–Front for a Country in Solidarity)	23.1	35/25
Justice Party (JP)	37.5	66/40
Action for the Republic (AR)	7.2	8/1

Bolivia

2005 Chamber of Deputies and Chamber of Senators Elections

Party	Percentage	Number of Seats (Deputies/Senators)
Movement Toward Socialism (MAS)	53.7	72/12
Social and Democratic Power (PODEMOS)	28.6	43/13
National Unity Front (FUN)	7.8	8/1
Nationalist Revolutionary Movement (MNR)	6.5	7/1

2002 Chamber of Deputies and Chamber of Senators Elections

Party	Percentage	Number of Seats (Deputies/Senators)
Nationalist Revolutionary Movement/Free Bolivia (MNR)	26.9	36/27
New Republican Force (NFR)	26.5	25/2
Movement of the Revolutionary Left (MIR)	19.8	26/5
Socialist Movement (MAS)	11.9	27/8

Brazil

2006 Chamber of Deputies and Federal Senate Elections

Party	Percentage (Deputies/Senators)	Number of Seats (Deputies/Senators)
Workers' Party (PT)	15.0/19.2	83/11
Brazilian Democratic Movement Party (PMBD)	14.6/12.0	89/15
Brazilian Social Democratic Party (PSDB)	13.6/12.5	65/15
Party of the Liberal Front (PFL)	10.9/25.7	65/18

2002 Chamber of Deputies and Federal Senate Elections

Party	Percentage (Deputies/Senators)	Number of Seats (Deputies/Senators)
Workers' Party (PT)	18.4/—	91/14
Brazilian Social Democracy Party (PSDB)	14.3/—	71/11
Party of the Liberal Front (PFL)	13.4/—	84/19
Brazilian Democratic Movement Party (PMBD)	13.4/—	74/19

Chile

2005 Chamber of Deputies Election

Party	Percentage	Number of Seats
Democratic Agreement (CD)	51.8	65
Alliance for Chile	38.7	54

2005 Senate of the Republic Election

Party	Percentage	Number of Seats
Democratic Agreement (CD)	55.7	20
Alliance for Chile	37.3	17

2001 Chamber of Deputies Election

Party	Percentage	Number of Seats
Democratic Agreement (CD)	47.9	61
Alliance for Chile	44.3	56

2001 Senate of the Republic Election

Party	Percentage	Number of Seats
Democratic Agreement (CD)	51.3	9
Alliance for Chile	44.0	9

Colombia

2006 Chamber of Representatives Election

Party	Percentage	Number of Seats
Liberal Party (PL)	19.0	35
Social National Unity Party (PSUN)	16.7	29
Colombian Conservative Party (PC)	15.8	29
Radical Change (CR)	10.7	21

2006 Senate of the Republic Election

Party	Percentage	Number of Seats
Social National Unity Party (PSUN)	17.5	20
Colombian Conservative Party (PC)	16.1	18
Liberal Party (PL)	15.5	18
Radical Change (CR)	13.4	15

2002 Chamber of Representatives Election

Party	Percentage	Number of Seats
Liberal Party (PL)	31.3	54
Colombian Conservative Party (PCC)	11.0	21

2002 Senate of the Republic Election

Party	Percentage	Number of Seats
Liberal Party (PL)	30.6	28
Colombian Conservative Party (PCC)	10.0	13

Costa Rica

2006 Legislative Assembly Election

Party	Percentage	Number of Seats
National Liberation Party (PLN)	36.5	25
Citizen Action Party (PAC)	25.3	17
Libertarian Movement Party (PML)	9.2	6
Christian Social Unity Party (PUSC)	7.8	5

2002 Legislative Assembly Election

Party	Percentage	Number of Seats
Christian Social Unity Party (PUSC)	29.7	19
National Liberation Party (PLN)	27.1	17
Citizen Action Party (PAC)	21.9	14

Dominican Republic

2006 Chamber of Deputies and Senate Elections

Party	Percentage	Number of Seats (Deputies/Senators)
Dominican Liberation Party (PLD)	46.4	96/22
Dominican Revolutionary Party (PRD)	31.1	60/7
Social Christian Reformist Party (PRSC)	10.9	22/3

2002 Chamber of Deputies and Senate Elections

Party	Percentage	Number of Seats (Deputies/Senators)
Dominican Revolutionary Party (PRD)	41.9	73/29
Dominican Liberation Party (PLD)	29.1	41/2
Social Christian Reformist Party (PRSC)	24.3	36/1

Ecuador

2006 National Congress Election

Party	Percentage	Number of Seats
Institutional Renewal Party of National Action (PRIAN)	24.5	27
Patriotic Society Party (PSP)	17.2	23
Social Christian Party (PSC)	13.5	12
Joint List of Proud and Sovereign Fatherland Movement (MPAIS) and Socialist Party–Broad Front (PS-FA)	12.4	11

2002 National Congress Election

Party	Percentage	Number of Seats
Ecuadorian Roldosista Party (PRE)	NA	15
Party of the Democratic Left (ID)	NA	13
Institutional Renewal Party of National Action (PRIAN)	NA	10
Joint List of Patriotic Society Party (PSP) and Pluri-National Pachakutik Movement–New Country (MUPP-NP)	NA	6

El Salvador

2006 Legislative Assembly Election

Party	Percentage	Number of Seats
National Republican Alliance (ARENA)	39.4	34
National Liberation Front Farabundo Martí (FMLN)	39.7	32
Party of National Conciliation (PCN)	11.0	10
Christian Democratic Party (PDC)	6.8	6

Guatemala

2007 Congress of the Republic Election

Party	Percentage	Number of Seats
National Unity of Hope (UNE)	22.8	48
Grand National Alliance (GANA)	16.5	37
Patriotic Party (PP)	15.9	30
Guatemalan Republican Front (FRG)	9.8	15

2003 Congress of the Republic Election

Party	Percentage	Number of Seats
Grand National Alliance (GANA)	24.3	47
Guatemalan Republican Front (FRG)	19.7	43
National Unity of Hope (UNE)	18.4	32
National Advancement Party (PAN)	10.9	17

Haiti

2006 Chamber of Deputies and Senate Elections

Party	Percentage	Number of Seats (Deputies/Senators)
Front for Hope (FL)	19.0	23/13
Fusion of Haitian Social Democrats	9.9	17/4
Christian National Union for the Reconstruction of Haiti	4.3	12/2
Fanmi Lavalas	8.1	2/1

2000 Chamber of Deputies and Senate Elections

Party	Percentage	Number of Seats (Deputies/Senators)
Fanmi Lavalas	NA	73/26
Christian National Union for the Reconstruction of Haiti	NA	3/0
Pati Louvri Bayré	NA	2/1

Honduras

2005 National Congress Election

Party	Percentage	Number of Seats
Liberal Party of Honduras (PLH)	44.8	62
National Party (PN)	40.4	55

2001 National Congress Election

Party	Percentage	Number of Seats
National Party (PN)	46.5	61
Liberal Party of Honduras (PLH)	40.8	55

Mexico

2006 Chamber of Deputies and Chamber of Senators Elections

Party	Percentage (Deputies/ Senators)	Number of Seats (Deputies/Senators)
National Action Party (PAN)	33.4/33.6	206/52
Coalition for the Good of All (PRD, Convergencia, PT)	29.0/29.7	157/36
Alliance for Mexico (PRI, PVEM)	28.2/28.0	123/39

2003 Chamber of Deputies Elections

Party	Percentage	Number of Seats
Institutional Revolutionary Party (PRI)/ Ecologist Green Party of Mexico (PVEM)	34.6	241
National Action Party (PAN)	23.1	149
Party of the Democratic Revolution (PRD)	17.6	97

Nicaragua

2006 National Assembly Election

Party	Percentage	Number of Seats
Sandinista National Liberation Front (FSLN)	37.6	38
Constitutionalist Liberal Party (PLC)	26.5	25
Nicaraguan Liberal Alliance (ALN)	26.7	23

2001 National Assembly Election

Party	Percentage	Number of Seats
Constitutionalist Liberal Party (PLC)	52.6	48
Sandinista National Liberation Front (FSLN)	42.6	41
Conservative Party of Nicaragua (PCN)	4.8	1

Panama

2004 Legislative Assembly Election

Party	Percentage	Number of Seats
Democratic Revolutionary Party (PRD)	37.8	41
Arnulfista Party (PA)	19.2	17
Solidarity Party	15.7	9

1999 Legislative Assembly Election

Party	Percentage	Number of Seats
Democratic Revolutionary Party (PRD)	NA	34
Arnulfista Party (PA)	NA	18
Christian Democratic Party (PDC)	NA	5

Paraguay

2003 Chamber of Senators Election

Party	Percentage	Number of Seats
Republican National Alliance/Colorado Party (ANR)	32.9	16
Authentic Radical Liberal Party (PLRA)	24.3	12
Beloved Fatherland Movement (MPQ)	15.2	7
National Union of Ethical Citizens (UNACE)	13.7	7

2003 Chamber of Deputies Election

Party	Percentage	Number of Seats
Republican National Alliance/Colorado Party (ANR)	35.3	37
Authentic Radical Liberal Party (PLRA)	25.7	21
Beloved Fatherland Movement (MPQ)	15.3	10
National Union of Ethical Citizens (UNACE)	14.7	10

1997 Chamber of Deputies Election

Party	Percentage	Number of Seats
Republican National Alliance (ANR)	53.8	45
Democratic Alliance (AD)	42.7	35

1997 Chamber of Senators Election

Party	Percentage	Number of Seats
Republican National Alliance (ANR)	51.7	24
Democratic Alliance (AD)	42.1	20

Peru

2006 Congress of the Republic Election

Party	Percentage	Number of Seats
Union for Peru (UPP)	21.2	45
Peruvian Aprista Party	20.6	36
National Unity Party (UN)	15.3	17
Alliance for the Future	13.1	13

2001 Congress of the Republic Election

Party	Percentage	Number of Seats
Possible Peru (PP)	26.3	45
Peruvian Aprista Party	19.7	26
National Unity Party (UN)	13.8	17
Independent Moralizing Front	11.0	11

Uruguay

2004 Chamber of Deputies and Chamber of Senators Elections

Party	Percentage	Number of Seats (Deputies/Senators)
Progressive Encounter–Broad Front (EP)	51.7	52/17
National Party–Whites (PN–B)	35.1	36/11
Colorado Party (PC)	10.6	10/3

1999 Chamber of Deputies and Chamber of Senators Elections

Party	Percentage	Number of Seats (Deputies/Senators)
Progressive Encounter–Broad Front (EP–FA)	38.5	40/12
Colorado Party (PC)	31.3	32/10
National Party–Whites (PN–B)	21.3	22/7

Venezuela

2005 National Assembly Election

Party	Percentage	Number of Seats
Movement for the Fifth Republic (MVR)	60.0	116
For Social Democracy	8.2	18
Fatherland for All (PT)	6.8	10
Communist Party of Venezuela (PCV)	2.7	7

2000 National Assembly Election

Party	Percentage	Number of Seats
Movement for the Fifth Republic (MVR)	NA	76
Democratic Action (AD)	NA	29
Movement toward Socialism (MAS)	NA	21
Project Venezuela (ProVen)	NA	7
Social Christian Party (COPEI)	NA	5

Sources: Georgetown University and Organization of American States Political Database of the Americas, http://www.georgetown.edu/pdba/. Derksen, Wilfried. Elections Around the World, http://www.electionworld.org/.

AUTHORS AND CONTRIBUTORS

Authors

Gary Prevost is Professor and Chair, Department of Political Science, St. John's University/College of Saint Benedict, Minnesota. He received his Ph.D. in political science from the University of Minnesota and has published widely on Latin America and Spain. His books include *Democracy and Socialism in Sandinista Nicaragua*, coauthored with Harry E. Vanden; *The 1990 Nicaraguan Elections and Their Aftermath*, coedited with Vanessa Castro; *The Undermining of the Sandinista Revolution*, coedited with Harry E. Vanden; *Cuba: A Different America*, coedited with Wilber Chaffee; *The Bush Doctrine and Latin America*, coedited with Carlos Oliva Campos; *Revolutionaries to Politicians*, coedited with David Close and Kalatowie Deonandan; and *United States-Cuban Relations—A Critical History*, coauthored with Esteban Morales, in addition to numerous articles and book chapters on Nicaragua and Spanish politics. His research on Latin America has been supported by a number of grants, including a Fulbright Central American Republics Award.

Harry E. Vanden is Professor of Political Science and International Studies at the University of South Florida, Tampa. He received his Ph.D. in political science from the New School for Social Research and also holds a graduate Certificate in Latin American Studies from the Maxwell School of Syracuse University. He has lived in several Latin American countries, including Peru, where he was a Fulbright Scholar and later worked in the Peruvian government's National Institute of Public Administration, and in Brazil, where he held a second Fulbright and taught at the State University of São Paulo. His scholarly publications include numerous articles and book chapters and the following books: *Mariátegui, influencias*; *National Marxism in Latin America*; *A Bibliography of Latin American Marxism*; *Democracy and Socialism in Sandinista Nicaragua*, coauthored with Gary Prevost; *The Undermining of the Sandinista Revolution*, coedited with Gary Prevost; *Inter-American Relations in an Era of Globalization. Beyond Unilateralism?* edited wiith Jorge Nef; and *Latin American Social Movements in the Twenty-First Century*, edited with Richard Stahler-Sholk and Glen Kuecker.

Contributors

Wilber Albert Chaffee is Professor Emeritus at Saint Mary's College of California and presently lives in Brazil. He has been a Senior Research Associate at the Instituto

607

Universitário de Pesquisas do Rio de Janeiro and a Fulbright scholar. He received his Ph.D. in government from the University of Texas, Austin. In addition to his numerous articles and book chapters, he has published *The Economics of Violence in Latin America; Cuba, A Different America*, coedited with Gary Prevost; and *Desenvolvimento: Politics and Economy in Brazil*. He is currently working on a study of institutional change in Brazil.

Nora Hamilton is Professor of Political Science at the University of Southern California. She received her Ph.D. in sociology from the University of Wisconsin. She has published *The Limits of State Autonomy: Post-Revolutionary Mexico; Crisis in Central America* (editor); *Modern Mexico, State Economy and Social Conflict*, coedited with Timothy Harding; and several articles and book chapters on political and economic change in Mexico and Central America. She has also published on Central American migration and recently published *Seeking Community in a Global City: Guatemalans and Salvadorans in Los Angeles*, coauthored with Norma Chinchilla.

Susanne Jonas is Professor of Latin American and Latino Studies at the University of California, Santa Cruz. She received her Ph.D. in political science from the University of California, Berkeley, and has been an expert on Central America, particularly Guatemala, and on U.S. policy in the region, for 38 years. Her most recent book is *Of Centaurs and Doves: Guatemala's Peace Process*. Among her other recent books are *Immigration: A Civil Rights Issue for the Americas, Beyond the Neoliberal Peace: From Conflict Resolution to Social Reconciliation, Latin America Faces the 21st Century*, and *The Battle for Guatemala*. She has also written seventy major journal articles and book chapters as well as op-ed articles for major U.S. newspapers. She is currently coauthoring a book on Guatemalan migrant communities in the United States with Nestor Rodriguez.

Eduardo Silva is Professor of Political Science and a Fellow of the Center for International Studies at the University of Missouri–St. Louis. He received his Ph.D. in political science from the University of California, San Diego. He is author of *The State and Capital in Chile: Business Elites, Technocrats and Market Economics*, and coeditor of *Organized Business, Economic Change and Democracy in Latin America* and *Elections and Democratization in Latin America, 1980–1985*. He has also published over thirty articles that have appeared in professional journals, edited volumes, and public affairs outlets.

Aldo C. Vacs is Professor and Chair of the Department of Government, Skidmore College, a Research Associate at the University of Pittsburgh, and a contributing editor for the *Handbook of Latin American Studies*. He holds a Ph.D. in political science from the University of Pittsburgh. Dr. Vacs has published many articles and book chapters and has authored *Discreet Partners: Argentina and the USSR since 1917; The 1980 Grain Embargo Negotiations: The U.S., Argentina and the USSR*; and *Negotiating the Rivers*. He is currently researching political democratization, economic liberalization, and the process of political economic transformation in Latin America.

John C. Dugas is Associate Professor and Chair of the Department of Political Science at Kalamazoo College. He received his Ph.D. in political science from Indiana University. He has worked for over a decade on issues of political reform in Colombia and is the coauthor of *Los Caminos de la Descentralización: Diversidad y retos* *de la transformación municipal* and editor of *La Constitución de 1991: ¿Un pacto político viable?*, both published by the Universidad de los Andes in Bogotá, Colombia. He has also published articles in the *Journal of Latin American Studies*, the *Latin American Research Review*, *Third World Quarterly*, and *America Latina Hoy*.

Daniel Hellinger is Professor of Political Science at Webster University in St. Louis, Missouri. He received his Ph.D. in Political Science from Rutgers University and has authored *Venezuela: Tarnished Democracy* (Westview, 1991), many scholarly articles on Venezuela and Latin America, and coedited (with Steve Ellner) *Venezuelan Politics in the Chávez Era: Class, Polarization and Conflict.* He is presently working on a comparative study of the nationalizations of copper in Chile and oil in Venezuela.

Waltraud Q. Morales is Professor of Political Science at the University of Central Florida. She received her M.A. and Ph.D. from the Graduate School of International Studies of the University of Denver. She has published articles on Bolivian domestic and foreign policies, women and gender in Latin America and the Third World, the Andean drug war, Andean indigenous peoples, and sustainable development and human security. Recent publications include *A Brief History of Bolivia* (2005), and "Responding to Bolivian Democracy: Avoiding the Mistakes of Early U.S. Cuban Policy," *Military Review* (July–August 2006). She has been the recipient of grants from the National Endowment for the Humanities and Fulbright teaching, research, and study grants to Bolivia in 1990 and 2004.

INDEX

INDEX